Religious Diversity in the

Employees bring their beliefs and religious values to work, and this can be a source of either positive performance or negative conflict. Social conflicts around religion impact more than societies and communities. They also impact organizations. "Anti-religion" sentiments tend to be based on the perception that religion can be neatly separated from the "more acceptable/palatable" spirituality, but this ignores the fact that – for most people – the two are intimately intertwined and inseparable. As religious identity is salient for a majority of the world's population, it is thus an important aspect of organizations – particularly those with a large and diverse body of employees. This handbook provides a timely and necessary analysis of religious diversity in organizations, investigating the role of national context, the intersections of religion with ethnicity and gender, and approaches to diversity management.

JAWAD SYED is Professor of Organizational Behavior and Dean of Suleman Dawood School of Business, Lahore University of Management Sciences. Professor Syed is an Academic Fellow of the Chartered Institute of Personnel and Development (CIPD), UK, and Program Co-Chair of European Academy of Management's (EURAM) Gender, Race, and Diversity in Organizations (GRDO) Special Interest Group. He is one of the directors of the Global Centre for Equality and Human Rights (GCEHR). He has edited/authored eight books and written more than 75 journal articles and book chapters, including his articles in the *British Journal of Management*, *Business Ethics Quarterly* (Cambridge), the *International Journal of Human Resource Management*, and *Gender, Work and Organization*.

ALAIN KLARSFELD is Senior Professor at Toulouse Business School, University of Toulouse, France, where he created and managed (2003–15) the Human Resource Management Specialized Masters program, and acted as Department Head from 2012 to 2016. He co-founded the competence management Special Interest Group (SIG) and the equality-diversity SIG within the French-speaking HR society (AGRH) and has published extensively in both these fields in various French-speaking and international journals, including *Cross-Cultural and Strategic Management*, *Equality Diversity and Inclusion*, the *European Journal of Industrial Relations*, the *European Management Journal*, and the *International Journal of Human Resource Management*.

FAITH WAMBURA NGUNJIRI is Associate Professor of Ethics and Leadership at Concordia College, Minnesota. She is also Director of the Lorentzsen Center for Faith and Work at the Offutt School of Business of Concordia College. She is the author of *Women's Spiritual Leadership in Africa: Tempered Radicals and Critical Servant Leaders* (2010), coauthor of *Collaborative Autoethnography* (2013), and coeditor of *Women as Global Leaders* and *Women and Leadership around the World* (2014 and 2015, respectively). Her research has been published in various academic journals, including the *Journal of Management, Spirituality and Religion*, the *International Journal of Qualitative Studies in Education*, and *Advances in Human Resource Development*.

CHARMINE E. J. HÄRTEL is Professor and Chair of Occupational Health and Work Psychology for The University of Queensland Business School in Brisbane, Australia. Recently, in her role as Senior Editor (Invited Contributions and Special Issues) for the *Journal of Management & Organization* (Cambridge), she commissioned the special issue "Contextualizing diversity within Islam: Interpretations, understandings and implications for management and organizations."

Religious Diversity in the Workplace

Edited by

JAWAD SYED
*Suleman Dawood School of Business,
Lahore University of Management Sciences, Pakistan*

ALAIN KLARSFELD
Toulouse Business School, University of Toulouse, France

FAITH WAMBURA NGUNJIRI
Concordia College, US

CHARMINE E. J. HÄRTEL
University of Queensland, Australia

CAMBRIDGE
UNIVERSITY PRESS

University Printing House, Cambridge CB2 8BS, United Kingdom

One Liberty Plaza, 20th Floor, New York, NY 10006, USA

477 Williamstown Road, Port Melbourne, VIC 3207, Australia

314–321, 3rd Floor, Plot 3, Splendor Forum, Jasola District Centre, New Delhi – 110025, India

79 Anson Road, #06-04/06, Singapore 079906

Cambridge University Press is part of the University of Cambridge.

It furthers the University's mission by disseminating knowledge in the pursuit of education, learning, and research at the highest international levels of excellence.

www.cambridge.org
Information on this title: www.cambridge.org/9781107136038
DOI: 10.1017/9781316477106

© Cambridge University Press 2018

This publication is in copyright. Subject to statutory exception and to the provisions of relevant collective licensing agreements, no reproduction of any part may take place without the written permission of Cambridge University Press.

First published 2018
3rd printing 2018

Printed in the United Kingdom by Clays, St Ives plc

A catalogue record for this publication is available from the British Library.

Library of Congress Cataloging-in-Publication Data

Names: Syed, Jawad, editor.
Title: Religious diversity in the workplace / edited by Jawad Syed, Lahore University of Management Sciences, Pakistan, Alan Klarsfeld, Toulouse Business School, Faith Wambura Ngunjiri, Concordia College, Charmine E.J. Härtel, University of Queensland.
Description: First [edition]. | New York : Cambridge University Press, 2018. | Includes bibliographical references and index.
Identifiers: LCCN 2017042274 | ISBN 9781107136038 (hardback : alk. paper)
Subjects: LCSH: Religion in the workplace. | Cultural pluralism—Religious aspects.
Classification: LCC BL65.W67 R45 2017 | DDC 204/.4—dc23 LC record available at https://lccn.loc.gov/2017042274

ISBN 978-1-107-13603-8 Hardback
ISBN 978-1-316-50173-3 Paperback

Cambridge University Press has no responsibility for the persistence or accuracy of URLs for external or third-party internet websites referred to in this publication and does not guarantee that any content on such websites is, or will remain, accurate or appropriate.

Contents

List of Figures	*page* viii
List of Tables	ix
List of Boxes	x
Notes on Contributors	xi

Introduction: *The Complex Interface of Work and Religion* 1
JAWAD SYED, ALAIN KLARSFELD, FAITH WAMBURA NGUNJIRI, AND CHARMINE E. J. HÄRTEL

Part I General Frameworks and Sources of Reflection 35

1 A Relational Perspective on Religious Diversity at Work 37
JAWAD SYED

2 Religious Diversity, Identity, and Workplace Inclusion 60
CHARMINE E. J. HÄRTEL, JASMIN C. R. HÄRTEL, AND PREM RAMBURUTH

Part II Religious Approaches 81

3 The Christian Faith and the Preservation of Personal Identity 83
TIMOTHY EWEST

4 An Islamic View of Diversity: *Implications for the Business World* 105
ABBAS J. ALI

v

5	The Untold, the Unseen, and the Forgettable: *Jewishness, Jews, and Judaism in Diversity Management Scholarship* ALAIN KLARSFELD	123
6	National Perspectives on Jews at Work: *Contrasting Australia, France, Israel, and the UK* ALAIN KLARSFELD, DIANE BEBBINGTON, AVI KAY, LUCY TAKSA, FEI GUO, AND PHILIP MENDES	145
7	Hinduism, Religious Diversity, and Spirituality at Work in India RADHA R. SHARMA AND RANA HAQ	177
8	Buddhist *Brahmaviharas* and Religious Diversity at Work EDWINA PIO	198
	Part III Regional Approaches	**221**
9	Spirituality and Workplace Diversity Practices in Africa KURT A. APRIL, THABO MAKGOBA, AND DION A. FORSTER	223
10	The French Principle of *Laïcité* and Religious Pluralism in the Workplace: *Main Findings and Issues* PATRICK BANON AND JEAN-FRANÇOIS CHANLAT	264
11	Lessons from the Academy: *Concordia College's Journey toward Religious Pluralism* JACQUELINE BUSSIE AND MICHELLE LELWICA	305
12	Religious Diversity in the Canadian Workplace: *The Case of Muslims* HANIFA ITANI AND YUSUF M. SIDANI	331
13	Religious Diversity at Work in the Asia-Pacific Region EDWINA PIO AND TIMOTHY PRATT	354

| | Part IV Organizational Approaches | 387 |

14 Organizational Approaches to Religious Diversity in the Workplace — 389
TIMOTHY EWEST

15 From Diverse Frameworks to Diverse Attitudes towards Religion at Work: *Focus on the French Case* — 416
GÉRALDINE GALINDO AND HÉDIA ZANNAD

16 Resilient Leadership and Tempered Radicalism: *Navigating the Intersections of Race, Gender, Nationality, and Religion* — 441
FAITH WAMBURA NGUNJIRI AND
KATHY-ANN C. HERNANDEZ

Index — 471

Figures

1.1	A relational perspective on religious diversity at work	*page* 51
9.1	Spirituality continuum within organizations	252
13.1	Religious affiliation in Asia-Pacific 2010	360
15.1	The different levels of the principles for managing religious issues in the workplace	423
15.2	The phases of the religious French guides project	428

Tables

0.1	The book at a glance: Regions, religions/spiritualities, and theoretical categories of the chapters	page 25
3.1	Basic Christian beliefs	87
4.1	Foundations of diversity and their implications	117
6.1	Summary table contrasting Australia, France, Israel and the United Kingdom	171
7.A1	List of annual gazetted and restricted holidays in India	193
9.1	The dimensionality of spirituality	226
9.2	Key features of the three conceptualizations of spirituality in the workplace	233
12.1	Facilitating integration of Muslim workers and diversity: What Muslim workers need to do	347
12.2	Facilitating integration and diversity of Muslim workers: What employers need to do	348
13.1	The sub regions and countries of Asia-Pacific	356
14.1	Equal opportunity commissions claims based on religious grounds	391
14.2	A pattern of organizations observing human rights issues	396
14.3	Organizational frames for faith and work	397
14.4	Faith-friendly scorecard	399
14.5	Charter of secularism adopted by a French recycling company	405
14.6	Comparison of employees' attitudes in a faith-friendly company and in a random sample	408
15.1	Levels and uncertainty of the frameworks used by firms to manage religious issues	422
15.2	Typology of faith-orientations and their implications in the workplace	425
15.3	Profile of French firms of our research	428
15.4	The arguments presented in French corporate guides	432

Boxes

12.1 Najat   341
12.2 Hamada   342
15.1 The French and *Laïcité*   426

Contributors

Abbas J. Ali, PhD, is Distinguished University Professor and Professor of Management, Director, School of International Management, Eberly college of Business, at Indiana University of Pennsylvania. He serves as the Executive Director of the American Society for Competitiveness. Ali has served as visiting professor at King Saud University, University of Sharjah, and as senior Fulbright Scholar at the University of Jordan. His research interests include global business leadership, strategy, business ethics, foreign policy, comparative management, competitiveness issues, organizational politics, and international management. He has published more than 160 scholarly journal articles and more than 20 chapters in scholarly books. His articles have been published in such journals as *Academy of Management Executives*, *Business Horizon*, the *Journal of Business Ethics*, the *Journal of Psychology*, the *Journal of Social Psychology*, *International Studies of Management & Organization*, the *Journal of Small Business Management*, *Organization Studies*, and *Personnel Review*, among others. In addition, he has delivered more than 500 presentations at professional and academic meetings. He has authored or coauthored nine books, including the *Handbook of Research on Islamic Business Ethics* (2015); *Business Ethics in Islam* (2014); *Strategic Management: Concepts and Cases* (2011); *Islamic Perspectives on Management and Organization* (2005); and *Business and Management Environment in Saudi Arabia: Challenges and Opportunities for Multinational Corporations* (2008).

Kurt A. April, PhD, lectures and researches in the areas of leadership, diversity, and inclusion at the Graduate School of Business, University of Cape Town (South Africa). He is also Orchestrator/Educator for DukeCE (USA), Associate Fellow of Saïd Business School at the University of Oxford (UK), Research Fellow of Ashridge-Hult (UK), and Visiting Professor for London Metropolitan University (UK). Outside of academia, Kurt sits on a number of boards and advisory boards as a Non-Executive Director: Novartis International AG (Switzerland), Power Group (South Africa), Leicester University's Diversity, Inclusion and Community Engagement (DICE) Unit (UK), Achievement Awards Group (South Africa), and the International School of Cape Town (South Africa), as well as serving on the editorial boards of a number of academic journals globally. He has authored and coauthored 145 academic articles and eight books with various world-renowned publishers around the globe.

Patrick Banon is a French writer, specializing in religious sciences and systems of thought (at the École Pratique des Hautes Études), research associate at the Chaire Management, Diversités et Cohésion Sociale, Université Paris-Dauphine, lecturer at the Université d'Orléans, and Director of the Institut des Sciences de la Diversité, a think tank devoted to the study of systems of contemporary thought and intercultural and religious relations. He has published numerous books, studies, and articles on the history of religions, the impact of religious traditions on societies, and the management of religious expression in the workplace. His essay "Osons la Mixité, L'entreprise au féminin masculin" received the Femmes de l'Économie 2015 Prize. Patrick Banon has recently published *Marianne en péril: Religions et laïcité, un défi français* (2016), and the *Guide du Mieux Vivre-Ensemble: Ma laïcité, ma religion, mon identité* (2016).

Diane Bebbington is Director of Knowledge Perspectives Ltd., an independent research company specializing in equality issues. She holds a PhD in sociology from the University College London's Institute of Education. Diane was Diversity Advisor to the Leadership Foundation for Higher Education from 2008 to 2016, where she was responsible for developing and implementing the organization's diversity strategy. She has extensive experience in project management, research, and writing for publication. Her most recent paper was a collaboration with Drs Victoria Showunmi and Doyin Atewologun on ethnic, class, and gender intersections in British women's leadership experiences.

Jacqueline Bussie is Director of the Forum on Faith and Life and Professor of Religion at Concordia College in Moorhead, Minnesota, where she teaches courses in theology, compassion, the problem of evil, Christian ethics, interfaith studies, and faith and life. Dr Bussie's first book, *The Laughter of the Oppressed* (2007), won the national

Trinity Prize. Her second book, *Outlaw Christian: Finding Authentic Faith by Breaking the Rules* (2016), received a coveted starred review from *Publishers Weekly*. Dr Bussie has served as project director and/ or primary investigator on grants from the Lilly Endowment, the Teagle Foundation, Interfaith Youth Core, and the Wabash Center for Teaching and Learning; most recently, Dr Bussie received a grant from the James S. Kemper Foundation and Interfaith Youth Core to research religious diversity in professional settings.

Jean-François Chanlat has a PhD in sociology from the University of Montréal. He was a full time faculty member at HEC Montréal from 1979 to 1997 and a part-time faculty member of HEC Montréal and University Robert Schuman of Strasbourg from 1997 to 2001. He has been Professor at the University of Paris-Dauphine since then. His main domains of teaching and research are organization theory, organizational behavior, anthropology of organizations, sociology of business firms, cultures, diversity and organizations, critical management thinking, and organizational stress. Professor Chanlat has published 15 books and numerous articles and book chapters in French, English, Spanish, Portuguese, and Arabic. Some of them are considered as classics among the Francophone, Hispanophone, and Lusophone worlds. He is regularly invited to give seminars, courses, and conferences in Latin America, Africa, Canada, Asia-Pacific, and Europe on these topics. He was president of the research committee Sociology of Organizations, of the International Sociology Association, between 1994 and 2006. He was co-chair of the French-speaking network Business and Societies, of the International Association of the French Speaking Sociologists, from 1995 to 2008. He was also very involved for several years in the Society for the Advancement of Socio-Economics. He is presently associate editor of *Management International* (Montréal) as well as a member of several editorial boards of French- and English-speaking journals.

Timothy Ewest has worked in higher education since 2002 on corporate social responsibility, social entrepreneurship, management, and leadership. His research interests include: issues surrounding faith and work, leadership and pro-social behavior, and leadership in social entrepreneurship. He has published numerous journal articles, conference presentations, and contributed to numerous leadership books and books on workplace spirituality. He also consults with nonprofit organizations, focusing on strategy, fundraising, ethics, and leadership development. In addition to his duties at Houston Baptist University, he is currently working as a visiting research collaborator with David Miller at Princeton University's Faith and Work Initiative, exploring the integration of faith (spirituality and religion) within the workplace.

Dion A. Forster is a senior lecturer in systematic theology and ethics, with a focus on public theology, at the University of Stellenbosch. He is the Head of Department, Systematic Theology and Ecclesiology and the Director of the Beyers Naudé Centre for Public Theology. He holds a PhD in theology and science (2006) and post-graduate qualifications from the University of Stellenbosch Business School (2009) and Rhodes University (1997, 2001). Dion received a scholarship to complete a second PhD at Radboud University, the Netherlands (2014–17). He is chair of the Global anti-corruption campaign, "EXPOSED – Shining a light on corruption." He serves on the World Economic Forum's "Expert Network" (Religion and Africa) and is the author and editor of eight books and numerous scholarly articles.

Géraldine Galindo is an Associate Professor in the Strategy, Organizational Behavior, and Human Resources Department at ESCP Europe Paris where she teaches Human Resources Management (HRM). She is in charge of French HRM classes and the HR option in the Masters in International Management program. She graduated from Ecole Normale Supérieure Cachan, where she passed the competitive national examinations in Economics and Management. After obtaining her PhD in management sciences at the University of Paris Sud, she taught for 12 years and continued her research as associate professor at the University. Her research focuses on HRM, innovation, and diversity management – she has conducted research on religious diversity management practices in French companies in several areas: the emergence of this subject in management in France (with Joëlle Surply), the attitudes of different companies, the role of managerial guides, and the different levels of this issue (with Hedia Zannad). She has been scientific moderator of a group of HR directors focused on this topic since 2016.

Fei Guo is Deputy Head and Research Coordinator in the Department of Marketing and Management, Macquarie University. Her main research interests include skilled migration, return migration, and student migration in the Asia Pacific region, internal migration and migrant communities in China, and impacts of population ageing on labor supply in China. She conducted an Australia Research Council funded project on rural migrant labor in large Chinese cities, and is currently working on another investigating "Affinities in Multicultural Australia" with Ellie Vasta and Lucy Taksa. She has widely published in such journals as *International Migration Review*, *Asian and Pacific Migration Review*, *Habitat International*, *China Perspectives*, and the *Journal of Asian Public Policy*. Recently she guest-edited a special issue, "New Developments in Australia's Skilled Migration Flows" (with Massimiliano Tani and Graeme Hugo), for the *Asian and Pacific Migration Review*. She is currently an associate editor of *International Migration Review*.

Rana Haq is Assistant Professor at the Department of Marketing and Management in the Faculty of Management at Laurentian University in Sudbury, Ontario, Canada. She teaches undergraduate and graduate courses in the Organizational Behavior and Human Resource Management (OB/HRM) stream, both on campus and online. Her research interests are in the field of organizational behavior and human resource management, managing diversity, equality and inclusion in the workplace, international comparative human resource management, and cross-cultural communications. She has several peer-reviewed conference presentations, cases, book chapters, and papers published on these topics.

Charmine E. J. Härtel is Professor and Chair of Occupational Health and Work Psychology for The University of Queensland Business School in Brisbane, Australia. She is an acknowledged preeminent scholar-practitioner of Human Resource Management and Organizational Behavior, evidenced by election to the Australian Academy of Social Sciences, the Society for Organizational Behavior in Australia, award by the Australian Psychological Society of the Elton Mayo Award for scholarly excellence, Fellowship of the (US) Society for Industrial and Organizational Psychology (SIOP) and the Australian and New Zealand Academy of Management (ANZAM), over 200 publications, award of some AUD$3million in Australian Research Council (ARC) grants and AUD$1 million for commissioned research. She is passionate about promoting and facilitating international perspectives on gender and diversity and the research, teaching, and practice contributions needed to advance inclusion globally. For example, as Division Chair of the Gender and Diversity in Organizations Division of the (U.S.) Academy of Management (comprising 770 U.S. members & 401 non-US members), she initiated the review and development of guidelines for better representing international perspectives in committees and doctoral and early career academic consortia; the International Corner in the GDO newsletter; internationally assessable language guidelines for all communications; and trialing webinars showcasing diversity research, education, and practice outside English speaking countries. During her term on the Board and as President of ANZAM, she initiated recruitment of the first Indigenous doctoral representative, introduction of the Indigenous Management Interest Group, and rebadging of the Gender and Diversity conference track as the Gender, Diversity and Indigeneity track. Recently, in her role as Senior Editor (Invited Contributions and Special Issues) for Journal of Management & Organization (Cambridge University Press), she commissioned the special issue "Contextualizing diversity within Islam: Interpretations, understandings and implications for management and organizations" (to appear in print at the end of 2017).

Jasmin C. R. Härtel is a Research Assistant in The University of Queensland Business School, Brisbane Australia. She attended The University of Queensland and Monash University, completing in 2015 her Bachelor of Science with a double major in Zoology and Marine and Freshwater Biology. Currently she is completing a Masters of Science (Ecosystem Science) degree at The University of Melbourne, specializing in Urban Ecology. She has undertaken field research in both the social and biological sciences and in her current role provides research assistance in the areas of management, social marketing, and psychology. Her research interests relate to harmonious relationships between humans, organizations, and the environment, with particular focus on the sustainability and conservation of marine species and native Australian wildlife, including writing science communications targeted at policy makers and the general public.

Kathy-Ann C. Hernandez, PhD is Professor of Educational Psychology and Research Methods at Eastern University (Pennsylvania, USA). She is also CEO of Nexe Consulting and regularly consults with school districts, churches, schools, government offices, and colleges and universities nationally and internationally. She is an author/presenter on several autoethnographically related scholarly projects and her work has appeared in the *Handbook of Autoethnography*, *The International Journal of Qualitative Studies in Education*, and *The Journal of Research Practice*. Her research is focused on the black diaspora and the salience of race/ethnicity, gender, and social context in identity formation, leadership development, and social and academic outcomes. She is coauthor of *Collaborative Autoethnography* (2013, with Heewon Chang and Faith Wambura Ngunjiri) and is currently working on her next book, *Black Men and the Black Church*. She earned a PhD in Educational Psychology from Temple University.

Hanifa Itani is a freelance researcher based in Abu Dhabi, United Arab Emirates (UAE). Prior to moving to the UAE, she lived in Canada (Mississauga, Ontario) where she blended into the country's cultural mosaic through various social activities and artistic explorations, such as teaching French, creative writing, mindfulness, art media, and even training as a professional barista. She also volunteered with Amnesty International's Toronto Francophone Chapter. She holds an MBA in marketing and a BBA in operations and information systems and accounting, both from the American University of Beirut. Her research contributions focus on female entrepreneurs, their motivations and frustrations. She has published works in journals including, "*Diversity and Inclusion: An International Journal*," and more recently her coauthored paper won a best paper award at the Academy of Management, Gender and Diversity in Organizations Division.

Avi Kay is an Associate Professor in the Faculty of Management at the Lev Academic Center in Jerusalem, where he also serves as the Director of the Schuman Center for Entrepreneurship. Following a six-year stint as the chair of the Department of Management, one focus of Avi's research program focuses on the juxtaposition of religion and spirituality and the workplace. His publications in the area have addressed the place of traditional Jewish sources in contemporary management issues, the occupational behavior of Ultra-Orthodox Jews (Israel's fastest growing population), and the impact of technology on traditional work-related attitudes.

Alain Klarsfeld is Senior Professor at Toulouse Business School, Toulouse, France. He has been doing research on skill-based management, corporate social responsibility, international human resource management, and equality, diversity and inclusion. He has co-founded the competence management Special Interest Group (SIG) and the equality-diversity SIG within the French-speaking HR society (AGRH) and published extensively in both these fields in various French-speaking and international journals. Alain Klarsfeld founded and managed his institution's specialized masters in Human Resource Management from 2003 to 2015. From 2012 until 2016, he also served as Department Chair of HR and Corporate Social Responsibility at Toulouse Business School. His present research includes talent management, gendered careers, the gender pay gap, comparative equality and diversity management, and the management of religious diversity.

Michelle Lelwica is Professor of Religion at Concordia College in Moorhead, Minnesota, where she teaches courses related to religion, gender, culture, and the body. She did her graduate work at Harvard Divinity School, where she received a Masters of Theological Studies in Christianity and Culture (1989) and a Doctorate of Theology in Religion, Gender, and Culture (1996). She is the author of *Shameful Bodies: Religion and the Culture of Physical Improvement* (2017), *The Religion of Thinness: Satisfying the Spiritual Hungers behind Women's Obsession with Food and Weight* (2009), and *Starving for Salvation: The Spiritual Dimensions of Eating Problems among American Girls and Women* (1999), as well as scholarly articles and popular blogs relating to women's conflicted relationships with their bodies. She has also published articles and taught courses that focus on embodied pedagogy and mindfulness practice.

Thabo Makgoba is the Archbishop and Metropolitan of the Anglican Church of Southern Africa. Among others, he holds the degrees of BSc (University of Witwatersrand) and PhD (University of Cape Town). Formerly he was Bishop Suffragan (2002) and Bishop of the Grahamstown Diocese (2004). Since 2008 he has been the Anglican Archbishop and Metropolitan of the Anglican Church of Southern Africa. He is the former Chair of the Anglican Communion Environmental Network, and a former Commissioner of the Press Freedom Commission. Since 2012 he has served as the Chancellor of the University of the Western Cape. He is the recipient of various awards and honors including the Cross of St Augustine (Archbishop of Canterbury); Doctor of Divinity, honoris causa (General Theological

Seminary, Episcopal Church, NY, 2009); Doctor of Divinity, jure dignitatis (Huron University College, Ontario, 2013); Doctor of Divinity, honoris causa (University of the South, Sewanee, TN, 2015); Doctor of Literature, honoris causa (University of the Witwatersrand, 2016); and a recipient of the Ernest Oppenheimer Memorial Trust Scholarship. He is a Procter Fellow, EDS, Cambridge, USA and Adjunct Professor at the Graduate School of Business (GSB), Allan Gray School for Values. He is a pastor, teacher, author, and servant of peace with justice.

Philip Mendes is the Director of the Social Inclusion and Social Policy Research Unit in the Department of Social Work at Monash University, and also holds an honorary appointment with the Monash University Centre for Jewish Civilization. He is the author or coauthor of 10 books including *The New Left, the Jews and the Vietnam War, 1965–72* (1993), jointly edited with Geoffrey Brahm Levey; *Jews and Australian Politics* (2004); and *Jews and the Left: The Rise and Fall of a Political Alliance* (2014).

Faith Wambura Ngunjiri is Associate Professor of Ethics and Leadership at Concordia College, Minnesota. She is also Director, Lorentzsen Center for Faith and Work at the Offutt School of Business of Concordia College. She is the author of *Women's Spiritual Leadership in Africa: Tempered Radicals and Critical Servant Leaders* (2010) and coauthor of *Collaborative Autoethnography* with Heewon Chang and Kathy-Ann Hernandez (2013). She is coeditor of *Women as Global Leaders* and *Women and Leadership around the World* with Susan R. Madsen and Karen A. Longman (2014 and 2015, respectively). Dr Ngunjiri is coeditor of two book series: *Women and Leadership: Theory, Research and Practice* and *Palgrave Studies in African Leadership*. Her research on women and leadership, spirituality in organizations, and qualitative methods/autoethnography has been published in various academic journals, including the *Journal of Management, Spirituality and Religion*, the *International Journal of Qualitative Studies in Education*, and *Advances in Human Resource Development*. She earned a doctorate in leadership studies from Bowling Green State University, USA.

Edwina Pio is University Director of Diversity at the Auckland University of Technology, in a position annexed to her substantive role as professor in the Faculty of Business, Economics, and Law and leader of the research group Immigration and Inclusion. She is New Zealand's first Professor of Diversity, a Fulbright alumna, recipient of a Duke of Edinburgh fellowship and widely published. Her accolades include Visiting Professor at Boston College, USA; research fellowship at Jonkoping International Business School, Sweden; Visiting Academic at Cambridge University, UK; Fellow of the New Zealand India Research Institute, New Zealand; and Co-Director of the Global Centre for Equality and Human Rights, UK. Edwina is a thought leader and knowledgeable interpreter in the area of diversity in business, communities, and education and her passion for interdisciplinary scholarship and social justice encompass the intersections of work, ethnicity, religion, and pedagogy.

Timothy Pratt leads the Interchurch Council of Hospital Chaplains who have a contract with the Ministry of Health to deliver Chaplain services in all District Health Boards within New Zealand. Prior to that, he was a Vice Chancellor's Doctoral Scholar in the Management Department at Auckland University of Technology where he also taught Change Management to MBA students. His doctoral research explored collaboration of New Zealand's civil society organisations amidst neo-liberalism and for his masters he examined Transitional (intentional Interim Ministry) within the Christian church. His academic interests are derived from an initial vocation as a minister of religion and then as chief executive, consultant and chair for national and international non-government organisations. His interests lie in enhancing the effective management, leadership and governance of organisations focused on youth development and/or religion.

Prem Ramburuth is President of the Academic Board at the University of New South Wales (UNSW) and Professor in International Business. Her leadership positions at UNSW include Associate Dean Education, Associate Dean Undergraduate Programs, Head of the School of Management, and Foundation Director of the Business Faculty's Education Development Centre. Professor Ramburuth researches and teaches in cross-cultural and diversity management in business and higher education and has published in high ranking business and higher education journals across these areas. She has gained national and international recognition for her work and is the recipient of several teaching excellence awards. Professor Ramburuth is on the editorial board of the *Academy of Management Learning and Education*, the *Journal for Multicultural Education*, the *International Journal of Emerging Markets*, and *Chinese Management Studies*. She has been a Visiting Professor at Vietnam National University (VNU) Hanoi Business School, VNU International University, University of Colorado (Denver), Universiti Tunku Abdul Rahman(UTAR) (Malaysia), and University of Hawaii.

Radha R. Sharma is Dean, Centres of Excellence, Case Centre, Hero MotoCorp Chair Professor, and Professor of Organizational Behavior and Research at Management Development Institute, India. Radha Sharma is an alumnus of the Global Colloquium on Participant-Centered Learning from Harvard Business School and has CSR certifications, World Bank Institute, the British Council, and New Academy of Business, UK. Her research has been supported by the World Health Organization; the McClelland Centre for Research & Innovation; and Academy of Management. Her research interests include emotional/social intelligence, workplace spirituality, burnout, well-being, gender equity, change management, organizational transformation, humanistic management, and social responsibility. She has been Visiting Professor to European countries for global MBA programs. She has published 14 books and articles in *Frontiers in Psychology*, *Cross Cultural Management*, the *Journal of Management Development*, and *Global Management Review*, among others.

Yusuf M. Sidani is Professor of Leadership and Business Ethics and the chairperson of the Management, Marketing, and Entrepreneurship Track at the Olayan School of Business, American University of Beirut. He has a PhD in organization behavior (leadership) from the University of Mississippi, an MBA from Indiana University at Bloomington (accounting), and a BBA from the American University of Beirut. Professor Sidani's research and teaching focus on business ethics/Corporate Social Responsibility and gender and diversity in organizations, with special focus on the Arab region. He has dozens of contributions to international refereed academic journals, conferences, and professional journals. His research has appeared in leading international peer-reviewed academic journals such as *Human Resource Management Review*, *Business Ethics Quarterly*, the *Journal of Business Ethics*, the *Journal of World Business*, and the *International*

Journal of Human Resource Management. Dr Sidani was awarded the prestigious 2015 *Abdul Hameed Shoman Award* for Arab Researchers.

Jawad Syed, PhD, is Professor of Organizational Behavior and Dean of the Suleman Dawood School of Business, Lahore University of Management Sciences. Professor Syed is an Academic Fellow of the Chartered Institute of Personnel and Development (CIPD), UK, and Program Co-Chair of European Academy of Management's (EURAM) Gender, Race, and Diversity in Organizations (GRDO) Special Interest Group. He is one of the directors of the Global Centre for Equality and Human Rights (GCEHR). He has edited/authored eight books and written more than 75 journal articles and book chapters, including his articles in the *British Journal of Management, Business Ethics Quarterly* (Cambridge), the *International Journal of Human Resource Management*, and *Gender, Work and Organization*.

Lucy Taksa is Associate Dean (Research) in the Faculty of Business and Economics at Macquarie University, after nearly six years as Head of the Department of Marketing and Management. She has published extensively on migrant employees, diversity management in Australia, multiculturalism, and gendered cultures. She has been a member of the Equal Opportunity Division of the NSW Administrative Decisions Tribunal (1996–2007), Chair of the Board of the New South Wales State Archives (2007–12) and she is currently an Independent Board member of the not-for-profit Settlement Services International Ltd. She is currently working on an Australian Research Council funded project investigating "Affinities in Multicultural Australia" with Ellie Vasta and Fei Guo, and on a Catholic Education Commission funded project on "Historical Patterns of Schooling, Religion, and Socio-demographics of Australia's Population," with Nick Parr and Nikki Balnave.

Hédia Zannad trained in management, psychology, and sociology, and is currently associate professor in NEOMA Business School. Her areas of research and publications focus mainly on discrimination and diversity: How to measure them? How to manage religious diversity? To what extent is it possible to become a top leader without a "Grande Ecole" degree in France? How to break the glass ceiling encountered by women? What are the factors of socio-professional integration for refugees in France?

Introduction: The Complex Interface of Work and Religion

JAWAD SYED, ALAIN KLARSFELD,
FAITH WAMBURA NGUNJIRI, AND
CHARMINE E. J. HÄRTEL

Religions and Tensions around the World

Despite extensive scholarship and developments in the field of management over the last century, and plentiful evidence of the worldwide increase in religious diversity (Alesina et al., 2002; Pew Research Center, 2014), not much attention has been paid to religious diversity and its role in the workplace.

Religion has been traditionally seen as a private matter with little or no consideration given to religious diversity in the workplace. Today, given the re-emergence or revival of religious identities and sentiments in the Middle East, Europe, North America, South Asia, and other parts of the world, it is crucial for policymakers and employers to develop better understanding and management of religious diversity. This is particularly important in the global marketplace, given that companies are increasingly interacting with diverse religions, cultures, and stakeholders (Syed & Ozbilgin, 2015).

In the last three decades, there has been a growing number of courses in academia and corporate training, and an exponential increase in publications in the areas of diversity, equality, and social responsibility. These avenues have raised the issue of diversity, but the discussion on religious diversity has been somewhat superficial and limited. Leaders and managers are interested in pre-empting or resolving religious conflicts and tensions while trying to harness diversity for enhanced individual and team performance, productivity, and other organizational benefits. However, it is unclear how to go about doing this. Thus far, the rise of the "faith at work" or "God at work" movement has primarily targeted workers of Christian affiliation (Miller, 2007). There the focus has been on integrating faith and making sense of religious beliefs in the workplace, but the issue of potential conflict from religious diversity has not been adequately addressed (Miller, 2007).

However, in the past two decades, the "spirituality at work" scholarship has attempted to describe, measure, and assess the challenges and opportunities of spirituality and religion in the workplace (Fry, 2013; Karakas, 2010).

Employees from varied ethnic or racial groups usually bring together a variety of ideologies and practices (Gebert et al., 2014), some of which may be useful for evoking alternative approaches to management and innovation. Employees that are exposed to different cultures are more likely to adapt to diverse situations and people (Gebert et al., 2014). The cultural expertise of employees and managers can benefit organizations, especially those that operate globally (SHRM, 2015), for example, by better understanding the religious and ideological preferences and sensitivities of people of diverse backgrounds (Hambler, 2015).

Organizations have begun to appreciate the value of religious and cultural diversity while incorporating equality and diversity into their core values. For example, local and multinational corporations in Brunei are expected to consider the notion of Melayu Islam Beraja (Malay Muslim Monarchy), a national ideology which embraces the Brunei Malay culture, Islamic values, and the history and role of monarchy. The notion of Melayu Islam Beraja promotes the idea that people, both within and outside organizations, should be treated like family members, as is consistent with Islamic religious and local cultural values (Low & Mohd Zain, 2008). Similarly, Alliance Bank Malaysia integrates cultural diversity into its core values and seeks to build a strong workforce while achieving business goals (Alliance Bank, 2014). A similar commitment to religious diversity is evident in Ireland, where Community National Schools with diverse religious, denominational, and cultural ideologies are encouraged. Recently, Education Minister Richard Bruton reiterated his strong support for the growth of Community National Schools as a way of offering parents more choice. It has been stated that these schools offer a multi-denominational approach to religious education, catering for all beliefs in the school day. In practice, they are like a hybrid between the traditional, religion-led schools, and the growing "Educate Together" model that provides for no religious teaching inside the school (Donnelly, 2017).

While religion usually entails adhering to a structured belief system or dogma, spirituality is concerned with growing into and experiencing the Divine consciousness. Loosely speaking, the traditions of Sufism in Islam (both Sunni and Shia Islam) and Kabbalah in Judaism may be seen as spiritual in their orientation, concerned with explaining the mystical content of the universe and humanity's relationship to God's creation, while seeking the refinement of the soul and intimacy with God (Schwartz, 2011).

Religion places importance on intellectual beliefs (Byrd & Scott, 2014) while spirituality emphasizes a personal connection with the universe and its constituents. Spirituality-oriented workplaces are known to have a more accepting and reconciliatory approach towards demographic and ideological differences (Gröschl, 2016). An egalitarian and inclusive perspective and practice of religion and spirituality may provide a feeling of purpose, a sense of connection, and positive social relations between people, and enhance the ability to work with one another without conflicts (Byrd & Scott, 2014).

Scholars (e.g., Kirton & Greene, 2015; Messarra, 2014) suggest that religious and spiritual diversity has become a catchphrase that is generally acknowledged but rarely instituted until conflicts appear. Although preemptive policies exist particularly in Western countries to eliminate religious discrimination, organizations usually take a less proactive approach to addressing such issues (Kirton & Greene, 2015).

As organizations are becoming more diverse, religion is often an issue in the workplace. Problems usually arise due to conflicts between organizational policies and employees' religious practices (Mathis et al., 2016). For example, some organizations may require their employees to dress in a certain way. However, this may not be acceptable to some men and women for religious reasons, as may be the case with headgear such as the turban for Sikhs and the hijab/headscarf for some Muslim women. Similarly, some employees may struggle to work on particular days and times due to religious obligations such as Sabbath and Ramadan (Hambler, 2015).

Religious discrimination is an issue that continues to fester in Western workplaces, affecting people of diverse beliefs, such as Muslims, Sikhs, and Jews (Moodie, 2016). The problem often stems from lack of understanding of different religious and cultural values, which may lead to misunderstandings and resentment. As a result, employees may experience conflicts not only amongst themselves but also between their religious obligations and employment (Byrd &

Scott, 2014). Some of the discriminatory or non-inclusive practices or behaviors may not be deliberate and malicious, but may reflect a lack of diversity awareness in the workplace (Mor Barak, 2014). Often these issues merely scratch the surface of deeper issues, i.e., behavioral outcomes that may affect organizational performance as well as employee commitment and engagement (Bendl et al., 2015).

Previous research suggests that if it is not appropriately understood and managed, religious diversity can potentially trigger serious conflicts in the workplace (Byrd & Scott, 2014; Gebert et al., 2014). For example, Christians may not be willing to work on their traditional religious or festive holidays, while practicing Muslims may require one to three short breaks per day for obligatory prayers (Chapman et al., 2014; Yasmeen & Markovic, 2014). Thus, it is not only an issue of diversity management but also organizational flexibility in accommodating religious diversity at work.

The resolution of some of the religion-related issues may require an understanding of the laws and religious obligations, and balancing organizational needs and employees' preferences regarding practicing their religion at work (Bendl et al., 2015). In view of anti-discrimination legislation across several countries and jurisdictions, organizations, particularly in Western countries, are interested in devising strategies and management interventions to mitigate negative organizational and personal consequences of religious discrimination in the workplace (Chapman et al., 2014; Messarra, 2014).

Despite such efforts being made, inequalities continue to exist between majorities and minorities (Gröschl, 2016), and at times, there may be a clear religious penalty for people of certain religious backgrounds, such as Muslims in the post-9/11 world. The fatal flaw of many corporate and social policies is that they neglect the extent of religious and ethnic inequalities within and outside the workplace (Chapman et al., 2014). Justice is concerned not only with socioeconomic and legal inequalities at the level of the individual, but also with persistent patterns of collective discrimination and disadvantage (Yasmeen & Markovic, 2014).

Often, negative attitudes and behaviors in the workplace include prejudice, stereotyping, and discrimination, which may also occur when recruiting and hiring staff (Messarra, 2014). Discriminatory and negative behaviors may have significant implications for organizational culture because these may harm working relationships and damage morale and productivity (Gebert et al., 2014).

Religious tensions and conflicts are commonplace in the world today, not only in the Middle East, but also in parts of South and South East Asia, Africa, Europe, and the Americas. Today, reference to religion and religious pluralism, often perceived as a threat by certain segments of the populace, is commonplace in the run up to any election, as witnessed in the recent campaigns for the US and French presidencies, and the German regional elections. Such tensions and conflicts are found not only on an inter-religious level, for example between Muslims and Jews, Hindus and Christians, Muslims and Buddhists, but are also evident at an intra-religious level, for example between Protestants and Catholics, Sunnis and Shias, Salafis/Wahhabis and Sufis, Reform and Orthodox Jews. Tensions are also found between people of faith and those who do not identify with a religious faith, e.g. atheists. Such tensions are manifested in all aspects of everyday life, such as employment, political and other institutions, media, education, and wider society.

In light of recent high-profile religion-based conflicts (e.g. the Paris and Nice killings in France, the Israel-Palestine conflict, the rise of the so-called "Islamic State" in Iraq and Syria, the emergence of radical Salafi and Deobandi Islamism, as well as Islamophobia and anti-Semitism), there is a need to more deeply examine how religion-based tensions impact people, work, employment, and organizations.

There are several examples of how religious diversity may affect individuals in the workplace. In 2016, US food processing company Cargill fired 150 Muslim workers from its beef processing plant in Colorado after a dispute over prayer breaks. After facing protests about the layoffs, the company changed its hiring policy allowing the fired employees to reapply for their jobs (Moodie, 2016). This suggests that some organizations are still unwilling to accommodate employees' religious beliefs. Similarly, the US Supreme Court heard a case in 2015, filed by a Muslim plaintiff, Samantha Elauf, who argued that a clothing retailer, Abercrombie & Fitch, denied her a job because she wore a hijab. After a thorough investigation, it was confirmed that Ms Elauf was not hired because of her religious dress, and as a result she won the case (Kaur, 2015).

Similarly, a well-qualified Sikh applicant tried to obtain a job as a salesperson at a car dealership. During a group interview, the recruiter allegedly asked the applicant if he would be willing to shave his beard for the job. He explained that this was not possible because of his religious beliefs and as a result he was denied the job. The complainant won his case for being treated unfairly (Kaur, 2015).

In another similar case, a British Airways (BA) employee suffered discrimination for her Christian beliefs. Nadia Eweida took her case to the European Court of Human Rights (ECHR) after BA asked her to stop wearing a white gold cross visibly. The court ruled that BA had not struck a fair balance between Ms Eweida's religious beliefs and the company's corporate image. As a result, the company was ordered to pay Ms Eweida 2,000 euros (£1,600) in damages and 30,000 euros (£25,000) in costs (Pigott, 2013).

Events happening outside of work can have an impact on the treatment of religious minority employees within the workplace. For example, since . . . the terrorist attacks by Deobandi/Salafi Islamists in 2015 in San Bernardino, the Anti-Discrimination Committee has received more than a dozen phone calls from Muslim Americans locally reporting a variety of workplace discrimination and harassment. One of them was from Terry Ali, a 48-year-old medical receptionist, who was suing her employer, Livonia Dermatology, claiming that the clinic fired her two days after the deadly shootings due to her religious beliefs (Baldas, 2015).

There are also organizational examples of how religious diversity may be promoted in the workplace. Accounting giant EY (formerly Ernst & Young) is seeking to build an inclusive environment for its workers. The firm has created quiet rooms at its New York headquarters and in all of its Canadian offices, which are open to all employees either to take quick breaks or to pray, or for meditation purposes. The company also accommodates major religious and cultural holidays for its diverse employees.

Although the initial focus of this book project was on tensions and conflicts, the editors early on acknowledged the need to examine how societies and organizations could develop an inclusive and pluralistic environment in which people of diverse faiths and cultures feel equally valued and are able to be productive members of the society. Beyond this, they have sought out contributions where religious management practices as well as individual spirituality have been shown to lead to improved individual and collective performance, and this is reflected in several chapters of the present volume as will be outlined below.

Aim of the Present Volume: Addressing the Need to Manage Religious Diversity

While religion has recently received some attention in academic scholarship (e.g., McKim, 2001, 2012; Meister, 2010; Miller, 2007; Paloutzian & Park, 2013; Tilley, 2007; Wiggins, 1996), barring very few exceptions (Giacalone & Jurkiewicz, 2003; Gröschl & Bendl, 2013; Neal, 2013), the implications of religious diversity in the workplace remain largely underexplored.

The aim of the present volume is to advance and disseminate the latest and most relevant knowledge in the area of religious diversity at work. It seeks to provide researchers, academics, students, and practitioners with a multidisciplinary view of religious diversity at work from a global perspective, taking into account the sources and arenas of religious tensions in the world today, and also the possibilities for constructive engagement and harmonization of religious differences for individual, social, and organizational good.

This book also takes into account how religious perspectives have contributed to the development of management theory, and how religious ideologies can provide useful lenses by which to interpret and extend management theory, e.g., Greenleaf's (1977) servant leadership theory, which can be found in many religious texts, although the philosophy itself transcends any particular religious tradition.

This book offers an intersection of theory and practice on this topic, with a particular focus on the implications of religion for work and employment, but also taking into account wider societal, cultural, and institutional contexts. It is an interdisciplinary book, integrating contributions and insights from management, sociology, economics, politics, law, psychology, and religion. It also integrates the views on managing religion from diverse regional perspectives: North America, but also Africa, Asia, Europe, and the South Pacific. It features forward-looking essays from thought leaders and practitioners in the field.

Increasingly, policymakers and leaders around the globe are realizing the need to attend to the potential threat that religion-based tensions may pose to individuals, communities, and organizations (Syed et al., 2016), even though in some instances the threat may not be apparent or imminent (Reuters, 2016). In many instances, political, religious, and cultural biases may infiltrate organizational boundaries, thus replicating the societal stereotypes and *othering*. Within the domain of work and employment, individuals may suffer from overt or covert forms of hatred, prejudice, and discrimination, and this may affect their well-being and performance (Chickering et al., 2006). They may be under direct or indirect pressure to refrain from exposing their religious identity for the fear of othering (Crossmann, 2015; Hecht & Faulkner, 2000), which might result in lower well-being, organizational commitment, and individual performance (Yoshino & Smith, 2013, 2014), as well as negative personal outcomes in some contexts (Rosh & Offermann, 2013). Christerson and Emerson (2003) suggest that the same social dynamics that enforce or encourage internal homogeneity also produce high personal costs to belonging to minority ethnic or religious groups.

However, as suggested by Allport (1954) long ago, the workplace can and should provide a forum for inclusion, lowering of prejudice, and the overcoming of identity-based differences, thus improving people's well-being and alleviating tensions by bringing them together in pursuance of common work goals. Thus, there is not only an ethical and social responsibility to manage religious diversity well, but also a performance rationale. Hicks (2002) suggests that the task of effective organizational leadership is to create an inclusive structure and culture in which leaders and followers can respectfully negotiate religious and spiritual diversity alongside other forms of difference such as ethnicity, gender, age, familial obligations, and ability. Bouma et al. (2003), for instance, show that there is no inherent conflict between Islamic doctrine and modern workplaces, and therefore potential areas of friction between religion and contemporary human resource management (HRM) practices can and should be managed effectively. An example of this is provided by the chapter by Itani and Sidani in the present volume.

Indeed, chapters in this book offer up-to-date international scholarship on religious diversity at work addressing issues of conflict, harmony, and performance. They have been gathered by a diverse team of editors, who have paved the way for the diversity of chapters of this book, by contributors from a wide range of geographic regions, ethnicities, nationalities, and religious affiliations.

The Diversity of the Editorial Team

The editors form a diverse team, in terms of ethnicity, gender, and religion. They all experience or have experienced a nexus of contradictory and simultaneous "majority" and "minority" statuses, or "relatively privileged" and "relatively deprived" positions. We collectively represent life as management academics at the intersections of race, gender, ethnicity, religion, and nationality, not to mention the differences in our geospatial locations in France, England, the United States, and Australia.

Alain Klarsfeld is a French secular Jew born and brought up in France by parents who had emigrated from Romania, so that his migrant-descendent status intersects with minority ethnicity status. Frequently being exposed to English-speaking academia gives Alain yet another minority (French) standpoint as opposed to mainstream North-American scholarship. At the same time, Alain experiences being a White male in a country with a White majority, and in a professional context where White males are a majority (full professors in management). He also experiences being an agnostic in a country where this religious affiliation is the majority affiliation.

Jawad Syed was born and grew up in Pakistan in the majority religion (Islam) but in a mixed-sect family, representing the majority Sunni Islam (on his maternal side and part of his paternal side) and minority Shia Islam (part of his paternal side). He thus recognizes the artificial and inflated nature of the Sunni-Shia binary in the mainstream media and academic discourse. He completed his higher studies in Australia, and lived and worked in the United Kingdom. In both countries, he has experienced Islam as a minority religion, in contexts where there is a low level of awareness and knowledge about the distinction between largely peaceful mainstream traditions of Islam (Sunni and Shia) and the patterns of violence and extremism within some hard-line sections of the Salafi (Wahhabi) and Deobandi groups. In both countries, Islam intersects with color of skins as both Australia and the United Kingdom are predominantly White, with a strong historical Christian background. Like Alain, Jawad enjoys a privileged male status when it comes to joining the ranks of full professorship in the UK. Since late 2016, Jawad has relocated to Pakistan where he is a full professor at a local university.

Faith Ngunjiri was born and raised in Kenya in the Christian faith, the majority faith in the country. She moved to the USA where she completed her doctoral education and where she now resides and works. In both Kenya and the USA, she is in the majority in terms of being a Christian; however, in both contexts, gender has been a source of conflict and discrimination. Furthermore, in the USA, she experiences oppression and microaggressions at the intersections of race/ethnicity and gender, in both the religiously affiliated institutions where she presently works and the secular institutions she has worked or studied in previously. Thus she arrived in the USA with no racial identity, and has needed to develop a racial identity and learn to navigate the racialized context of the USA. Further, in spite of the "majority" status conferred by her Christian faith, her strong social justice ideals as a Quaker make her a minority within that larger context – and often place her at odds with others whose values differ significantly, especially around the question of women and leadership in the church.

Charmine Härtel is a White American who grew up in a predominantly aboriginal community in Alaska, so she represents a minority within a minority. She was brought up in a rather secular immediate family environment but she was exposed to aboriginal spirituality that permeated life in the community where she lived, including that of her own family. She moved to a more mainstream US environment when she was 17, and felt foreign to this mainstream society that she came to know relatively late. She is a woman in the highly competitive, male-dominated profession of academia. At the same time, she also has experienced or experiences being White in two countries where Whites are a majority: Australia and the USA.

As a team then, we form a microcosm of the issues discussed in this book at the intersections of social identities and organizational life; we personify the very diversity that this book aims to explore.

Overview of the Book

The book is organized in a manner that not only covers main regions and religions but also, within many chapters (where possible and appropriate), there is a specific focus on organizational approaches, experiences, challenges, and opportunities with regard to religious diversity.

The chapters in this book offer a combination of theoretical and empirical contributions to interrogate and explore the question of religious diversity in the workplace. Interdisciplinary studies and emergent research designs such as autoethnography (Chang et al., 2013) are included where relevant. Before going into the substance of each chapter, we will try to outline the takeaway from this chapter in relation to transverse questions: religion as a source of tensions at the workplace, religion as a source of performance at the workplace, the role of national context in shaping the view of the religion/tension/performance relationship, and the need to address intersectionality between religion and other identity traits such as ethnicity and gender. These questions are examined in the following section, with examples from different authors and countries/regions.

Religion: A Source of Tensions?

All authors in the present volume share the view that demands for religious accommodation are on the rise in most countries around the world, but this is also where consensus ends. Despite our insistence as editors on religion as a potential source of conflict as well as performance, some authors in this volume (Ewest; Syed; Itani & Sidani; Sharma & Haq) argue in favor of religious accommodation in response to these rising requests to bring one's whole self to work. They support the view that religion (or faith, or spirituality, terms that are sometimes used synonymously with religion, a point that can of course be debated) has positive implications for the workplace if managed properly. Accommodations are at the same time a moral imperative (Syed; Itani & Sidani) and a stable cultural feature in some countries like India and South-East Asia and the Pacific more generally (Sharma & Haq; Pio & Pratt). This is likely to create a faith-safe or even better, a faith-friendly environment that will favor well-being and ultimately, performance (Ewest; Syed; Itani & Sidani), provided managers are given the appropriate training and priming. Not only should managers be trained to accommodate religion, but employees should also be trained in how to request accommodation and to take into account their employer's business needs (Itani & Sidani). This view is not so often publicized, although it is perfectly consistent with Berry's work (1997) on acculturation practices.

Other authors (see section below) writing specifically on the implications of different religions for organizations and the workplace suggest that there are positive takeaways from the religions under study. Some authors (Galindo & Zannad), however, do not take a stance, but instead observe that for corporations there are a variety of possible responses to these accommodation demands, ranging from acceptance to refusal through compromise. It seems that a majority of firms (in France, for example) are taking the middle road of compromise

(Galindo & Zannad). Other French authors (Banon & Chanlat) point to the dangers of the dissolution of the collective workplace under the pressure of competing requests, some of which contradict, according to them, the necessities of smooth business operation and of "living together." The best response, according to these authors, is to extend the principle of "laïcité," which is understood as a complete banning of religious presence and visibility from the public sphere, of which businesses and workplaces form a part.

Religion: A Source of Performance?

Whilst there is ample evidence from the media of religion being a source of tension, it seems interesting to focus on managerial practices or wisdom that can be derived from religious precepts, and several chapters in this book devote all or part of their content to drawing key lessons from various religious traditions. Commonalities can be found across different religions (as per the chapters on Buddhism (Chapter 8), Christianity (Chapter 3), Islam (Chapters 4 and 12), and Judaism (Chapters 5 and 6), and Chapter 2, on theorizing religion, which devotes a section to indigenous religions) in the present volume.

First, attention is given to the well-being and fairness of treatment of employees across several religions. For instance, the Christian-derived concept of servant leadership focuses on imitating Jesus Christ in his devotion to serving and healing, and workers of Christian faith are exhorted to imitate Christ (Ewest). The Christian worker should not just comply with prescribed "ethical" norms of behavior, but should be always questioning how Jesus would have acted in situations encountered in the work setting (Ewest). Buddhism stresses equanimity and the importance of compassion for workers as a pre-condition for a sustainable business and, beyond this, proposes many sets of principles that can be applied when managing organizations (Pio). In Islam, the principle of *ehsan* emphasizes advancing societal welfare by being generous, forgiving, and tolerant. Public interest and moderation understood as the avoidance of extremes are equally important principles. This supports a socially responsible view of management (Ali). Judaism stresses the importance of equitable treatment; for instance, the Torah stipulates that salaries paid to workers and contractors alike should be paid in a timely manner and allow them to make a decent livelihood. Walking humbly, doing justice, showing courage, and delegating responsibility are other key precepts available from the Torah (or Pentateuch) and Talmudic sources that are commentaries on the Torah (Klarsfeld). Indigenous traditions are infused with the centrality of relational knowledge, the importance of public discussion taking into account all views before decision-making, and the sense of an obligation to create well-being and sustainability for all, thereby fostering social performance rather than financial performance (Härtel, Härtel & Ramburuth). Bussie and Lelwica provide an illustration of how integrating multiple faiths into higher education has benefits for both students and staff. Therefore, it can be concluded that religions under study in this handbook can be tapped into as sources of teachings relevant to the workplace and leadership, and therefore for sustainable individual, corporate, and educational performance.

Managing Religious Diversity: A Matter of National Context?

Religions and national contexts intersect closely. Specifically, 97% of Hindus, 87% of Christians, 73% of Muslims, and 71% of the unaffiliated live in countries where their affiliation (or non-affiliation) is that of the majority of the population. Therefore, the chances are that being affiliated with any of these groups generally confers some sort of "majority" status for the greater proportion of those concerned. Whereas the majority (59%) of Jews live in countries where they are but a tiny minority, while the rest live in Israel where they are an overwhelming majority. Additionally, only 28% of Buddhists live in a country where they are in a majority situation, and 72% are in countries where their faith is a minority one (Pew Research, 2012).

The views of religions explored above clearly follow national patterns (be they termed cultural or institutional). Authors from France, where non-affiliation is the dominant affiliation, tend to depict religious diversity at work as problematic. One of the editors of this volume (Klarsfeld) was prompted to start this very book project as the result of the escalating interfaith tensions, exclusionary processes, and murderous violence conspicuous in France during the last five years. As mentioned earlier, the continuum of managing religious diversity presented by Galindo and Zannad ranges from acceptance to refusal through compromise, when it comes to categorizing employers' religious management policies. In any event, religion is an element external to the firm that is at best tolerated, and not a foundation or a resource that may be proactively encouraged, supported, or tapped into, as suggested by other authors in this volume who also happen to come from other regions. Banon and Chanlat make a vivid presentation of "laïcité," the French version of the concept of secularism, providing many illustrations by showing corporate and case law examples. Banon and Chanlat view freedom and equality as foundational but contradictory principles of modern democracies, between which countries have to make a choice. According to them, France is currently assumed to have chosen equality (achieved through separation from religion in the public sphere, i.e. "laïcité"), while Anglo-Saxon countries are assumed to have chosen freedom (achieved through accommodating religious requests). In short, according to Banon and Chanlat, equality is acquired at the cost of freedom of religious expression, while freedom of religious expression is acquired at the cost of treating everyone equally, which is arguably a core foundation for maintaining social cohesion.

In contrast, Haq and Sharma's depiction of India is that of a country where the visibility and presence of different religions are part of the normal day-to-day work setting and the work culture. The 14 mandatory Indian holidays include three national (non-religious) holidays, but also two Hindu holidays, three Muslim ones, two Christian ones, a Buddhist one, a Sikh one, and a Jain one. There are also provisions for a variety of holidays for various Hindu denominations, Hinduism being itself very diverse. Haq and Sharma generally tend to depict this religious landscape at work as a positive feature of India, and consciously contrast this state of affairs to which they refer to as "secularism," with the French "laïcité" as put forward by Banon and Chanlat. Pio and Pratt, who look at the Asia-Pacific region more globally, also convey the idea that religious pluralism is almost a defining attribute of the region, through examining the cases of countries as different as Australia, Japan, New Zealand, the Pacific Islands, and South Korea.

Ewest's (North American) continuum of organizational approaches to managing religious diversity (the Faith Integration framework) seems to span the categories explicitly or implicitly underlying the work of his French (Banon & Chanlat; Galindo & Zannad), Indian (Haq & Sharma), and Asia-Pacific (Pio & Pratt) colleagues. The approaches range from the faith-based and faith-friendly approaches commonplace in India and more generally the Asia-Pacific region, to the faith-avoiding firm more representative of the French ideal-type of "laïcité," an ideal-type that can also be found in other European countries. It would thus seem that the North-American work setting offers more variations in terms of approaches to how to manage religious diversity, than those which predominate in France (and much of continental Europe), on the one hand, and India and the Asia Pacific, on the other hand. This might be a reflection of North America being itself built on immigrant influences drawn from all over the world, on top (and out) of having based its own early identity upon religious freedom. It is also reflective of the fact that the USA has legal protections in place against religious discrimination and harassment in employment, and a requirement that firms make reasonable accommodations to their employees' religious needs, such as religious holidays and clothing. However, this doesn't always translate into full freedom of expression for religious minorities, as is evidenced by the increase in cases at the Equal Employment Opportunity Commission in the USA (Morgan, 2016).

How Does Religion Intersect with Ethnicity and Gender?

Beyond national contexts, it is important to take into account the intersectionality of religion with other dimensions of identity such as gender and ethnicity. In many instances, religion is intertwined with ethnicity, thus making it difficult to neatly differentiate the religion-based tensions from ethnic tensions, as is the case for Jews whose identities can be religious or non-religious (Hecht & Faulkner, 2000). Ethnicity often intersects with religion, as is the case in most countries and communities, where the majority ethnic group of the population shares the same religious background, and a different background from other, minority ethnic groups (Chua, 2004). A secular Jew may be discriminated against based on religious prejudice. Similarly, an Arab may be discriminated against based on Islamophobic prejudice, as Arab minorities often happen to be Muslim minorities as well. As such, a Muslim may be discriminated against based on anti-Arab prejudice. In South-East Asian countries, ethnic minorities often tend to be of a different religion than the majority. Such is the case for the Hindu/Indian minority and the Malay/Muslim minorities in Singapore, or the Chinese/Confucian minorities in Indonesia, Malaysia, and the Philippines (Chia & Lim, 2010; Chua, 2004). In this volume, chapters by Klarsfeld, by Klarsfeld, Bebbington, Kay, Taska, Guo, and Mendes, by Ngunjiri and Hernandez, by Pio, by Pio and Pratt, and by Syed devote at least part of their content to the intersecting nature of religious and ethnic identities.

There is also the issue of how religion intersects with gender and/or class and/or ethnicity, adding to the complex and multi-layered nature of discrimination and intolerance in society and the workplace. The extent of religious practice, too, may add to the visible identity of an individual, such as a Muslim woman with a hijab or a Jewish man (and woman, among Reform Jews) wearing a kippah. An intersectional approach allows for the investigation of individuals' experiences at work at the nexus of religion and other social identities, including race, ethnicity, and gender. It recognizes the problematic nature of the matrix of domination for minoritized individuals in organizational contexts as well as in society (Cho et al., 2013; Collins, 2004; Hernández, 2008). However, most intersectionality studies focus on race, class, and gender (Holvino, 2010), often ignoring religion as a marker of social identity and source of discrimination at work. In this volume, chapters by April, Makgoba, and Forster, and by Ngunjiri and Hernandez, address the intersection of religion or spirituality with gender and ethnicity.

Overview of Chapters

This section is devoted to presenting a summary of each chapter. Chapters have been ordered as much as possible to reflect the thematic proximity between them.

The first two chapters are intended to provide *general frameworks and sources of reflection*, which can be drawn on while reading subsequent chapters. It must be noted, however, that many of the other chapters also refer to generic frameworks or implications that may be applied to a variety of geographical and religious contexts.

In his chapter titled *A Relational Perspective on Religious Diversity at Work*, Jawad Syed offers a relational, multilevel perspective on theorizing and managing religious diversity at work. The chapter explains that in order to understand and manage religious diversity in organizations, a holistic approach is needed, taking into account the macro-national, meso-organizational, and micro-individual level factors that are often interrelated and overlapping. At the macro-national level, the chapter highlights the implications of socio-cultural context, laws, and demography on approaches to religious diversity. At the organizational level, it takes into account issues such as organizational vision and culture, allocation of resources, and procedures. At the individual level, it considers issues of individual identity, intersectionality, and agency.

Härtel, Härtel, and Ramburuth's chapter, titled *Religious Diversity, Identity, and Workplace Inclusion*, provides a theoretical analysis of the paradox and possibilities of religious diversity bringing people together or pushing them apart. Faith-related identity development is an ongoing process, and religious identity may change several times throughout life. Religious attitudes are becoming increasingly diverse worldwide, and this diversification is mirrored in the workplace. The authors explore the background literature on increasing global religious diversity, including its intersectionality with other identity-based differences. Then, they examine and problematize definitions of religious diversity, and develop an integrated definition of religious diversity. Next, they utilize Paradox Theory to support why and how religious diversity needs to be managed. They illustrate how religious diversity can inform the management of diversity paradoxes through the lens of indigenous people's traditional belief systems. The chapter concludes with a discussion of pluralistic organization design and practical suggestions on how to promote an inclusive culture for religious diversity.

The next six chapters are devoted to *religious approaches*. Christianity, Islam, Judaism, Hinduism, and Buddhism are presented.

In *The Christian Faith and the Preservation of Personal Identity*, Tim Ewest provides a brief summary of the historical emergence of Christianity, surveys the major Christian subgroups, summarizes the basic tenets of Christianity, considers Christian tensions in the pluralistic world, and then considers how Christians integrate their faith into the workplace. Finally, Ewest considers how the preservation and enhancement of Christian religious identity is a primary motivator for Christians who seek to integrate their faith into the workplace. To illustrate the concepts, the chapter presents the case of Chick-fil-A as an example of how individual Christian beliefs can impact an organization, and Nadia Eweida as an example of how an organization can impact the individual Christian. Both are examples of how Christian beliefs are internalized and how individuals create normative behavior in order to maintain a Christian identity.

In Abbas Ali's *An Islamic View of Diversity: Implications for the Business World* chapter, three objectives are sought: articulating the genuine concept and practice of diversity, reflecting on the practice of diversity in contemporary businesses in countries with Muslim majorities, and proposing certain implications for institutions in today's world. The focus is on principles and what amounts to an ideal in an environment that is heavily influenced by global capitalism, where the quest for profit is a driving force. The author suggests that this added complexity, while encouraging deviation from religious precepts, underscores the fact that imprudent merging of developing countries, including Muslim ones, into the global capitalist system may constitute a threat.

In his chapter titled *The Untold, the Unseen, and the Forgettable: Jewishness, Jews, and Judaism in Diversity Management Scholarship*, Alain Klarsfeld points out that diversity management scholarship on Jewishness, Jews, and Judaism is remarkably absent. This is in spite of the continued flourishing of both anti-Semitism and social research on Jewish studies in non-workplace related fields such as religious practice, marriage, and the upbringing of children. He proposes explanations for why this might be the case based on the available literature, exploratory interviews, informal conversations with Jewish colleagues active in higher education in France, the UK, the USA, and Israel, and personal reflection. The objective is to feed this reflection into a wider research project involving other Jewish and non-Jewish scholars alike. Klarsfeld then turns to positive arguments in favor of diversity research about Jewishness/Jews/Judaism. The interest of research on Jewishness, Jews, and Judaism for diversity management scholarship in particular is discussed. Some managerial implications for Jews, Jewishness and Judaism are proposed. Avenues for future research questions are offered in the final section.

As a follow-up to this call for contextualized research on Jewishness, Jews, and Judaism in the workplace, Klarsfeld, Bebbington, Kay, Taksa, Guo, and Mendes, in their chapter titled *National Perspectives on Jews at Work: Contrasting Australia, France, Israel, and the UK*, have deliberately chosen to study Jews from national perspectives in countries where they can be considered "privileged" if only by being present in significant numbers. This is in contrast to countries where even small numbers of Jews are hard to find , such as Eastern Europe, the Middle East, and Asia. Each country section attempts to provide a brief history and demographics of Jews in the respective country, data

Introduction: The Complex Interface of Work and Religion 19

on their socioeconomic status and occupations, literature on Jewish experience at the workplace, and challenges and opportunities facing them. Israel aside, authors agree that there is a lack of research on Jewishness, Jews, and Judaism in the workplace in each of their respective countries. A conclusion attempts to place the four states on a continuum ranging from the most "Jewish faith-based" (to use Ewest's typology in this volume) to the most "Jewish faith-avoiding," again in the words of Ewest's framework.

In their chapter, *Hinduism, Religious Diversity, and Spirituality at Work in India*, Sharma and Haq take a dual focus on a particular religion (Hinduism) and on a particular country (India). India is a highly religious and spiritual country where religion constitutes an integral, integrated, and essential part of daily life. Although Hinduism is the dominant religion, Islam, Christianity, and Judaism are also practiced. In addition, India is the birthplace of three other religions: Buddhism, Jainism, and Sikhism. Regardless of which particular religion one follows in India, religious practices and rituals are ubiquitously incorporated into everyday activities and celebrated every day in Indian society. The aim of this chapter is to advance understanding of the complexity of multi-religious and multi-cultural diversity in India and efforts to respectfully accommodate religion in Indian workplaces. It contributes to the literature on religion and spirituality in the workplace by providing insights into Hinduism in particular and its influence on religious diversity in Indian society and workplaces.

Buddhism is followed by numerous individuals around the world and there are many famous individuals associated with this religion. In her chapter titled *Buddhist* Brahmaviharas *and Religious Diversity at Work*, Edwina Pio focuses on Buddhism at work to present the multiple interpretations and heterogeneity in the performance of Buddhist principles at work. The conceptual foundation of the Buddhist *brahmaviharas* or life-affirming organizational possibilities – *metta* or love, *karuna* or compassion, *mudita* or empathy, and *upekkha* or equanimity is presented to create and sustain inclusive and equitable places of work. This is followed by an explication of some of Buddhist beliefs in order to contextualize its practice in the workplace. Work in organizations encompasses aspects such as leadership and decision-making, gender, mindfulness, and enlightened workplaces. In the context of religious diversity, work also embraces how various religions are viewed and how, for example, Buddhism views other religions.

The following chapters are devoted to *regional approaches* to religious diversity: Africa, Europe, North America, and Asia-Pacific.

Africa. The intersection of spirituality and diversity management in the workplace forms a rich location for an investigation into individual and social identity as it relates to the flourishing of human persons and social structures (such as economic entities). In the chapter titled *Spirituality and Workplace Diversity Practices in Africa*, April, Makgoba, and Forster engage this intersectional space from the perspective of African spirituality and the complexity of diversity for Africa and Africans. The notion of spirituality in the workplace is engaged through a literature review that identifies three categories of spirituality relevant for analysis in the African context and beyond: palliative spirituality, via-media spirituality, and transformative spirituality. While palliative spirituality mainly operates at the individual level, via-media spirituality connects the individual with his or her broader religious community, and transformative spirituality distances itself from the imprint of religion. Transformative spirituality pre-supposes a critical stance towards the status quo in society, and confers the will and the energy to act as a change agent within a dysfunctional societal context. Three case studies of African female leaders are provided to explicate a nuanced and textured understanding of the characteristics of these three categories of spirituality for Africans and the African context.

Europe. In their chapter titled *The French Principle of Laïcité and Religious Pluralism in the Workplace: Main Findings and Issues*, devoted to the contested interpretation of secularism in France, Banon and Chanlat argue that the singularly French principle of "laïcité" (a French word meaning "secularism") is often misunderstood abroad. Yet, secularism is well researched and exists to various degrees in most democracies. Public service neutrality leading to restriction of religious expression in the workplace often causes criticism. But are these criticisms justified? What are the motivations behind the French principle of "laïcité"? What does the jurisprudence in France, in Europe, say on this issue? What about the United States and Canada? The authors distinguish two different philosophies, which are arguably complementary. The French model places equality as a precondition of an ethical society, while the United States, Great Britain, and Canada all consider freedom to be a precondition of democracy. This text is based on a comparative analysis of both models, and an analysis of justice decisions in this field. In their conclusion, the authors identify the impact of the "laïcité" principle on a pluralist society, highlighting the risk of a spread of religious-driven companies in coming years. They also highlight the risk of considering "laïcité" as yet another religious belief.

North America. In their chapter *Lessons from the Academy: Concordia College's Journey toward Religious Pluralism*, Bussie and Lelwica define religious pluralism as the intentional and active engagement of religious diversity to positive ends. Concordia College is a small, liberal arts college of the ELCA (Evangelical Lutheran Church in America). Its intentional commitment to fostering interfaith understanding among the college's constituents illustrates how institutions, organizations, and companies can constructively engage religious diversity in the workplace – not only to pre-empt or navigate conflicts that emerge among people who orient to religion differently, but also to harness its creative potential to advance institutional or organizational goals. This case study describes ten deliberate steps Concordia College took in its efforts to promote interfaith literacy and skills for dialogue. Shaped by specific challenges and opportunities in the academy, Concordia's interfaith journey has implications for any organization, business, or institution that seeks to create a workplace that flourishes, not in spite of, but because of religious diversity.

In the chapter titled *Religious Diversity in the Canadian Workplace: The Case of Muslims*, Itani and Sidani tackle the challenges faced by Muslims in the Canadian workplace. Most Muslims belong to the "visible minority" group in Canada. This makes them subject to similar challenges and pressures faced by those belonging to other visible minorities. Yet, recent political events have implications for how Muslims are perceived. This could lead to negative implications in terms of their integration in the workplace. Although Canadian workplaces are generally inclusive and diverse, more so than in other Western countries, some challenges have still been reported. Media reports tell stories of continuous challenges that often differ in intensity and frequency from one Canadian province to another, but also from one degree of affiliation to another. For Muslims who do not show signs of visible religious affiliation or religiosity, things tend to be easier. To those, other problems may emerge that are not particular to their religions or levels of religiosity but relate more to their ethnic origins and skin colors. Specific difficulties pertain to veiled Muslim women because their religious affiliation is clearly detectable.

Implications both for Muslim employees and Canadian employers are explored. Following Berry's (1997) acculturation model, Canadian HR guidelines encourage both employers and employees to mutually understand each other.

Asia Pacific. The chapter *Religious Diversity at Work in the Asia-Pacific Region*, by Pio and Pratt, is dedicated to a vast geographical area spanning 58 countries from Mongolia in the North East to New Zealand in the South West. The area comprises 60% of the global population. The region has been defined as the most religiously diverse geographical area of the globe. Around 80% of the population affiliate with at least one of many faiths, and interacting with persons of different beliefs is increasingly the norm. Having briefly overviewed some of the characteristics of the region, the authors summarize the beliefs of a sample of its religions. Next, they overview some of the recent academic literature that grapples with the integration of different faiths into concerns of residents, such as those related to employment, healthcare, and community participation. Pio and Pratt undertake this review in five countries (Australia, Japan, New Zealand, the Pacific Islands, and South Korea), to find that religious diversity calls into question the distinction between that which is sacred and that which is secular. The chapter concludes by identifying five organizational policies that have relevance in negotiating religious diversity.

Having mapped out specific regional approaches, the next two chapters reflect a more *ethnicity-based angle*, contrasting two Western organizational approaches to the management of religion at the workplace. While the first contribution proposes a typology elaborated in the North American context, the second one proposes a typology conceptualized in the French context, the first of its kind. It is interesting to see how both these typologies overlap and yet present distinctive features.

In his chapter *Organizational Approaches to Religious Diversity in the Workplace*, Ewest presents a religious diversity workplace integration framework building upon those proposed by Ashforth and Pratt (2010), Giacalone and Jurkiewicz (2003), and Mitroff and Denton (1999). The proposed Faith Integration Framework posits four frames to assess how well an organization manages religious diversity. The four frames within the framework are: faith avoiding, faith based, faith safe, and faith friendly. These frames are placed within an assessment rubric assessing organizational policy, religious, or faith accommodation requests, and employee well-being. The chapter also presents two case studies as a means to understand this framework in a diagnostic fashion, and early analyses of empirical data suggesting that the "faith-friendly" approach leads to better individual outcomes for employees of faith.

In the chapter *From Diverse Frameworks to Diverse Attitudes towards Religion at Work: Focus on the French Case*, Galindo and Zannad contend that the expression of religious beliefs has become a shared concern. In the face of these more or less pressing employee expectations, it is important to study how firms can respond to them and what they can base their responses on. They discuss why firms respond in very different ways to their employees' expectations in terms of religious expression. More specifically, Galindo and Zannad investigate the legal and informal foundations upon which companies base their responses. Their research is focused on the French context, and includes a study of 25 managers and of managerial guidelines produced by major French firms for use by their line managers. Based on an analysis of their empirical data, the authors have identified a continuum of three possible corporate responses to religious requests in the French context: acceptance, accommodation, and refusal. Galindo and Zannad suggest that the accommodation approach is becoming the most adopted one. Their framework interestingly complements the previous chapter, as the accommodation approach does bear some similarities with both the faith-safe and the faith-friendly approaches proposed by Ewest. Their investigation of the different levels of analysis (legal, organizational, and individual) shows the limitations of each level taken alone and also the difficulty of reconciling them.

Finally, the last chapter brings the different elements of diversity and religion together. Titled *Resilient Leadership and Tempered Radicalism: Navigating the Intersections of Race, Gender, Nationality, and Religion*, it takes a first person approach by using an auto-ethnographic methodology to provide insights on how religion (here, the Christian faith) can act as a resource for individuals faced with stereotyping, prejudice, and discrimination. Ngunjiri and Hernandez use collaborative auto-ethnography to interrogate their experiences at the nexus of race, ethnicity, gender, nationality, and religion. As immigrant black faculty in predominantly white institutions in the USA, the authors employ their religious identity and deep spirituality in navigating the racist, sexist, and ethnocentric micro-aggressions directed at them. They do this not only to survive, but to thrive and be productive academic leaders acting as tempered radicals. Their religious identity and transformative (April et al., in this volume) spiritual practices are critical to their ability to perform effectively as professors, leaders, and agents of change, as they advocate for more just social arrangements for themselves and other minorities in their institutional contexts. Table 0.1 offers a summary of regions, religions, spiritualities, and theoretical categories covered in various chapters in this book.

Concluding Thoughts

This book is unique in terms of its emphasis on religion, in addition to the Anglo-American view on spirituality and faith, without setting religion aside as divisive. Much of the extant literature is about spirituality at work; Hicks (2002), for example, says religion is inappropriate in organizations, Mitrof and Denton (1999) talk about managers' discomfort with religion. It is important to recognize that people do bring their religious values to work, and that can be either a source of positive performance or negative conflicts. The various social conflicts around religion are not limited to their impacts on societies and communities; they also have an impact on the world of organizations. Miller (2007) argues that the "anti-religion" sentiments tend to be based on the perception that religion can be neatly separated from the "more acceptable/palatable" spirituality, ignoring the fact that for most people, the two are intimately intertwined and inseparable. Thus where authors urge the "unifying" element of spiritual values, they fail adequately to take into consideration that religions can have unifying values too … as well as discordant practices that cause conflict. So, focusing on religion is timely and necessary because religious identity is salient for a majority of the world's populations (salient enough to be a source of conflict if people feel that this part of their identity is being disrespected).

Taken together, the chapters in this volume offer the reader a wide variety of theoretical frameworks, research approaches, and practical implications for the role of religion in social and organizational life – whether it is seen as a cause of conflict or a source for enhancing performance. One can deduce that the best way to engage with the question of religion in the workplace is to use a positive approach,

Table 0.1 *The book at a glance: Regions, religions/spiritualities, and theoretical categories of the chapters*

Author/s and chapter title	Country or region	Religion and/or spirituality	Theoretical categories
0. Syed, Klarsfeld, Ngunjiri, & Härtel: Introduction: The Complex Interplay of Work and Religion	NA	NA	Overview of the book and explanation of its focus and key themes
1. Syed: A Relational Perspective on Religious Diversity at Work	NA	NA	Macro-national level, meso-organizational level, micro-individual level
2. Härtel, Härtel, & Ramburuth: Religious Diversity, Identity, and Workplace Inclusion	NA	Indigenous	Paradox theory, relational knowledge in indigenous spiritualities
3. Ewest: The Christian Faith and the Preservation of Personal Identity	NA	Christianity	Normative ethical behavior; Christian ethical behavior
4. Ali: An Islamic View of Diversity: Implications for the Business World	NA	Islam	Goodness-generosity, moderation, public interest
5. Klarsfeld: The Untold, the Unseen, and the Forgettable: Jewishness, Jews, and Judaism in Diversity Management Scholarship	NA	Judaism	Mending the world, Mosaic leadership, workplace justice, full strength engagement

(*cont.*)

Table 0.1 (*cont.*)

Author/s and chapter title	Country or region	Religion and/or spirituality	Theoretical categories
6. Klarsfeld, Bebbington, Kay, Taksa, Guo, & Mendes: National Perspectives on Jews at Work: Contrasting Australia, France, Israel, and the UK	Australia, France, Israel, UK	Judaism	Jewish-based, Jewish-safe, Jewish-avoiding (see also Ewest's organizational approaches chapter)
7. Sharma & Haq: Hinduism, Religious Diversity, and Spirituality at Work in India	India	Hinduism, Islam, Jainism, Sikhism, Parsi	Integration of faith and work, Indian secularism
8. Pio: Buddhist *Brahmaviharas* and Religious Diversity at Work	NA	Buddhism	Love, compassion, empathy, equanimity
9. April, Makgoba & Forster: Spirituality and Workplace Diversity Practices in Africa	Africa	Spirituality, Religion, Christianity	Palliative spirituality, via-media spirituality, transformative spirituality
10. Banon & Chanlat: The French Principle of Laïcité and Religious Pluralism in the Workplace: Main Findings and Issues	Europe and North America	Christianity, Islam, Judaism, Sikhism	French secularism or "laïcité," freedom vs equality, living together or "vivre-ensemble"

11. Bussie & Lelwica: Lessons from the Academy: Concordia College's Journey Toward Religious Pluralism	USA	Multiple religions	Religious pluralism in higher education and 10 steps to achieve it
12. Itani & Sidani: Religious Diversity in the Canadian Workplace: The Case of Muslims	Canada	Islam	Integration strategy in Berry's (1997) acculturation framework
13. Pio & Pratt: Religious Diversity at Work in the Asia-Pacific Region	Australia, Japan, New Zealand, Pacific Islands, South Korea	Buddhism, Christianity, Islam, Sikhism, Zoroastrianism	Religious pluralism
14. Ewest: Organizational Approaches to Religious Diversity in the Workplace	Western countries (USA focus)	NA	Faith-avoiding, faith-safe, faith-friendly, faith-based
15. Galindo & Zannad: From Diverse References to Diverse Attitudes towards Religion at Work: Focus on the French Case	Western countries (France focus)	NA	Refusal, accommodation, acceptance as corporate responses to religious requests
16. Ngunjiri & Hernandez: Resilient Leadership and Tempered Radicalism: Navigating the Intersections of Race, Gender, Nationality, and Religion	US immigrant perspectives (Kenya, Trinidad and Tobago)	Christianity	Tempered radicalism, resilient leadership

whether it is basic accommodation or more proactively determining how best to become religion-friendly (or faith-friendly, as per Ewest in this volume), while at the same time providing a common ground of rules for "living together" (Banon & Chanlat in this volume). Those organizations that are proactively friendly to religion craft appropriate policies and create structures that enable people who affiliate with religion, as well as those who don't, to bring all of who they are to the workplace, including their religious identity (Ewest, this volume; Morgan, 2016), without imposing undue hardship on their employers and colleagues (Berry, 1997; Itani and Sidani in this volume). In the ever-increasingly diverse globalized world and pluralistic organizational context, it is imperative to make room for religious diversity, and it is possible to do so while at the same time preserving common values. Some have suggested that this is the era for religious diversity management, just as previous eras have involved women in the workplace, minorities in the workplace, and LGBTQ in organizations (Miller & Ewest, 2013).

One of the implications that we can draw from these chapters is the continued need for conceptual and empirical studies of religious diversity in organizations. As far as diversity and inclusion studies go, religious diversity appears to receive the least amount of focus in the literature (King, 2008; King et al., 2009). Yet, again as demonstrated through these chapters, this is an area that can either be a source of conflict or provide the possibility for enhanced performance. The more studies that can be published in the area, the better informed both scholars and practitioners can be on best practices for managing this type of diversity.

We are concluding this chapter at the end of the most contentious election (2016) the United States has seen in recent memory; one where the newly elected president chose to use language that pitted all kinds of minorities – racial, religious, ethnic, ability, and even gender – against the white, male majority, and apparently won the election on that platform. Much remains to be seen as to how the aftermath of this election will play out within the United States, and in US-global relations, particularly with Muslim-majority countries. Mr Trump has suggested that Muslims in the USA should be registered – with some suggesting that the internment of Japanese-Americans after World War II serves as the precedent. Indeed, not unlike his predecessors, he fails to distinguish the majority of peaceful Sunni and Shia

Muslims from the violent Salafi, Wahhabi, and Deobandi militants who are responsible for almost all incidents of Islamist violence and terrorism in the USA and elsewhere in recent decades. In this kind of climate that adds fuel to the fire of the many terror attacks experienced around the globe, it is imperative that scholars provide some way, some direction, as to how to better manage diversity, how to create organizations and societies that are truly inclusive, and most urgently, how religion and religious identities can be a source of personal meaning as well as organizational and social cohesion rather than conflict. This volume could not be any more timely.

References

Alesina, A., Devleeschauwer, A., Easterly, W., Kurlat, S., Wacziarg, R. (2002). *Fractionalization*. Harvard Institute of Economic Research Discussion Paper.

Alliance Bank (2014). Annual report. *Alliance Financial Group Berhad*. Retrieved from: www.alliancebank.com.my/images/AFGB_AR2014/files/assets/common/downloads/AFGB%20AR2014.pdf.

Allport, G. (1954). *The nature of prejudice*. Cambridge, MA: Perseus Books Ltd.

Ashforth, B. E., & Pratt, M. G. (2010). Institutionalized spirituality: An oxymoron? *In* R. A. Giacalone & C. L. Jurkiewicz (eds.). *Handbook of workplace spirituality and organizational performance*. Armonk: M. E. Sharpe, 93–107.

Baldas, T. (2015). Workplace bias complaints pour in from Michigan Muslims. *Religion News*, December 27. Retrieved from: http://religionnews.com/2015/12/27/workplace-bias-complaints-pour-in-from-michigan-muslims.

Bendl, R., Bleijenbergh, I., Henttonen, E., & Mills, A. (2015). *The Oxford handbook of diversity in organizations*. Oxford: Oxford University Press.

Berry, J. W. (1997). Immigration, acculturation, and adaptation. *Applied Psychology*, 46(1), 5–34.

Bouma, G., Haidar, A., Nyland, C., & Smith, W. (2003). Work, religious diversity and Islam. *Asia Pacific Journal of Human Resources*, 41(1), 51–61.

Byrd, M., & Scott, C. (2014). *Diversity in the workplace: Current issues and emerging trends*. London: Routledge.

Chang, H., Ngunjiri, F., & Hernandez, K. A. C. (2013). *Collaborative authoethnography*. Walnut Creek, CA: Left Coast Press.

Chapman, G., White, P., & Myra, H. (2014). *Rising above a toxic workplace: Taking care of yourself in an unhealthy environment.* Chicago, IL: Northfield Publishing.

Chia, A., & Lim, A. (2010). Singapore: Equality, harmony and fair employment. *In* Klarsfeld, A. (ed.), *International handbook on diversity management at work: Country perspectives on diversity and equal treatment.* Cheltenham: Edward Elgar Publishing, 198–214.

Chickering, A. W., Dalton, J. C., & Stamm, L. S. (2006). *Encouraging authenticity and spirituality in higher education.* San Francisco, CA: John Wiley and Sons.

Cho, S., Crenshaw, K. W., & Mccall, L. (2013). Toward a field of intersectionality studies: Theory, applications, and praxis. *Signs,* 38, 785–810.

Christerson, B., & Emerson, M. (2003). The costs of diversity in religious organizations: An in-depth case study. *Sociology of Religion,* 64(2), 163–81.

Chua, A. (2004). *World on fire: How exporting free market democracy breeds ethnic hatred and global instability.* New York: Anchor books.

Collins, P. H. (2004). Learning from the outsider-within: The sociological significance of black feminist thought. *In* Harding, S., *The feminist standpoint theory reader: Intellectual and political controversies.* New York and London: Routledge, 103–26.

Crossman, J. E. (2015). Being on the outer: The risks and benefits of spiritual self-disclosure in the Australian workplace. *Journal of Management & Organization,* 21(6), 772–85.

Donnelly, K. (2017). "Religious identity is explicitly not left at the school gate" – Minister pledges strong support for community national schools. *The Independent,* January 27. Retrieved from: www.independent.ie/irish-news/education/religious-identity-is-explicitly-not-left-at-the-school-gate-minister-pledges-strong-support-for-community-national-schools-35402891.html.

Fry, L. (2013). Spiritual leadership and faith and spirituality in the workplace. *In* J. Neal (ed.), *Handbook of faith and spirituality in the workplace*: New York: Springer, 697–704.

Gebert, D., Boerner, S., Kearney, E., King Jr., J. Zhang, K., & Song, L. (2014). Expressing religious identities in the workplace: Analyzing a neglected diversity dimension. *Human Relations,* 67(5), 543–63.

Giacalone, R. A., & Jurkiewicz, C. L. (2003). *Handbook of workplace spirituality and organizational performance.* Armonk, NY: M.E. Sharpe.

Greenleaf, R. (1977). *Servant leadership.* Mahwah, NJ: Paulist Press.

Gröschl, S. (2016). *Diversity in the workplace: Multi-disciplinary and international perspectives.* London: Gower.

Gröschl, S., & Bendl, R. (2013). *Managing religious diversity in the workplace*. Farnham: Gower.
Hambler, A. (2015). Managing workplace religious expression within the legal constraints. *Employee Relations*, 38(3), 406–19.
Hecht, M. L., & Faulkner, S. L. (2000). Sometimes Jewish, sometimes not. *Communication Studies*, 51(4), 372–87.
Hernández, T. K. (2008). The Intersectionality of lived experience and anti-discrimination empirical research. *In* Nielsen, L. B., & Nelson, R. L. (eds.), *Handbook of Employment Discrimination Research*. Springer New York: Springer, 325–35.
Hicks, D. A. (2002). Spiritual and religious diversity in the workplace: Implications for leadership. *The Leadership Quarterly*, 13(4), 379–96.
Holvino, E. (2010). Intersections: The simultaneity of race, gender and class in organization studies. *Gender, Work & Organization*, 17, 248–77.
Karakas, F. (2010). Spirituality and performance in organizations: A literature review. *Journal of Business Ethics*, 94(1), 89–106. doi:10.1007/s10551-009-0251-5.
Kaur, G. (2015). Abercrombie religious discrimination case less than cool for supreme court, Sikh Americans. *The Huffington Post*, February 3. Retrieved from: http://www.huffingtonpost.com/gurjot-kaur/abercrombie-religious-discrimination_b_6772732.html.
King, J. E. (2008). (Dis)Missing the obvious: Will mainstream management research ever take religion seriously? *Journal of Management Inquiry*, 17(3), 214–24. doi:10.1177/1056492608314205.
King, J. E., Bell, M. P., & Lawrence, E. (2009). Religion as an aspect of workplace diversity: An examination of the US context and a call for international research. *Journal of Management, Spirituality & Religion*, 6(1), 43–57. doi:10.1080/14766080802648631.
Kirton, G., & Greene, A. (2015). *The dynamics of managing diversity: A critical approach*. London: Routledge.
Low, K. C. P., & Mohd Zain, A. Y. (January 8–9, 2008). Creating the competitive edge, the father leadership way. *Paper presented in the international conference on business and management*. Brunei Darussalam: Universiti Brunei Darussalam.
Mathis, R., Jackson, J., & Valentine, S. (2016). *Human resource management: Essential perspective*. Boston, MA: Cengage Learning.
McKim, R. (2001). *Religious ambiguity and religious diversity*. Oxford: Oxford University Press.
  (2012). *On religious diversity*. Oxford: Oxford University Press.
Meister, C. V. (2010). *The Oxford handbook of religious diversity*. Oxford: Oxford University Press.

Messarra, L. (2014). Religious diversity at work: The perceptual effects of religious discrimination on employee engagement and commitment. *Contemporary Management Research*, 10(1), 59–80.

Miller, D. W. (2007). *God at work: The history and promise of the faith at work movement.* Oxford: Oxford University Press.

Miller, D., & Ewest, T. (2013). The integration box (TIB): An individual and institutional faith, religion, and spirituality at work assessment tool. In Neal, J. (ed.), *Handbook of faith and spirituality in the workplace.* New York: Springer, 403–17.

Mitroff, I., & Denton, E. (1999). *A spiritual audit of corporate America: A hard look at spirituality, religion, and values in the workplace.* San Francisco, CA: Jossey-Bass Inc.

Moodie, A. (2016). Are US businesses doing enough to support religious diversity in the workplace? *The Guardian*, January 28. Retrieved from: www.theguardian.com/sustainable-business/2016/jan/28/religious-diversity-us-business-muslim-hijab-discrimination-equal-employment-eeoc.

Mor Barak, M. (2014). *Managing diversity: Toward a globally inclusive workplace.* London: Sage Publications.

Morgan, J. F. (2016). Faith (re)engages with business: Cultural, legal, and managerial dimensions. *International Journal of Law and Management*, 58(4), 444–67. doi:10.1108/IJLMA-08-2015-0048.

Neal, J. (2013). *Handbook of faith and spirituality in the workplace: Emerging research and practice.* New York: Springer.

Paloutzian, R. F., & Park, C. L. (2013). *Handbook of the psychology of religion and spirituality.* New York: The Guilford Press.

Pew Research Center. (2012). Global diversity landscape, December 18. Retrieved from: www.pewforum.org/2012/12/18/global-religious-landscape-exec/.

(2014). Global religious diversity, April 4. Retrieved from: www.pewforum.org/2014/04/04/global-religious-diversity.

Pigott, R. (2013). British Airways Christian employee Nadia Eweida wins case. *BBC News*, January 15. Retrieved from: www.bbc.co.uk/news/uk-21025332.

Reuters (2016). Religious extremism is spreading to inland China: Official. *Reuters*, November 28. Retrieved from: www.reuters.com/article/us-china-security-xinjiang-idUSKBN13N12P.

Rosh, L., & Offermann, L. (2013). Be yourself, but carefully, *Harvard Business Review*, October. Retrieved from: www.hbr.org/2013/10/be-yourself-but-carefully/ar/1.

Schwartz, S. (2011). Islamic Sufism and Jewish Kabbalah: Shining a light on their hidden history. *The Huffington Post*, October 10. Retrieved from: www.huffingtonpost.com/stephen-schwartz/sufism-and-kabbalah_b_989875.html.

SHRM (2015). Accommodating religion, belief, and spirituality in the workplace. Retrieved from: www.shrm.org/resourcesandtools/tools-and-samples/toolkits/pages/accommodating-religion,-belief-and-spirituality-in-the-workplace.aspx.
Syed, J., & Ozbilgin, M. (2015). *Managing diversity and inclusion*. London: SAGE Publications.
Syed, J., Pio, E., Kamran, T., & Zaidi, A. (2016). *Faith-based violence and Deobandi militancy in Pakistan*. Basingstoke: Palgrave Macmillan.
Tilley, T. W. (2007). *Religious diversity and the American experience: A theological approach*. London: Bloomsbury.
Wiggins, J. (1996). *In praise of religious diversity*. New York: Routledge.
Yasmeen, S., & Markovic, N. (2014). *Muslims citizens in the West: Spaces and agents of inclusion and exclusion*. Surrey: Ashgate Publishing Ltd.
Yoshino, K., & Smith, C. (2013). *Uncovering talent, a new model of inclusion*. New York: Deloitte University.
Yoshino, K., Smith, C. (2014). Fear of being different stifles talent, *Harvard Business Review*, March. Retrieved from: http://hbr.org/2014/03/fear-of-being-different-stifles-talent/ar/1.

PART I

General Frameworks and Sources of Reflection

1 A Relational Perspective on Religious Diversity at Work

JAWAD SYED

Introduction

This chapter offers a relational, multilevel perspective on theorizing and managing religious diversity at work. It explains that in order to understand and manage religious diversity in organizations, a holistic approach is needed which takes into account the macro-national, meso-organizational, and micro-individual level factors that are often interrelated and overlapping. At the macro-national level, the chapter highlights the implications of socio-cultural context, laws, and demography on approaches to religious diversity. At the organizational level, it takes into account issues such as organizational vision and culture, allocation of resources, and procedures. At the individual level, it considers issues of individual identity, intersectionality, and agency.

Religious Diversity at Work

The term religious diversity refers to "distinct faith traditions and their internal variations found within a country" (Beckford, 2012, p. 111). In the context of workplace, it refers to diverse beliefs and faith practices of employees (Basinger, 2012; Furness & Gilligan, 2014). Mainly due to immigration and other demographic changes, the workforce in developed or industrialized countries is becoming more diverse in terms of religious and cultural backgrounds. Increasingly, policymakers and leaders around the globe are realizing the need to attend to the potential challenges and opportunities that religious diversity may offer to individuals, organizations, and communities. Often, political and socio-cultural attitudes infiltrate the organizational domain thus replicating societal stereotypes and othering of the minority communities. Within organizations, individuals may suffer from refined or blatant discrimination, which may affect their well-being and performance (Böhm et al., 2014; Day, 2005). At the same time, religious diversity also has a business case, which means that if properly managed, it may add value to organizations in terms of skill, innovation, marketing, customer service, etc. Indeed, the workplace can and should provide a forum for inclusion and the overcoming of identity-based differences (Allport, 1979), thus improving employees' well-being and enabling a productive environment.

This chapter seeks to develop a relational, multilevel approach to religious diversity, taking into account not only an ethical and social responsibility rationale but also a business performance rationale. There is support for a relational perspective not only in the literature on management and organizations but also in fields as diverse as sociology, psychology, culture, and religion.

In the context of culture and psychology, Erez and Gati (2004) argue that culture comprises structural and dynamic characteristics that explain the interplay between various levels of culture. The structural dimension represents the nested structure of culture from the most macro level of a global culture, through national, organizational, and team cultures, and down to the individual level. The dynamic nature of culture conveys the top-down and bottom-up processes where one level affects changes in other levels. Specifically, Erez and Gati argue, globalization affects, through top-down processes, behavioral changes of members in various cultures. Reciprocally, behavioral changes at the individual level, through bottom-up processes, become shared behavioral norms and values, modifying the culture of teams, organizations, and societies.

The above theorization is similar to Giddens' (1984) structuration theory, which seeks to reconcile the long-standing divisions between two differing perspectives held by social theorists. Giddens argues that structuralists and functionalists have provided macro-level explanations of social behavior in terms of structural forces that limit individual's capability to do things in their own way, while studies focusing on the individual as the salient factor (hermeneutics, phenomenology) explain the social life by generally ignoring the influence of external entities. Giddens argues that both perspectives are interlinked, in that social life is neither simply a micro-level activity nor can it be studied by purely macro-level approaches. He refers to this balancing of agency and structure as the duality of structure.

In a similar fashion, theorizations about religion or secularism are based on three levels (Tschannen, 1991), i.e., social differentiation at the macro-level, the decline or contested role of religion in organizations at the meso-level, and differences in levels of practice, belief, or affiliation at the micro-level. More often than not, influences, practices, and perceptions from one level permeate into other levels, thus creating a multi-layered and interconnected phenomenon. Next, a detailed discussion on each level of analysis is offered.

Macro-level

Globalization and immigration have an important role in shaping religious and racial diversity in societies and workplaces (Dolansky & Alon, 2008). Accordingly, religion has an important role in both public and private sector organizations. The role of religion in employment and other domains of life has been a topic of numerous studies and debates. Durkheim (1964) suggested that the social division of labor and the resulting social differentiation would lead to the separation of religious and secular realms. He posited that gradually the collective conscience generated by religious participation would erode, and the functions performed by religion would be taken over by secular institutions, such as the nation-state, education system, and industry (Wallwork, 1984). Weber (1958) argued that the increasing dominance of instrumental rationality in economic and political institutions would eventually enable the eclipse of religious reason. Marx saw religion a repressive, ideological system for the justification and perpetuation of class domination, arguing that with the advancement of class-consciousness and materialism, religion would disappear (McKinnon, 2005).

Despite the ascendancy of secularism in recent centuries and the corresponding church-state separation, at least some of the mechanisms proposed by secularization theorists seem to remain obscure, and the evidence in practice is somewhat sketchy. For example, indicators of secularization (such as faith-based regulations, provisions, or norms) may be high in some modern societies, e.g. in Western Europe, but lower in others such as the USA. Similarly, some countries that are far less developed than the Western industrial democracies are more irreligious, e.g., the Czech Republic and Estonia (Pew Research Center, 2012). Berger (1967) acknowledges that we live in an age of exuberant religiosity, not secularization. Indeed, some social scientists have been proposing the religious economy model, taking into account the influence of religion in everyday life including work and beyond.

Scholars have identified the influence of church-state institutions on secular institutions across societies (Roccas & Schwartz, 1997). Political mobilization on the basis of religion is often triggered by the efforts of political elites to extend governmental authority into domains previously organized by religious organizations. Indeed, state regulation or penetration into areas once dominated by religion has, historically, provoked conflict and contentions (Knill & Preidel 2015; Koterski, 2011).

In their discussion of Religious Market Theory, Stark and Bainbridge (1985) argue that there will always be a demand for religion, and when real rewards are not available, people turn to religion for metaphysical rewards, such as promises of paradise. Stark and Bainbridge suggest that religion in several countries across Europe is declining because of domination of one religion, i.e., Christianity comprising Catholic and Protestant traditions. They argue that a greater variety of religion may result in an improvement in the services that religions offer and in turn may lead to greater religiosity.

The economics of religion uses socioeconomic theory to explain the religious behavior patterns of individuals, groups, and communities and the social consequences of such patterns. An example of religious behavior patterns is Adam Smith's analysis of the effect of competition and government regulation of religion on the quantity and quality of religious services (Anderson, 1988). An example of social consequences is Max Weber's (1958) thesis that the Protestant ethic promoted the rise of capitalism.

The economics of religion implies that religion will be more vibrant where it is less regulated and hence more competitive. However, Chaves and Cann (1992) argue that the hypothesis is weakened by the use of religious pluralism as a proxy measure for the extent to which the religious market is subsidized or regulated. In their study on the regulation of religious markets in 18 Western democracies, the authors provide strong support for the connection between religious competitiveness and vitality. Their study shows that the relationship between subsidized religion and religious participation holds in both Protestant and Catholic countries, and its explanatory power is far superior to that of religious pluralism alone.

From an economic and labor market perspective, forces for or opposed to certain or all religions can also influence employability and equal opportunity. Indeed, it is important to consider the negative impact that social and institutional perceptions and stereotyping may have upon individual employability and expected performance (Ghumman & Jackson, 2010). Religious discrimination refers to those prejudiced behaviors that are experienced by employees on the grounds of their religious belief, including stereotypes and assumptions, such as those of being fanatics, barbaric, terrorists, followers of demon and evil, and oppressors of women (Ghumman & Jackson, 2010). The issue encompasses the concern that employees may be ridiculed, discriminated against, or segregated on the basis of their religious identity or practices (Armitage, 2007). The complexity of stereotyping in the workplace confirms the need to tackle this issue adopting a multilevel approach (Syed & Kramar, 2009).

In terms of the overlapping and inter-related nature of the multiple levels, the macro-level influence of social dimensions of stigma on individual identity at the micro-level is crucial, given that such influences can change through decades and generations of interventions (Beatty & Kirby, 2006). With a few exceptions where markers are obvious, such as the kippah and hijab, religion may be generally categorized among invisible yet stigmatized dimensions of diversity. At the meso-level, the consequences of social stigma may include increased stereotyping and levels of stress and anxiety, difficulties in terms of employment and career progression, isolation, and increased levels of labor turnover (Clair et al., 2005). The neglect of such issues may reinforce interpersonal discrimination and frictions in the workplace, having important costs such as the loss of talent due to disengagement and employee turnover (Muñoz & Thomas, 2006).

Religious stereotypes continue to exist and continue to affect people's behaviors and attitudes. For example, Catholic individuals may be stereotyped as being homophobic. Adverse stereotypes may also exist against other religions, e.g., Jews may be perceived as hoarders, which may be explained by their history. Islam is arguably the strongest religious stereotype; perhaps most commonly discriminated against in recent years, especially since the 9/11 terror attacks in America. Islam currently suffers from a negative reputation as being a religion of hatred, violence, and women's oppression. This prejudice, hatred, or fear of Muslims or of ethnic groups perceived to be Muslim may be referred to as "Islamophobia." Islamophobia is the fear or dread of Islam or Muslims (Abbas, 2004). There are many stereotypes about Muslims, e.g., commonly held assumption that all Muslims are intolerant or violent. The media can be accused of Islamophobia and antisemitism as it is a large source of information that can spread the stereotype and discrimination worldwide.

Also it is important to consider the historical and colonial influences on religious and sectarian divisions and vilifications. It is, for example, a fact that antisemitism was exported to parts of Asia, Africa, and Latin American as a result of deeply anti-Jewish prejudices of British, Spanish, Portuguese, and other colonial powers. The British policies of divide and rule can also be used to explain the Hindu-Muslim communal violence and hatred during and after the British Raj in South Asia. Similarly, the usual representations of Muslims in media and academic scholarship ignore their internal heterogeneity, and at times misleading binaries such as Sunni vs. Shia are invoked, ignoring or obfuscating the fact that from South Asia to Middle East and from Europe to North America, almost all incidents of Islamist terrorism are the handiwork of Salafi (Wahhabi) and Deobandi militants who have spared no community including Sunni, Shia, Christian, Jew, and atheist from their violence.

Cross-nationally, the treatment of people with different religious beliefs or values varies dramatically. The perpetrator of faith-based discrimination in one country may be the sufferer in another country. Accordingly, it is a challenge for organizations as well as governments to stop discrimination or harassment and overcome adverse stereotypes to develop a productive and harmonious workforce.

Legislation is a common intervention used by countries to address faith based and other forms of discrimination. The number of lawsuits concerning religious discrimination is increasing exponentially as employees believe that they cannot express or practice their religion freely in their workplace (Borstorff & Arlington, 2011). For example, in the UK, the Equality Act 2010 protects individuals from being discriminated against, harassed, or victimized due to their religious beliefs or rational beliefs (EDF, 2010). However, while members of all religions are protected by the Equality Act 2010, there are still reports of religious discrimination and stereotyping.

In the USA, the federal law agency, the Equal Employment Opportunity Commission (EEOC), has created guidelines for religious expression and accommodation at work. It has provided recommendations on how to deal with religious expression in a correct manner and how to avoid discrimination against people's religion (Bell, 2011).

However, the decision to promote religious diversity in the workplace may be conflictive given that the historic complexity of patriarchal norms underpinning certain religious practices may result in indirect, direct, and perceived hostilities towards other disadvantaged groups such as women, LGBT individuals, and people of color (Whitman & Bidell, 2014).

Meso-level

The macro-societal perceptions and attitudes of religion also permeate into the organizational space. For example, based on her study of the impact of religion and ethnicity on employment and earnings in the UK, Lindley (2002) examines whether religious divisions have a greater impact on employment and earnings than being a member of a particular ethnic group. She notes that using conventional ethnic group classifications does not capture important differences within nationalities, e.g., between Indian Sikhs and Hindus, as well as between Muslims and the other religious groups. However, after controlling for religion, substantial ethnic labor market disadvantage is still apparent. Lindley's study indicates a substantial disadvantage to Muslims, relative to all other non-whites, which can be at least partially described as "pure Islamic penalty," i.e., faith-based discrimination.

A number of institutional interventions, regulations and guidelines in the shape of labor laws and business guidelines shape the way religious diversity is treated and managed in the workplace, for example, the extent to which religious discrimination is even acknowledged in employment regulations and the mechanism for redress.

In several countries, employers are legally required to accommodate religious expression in the workplace. Indeed workers expect more from their job than just a salary, e.g., freedom to express and practice their cultural and faith identity (Kelly, 2008). Moreover, managers who are able to understand and accommodate diverse religions and beliefs have the ability to form a motivated and diverse workforce. Indeed, some religions differ in their dietary needs, worship, and clothing appearance. For example, Muslims are forbidden to eat pork and to drink alcohol, whereas some practicing Jews may not eat anything that is not kosher (XpertHR, 2014).

Reasonable accommodation may be defined as a "mechanism of response by employers to employees' request for flexibility in relation to their religious practices" (Beaman, 2012, p. 2). This constitutes a legal duty in the USA and Canada, whilst in the UK the Equality Act 2010 does not impose a similar legal duty apart from the case of disability, which warrants reasonable adjustment (Kumra & Manfredi, 2012). The key areas to cover for accommodating religious practices in the workplace may include time of prayers, diet, and fasting, holy festivals, and dress (CMI (Charted Management Institute), 2012).

A survey in the UK has shown that managers usually tend to hire workers with similar characteristic backgrounds to their own (Roberts, 2014). This may lead to a decrease in hiring talented workers of different religious backgrounds, which is a lose-lose situation, not only for the diverse workers but also for the employer.

Religious diversity at work may also pose a dilemma, such as the extent to which employers can allow employees' needs of religious expression without disregarding other stakeholders' interests (Adams, 2012). For example, proselytizing (tabligh or dawa in Arabic) in the workplace may be perceived as harassment and disparate treatment by other religious and atheist employees (Ghumman et al., 2013; Olasky 2003). Traditionally, discussing religion in the workplace has been considered to be a taboo (Morgan, 2005). However, with a diverse workforce, there is no escaping this topic.

In the UK context, a British Airways (BA) employee, Nadia Eweida, was dismissed from her job for wearing a Christian cross on a necklace (Newcombe, 2013). It took almost seven years for Eweida to have the dismissal revoked. In the aftermath of this case, BA revised their dress code by allowing all employees to reveal any religious symbols or jewelry on their uniform (Bowcot, 2013). However, religion is still considered one of the most sensitive topics to discuss openly in the workplace (Newcombe, 2013).

In contrast, there are cases where it is considered acceptable for employers to take a stand on official uniform if it is supported by a strong reason. An example of this is the case of a National Health Service (NHS) nurse, Sherly Chaplin, who wanted to wear crosses as dangling earrings. However, the case was dismissed as NHS policies prohibit any kind of jewelry, due to risks of infection (Brown, 2013).

In the USA, the EEOC has supported several cases against religious discrimination. For example, one of the cases discussed was how two employees of telecommunications company American Telephone & Telegraph (AT&T) were unlawfully dismissed for attending the

Convention of Jehovah's Witnesses, a three-day course related to their religion. The two workers had attended the convention in previous years in the same company. They were denied permission for leave even after submitting an application six months in advance; they were suspended and later on discharged for attending the function (Bell, 2011).

Micro-level

Scholars suggest that the best way to deal with religious diversity is to develop a nuanced understanding of faith, the variety of individual practice, and how faith intersects with other forms of individual identity (Banton, 2011). Employers ought to take into account the heterogeneity of their employees and allow flexibility to accommodate certain religious needs. For example, a Muslim worker who fasts in the month of Ramadan from dawn to sundown may be relieved an hour earlier in exchange for work during their lunch break (Mooney, 2013).

Also it is important to consider individual agency and discretion in believing in and practicing or not practicing a faith. While some choices may not be readily available given the restrictions on women and LGBT individuals in conservative faith-based communities, in most industrialized countries, a greater level of individual freedom and choice is available. Thus, bracketing all people of a certain faith into one category may not be advisable. Similarly the visible expression or practice of faith, e.g., kippah or hijab, may reveal the religious identity of the individual, making her or him vulnerable to discrimination.

Also it is important to examine and highlight examples of success, i.e., members of diverse faith and minority ethnic groups including women who use their agency, unique skills and coping strategies to overcome the multilevel challenges in the way of their careers.

It is not only the people of faith or minority faith who may face discrimination or harassment at work; atheists, too, may be victims due to their non-belief. In faith-dominated societies, attitudes towards non-believers or atheists are usually negative. According to one estimate, 85% of people in the USA are part of a religious group, leaving the remainder as non-believers (Bell, 2011). Atheists may be seen as a small minority in contrast to religious people, and be recipients of negative attitudes (Cragun et al., 2012). Workers who identify themselves as atheists may have issues with their employers or coworkers who are considered to be somewhat religious, as it immediately creates issues of judgment, as atheists not only have no religion, but also doubt the existence of "God" (Cragun et al., 2012). Similar challenges may also arise between other groups. For example, a worker in HP (Hewlett Packard, a multinational information technology firm) filed a lawsuit against the firm where he alleged that it targeted Christian workers to forcefully accept homosexuality by displaying related posters. He stated that the firm had been treating him differently as they had not accommodated his beliefs in a reasonable manner (Bell, 2011).

In terms of intersectionality, it is important to consider that persons of religion, like all other persons, have multiple and intersecting identities. Often religion is intertwined with ethnicity, thus making it difficult neatly to differentiate religion-based tensions from ethnic tensions, as is the case for Jews, whose identities can be religious or non-religious (Hecht & Faulkner, 2000). Ethnicity interacts with religion, particularly in contexts where the majority ethnic group of the population shares the same religious background.

There is also the issue of how religion intersects with gender or/ and class, thus adding up to the complex and multilayered nature of discrimination and intolerance in the society and the workplace. For example, a blue-collar Muslim worker may be relatively more drained of energy during fasting in Ramadan than one who works in an office (Mooney, 2013).

Bender et al. (2012) highlight the important of considering religious self-constitution as a relational and embodied process. Such a consideration helps in decentering the emphasis on belief in the commonly used category of the religious self, and recenters it on an approach that studies the self as an embodied process contextualized in ongoing social relations. Bender et al.'s study suggests that there is a need to consider multiple dimensions of the embodied space in which religious selves develop: the importance of collective practice, the relation to the body, and the engagement with the material environment.

Country Example: Religious Diversity in the UK

The UK has "one of the most religiously diverse populations in the European Union" (Purdam et al., 2007, p. 147). According to 2011 census, the following is the faith-wise break-up of the country's population: Christianity (59.5%), Islam (4.4%), and Hinduism (1.3%). Moreover, 25.7% indicated that they had no religious belief, whereas 7.2% did not state their religion or did not respond. A significant change that the country has experienced is an increase in the population reporting no religion, a decrease in percentage of Christians and an increase in percentage of Muslims (ONS (Office for National Statistics), 2012). An awareness of current demographics is important to understand the complexity involved in accommodating religious practices in the workplace (Farnham, 2010).

Before the Equality Act 2010, the main legislation in the field was the Employment Equality (Religion and Belief) Regulations 2003 (CMI (Charted Management Institute), 2012). The types of discrimination currently covered by the Equality Act 2010 are direct and indirect discrimination, perception discrimination, harassment and harassment by a third party, and victimization (ACAS (Advisory, Conciliation and Arbitration Service), 2011).

The British media has often been accused of Muslim activists and community groups of persistent negative coverage, by generically and stereotypically associating acts of violence and intolerance with all Muslims. Indeed, ultra-nationalist right-wing parties and media persons have contributed to the rise of Islamophobia in the country, which has been further exacerbated by the ongoing violence and wars in the Middle East.

Religion as a legally protected characteristic also includes a lack of religion, as well as any type of religious affiliation that follows a clear structure and belief system. The Equality Act covers "any religious or philosophical belief or lack of such belief," involving at the same time the requirement that the belief must be a "weighty and substantial aspect of human life and behavior" (ACAS (Advisory, Conciliation and Arbitration Service), 2011, p. 7; Equality Act, 2010). In line with its approach to positive action, to counteract the negative effects of discrimination and remedy previous inequalities, the Act provides the possibility to encourage particular religions that are underrepresented in certain roles or organizations, but without violating merit (ACAS (Advisory, Conciliation and Arbitration Service), 2011). Additionally, an exception for lawful disparate treatment is given to religious organizations such as churches that need employees or clergy to perform religious functions (Ghumman et al., 2013).

Weller (2011) notes that since 2003, the number of Employment Tribunal cases has increased, which may represent an increase in the number of discriminatory episodes as well as a "greater awareness of potential legal remedies" (p. 7). Borstorff and Arlington (2011) assert that these figures can be seen as indicating that employers are failing to meet employees' religious needs.

According to a study commissioned by the Equality and Human Rights Commission (Equality and Human Right Commission (EHRC), 2010), the most significant employment gap in the UK is represented by the low rates of employment of Muslims in comparison with the reference group, i.e., white Christian men. Further, the pay gap experienced by Muslim men is 17% and 24% for Muslim and Sikh women in comparison with the reference group (Equality and Human Right Commission (EHRC), 2010). This indicates the impact of intersection of gender and religion. Moreover, an analysis of the census data reveals that despite an increased level of education over the 10 years (2001–11), Muslims have a higher rate of unemployment than the average. The analysis notes that Muslims face a double penalty – racial and religious discrimination – in entering the labor market. At the macro-level, the report also takes into account the social deprivation, e.g., the high Muslim proportion of the prison population (13%) and the proportion of Muslims in social housing (28%) (Ridley, 2015). Muslim women, in particular those of Pakistani and Bangladeshi descent, are most disadvantaged in terms of highest unemployment rates and gender pay gaps in the UK.

As earlier mentioned, the case of Nadia Eweida in British Airways highlights the complexity of religious discrimination in the workplace. The case reached the Employment Appeal Tribunal (EAT) in 2008. Eweida claimed that she was discriminated against on the basis of her religion when she was disciplined due to wearing a cross on a necklace (Dineley, 2009). The EAT ruled that the case was not a genuine case of religious discrimination due to the lack of evidence of group disadvantage (Javaid, 2008). However, since then British Airways changed its uniform policy to allow employees wear religious symbols (Dineley, 2009). Eweida finally won her case in the European Court of Human Rights due to the violation of the Article 9 of the European Convention of Human Rights (Eweida and Others v. The United Kingdom, 2013) (Newcombe, 2013).

Another example of discrimination in the workplace is the case of NIC Hygiene Ltd. in Bradford. It was the first case won by an employee under the religious discrimination legislation of 2003 (Hope, 2005). Mr Khan, a cleaner for NIC Hygiene Ltd. in Bradford, asked his employer if he could use his 25-day annual holiday entitlement, and another week's unpaid leave, to make an Islamic pilgrimage to Mecca. When his employer did not respond to his request, his manager told him he should assume he could go. However, on his return to work, he was suspended and subsequently dismissed. He brought claims of unfair dismissal and religious discrimination. A Leeds employment tribunal upheld Khan's claims and awarded him compensation in the region of GBP 10,000 (Personnel Today, 2005).

In terms of examples of best practice, an organization that shows commitment to faith diversity in the workplace is Sodexo UK and Ireland, a multinational corporation of food services. The company was given an award in 2010 by the Employers Forum on Belief (Sodexo, 2010). The company raises awareness within the workplace by, for example, distributing information about festivals relating to different religions. Additionally, in its marketing and promotion packs, the company provides information about restaurants that provide vegetarian and Halal menus (ENEI (Employers Network for Equality and Inclusion), 2010a).

Another important example of effective religious diversity management is the London Borough of Lambeth. The organization implemented the Equality Exchange Programme to promote an open organizational environment of debate on diverse religions in the workplace. Furthermore, to increase employees' awareness of diverse faiths, the organization launched the Multi Faith Forum and also provided multi-faith prayer rooms. Through such provisions, the organization seeks to develop an inclusive organizational culture (ENEI (Employers Network for Equality and Inclusion), 2010b; Lambeth, 2013).

Brief Example: Pakistan

A similar example of multilevel influences on religious diversity can be seen in the form of Pakistan. The country's very genesis in 1947 was rooted in a communal struggle by Muslims of the Indian Subcontinent to have a separate homeland. At the legal level, the constitution declares Pakistan as an Islamic Republic and declares that no laws shall be made contravening the fundamental teachings of the Quran and the Hadith (traditions of Prophet Muhammad). While the constitution ensures equality, it also discriminates against non-Muslims. For example, no non-Muslim can become a president or prime minister.

In 1974, the Pakistan parliament, through its Second Amendment, declared the Ahmadi sect to be non-Muslims, relegating them to a religious minority, a step that was followed by numerous anti-Ahmadi laws and regulations in subsequent years. It is not unusual in Pakistani markets and even offices to come across posters and literature blatantly insulting and discriminating against Ahmadis and their beliefs.

Discussion

The chapter has treated religious diversity at work at multiple, relational levels (Syed & Özbilgin, 2009), i.e., in the context of society, organization, and individual identity. It has taken into account the complexities presented by religion, gender, class, and other dimensions of individual identity, and their continuous interplay with various macro-societal and meso-organizational level variables. The approach is consistent with the previous studies that have highlighted the need to develop a contextual and relational understanding of diversity and management, e.g., Syed's (2009) contextual approach to diversity management and Tsui's (2004) perspective on indigenous research.

The chapter has highlighted the need to focus on a range of imagined and real connections and disconnections and levels of choice that breach national and ethnic boundaries (Shukla, 2001). A multilevel approach (Figure 1.1) may enable us to think about the wider networks of material and symbolic relations within, and through which, equality, diversity, and inclusion may be theorized, aspired to, perceived, and experienced in particular locales.

Effective religious diversity management may also help in improving organizational reputation in the labor market and wider society, leading to enhanced employee attraction and retention, as well as increased support from other stakeholders (ACAS (Advisory, Conciliation and Arbitration Service), 2005). The reduction of the risk of cases being taken to a court of law can imply an additional financial benefit for organizations. Overall, these factors can have a knock-on effect of improving levels of performance and profitability (CMI (Charted Management Institute), 2012). Additionally, diversity is linked with performance through productivity and innovation in the sense that it can provide market expansion and a more diverse customer and partnership pipeline (Kamenou & Syed, 2012).

A Relational Perspective on Religious Diversity at Work 51

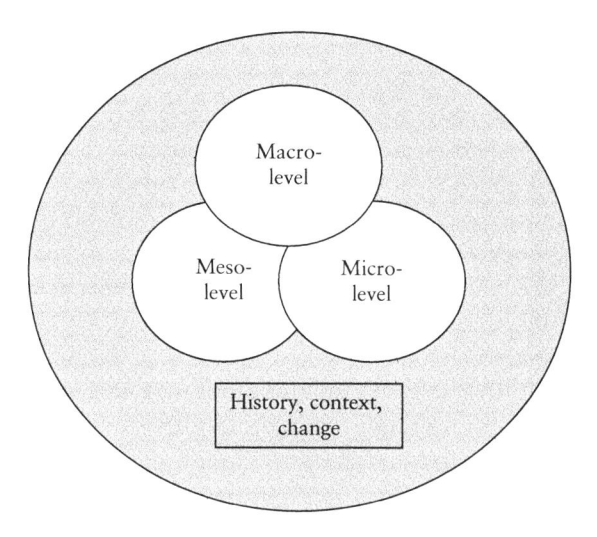

Figure 1.1 A relational perspective on religious diversity at work

The development of organizational strategies that can contribute to effective management of religious diversity is important, given that direct or indirect discrimination can negatively affect employees' performance (CMI (Charted Management Institute), 2012). While the business case for religious diversity encompasses the improvement and enhancement of employee morale (Paludi et al., 2011) in terms of levels of engagement, commitment, and motivation of the workforce, it is important to also take into account the social justice and ethical aspects of diversity and equality. Prevention strategies to avoid religious discrimination may include training programs for managers and employees to increase awareness and deal with stereotypes, and counseling services for past victims of discrimination or harassment (EEOC (US Equal Employment Opportunity Commission), 2008). Diversity policies and procedures may be monitored to audit their effectiveness over time and detect inconsistencies in practice through tools such as climate surveys (Paludi et al., 2011).

Consultation with relevant faith groups and other stakeholders on the best ways to respond to employees' requests for accommodation may be useful to reduce bias among managers and employees that can exist due to assumptions and stereotypes (EEOC (US Equal Employment Opportunity Commission), 2008).

At the meso-level, organizations may resort to positive action to beat adverse faith-based stereotypes. At the macro-level, governments and business associations may encourage "positive action" to implement legally permissible measures designed to counteract the effects of past discrimination. Such interventions may be used to encourage people within a minority group to take opportunities available to them, such as training, work experience schemes, or applying for particular job roles. This can only be done if the minority group has been under-represented in a certain area of employment, yet at the same time the treatment should be on merit, within the remit of national legislation. At the micro-individual level, organizations may enable the voice and participation of diverse employees in decisions affecting their work and employment. Managers may carefully decide about possible religious accommodations, taking into account the heterogeneity of individual belief, practice, and intersectionality. As a matter of fact, employees are not necessarily entitled to accommodations of their choice and the accommodation does not have to be cost-free to the employee. Although managers have the final say on allowing for accommodations, it is important to adhere to their ethical and legal obligations, and also exercise benevolence where possible.

In order for organizations effectively to manage and tackle discrimination in the workplace, it is important to consider and moderate generalized and stereotypical views about religion. The best method of doing this is through training. Training can also be used by the organization to show how seriously discrimination is taken and that it will not be tolerated. Unfortunately, religious discrimination and generalizations happen on a daily basis at multiple levels. While it may not be possible fully to overcome this discrimination, it is important that organizations do whatever they can to create an inclusive and productive workplace.

Although there is a greater interest among organizations in addressing employees' religious needs in the workplace, the increasing number of religious discrimination claims represents a challenge for not only for employers but also for governments and community groups (Weller, 2011). Informal practices and accommodations may require formalization, with the risk of raising complex issues and challenges for employers and managers (Ghumman et al., 2013).

Employees' freedom to express and openly live their personal faith is not something that is straightforward in the workplace. Organizations, employers, and managers, as well as government policy makers and community groups need to understand the benefits both to individuals and the business of promoting a culture of inclusion, integration, trust, and mutual respect. Thus, an awareness of or compliance with legislation and regulations in the field is not sufficient to ensure the effective management of religious diversity in organizations (CMI (Charted Management Institute), 2012). Equality of opportunities and the organizational climate need to be constantly assessed, given that effectively managing religious diversity in the workplace is not only a matter of harnessing business benefit but also an ethical obligation. In addition to legal compliance, organizations can be positive action oriented and commit to religious diversity in their overall strategy. Furthermore, it is important to have an open communication network to allow religious freedom and dialogue at work (CIPD, 2013), thus moderating any stereotypes and misperceptions that might exist in domains outside the workplace.

Acknowledgements

Thanks to Al-Busaidi, Hind, and Panebianco for their assistance in the literature review.

References

Abbas, T. (2004). After 9/11: British South Asian Muslims, Islamophobia, multiculturalism, and the state. *American Journal of Islamic Social Sciences*, 21(3), 26–38.

Adams, R. (2012). Balancing employee religious freedom in the workplace with customer rights to a religion-free retail environment. *Business and Society Review*, 117(3), 281–306.

ACAS (Advisory, Conciliation and Arbitration Service) (2005). Religion or belief and the workplace. Retrieved from: www.acas.org.uk/media/pdf/f/l/religion_1.pdf.

(2011). *The Equality Act: What's new for employers?* London: ACAS. Retrieved from: www.acas.org.uk/media/pdf/8/a/Equality-Act-2010-guide-for-employers.pdf.

Allport, G. W. (1979). *The nature of prejudice*. Cambridge, MA: Perseus Books.

Anderson, G. M. (1988). Mr. Smith and the preachers: The economics of religion in the Wealth of Nations. *Journal of Political Economy*, 96(5), 1066–88.

Armitage, R. N. (2007). *Issues of religious diversity affecting visible minority ethnic police personnel in the workplace.* PhD Thesis. Department of Theology and Religion, School of Historical Studies. Birmingham: The University of Birmingham.

Banton, M. (2011). Religion, faith, and intersectionality. *Ethnic and Racial Studies*, 34(7), 1248–53.

Basinger, D. (2012). Religious diversity (pluralism). Retrieved from: http://plato.stanford.edu/cgi-bin/encyclopedia/archinfo.cgi?entry=religious-pluralism.

Beaman, L. (2012). Exploring reasonable accommodation. *In* Beaman, L. (ed.), *Reasonable accommodation: Managing religious diversity.* Vancouver: University of British Columbia (UBC) Press, 1–12.

Beatty, J., & Kirby, S. (2006). Beyond the legal environment: How stigma influences invisible identity groups in the workplace. *Employee Responsibilities and Rights Journal*, 18(1), 29–44.

Beckford, J. (2012). Public responses to religious diversity in Britain and France. *In* Beaman, L. (ed.), *Reasonable accommodation: Managing religious diversity.* Vancouver: University of British Columbia Press, 109–38.

Bell, M. (2011). *Diversity in organizations.* 2nd edn. Nashville, TN: South-Western.

Bender, C., Cadge, W., Levitt, P., & Smilde, D. (2012). *Religion on the edge: Decentering and recentering the sociology of religion.* Oxford: Oxford University Press.

Berger, P. L. (1967). *The sacred canopy.* New York: Anchor Books.

Böhm, S. A., Dwertmann, D. J., Kunze, F., Michaelis, B., Parks, K. M., & McDonald, D. P. (2014). Expanding insights on the diversity climate–performance link: The role of workgroup discrimination and group size. *Human Resource Management*, 53(3), 379–402.

Borstorff, J., & Arlington, K. (2011). Protecting religion in the workplace? What employees think. *Journal of Legal, Ethical and Regulatory Issues*, 14(1), 59–70.

Bowcott, O. (2013). Cross ban did infringe BA worker's rights, Strasbourg court rules. Retrieved from: www.theguardian.com/law/2013/jan/15/ba-rights-cross-european-court.

Brown, A. (2013). The BA Christian case was judged rightly, and a true test of tolerance. Retrieved from: www.theguardian.com/commentisfree/2013/jan/15/ba-christian-case-judged-rightly.

CMI (Charted Management Institute) (2012). Best practice: Religion and belief in the workplace – Guidance for managers. Retrieved from: www.managers.org.uk/page/best-practice-religion-and-belief-workplace-guidance-managers.

Chaves, M., & Cann, D.E. (1992). Regulation, pluralism, and religious market structure: Explaining religion's vitality. *Rationality and Society*, 4, 272–90.
CIPD. (2013). Diversity in the workplace: An overview. Retrieved from: www.cipd.co.uk/hr-resources/factsheets/diversity-workplace-overview.aspx#link_2.
Clair, J., Beatty, J., & Maclean, T. (2005). Out of sight but not out of mind: Managing invisible identities in the workplace. *Academy of Management Review*, 30(1), 78–95.
Cragun, R. T., Kosmin, B., Keysar, A., Hammer, J. H., and Nielsen, M. (2012). On the receiving end: Discrimination toward the non-religious in the United States. *Journal of Contemporary Religion*, 27(1), 105–27.
Day, N. E. (2005). Religion in the workplace: Correlates and consequences of individual behavior. *Journal of Management, Spirituality and Religion*, 2(1), 104–35.
Dineley, R. (2009). Christian beliefs not allowed to "trump" others' rights. *People Management*. Retrieved from: www.peoplemanagement.co.uk/pm/articles/2009/12/christian-beliefs-not-allowed-to-trump-others-rights.htm.
Dolansky, E., & Alon, I. (2008). Religious freedom, religious diversity, and Japanese foreign direct investment. *Research in International Business and Finance*, 22(1), 29–39.
Durkheim, E. (1964 [1893]). *The division of labor in society*. New York: Free Press.
EDF. (2010). Equality act 2010: What do I need to know? A quick start guide on religion or belief discrimination in service provision for voluntary and community organizations. Retrieved from: www.gov.uk/government/uploads/system/uploads/attachment_data/file/85027/vcs-religion-belief.pdf.
EEOC (US Equal Employment Opportunity Commission). (2008). Best practices for eradicating religious discrimination in the workplace. Retrieved from: www.eeoc.gov/policy/docs/best_practices_religion.html.
ENEI (Employers Network for Equality and Inclusion). (2010a). EFB award overall private sector. Retrieved from: www.enei.org.uk/data/files/Awards_2007_2010_Case_Studies/Sodexo_EFB_Award_Overall_Private_Sector.pdf.
 (2010b). EFB award overall public sector. Retrieved from: www.enei.org.uk/data/files/Awards_2007_2010_Case_Studies/Lambeth_EFB_Award_Overall_Public_Sector.pdf.
Equality Act UK. (2010). *Equality Act*. London: The Stationery Office Limited. Retrieved from: www.legislation.gov.uk/ukpga/2010/15/pdfs/ukpga_20100015_en.pdf.

Equality and Human Right Commission (EHRC). (2010). *How fair is Britain? Equality, human rights and good relations in 2010: The first Triennial Review*. London: Equality Human Rights Commission. Retrieved from: www.equalityhumanrights.com/uploaded_files/triennial_review/how_fair_is_britain_-_complete_report.pdf.

Erez, M., & Gati, E. (2004). A dynamic, multi-level model of culture: From the micro level of the individual to the macro level of a global culture. *Applied Psychology: An International Review*, 53, 583–98.

Farnham, D. (2010). *Human Resource Management in context: Strategy, insights and solutions*. 3rd edn. London: CIPD.

Furness, S. and Gilligan, P. (2014). "It never came up": Encouragements and discouragements to addressing religion and belief in professional practice—what do social work students have to say? *British Journal of Social Work*, 44(3), 763–81.

Ghumman, S., & Jackson, L. (2010). The downside of religious attire: The Muslim headscarf and expectations of obtaining employment. *Journal of Organizational Behavior*, 31(1), 4–23.

Ghumman, S., Ryan, A. M., Barclay, L. A., & Markel, K. S. (2013). Religious discrimination in the workplace: A review and examination of current and future trends. *Journal of Business and Psychology*, 28(4), 439–54.

Giddens, A. (1984). *The constitution of society: Outline of the theory of structuration*. Berkeley, CA: University of California Press.

Hecht, M. L., & Faulkner, S. L. (2000). Sometimes Jewish, sometimes not: The closeting of Jewish American identity. *Communication Studies*, 51(4), 372–87.

Hope, K. (2005). First employee win under religion law. *People Management*, 11(2), 10.

Javaid, M. (2008). Eweida v British Airways plc. *People Management*, 11 December. Retrieved from: www.peoplemanagement.co.uk/pm/articles/2008/12/eweida-v-british-airways-plc.htm.

Kamenou, N., & Syed, J. (2012). Diversity management. In Kramar, R., & Syed, J. (eds.), *Human Resource Management in a global context: A critical approach*. Hampshire: Palgrave McMillan, 75–94.

Kelly, E. (2008). Accommodating religious expression in the workplace. *Employee Responsibilities and Rights Journal*, 20(1), 45–56.

Knill, C. and Preidel, C. (2015). Institutional opportunity structures and the Catholic Church: Explaining variation in the regulation of same-sex partnerships in Ireland and Italy. *Journal of European Public Policy*, 22(3), 374–90.

Koterski, J. W. (2011). Church, state, and society. *International Philosophical Quarterly*, 51(2), 272–74.

Kumra, S., & Manfredi, S. (2012). *Managing equality and diversity: Theory and practice*. Oxford: Oxford University Press.

Lambeth. (2013). Faith in Lambeth. Retrieved from: www.lambeth.gov.uk/Services/CommunityLiving/FaithInLambeth/.

Lindley, J. (2002). Race or religions? The impact of religion on the employment and earnings of Britain's ethnic communities. *Journal of Ethnic and Migration Studies*, 28(3), 427–42.

McKinnon, A.M. (2005). Reading "opium of the people": expression, protest and the dialectics of religion. *Critical Sociology*, 31(1/2), 15–38.

Mooney, J. (2013). Accommodating Muslim employees during Ramadan. Retrieved from: www.shrm.org/hrdisciplines/Diversity/Articles/Pages/Accommodating-Muslim-Employees-During-Ramadan.aspx.

Morgan, J.F. (2005). Religion at work: a legal quagmire. *Managerial law*, 47(3/4), 247–59.

Muñoz, C., & Thomas, K. (2006). LGBTQ issues in organizational settings: What HRD professionals need to know and do. *New Directions for Adult and Continuing Education*, 112, 85–95.

Newcombe, T. (2013). "This is a victory for equality and religious freedom," says HR director on BA Christian cross case. Retrieved from: www.hrmagazine.co.uk/hro/news/1075958/-this-victory-equality-religious-freedom-hr-director-ba-christian-cross.

Olasky, M. (2003). Christophobia and the American future. In Dunn, C. (ed.), *Faith, freedom and the future: Religion in American political culture*. Maryland, MD: Rowman and Littlefield Publishers Inc., 40–54.

ONS (Office for National Statistics). (2012). *Religion in England and Wales 2011*. London: The National Archives. Retrieved from: www.ons.gov.uk/ons/dcp171776_290510.pdf.

Personnel Today. (2005). Religious discrimination victory is a wake-up call. *Personnel Today*, February 8. Retrieved from: www.personneltoday.com/hr/religious-discrimination-victory-is-a-wake-up-call/.

Pew Research Center. (2012). Table: Religious composition by country, in percentages. Pew Research Center, December 18. Retrieved from: www.pewforum.org/2012/12/18/table-religious-composition-by-country-in-percentages/.

Paludi, M., Ellens, H., & Paludi, A. (2011). Religious discrimination. In Paludi, M., Paludi, C., & DeSouza, E. (eds.), *Handbook on understanding and preventing workplace discrimination*. Santa Barbara, CA: Praeger, 157–82.

Purdam, K., Afkhami, R., Crockett, A., & Olsen, W. (2007). Religion in the UK: An overview of equality statistics and evidence gaps. *Journal of Contemporary Religion*, 22(2), 147–68.

Ridley, L. (2015). British Muslims among the most deprived in the country, finds landmark report. *The Huffington Post UK*, February 13. Retrieved from: www.huffingtonpost.co.uk/2015/02/12/british-muslims-facts_n_6670234.html.

Roccas, S., & Schwartz, S. H. (1997). Church-state relations and the association of religiosity with values: A study of Catholics in six countries. *Cross-Cultural Research*, 31(4), 356–75.

Roberts, H. (2014). Reliance on recruitment intuition harms diversity. Retrieved from: www.hrmagazine.co.uk/hro/news/1143025/reliance-recruitment-intuition-harms-diversity.

Shukla, S. (2001). Locations for South Asian diasporas. *Annual Review of Anthropology*, 30, 551–72.

Sodexo. (2010). Sodexo named as leading private sector organization for diversity and inclusion programme. Retrieved from: http://uk.sodexo.com/uken/media-centre/press-releases/efa-diversity-award.asp.

Stark, R., & Bainbridge, W. S. (1985). *The future of religion: Secularization, revival, and cult formation*. Oakland, CA: University of California Press.

Syed, J. (2009). Contextualising diversity management. *In* Özbilgin, M. (ed.), *Equality, diversity and inclusion at work: A research companion*. Cheltenham: Edward Elgar, 101–11.

Syed, J., & Kramar, R. (2009). Socially responsible diversity management. *Journal of Management and Organization*, 15(5), 639–51.

Syed, J., & Özbilgin, M. (2009). A relational framework for international transfer of diversity management practices. *International Journal of Human Resource Management*, 20(12), 2435–53.

Tschannen, O. (1991). The secularization paradigm: A systematization. *Journal for the Scientific Study of Religion*, 30, 395–415.

Tsui, A. (2004). Contributing to global management knowledge: A case for high quality indigenous research. *Asia Pacific Journal of Management*, 21(4), 491–513.

UK Government. (2013). Disability rights employment. Retrieved from: www.gov.uk/rights-disabled-person/employment.

Wallwork, E. (1984). Religion and social structure in the division of labor. *American Anthropologist*, 86, 43–64.

Weber, M. (1958 [1904–5]). *The Protestant ethic and the spirit of capitalism*. New York: Scribner's.

Weller, P. (2011). *Religious discrimination in Britain: A review of research evidence, 2000–2010. Research report number: 73*. Manchester: Equality and Human Rights Commission. Retrieved from: www.equalityhumanrights.com/uploaded_files/research/research_report_73_religious_discrimination.pdf.

Whitman, J. S., & Bidell, M. P. (2014). Affirmative lesbian, gay, and bisexual counselor education and religious beliefs: How do we bridge the gap? *Journal of Counseling & Development*, 92(2), 162–9.

XpertHR. (2014). Take steps to ensure that the workforce is inclusive of people of different religions and beliefs. Retrieved from: www.xperthr.co.uk/tasks/take-steps-to-ensure-that-the-workforce-is-inclusive-of-people-of-different-religions-and-beliefs/151731/.

2 | Religious Diversity, Identity, and Workplace Inclusion

CHARMINE E. J. HÄRTEL, JASMIN C. R. HÄRTEL, AND PREM RAMBURUTH

Introduction

Exposure to religious institutions and attitudes toward faith and spirituality, including atheism and secularism, is ubiquitous to human society. Many children will carry into adulthood an identity ingrained with religion and spirituality learned from their parents (Lees & Horwath, 2009; Rymarz & Graham, 2005). This is especially so if, as children, they expressed religious values and practices (Lees & Horwath, 2009; Rymarz & Graham, 2005). Others will engage in identity work that leads them to adopt a different religious or spiritual orientation. Irrespective of the path taken, in all cases and at any given time, humans will hold attitudes toward religiosity and beliefs about the metaphysical world.

This chapter provides a theoretical analysis of the paradox and the possibilities of religious diversity bringing people together or pushing them apart. We begin with the global backdrop of rising religious diversity generally and workplace religious diversity and discrimination, illustrated by the example of changes in the variety of beliefs represented by the religious diversity spectrum in the US context. Next, after examining and problematizing definitions of religious diversity, we develop an integrated definition of religious diversity that incorporates atheism, secularism, spirituality, and religiosity. We then draw on Paradox Theory to lay out the case for why and how religious diversity needs to be strategically managed on an ongoing basis. We also illustrate how religious diversity itself can inform the management of diversity paradoxes, using the lens of Indigenous people's traditional belief systems. We conclude our chapter by considering practical ways to promote an inclusive and positive workplace environment for religious diversity.

Trends in Religious and Spiritual Diversity, Discrimination, and Accommodation

Increasing global mobility brings with it collisions and juxtapositions of different faith orientations and activities. For example, changes in immigration trends in the UK have both broadened the range of religious groups and increased the proportion of people identifying with non-Christian religions (Webly, 2011). Secularization does not always lead to disbelief, but often results in a diversity of spiritual and paranormal beliefs and practices or disinterest in religion (apatheism) or skepticism toward religion (analytical atheism) (Norenzayan, 2016).

The growth and changing profile of religious diversity in populations around the world is mirrored, to a greater or lesser degree, in their workforces. Among the identity characteristics that people bring into the workplace is their religious identity (Hicks, 2003; see Miller & Thoresen, 2003, for a review). Religious diversity is worthy of deliberate contemplation by organizational scholars and managers because the way that people relate to others is based on how similar or different they perceive them to be (Chan-Serafin et al., 2013). For example, using an experimental method, Härtel et al. (1999) showed that between two equally qualified job applicants, the one that was perceived as most similar to the rater was evaluated most favorably. In the context of religious diversity, Cunningham (2010) showed that when workers perceive another as religiously dissimilar, they also perceive that person to have different values from them. Also, he showed that perceiving religious differences in one's workgroup leads to reduced job satisfaction.

The severity of discrimination appears to be associated with religious distance from the majority religion and the visibility of one's faith-related identity (Basford, 2010; Dupper et al., 2015). For example, discrimination against atheists tends to be highest in contexts where there are religious majorities (Gervais & Norenzayan, 2013). In another study, Ghumman and Ryan (2013) showed evidence of discrimination in job application outcomes for Muslim women wearing a headscarf (Hijabis) in contexts where they were perceived as dissimilar to the organization's employee profile. This research highlights the importance of taking into account contextual factors in studies of religious diversity (cf. Härtel, 2014; Härtel & O'Connor, 2014).

In a process referred to as social categorization, people assign themselves to social group categories (e.g., ethnicity, social class) to identify their group membership and distinguish their in-group from other group memberships. Research about the effects of this process, based on social identity theory (Tajfel, 1978) and self-categorization theory (Turner et al., 1987), shows that individuals are more likely to collaborate with members of their in-group than members of out-groups. Furthermore, neuroscience research shows that the process of favoring one's in-group is an automatic process (Scheepers & Derks, 2016).

Unconscious in-group bias plays out in very real ways, and provides a partial explanation for the reports of destructive workplace conflicts and discrimination between individuals and groups holding different perspectives on religion and faith (e.g., Webly, 2011). For example, people highly identifying as Christian (vs. low identification levels) showed more favoritism to their religious in-group (Christians) and more negative attitudes toward out-groups whose values conflicted with their religious values (Johnson et al., 2012). This effect was replicated for individuals with a low level of identification as Christian when their Christian identity was experimentally primed (Johnson et al., 2012). The data collected on out-groups in this study included atheists and Muslims, with the findings showing that negative attitudes toward atheists were higher than those toward Muslims (Johnson et al., 2012).

A variety of different institutional responses to problems associated with religious diversity are evident around the world. For example, in the United States and Canada, employers are legally obliged to provide "reasonable accommodation" for religious differences. Implementing so called "reasonable accommodation" is subjective, however, and does not always grant accommodation to certain religious needs. Europe, in contrast, has no legal requirement obliging employers to make "reasonable accommodation" for an employee's religious beliefs, observances and practices. Nonetheless, liberal-democratic states in Europe are facing increasing pressure to accommodate religious diversity and expression (Bader et al., 2013).

We illustrate next, with the case of the United States, the dynamic nature of religious diversity over time and examples of the types of discrimination that may be associated with religious diversity.

Country Example: The United States

We choose to profile the United States as emblematic of growing religious diversity and discrimination because the freedom to choose one's religious affiliation and how to express it was a foundation stone for the United States as a country (Bellah, 1988). Ever since, religious freedom has prominently figured in public, legal, and political debate in US culture (Mead, 2006). The visibility of religious diversity in the US and international media also provides a vivid example of how different perspectives on religion and faith manifest themselves sometimes in destructive ways and at other times constructively. September 11, 2001, exemplifies this; on the one hand exposing religious perspectives as a motivator for terrorism and prejudice, and on the other hand as a motivator for compassion and a source of comfort and hope (Kelly, 2008). Additionally, there are well-documented examples in the United States of intra-religious diversity, including the radicalization of belief. For example, the legal activism of anti-abortion Christians is contrasted with the violent attacks by fundamentalist Christians on abortion clinics and providers (Winter, 2015).

A report by the Pew Research Center (2015), titled "America's Changing Religious Landscape," provides revealing insights into trends on numbers and distribution of religious groups, demographic composition of religious groups, religious switching and intermarriage, religious practices, and discrimination from its latest 2014 survey in the United States. We highlight some of the trends identified in its 2014 Religious Landscape Study in the sections that follow.

Changing Religious Demographics and Intragroup Religious Affiliations

- The 2014 survey data (Pew Research Center, 2015) indicate that the number of adults in the United States who describe themselves as having no affiliation with an organized religion or atheist or agnostic is approximately 56 million, a proportion greater than Catholics and mainline Protestants, and second in size only to evangelical Protestants. It also suggests that among the non-affiliated, the number of people identifying as agnostic or atheist has grown from 25% to 31%.

- Further analyses of changing religious affiliations indicate that identification with non-Christian faiths also has increased from 4.7% in 2007 to 5.9% in 2014. Of these, Muslims, Hindus, and Jews accounted for the most growth, with percentage changes of 0.5%, 0.3%, and 0.2%, respectively, with other world religions in this category including Sikhs, Baha'is, Taoists, Jains, Rastafarians, Zoroastrians, Confucians, and Druze.
- The 2014 survey data (Pew Research Center, 2015) also suggest that 1.5% of adults in the United States identify with non-traditional faiths, including Native American religions, Pagans, Wiccans, New Agers, Deists, Scientologists, Pantheists, Polytheists, Satanists, and Druids.
- It seems that the geographic distribution of religiously affiliated (or non-affiliated) groups varies, with some religions being concentrated in certain areas. For example, large numbers of Protestants and evangelicals are concentrated in the South of the United States, while the majority of Jewish and Catholic citizens are concentrated in the Northeast, and most Mormons and unaffiliated people reside in the West.
- There is evidence of intra-religious group diversity being high in some organized religious groups, for example, in Protestantism, where there are more than a dozen major denominations.

Changing Intersectionality in Faith, Spiritual, and Religious Orientations

The demographic composition of religious groups is changing as well, along lines such as race, ethnicity, age, education, class, sexual orientation, and gender. These changing trends indicate that the racial and ethnic diversity of Christians in the United States is growing, with two-thirds of immigrants arriving in the United States being of the Christian faith.

- Furthermore, 41% of survey respondents identifying themselves as gay, lesbian, or bisexual report being religiously unaffiliated, 48% identify as Christians, and 11% with non-Christian faiths.
- On the basis of age, approximately 35% of young adults aged between 18 and 33 years are religiously unaffiliated, compared to approximately 25% of Generation Xs (around 36–46 years), with

the data indicating a significant increase of religiously unaffiliated people in the younger age bracket.
- The finding that 24% of all college graduates report being unaffiliated complements the finding that approximately 25% of Generation Xs report being unaffiliated.
- In terms of education and related income, the data (Pew Research Center, 2015) indicate that those of the Hindu and Jewish faiths continue to be the most highly educated religious group category, with 77% of Hindus and 59% of Jews being college graduates. This is significantly higher when compared with 27% of all US adults.
- Furthermore, a greater proportion of Hindus and Jews have above-average household incomes, with 44% of Jews and 36% of Hindus reporting an annual family income in excess of $100,000 (compared with 19% of all US adults).
- On the basis of gender, the majority of those with no religious affiliation are men, and the figure has increased from 20% in 2007 to 27% in 2014. However, the percentage of women reporting as non-affiliated indicates an increasing trend from 13% in 2007 to 19% in 2014. Further analyses of the data on the basis of gender indicate that the majority in every Christian group are women.

Religious Switching and Intermarriage

Factors such as religious switching (including intermarriage) also influence the dynamics in religious group affiliations.

- The Pew Research Center (2015) indicates that 39% of US adults married since 2010 report being in religiously mixed marriages, with some 20% being marriages between an unaffiliated and Christian spouse.
- Switching religious affiliation is common in the United States, but low among Hindus, Muslims, and Jews, with 80%, 77%, and 75%, respectively, maintaining their childhood religious identity.

Religious Diversity Awareness and Integration of Faith Practices in the Workplace

Religiosity and religious group affiliation bring diversity to the workplace and influence interpersonal interactions and group dynamics.

This dimension of diversity needs to be recognized and included in the workplace as part of a healthy organizational culture. The Pew Research Center (2015) indicates that 61% of US workers believe greater religious awareness would benefit the workplace. Other studies indicate that:

- US employers are increasingly recognizing the presence of religious diversity in the workforce and the need to update their human resource management (HRM) policies and practices to reflect the diversity (Grossman, 2008; Webly, 2011) in order to maintain a satisfied workforce (King & Williamson, 2005) and reduce legal liability and cost (Morgan, 2005).
- Human resource (HR) managers are increasingly dealing with requests to accommodate religious identity and expression, including prayer time, religious study, observance of religious holidays, and displaying religious materials (Cash et al., 2000; Dobson, 2010; King, 2008; Rollins, 2007).
- Although US workplaces are typically secular (Kelly, 2008), some workers may not view work as secular (Morgan, 2004) and thus view religious expression at work as a right.
- With the bulk of the consumer population residing outside the United States, it has been imperative for US companies to develop overseas customer relationships and subsidiaries (Rollins, 2007).

Religion-based Tensions and Discrimination in the Workplace

Religious diversity will bring with it aspects difference, which if not well understood and well managed could lead to workplace tensions and conflict. Evidence provided below indicates that:

- Increasing religious diversity in the US workforce has, in some cases, led to conflict and intolerance (Ghumman et al., 2013; Kelly, 2008).
- Claims of religious discrimination and harassment, as well as requests for reasonable accommodation of religious diversity have increased with the relevant US government's enforcement body, namely, the Equal Employment Opportunity Commission (King, 2008).
- US work policies and practices typically align with Christian practices, the dominant religious affiliation in the United States (American

Religious Identification Survey, 2009). Consequently, workers from other faiths or lifestyles (e.g., homosexuals, unwed mothers) may become targets of harassment, marginalization, and discrimination (Anti-Defamation League, 2011; Ghumman et al., 2013).
- Employers are challenged to balance religious accommodation with discrimination or harassment of others (Anti-Defamation League, 2011) and may not be well equipped to deal with facilitating or managing this balance.

The trends highlighted above belie the vastness of the religious diversity spectrum. Any definition of religious diversity must, therefore, address not only identification with an organized religion, but also disbelief, indecision, and apathy about religion and faith. Moreover, it is possible for intra-religious diversity to be greater than inter-religious diversity. It is also apparent from the US data that attitudes toward religion and faith also intersect with other identities, including gender, culture, education, income, ethnicity, and age. The intersection of identities has implications for the likelihood of switching one's orientation to religion as well as the likelihood of marrying outside one's personal belief system. Current definitions of religious diversity are unable to embrace the features of religious diversity in contemporary society. In the next section, we take up this issue and attempt to develop a workable solution.

Problematizing Religious Diversity and Developing an Integrated Definition

In general, diversity can be separated into two categories: surface-level or deep-level (Ancarani et al., 2016). Surface-level diversity refers to the more obvious and usually physical traits, such as gender and race. Deep-level diversity refers to psychological traits, such as one's values and beliefs; this includes religion, or non-religion. The two diversity categories can overlap when one's religion is assumed from one's appearance, whether the two coincide or not. For example, some people wear religious dress, or jewelry, making their religious identity obvious to others without their having to ask. On the other hand, some may assume that because an individual is Indian, they must be Hindu, even if this is not the case.

Religious identity is often concealable and thus may remain undisclosed to others (King & Williamson, 2005). People with concealable identities are least likely to disclose their identity if they perceive that it is stigmatized. Research shows that when individuals conceal a stigmatized identity, they experience less discrimination (Jones et al., 1984; Trau & Härtel, 2007). This feature of religious identity may lead some to the conclusion that, since expressing identity is within their control, they should conceal it in the workplace (Moran, 2007). However, suppressing an important aspect of one's identity has detrimental effects (Trau & Härtel, 2007). Evidence of this in the context of religious diversity is provided by King and Williamson's (2005) study, which shows that individuals high in religiosity, who believe that they should be able to express their religion at work, have reduced job satisfaction in organizations that they perceive disapprove of religious expression.

Religious Identity Development

Religious identity development consists of four dimensions: (1) affiliation and belonging, (2) behaviors and practices, (3) beliefs and values, and (4) religious and spiritual experiences (Hemming & Madge, 2012). An individual may have a stronger religious identity in some of these aspects, and less so on others (Forrest-Bank & Dupper, 2016; Hemming & Madge, 2012). Children whose religious identity is high in all four dimensions are less likely as adults to leave or switch their childhood religion and more likely to be dedicated to expressing their religious identity through its associated rituals and ceremonies.

There is a variety of underlying mechanisms suggested to explain religious identity development (Norenzayan, 2016). For example, the ritualization of behavior is one mechanism through which individuals develop a specific set of supernatural beliefs and connect these with a religious identity (Legare & Watson-Jones, 2015; McCauley & Lawson, 2002).

There is increasing evidence that religious beliefs help to ease certain anxieties, and that when these anxieties are intensified, these religious beliefs are also intensified (Atran, 2002; Kay et al., 2009). As a result of this, communities that are prone to greater threats and fears, such as poverty, natural disasters, and hunger, are more commonly religious (Norris & Inglehart, 2004). Similarly, when people lack self-confidence or are in a period of transition, their religious identity may be shaped by prestige bias in order to ease their anxieties. Prestige bias is the tendency to adopt the beliefs and behaviors a person believes are associated with skill and/or success (Chudek et al., 2015). An example of the effect of prestige bias on religious identity development is when people adopt a specific religious identity they associate with high-profile occupations and businesses.

Another possible mechanism underpinning religious identity development is conformist bias Norenzayan (2016) or the tendency people have to adopt the beliefs and behaviors held by the majority of people in their community, society, or social group. Conformist bias is particularly evident in children and adolescents who take on a religious identity to be like their parents or to fit in with peers.

People's traits may also play a role in religious identity development. For example, Willard and Norenzayan (2013) found that mentalizing tendencies (a set of cognitive tendencies to sense and come to conclusions about what others are thinking) increase mind-body dualism (the intuition that the mind can exist apart from the body) and teleological bias (the intuition that people, things, and events all serve a specific purpose, e.g., everything happens for a reason). Consequently, mentalizing tendencies are associated with an increase in religious, spiritual, and supernatural beliefs, such as God(s), psychics, and aliens, as well as the belief that there is a purpose to life.

Definitions of Religious Diversity

Dow et al. (2016) define religion as consisting of not only a set of principles or doctrines, but also the shared set of beliefs and behaviors of those from the same religious group. Durkheim (1912) had a more restricted definition, saying that religion is a system that consists of beliefs and practices related to sacred things. Walker et al. (2004) attempt to distinguish religion from spirituality, saying that religion is more organizational, ritual, and ideological, whereas spirituality is based more on experiences and emotions, and is more personal, inasmuch as spirituality differs from person to person (as opposed to religion having a set of broad rules) (Pargament, 1999; Richards & Bergin, 1997).

Norenzayan (2016) constrains his definition of religious diversity to belief, separating non-belief. He uses the term theodiversity to describe religious diversity, explaining it as diversity in religious beliefs, behaviors, rituals, and traditions. In contrast, he uses the term atheodiversity to refer to the diversity of non-belief in religions, including atheism and belief in the paranormal in this category.

Scholars of diversity at work largely agree that diversity comprises individual- and group-level differences that may result in people viewing another person as different from themselves (Härtel, 2004; Härtel & Fujimoto, 2000). This perspective highlights the need to include both formally recognized or organized religious groups (the group level) and faith orientations that are idiosyncratic to the individual (individual level) within an integrated definition of religious diversity.

An Integrated Definition of Religious Diversity

Synthesizing the above definitions of religious diversity, we propose an integrated definition of *religious diversity* as "differences in cognitions, emotions, and behaviors relating to supernatural explanations at the individual and group level, which may be visible or invisible to others and whose evolution rates may be slow or rapid." This new definition is multi-level, multi-faceted, and incorporates time dimensions as well as belief and non-belief.

The Why and How of Religious Diversity Management: A Paradox Theory Analysis

Paradox theory considers a paradox to consist of two or more components that are conflicting, yet connected in nature (Guerci & Carollo, 2016). Taken separately, each component seems irrefutable. However, taken together, the components seem inconsistent and incompatible. Paradoxes are considered to be inherent in organizations, and may result in either vicious or virtuous cycles, depending on how they are dealt with (Guerci & Carollo, 2016).

Vicious cycles emerge from paradoxes when the organization focuses only on a single component and neglects the other. This blinkered perspective worsens the tensions already present within the organization, and is linked to overlooking alternative perspectives and organizational inertia (Guerci & Carollo, 2016). Either/or thinking drives vicious cycles (Miron-Spektor et al., 2011), for example, when an organization responds to the paradox of religious diversity by taking a strict secular stance or religious expression exclusive to one denomination. Conversely, virtuous cycles result from a paradox when the organization creates awareness of the inherent paradoxical tensions, and focuses on all components of the paradox, although it may be viewed as impractical or counterintuitive (Guerci & Carollo, 2016). Both/and thinking drives virtuous cycles (Miron-Spektor et al., 2011), for example, when an organization responds to the paradox of religious diversity by integrating secular and religious perspectives. Such cycles are beneficial as they promote innovation, which helps the survival of the organization in the long term.

It is a vital skill for the manager to "stay with the paradox," as it produces innovation by challenging the organization's actors to come up with creative solutions to the seemingly conflicting elements present (Guerci & Carollo, 2016). Managing paradoxes within organizations improves efficiency because elements perceived as conflicting are accepted and thus managed rather than dismissed or ignored. Organizations able to deal with paradoxes are the most successful and long-lived, in comparison to those who only deal with one of the components of the paradox, while ignoring the others (Guerci & Carollo, 2016).

A review of the literature reveals a number of organizational and individual-level characteristics that are likely to facilitate staying with the paradox. Beginning with Mazumdar and Mazumdar's (2005) four-part typology of the relationship between organizations and religious diversity, we can hypothesize the organizational contexts that are likely to support or inhibit constructive religious diversity management. They label organizations that intertwine religion and business as Religion Dominant Organizations, which are businesses that produce and sell faith-related material for a specific religion. They label organizations whose products and services are primarily secular but place religion central to the lives of the owner and employees as Religion Included Organizations. Their Religion Accommodating Organizations category refers to organizations that deal with secular products and services but cater to the religious-expression expectations of their religiously diverse workforce and customers. Secular organizations that demonstrate disrespect or perceived sacrilege in their use of faith-related material are termed Religion Insensitive Organizations. Based on their typology, we propose that the religion insensitive organizational stance is likely to be most vulnerable to vicious cycles while the religion accommodating organizational stance is most likely to foster virtuous cycles.

Managers also must be aware of the religious distance between the country they reside in, and the target countries of the organization.

They must be aware of the possible tensions and issues associated with these differences, which in turn will help them to develop methods of dealing with, or minimizing any negative effects (Dow et al., 2016). Cognitively complex managers are likely to be better equipped to identify and deal with potential tensions.

Dow et al. (2016) suggest that individuals whose cognitive complexity is low in regards to religion are simply aware of religion, with no knowledge or understanding beyond that. Conversely, individuals whose cognitive complexity is high in regards to religion have an extensive knowledge of religions, and are aware of the subtle differences in religious denominations, sects, and branches. This suggests that the former individual may be ignorant of behaviors that may be deemed offensive to certain religious people, which may result in lower trust, misunderstandings, and overall tension. Dow et al. (2016) also suggest that bicultural individuals are more likely to have higher religious cognitive complexity, as they are exposed to/aware of cultural and/or religious differences. Likewise, they argue that those who live in a religiously diverse country are more likely to have high religious cognitive complexity. Following on from this line of reasoning, it is logical to expect that managers who have high cognitive complexity in regards to religious diversity may also be able to predict the impact of the different religious orientations in their workforce (e.g., tension and miscommunication), and thus possess greater knowledge of how to deal with such matters.

Besides the academic literature, we can gain ideas for effective religious diversity management from considering what characteristics of various worldviews and faith traditions would foster virtuous cycles out of differences. We illustrate this by considering some of the defining features of indigenous faiths.

Managing Diversity Paradoxes from the Lens of Indigenous Worldviews and Traditions

Religious diversity represents different worldviews. A characteristic shared among indigenous peoples around the world is pattern thinking or viewing all things as connected and belonging within the larger pattern of the universe (Härtel, 2015). Pattern thinking also may be evident among other world religions as well as those who identify as non-religious or spiritual.

Another distinctive feature of indigenous traditions is relational knowledge, or the acceptance and co-existence of different points of view. Relational knowledge allows the co-existence of differences in an environment of trust, collaboration, and respect (Härtel, 2015). This is evident in the inclusiveness of the traditional problem-solving processes of Australian Aboriginal peoples in which the whole kinship structure is involved in a public discussion (Härtel, 2015).

The emphasis of relational knowledge is not on the individual, but on relationships and helping each other (Härtel, 2015). Thus, one cannot take unless the taking is transformed into benefit for others. The Maori concept of Kaitiakitanga or stewardship illustrates this. In the Maori worldview, one's well-being (mauri ora) is connected to the well-being of all aspects of creation. Thus, everyone has an obligation and power to create mauri ora (well-being) for all (Spiller et al., 2011), and this includes organizations (Härtel, 2015; Spiller et al., 2011). Management decisions in Maori organizations are value-based and evaluated against Maori values. These include respect (manaaki), empathy (aroha), fostering unity (kotahitanga), seeking knowledge and understanding (mātauranga), just behavior (tika), relational/interconnected view of all creation (whakapapa), and uplifting others (hāpai) (Härtel, 2015; Spiller et al., 2011).

Pattern thinking and relational knowledge are also evident in the concept of indigenous capitalism, defined as the accumulation and redistribution of wealth by indigenous corporations within indigenous communities, with the objective of ecological, social, spiritual, and cultural stewardship (Härtel, 2015). It prioritizes relationships with people and the environment, with an emphasis on stewardship and sustainability instead of economic growth (Härtel, 2015).

Our illustrative case of indigenous faiths shows how clues for effective diversity management may be extracted from analyzing belief systems. Our analysis suggests that virtuous cycles may be achieved in religious diversity management by enacting practices that reflect pattern and relational thinking and the values that underpin them, such as respect, empathy, and seeking to learn and understand another's point of view. A methodology that may be useful in applying these concepts in the workforce is Organizational Diversity Learning Framework (Fujimoto & Härtel, 2017). This practical framework lays out an intervention that provides structured positive interaction opportunities between employees from different backgrounds and worldviews, supporting inter-group understanding and inclusive decision-making.

Discussion

In this chapter, we have described the dynamic growth in religious diversity around the world, introduced and problematized an integrated definition of religious diversity, and examined religious diversity management from the perspectives of Paradox Theory and Indigenous Worldviews. In so doing, we have highlighted religion-based tensions and differences in the workplace as opportunities for dialogue, mutual discovery, understanding, and respect. As well as this, we have illustrated how a consideration of the variety of beliefs represented by the religious diversity spectrum may inform effective means for managing differences in religious perspectives. We also have identified the Organizational Diversity Learning Framework (Fujimoto & Härtel, 2017) as a potentially useful method for the "doing" of religious diversity management. We now conclude our chapter by suggesting a number of ways to promote an inclusive and positive work environment for religious diversity.

First, given the nature of the contemporary landscape, it is imperative that managers and HR professionals be proactive in promoting accurate knowledge of the full spectrum of religious diversity in their organization as well as the organizational policies that define the scope and accommodation of religious expression at work, and what constitutes discriminatory acts. Second, developing and encouraging the use of perspective-taking and empathy supports acceptance of dissimilar identities and decreases people's tendency to stereotype (Galinsky & Moskowitz, 2000). Doing so will reduce unintended offence and normalize the presence and appropriateness of religious diversity (cf. Forrest-Bank & Dupper, 2016).

Third, research demonstrates that sharing and emphasizing a group identity (collective identity) facilitates supportive behavior toward colleagues, feedback acceptance, shared understanding, and effective communication (Haslam & Reicher, 2006; Haslam et al., 2012; Stevenson & Sagherian-Dickey, 2016). Thus, organizational newcomers whose orientation toward religion and faith differs from their colleagues are likely to feel anxious about being accepted (Iyer et al., 2009). Managers can support their transition by fostering shared group goals and structuring a positive introduction to other group members (Chatman et al., 1998; Stephan, 2014). Providing ample opportunity for positive contact is important too, as intergroup contact theory research shows that increased levels of contact between two religious groups decreases levels of prejudice and results in improved intergroup relations (Hewstone et al., 2008; for a review see Pettigrew, 1998). This holds true in cases of both direct and indirect intergroup contact (Paolini et al., 2004) as long as individuals have equal status to other members of their team and the team has common goals (cf. Pettigrew, 1998).

Fourth, borrowing successful approaches from research on integrating religion and spirituality into psychological counseling and therapy (Walker et al., 2004) may be useful in the workplace. One such approach is the direct method, which directly incorporates religious and spiritual resources, such as prayer, sacred texts, and representatives from the various perspectives toward faith within the organization (Tan, 1996). The direct method is apparent in countries such as Indonesia, the Philippines, India, and Tanzania, where acceptance and official accommodation of religious diversity is quite commonplace (Gröschl & Bendl, 2015). Another method of integration is not to explicitly focus on or discuss religion or spirituality, but instead to focus on the beliefs and values derived from the specific religion or spirituality (Tan, 1996). Managers and organizations in secular nations may prefer the indirect method.

To conclude, the key to effective religious diversity management is creating a psychologically safe environment where people can bring their identity orientation toward religion to work without fear of being negatively viewed or excluded (cf. Avery, 2011; Härtel, 2004) and where people accept, embrace, and see the value in different worldviews (Härtel, 2004; Härtel & Fujimoto, 2000). Organizations that do so will reap the benefits in recruitment, retention, performance, and innovation outcomes (Miller, 2015).

References

American Religious Identification Survey. (2009). ARIS 2008 Summary Report. Retrieved from http://www.americanreligion.

Ancarani, A., Ayach, A., Di Mauro, C., Gitto, S., & Mancuso, P. (2016). Does religious diversity in health team composition affect efficiency? Evidence from Dubai. *British Journal of Management*, 27(4), 740–59.

Anti-Defamation League. (2012). Anti-Semitism in the United States: ADL Audit of Anti-Semitic Incidents in 2011. Retrieved from http://www.jewishvirtuallibrary.org/2011-adl-audit-of-anti-semitic-incidents-in-u-s.

Atran, S. (2002). The Neuropsychology of Religion. *In* Joseph, R. (ed.), *NeuroTheology: Brain, science, spirituality & religious experience*, California: University Press California.

Avery, D. R. (2011). Support for diversity in organizations: A theoretical exploration of its origins and offshoots. *Organizational Psychology Review*, 1(3), 239–56.

Bader, V., Alidadi, K., & Vermeulen, F. (2013). Religious diversity and reasonable accommodation in the workplace in six European countries: An introduction. *International Journal of Discrimination and the Law*, 13(2–3), 54–82.

Basford, L. (2010). From headphones to hijabs: Cultural and religious experiences of Somali youth in US schools. *Proceedings of Intercultural Competence Conference August*, 1, 1–26.

Bellah, R. N. (1988). Civil religion in America, *Daedalus*, 117(3), 97–118.

Cash, K. C., Gray, G. R., & Rood, S. A. (2000). A framework for accommodating religion and spirituality in the workplace. *The Academy of Management Executive*, 14(3), 124–34.

Chan-Serafin, S., Brief, A. P., & George, J. M. (2013). Perspective – How does religion matter and why? Religion and the organizational sciences. *Organization Science*, 24, 1585–600.

Chatman, J. A., Polzer, J. T., Barsade, S. G., & Neale, M. A. (1998). Being different yet feeling similar: The influence of demographic composition and organizational culture on work processes and outcomes. *Administrative Science Quarterly*, 43(4), 749–80.

Chudek, M., Muthukrishna, M., & Henrich, J. (2015). Cultural evolution. *In* Buss, D. M. (ed.), *Handbook of evolutionary psychology*, Vol. 2. Hoboken, NJ: Wiley, 1–21.

Cunningham, G. B. (2010). The influence of religious personal identity on the relationships among religious dissimilarity, value dissimilarity, and job satisfaction. *Social Justice Research*, 23(1), 60–76.

Dobson, S. (2010). Calm amidst the storm, reflection rooms provide privacy, peace and religious accommodation at work. *Canadian HR Reporter*, 23(17), 23.

Dow, D., Cuypers, I. R. P., & Ertug, G. (2016). The effects of within-country linguistic and religious diversity on foreign acquisitions. *Basingstoke*, 47(3), 319–46.

Dupper, D., Forrest-Bank, S., & Lowry-Carusillo, A. (2015). Experiences of religious minorities in public school settings: Findings from focus groups involving Muslim, Jewish, Catholic, and Unitarian Universalist Youths. *Children & School*, 37(1), 37–45.

Durkheim, E. (1912). *The Elementary Forms of Religious Life*. New York: The Free Press.

Forrest-Bank, S. S., & Dupper, D. R. (2016). A qualitative study of coping with religious minority status in public schools. *Children and Youth Services Review*, 61, 261–70.

Fujimoto, Y., & Härtel, C. E. J. (2017). Organizational diversity learning framework: Going beyond diversity training programs. *Personnel Review*, 46(6), 1120–41.

Galinsky, A. D., & Moskowitz, G. B. (2000). Perspective-taking: Decreasing stereotype expression, stereotype accessibility, and in-group favoritism. *Journal of Personality and Social Psychology*, 78(4), 708–24.

Gervais, W. M., & Norenzayan, A. (2013). Religion and the origins of anti-atheist prejudice. *In* Clarke, S., Powell, R., & Savulescu, J. (eds.), *Intolerance and Conflict: A Scientific and Conceptual Investigation*. Oxford, UK: Oxford University Press, 126–45.

Ghumman, S., & Ryan, A. M. (2013). Not welcome here: Discrimination towards women who wear the Muslim headscarf. *Human Relations*, 66, 671–98.

Ghumman, S., Ryan, A. M., Barclay, L. A., & Markel, K. S. (2013). Religious discrimination in the workplace: A review and examination of current and future trends. *Journal of Business and Psychology*, 28(4), 439–54.

Gröschl, S., & Bendl, R. (2015). *Managing Religious Diversity in the Workplace*. London & New York: Routledge.

Grossman, R. J. (2008). Religion at work-weaving religion or spirituality into company culture poses legal and managerial challenges galore. *HRMagazine*, 53(12), 26.

Guerci, M., & Carollo, L. (2016). A paradox view on green human resource management: Insights from the Italian context. *The International Journal of Human Resource Management*, 27(2), 212–38.

Haslam, S. A., & Reicher, S. (2006). Stressing the group: Social identity and the unfolding dynamics of responses to stress. *Journal of Applied Psychology*, 91, 1037–52.

Härtel, C. E. J. (2004). Towards a multicultural world: Identifying work systems, practices and employee attitudes that embrace diversity. *The Australian Journal of Management*, 29(2), 189–200.

(2014). Advancing organizational behavior through context considerations. *Journal of Management & Organization*, 20(4), 415–16.

(2015). Indigenous management styles. *In* Wright, J. D. (ed.), *International encyclopedia of the social and behavioral sciences*, 2nd edition. Oxford, UK: Elsevier, 784–7.

Härtel, C. E. J., Douthitt, S. S., Härtel, G., & Douthitt, S. Y. (1999). Equally qualified but unequally perceived: Openness to perceived dissimilarity as a predictor of race and sex discrimination in performance judgments. *Human Resource Development Quarterly*, 10(1), 79–89.

Härtel, C. E. J., & Fujimoto, Y. (2000). Diversity is not a problem to be managed by organisations but openness to perceived dissimilarity is. *Journal of Australian and New Zealand Academy of Management*, 6(1), 14–27.

Härtel, C. E. J., & O'Connor, J. M. (2014). Contextualizing research: Putting context back into organizational behavior research. *Journal of Management & Organization*, 20(4), 417–22.

Haslam, S. A., Reicher, S. D., & Levine, M. (2012). When other people are heaven, when other people are hell: How society determines the nature and impact of social support. *In* Jetten, J., Haslam, C., & Haslam, S. A. (eds.), *The social cure: Identity, health, and well-being*. London & New York: Psychology Press, 157–74.

Hemming, P. J., & Madge, N. (2012). Researching children, youth and religion: Identity, complexity and agency. *Childhood*, 19(1), 38–51.

Hewstone, M., Kenworthy, J. B., Cairns, E., Tausch, N., Hughes, J., Tam, T., Voci, A., Von Hecker, U., & Pinder, C. (2008). Stepping stones to reconciliation in Northern Ireland: Intergroup contact, forgiveness, and trust. *In* Nadler, A., Malloy, T. E., & Fisher, J. D. (eds.), *The Social Psychology of Intergroup Reconciliation*. Oxford: Oxford University Press, 199–266.

Hicks, D. A. (2003). Religion and respectful pluralism in the workplace: A constructive framework. *Journal of Religious Leadership*, 2(1), 23–51.

Iyer, A., Jetten, J., Tsivrikos, D., Postmes, T., & Haslam, S. A. (2009). The more (and the more compatible) the merrier: Multiple group memberships and identity compatibility as predictors of adjustment after life transitions. *British Journal of Social Psychology*, 48(4), 707–33.

Johnson, M. K., Rowatt, W. C., & LaBouff, J. P. (2012). Religiosity and prejudice revisited: In-group favoritism, out-group derogation, or both? *Psychology of Religion and Spirituality*, 4(2), 154.

Jones, E. E., Farina, A., Hastorf, A. H., Markus, H., Miller, D. T., & Scott, R. A. (1984). *Social Stigma: The Psychology of Marked Relationships*. New York: Freeman.

Kay, A. C., Whitson, J. A., Gaucher, D., & Galinsky, A. D. (2009). Compensatory control achieving order through the mind, our institutions, and the heavens. *Current Directions in Psychological Science*, 18(5), 264–8.

Kelly, E. P. (2008). Accommodating religious expression in the workplace. *Employee Responsibilities and Rights Journal*, 20(1), 45–56.

King, J. E. K. (2008). (Dis)missing the obvious. *Journal of Management Inquiry*, 17(3), 214–24.

King, J. E., & Williamson, I. O. (2005). Workplace religious expression, religiosity and job satisfaction: Clarifying a relationship. *Journal of Management, Spirituality & Religion*, 2(2), 173–98.

Lees, J., & Horwath, J. (2009). "Religious parents . . . Just want the best for their kids:" Young people's perspectives on the influence of religious beliefs on parenting. *Children & Society*, 23(3), 162–75.

Legare, C. H., & Watson-Jones, R. E. (2015). The evolution and ontology of ritual. *In The handbook of evolutionary psychology*, Part VI, 34, 1–19.

Mazumdar, S., & Mazumdar, S. (2005). How organizations interface with religion: A typology. *Journal of Management, Spirituality & Religion*, 2(2), 199–220.

McCauley, R. N., & Lawson, E. T. (2002). *Bringing Ritual to Mind: Psychological Foundations of Cultural Forms*. Cambridge: Cambridge University Press.

Mead, W. R. (2006). Religion and US foreign policy. *Foreign Affairs*, 85(5), 24–43.

Miller, B. (2015). Entitlement and conscientiousness in the prediction of organizational deviance. *Personality and Individual Differences*, 82, 114–9.

Miller, W. R., & Thoresen, C. E. (2003). Spirituality, religion, and health. An emerging research field. *American Psychology*, 58(1), 24–35.

Miron-Spektor, E., Gino, F., & Argote, L. (2011). Paradoxical frames and creative sparks: Enhancing individual creativity through conflict and integration. *Organizational Behavior and Human Decision Processes*, 116(2), 229–40.

Moran, C. D. (2007). The public identity work of Evangelical Christian students. *Journal of College Student Development*, 48(4), 418–434.

Morgan, J. F. (2004). How should business respond to a more religious workplace? *SAM Advanced Management Journal*, 69(4), 11.

(2005). Religion at work: A legal quagmire. *Managerial Law*, 47(3/4), 247–59.

Norenzayan, A. (2016). Theodiversity. *Annual Review of Psychology*, 67, 465–88.

Norris, P., & Inglehart, R. (2004). *Sacred and Secular: Religion and Politics Worldwide*. Cambridge: Cambridge University Press.

Paolini, S., Hewstone, M., Cairns, E., & Voci, A. (2004). Effects of direct and indirect cross-group friendships on judgments of Catholics and Protestants in Northern Ireland: The mediating role of an anxiety-reduction mechanism. *Personality and Social Psychology Bulletin*, 30, 770–86.

Pargament, K. I. (1999). The psychology of religion and spirituality? Yes and no. *The International Journal for the Psychology of Religion*, 9(1), 3–16.

Pettigrew, T. F. (1998). Intergroup contact theory. *Annual Review of Psychology*, 49, 65–85.

Pew Research Center. (2015). *America's changing religious landscape*. Pew Research Centre, May 12. Retrieved from: www.pewforum.org/2015/05/12/americas-changing-religious-landscape/.

Richards, P. S., & Bergin, A. E. (1997). *A spiritual strategy for counseling and psychotherapy*. Washington, DC: American Psychological Association.

Rollins, G. (2007). Religious expression in the growing multicultural workplace. *Journal of Diversity Management*, 2(3), 1–12.

Rymarz, R., & Graham, J. (2005). Going to church: Attitudes to church attendance amongst Australian core Catholic youth. *Journal of Beliefs & Values*, 26(1), 55–64.

Stephan, W. (2014). Intergroup anxiety: Theory, research, and practice. *Personality and Social Psychology Review*, 18(3), 239–55.

Stevenson, C., & Sagherian-Dickey, T. (2016). Collectively coping with contact: The role of intragroup support in dealing with the challenges of intergroup mixing in residential contexts. *British Journal of Social Psychology*, 55(4), 681–99.

Scheepers, D., & Derks, B. (2016). Revisiting social identity theory from a neuroscience perspective. *Current Opinion in Psychology*, 11, 74–8.

Spiller, C., Pio, E., Erakovic, L., & Henare, M. (2011). Wise up: Creating organizational wisdom through an ethic of Kaitiakitanga. *Journal of Business Ethics*, 104(2), 223–35.

Tajfel, H. (1978). Social categorization, social identity, and social comparison. *In* H. Tajfel (Ed.), *Differentiation between social groups: Studies in the social psychology of intergroup relations* (pp. 61–76). London: Academic Press.

Tan, S. Y. (1996). Religion in clinical practice: Implicit and explicit integration. *In* Shafranske, E. P. (ed.), *Religion and the Clinical Practice of Psychology*. Washington, DC: American Psychological Association, 365–87.

Trau, R. N. C., & Härtel, C. E. J. (2007). Contextual factors affecting quality of work life and career attitudes of gay men. *Employee Responsibilities and Rights Journal*, 19(3), 207–19.

Turner, J. C., Hogg, M. A., Oakes, P. J., Reicher, S. D., & Wetherell, M. S. (1987). *Rediscovering the Social Group: A Self-Categorization Theory*. Oxford: Blackwell.

Walker, D. F., Gorsuch, R. L., & Tan, S.-Y. (2004). Therapists' integration of religion and spirituality in counseling: A meta-analysis. *Counseling and Values*, 49, 69–80.

Webley, S. (2011). *Religious practices in the workplace*. London: Institute of Business Ethics.

Willard, A., & Norenzayan, A. (2013). Cognitive biases explain religious belief, paranormal belief, and belief in life's purpose. *Cognition*, 129, 379–91.

Winter, M. (2015, November 12). The Stealth Attack on Abortion. *New York Times*, p. A.35.

PART II
Religious Approaches

3 | *The Christian Faith and the Preservation of Personal Identity*

TIMOTHY EWEST

Introduction

Presently, the Christian religion has the most adherents globally, at least until 2050 when Islam is predicted to have an equal percentage of global adherents (Hackett et al., 2015). And, while Christianity may appear as a great edifice, centered around a common set of core beliefs and practices, in reality there are multiple nuances of these beliefs and practices, creating a mosaic of Christian subgroups or sects. These Christian sects, historically, have collaborated (e.g., in the Arts) and at other times been in conflict with one another (e.g., during the crusades). Yet, Christians also share common struggles due to their convictions.

One common struggle among Christians centers on ethical considerations relating to how the Christian faith obligates, confines, or enhances their actions in the workplace. Correspondingly, Christians must also navigate real, and in some cases, perceived barriers within organizations, facing both positive and negative consequences resulting from the manifestation of their faith. Yet, what is paramount for many people of faith is not letting these considerations and barriers marginalize what is a significant contributor to their personal identity.

This chapter will provide a brief summary of the historical emergence of Christianity, survey the major Christian subgroups, summarize the basic tenets of Christianity, consider Christian tensions in the pluralistic world, and then consider how Christians integrate their faith into the workplace. Finally, this chapter considers how the preservation and enhancement of Christian religious identity is a primary motivator for Christians who seek to integrate their faith into the workplace. To illustrate the concepts, this chapter presents the case of Chick-fil-A as an example of how individual Christian beliefs impact an organization, and Nadia Eweida as an example of an organization that impacts the individual Christian. However, both are examples of how Christian beliefs are internalized and normative behavior is created by individuals in order to maintain a Christian identity.

The Historical Emergence of the Christian Faith

According to the Christian Bible (Acts 11:26), those who believed in the work and person of Jesus of Nazareth and followed his teaching, were first regarded as Christians in Antioch circa 5 AD after a visit by the Apostle Paul, an early Jewish convert to the teaching of Jesus. However, for Christians, the origins of the Christian faith predate the person of Christ, whom they regard as the fulfillment of a Hebrew prophecy of the promised Hebrew Messiah. This is visible in the etymology of the name Christian. The word Christian comes from the Greek word Χριστιανός, which means "one who follows Christ." The Greek word for Christ, Χριστός means "anointed one," a translation of the Hebrew word "Messiah" or "Anointed one." The "anointed one" was the individual who would fulfill specific ancient Hebrew prophecy. The person who would fulfill this prophecy was regarded as the Messiah (Hebrew) or the Christ (Greek). Jesus of Nazareth, was given the title "Christ," which is a direct reference to the Hebrew ideal of the person who is a physical descendant of King David and who would reunify the nation of Israel and bring about global peace. For Christians, Jesus's death, burial, resurrection and pending his second coming to earth fulfills the ancient Hebrew prophecies, although most Jews do not recognize Jesus as the anointed one, the Messiah.

Martin Buber (1956), an Israeli Jewish philosopher, captures the tensions between the Christianity and Judaism:

Pre-messianically, our destinies are divided. Now to the Christian, the Jew is the incomprehensibly obdurate man who declines to see what has happened; and to the Jew, the Christian is the incomprehensibly daring man who affirms in an unredeemed world that its redemption has been accomplished. This is a gulf which no human power can bridge. (p. 276)

Jesus followers regarded him as the incarnate Son of God and the Jewish Messiah who would usher in a new earthly kingdom, but more importantly, through his atoning death and resurrection, offer the forgiveness of sins and eternal life. Jesus, who was regarded by some of his followers as a Jewish rabbi or teacher, interpreted Jewish scriptures for a largely Jewish audience and correspondingly those who first followed Jesus were viewed as a sect of Judaism. Christianity grew within context of the immensity of the Roman Empire, which provided a commonly spoken language (Koiné Greek), and safe and easy travel. Christianity, when adopted by the emperor Constantine in 312 CE brought the Roman Church into being (Cunningham & Reich, 2009).

The Roman Catholic Church professes to have been established by Christ, who appointed the first leader of the Church, his follower Simon Peter. The Roman Catholic Church was the first organized Christian church until 1064 CE, when a schism occurred, and the Churches from the Constantinople or Eastern Orthodox Church were established. Finally, Protestantism emerged in the sixteenth century and "protested" specific Roman Catholic doctrines. For example, the Protestants protested papal authority, the sacraments, and ascetic traditions. Today there still remain these three primary established Christian branches: Roman Catholic; Eastern Orthodox; and Protestant (Pelikan, 1992; Walker, 2004b).

Today, these three major branches, and numerous other smaller sects of Christianity, comprise approximately 2.18 billion worldwide, representing nearly a third of the world's population. Globally a quarter of all Christians live in Europe (26%), a third live in the Americas (37%), a quarter live in sub-Saharan Africa (24%), and about an eighth live in Asia and the Pacific (13%) (Christianity, 2011).

Basic Faith Tenets of Christianity

The scope of the Christian faith, accurately depicting or codifying the tenets of the Christian faith is a daunting if not insurmountable task. Yet, there are certain historical beliefs the Church has maintained and are preserved in the creeds. Specifically, The Nicene Creed, which was written in the fourth century as a means to unite the Christian church, is accepted by Roman Catholics, Orthodox Christians, and Protestants (Burn, 1909).

The Nicene Creed

> We believe in one God,
>> the Father almighty,
>> maker of heaven and earth,
>> of all things visible and invisible.

And in one Lord Jesus Christ,
   the only Son of God,
   begotten from the Father before all ages,
      God from God,
      Light from Light,
      true God from true God,
   begotten, not made;
   of the same essence as the Father.
   Through him all things were made.
   For us and for our salvation
      he came down from heaven;
      he became incarnate by the Holy Spirit and the virgin Mary,
      and was made human.
   He was crucified for us under Pontius Pilate;
   he suffered and was buried.
   The third day he rose again, according to the Scriptures.
   He ascended to heaven
   and is seated at the right hand of the Father.
   He will come again with glory
   to judge the living and the dead.
   His kingdom will never end.
And we believe in the Holy Spirit,
   the Lord, the giver of life.
   He proceeds from the Father and the Son,
   and with the Father and the Son is worshiped and glorified.
   He spoke through the prophets.
   We believe in one holy catholic and apostolic church.
   We affirm one baptism for the forgiveness of sins.
   We look forward to the resurrection of the dead,
   and to life in the world to come. Amen.

Correct belief, or orthodoxy, has been a historical as well as contemporary means to determine whether a person or community is adhering to the Christian faith. And, while creeds are an important aspect of determining orthodoxy, formal doctrinal and theological statements or catechisms are also crucial elements of the Christian Church (McGrath, 2005). Table 3.1 offers a typical sample of these Christian doctrinal or catechumenal statements of belief.

These beliefs are the basis of and are intended to be a primary motivator for Christian behavior, acting as a guide for Christians who regard their faith as a significant contributor to forming their personal identity (Emmons, 2003; Wuthnow 2011). Again, Christians also have

Table 3.1 *Basic Christian beliefs*

- One God, eternally existing in three persons: Father, Son, and Holy Spirit.
- God is creator and sustainer of all created things.
- Humans have sinned, or transgressed against God's law, or design and purpose for human life and are not able to restore themselves.
- The death, burial, and resurrection of Jesus the Son of God, is the means to atone for man's sin.
- Those who have received the atonement for their transgressions provided by Christ's death, burial, and resurrection are promised life eternal after death.
- The role of Holy Spirit as a guide, restorative, and indwelling presence for God's people.
- The importance of church sacraments, which can include baptism and the Lord's Supper (Eucharist), either as a direct means of receiving Christ's atoning work or as a symbol of what has been received through belief.
- The authority of sacred texts, which include the Old and New Testaments, and for some Christian traditions church teaching, ecclesial authority of church overseers who preserve and interpret tradition, and extra-biblical writings (e.g., apocrypha).

to navigate barriers within organizations, facing both positive and negative consequences, whilst not letting these tensions marginalize a central aspect of their humanity.

Christian Tensions in the Pluralistic World

Christians use their religious faith as a primary means for ethical self-expression (Wuthnow, 2011) and personal identity (Emmons, 2003). Religion is regarded, along with ethnicity, gender, and age, as being an essential and endemic human right. This is recognized by numerous national and global initiatives and laws including: The Universal Declaration of Human Rights, Title VII of the Civil Rights Act (US), and the Employment Equality Framework Directive (EU).

Yet, Christians still face numerous challenges when seeking to integrate their faith in the workplace, particularly because of the overwhelming assumption that there should "be a wall of separation between a person's beliefs and the workplace" (Kelly, 2008, p. 42). Many organizations seek to remain neutral regarding religion, believing that creating and maintaining an environment that is devoid of religion creates a place safe from harassment, and also prevents religion from being disruptive to work processes (Ashforth & Vaidyanath, 2002; King, 2007). Intentional secularization within the workplace stands in contrast to a society where religion still finds a voice and has a noted impact (Ashforth & Vaidyanath, 2002; Goldblast, 2000; Seales, 2012). But some organizations go beyond the championing of secular neutrality, and actually outwardly resist Christians who choose to express their faith in the workplace (Bradley & Kauanui, 2003; Lund Dean et al., 2003).

Yet, regardless of organizational context, Christians may be stigmatized and have societal stereotypes projected onto them (Bryant, 2011). These stereotypes include depicting Christians as being narrow minded, and having outdated values and exclusive beliefs (Willard, 1992). There are varying consequences when a Christian, or any religion's adherent, has their faith intentionally suppressed by individuals stigmatizing them by projecting stereotypes onto them.

Thomson (2016) conducted qualitative research on the power of stigma in the workplace, to better determine what the religious person's perspective and strategic thought process were as they sought to maintain their religious identity in the workplace. Thomson used Stigma Theory, which defines stigma as "an individual attribute viewed by others as a personal flaw within a social context" (Ragins, 2008, p. 196). Thomson's research considered the question, "What identity management strategies do individuals use with regard to their religious belief?" (p. 38). He found individuals who wished to preserve their religious identities, felt required to navigate real and perceived organizational stigmatisms, and did so as a means to preserve their personal religious identity. Thomson found, "participants revealed that their strategy to manage religion in the workplace was contextual and factors that influence their decisions occurred on the individual, organizational and national levels" (p. 217). The reality is that many religious individuals feel the need to develop strategies to integrate their faith into a resistant workplace.

Practices of Integrating Faith into the Workplace

As mentioned earlier, Christian beliefs require of the individual specific corresponding behaviors, and whether these behaviors are expressed or suppressed, is determined based on the individual perception of the Christian understanding of an organization's existing policy and the organizational culture – thus personal strategies emerge (Thomson, 2016). Thomson found that individuals used three integration strategies as means to integrate or suppress faith into the workplace: an awareness of religious differences in the marketplace, leading to expression; an awareness of the positive benefits of their religion at work, which led to integration; and the connection of religious faith to spirituality, which led to integration. A fourth strategy of suppression happens when the religious people perceive barriers to their religious expression.

But other strategies have also been observed. Miller (2007), and later Miller and Ewest (2013), observed that Christians (people of faith) integrate their faith in four distinct strategic ways, including: individual and organizational behaviors focused on ethical concerns, expressing religious faith verbally or through symbols and religious garb, enriching faith through personal or communal spiritual activities, and seeing work as an experience of personal calling or organizational impact.

But for many Christians, the only means for Christian faith integration is ethics. Ethics or morals refers to innate knowledge of right and wrong, which transcends culture and time, and can be based on multiple personal, cultural, societal, and religious sources that are concerned with the expectations of how individuals ought to live (Ewest, 2016; Gill, 2014; Stackhouse, 1995). So, if ethics is understood as expectations of how one should live, and the source for some is religious expectations of how they ought to live the life of faith, then ethics can supersede other forms of religious expression.

Thus, the nature of religion is that beliefs ethically direct, confine, and mandate individual and communal practices, and thus ethics based in religion has been understood as representative of "alternative paradigms for evaluating the meaning and methods of business behavior" (Epstein, 2002, p. 66). Thus religious perspectives are suggested to preface judgment, guidance, and inspiration related to ethical decision-making (e.g., Fernando & Jackson, 2006). Moreover, religion is regarded not just as a simple human right, but as a means of "upholding of human dignity and moral order in a world dominated by voracious state bureaucracies and sprawling transnational corporations that are neither effectively accountable to national law nor effectively answerable to well-established codes of behavior" (McClay, 2000, p. 56). Therefore, religion and correspondingly Christianity's ability to influence individuals in ethical and organizational settings has been well established (Dyck & Wiebe, 2012; Stackhouse, 1995).

Christian Ethics Confined to Ill-Aligned Normative Ethics

Christianity is misunderstood, however, and consequently ill-aligned within organizational research. Prior to the recent emergence of the field of business ethics, religious moralists preached Christian morality in business, and since then, the field has been taken over by moral ethicists framing the conversation in terms of normative rational philosophical arguments, which indirectly deny or marginalize theological ethics (De George, 1986). Arguably, ethics is the primary attempt made by Christians, management scholars, and organizational leaders, to integrate Christian belief into organizational life. Specifically, for management scholars and organizational leaders, the primary means of integrating Christianity into organizational life is done by attempting to align Christian beliefs and their corresponding ethical codes with the predominant governing ethical theory, the Normative Ethical approach. The Normative Ethical approach, rooted in Modernism, assumes that individuals are and/or need to be rational agents when engaging in ethical decisions (De Cremer et al., 2011).

First, while this assumption is myopic and reductionist, demonstrating a misconception of the Christian religion, it is nonetheless synchronous with the governing economic assumption that humans making economic decisions do so as rational decision makers. This condition has produced two phenomena. Ulrich (2002) notes both: The first suggests economics is assumed to be unlike the rest of life because it is in the reality of pure and autonomous business transactions; where organizational behavior is distinct from other types of behavior and business organizations are distinct from other organizations (since it is suggested the primary goals for business organizations is profit). The second phenomenon flows out of the first, wherein ethical training is done best by developing rational decision makers using the Normative Ethical decision-making approach and processes (Rest et al., 1999; Trevino & Weaver, 1994; Weaver, 2001).

This is demonstrated by the majority of ethical decision making models or processes which all contend for the central and dominant role of reason and cognition for appropriate ethical outcomes (Cooper, 1998; Day, 2003; Kidder, 1995;). The majority of ethical decision making models emphasize ethical decision making as a rational choice, indicating that if a person knows the good, they will do the good (c.f. Plato in Jostein Gardner's 1991 novel *Sophie's World*). Thus the goal for Normative Ethics is to capitalize on the assumption that people in organizations are basically rational in regards to actions in the marketplace (weighing costs verses benefits) and rational when making ethical decisions (De Cremer et al., 2011; Ulrich, 2002).

However, there is a growing body of research that shows a weak or moderate association between moral reasoning and moral action or behavior (Bergman, 2004; Blasi, 1983; Hoffman, 2000; Walker, 2004a). Moreover, other research suggests that other personal motivators may be active beyond reasoning when making ethical decision, including: emotions (Eisenberg, 1986; Hoffmann, 2000), intuitions (Haidt, 2001), and, specifically, religion (Blasi, 1983; Vitell, 2009; Weaver & Argle, 2002). This suggests there are other motivational aspects involved in the ethical decision making process, and that moral reasoning is not central, but is instead one important aspect among many in ethical decision making.

Secondly, the Normative Ethical theory posits that if ethics are to be effective they must be stable over time, rather than shifting for expediency's sake. Yet, Bay et al. (2010) examined the history of Christian normative principles with respect to business, tracing this relationship through five distinct time periods: early Christianity, the Patristic period, the Dark and Middle Ages, the Reformation, and the Enlightenment. They examined five practices informed by the Christian faith in each period: the purpose of work, ownership of land, amassing wealth, charging interest on loans, conducting trade, and making a profit (p. 655). Their research shows that each of the five Christian practices were initially regarded as prohibited and immoral, but over time became acceptable and in some cases admired.

This overview suggests that regarding Normative Ethical theory as a solution for integrating the Christian faith into organizational life is problematic, fostering reductionism, because it is ill fitted to a Christian religious experience which is phenomenological and multi-dimensional, leaving Christians who want to integrate their faith into their work confined to normative expressions (Stefan, 2008). Since normative theories poorly represent religion, religion proper has all but disappeared from the discussion of business ethics (Ferrell, 2005; Quddus et al., 2009) and there remains only a nostalgic appreciation, and a malaise in regards to organizational fit for business students and workplace employees who have their ethics grounded in a faith or religion (Quddus et al., 2009).

This chapter suggests that for Christian ethics to be understood correctly, they must be understood as an extension of Christians forming and maintaining their personal identity, and this process of identity formation is rooted in the work and person of Christ. Leahy (1986) suggests two orientations within theology, the first being the orthodox model, which aligns itself philosophically with normative ethics. Here the orthodox theologian searches their tradition for moral norms and applies them to business cases. However, Leary argues that this theological orientation is problematic because the Christian ethic is an "embodied ethic," which he describes as having a meaning, a systematic framework, an investment of the person's spirit, an ethos which includes the physical body. Stefan (2008) addresses the multidimensionality of a Christian ethic which concerns itself first with the person of Christ – specifically the waters of baptism, whereby the Christian is united with Christ and his or her actions become a means to express this life of faith; from this union, behaviors and belief flow, which become norms.

The Way Forward: Christianity Is about Personal Identity

Identity is regarded as important if not endemic to religion and understanding religion. Specifically Christianity, as the pursuit and preservation of the formation of personal identity, would provide researchers and organizational leaders with insight into Christian behaviors in the workplace. Emmons (2003) who understands religion as instrumental to an individual's identity formation, specifically in regards to an individual's personality, suggests that "People construct a life story often rooted in a religious ideology that gives a unique meaning to their life" (p. 134). Wuthnow (2011) concurs, understanding religion as a central human activity whereby people create meaning for themselves (p. 273). Moreover, Richards and Bergin (1997) state that "if we omit religious and spiritual realities from our account of human behaviour, it won't matter much what we keep in, because we will have omitted the most fundamental aspect of human behaviour" (p. xi).

Tracy et al. (2014) and Mele and Naughton (2011) suggest that the most obvious connection organizations can have to religion, is how individual identities approximate expectations associated with organizational roles. Fundamentally, the literature on identity concerns itself with how individuals and groups answer two fundamental questions: "Who am I?" and "Who are you?" (p. 9). Identity is an active research topic across social disciplines, but only just emerging within management studies. Specifically, identity theories can help explain the place of religion within organizations. For example, Social Identity Theory understands the individual's identity to consist of abilities, interests, and psychological traits, and these dynamics interact with social structures, creating salient group classifications (Ashforth & Mael, 1989). These theories are widely applied to religion within the disciplines of sociology and psychology (Tracy et al., 2014).

Examples of this exploration of religious identity within organizational life are limited, but do exist. Weaver and Agle (2002) suggest a Symbolic Interactionist Perspective, which states that work behavior will align itself with role expectations based on personal identity and religious identity. Wimberley (1989) conducted research on religious identity and a person's role expectations. Similarly, Werner (2008) explored the role of Christianity as an intermediary institution and identity creating context. The study examined how Christian religious identity impacted the way business activity was carried out. The research found that Christian identity did impact business practices, but the business environment is just one behavioral context where the identity may be used. Ashforth and Mael (1989) and Hogg and Terry (2000) suggest that workers' spirituality will drive behavior at work based on how they classify or identify themselves. Finally, Walker (2004a) argues that for some workers, moral views are framed by their religion/spirituality.

The exploration of personal identity within organizations appears to align better with the phenomenon and existential nature of religion. While many scholars continue to misunderstand the logics of Christianity, Christian scholars are working within similar theories, using much the same philosophical underpinnings and understandings from within their discipline to depict how personal identity is also foundational to Christian ethical identity.

Christian Identity and Christian Ethics

Religion, whether formalized in adhering to a Church or religious community, or expressed as individual belief or spirituality, or apprehending a revealed supernatural truth, creates for itself as well as follows its own logics (Varga, 2010). These logics, while internally consistent for those within the religious tradition, remain opaque to those outside. These internal logics resist reductionism, whether in regards to the two aforementioned means or other philosophical tendencies imposed on them from outside.

This phenomenon is understood by both Protestants and Catholics (Orthodox withholding). The Second Vatican Council recommended that moral theology become more "Christocentric," recognizing that the work of some Catholic theologians of the Postconciliar period focuses on creating normative rules and denies or ignores some important Christian teachings (Mealey, 2009). Further, Dierksmeier (2012) captures Pope Benedict XVI's insight, commutated in the Caritas in Veritate, which envisions a new hermeneutic. "Instead of treating ethics as an intangible externality of economics, the Pope ponders what can be done in order to visualize and then internalize the positive as well as negative effect of current business models through a new economic hermeneutic" (p. 12). Protestant theologians have also recognized the misalignment.

Hauerwas (2001) argues there is a tendency for theologians to devote too much time trying to translate theological language into normative terms that are comprehensible and meaningful for secular audiences. Peterson and Seligman (2004) support this claim by stating that "although archival and empirical data suggest a link between religiousness, spirituality, and a range of prosocial outcomes, there is a need for greater attention to the specific theological (i.e., doctrinal) beliefs that are central in producing these outcomes" (p. 621).

The assumption that religion is a means to create personal meaning and identity (Emmons, 2003; Wuthnow, 2011) which is at the center of not only Social Identity Theory, but also an emerging perspective among theologians. Mealey (2009) considers the works of Fuchs (1970), as well as Hauerwas (2001) and Ricoeur (2007), who all attempt to redirect Christian ethics back to the centrality of Christ's work and tenets of faith – while honoring the multidimensionality of Christian Ethics (Leahy, 1986; Stefan, 2008).

Hauerwas (2001) understands that, for Christians, biblical narratives identify who they are and enable them to understand and learn universal virtues. Hauerwas suggests that morality is a connected to a person's religious tradition and it provides a context for the virtues being pursued, as well as a guide in the direction of the good one wishes to pursue. Thus, moral development is contextualized within an identity guided by the narrative within tradition, which provides meaning.

Fuchs (1970) argues against a moral theology that is objectified as a set of rules and principles that can be distilled and taught (e.g., Normative Ethical Theory). Instead, Fuchs argues that a moral pursuit for Christians is the joyful message of Christ's call to people, the "vocation of being believers in Christ" (p. 8). The intent is for Christians to live their lives as a calling to follow Christ, whom they regard as "the prototype to whose pattern we are all created and must conform" (p. 5).

Synthesizing the aforementioned theologians around the philosophy of Ricoeur (2007), Mealey (2009) argues that Christian morality has a distinctive identity because it is determined or arrived at by using the Christian tradition. And, in some regards, Christians may arrive at the same moral positions as humanists, or people from another faith, but Christians' moral decisions derive from their Christian tradition. Thus Christian moral theology, like Social Identity Theory, asks two questions: "Who am I?" and "What should I do now as that person?" (p. 37). A Christian can act morally without regard or reference to their religion, but when they act out of or because of their Christianity, they do so with the desire to imitate Christ and/or honor him.

Christian Identity as a Primary Means of Faith Integration

Meeks (1993) points toward the idea that early Christians regarded themselves as having a unique identity, rather than being adherents to a stringent set of moral codes. Christian moral codes, Meeks suggests, were consistent with Jewish morals (not specific Jewish practices), the major difference being that they saw themselves as belonging to God and part of his action in history through Jesus Christ. So, when a Christian behaves, they not only desire good moral actions, but more importantly they try to act in ways that are consistent with honoring God and preserving or enhancing their distinctive Christian identity. For example, numerous employees may intentionally seek to serve customers so they are satisfied, but those who have their Christian identity as central to their lives, are caring for others because they want to imitate Christ's love for them. While this may be indistinguishable to the customer or fellow employees, it is nonetheless central to the employee who holds their Christian faith as an important or central part of their identity.

Meeks depicts Ricoeur's (2007) emphasis on narrative in this process since the history as described in the sacred text allows Christians to be informed about their own moral choices and ensuing personal identity, based on the identity of other Christians provided in the narrative of the text. Drawing on an Aristotelian understanding of ethics, it is the Christian narrative that guides the pursuit of virtue and moral happiness; the narrative does not replace reason but enables Christians to imagine the good to be sought within the context of their current circumstances. Thus while ethical expectations are the same for everyone, researchers and organizational leaders must understand the importance of the individual's Christian identity being formed and pursued within the community of Christian faith.

Take as an illustration the confusion for some academic scholars and organizational leaders regarding sacred scriptures. Researchers and organizational leaders must understand that when Christians reference sacred scripture, it is done with the intent of being moral in behavior (following normative rules), but more importantly to have their actions imitate Christ. Mealey (2009) suggests that rationality still plays a part of moral decision making, but that those decisions are placed within the narrative of Christianity as individual Christians seek to preserve their Christian identity.

Primary among the many Christian narratives that can be drawn upon to provide personal identity, is the central Christian narrative concerning the sacrificial death of Christ on the cross, by which Christians understand the nature of God's love for them. Melé and Dierksmeier (2012) capture this succinctly by stating, "Charity is the central value of Christian morality overall" (p. 10). This act of Christ's love demonstrated on the cross should be the central narrative that confines all Christian actions in and out of the workplaces, being a primary motivation for behavior. Pope Benedict XVI states,

> Just as a family does not submerge the identities of its individual members, just as the Church rejoices in each "new creation" (Gal 6:15; 2 Cor 5:17) incorporated by Baptism into her living Body, so too the unity of the human family does not submerge the identities of individuals, peoples and cultures, but makes them more transparent to each other and links them more closely in their legitimate diversity (Benedict XVI, 2009).

Whatever ethical workplace norms Christians adhere to, they are to be motivated and given meaning by a love for others that is independent and not contingent on reward, praise, or personal cost, because this is how Christians were loved by Christ and in acting, they identify with Christ and his love for them.

Cases for Discussion

The two cases that follow both depict examples of how Christian faith plays a significant role in the integration of faith in the workplace. Both cases represent individuals who act as a means to solidify their identity as Christians. The first case, Chick-fil-A, illustrates how individual Christian identity formation is projected onto the entire organization. The second case illustrates how organizations can inhibit individual Christian identity formation.

Case Study Chick-fil-A

In 1946, S. Truett Cathy, a Christian businessman, opened his first restaurant, the Dwarf House, in Atlanta and invented a new style of chicken sandwich a few years later. In 1967, Cathy opened his first Chick-fil-A at a mall. Today Chick-fil-A has over 1,600 restaurants, $4 billion in sales, and has been voted America's healthiest fast food chain. A remarkable accomplishment especially for a restaurant that only operates six days out of the week (https://www.chick-fil-a.com/About/History).

Chick-fil-A has a companywide Closed on Sunday policy. Every Sunday, all 1,605 restaurants are closed. Cathy says that it is one of the best business decisions he has ever made, and has been established since his start in 1946. The Closed on Sunday policy is a testament to Cathy's faith in God, and as a Christian he did not want to deal with money on the Lord's day. The policy is also consistent with the corporate purpose of Chick-fil-A, which states:

To glorify God by being a faithful steward of all that is entrusted to us. To have a positive influence on all who come in contact with Chick-fil-A. The Closed on Sunday policy allows employees to be with family, worship, be in fellowship, or rest (Chick-fil-A's Closed on Sunday Policy, 2012).

This policy, according to Chick-fil-A, attracts people who have values, are purpose driven and seek balance between work and family. Cathy states that it is a financially sound decision because Chick-fil-A is blessed by the Lord with the great success they have had (Chick-fil-A's Closed on Sunday Policy, 2012).

The main motivation for the Closed on Sunday policy comes from a Biblical scripture passage from the book of Exodus, which states "Remember the Sabbath day by keeping it holy, six days you shall labor and do your work, but the seventh is the Sabbath to the Lord, your God, on it you shall do no work" (Exodus 20:8). Since Cathy identifies as a Christian, he believes that it is his responsibility to honor the Sabbath (Sunday); but for non-Christians it may be seen as simply a time for family or relaxation. While the company is founded on Cathy's Christian values, it is not religiously exclusive. Chick-fil-A seeks to identify with many different people on the basis of common values and morals.

Wheaton (2010) quotes S. Truett Cathy: "we feel like it's a fundamental business issue to us ... and we're not tempted to open on Sunday. Ironically, a lot of people respect the fact that we put something ahead of making another dollar in life." Chick-fil-A doesn't seem to be suffering financially from this Closed on Sunday policy, with average sales per restaurant in 2014 at $3.1 million (Schoffman et al., 2016).

Case Study Nadia Eweida

Nadia Eweida worked at the British Airways check-in counter at London's Heathrow Airport. Nadia was a Christian. Earlier in the year, she attended an employee diversity training program where she was instructed about the company's diversity and tolerance policy, which emphasized respect for minorities. After this meeting, she began to wear a small silver cross pendant, which allowed her to show others she identified as a Christian.

But, on September 20, 2006, while wearing her cross at work, she was told by supervisors to remove the pendant because it was an important symbol of her Christian faith. While British Airways offered her another job where she would not be confined to the uniform policy, she refused and shortly therefore she was suspended. Later, Nadia Eweida filed a lawsuit in British courts claiming religious discrimination, and was vindicated. Today, British Airlines now has a new uniform policy in place (Hill, 2013).

Conclusion

This chapter provided a brief summary of the historical emergence of Christianity, surveyed the major Christian subgroups, summarized the basic tenets of Christianity, considered Christian tensions in the pluralistic world, and then, germane to this publication, considered how Christians integrate their faith into the workplace. Finally, this chapter considered how the preservation and enhancement of religious identity is a primary motivator for Christians who seek to integrate their faith into the workplace. The chapter resolved by presenting an alternative theoretical means to frame Christian ethics, suggesting theoretical consensus between social identity theory and Christian Moral Identity hermeneutical theories as posited by Fuchs (1970), Hauerwas (2001), and Ricoeur (2007), as a means to more accurately embrace the essence of an embodied Christian ethic (Leahy, 1986).

Implications/directions for Future Research and Practice

The purpose of this chapter is to suggest the need for identity formation theory as a means to better align the use of the Christian religion as a resource for moral behavior within organizations. Moreover, while this approach is not conclusive, it endeavors to approach religion with a "thicker" (Dadze-Arthur, 2017) understanding to provide an accurate descriptive analysis, in what Berger (2011) calls the Symbolic Universe, the body of theological tradition. Berger suggests that religion should be understood as a grouping of symbols "which shape ideas, knowledge and human life, determine right and wrong and structure human relationships and actions" (p. 147). When researchers and organizational leaders are able to understand and observe religion as it occurs, and not as configurations of socioeconomic basis, they may then begin to understand the ways in which religious ethics can contribute to the betterment of organizations and the greater world.

If organizational researchers and leaders can understand the real essence of the Christian religion and based on this awareness choose the right custodial theory to explore the significance of religious integration in the workplace, without reducing or confining it, they not only honor the phenomenon of Christian (religious) belief, but also act with integrity in regards to their role as social scientists.

References

Ashforth, B.E., & Mael, F. (1989). Social identity theory and the organization. *Academy of Management Review*, 14, 20–39.

Ashforth, B., & Vaidyanath, D. (2002). Work organizations as secular religions. *Journal of Management Inquiry*, 11(4), 359–70.

Bay, D., McKeage, K., & McKeage, J. (2010). An historical perspective on the interplay of Christian thought and business ethics. *Business & Society* 49(4), 652–76.

Benedict XVI (2009). Encyclical Letter "Caritas in veritate." Retrieved from: www.vatican.va/holy_father/benedict_xvi/encyclicals/documents/hf_ben-xvi_enc_20090629_caritas-in-veritate_en.html.

Bergman, R. (2004). Identity as motivation: Toward a theory of moral self. *In* Lapsley, D. K., & Narvaez, D. (eds.), *Moral development, self and identity*, London, England. Psychology Press, 21–46.

Berger, P. L. (2011). *The sacred canopy: Elements of a sociological theory of religion*. New York: Open Road Media.

Blasi, A. (1983). Moral cognition and moral action: A theoretical perspective. *Developmental Review*, 3, 178–210.

Bradley, J., & Kauanui, S. (2003). Comparing spirituality on three southern California college campuses. *Journal of Organizational Change Management*, 16(4), 448–62.

Buber, M. (1956). The two foci of the Jewish soul. *In* Herberg, W. (ed.), *The writings of Martin Buber*. New York: Meridian Books.

Burn, A. E. (1909). *The Nicene Creed*. Edwin, S. Gorham. Charelston, NC: BiblioLife Publishers, 23–34.

Bryant, A.N. (2011). Evangelicals on campus: An exploration of culture, faith, and college life. *In* Waggoner, M. D. (ed.), *Sacred and secular tensions in higher education*. New York: Routledge, 108–33.

Chick-fil-A's Closed on Sunday Policy. (2012). Retrieved from: www.chick-fil-a.com/Pressroom/Fact-Sheets#?release=Sunday2012.

Cooper, T.C. (1998). *The responsible administrator* (4th edn.). San Franscio, CA: Jossey Bass.

Cunningham, L. S., & Reich, J. J. (2009). *Culture and values: A survey of the humanities.* Boston, MA, Cengage Learning.

Day, L. A. (2003). *Ethics in media communications. Cases and controversies* (4th edn.). Belmont, CA: Wadsworth Thompson Learning.

Dadze-Arthur, A. (2017). *The Interpretation of Cultures.* Boca Raton, FL: CRC Press.

De Cremer, D., Van Dick, R., Tenbrunsel, A., Pillutla, M., & Murninghan, J.K. (2011). Understanding ethical behavior and decision making in management: A behavioral business ethics approach. *British Journal of Management,* 22(1), 1–12.

De George, R. (1986). Theological ethics and business ethics. *Journal of Business Ethics,* 5(6), 421–32.

Dierksmeier, C. (2012). Deconstructing the neoclassical economic paradigm. *In* Melé, D., & Dierksmeier, C. (eds.), *Human development in business. Values and humanistic management in the in the encyclical "Caritas in Veritate."* New York: Palgrave MacMillan.

Dyck, B., & Wiebe, E. (2012). Salvation, theology and organizational practices across the centuries. *Organization,* 19(3), 299–324.

Eisenberg, N. (1986). *Altruistic emotion, cognition, and behavior.* Hillsdale, NJ: Erlbaum.

Emmons, R. (2003). *The psychology of ultimate concerns: Motivation and spirituality in personality.* New York: Guilford Press.

Epstein, E. M. (2002). Religion and business–the critical role of religious traditions in management education. *Journal of Business Ethics,* 38(1), 91–6.

Ewest, T. (2016). Leadership and moral behavior. *In* Marques, J., & Dhiman, S. (eds.), *Leadership today: Practices for personal and professional performance.* New York: Springer.

Fernando, M., & Jackson, B. (2006). The influence of religion-based workplace spirituality on business leaders' decision-making: An inter-faith study. *Journal of Management & Organization,* 12(1), 23–39.

Ferrell, O. C. (2005). A framework for understanding organizational ethics. *Business ethics: New challenges for business schools and corporate leaders,* 3–17.

Fuchs, J. (1970). *Human values and Christian morality,* trans. Heelan, M. H., McRedmound, M., Young, E., & Waston, G. Dublin, Ireland: Humanities Press, Ex-Monastery Library edition.

Gill, R. (2014). *A textbook of Christian ethics.* New York. Bloomsbury Publishing.

Global, Christianity, (2011). A report on the size and distribution of the world's Christian population. PDF Retrieved www.pewforum.org/2012/12/18/global-religious-landscape-christians/, 12–29.

Gonzalez, J. L. (1984). *The story of Chrisfianity. Vol. 1: The early Church to the dawn of the Reformafion.* San Francisco, CA: HarperOne.

Hackett, C., Stonawski, M., Potančoková, M., Grim, B. J., & Skirbekk, V. (2015). The future size of religiously affiliated and unaffiliated populations. *Demographic Research*, 32, 829.

Haidt, J. (2000). The positive emotion of elevation. *Prevention and Treatment*, 3(3), 2–7.

Hauerwas, S. (2001). On keeping theological ethics theological. *In* Berkman, J., & Cartwright, M. (eds.), *The Hauerwas reader*. Durham, NC: Duke University Press, 51–74.

Hill, M. (2013). Religious symbolism and conscientious objection in the workplace: An evaluation of Strasbourg's judgment in Eweida and others v. United Kingdom. *Ecclesiastical Law Journal*, 15(02), 191–203.

Hoffman, M.L. (2000). *Empathy and moral development: Implications for caring and justice.* New York: Cambridge University Press.

Hogg, M. A., & Abrams, D. (1990). Social motivation, self-esteem and social identity. *Social Identity Theory: Constructive and Critical Advances*, 28, 47.

Kelly, E. P. (2008). Accommodating religious expression in the workplace. *Employee Responsibilities and Rights Journal*, 20(1), 45–56.

Kidder, R. M. (1995). *How good people make tough choices: Resolving the dilemmas of ethical living.* New York: Fireside.

King, S. M. (2007). Religion, spirituality, and the workplace: Challenges for public administration. *Public Administration Review*, 67(1), 103–14.

Leahy, J. (1986). Embodied ethics: Some common concerns of religion and business. *Journal of business Ethics.* 5, 466–72.

Lund Dean, K., Fornaciari, C. J., & McGee, J. J. (2003). Research in spirituality, religion, and work: Walking the line between relevance and legitimacy. *Journal of Organizational Change Management*, 16(4), 378–95.

McClay, W. M. (2000). Two concepts of secularism. *The Wilson Quarterly*, 24(3), 54.

McGrath, A. E. (2005). *Iustitia Dei: A history of the Christian doctrine of justification.* Cambridge, England, Cambridge University Press.

Mealey, A.M. (2009). *Identity of Christian morality.* Abingdon: Ashgate Publishing Ltd.

Meeks, W. (1993). *The origins of the first Christians: The First two centuries.* London and New Haven, CT: Yale University Press.

Melé, D., & Dierksmeier, C. (2012). *Human development in business. Values and humanistic management in the in the encyclical "Caritas in Veritate."* New York: Palgrave MacMillan.

Mele, D., & Naughton, M. (2011). The encyclical-letter "Caritas in Veritate": Ethical challenges for business. *Journal of Business Ethics*, 100, 1–7.

Miller, D. W. (2007). *God at work: The history and promise of the faith at work movement.* Oxford, England: Oxford University Press.

Miller, D., & Ewest, T. (2013). The integration box (TIP): An individual and institutional faith, religion, and spirituality at work assessment tool. *In Handbook of Workplace Spirituality.* Springer Publications, 403–17.

Pelikan, J. (1992). *The Christian tradition: A history of the development of doctrine (Vol. 1).* Chicago, IL: University of Chicago Press.

Peterson, C., & Seligman, M. (2004). *Character strengths and virtues: A handbook and classification.* Oxford, England: Oxford University Press.

Quddus, M., Bailey, H., & White, L. (2009). Business ethics: Perspectives from Judaic, Christian and Islamic scriptures. *Journal of Management*, 6(4), 323–34.

Ragins, B. R. (2008). Disclosure disconnects: Antecedents and consequences of disclosing invisible stigmas across life domains. *Academy of Management Review*, 33(1), 194–215.

Rest, J. R., Narvaez, D., Bebeau, M., & Thoma, S. (1999). A neo-Kohlbergian approach: The DIT and schema theory. *Educational Psychology Review*, 11(4), 291–324.

Richards, P. S., & Bergin, A. E. (1997). *A spiritual strategy for counseling and psychotherapy.* Washington, DC: American Psychological Association.

Ricoeur, P. (2007). *The conflict of interpretations: Essays in hermeneutics.* Evanston, IL, Northwestern University Press.

Schoffman, D. E., Davidson, C. R., Hales, S. B., Crimarco, A. E., Dahl, A. A., & Turner-McGrievy, G. M. (2016). The fast-casual conundrum: Fast-casual restaurant entrées are higher in calories than fast food. *Journal of the Academy of Nutrition and Dietetics*, 116(10), 1606–12.

Stackhouse, M. (1995). Introduction: Foundations and purposes. *In* Stackhouse, M., McCann, D., Roels, S., & Williams, P. (eds.), *On moral business: Classical and contemporary resources for ethics in economic life.* Grand Rapids, MI: Eerdmans Publishing Co.

Stefan, F. (2008). Christian ethics and the ethics of contemporary man. *HEC Forum*, 20(1), 61–73.

Thomson, S. B. (2016). *Religion and organizational Stigma at work.* New York: Springer.

Tracy, P., Nelson, P., & Lousnbury, M. (2014). *Taking religion seriously in the study of organizations. Religion and Organizational Theory, Research*

in the sociology of organization, vol. 41, Bingley, West Yorkshire, England, Emerald books.
Trevino, L. K., & Weaver, G.R. (1994). Business ethics/business ethics: One field or two? *Business Ethics Quarterly*, 4, 113–28.
Ulrich, P. (2002). Ethics and economics. *In* Zsolnai, L. (ed.), *Ethics in the economy. Handbook of business ethics*. Bern: Peter Lang Academic Publishers, 9–36.
Underwood, L. G. (eds.), *The science of compassionate love: Theory, research, and applications*. West Sussex: Wiley-Blackwell, 81–120.
Varga, I. (2010). George Simmel: Religion and spirituality. *In* Flanagan, K., & Jupp, J. (eds.), *A sociology of spirituality*. Burlingon, VT: Ashgate Publishing, 145–60.
Vitell, S. (2009). The role of religiosity in business ethic and consumer ethics: A review of the literature. *Journal of Business Ethics*, 90, 155–67.
Walker, L. J. (2004a). Gus in the gap: Bridging the judgment-action gap in moral functioning. *In* Lapsley, D.K., & Narvaez, D. (eds.), *Moral development, self and identity*, 341–68.
Walker, W. (2014b). *History of the Christian church*. New York. Simon and Schuster.
Weaver, G. (2001). Ethics programs in global businesses: Culture's role in managing ethics. *Journal of Business Ethics*, 30, 3–15.
Weaver, G. R., & Agle, B.R. (2002). Religious and ethical behavior in organizations: A symbolic interactionist perspective. *Academy of Management Review*, 27, 77–97.
Werner, A. (2008). The influence of Christian identity on SME owner-managers conceptualizations of business practice. *Journal of Business Ethics*. 19, 450–62.
Wheaton, K. (2010). Chick-fil-A for Sunday lunch? Still not happening. *Advertising Age*, 81(27), 3.
Willard, D. (1992). Being a Christian in a pluralistic society. *In The student*. Nashville, TN: Southern Baptist Convention. Retrieved, www.dwillard.org/articles/artview.asp?artID=17.
Wimberley, D. (1989). Religion a role identity: A structural symbolic interactionist conceptualization of religiosity. *Sociological quarterly*, 302(2), 125–42.
Wuthnow, R. (2011). *America and the challenges of religious diversity*. Princeton, NJ: Princeton University Press.

4 An Islamic View of Diversity: Implications for the Business World

ABBAS J. ALI

Unlike other religions, Islam, during its early days of inception, articulated in specific messages and instructions its vision of diversity. While organizational diversity in today's world might be regarded as good practice, in Islam it was and has been treated as a mandatory principle that gives meaning to the nature of relationships among people and is considered a foundation for a moral society (Ali, 2005). This view places emphasis on both the practical and moral dimensions of diversity and, in the first seven centuries of Islam, it gave minorities a sense of self-confidence and equality. More importantly, the Islamic perspective on diversity, in the early years of the inception of Islam, enhanced dynamism and enthusiasm in the emerging community, while profoundly changing the prevailing ethos at a time when the elite had a free hand in oppressing and alienating minorities.

While the issue of diversity has been extensively discussed in western academic circles, in countries with Muslim majorities (CMM) the subject has not until recently gained comparable attention. This is the result of various factors. Chief among these factors are: business schools have thrived only in the last decade or so; markets have been dominated only by small and medium sized enterprises; a lack of serious research in the business field; avoidance of any controversial research subject by scholars; policymakers showing no interest in the concept, its dimensions, and the implications of diversity; and the limited number of foundations and or private institutions that promote diversity.

However, of late there have been gradual changes in CMM societies. These changes have been brought about not only by globalization of business and the flourishing of western corporations, including consultants, but also by other indigenous factors. Scholars have become, although not on a large scale, aware of their social and moral responsibilities. Likewise, competition has induced many senior executives to look for ways to improve performance and subsequently attract talent, irrespective of the candidates' backgrounds (Ali, 2013). More importantly, the public in general has become more critical of business opportunities that are limited only to certain groups. The questioning of income inequalities associated with the increasing rate of women's and other minorities' graduation from colleges and universities has made these groups sensitive to their roles in business and society in general.

In this chapter, three objectives are sought: articulating the genuine concept and practice of diversity, reflecting on the practice of diversity in contemporary businesses in CMM, and proposing certain implications for institutions in today's world. The focus is on principles and what amounts to an ideal in an environment that is heavily influenced by global capitalism, where the quest for profit is a driving force. This added complexity, while encouraging deviation from religious precepts, underscores the fact that imprudent merging of developing countries, including Muslim ones, in the global capitalist system may weaken traditional and religious beliefs and values. This is not only true of CMM societies. In his visit to South America, Pope Francis in 2015 stated "Let us say no to an economy of exclusion and inequality, where money rules, rather than service. That economy kills. That economy excludes" (quoted in Yardley & Neuman 2015).

Why Diversity?

In recent years, business organizations have given considerable attention to the subject of diversity. This has been primarily the outcome of an ongoing global demographic trend, but mostly in the United States. Once such a trend is recognized, diversity takes on an added value (Roberson & Kulik, 2007). This is because the trend has created opportunities for business organizations to seize and take advantage of it. If this opportunity is left to chance and diversity is not adequately managed, there will be a high possibility that a company may face threats in terms of discrimination, high turnover, and missed opportunities to attract the best talent in the global market, thus endangering the very survivability of an organization.

Aside from this potential problem, researchers have underlined the advantages and benefits of diversity. For example, Martin-Alcazar et al. (2012) have emphasized the practice of diversity in regards to business and social justice. Others have underlined the financial benefits. Marquis et al. (2008) have indicated that diversity improves a company's bottom line and enhances the work environment. In a global study, McKinsey and Company found companies and institutions practicing diversity are achieving better performance than other companies (see Hunt et al., 2015). The importance of diversity in an organization stems primarily from the acknowledgment and recognition of the centrality of the workforce in achieving a competitive advantage in the marketplace. This is especially true in a globalized world where competition, rapid change, and innovation have become the primary traits of business affairs. Likewise, diversity enhances creativity and the search for a better solution for mounting market problems and pressures. In fact, in the long term, it has become impossible to achieve a competitive market position without optimal utilization of human resources. That is, sustainability of competitive advantage and positioning a company strategically are hard to sustain when diversity is not managed to the satisfaction of the employees.

Diversity in Islamic Thinking

Tackling diversity is, in its historical context, an insightful development and evolution. In fact, this evolution highlights the richness of the concept and its limitations across centuries. Inclusiveness in early Islamic thinking is not only a given reality, but the principles of the religion also consider diversity to be a source of strength that can be leveraged to motivate people, enhance commitment, and actively perform duties.

Generally, in Islamic thinking, two issues stand out as most prominent in expressing diversity: differences in thinking and variances in behavior (Ali, 2014). The Prophet asserted that innovation and fruitful discourse was beneficial to society (Imam Al-Ghazali, 2006, died 1111, p. 394). He declared, "The differences [of opinion] among the thinkers of my community are a blessing" (see Ali, 2007) and stated that even if thinkers made mistakes when exercising their right to think about matters of religious law, they would be rewarded, stating, "He who arrives at the right opinion receives two rewards and he who errs receives one" (Sahih Muslim, Hadith #1716, n.d., p. 493). While this message enhances competition to pursue what is good and useful, it also promotes creative thinking and tolerance for reaching a wrong conclusion.

In terms of practice and behavior, differences are the norm rather than the exception. The Quran (5:48) instructs, "To each among you have we prescribed a law and an open way. If God had so willed, He would have made you a single people, but (His plan is) to test you in what He hath given you: so strive as in a race in all virtues." Al-Mawardi, an Islamic Jurist (2002, died 1058, p. 11), observed that "Though people differ in their aspirations, abilities, needs, and objectives, God has made it possible for them to work together." Similarly, the *Ikhwan-us-Safa* (Brothers of Purity), who rose to prominence in the tenth century in the Muslim World, asserted that people are different in behavior, thinking, aspirations, and goals. Thus, the methods they utilize for achieving their goals are different.

In the early days of the Islamic community, the meaning of diversity encompassed gender, race, religious beliefs, and social class. At that time, as in the present, these issues dominated the public discourse, despite the clear instructions by the Prophet on where one should stand. For example, in Saudi Arabia all senior positions are held by the ruling family and women face political and social restrictions. Indeed, the subjects of power, equality, rightfulness, and exploitation have long been intertwined with societal progress and setbacks. In times of progress and prosperity, enlightenment is in ascendance and thus optimism and positivist ideologies on these issues shape societal affairs. In contrast, when CMM experience political and economic setbacks, society becomes intolerant and unreceptive to optimistic outlooks.

In recent years, CMM have experienced an increase in unenlightened thinking and, politically, authoritarian regimes have managed to solidify their power and dictate their perspectives on a variety of issues, including diversity. This has happened despite the relative economic progression that some countries have witnessed. This has further confused the public, intensified closed mindedness and obstructed a progressive outlook. In business organizations, however, diversity policies have taken different forms, due to variations in outlook and development strategies for CMM, but these policies are neither shared nor adequate.

For example, countries that once were characterized as being progressive and which witnessed inclusive diversity policies have in recent years experienced setbacks (e.g., Syria, Iraq, Egypt, Yemen).

Furthermore, countries that have merged into the global capitalist system have been complicit in various forms of exploitation or limitations of the rights of religious and ethnic minorities and poor laborers (be they citizens or migrant) (e.g., Turkey, Qatar, United Arab Emirates, Saudi Arabia, Malaysia, Afghanistan). For example, Amnesty International (2015) has stated that foreign workers are routinely abused in Qatar: "Through multiple on-the-ground investigations in Qatar, Amnesty International has documented human rights abuses by employers and the failure of the government to protect workers from abuse" (p. 1).

Therefore, in this chapter, priority is given to the articulation of genuine religious precepts on diversity, while incorporating practical cases both from the past and current history. The reason for underscoring religious prescriptions found in the Quran or the sayings of the Prophet is that there are many scholars and managers who either lack access to the original writings or have no understanding of the nature of their religion and the necessity to move forward in preventing harm and acquiring benefits for mankind. The chapter is guided by the ethical foundations of Islam, which encompass three elements: public interests (acquisition of benefits and repulsion of harm), moderation (avoidance of extreme positions), and *ehsan* (advancing societal welfare by being generous, forgiving, and tolerant) (Ali, 2014).

These ethical foundations set the stage for envisioning diversity policies that optimize the well-being of society and create an environment in the workplace that makes harmonious relationships among employees not only a possibility but practical and beneficial. More importantly, they can enable corporations to act in a socially responsible way by devising HR policies that are in line with economic development and universal standards. Achieving this task, however, is almost impossible, not only because many Muslims are not aware of the teachings of their faith regarding diversity and other organizational issues, but because many CMM have been merged into global capitalism and have adopted an ethos which is different from the principles of the religion. However, in spite or more directly because of these obstacles, the need for a clarification of diversity and its meaning and practice is a worthy cause, intellectually and practically.

Diversity as a Natural Aspect of Life

While the debate on diversity has often been depicted as a new thinking and practice, the fact remains that the subject has long been addressed in religion as a natural way of life. This, we assume, is a qualitative development that has far-reaching implications for business and other fields. Indeed, the dialectic relationship between diversity and human beings and between the latter and the environment and organizations presents a convenient and suitable way to minimize harm to others, including organizations and environment. This, however, should not obscure the fact that there are other factors in life, like greed, jealousy, and selfish interests that render the concept of diversity in Islam a distant reality. For centuries these factors have been pivotal in obstructing any progress toward a sound application of diversity, despite the clarity of instructions in the Quran and the Prophet's saying and practices.

The Quran articulates the natural aspect and reality of diversity in its statement (5:48) "If God has so willed, he would have made you a single people, but (His plan is) to test you in what He hath given you: so strive as in a race in all virtues" and (11:118) "If thy Lord had so willed, He could have made mankind one people: but they will not cease to differ." That is, human diversity is a divine design.

The Prophet Muhammad, in his last sermon to the pilgrims of Makkah, described what could be called the basis of equality and diversity in Islam:

[A]n Arab has no superiority over a non-Arab nor a non-Arab any superiority over an Arab; also a white has no superiority over a black nor a black any superiority over white, except by piety and good action. (Quoted in Antepli, 2012)

The Quran further states that regardless of the gender, it is the actions and attitudes of a person that matters. It states (3:195), "Never will I suffer to be lost the work of any of you, be he/she male or female: you are members one of another." Also, the Quran (4:124) instructs, "If any do deeds of righteousness, be they male or female, and have faith, they will enter paradise and not the least injustice will be done to them." All the while, the Quran acknowledges that people have been created with different natures, desires, and outlooks (Quran 40:35; 39:9; 49:11). These and other religious instructions set the groundwork for a diversity that is sanctioned. It affirms that those that differ should be treated according to their performance and behavior. In a letter that Abu Othman Ibn Omer Al Jahiz (2000, vol. 1, p. 84), who died in 868 AD, sent to Mohamed Ibn Dawad, a Judge of Baghdad, he stated:

Beware that you will associate with people that differ in their status and state. All of them are useful in various aspects and each will provide benefits that no others above them provide. So they all might advise you and sincerely feel they are of help to you. Some you need for vision and advice, others for trustworthiness affairs, others are needed for toughness and straighten others, and some you need to carry out profession related tasks. All of them provide service according to their capabilities.

Al Jahiz continued, stating,

Do not leave anyone of them, irrespective of greatness or low status, from your caring and your assurance that reward is given for good achievement and remind those who fail to deliver so they know that you are aware of what they are doing. And do not permit any to perform what is not in his mandate and do not let him responsible for issues that he is not qualified for so he can upright his situation and behaves orderly.

Diversity, however, necessitates a policy of equality among people. This emerges, as we will note shortly, from a society built on justice and concern for the welfare of others. The absence of justice and overlooking the requests or situations of those who are at a disadvantage can be a source of discontent and corruption. The Prophet, when he sent Imam Ali (his cousin and son-in-law) to certain areas, stated, "I am sending you, and am fully trusting you, to interact with people; give priority to the those of low status over nobles, the weak over the strong, and women over men." Similarly, the second Caliph, Omer, instructed one of his representatives, Abu Musa, to "Treat people the same in your presence, whether you were secluded or not, so no strong person will take advantage of your decision, and no weak will give up on your justice" (Quoted in Al Jahiz, 2000, vol. 2, p. 23). Likewise, Imam Ali, the fourth Caliph (656–61), in a letter to his governor of Egypt, around 660, succinctly stated the essence of equality when he wrote, "They [People] are either brothers in religion or counterparts in creation." Therefore, he instructed his governor to be kind and attentive to everyone, irrespective of their ethnicity or religion.

The underlying philosophy of the Islamic view on diversity is, therefore, whatever serves people serves God. That is, people are created in different shapes and colors, capabilities, and outlooks and thus discrimination, whether at work or in personal interaction, is contrary to the faith. The important issue is that a person must not harm others. The Quran (16:97) states, "Whoever works righteousness, man or woman, and has faith, verily to him will We give a life that is good and pure and We will bestow on such their reward according to the best of their actions."

Diversity Practices

Throughout Islamic history, the practice of diversity has varied and commitment to it changed. For practical reasons, and to have clear understanding of the practice of diversity, we address two eras: the first seven centuries of Islam and contemporary times. The first seven centuries placed a different emphasis on diversity. Three distinctive practices emerged according to the specific era: the Prophet and the Rightly Guided Caliphs era (610–61), The Ommeyade (Era (661–749), and The Abbasid Era (749–1258).

During the first era (610–61), especially when the Prophet was alive, diversity had a special meaning. It was inclusive and knew no bounds, as it was based on a spiritual understanding that people are equal regardless of their ethnicity or gender. At that time, diversity had social and faith significance. Before Islam, Arabian society was dominated by the Arab aristocracy, who not only exploited minorities and those from other regions but also looked down on them and denied them any useful roles, socially or politically. The Prophet profoundly changed this culture. He appointed an Ethiopian, Bilal, to lead the call for prayer (azaan) and in a symbolic gesture held the hand of Sulyman Al-Farsi, a Persian, saying "Sulyman is a member of my family." In his last sermon said, "there is no preference of an Arab over a non-Arab" and that "a white has no superiority over a black nor a black any superiority over white except by piety and good action." Among other leading minorities at the time of the Prophet (Africans, Persians, Christians, Jews, etc.) who represented the Islamic instructions are Saeed ibn Jubar (black) and Al Mugdad Ibn Omer Al Kindy (black), all from Southern Arabia. The latter was among the four people (two of them were minorities) of whom the Prophet stated, "God instructed me to

An Islamic View of Diversity 113

love four as He loves them: Ali, Al Mugdad, Abu Thar (a person with no wealth), and Sulyman" (quoted in Al Jahiz, 2000, vol. 1–2, p. 126).

The ascendency of the Ommeyade clan to power (661–749) philosophically represented a setback for the inclusive message of the previous era. Ruling members of the Ommeyade utilized Arab solidarity to solidify their power. The ruling elite focused on tribal power and alliances to protect their claims and expand the state. However, by excluding other ethnicities and the poor, the Ommeyade elite isolated themselves from the richness of cultural perspectives essential for building a state based on justice and equality. Despite their phenomenal geographic and political expansion, the Ommeyade relied on Arabs to head the new regions. Tribal relationship, personal trust, and loyalty were instrumental in hiring regional leaders, judges, and heads of military (Al-Masudi, n.d.). Governing vast and rich regions through tribal loyalty incited other ethnic groups to uprise. This eventually accelerated the demise of the Ommeyade state and the end of its era.

During the early Abbasid Era (749–1258), the Abbasids not only relied on religion to justify their claim to power, but also inclusive policies that placed ethnic individuals from different regions in leadership positions. The Abbasid elite recognized that it was the discontent of ethnic groups that paved the way for them to establish their state. Therefore, consolidating their political power dictated that Persians, Turks, Barbers, and Africans should assume powerful positions in the new state.

The collapse of Abbasid State in 1258 had created chaos in various parts of the Muslim World. Many states emerged in Egypt, Central Asia, and Africa. These states neither coordinated their affairs nor addressed diversity issues. Even after the establishment of Ottoman Empire in Turkey in 1299 and that of the Safavid in 1501 in Iran, stability was never the norm in the Muslim World. The Western invasion during various periods constituted a turning point in that part of the World and was characterized by fragmentation and backwardness. This has created fertile conditions in many CMM to seek and gain independence.

Contemporary Era

In this contemporary era, there has been intense discussion about diversity. This, however, has not guaranteed that there is a uniformity of understanding of the concept and its practice. In countries that are not resource-rich in terms of workforce, like the Gulf region, it is normal for the workforce to come from all walks of life. Minorities, irrespective of gender or ethnicity, work together and have relatively similar but limited opportunities. However, in the Gulf area and some other countries, workers are abused and experience discrimination not only in salary but also in treatment. This is primarily attributed to the fact that in traditional societies there are intense social interactions sanctioned by faith. Furthermore, in traditional societies, as in countries with Muslims majorities, people know each other, and harm to any can have social consequences. This does not imply, however, an absence of discrimination or abuse. In Lebanon, for example it has been reported that many foreign maids are being tortured and often raped (Nazal, 2014). Furthermore, narrow interpretations of Islam place certain restrictions on the full participation of women in the workplace. In countries such as Saudi Arabia and Afghanistan, rigid interpretations of Islam have conspicuously limited the role of women in the business world. Likewise, in traditional societies most senior management positions are held by men. Indeed, women in the workplace, despite their achievements and potential, have been relegated to working as clerks and placed in non-supervisory roles.

In the Gulf States and some other countries that rely, to varying degrees, on foreign labor, diversity is common, but it is accompanied by deep forms of discrimination and abuse. Until recently, the policy in the Gulf was to compensate western expatriates much more highly than those from South Asia or Africa. The same is also true for their own citizens whose salaries are higher than other employees from non-western countries. Furthermore, in the Gulf States, discrimination against women and foreign labor is found in almost every economic sector. Amnesty International (2010) reported that in the UAE, women "have continued to suffer discrimination in law and practice. Foreign migrant workers, who make up a large proportion of the UAE's workforce and many of whom are employed in construction, face exploitation, abuse and poor living conditions." Similarly, in the context of Qatar, Amnesty International (2013) stated that foreign migrant workers, who "comprised more than 90% of Qatar's workforce, continued to be exploited and abused by employers despite protective provisions set out in the 2004 Labour Law and related decrees, which the authorities failed to adequately enforce." In Jordan, Human Rights

Watch (2009) reported "abuses against Asian migrants working in Jordan's Qualified Industrial Zones, including late payment of wages, withholding of passports, unsanitary lodging conditions, and police breaking up impromptu strikes." These examples demonstrate that the gap between Islamic instructions and diversity practice is difficult if not impossible to bridge.

Foundations of Diversity

As indicated earlier, diversity in Islam is a natural fact of life; it is a norm and its practice represents a fulfillment of religious instructions. Human beings are perceived as God's vicegerents on earth (Quran, 2:30): "Behold, thy Lord said to the angels: 'I will create a vicegerent on earth'." As vicegerents, human beings have obligations as custodians of the universe and duties toward each other. This is the very reason that everything on earth is created to serve mankind. The Quran (45:12–13) states, "It is God who has subjected the sea to you that ships may sail through it by His command that ye may seek of His bounty and that ye may be grateful. And He has subjected to you as from Him all that is in the heavens and on earth: behold in that are signs indeed for those who reflect." Furthermore, the Prophet observes, "The closest people to God are those who serve people" and "whatever the believers consider a good act, then it is good in the eyes of God. And whatever they deem bad, God treats as bad" (quoted in Al-Maki, 1995, p. 551). The Prophet too instructs people to appreciate others and be kind to them, stating that "He who does not thank people, does not thank God" (Al-Mawardi, 2002, p. 333). In interactions with those who are under one's supervision, the Prophet instructs, "Your maids are your brethren, God has placed them under your supervision; so whoever has his brother under his control should feed him from the same food he eats and should give him clothes to wear from whatever he wears, and should not impose on them a task which overpowers them" (quoted in Muhammad Ali, 1988, p. 383). Since these instructions are addressed to all human beings, irrespective of time and geography, diversity implies equality in treatment and that no person should experience harm or oppression. Indeed, the fourth Caliph, Imam Ali, summed up equality and rejection of discrimination when a Muslim woman complained that her share of the public fund was the equivalent to that of a Jewish woman's. His response was that the Quran does not discriminate between the sons of Ismael and those of Isaac.

The above Quranic instructions and the Prophet's sayings set a sound foundation for diversity and serve the people as a reference guide for judging their behavior and relations with others. Three philosophical logics, *Maslaha Aamah* (public interest), *Etidal* (moderation), and *Ehsan* (goodness and generosity in interaction and conduct) all constitute the foundations for ethical and responsible action. They represent the theoretical framework that guides the faithful in conducting their affairs. This perspective presents diversity not only as something that must be promoted but also as a desired action and application for morally guided individuals and organizations. The first, *Maslaha Aamah* (public interest), situates the interests of the people at the heart of any ethical action and the practice of diversity as serving the organization and the public at large. This is because diversity implies cooperation, tolerance, openness, and creative involvement. Public interest, however, should be given priority in a way that optimizes the welfare of the organization and society. As Table 4.1 shows, public interest has two elements: acquisition of benefits and repulsion of harm. The first conveys that any action that is taken must either advance or create benefits to society and the organization. Furthermore, diversity implies that differences in thinking among members of an organization stimulate creativity and shed light on issues that might be overlooked.

The benefits that result from diversity are numerous. The most important ones are exposure to different ideas, creative participation in the affairs of the company, satisfaction and commitment to organization goals, and a positive image within society. While these benefits are mostly notable for their immediate outcomes, the survivability and growth of the organization may take years to recognize as a testament of deeply rooted diversity beliefs and practices.

The second element, repulsion of harm (*Dafe Almfsada*), is tied to the first. It conveys a strong message that lack of diversity is not only bad practice, but is contrary to the faith. Among the harms that might exist because of the absence of an articulated diversity policy are discrimination, abuse, bigotry, preventing the organization from utilizing available talent, and hindering its ability to compete effectively in the marketplace. Repulsion of harm is broad and conveys the psychological and physical abuses that have undesirable consequences, leading to the alienation of people and generating discontent. Most

Table 4.1 *Foundations of diversity and their implications*

Foundational elements	Implications
Public Interest (*Maslaha Amah*) • Acquisition of benefits (*Jalb al Manfa*) • Repulsion of harm (*Dafe al Tharar* or *Almsada*)	Situating the interests of the people at the heart of any action; the practice of diversity serves the organization and the public at large. Diversity has immediate benefits for both the organization and its employees. Diversity is a powerful instrument for aligning organizational goals with that of society. Individuals are intrinsically motivated and are willing to cooperate in a way that deepens diversity and sound practice. Varieties of perspectives exist on how to solve certain organizational problems. Psychological, economic, and physical abuses contradict religious principles and lead to setbacks for the organization in the marketplace. Employees who experience abuses will be less motivated and less involved in organizational life.
Moderation (*Etidal*)	Diversity policies should be flexible to achieve optimum inclusiveness. However, flexibility must not be an avenue to be taken advantage of by powerful persons within an organization. Diversity entails that both employees and organizations should gain benefits and that it is the responsibility of the two to make sure that an organization is a place where prejudice is not promoted.
Goodness/Generosity (*Ehsan*)	The organization is an attractive place to work in; talent is attracted; and survivability and growth of the organization are more likely to be the norm.

importantly, repulsion of harm enhances hope and optimism. While optimism takes various forms (e.g., outlook, commitment to work, feeling good, hopefulness), the Prophet placed emphasis on a positive outcome. He stated "Optimism is saying a good word" and "Optimism is better than pessimism." He further equated positive expression to charity saying that "every good deed is charity, and it is a good deed that thou meet thy brother with a cheerful countenance" (quoted in Muhammad Ali, 1988, p. 211). Furthermore, he stated, "There should be no transgression and pessimism. I am inclined toward optimism." By highlighting transgression and pessimism as bad qualities that should be avoided, the Prophet intended to ensure that there is no ill feeling and fear among people and that relationships among them must be based on tolerance and doing what is good for individuals and groups. Preventing harm is essential for building sound relationships and enhancing the well-being of employees. Indeed, in an environment where employees sense that no unjust actions will be taken against them, they value their association with their company and possibly improve the quality and productivity of their activities.

Though the repulsion of harm principle is intended to be application based, in today's world it is idealistic. Companies and even individuals may find it difficult to follow. This is because diversity is directed toward minimizing if not avoiding any possible harm to others or society at large, now or in the future. The application of this principle is not only complex but also makes the consideration of diversity goals part of senior management responsibility, where various options have to be entertained. However, most senior managers are neither futurists who can imagine possible harm, nor are they closely familiar with their faith and principles. For these reasons, preventing possible harm may not be widely practiced.

Moderation is the second foundation for diversity. It means that the application of diversity should be carried out realistically and beneficially. It conveys the message of inclusion and the avoidance of favoritism. Al-Andelesy (1996, p. 61) stated, "Do not be too lenient to be taken advantage of and do not be rigid that people stay away from you. Be in the Middle Way is the safest action." This implies that a diversity policy should be flexible, but should not be taken advantage of by powerful persons within an organization. It should be noticed that in the early years of the first century of Islam, moderation was inspired by principles of the faith. In the later stages, it was seldom practiced optimally, as the State either relied almost exclusively on Arabs (as in the Ommeyade era) or on non-Arabs (e.g., during the Abbasid era). Moderation in diversity, in Islamic thinking, entails that both employees and organizations should benefit and that it is the responsibility of the two to make sure that the organization is a place where prejudice is not promoted.

Moderation, in the context of diversity, is an applied concept. Violating it means deviation from a moral standard. As was stated before, moderation implies inclusiveness and avoidance of any excessive reliance on a particular group at the expense of others. For example, when a ruling party or a ruling family allocates senior positions jobs to its members, it does disservice to the organization or the state and alienates others. More importantly, this practice violates religious precepts. Moderation is linked to the principle of avoidance of inflicting harm on others. That is, in recruiting, qualified applicants must be given equal consideration. But again, is equal consideration possible in today's business? It might be a hard-to-reach objective, rendering its application, at least in the near future, impossible.

The third element, *ehsan*, conveys goodness, generosity, and kindness, be it in an organization or in society. The philosophy of *ehsan* is embedded in the recognition that humanity, in order to survive and thrive, has to be inclusive and tolerant, responsive and appreciative to changes and emerging needs. According to a tenth century Jurist, Al-Maki (1995, p. 561), *ehsan* is much broader than justice. He stated, "Justice is to take what is right for you and give what is right to others. *Ehsan* is to absolve part of your right and give more than what you owe to others to be among those who do the right things" (1995, p. 561). This meaning conveys that for an organization or a community to thrive, members must not only be fair and pleasant in their relations with others but also willing to go out of their way to reduce the burden of others, lift their spirits, and avoid harm, be it psychological, economic, or physical. Ali (2014) argued that since *ehsan* places considerable emphasis on relationships among actors in the marketplace and organizations, judging whether any action or conduct is right or wrong must stem primarily from the assurance that no market participants are hurt or that their rights or those of the society as a whole are ignored. In other words, the philosophy of *ehsan* does not compartmentalize the rights of members of an organization as competing rivals and as allies, but as significant actors in a worthy and religiously sanctioned cause.

In contemporary business, the concept of *ehsan* may be difficult to implement. That is, in a business world where organizations are primarily driven by profit and wealth accumulation, *ehsan* may have difficulty flourishing. For example, guided by the logic of *ehsan*, human resource management may be deterred from firing people. In terms of diversity, *ehsan* requires not only that it is actively pursued, but that management, too, must create an organizational environment where employees, irrespective of their ethnicity, gender, or orientation, find a place to utilize their potential and feel that they are vital members in the organization. Most importantly, *ehsan* implies that interactions in the marketplace and within organizations are treated primarily as relationships among equals who seek to offer benefits beyond self and immediate interests. However, equality these days is a distant dream and, in fact, the more that CMM adopt global capitalism, the fewer the possibilities that they will practice equality.

Conclusion

In this chapter, the subject of diversity is discussed in the context of religious prescriptions and today's practices. There was an understanding in the early years of the Islamic state that tolerance and inclusiveness at the workplace were moral duties and necessary for the motivation and commitment to build sound institutions. By viewing diversity as a religiously sanctioned concept and practice, diversity was treated as a moral duty essential for sound conduct. This was a qualitative advancement in a society where, at the time, there was oppression and submission of those who were in disadvantaged positions.

This chapter reflects on the importance of diversity, its normative aspects and how the concept is mostly disregarded in CMM. These countries have been merged in the global capitalism system and most people who are living in these societies are either driven by greed or are unfamiliar with the principles of their religion. Most importantly, the chapter outlines the foundations of diversity. It specifies three foundations: public interest (acquisition of benefits and repulsion of harm), moderation, and *ehsan*. Implications for these foundations of diversity are briefly outlined.

Furthermore, the chapter highlights the difficulties in applying diversity and its foundations in today's world. In particular, repulsion of harm and the principles of *ehsan* are not in line with immediate concerns for wealth accumulation and some other pillars of global capitalism (e.g., cost cutting, the primacy of shareholders' interest). Both repulsion of harm and forsaking one's own rights to help others in need contradict selfishness and gaining profits at any expense. Nevertheless, diversity from an Islamic perspective offers human resource management and senior managers an enlightened principle with which to reconcile the demands of individuals, organizations, and society.

References

Al Jahiz, A. O. O. B. (2000). *Letters of Al Jahiz, vol. 1–2. (Selected by Imam Abiedallah ibn Hassaan)*. Beirut: Dar al-kotab al-ilmiyah.
Al-Andelesy, A. (1996). *The unique necklace (Al Iqd Al Farid), vol. 3*. Beirut: Dar Iheah Al Tarath Al Islami.
Al-Ghazali, A. H. (2006). *Collection of letters*. Beirut: Dar Al-Fikr.
Al-Maki, A. T. (1995). *Guot al-Gwlob (Nourishment of hearts), part 2*. Beirut: Dar Sader.
Al-Masudi, A. A-H. (n.d.). *Muroj Al-thahib [prairies of gold], vol. 3*. Beirut: Dar-Almarifa.
Al-Mawardi, A. (2002). *Kitab aadab al-dunya w'al-din (The ethics of religion and of this world)*. Damascus: Dar Ibn Khather.
Ali, A. J. (2005). *Islamic perspectives on management and organization*. Cheltenham: Edward Elgar Publishing.
   (2007). Schism in Islam: Myths and continuing misconceptions regarding the Sunni-Shia split, world security network. Retrieved from: www.worldsecuritynetwork.com/Broader-Middle-East/abbas-ali-1/Schism-in-Islam-Myths-and-Continuing-Misconceptions-Regarding-the-Sunni-Shia-Split.
   (2013). "Talent management and change in the Gulf region." Presented at Innovation and Development: The Role of Human Capital Seminar, Bahrain, September 26.
   (2014). *Business ethics in Islam*. Cheltenham: Edward Elgar.
Amnesty International USA. (2010, May 28). *Annual report: United Arab Emirates 2010*. Retrieved from: www.amnestyusa.org/research/reports/annual-report-united-arab-emirates-2010?page=2.
   (2013, May 23). *AnnualrReport: Qatar 2013*. Retrieved from: http://www.amnestyusa.org/research/reports/annual-report-qatar-2013.
   (2015, July 15). *Amnesty International USA highlights worker abuses in Qatar at FIFA hearing*. Retrieved from: www.amnestyusa.org/news/press-releases/amnesty-international-usa-highlights-worker-abuses-in-qatar-at-fifa-hearing.
Antepli, A. (2012, February 3). The last sermon of the Prophet Muhammad, *The Huffington Post*. Retrieved from: www.huffingtonpost.com/imam-abdullah-antepli/the-last-sermon-of-prophe_b_1252185.html.
Human Rights Watch (2009). *Jordan events of 2009*. Retrieved from: www.hrw.org/world-report/2010/country-s/jordan.

Hunt, V., Layton, D., & Prince, S. (2015, January). *Why diversity matters.* McKinsey & Company. Retrieved from: www.mckinsey.com/insights/organization/why_diversity_matters. September 27, 2015

Ikhwan-us-Safa (1999), *Letters of Ikhwan-us-Safa, 3.* Beirut: Dar Sader.

Marquis, J. P., Lim, N., Scott, L., Harrell, M. C., & Kavanag, J. (2008). *Managing diversity in corporate America.* Santa Monica, CA: Rand Corporation.

Martın-Alcazar, F., Romero-Fernandez, P. M., & Sanchez-Garde, G. (2012). Transforming human resource management systems to cope with diversity, *Journal of Business Ethics*, 107(4), 511–31.

Muhammad Ali, M. (1988). *A manual of Hadith*, Ithaca, NY: Olive Branch Press.

Nazal, M. (2014, March 25). The tormentor teaches a foreign worker manners by raping her. *Al-Akhbar.* Retrieved from: www.al-akhbar.com/print/203270.

The presidency of Islamic Research and Guidance. (1989). *Holy Quran: English translation of the meanings and commentaries.* Al-Madinah Al Munawarah: King Fahid Holy Quran Printing Complex.

Roberson, L., & Kulik, C. T. (2007). Stereotype threat at work. *Academy of Management Perspectives*, 21(2), 24–40.

Sahih, Muslim (n.d.). (*Abul Husain Muslim Bin al-Hajjaj al-Qushayri al-Nisapuri*). Cairo: Dar Al Shab.

Yardley, J., & Neuman, W. (2015). In Bolivia, Pope Francis apologizes for church's "grave sins". *New York Times*, July 9. Retrieved from: www.nytimes.com/2015/07/10/world/americas/pope-francis-bolivia-catholic-church-apology.html?_r=0.

5 | The Untold, the Unseen, and the Forgettable: Jewishness, Jews, and Judaism in Diversity Management Scholarship

ALAIN KLARSFELD

Introduction

Jews are a small ethnic/religious minority representing 14.2 million people or about 0.2% of the world's population, more than 80% of whom reside in approximately equal numbers in Israel (6 million) and the USA (5.7 million), the rest residing mainly in Europe, which is home to about 1.5 million Jews (Della Pergola, 2014). Even though Jews are but a small ethnic/religious group, there is a wide diversity of ways of being Jewish, as evidenced by research undertaken in the USA (Pew Research Center, 2013). Some involve religion, some not, as a significant number of Jews identify as Jews through ethnic/cultural heritage rather than through religion. Some involve believing in God, some not. Some involve observing *kosher* (dietary prescriptions) and other rituals, some not. As there is no central Jewish religious authority, religious affiliation itself is extremely diverse and generally falls under one of the following movements: ultra-orthodox or *Haredi*, orthodox, conservative, reform, and reconstructionist – this list being non-exhaustive. Within these movements, there are variations, and developments are perpetually unfolding. The *Bund*, particularly active in Poland, Russia and/or Lithuania before World War I and World War II, or Humanistic Judaism in Western countries, are both secular Jewish movements promoting socialist and/or Human Rights ideals (Goldberg, 1993).

Yet, diversity and management scholarship on Jews/Judaism/Jewishness is remarkably absent, in spite of anti-Semitism continuing to flourish (Anti-defamation league, 2003; Fundamental Rights Agency, 2013) and in spite of social research on Jewish studies flourishing in non-workplace related fields (Chalmer & Cohen, 2014). Most research on Jews and Judaism focuses on Jewish history, demographics, marriage and intermarriage, religious affiliation and practice, political attitudes and attitudes towards Israel, Jewish identity, and Jewish upbringing, but not workplace (Chalmer & Cohen, 2014; Pew Research Center, 2013) with virtually no papers involving the intersection of "Jew," "Jewishness," and "Judaism" and the modern workplace but for notable exceptions (Hersh, 2010; Kehat, 2012; Kletz et al., 2012; Sharabi, 2012). There is research undertaken in Israel (where the notion of Jewishness is clearly associated with that of the majority rather than as that of minority), where there is strong interest in studying the *Haredi* (orthodox) Jewish minority and comparing attitudes between Jewish and Arab and/or Muslim (here the minority) workers.

In this paper, I will try to outline why this might be the case, based on the available literature, exploratory interviews, informal conversations with Jewish colleagues active in higher education in France, the UK, the USA, and Israel, and personal reflection. The objective is to feed this reflection into a wider research project involving other Jewish and non-Jewish scholars alike. I identify the tempered radical dilemma raised in previous literature, here broken down in various components; I then turn to positive arguments in favor of diversity research about Jews.

Why So Little Work-Related Research on Jews/Judaism/Jewishness in Diversity Management?

The Tempered Radical Dilemma

"Tempered Radicals are individuals who identify with and are committed to their organizations, and are also committed to a cause, community, or ideology that is fundamentally different from, and possibly at odds with the dominant culture of their organization" (Meyerson & Scully, 1995, p. 586).

Jewish diversity scholars are often caught, as are many diversity scholars, in the "tempered radical" dilemma. Indeed, diversity scholars often engage in diversity studies with a passion and a leaning towards social justice, and see in it a possibility to act as a tempered radical (Meyerson & Scully, 1995) in order to bring about a more just society. This posture is fraught with difficulties and ambivalence as the type of change advocacy that diversity scholars support often challenges the dominant values of the organizations/societies that they participate in. Therefore diversity scholars may find themselves torn between doing research that engages them emotionally, which can only benefit themselves and the research community (Bell, 2009), and a push towards doing research that will be valued by their institutions and avoiding possible negative consequences attached to being identified as a researcher engaged in gender, race, ethnic studies, as suggested by Meyerson and Scully (1995). Strategies may range from total silence, i.e., not doing any research to which one is emotionally linked to pursuing more risky strategies of being open about a very specific diversity research agenda (such as a focus on homosexuality, or on black women) and the personal connection with this research agenda.

What little self-reflective intersectional research on diversity tempered radicals exists reveals a variety of situations and experiences. This has been highlighted for white women and black women researchers whose perspectives and voices on "diversity," "race," or "gender" can be different (Edmonson-Bell et al., 2003). Auto-ethnographic, self-reflective accounts include accounts by women, by Blacks (Edmonson-Bell et al., 2003), by homosexuals (Roberts, 2014), by men (Styhre & Tienari, 2014), but not by Jews as Jews. The tempered radical dilemma will play out with some resemblance and some specifics as regards research on Jews/Jewishness/Judaism. I identify the marketing argument, the career argument, the secularism argument, the "bad reminiscence" argument, the "what if results fall in the wrong hands" argument, the "there are no more problems" argument, and the sampling argument.

The Marketing Argument

As Meyerson and Scully (1995) pointed out, a first possible explanation is that as a scholar, whether Jewish or non-Jewish, you want to address issues that will be of interest to a large audience. Jews are a tiny proportion of the world population (or below 0.2%), and a small minority even in the country where they are to be found in the largest proportion outside of Israel, the USA, where Jews make up less than 2% of the population by the most generous estimates (Pew Research Center, 2013). Therefore researching Jews might raise the fear of rejection by publication outlets and by colleagues. Why do research that is of interest to only 0.2% of the world's population and 2% of the

US one? This argument does not take into account the fact that studying a small minority does not make said research less interesting. For instance, although LGBT people are a small minority, there is diversity research on LBGT issues, and this only enhances our understanding of diversity issues and the complexities of accommodating multiple diversity strands (such as sexual orientation and religion) in organizations and societies. That the population under study is a "small" (but then, where does "small" start?) minority should not be a sufficient reason not to research this particular minority. However, embarking on this is a difficult and risky venture given the marketing argument.

The Career Argument

A second explanation, linked to the previous one, is that of the possible encounter with hostile reactions of colleagues that might occur in one's professional environment (business schools), and even within the equality, diversity, and inclusion scholarly community. Fear of being faced with hostility is a common thread that runs through accounts of the early stages of gender and diversity research in academia, as has been pointed out in the tempered radical literature. This means that, however open the diversity scholarly community may purport to be towards people who experience hatred or discrimination, disclosure of one's Jewishness to a wide audience, particularly through written and published work, may pose a problem to many Jews. Research indeed shows that Jews often "closet" or cover their Jewish identity, when they do not feel it is entirely safe for them to disclose it, even in the one country in the world where religious freedom is a core foundational value, the USA, and where the Jewish community could be considered to be most thriving, or at least at its highest possible numerical presence outside of Israel (Hecht & Faulkner, 2000).

For instance, during the organization conference dedicated to equality, diversity, and inclusion in 2015 in Israel, a boycott was initiated by an equality, diversity, and inclusion scholar against this conference location. Although some boycotters did try to disassociate themselves from anti-Semitism (Israel was pointed to, not the Jews), the "Israel is the worst of nations" argument raised by a few signatories seemed exaggerated in the face of the many scientific events that take place in countries having contested practices in terms of equality/human rights and/or their foreign policy. For instance, a conference dedicated to equality and diversity was held in Turkey in 2009 without triggering any boycott attempt, yet many object to this country's drift away from secular values, its fierce repression of the Kurds, and its ruling party's links with radical Salafi/Wahhabi jihadist militant groups in Syria and Iraq. Scientific conferences are also regularly held in other states, such as Russia, Bahrain, or Qatar, again countries where state policies can be deemed debatable or even murderous as regards the rights of women, freedom of expression, or the treatment of migrant labor. Singling out Israel as "the worst nation" is therefore a "double standard" that deserves to be identified and warrants investigation.

Many Jews grew up either with direct experience of anti-Semitism, or surrounded by stories of it. As a result, Jewish scholars may want to reduce the risk of being faced with Jewish-related rejection, if not by outright anti-Semitism. Again, the negatives of such a stance should not be underestimated: by turning away from doing diversity research about Jews, Jewish and non-Jewish scholars alike leave the door open to non-scientific, unconfronted, hate-laden discourse that can only pollute real issues with imaginary ones. They also maintain the silence around present-day injustices.

The Secularism Argument

Jews active in social sciences (which includes management science) may adhere to (or feel constrained by) an ideal of society where Jewish and other religious identities are perceived as a threat to universal values and therefore undervalued (see the chapter titled "Christian faith and the preservation of personal identity" by Timothy Ewest in this edited book). Such an ideal is commonplace in social science and in particular in management. Beyond the career argument, they sometimes themselves personally reject their heritage as something obsolete and opposed not only to secular values predominant in academia but to their own personal values, as was the case with Claude Lévi-Strauss or Emile Dürkheim in France (Birnbaum, 2004) or of Georg Simmel and Franz Boas in Germany (Birnbaum, 2004; Morris-Reich, 2008). Such a stance is particularly paradoxical in ethnology and anthropology, where cultural differences are of paramount importance and at the core of the object of study. Because some Jewish scholars adhere to a universalist and secularist ideal, they distance themselves from Judaism which, for some among the earliest of them such as Marx, is bound to disappear in a "reconciled humanity" (Birnbaum, 2004). We suspect that what has been uncovered for major figures of sociology and anthropology holds true for other fields in social science.

Bad Memories of Former Justifications for Oppression

Thirdly, a lot of research dedicated to equality, diversity, and inclusion builds evidence of inequality based on representation statistics. Such concepts as "underrepresentation" and "overrepresentation" are essential for analyzing inequalities. However, statistics also carry bad memories for many Jews. While Jews might feel at ease demonstrating the "underrepresentation" of other disenfranchised groups, by gathering even secondary socioeconomic data on Jews, a Jewish researcher might fear that these data could be used by hostile hands to only confirm the stereotype of the "privileged" Jew, and that just raising the question might lead readers to assume you are an anti-Semite (Hersh, 2010). Indeed, what data exists suggests that even though there are many Jews found among the poorest groups (which runs counter to the stereotype that holds that all Jews are rich), they are found in larger than average proportions among the middle and upper income classes in some nations (Fundamental Rights Agency, 2013; Pew Research Center, 2013; Chua & Rubenfeld, 2014), which partially confirms the stereotype, notwithstanding the case of Israel, where 45% of Jews live, which ranks among the poorest of the OECD countries.

Statistics were available for instance in Tsarist Russia, as evidence in census data dating back to 1897 (Spitzer, 2012), and in the writings of a late nineteenth century Australian-born statistician, Joseph Jacobs (1891), based on German statistics. Such statistics could be used to justify anti-Semitic measures such as "numerus clausus," barring many able Jews from higher education. There are many examples of German Jews either converting or leaving Germany for the USA throughout the nineteenth century in order to be accepted as academics (Birnbaum, 2004).

Comparisons of Jews with other identity groups on various socioeconomic variables may therefore trigger hurtful memories for Jews, particularly when they originate from Central Europe. Raising the subject is touchy (Chua & Rubenfeld, 2014), and thus rarely found in modern literature, as has been stated by an American mathematician eager to understand representation of Jews in his profession in his country (Hersh, 2010). Whatever the statistical evidence, the status of the Jews should not be reduced to income or wealth statistics, and this in turn should not be confused for absence of discrimination. For instance, "higher than average income" does not mean "absence of discrimination against Jews." It has been argued that although Asian-Americans have higher-than-average incomes, they earn less when educational attainment is factored in (Wise, 2010). Again, by failing to address these complex statistical issues, scholars give free reign to defamation and hate-speech.

Another objection to this stance (but less of a challenge) is that diversity research is not all about income and assets. Research on women or LGBT people in organizations, for instance, points to other forms of discrimination than pay discrimination, such as sexist discourse, harassment, and subtle, indirect forms of rejection and othering. In spite of whatever "privilege" Jews may be thought to enjoy based on economic statistics, the mere fact that closeting occurs even in the USA (Hecht and Faulkner, 2000), a country where Jews are supposed to enjoy the greatest power, wealth, freedom, and ability to express their belonging, is a sign that affirming one's Jewish identity still attracts potential hostility and challenges anywhere in the world, except perhaps for Israel.

The "What If Results Fall into the Wrong Hands?" Argument

Given that Jews are a tiny minority, they may fear that whatever is written about Jews may be used against Jews. This perhaps goes back to a long tradition of Jewish sources being used against Jews. Indeed, many passages of the "Tanakh"[1] or Ancient Testament could nurture criticism of Jews. These fundamental sources often depict the Jewish people as doing something wrong in the eyes of God. Starting with the Exodus, the Jewish people fall prey to idolatry of the Golden Calf, such that Moses breaks the tables of the Law and perpetrators are sentenced to death. This and other transgressions, such as refusing to enter the Promised Land, result in a whole generation wandering and dying in the desert. Subsequently, the Torah abounds with accounts of periods when Jews are said not to act consistently with the precepts of the Torah and therefore encounter all kinds of

---

[1] Composed of the "Torah" or Pentateuch, the "Nevi'im" or Prophets, and the "Ketuvim" or Writings.

misfortunes. The Prophets are only the continuation of this critical dialogue internal to Judaism itself. Christianity and Islam can be seen as continuing this originally (self) critical literature. "Stiff-necked people," who "have eyes, but do not see," who "have ears, but do not hear," whose "heart is hardened," or is "uncircumsized," all these negative traits have their roots in what, originally, was written by Jews referring to Jews. It is of little surprise that, as Christianity and Islam grew as rival religions to Judaism in search for arguments to demean Jews, they found abundant material to use when referring to Jews in a strongly negative manner, provided by Jewish tradition and sources themselves.

Anecdotal evidence from many conversations held by the author of these lines with relatives or friends suggests that for many Jews, even today, too much is written about Jews and Jews are all too visible and should not be so as this can only harm them. From this perspective, any research effort aimed at addressing Jews, Jewishness and Judaism, and destined to be published, may be seen as threatening. However, we contend silence is bound to fail. Anti-Semitic hatred is not *caused* by any possible knowledge about Jews but pre-exists such knowledge. In the absence of any knowledge, anti-Semites will always build stories to cling to – possibly borrowing elements of the truth – in order to make Jews appear overpowered, privileged, sly, money-loving, treacherous, and traitorous. Whatever the information (true or false), what matters is its interpretation, as portrayed in this famous joke: During times of rationing somewhere in Europe, Jews are queuing alongside other minority groups (say, Armenians) and the majority group to buy bread. The baker comes out and shouts: "Jews, go home, no more bread for you, the others can stay in the queue." One hour later: "Armenians, go home, no more bread for you, the others can stay in the queue." One hour later: "everybody, go home, no more bread anyway for anyone!" Some of the remaining [majority group] people then comment: "those privileged Jews! They got the news before everyone else!." From a situation where it seems evident that Jews were treated worst, it is therefore possible to build a narrative that depicts Jews as benefiting from undue "first served" status.

This view is supported by constant research on cognitive processes. In its quest for maintaining its routine of thought, our brain builds narratives that allow its stereotypes to survive, whatever the evidence, statistical or otherwise (Kahneman, 2011).

The "There Are No More Problems" Argument

Fourthly, Jewish and non-Jewish scholars may be inclined to sit content with the present-day condition of Jews. After all, things have been so much worse in the past (compared to, say, in the present day in the USA and Western Europe), so why care about the "micro"-problems of the present, endured by a micro minority living in a handful of privileged economies? The underlying argument is that other minorities are suffering more, and they should be given the priority over the Jews, who are part of the "privileged whites" majority, or even a "privileged subset" within that. The conviction that other minorities suffer more than the Jews is actually supported by American Jews themselves (Pew Research Center, 2013) and probably in other countries, too. But if this were true, then why keep on researching on women, LGBT people, or people of color, since the condition of women, LGBT people, and people of color is supposedly better than it used to be, say, 70 years ago? This stance denies any interest in studying the present day issues faced by any minority or by women, whenever there has been an improvement, something that does not hold true, and that silences subtle or less subtle of forms of mistreatment. Besides, "there are no more problems" is an affirmation that should come under close scrutiny when one looks at the few rigorous studies of anti-Semitism (Fundamental Rights Agency, 2013; Anti-Defamation League, 2014). Violent anti-Semitic content is to be found everywhere on the Internet. Anti-Semitic feelings and hate speech are quick to surface whenever there is war in the Middle East between Israel and Palestinians, and the streets of Paris and other European capitals resonated with "death to the Jews" in the summer of 2014 during the "Gaza and rockets" war. Mostly Europe and in particular France have seen the bloodshed and murder of "Jews as Jews" perpetrated on at least six occasions since 1975. These include the Paris shootings of rue Copernic (1980) and rue des Rosiers (1982), the Buenos Aires bombing of 1994, the kidnapping and one-month-long torturing and murder of 23-year-old, Ilan Halimi, near Paris (2006), the shootings (including children of school age) of Toulouse (2012), of the Brussels Jewish Museum (2014), of the Paris Hypercacher supermarket (2015), the double shootings in Copenhagen (2015), and the mass-shooting of November 2015 at the Bataclan, a Paris theatre, which the attackers (wrongly) believed to belong to a Jew.

The Sampling Difficulty Argument

A further difficulty plagues the attractiveness of research involving Jewish participants: that of the difficulty of gathering large samples. This of course does not apply to Israel, where Jews are a majority. As mentioned above, Jews in any country form a maximum of 2% of the general population, and more often than not it is 1% or less. Therefore, constituting large samples of Jews may prove problematic. A way around this can be working in areas where Jews are found in large numbers, such as New York City, London, or Paris. Yet other difficulties may make sampling difficult. First, as Hecht and Faulkner (2000) stated, many Jews will not readily disclose being Jewish. Second, Jewish participants may also share the apprehensions as mentioned above: i.e., they may disapprove of the research project altogether for being reminiscent of a painful past, they may object that "there is no more problem," so why investigate, and they may fear being identified for reasons related to their own careers and "marketing of themselves" to wider society, as applies for tempered radical scholars. However, this obstacle can be overcome by focusing on places where Jews dwell in large numbers, and through activating networks and using a snowball sampling method.

Why Researching about Jews Can Be of Interest for Equality and Diversity Scholars and the Management Scholarly Community at Large

Giving a Voice to Unheard Voices

Beyond refuting the reasons for not doing any EDI research on Jews/Judaism/Jewishness, researching these three themes contributes to filling a gap and giving a voice to untold forms of modern sufferings of Jews who are supposed to at last be benefitting from a 70-year-long period without killings and overt forms of oppression almost anywhere in the world (except for spectacular acts of terrorism). This should not erase the present day reality not only of crimes perpetrated against Jews as Jews in France and Belgium, but of other forms of demeaning and oppression, such as being subjected to insults, threats, overt hate speech on the Internet, and even assaults (Fundamental Rights Agency, 2013), or living as a "survivor" in the aftermath of several killings that have affected people sharing the same identity. But beyond these arguments, research about Jews is a contribution to the literature on intersectionality and of challenging forms of intersections.

The Intersection of Religion and Ethnicity

For many scholars, intersection means intersecting two particular dimensions that exist separately (such as gender and race, or race and religion). However, the notion of Jewishness ambiguously and simultaneously sits at the confluence of ethnicity and religion and questions the very categorizations of ethnicity and religion themselves. For Jews, in all contexts but in Israel, being potentially seen – and seeing oneself – as both an ethnic and/or a religious minority is ingrained in the very notion of Jewishness itself. The Jewish identity is therefore a complex one, with which one can identify based on religious grounds, but also on cultural/ethnic grounds, or on both grounds. For instance, in the USA, it was found that "32% [of young Jews and 22% of all Jews] describe themselves as having no religion and identify as Jewish on the basis of ancestry, ethnicity or culture" (Pew Research Center, 2013, p. 7). More generally, it has been argued that there exists such a thing a secular Jewishness and that Judaism may not be a precondition of Jewishness (Shapiro, 2014). In comparison with religious voices, non-religious Jewish voices are more difficult to hear and such intersectional literature could therefore give voice to these non-traditional and less visible Jewish identities.

The Intersection of the Oppressed and the Privileged

Research about Jews contributes to the emerging literature on race and ethnic privilege. Stereotypically, Jews may be portrayed as quintessentially privileged, or even, in the most caricatured stereotypes, as a domineering conspiratorial sect planning to rule the world – as rendered by the Russian pamphlet *The protocols of the Elders of Zion*, a violently anti-Semitic document available for open access consultation on the Internet.[2] Where such literature is of course a gross and hateful caricature, statistics from the European Union (Fundamental Rights

---

[2] Retrieved from www.biblebelievers.org.au/przion1.htm#WHO.

Agency, 2013), the USA (Pew Research Center, 2013), and France (Schnapper et al., 2009) suggest Jews enjoy an above average economic standing in North America and Europe.

On the other hand, at least as far as Europe and the Americas are concerned, oppression culminating with the mass extermination of Jews under Nazi-ruled Europe is acknowledged and made widely available through the media, with the paradoxical consequence that even this recognition can sometimes be regarded as yet another form of privilege and manifestation of conspiratorial power. For instance, in many parts of the world, there is widespread belief that the depiction of the Shoah is inaccurate and exaggerated (Anti-Defamation League, 2014). Between these extreme narratives of the Jewish condition, modern day experience of moderate forms of oppression and exclusion are supposedly nowhere to be found. Yet, research undertaken outside of the sphere of work and management has documented the ripple effects of the Shoah on surviving children who had been hidden during World War II with no clear awareness of the situation at the time (Fohn et al., 2014). A clinical center in Paris provides specific care for survivors and descendants of survivors of the Shoah.[3] Even in the USA, non-disclosure of Jewish identities in modern times signals that all is not privilege for the Jews in this country traditionally seen as the ideal country for Jewish thriving and well-being (Chua & Rubenfeld, 2014; Hecht & Faulkner, 2000). In between extermination and "privilege," these intermediary forms of oppression and suffering are the subject of some research efforts in the fields of sociology, psychiatry, and ethno-psychiatry, but their ramifications in the world of work, employment, and management are not.

Therefore it can be claimed that Jewishness challenges the dichotomy of privilege and oppression. Where, in the context of modern, large, plural societies, and speaking from a racial and economic perspective, being Jewish might be conflated with belonging to the "large" group or to the "privileged" group of Whites, and to a group of privileged Whites at that, Jews may simultaneously be seen as a deprived minority when one zooms into smaller groups. For instance, among the Whites, Jews are a minority, not being Christian, and have been subjected to Christian-based anti-Semitism for almost 2,000 years, mainly in Europe.

---

[3] www.ethnopsychiatrie.net/.

Research work undertaken in the field of history has shown how immigrant Jews in the USA combined a working-class identity with aspirations to upward social mobility and independence, sometimes (but not always) built on the memory of their families' long-gone prosperity in Eastern Europe (Soyer, 2001). These Jews experienced a sort of "tempered radical" dilemma of their own, that of remaining true to their Bundist[4] (socialist) ideals while at the same time individually trying to emancipate themselves from the working class by creating their own businesses and accumulating wealth, thus becoming "traitors" to the working class they came from. In some ways this echoes tempered radical scholars who sometimes feel they are "traitors" to an identity group or an ideal when they distance themselves from it or do not speak up for it.

Beyond the study of Jews, such work also demonstrates that the borders of the working class were blurred and porous: one entered and exited paid labor and independent work more than once in one's life; small sub-contractors, although bosses, experienced exploitation by their clients and sometimes demonstrated alongside the workers against tough conditions; small bosses were often almost as poor as their employees; according to the phases in the economic cycle, salaried labor could pay more than being self-employed or the owner of a small business; many union activists who had become independent business owners remained involved in their union activities even though they were no longer salaried workers themselves (Soyer, 2001).

It can be contended that such form of Jewishness may provide a model for present-day EDI scholars and other tempered radicals, torn between an aspiration to a relatively "bourgeois" and independent way of life rendered possible by many jobs in Management Academia, while at the same time continuing to remain faithful to their ideals of emancipation and social change.

Seeing the Jews part of the "white dominant" majority has another major drawback: it silences the existence and experience of Black Jewishness, an all too often ignored reality. Work on the identities and fate of Black Jews may be found on Black Ethiopian Jews in Israel (Chehata, 2012), but also on Black Jews in the USA (Gold, 2003),

---

[4] The Bund refers to the Jewish socialist movement founded in Eastern Europe at the end of the nineteenth century.

and in South Africa (Tamarkin, 2011). Yet clearly there is a dearth of scholarship regarding Black Jewishness.

As Merriweather-Woodson and Ollier-Malaterre (2016) put it,

> intersectionality disrupts the tendency to see categories as mutually exclusive and can be applied to the intersection of several identities, regardless of oppression and privilege. Even though it has often been used to highlight the experiences of the multiply-oppressed, intersectionality theory can also be used to understand interlocking systems of privilege ... Therefore, future research would benefit from exploring the intersection of oppressed and privileged identities. (p. 84)

Jewish identities thus offer rich variations where oppressed and privileged identities intersect, and a rich field of investigations, one that can allow new kinds of Jewish voices to be heard: religious and non-religious Jewish voices, White and Black Jewish voices, voices of Jews in the workplace, voices that connect Jewish sources of faith and Jewish culture with modern workplaces. These voices can only help the Jews better understand and acknowledge themselves, and the non-Jews better understand not only their own categorizing, prejudice, and stereotyping towards the Jews but also the positive take-aways for management drawn from Jewish sources. Beyond fighting prejudice, Judaism (and hopefully, one day, Jewish tradition) can be an inspirational source for workplace practices and management, as suggested by Kletz et al. (2012) who led a whole special issue of the *Journal of Management Development* on this question, as described in the next section.

If the equality and diversity scholarly community does not tackle the challenge of the visibility and worthiness of the study of Jewish difference in its own ranks, it may be ill-equipped to help any community (be it work or non-work) deal with its own invisible minorities, be they Jewish or based on some other deep-level characteristic.

Judaism/Jewishness as a Source of Reflection for Managers and Leaders

Judaism being a religion where practice and concrete behaviors are deemed central to, on an equal footing with, or even prioritized above espoused beliefs and surface-level discourse, its sources (the Torah and the Talmud, built on commentaries and debated interpretations of the

Torah) may be used as a source of inspiration for management (Kletz et al., 2012). The covenantal tradition of permanently studying "given" rules through debating them rather than by blindly obeying them can for instance inspire compliance management in the modern corporation (Habisch, 2012). The banning of images could, somewhat similarly, be used to question the representation of firms through figures – the modern equivalent of the images of traditional managerial reporting, and the validity of learning in the absence of debates, as may be the case in some passive e-learning practices (Colas & Laguecir, 2012).

The sources of Judaism also stress the importance of fairness and justice, and offer teachings in managing the employer-employee relationship: the employer must pay wages in a timely manner; wages must provide for a decent living and wage disparities must not be excessive; not just employees, but subcontractors' employees must be cared for; while the employee on her/his side must make every effort in good faith and work to the fullest of his or her capacity, any time taken from working time for personal use being considered as theft (Schnall, 1993; Kay, 2012). Employees can even be held individually responsible for poor work and asked for compensation in case of damage, with some exceptions (Schnall, 1993). Doing justice, showing kindness, and walking humbly are core Jewish values that would bring benefit by being infused in the modern organization (Mostovicz & Kakabadse, 2012).

Leadership is also illuminated by Jewish tradition. Entrepreneurship and innovation (both technical and social) around the world can be found to be inspired by the philosophy of "tikkun olam" or repairing the world (Kahane, 2012). The story of Moses as a leader conveys lessons for ethical leadership. Moses is not extrinsically driven to leadership but becomes leader by accident, against his will; he accepts leadership as part of a community that will support him; he has a vision rather than a detailed, predefined plan; he acts as a caring shepherd; he teaches rather than merely commanding; he acts as a servant to the people he leads, dying before the realization of his vision, but after having prepared a capable successor (Ben-Hur & Jonsen, 2012). Mosaic leadership can also be interpreted as a leadership style that combines charisma and bureaucracy (Gottlieb, 2012). Leadership lessons for times of crisis can also be derived from the Talmudic accounts of the period surrounding the destruction of the Second Temple in 70 AD, which was caused by excessive righteousness combined with cowardice, i.e. an inability to challenge those in power (Kehat, 2012).

Therefore, Jewish tradition is a source of both good and bad practice examples that can inspire the leaders of today and of tomorrow.

Such attempts to explicitly translate Jewish wisdom into management literature remain scarce, a fact that is all the more intriguing given the long history of Talmudic debates and prescriptions as regards work and the employment relationship (to start with, the establishment of the compulsory weekly rest or Shabbat), and the now century-old presence of Jewish scholars in the fields of psychology, social psychology, organizational behavior, and management. We contend that such a void is yet another evidence of a form of subtle, self-inflicted oppression. Likely, it results from the dilemma of tempered radicalism as exposed above, as well as a fear amongst Jewish scholars of discussing Jewishness and Judaism for the above-mentioned reasons, and others, yet to be uncovered.

Conclusion and Research Agenda

As scholars, Jews have often been engaged in equality work and activism, starting with Karl Marx, whose family had only recently converted from Judaism to Christianity as part of their desire to fully integrate into German society, where conversion was a common mode of assimilating. While some authors, such as Karl Marx, have highlighted class as the primary dimension worthy of being studied and acted upon, many have been engaged in studying and standing up for other oppressed categories and identities such as women and minorities, be they sexual, ethnic, or religious, as well as the underlying mechanisms of social categorization, prejudice, and stereotyping, as witnessed by the very general work of Henry Tajfel on social identity (see Tajfel, 2010 for a re-edition). For reasons that can be understood (some of which have been proposed for discussion in the above sections) there has not been much translating of this into empirical research about the real experience of Jews and Jewishness in the modern workplace as these scholars were targeting more general questions of interest to a wider audience.

We suggest that such silence renders this previous work, however rigorous and useful, incomplete. It seems that, in fighting for what matters most for them as male or female, social activist, or sexual minority, Jewish diversity scholars and their equality ancestors have, consciously or not, forgotten to care about what should matter for them as well as for their audiences: being exemplary in studying, voicing, and standing up for where they come from, however much they may be tempted to reject this provenance in the untold, the unseen, and the forgettable.

Such silence may be attributable to multiple factors (Birnbaum, 2004; Morris-Reich, 2008). In German society, scholars such as Karl Marx, Franz Boas, and Georg Simmel had to convert to a Christian denomination (Catholic or Protestant) in order to be accepted in the mainstream German society of their time – there was no other option. Conversion was a precondition to being hired in German universities. Erasing their Jewishness publicly was therefore a constraint of the German model of "emancipating" Jews. In France, social science scholars such as Emile Dürkheim and Claude Lévi-Strauss were not explicitly forced to convert or silence their Jewishness. They personally adhered to a secular model of society where past religious affiliations were to be put in the backyard, or even rejected as obsolete forms of solidarity and spirituality, and where new intermediary institutions such as the modern secular State, trade unions, and the modern "socially responsible" corporation were to become the major mechanisms of solidarity and bonding together people of all creeds and origins. In the USA, where there is a track record of Jewish scholars explicitly addressing the study of Jewish immigrants in the late nineteenth century and early twentieth century, slowly abandoning the study of Jews in order to turn to the study of other marginalized identity groups such as African Americans signaled not only a self-perceived successful assimilation of said Jewish scholars into American mainstream society but also the growing awareness of the particular ordeal faced by African Americans and other stigmatized identity groups in US society (Birnbaum, 2004).

But how can Jewish and non-Jewish scholars alike work on a multiplicity of forms of otherings, with the exception of the othering of Jews in the modern, "softer" world? This challenge is indeed faced by many oppressed identities anywhere in the world, and there is no higher goal for the equality, diversity, and inclusion agenda than to encourage these unheard voices to emerge into broad daylight. Jews and Judaism should therefore no longer be relegated to the silent fringes of management science.

There are parallel implications for all "othered" groups. The silence of scholars of all types of identity groups implies as a consequence that their identity group is understudied or even unheard of in the wider social conversation. For instance, who better than African American female scholars could have articulated the particular experience of other, less privileged African American women in the workplace and the wider society (Crenshaw, 1991; Edmonson-Bell et al., 2003)? By this we do not want to imply that belonging to a particular identity group is a necessary precondition for undertaking research on this particular group. Such a view would entail essentializing the qualities required to undertake legitimate research on any group, which would inevitably lead to a form of discrimination. Rather, we contend that stemming from a particular identity group confers a particular responsibility towards this particular identity group as a scholar. Another implication derives from the previous one: beyond studying the particular forms of otherings of their own identity group lest they be overlooked in the public debate, scholars dedicated to equality and diversity should be on permanent lookout for silent, marginalized groups with little or no access to academic professions.

In the following section we provide a list of questions worthy of future investigation.

We know the complexities of the formation of Jewish identity from social science research. Yet, what is the experience of Jews at work? How do they bring or not bring their Jewish identity to work, and what is that Jewish identity?

How do they disclose or not disclose their identity in their particular work setting? How do they see non-Jews at work? How do they relate to them?

How do Jews connect or not their sense of Jewish identity with what they do at work? Given the importance of the notion of "work" and "repairing the world" (Weiss, 2008) in the Jewish tradition (work and worship are one and the same word, "avoda," and "tikkun olam," or repairing the world, is a central concern), how is this enacted or not by Jews with different Jewish traditions?

How do non-Jews see the manifestation of Jewish identities at work, be they religious or not? How open or ready are they to want to know about the Jewish identity of coworkers? What are their attitudes towards them if they become aware of this Jewish identity?

What is the potential contribution of Judaism to the workplace in terms of ethics, quality management, customer relations, accounting standards, human resource management, labor relations?

Are Jewish-owned businesses run in a different way than non-Jewish owned ones? What is the contribution of Jewish leaders? Is there such a thing as a "Jewish" leadership?

Is there such a thing as a contribution to leadership and management studies, and in particular equality, diversity, and inclusion, that is specific to Jewish scholars?

We believe these research questions will be addressed in the future, and fruitful dialogues between studies of an increasing variety of different identity groups at work will follow suit.

These questions can be dealt with using a variety of methods. It is first possible to explore existing research material where work is not a central question but is being dealt with. For instance, interviews with Jews about their identity may include portions where work is evoked by the interviewee, with or without the invitation of the interviewer. Such is the case with the work of Frischer (2008) on survivors of the Shoah and their descendants, for whom in many cases work acted as a protection against painful remembrance and even as a way to forget about their Jewishness.

Second, it is possible for Jewish scholars to interview colleagues and relatives about their relationship to Jews, Judaism, and Jewishness. Jewish scholars can add their own personal reflection as academic professionals, a strategy that can also be followed by non-Jewish scholars when it comes to their own relationship with Jews, Judaism, and Jewishness.

Third, it is possible to use surveys and quantitative methods devoted to anti-Semitism by including specific questions or criteria pertaining to the workplace when addressing anti-Semitism more broadly. For instance, surveys of anti-Semitism by the Fundamental Rights Agency of the European Union and the Anti-Defamation League could include a section on perception of Jews, Judaism, and Jewishness in the workplace, and how Jews perceive themselves to be treated there.

Reciprocally, surveys on general issues as ethnic or gender discrimination at work, such as situational testing, could include various Jewish-related criteria in the study of religious and ethnic discrimination at work, as was done by Valfort (2015). Notably, the Eurobarometer on Discrimination now includes a question on how people would react upon discovering one of their coworkers is Jewish, but this is only a very recent inclusion (European Commission, 2015). Asking such questions ought to become commonplace in the future.

References

Anti-Defamation League (2003). *Conspiracy Theories about Jews and 9/11 cause dangerous mutations in global Anti-Semitism*, September 2. Retrieved from: archive.adl.org/presrele/asint_13/4346_13.html#.VKBfV14AAA.

—— (2014). *ADL Global 100, an index of anti-Semitism*. Retrieved from: global100.adl.org/public/ADL-Global-100-Executive-Summary2015.pdf.

Bell, M. P. (2009). Effects of the experience of inequality, exclusion, and discrimination on scholarship. *In* Özbilgin, M. (ed.), *Equality, diversity, and inclusion, a research companion*, Cheltenham, UK: Edward Elgar.

Ben-Hur, S., & Jonsen, K. (2012). Ethical leadership: Lessons from Moses, *Journal of Management Development*, 31(9), 962–73.

Birnbaum, P. (2004). *Géographie de l'espoir: L'exil, les lumières, la désassimilation*, Paris: Gallimard.

Chalmer, S., & Cohen, S. M. (2014). The year in social research, on Jews & Jewish life, *Jewish Journal of Sociology and Berman Jewish Policy Archive*.

Chehata, H. (2012). Israel: Promised land of Jews ... as long as they are white? *Race & Class*, 53(4), 67–77.

Chua, A., & Rubenfeld, J. (2014). *The Triple Package*, New York: The Penguin Press.

Colas, H., & Laguecir, A. (2012). The banning of images: Questions arising in the field of management. *Journal of Management Development*, 31(9), 925–37.

Crenshaw, K. (1991). Mapping the margins: Intersectionality, identity politics, and violence against women of color, *Stanford Law Review*, 43(6), 1241–99.

Della Pergola, S. (2014). World Jewish Population, 2014. *In* Dashefsky, A., & Sheskin, I. M. (eds.) *The American Jewish Year Book, 2014, Vol. 114*. Dordrecht: Springer, 301–93.

Edmonson-Bell, E., Meyerson, D., Nkomo, S., & Scully, M. (2003). Interpreting silence and voice in the workplace: A conversation about tempered radicalism among black and white women researchers. *Journal of Applied Behavioral Science*, 39(4), 381–414.

European Commission. (2015). Eurobarometer on discrimination 2015: General perceptions, opinions on policy measures and awareness of rights. Retrieved from: ec.europa.eu/justice/fundamental-rights/files/factsheet_eurobarometer_fundamental_rights_2015.pdf.

Fohn, A., Heenen-Wolff, S., & Mouchenik, Y. (2014). Silence et reconnaissance sociale dans le processus de reconstruction d'anciens enfants juifs caches. *Neuropsychiatrie de l'enfance et de l'adolescence*, 62, 293–8.

Frischer, D. (2008). *Les enfants du silence et de la reconstruction*. Paris: Grasset.
Fundamental Rights Agency. (2013). *Discrimination and hate crime against Jews in EU Member States: Experiences and perceptions of anti-Semitism*. Vienna: Fundamental Rights Agency, 81.
Gold, R. S. (2003). The Black Jews of Harlem: Representation, identity and race, 1920–1939. *American Quarterly*. 55(2), 179–225.
Goldberg, S. A. (1993). *Dictionnaire Encyclopédique du Judaïsme*. Paris: Éditions du Cerf, 1635.
Gottlieb, E. (2012). Mosaic leadership: Charisma and bureaucracy in Exodus 18. *Journal of Management Development*, 31(9), 974–83.
Habisch, A. (2012). The broken tables of stone: A Decalogue approach to corporate compliance practice. *Journal of Management Development*, 31(9), 912–24.
Hecht, M. L., & Faulkner, S. L. (2000). Sometimes Jewish, sometimes not. *Communication Studies*, 51(4), 372–87.
Hersh, R. (2010). Under-represented then over-represented: A memoir of Jews in American mathematics. *The College Mathematics Journal*, 41(1), 2–9.
Jacobs, J. (1891). *Studies in Jewish statistics: Vital, social and anthropometric*. London: Nutt.
Kahane, B. (2012). Tikkun Olam: how a Jewish ethos drives innovation. *Journal of Management Development*, 31(9), 938–47.
Kahneman, D. (2011). *Thinking, fast and slow*. London: Macmillan.
Kay, A. (2012). Pursuing justice: Workplace relations in the eyes of Jewish tradition. *Journal of Management Development*, 31(9), 901–11.
Kehat, H. (2012). Leadership wisdom from the Jewish tradition models of leadership in times of crisis. *Society and Business Review*, 7(3), 277–88.
Kletz, P., Almog-Bareket, G., Habisch, A., Lenssen, G., & Loza Adaui, C. (2012). Practical wisdom for management from the Jewish tradition. *Journal of Management Development*, 31(9), 879–85.
Merriweather Woodson, T., & Ollier-Malaterre, A. (2016). An intersectional approach to diversity management in the United States and France. *In* Klarsfeld, A., Booysen, L., Castro-Christiansen, L., Ng, E., & Kuvaas, B. (eds.), *International thematic perspectives on Equality, Diversity and Inclusion*, Cheltenham: Edward Elgar, p. 69–88.
Meyerson, D. E., & Scully, M. A. (1995). Tempered radicalism and the politics of ambivalence and change. *Organization Science*, 6(5), 585–600.
Morris-Reich, A. (2008). *The quest for Jewish assimilation in modern social science*. New York: Routledge.
Mostovicz, E. I., & Kakabadse, N. K. (2012). He has told you, O man, what is good! *Journal of Management Development*, 31(9), 948–61.

Pew Research Center. (2013). *A portrait of Jewish Americans*. Retrieved from: www.pewforum.org/2013/10/01/jewish-american-beliefs-attitudes-culture-survey/.

Roberts, S. (2014). "Out" in the field. Reflecting on the dilemmas of insider status on data collection and conducting interviews with gay men. *Equality, Diversity and Inclusion: An International Journal*, 33(5), 451–61.

Schnall, D. (1993). Exploratory notes on employee productivity and accountability in classic Jewish sources. *Journal of Business Ethics*, 12, 485–91.

Schnapper, D., Bordes-Benayoune, C., & Raphaël, F. (2009). *La condition juive en France: La tentation de l'entre-soi*. Paris: Presses Universitaires de France, collection Le Lien Social, 140.

Sharabi, M. (2012). The work and its meaning among Jews and Muslims according to religiosity degree. *International Journal of Social Economics*, 39(11), 824–43.

Shapiro, E. S. (2014). The decline and rise of secular Judaism. *First Things: A Monthly Journal of Religion and Public Life*, March(241), 41–6.

Soyer, D. (2001). Class-conscious workers as immigrant entrepreneurs: The ambiguity of class among Eastern-European Jewish Immigrants to the United States at the turn of the 20th century. *Labor History*, 42(1), 45–59.

Spitzer, Y. (2012). *Occupations of Jews in the Pale of Settlement*. Retrieved from: http://yannayspitzer.net/2012/09/30/jewish-occupations-in-the-pale-of-settlement/.

Styhre, A., & Tienari, J. (2014). Men in context: Privilege and reflexivity in academia. *Equality, Diversity and Inclusion: An International Journal*, 33(5), 442–50.

Tajfel, H. (2010). *Social identity and intergroup relations*. Cambridge: Cambridge University Press.

Tamarkin, N. (2011). Religion as race, recognition as democracy: Lemba "Black Jews" in South Africa. *Annals of the American Academy of Political and Social Science*, 637, 148–64.

Valfort, M. A. (2015). *Discrimination religieuse à l'embauche, une réalité*. Paris: Institut Montaigne, 142p.

Weiss, A. (2008). Spiritual activism: A Jewish guide to leadership and repairing the world. *Jewish Lights*, May, 250p.

Wise, T. (2010). *Color Blind: The rise of post-racial politics and the retreat from racial equity*. San Francisco, CA: City Lights Books.

6 | *National Perspectives on Jews at Work: Contrasting Australia, France, Israel, and the UK*

ALAIN KLARSFELD, DIANE BEBBINGTON,
AVI KAY, LUCY TAKSA, FEI GUO, AND
PHILIP MENDES

Introduction

The following chapter is an attempt at identifying research and current trends about Jews and Judaism at work in four specific country contexts: Australia, France, Israel, and the United Kingdom. It is based on Klarsfeld's chapter in this volume titled "The untold, the unseen and the forgettable: Jewishness, Jews and Judaism in diversity management scholarship," which states that in spite of a flourishing anthropological and sociological literature, there is a dearth of research about Jews, Judaism, and Jewishness in the world of work, with the exception of Israel. It also answers the need for embedding religious or religion-related research in specific national contexts. In this chapter we can contrast Israel, where Jews are a majority, with Australia, France, and the United Kingdom, where Jews are a very small minority. We have deliberately chosen to study Jews in countries where they could be considered "privileged," in contrast to countries where even tinier proportions of Jews cannot be found, such as the countries of Eastern Europe and the Middle East, from which Jews were either exterminated or had to flee in order to shelter themselves from potential or actual violence. Each country section attempts to provide a brief history and demography of Jews in the relevant country, data on Jews' socioeconomic status and occupations, and literature on the Jewish experience at the workplace and the challenges and opportunities facing them. A conclusion attempts to place the four countries on a continuum.

Jews in Australia

History

Jewish people have been in Australia since the time of the British invasion. Fourteen arrived as convicts in 1788 with the First British Fleet. By the middle of the nineteenth century, Jewish numbers had reached 1,887 and by 1901 "the Australian Jewish population numbered 15,239." Following World War II their numbers "more than doubled to 32,019" (Medding, 2006). Only a few hundred were among the 170,000 European Displaced Persons who were accepted by Australia between 1947 and 1953. The majority of the 25,000 Jewish refugees who came to Australia were assisted by Jewish relief organizations (Australian Government, 2015). In 2001, the Jewish population was estimated to be "105,000–112,000, with some 50,000 in Melbourne, 45,000 in Sydney, and the rest mainly in Perth, Brisbane, and Adelaide" (Medding, 2006).

Jews have always enjoyed full civil and political rights in Australia and have played a significant role in employment, commerce and trade, the Arts, education, the professions, the development of industry and technology, and politics. The "A Tour of Jewish History in Australia" website (www.jewishhistoryaustralia.net/jha/) reports that a Jew was the first police constable, the first "printer of the original 'Australian' newspaper (in Sydney, in 1836) and … the composer of the first Australian opera." Many Jews have been elected as Members of State and Federal Parliaments. Two Governor-Generals (quasi-Heads of State) were Jewish. Sir Isaac Alfred Isaacs (June 6, 1855–February 11, 1948), the 3rd Chief Justice of Australia, was the first Australian-born Governor-General (Cowen, 1983). Sir Zelman Cowen, Dean of the University of Melbourne Law Faculty and Vice-Chancellor of Universities in NSW and Queensland, was appointed Governor-General in 1977 (Gordon & Grattan, 2011). Others have been leaders in various social movements pertaining to the environment, peace, Aboriginal rights, and gender and sexual equality, as well as engaging in support networks that provide leadership on a range of issues including opposing any manifestations of anti-Semitism and defending the State of Israel (Levey & Mendes, 2004; Rutland, 2005). The Chief Justice of the Supreme Court of NSW and the State's 20th Lieutenant Governor from 1998, James Spigelman, was prominent in the 1965 Freedom Ride organized by students from the University of Sydney, a project undertaken by students to throw light on discrimination and segregation experienced by Indigenous communities in NSW (Sarzin & Sarzin, 2010).

Demography

The following numbers are enumerated in various Australian censuses under the religious category, Judaism. However, the real number of Jews is likely to be 20–25% higher than the figure suggested by the Australian census religion question, as many Jews identify as secular (Goldlust, 2004).

The 2011 census estimated that the Australian Jewish population was around 112,000, which made it the ninth largest Jewish population in the world (Graham, 2014). A century earlier, the 1911 census recorded only 17,287 Jewish people. The increase of the Jewish population occurred after World War II when a large number of Jewish people came from Eastern and Western Europe. In 1951, more than 40,000 were enumerated in the census. By the 1966 census, more than 63,000 were in Australia. During the 1970s and 1990s, a large number came from the former Soviet Union and subsequently many came from South Africa (Australian Bureau of Statistics, 2015b).

Between 1946 and 1966 the growth rate of the Jewish population was around 3.34% per annum. After 1966, the growth slowed down; the number in the 1981 census was 62,000. Since 1981, the growth has picked up but only by around 1.5% – close to the growth rate of the Australian population as a whole (Graham, 2014).

Australian Jews live mainly in the major urban centers. In 2011, about 95% lived in capital cities and more than 84% lived in Sydney and Melbourne. At this time, the age structure of the Jewish population was slightly older than the general Australian population, with the median age of Jewish Australians at 42 years, which was slightly higher than that of the general Australian population, at 37 years (Graham, 2014), and the proportion aged 15 and under was 18%, which was similar to that for the general population (19%). Also in 2011, the proportion of working age Jewish people (aged 15–64) was 63%, while for the general population it was 67%. The major difference in age structure was for those aged 65 and above. The latter proportion was more than 19% but only 14% for the general Australian population (Australian Bureau of Statistics, 2015a, 2015b). According to the 2011 census, about 50% of Jews were born in Australia, with the major source countries for migrant Jews being Southern and East Africa (14%), Eastern Europe (11%), Israel (6.5%), United Kingdom (4.7%), North America (2.9%), and Western Europe (2.5%).

Sectors/professions Where Jews Are Likely to Be Employed

Overall, Jewish people have higher educational attainment than the general Australian population. According to the 2011 census, among those who had post-school qualifications, 44% of Jewish people had bachelor degrees – 20% more than the general Australian population. Similarly, a higher proportion of Jewish people had postgraduate qualifications (14%), compared with the general Australian population (6.5%). An age-specific analysis of the educational attainments of Jewish people in comparison with the general Australian population suggests that in all age groups Jewish people have a much greater proportion of people with higher education qualifications (Bachelor's Degrees, Graduate Diplomas, Graduate Certifications, and Postgraduate Degrees) than the general Australian population. This difference has been especially pronounced in the labor force participation age groups. For people aged 20–29, 46% of Jews obtained bachelor or higher degrees compared to 25% for the general Australian population. For people aged 30–39, these proportions were 67% and 33%, and for those aged 40–49, 59% and 25%, respectively. The 2011 census data also suggested that Jewish people were closing the gender gap in terms of higher education qualifications. For those Jews in their 60s, 31% of Jewish men had a bachelor or higher degree compared with 24% for women in this age group. However, for those in their 20s and 30s, women were more likely to obtain a bachelor's or higher degree than their male counterparts (Graham, 2014).

In Australia, Jewish people have tended to be concentrated in high-level professional and managerial occupations. According to the 2006 census, Jews were much more likely to be in professional occupations than the general Australian population, with 40% and 20%, respectively. Similarly, Jewish people were more likely to be in managerial positions than the general Australian population, with 19% and 13%, respectively. However, there have been notable gender differences. For Australians in the general population, more females (23%) than males (17%)

are in professional occupations, compared with around 40% for both Jewish males and Jewish females. For both Jewish people and the general Australian population, males have been almost twice as likely to be in a managerial positions as their female counterparts. For example, according to the Australian Bureau of Statistics a few years ago more than 24% of Jewish males were in managerial positions compared with only 13% for Jewish females. The proportion of Jewish people in other occupational categories has, however, been generally lower than in the general Australian population. The data from the 2011 census revealed a similar occupational distribution pattern for both Jewish people and the general Australian population (Australian Bureau of Statistics, 2015a, 2015b).

An examination of occupation data from the 2006 and 2011 censuses suggests that gender gaps among Jewish professionals and managerial personnel are more profound in a few occupations, and also differ more significantly from the general Australian population. For example, among Chief Executives (CEOs), General Managers (GMs) and Legislators, close to 5% of Jewish men are in this category while only 1% of Jewish women are. This gender gap extends to other occupational categories and is considerable when compared with the general Australian population. While 12 % of Jewish males are Specialist Managers and 13 % are Business, HR and Marketing Managers, Jewish women tend to be better represented in Health professions, and Legal, Social and Welfare Professions, which is also the case for the general Australian population. In 2006, a much greater proportion of Jewish females (11%) made up Educational Professionals than their male counterparts (4%), which is again similar to the general Australian population, with 7% and 3%, respectively. At the same time, far fewer Jewish people work in low skilled occupations, such as Automotive and Engineering Trades, Construction Trades, and other Trades. Data from the 2011 census revealed a similar pattern of occupational concentration and gender gaps for Jewish people (Australian Bureau of Statistics, 2015a, 2015b).

In 2006, Jewish managers were more likely to be concentrated in a few categories, namely CEOs, GMs, and Legislators (16%), Construction-related Managers (15%), and Retail Managers (16%). Comparatively, in the Australian general population, Managers were concentrated in Farmers and Farm Managers (15%), Construction-related Managers (15%), and Retail Managers (16%). A greater proportion of Jewish females were Retail Managers and Business Administration Managers, which is similar to the general Australian population. These patterns of concentration among Managers for Jewish people and the Australian general population did not change in the 2011 census (Australian Bureau of Statistics, 2015a, 2015b). In the 2006 Census, Jewish Professionals included School Teachers (11%), Medical Practitioners (10%), Legal Professionals (8%), and Accountants, Auditors, and Company Secretaries (8%). This pattern of professional occupational concentration for Jewish professionals did not change substantially in the data from the 2011 census (Australian Bureau of Statistics, 2015a, 2015b).

Experiences of Jews in the Workplace

Despite such representation of Jewish people in higher and better paid occupations, the conciliated case registers drawn from the Australian Human Rights Commission (AHRC) Conciliated Cases Reports and from the NSW Anti-Discrimination Board Conciliated Cases Reports (ADB) indicate that Jews have continued to experience a range of issues in the workplace. A number of cases provide some indication of the nature of such issues.

In its report for 2001–2, the Australian Human Rights Commission referred to a complaint from a person who claimed that "he was treated less favourably because he was from Israel and was Jewish" during his 5 year employment with a large federal government organization. According to the complainant, he had experienced "repeated anti-semitic comments, intimidation, isolation, threats of demotion and shift restrictions due to work related health problems." In addition, he alleged "that the comments he was subjected to included being greeted by a staff member who said 'Sieg Heil' and performed a 'Nazi' salute, being asked 'Why don't you go back to Israel?' and told 'I'll send you back to Israel.'" He also claimed "that his supervisors, harassment officers, a staff doctor and a union representative all subjected him to less favourable treatment while working at a particular work centre and that management failed to act upon his complaints." The claim was conciliated and the employer paid $9,000 in general damages (Australian Human Rights Commission, 2001–2).

A couple of years later in another case brought before this Commission, another "complainant claimed that he was discriminated against in his employment with a large manufacturing company because of his Jewish origin and religious beliefs." In this case the complainant "claimed that while other casual employees were made permanent and new employees were employed, his appointment as a permanent employee was delayed for several months." The claim also referred to the fact that the man's "computer username was changed from his surname to 'Hitler's failure,' and following this incident his wage payments were late and/or incorrect." While the company agreed that the latter incident occurred, it "denied that the complainant was treated less favourably by the company because of his race and/or religious beliefs. The complaint was resolved through a conciliation process, which recognized that 'the employment relationship had broken down' and the complainant accepted 'an ex-gratia payment of $12,500 and payment of accrued annual leave entitlements'" (Australian Human Rights Commission, 2003–4).

In New South Wales, a decade later, a Jewish man who was employed on a casual basis by a cleaning company in a position which required him to work at different locations had "told his employer he was unable to work beyond a certain distance from home on Fridays as he had to get home by sunset for ethno-religious reasons." Although "the company said they could offer the man a different job at another location," following a restructure, the Jewish man said he "felt he had to quit as he felt he had been blacklisted." Although he subsequently "applied for another job with the same company," he was informed that "he had been marked 'review suitability if reapplies.'" This complaint of race discrimination was settled by "a minor amount of financial compensation and the removal of the 'review suitability' on his file" (Anti-Discrimination Board NSW, 2014).

Challenges/opportunities Facing Jews at the Workplace

According to Thornton and Luker (2010, p. 18):

> 'Legislation variously making unlawful racial and religious vilification or racial hatred in the form of verbal or written statements, images or sounds in public places was introduced from 1989, but does not apply in the area of employment. Discrimination on the grounds of religious belief or activity is not proscribed under federal legislation, nor in New South Wales or South Australia, although courts in various jurisdictions have found Jews and Sikhs

to be included under the term "ethnic origin" and the term "ethno-religious origin" has been included in the definition of "race" in New South Wales and Tasmania'.

Nevertheless, little research has been done on experiences of discrimination, harassment, and vilification of Jewish people in the workplace. In a report for the Australia/Israel and Jewish Affairs Council produced in 2011, it was noted that:

'At various times over the past sixty years, when there has been anecdotal evidence that racism against any segment of Australian society is increasing there has been a concurrent increase in reports of crude and unthinking anti-Semitic comments made in the workplace, educational institutions and in public places towards individuals who were or were believed to be Jewish. This type of abuse is indistinguishable from that aimed at other minority groups such as Indigenous Australians, Asians and Muslims (Jones, 2011)'.

However, such reports focus attention on the media and mail incidents. Similarly, annual reports on anti-Semitism in Australia published by the Executive Council of Australian Jewry specifically exclude workplace incidents (Nathan, 2015, p. 20).

By contrast, interviews conducted with Jewish Australians for the New South Wales (NSW) Bicentennial Oral History Project include accounts of work experiences from the early twentieth century. These transcripts and sound recordings in the National Library and in the NSW State Library clearly indicate that Jewish working class migrants experienced anti-Semitism throughout the twentieth century (The Australian Bicentenary Authority, New South Wales Council, 1988).

For the most part the challenges facing Jewish employees can be gleaned from newspaper or related media reports and the conciliated case registers from various state and federal anti-discrimination and human rights bodies referred to earlier. These Conciliated cases provide an insight into the challenges facing the coexistence of Jews with non-Jews in the workplace. Interestingly, the Victorian Equal Opportunity and Human Rights Commission (2013) acknowledged such challenges in a six-page toolkit entitled: Cultural Diversity in the Workplace: A Guide for Employers Working with Jewish Employees, which "explains some common practices that may be relevant to Jewish people in the workplace" and identifies "ways to accommodate these practices" in order to enable employers to meet their obligations under the Victorian Equal Opportunity Act. Clearly the challenge is for further scholarly research to be conducted on experiences of Jews in employment and the management of their religious and ethno-cultural issues.

Jews in the United Kingdom

History

There has been a continuous presence of Jews in Britain for more than three centuries; in the eighteenth and nineteenth centuries this comprised of a mainly Sephardi community which then transformed into a community of Ashkenazi Jews that were more diverse, including in terms of class differences. The numbers of Jews in Britain expanded rapidly at the turn of the nineteenth and twentieth centuries with the immigration of Eastern European Jews into the UK.

Kahn-Harris and Gidley (2010) note that Jews in modern Britain have not suffered the large pogroms that Jews have experienced elsewhere. By the nineteenth century most legislative restraints on Jewish participation in social life had been removed and with an unbroken presence, British Jews have been able to establish an extensive network of institutions including the United Synagogue, the largest umbrella body of British Jews with over 60 affiliated synagogues, and the Board of Deputies, Anglo Jewry's representative body. It is through the Board of Deputies that the interests of the Anglo-Jewish community are made known to the British state.

With regard to the minority status of Jews in Britain, Kahn-Harris and Gidley point out that current day research on minorities tends to focus on racism and material disadvantage, these aspects of experience being largely unreflective of today's generally prosperous Jewish community. Whilst Jews may seem to integrate economically and socially into British society, they do no easily fit into the main categories used to define minorities including "faith," "ethnicity/race," and "people." Furthermore, Jews are now associated with "whiteness," which excludes them from dominant concepts within multicultural research. According to Kahn-Harris and Gidley (2010), "The lack of Jewish voice at the heart of social and cultural research in the UK is reflected in the lack of Jewish voices in public debates about multiculturalism and racism" (p. 7). They argue that Jewish communal leadership has emphasized secure British belonging rather than claiming its space within debates around multiculturalism. This has led to other minorities perceiving Jews as being part of the white mainstream.

Demography

Two UK censuses have now included a question on religion – in 2001 and 2011. This has enabled researchers to monitor change in the UK Jewish population over time. The analysis below is based on reports that refer only to England and Wales, not Northern Ireland and Scotland. This is due to the unavailability of data when the reports were written.

Jews are 0.5% of the total population of England and Wales, a percentage unchanged since 2001. However, beneath the headline statistic there have been notable changes in the UK Jewish population, including high birth rates amongst Orthodox Jews, in particular Haredim, low birth rates and ageing in the rest of the Jewish population, and some assimilation.

The UK has the fifth largest Jewish population in the world and the second largest population in Europe after France. It reached its peak in the 1950s at around 420,000 people. From then on the Jewish population declined but this seems to have stopped (Staetsky & Boyd, 2014). The 2011 census counted 263,346 Jews in England and Wales, a slight increase of 3,419 since 2001. This means that one in 200 people in England and Wales identified as Jewish. However, a number of people may not have responded to the religion question in the census and Jewish Policy Research (www.jpr.org.uk) estimates that this group is likely to be in the order of 21,000 people. This brings the adjusted total to 284,000 (Jewish Policy Research, 2012).

More detailed analysis of Jews in England and Wales indicate that in comparison with other religious groups, Jews are older on average (41 years compared with 39 years) but in the decade between the 2001 and 2011 censuses, the Jewish population became younger overall. This can be accounted for by the high increase in the numbers of Haredi births. The average age of Haredi Jews, who make up 15% of the Jewish population in England and Wales, is 27, while that of non-Haredi Jews is 44 years (Graham, 2013).

Jews are both concentrated and dispersed across England and Wales, with more religious Jews living in areas of high concentration and less religious Jews being more dispersed. 65.3% of all Jews in England and Wales live in London and nearby areas.

Sectors/professions Where Jews Are Likely to Be Employed

Data from the 2001 Census provides the most detailed information yet obtained about the work activities of British Jews including the occupations towards which they gravitate (Graham et al., 2007). Key findings from the Census regarding Jewish people's employment in Britain were that British Jews were found to be high achievers in the workplace and Jewish women in particular exhibited very high levels of success. Almost a third (30.5%) of economically active Jews were self-employed, more than double the proportion in the general population (14.2%). Jewish men were more likely to be economically active than women (79.9% compared with 59.7%) and much more likely to be working full-time than part-time (83.6% compared to 52.4%). In Islington, over 80% of Jews were economically active; by contrast, in Hackney, 47% were economically inactive, many of whom were looking after the family/home. 54.2% of Jews worked in just three industries: real estate and business activities; the wholesale/retail trade; and health and social work. This compared with 40.6% of the general population. Jewish women were much more likely than men to work in health and social work (15.7% compared to 6.5%) and education (14.5% compared to 5.3%). Occupationally, 25.1% of Jews were managers and senior officials compared with 15.1% among the general population. A quarter (23.7%) of Jewish women worked in administrative and secretarial occupations, compared with 5.7% of men. However, Jewish women were equally likely to be managers and almost twice as likely to be professionals as men in the general population. There appears to be no available analysis of data from the 2011 Census which would enable an examination of Jewish employment trends over time.

Experience of Jews in the Workplace

There appears to be limited research specifically on the experiences of Jews in the UK workforce; issues are tackled either as part of larger projects involving the major religions and beliefs or as one aspect of Jewish life. Loewenthal (2012) for example, notes various incidents that can have consequences for the mental health of Jews, including losing employment because of the need to observe the Sabbath.

Again, it appears that data on these topics are limited and if they are covered, this is as part of larger pieces of commissioned research. A report on religion in UK higher education (Equality Challenge Unit, 2011) noted that higher proportions of Jewish students and staff experienced no dietary provision in their universities (30.7% of students and 28.2% of staff) compared with other religions or beliefs. Comments made include the following demands for accommodation as regards food provided on site:

The university should make kosher food available on campus, but it does not at present.

Understandably there may not be a huge market for providing kosher food, however I fail to understand why the sandwiches not containing meat couldn't be supplied from a kosher supplier, and would still be the same, i.e. egg mayo but kosher! (p. 42)

The research noted some tensions between different religions where kosher food was available, but not halal.

In one college they banned halal food. Instead of taking a step forward they took a step back. They serve kosher food but they don't serve halal food. They say it's inhumane. They say halal food is barbaric. I felt quite angry about that. It doesn't make sense if they have kosher food. (p. 43)

The report notes that higher education institutions mainly organize their trimesters or semesters around the Christian calendar. This was evident in the accounts of some student respondents.

My first day of lectures was on Yom Kippur, which is the Day of Atonement and a most holy day for Jews. The day for moving into the halls was on Rosh Hashanah – Jewish New Year. I am not a very religious person apart from the two days of Rosh Hashanah and Yom Kippur. These are the three days when I come out of the woodwork and go to synagogue and I pray. Last year because it was the first year of university I had to come to university early but my first day of lectures I was caught between a rock and a hard place. Do I go to university or go to synagogue like I have for the last 18 years? It just didn't feel right. (p. 55)

Universities may make arrangements regarding the timetabling of examinations and lectures to accord with religious calendars. In spite of these efforts, Muslim and Jewish staff and students indicated that they sometimes had difficulties with events on certain days, including late on Fridays and Saturdays for Jewish students and staff. In some universities students were supervised by a religious person or an academic until they were able to sit an exam. This could seem punitive, as described by a Jewish academic:

If you can't sit an exam because of Shabbat or Shavuot and you can't do it on that particular day, then we will identify somebody who will literally lock you away during the time when you should have been sitting your exam. They release you in order to do the exam. Here we call it incarceration – it's very extreme! (p. 56)

Another area of tension was around the ways in which religious spaces were made for some religions but not others:

It irks me that some religions are catered for and others aren't. There is a prayer room, for Muslims only. What about Christians, Jews, Buddhists etc.? How is this equal? Why have certain religions been placed above others? (p. 61)

The vast majority of students and staff felt they had not experienced discrimination or harassment because of their actual or perceived religion or belief identity. Of staff that did indicate feeling discriminated or harassed, 16 Muslims (17.8% of Muslim respondents) reported this and four Jewish staff (10.3% of Jewish respondents). These proportions were larger than for the other religion or belief groups including Christian, Hindu and Sikh. Jewish students were more likely as a proportion of their group to say they felt discriminated or harassed on the basis of their religion – 26.7% compared with 16.7% of Sikh and 14% of Muslim students. A Jewish student wrote:

When discussing the Holocaust as part of a theology module, I felt another student was being insensitive, as she told me I needed to get out of the "Jew-box" when viewing the Holocaust. (p. 79)

A recommendation made by the report is that though there may be tensions between the desire to observe a religion or belief with the logistical requirements of institutional scheduling, provision for religious practice should be "carefully managed to ensure equal access by all religion or belief groups" (p. 109).

Challenges/opportunities Facing Jews at the Workplace

A number of reports highlight anti-Semitic incidents in the UK, but these rarely focus on anti-Semitism in the workplace. The Report on the All-Party Parliamentary Inquiry into anti-Semitism of February 2015 was commissioned due to an increase in anti-Jewish incidents in the UK following increasing tensions in the Middle East. This must be put in the context of British Jews generally experiencing very little anti-Semitism. The perception of a rise in anti-Semitism within the UK Jewish Community is backed up by media reports, for example, based on a survey by the Campaign Against anti-Semitism, the Independent reported that "More than half of British Jewish people fear Jews have no future in the UK" (The Independent, 2015). None of the anti-Semitic incidents mentioned in the All-Parliamentary report relate to anti-Semitism in the workplace.

The Community Security Trust (CST) reports on anti-Semitic incidents, noting that there were 473 such reported incidents in the UK in the first six months of 2015, a 53% increase on the first six months of 2014 (CST, 2015). The CST records six categories of incident: extreme violence; assault; damage and desecration to Jewish property; threats; abusive behavior; and anti-Semitic literature. Specific instances of anti-Semitism in the workplace are not included in the CST's reporting of incidents.

The Fundamental Rights Agency carried out an online survey in 2012 gathering Jewish people's experiences and perceptions of hate crime, discrimination and anti-Semitism across eight EU member states including the UK. 5,847 Jewish people over sixteen years of age responded (Fundamental Rights Agency, 2013). Most respondents, apart from those in Latvia and the United Kingdom, considered anti-Semitism to be a very big or fairly big problem. About half of the respondents in France and Hungary felt anti-Semitism was "a very big problem" in their countries today. The United Kingdom can therefore be considered a country where Jews experience greater acceptance compared with other countries in Europe.

The Fundamental Rights Agency survey asked about discrimination in a variety of situations, including when looking for work, and in the workplace, by people for whom or with whom the respondent worked. Of the nine situations, people were most likely to mention discrimination at work. While the responses are not broken down quantitatively by country, all three quotes in the report are from UK respondents.

I believe that if I did inform people I was Jewish when applying for a job it may put me at risk of being discriminated against (Woman, 25–9 years old, United Kingdom). (p. 55)

You have not asked about institutional racism in the workplace, e.g. the difficulty of going home early on Friday; yet all social events [take place] on Fridays, etc. (Woman, 60–69 years old, United Kingdom). (p. 55)

I left my job at the university where I was teaching because of explicit anti-Semitism at work, both from colleagues and from students. I am still traumatised by this and incapable of looking for another job (Man, 55–9 years old, United Kingdom). (p. 55)

In conclusion, Jews seem to enjoy a more peaceful environment in the United Kingdom compared with other European countries, and in fact the UK can be regarded as "best-in-class" in Europe in this respect. However, given the existence of such testimonials in the UK, British policy makers need to keep monitoring anti-Semitism and put in place more initiatives to ensure people of all faiths coexist harmoniously in the workplace.

Jews in France

History

Jews' presence in France dates back to the Roman Empire. For instance, Jewish presence is recorded in Marseille, Narbonne, and Lyon at the time of the Roman Empire (Dubnov, 1936; Johnson, 1989). When Clovis founded the kingdom of France, Jewish presence is attested to by the fact that measures were taken in order to encourage or force the conversion of Jews to Christianity and to limit the interactions of Christians with Jews, as early as 576. However, it is believed that in spite of these measures, the integration of Jews in France was generally good (Goldberg, 1993) at least up until 1096. Their continued presence in the Middle Ages is attested to by the fact that Jews were ordered to be expelled from a number of regions in the thirteenth century, and then from the whole of France, by a decree dating back to 1394 (Winock, 2004) – a decree that was never fully implemented. Rachi (1040–1105), one of the major commentators on the Torah, was born and spent most of his life in Troyes, a city 150 km east of Paris, where he grew wine. It is therefore reasonable to say that Jewish presence in France is as old, if not older, than France itself, contrary to the stereotype of the Jew as a "foreigner" to France.

French Jews were emancipated, i.e., acquired full equality, as a consequence of the French Revolution, in 1791. At the time, it is estimated that 50–60% of French Jews were living in the Alsace and Lorraine in the Northeastern corner of France and 10–15% in the southwest (Bordeaux and Bayonne). According to where they lived, Jews had very different conditions: in the south west, they enjoyed official rights and near equality with Christians. They could practice a variety of professions. In Alsace and Lorraine, they lived in ghettos, were an object of contempt, and could only exercise a limited number of professions, such as money-lenders (some of whom turned into bankers) and peddlers. Money-lending, long considered a profession of a Jewish "nature," was exercised by Jews not so much because of a "natural" gift but because of socially and culturally constructed restrictions: the Catholic doctrine forbade Christians from pursuing this profession, and in many places (such as Alsace), restrictions prevented Jews from entering other professions and/or owning land (Winock, 2004). Emancipation following the French Revolution meant that Jews could embrace fully all types of professions (see below). Where the first half of the nineteenth century is depicted as a somewhat rosy period for Jews in France (Winock, 2004), such is not the case in the second half, which culminates with the Dreyfus affair. Captain Dreyfus, a Jewish officer, was accused of treason in 1894 and sentenced to forced labor in French Guyana. This affair unleashed considerable anti-Semitic campaigns and debates all over French society. The occupation of France by Nazi Germany from 1940 to 1944 and the extermination of 75,000 Jews (25% of Jews present in France at the time) as a result created a trauma that still resonates until the present day with descendants of survivors (Frischer, 2008). It seems that work acted as a protection but was also instrumental in silencing their own Jewishness for many survivors and their descendants.

Demography of Jews in France

Estimates of any religion-based group is a difficult exercise in general, as there is no "objective" criterion along which one can assign a religion-based identity to anyone. Is the assignation based on parents' religion? Is it based on beliefs? On religious practice? On observing holidays? On one's name? On self-declaration ? This is particularly true of Jews, in all countries where they are present (Schnapper, 1987). In France, counting the Jewish population has to face one more hurdle: since 1872, censuses do not ask about religion. Therefore one has to rely on estimates provided by foreign sources. According to Della Pergola (2014) relying on self-declaration of self or by someone of the same household, there were 475,000 Jews in France in 2014, a sharp decline from 1970's estimate of 530,000, but still making France the country with the third largest presence of Jews in raw numbers in the world and the fourth in proportion (behind Canada), with a proportion of 0.74% (Della Pergola, 2014).

Fine grained data such as that available in Australia and the UK, where the national census included Jewish identity, is not available in France. In much research conducted on Jews in France, samples of Jews in France rely on snowball sampling and/or on family names, which, in spite of the best efforts made by researchers, cannot pretend to be representative (Bensimon & Della Pergola, 1986; Cohen, 2002; Schnapper et al., 2009). With all this said, the economic situation of Jews in the sample studied over the last 40 years has improved: the share of production operators decreased from 10.5% to 1%, and the share of managers ("cadres") and intellectual professions ("professions libérales et intellectuelles") increased from 25.5% to 44.5% (Bensimon & Della Pergola, 1986; Schnapper et al., 2009).

Sectors/professions Where Jews Are Likely to Be Employed

Throughout the nineteenth century, Jews progressively left the east of France towards Paris, where their population grew from 3,000 in the early 1800s to an estimated 40,000 at the end of the nineteenth century. Between banking and peddling, Jews embraced a vast diversity of profession now open to them: doctors, lawyers, magistrates, professors, civil servants, army officers, play-writers, actors, composers, journalists, publishers, members of parliament (as early as 1842), and members of the government as early as 1848. Their successful and visible integration also nurtured the resentment of all of those whose wealth and power declined in the same period that the fate of Jews improved, as well as the resentment of some of those intellectuals who were critical of the development of capitalism (Winock, 2004). However, for all the qualitative richness of the historic accounts of the diversification of professions accessible to Jews and of their visibility, there are no precise statistics on numbers of Jews in each profession, French identity (and Jewish identity) being built on the principle that the Republic ignores differences between communities and only defends the freedoms of individuals.

Experience of Jews at the Workplace

As there is a denial of religion in the public sphere in France, it is of little surprise that there is no research that addresses Jews as Jews and how they perceive themselves in the workplace. In order to start addressing this research gap, one of the authors has conducted seven interviews with Jews active in business higher education and presents in this section the common themes that emerged from this small group of interviewees drawn from a small subset of the French occupational scenery.

First common trait is the fact none of the interviewees discuss their religious identity at work. One does so but with a close circle of colleagues active in the field of equality, diversity, and inclusion, or with colleagues-turned-friends. This is very much in line with the conception of French secularism inherited from the French Revolution and emancipation depicted above and portrayed by historians (Winock, 2004): Jews were granted equality and freedom as individuals on the condition that they disappear as a community of difference. According to their names (only three interviewees have totally traditional French-sounding names and surnames), some interviewees tend to assume that their colleagues know about them being Jewish, without their ever being explicit about it.

A second commonality is that within their occupation as academics, no interviewee perceives they have been treated unfairly as a Jew or have been confronted with derogatory remarks about their Jewishness, with the exception of one, as will be outlined below. Most perceive management academia as a more Jewish-friendly environment than, as one interviewee says, for instance, "the civil service," or "society at large" for another interviewee, or "radical left" circles for yet another one.

However, one interviewee's thesis supervisor commented "I know why you got the job [in the prestigious business school], it is because you are Jewish" upon him being hired in this business school. This made the interviewee anxious and report the incident to the Head of the Department, who was invited to sit on the thesis panel in order to monitor and prevent possible subtle discrimination from taking place. Another interviewee with a Jewish sounding name discovered that one of her previous employers (outside of academia, i.e., prior to her joining academia) had hired her with the "political" intention of proving to some external stakeholder that he was not anti-Semitic. Soon after discovering this, she resigned from this employer.

In contrast to this generally rosy picture of how interviewees perceive their environment to be generally tolerant to Jews, one interviewee had been indirectly confronted with evocations of stereotypes, and even discriminatory behavior in the most extreme case. A colleague of his told him that, on an academic recruitment panel, one of the members said about one applicant, "not him, he is Jewish." There are also anecdotal reports of remarks made by panel members about interviewees whose CV suggest they have spent part or all of their professional life in Israel, suggesting that mentioning such experience is considered by an unknown proportion of recruiters as a stigma. These anecdotal accounts all emanate from "invisible Jews" whose name is totally "not Jewish sounding," or from non-Jews. This suggests that anti-Semitic discourse and behavior is more likely to occur when perpetrators perceive that they are not in the presence of Jews. Whether this translates into the workplace at large and in what proportion is as yet an under-researched area. For the time being and to our knowledge, only one situation testing study has been conducted about religion in France on a large sample of applications in the accounting profession, and it was published in October 2015. From this study, it comes out that in France, "visible" Jews (whose CV explicitly refers to them being Jews) are treated less favorably than Christians, but more favorably than Muslims, in the context of fictitious applications for an entry-level position in accounting. The probability of the Christian applicant being invited to a recruitment interview is 30% higher than that for the Jewish applicant, and 100% higher than that for the Muslim applicant (Valfort, 2015). This suggests the situation depicted in the interview does indeed happen elsewhere in French society and is not an exceptional case.

The last common statement across the interviews is that all interviewees perceive that the situation has worsened over the last fifteen years or so. The ones who have children of high school and university age report their children being confronted to anti-Semitic discourse in their age-group environment, something from which the interviewees themselves (all aged between 45 and 65) had been generally preserved in what three among them describe as a "golden parenthesis" where anti-Jewish discourse had been nearly eradicated and they could even feel some sympathy for Jews in their immediate environment. All but one are worried about the future. This is very much in line with results obtained on a larger scale by the Fundamental Rights Agency (2013), which will be outlined below.

Challenges/opportunities Facing Jews at the Workplace

Although there is a dearth of research on how Jews and non-Jews interact at the workplace, we will first refer here to stereotypes of Jews in the workplace as they were spread by the French post emancipation (i.e., post 1789) literature. Such novelists as Maupassant and more recently Irene Némirovsky (herself a Russian Jew by origin) have often included Jewish characters in their novels. What often comes out is that Jews are generally rich, or intensely pursuing the accumulation of wealth, and are at best cold-headed and calculating people, and at worst crooks and of sly character, all traits that conform to existing anti-Semitic stereotypes about Jews. This general tendency of the nineteenth- and early twentieth-century literature has been altered by post-World War II, post-creation of the state of Israel literature, where Jews started to appear in more varied depictions, if only as victims, survivors, subjects of traumas, resisters, fighters, or descendants thereof. Many Jews were drawn to the military (such as Captain Dreyfus), to political careers (such as Adophe Crémieux and Léon Blum), to education and science, to the civil service, to the medical and legal professions, to social work, to trade unionism, all activities that do not match the classic stereotype of the "wheeler-dealer," and this is generally absent from the literature. However, French literature has also proposed non-stereotypical Jewish figures alongside the stereotypical ones, and this should be acknowledged (Samuels, 2010; Savy, 2010). For instance, counter to the stereotype evoked earlier, Eugène Sue depicted the "wandering Jew" as both economically miserable and morally courageous (Sue, 1844–5, reedited 1983).

As in Britain, no research provides insight into how Jews are perceived by others or perceive others in the workplace, or how they interact with others in the workplace. What does, however, surface in recent research is a comparative literature on anti-Semitism, i.e. of how Jews are perceived by non-Jews (Anti-Defamation League, 2014) and of Jews' own perceptions about how they are treated and perceived (Fundamental Rights Agency, 2013). When considering anti-Semitism, France appears to be one of the "leaders" of Western Europe, second only to Greece (Anti-Defamation League, 2014) with 37% of the French population agreeing with six out of eleven stereotypes about Jews, in contrast with the lowest ranking countries of Western Europe: Denmark, the Netherlands, Sweden, and the UK, all of which score 9% or less on this same index, and in contrast with Western Europe as a whole, which scores 24% on average. As for perceived anti-Semitism by Jews themselves in their respective countries, France is again one of the European leaders, coming out top of the league, with Hungary, according to the Fundamental Rights Agency (2013).

Respondents were most likely to consider anti-Semitism to be either "a very big" or "a fairly big problem" in Hungary, France and Belgium (90%, 85% and 77%, respectively). In Hungary and France, about half of the respondents feel that anti-Semitism amounts to "a very big problem" in the country today (49% and 52%, respectively) (Fundamental Rights Agency, 2013, p. 15).

As regards perception of change (i.e., perception of an increase/decrease in anti-Semitism), France comes out first in Europe; 74% of respondents in France agreeing that there has been a large increase in anti-Semitism (Fundamental Rights Agency, 2013) – more than anywhere else in Europe. This does point to the necessity of a societal response to this high and growing feeling of unease.

Jews in Israel

Brief History of Israel

In a state in which both 75% of the population and the dominant culture are Jewish, the situation of the Jewish community in all avenues of life – including at work – is profoundly different than that of any other Jewish community. Thus, while Israel is a diverse, multi-cultural country in which there continues to exist on-going and animated discussions with regard to the exact nature and meaning of the "Jewishness" of the country, that "Jewishness" is at its core in all of its social, cultural, and economic institutions. One clear expression of the above is that in the economic sphere in general, and at the workplace in particular, it is "Jewish time" by which the days of work and leisure are arranged. The Jewish Sabbath on Saturday is the default day of rest and it is in accordance with traditional Jewish religious holidays that workplaces operate.

The creation of the State of Israel in 1948 can, perhaps, be best viewed as the end-result of an "ideological start-up." Building on historical yearnings to return to the Land of Israel and the political winds that swept across Europe in the nineteenth century, modern political Zionism was born. Central to the ideology that led to the establishment of the state were the socialist ideas of its leading founders, stressing the centrality, if not the nobility, of work – and particularly physical work – to Jewish renewal. The economic and political institutions of the state in the making and in the nascent state, itself, were clearly socialist in nature and part of an overall policy of creating a "workers' commonwealth." Not surprisingly, a central feature of economic policy was the creation of a strong Jewish proletariat and the protection of the rights of and equality among workers. In contrast to the relative invisibility of the relationship between work and Jewishness in Australia, the United Kingdom, and even more France, work and in particular manual work must be considered a central and highly visible concept in the short history of Israel.

Sectors/professions Where Jews Are Likely to Be Employed

Increased contact with – and desire for – a more consumer oriented society, along with a significant economic crisis in the 1980s, necessitated a fundamental change in Israeli economic policy that transformed Israel from an economy characterized by almost ubiquitous government intervention to one in which market forces became dominant. Concurrent with the rise of market forces, Israel has emerged as a central player in the high-tech sector and is currently widely seen as one of the most important epicenters of high-tech activity and innovation in the world. Accordingly, the dream of national economic success shifted from the toil of the rigorous laborer to the trials of the resolute technological entrepreneur. Regardless of these changes, the state and its institutions, the economy, and organizations are overwhelmingly influenced by the majority Jewish population.

The 6.3 million Jews in Israel currently comprise 75% of the total population of 8.46 million. "The Jewish population makes up 6,335,000 (74.9%); 1,757,000 (20.7%) are Arabs; and, those identified as 'others' (non-Arab Christians, Baha'i, etc) make up 4.4% of the population (370,000 people)" (Jewish Virtual Library, 2016). Both in terms of their sheer numbers and the nature of the relative educational and professional levels of various population groups in Israel, Jews dominate all fields except a number of lower paying fields such as construction (dominated by Arabs – almost all Muslims), agriculture, and care of the aged and invalid (dominated by – primarily – Asian foreign care workers).

With regard to non-Jewish labor, while discrimination does exist, so does extensive legislation protecting the religious accommodation rights of minority workers. Israeli law recognizes the Sabbaths of both the Muslim and Christian communities – as well as the rights of employees from those communities to operate according to them. Organizational adjustments are regularly made with regard to holidays and time needed to pray and observe other (non-Jewish) traditions, particularly in the case of Arab workers. Finally, within this context, it is common to find Arab physicians, nurses, pharmacists, etc. being overrepresented in shifts on the Jewish Sabbath and holidays. This suggests that accommodation rights, as practiced in Israel, are not only a source of difficulty as often depicted in the reasonable accommodation literature, but one of opportunity.

Challenges/opportunities Facing Jews in Israel

While the occupational Jew/non-Jew occupational segregation depicted above and that takes place – formally or informally – constitutes a first challenge in itself, other types of inequalities and challenges can be pointed to within the Jewish majority itself, and these challenges are specific to Israel, with no equivalent in the Western countries depicted above. While roughly 60% of the Jewish population is of "Sephardi" (sometimes termed "Mizrachi" in Israel) ancestry, which can be traced back to Muslim countries in North Africa and the Middle East, it is the

European "Ashkenazi" community that has traditionally dominated the Israeli economy, and particularly higher status and professional positions. Though the gaps between the two communities have gradually closed in recent decades, differences in education and income levels persist. It is the former, Sephardi/Mizrachi population that predominates in lower end jobs in such areas as sales, service, and semi-skilled crafts. Accordingly, the average wage of salaried Ashkenazi workers in 2014 was roughly 15% higher than that of their non-Ashkenazi counterparts (Swirski et al., 2015).

An additional within-Jews division that exists in Israel with regard to the workplace is that between the "general" population and the fastest growing population in Israel: the Ultra-Orthodox Jewish (or "Haredi") population, which presently comprises slightly more than 10% of the total Israeli population. Due to theological, social and political reasons, the Haredi population in Israel has exhibited unique attitudes and behavior within the workplace: men tend to refrain from working in order to study the Torah and Talmud, the Jewish main religious sources. Men tend to enter the labor force at a later stage in life than is customary in other populations – if at all. Women have been placed into the role of "breadwinners" to allow their male spouses to continue their religious studies. These women tend to be clustered in a few professions such as education, lower-level administration, and bookkeeping, in "spiritually safe" organizational frameworks (Friedman, 1991; Kay, 2012, 2015).

The above is changing due to both "push" factors (economic necessity driving Haredim to seek higher paying jobs) and "pull" factors (an increasing desire among Haredim to seek jobs commensurate with their skills and interests). As a result of the above, it is no longer unusual to find Haredi men and (particularly) women employed in a wide variety of organizations. This reality brings with it many challenges, both due to the nature of the traditional relationship between the Haredi population and other population groups and the nature of the Haredi lifestyle, characterized by stringent guidelines regarding a variety of matters, including: the accepted relationship between Haredim and others, norms regarding the roles of men and women and the nature of the social contact among them, as well as a variety of other matters related to dress, speech, "work/life" issues – and the overall role and meaning of work.

Research has shown that half of Haredi males who have entered the workplace prefer to work among only males, prefer to work for male managers, and have fears of being discriminated against. Similarly, women are urged by religious leaders to be careful with regard to their interactions with men at the workplace. Not surprisingly, a number of special "sex-segregated" organizational frameworks have emerged in the financial services industry, accounting, and computing, to accommodate Haredi preferences. Along with these developments, initial research concerning how Haredim are viewed at the workplace suggests that many employers have considerable reservations about hiring and promoting Haredim at the workplace. These concerns relate to possible difficulties with regard to both working in teams and meeting expected standards of work (Ono, 2010).

In closing, one of the central challenges of Israeli society in the coming years will be the fuller integration of Arab and Haredi workers into the workplace in a manner that will allow for both their personal benefit and that of the overall economy. The above is not only an economic necessity but in complete accord with both Israeli law and the Torah (Pentateuch) for, of the 613 commandments given, fourteen commandments deal directly with business practices, eleven deal with matters of property, and nineteen deal with employee relations. Acting according to those commandments will be one of the true measures of the distinct "Jewishness" of the Israeli workplace. An overview of some of the prescriptions of the Jewish religion for workplace matters is proposed in Klarsfeld's chapter, "The untold, the unseen, and the forgettable: Jewishness, Jews, and Judaism in diversity management scholarship," Chapter 5 in the present volume.

Conclusion

Presenting the situation of Jews in four countries allows the reader to contrast countries on two different criteria. The first is the contrast between Israel and the other countries based on the majority/minority criterion. Jews being the numerically dominant group in Israel, the literature and publicly available data tend to underscore the dominance of Jews rather than their oppression or feelings of being discriminated against, in contrast to the other three countries, where in spite of their economic success, a varying number of Jews feel oppressed. Israel also contrasts with the other countries in that it is a religiously grounded state. Its very *raison d'être* is the existence of Jews as a distinct, historically oppressed, religion-based identity group elsewhere. Also in contrast to the other countries, and in contrast to Orthodox Judaism as it was practiced in many European countries prior to World War II and is now by Haredi Jews, work is particularly important in the foundation and self-identity of Israel. In relation to this centrality, during the first 30 years of its existence, Israel was ruled by a party named the "Labor Party." In the Zionist ideology, the foundation of Israel went hand in hand with the willingness of many Jews to access professions and property rights they had long been denied in the Diaspora: that of owning land and being involved in agricultural production, in contrast with options offered to them in much of Europe until the end of the nineteenth century: being money-lenders, merchants, tailors, studying the Torah and Talmud, or having to face *numerus clausus* if they wanted to enter other professions opened to them. On another note, Israel now encounters specific workplace inequalities and challenges owing to different sets of differences: differences between Ashkenazi and Sephardi; differences between Haredi and "mainstream" Jews; differences between Jews and non-Jews. Israel is also a country where research on workplace Judaism abounds, if only around differences/inequality and the management thereof between the above-mentioned identity groups. This, contrasts Israel with the other three countries studied in the present chapter. Indeed, in Australia, France, and the United Kingdom, research explicitly addressing Jews, Judaism, and Jewishness in the workplace is scant.

A second possible contrasting of countries drawn from comparing Australia, France, Israel, and the United Kingdom can be based on the strength of secularism. Israel is clearly the least secular and most religious of all countries if only for the centrality of Judaism in its foundation and the functioning of its institutions, even in the context of a dominant secular Labor Party during its first 30 years of existence, but also in realizing the importance of its accommodation policies and acknowledgement of religious differences at the workplace. Australia and the United Kingdom sit somewhere in the middle of this continuum between Israel and France. While both can be termed secular societies, it is evident based on the country sections above that religiously observant Jewish workers in these countries either encounter or expect some form of accommodation to their dietary requests or weekly holidays, for instance, even when they cannot find it or are denied it in specific instances. Finally, France appears to be the country where Jews face the most difficult challenges for the time being. France has been the country with the worst track-record for the number of Jews killed as Jews in the world (leaving Israel aside, as a nation sporadically at war ever since 1948) in the last 10 years. Perceived anti-Semitism (by French Jews) and intention to leave the country, as measured by the Fundamental Rights Agency (2013), and anti-Semitism (among non-Jews in France), as measured by the Anti-Defamation League (2014) is the highest in Western Europe, where levels for both Australia and the United Kingdom are low. In the present state of the legislation, it also is the country where gathering statistical data on Jews, and particularly on Jews at the workplace, represents a huge challenge, in contrast to the other three countries, given the habit of invisibility taken on by many Jews in this country and the legislation restricting data collection on ethnic and religious-based identities. Future research will hopefully close these gaps. A summary of the data presented in this chapter is given in Table 6.1.

Table 6.1 *Summary table contrasting Australia, France, Israel and the United Kingdom*

	France	Australia	United Kingdom	Israel
Minority/majority status of Jews	Minority	Minority	Minority	Majority
Census of Jewish population by State	Not done	Done	Done	Done
% of Jews	0.7%	0.5%	0.5%	75%
Nature of state	Secular	Secular	Secular	Ethno-religious
Research on Jews in general	Weak	Weak	Weak	Strong
Research on Jews and the workplace	Non-existent	Non-existent	Non-existent	Strong
Accommodation of religion at workplace	Nascent	Established	Established	Established (inherent in nature of State)

(*cont.*)

Table 6.1. (cont.)

	France	Australia	United Kingdom	Israel
Anti-Semitism as measured among non-Jewish population	Strong	Weak	Weak	Not measured in Israel
Anti-Semitism as perceived by Jews	Strong	Weak	Weak	Not measured in Israel
Expression of intention to leave	Strong	Weak	Weak	Weak
Acts of fatal violence against Jews since 1980	5	0	0	Ongoing state of conflict

References

A tour of Jewish history in Australia. Retrieved from: www.jewishhistory australia.net/jha/.

Anti-Defamation League. (2014). ADL Global 100, an index of anti-Semitism. Retrieved from: www.global100.adl.org/public/ADL-Global-100-Executive-Summary2015.pdf.

Anti-Discrimination Board NSW. (2014). Jewish man's problems with work location (February), Anti-discrimination board conciliations – Race discrimination – Employment. Retrieved from: www.antidiscrimination .justice.nsw.gov.au/adb/adb1_equaltimeconciliation/conciliations_race .html.

Australian Bureau of Statistics. (2015a). 2006 Census of Population and Housing, TableBuilder. Retrieved from: www.abs.gov.au/websitedbs/ censushome.nsf/home/tablebuilder?opendocument&navpos=240.

(2015b). 2011 Census of Population and Housing, TableBuilder. Retrieved from: www.abs.gov.au/websitedbs/censushome.nsf/home/tablebuilder? opendocument&navpos=240.

Australian Government. (2015). Displaced Persons and Postwar Refugees. Retrieved from: www.australia.gov.au/about-australia/australian-story/changing-face-of-modern-australia-1950s-to-1970s.

Australian Human Rights Commission. (2001–2002). Racial Discrimination Act complaints: Conciliated outcomes – Complaint of racial discrimination in employment. Retrieved from: www.humanrights.gov.au/site-navigation.

   (2003–2004). Racial Discrimination Act complaints: Conciliated outcomes – Complaint of discrimination on the grounds of race and religion. Retrieved from: www.humanrights.gov.au/site-navigation.

Bensimon, D., & Della Pergola, S. (1986). *La population juive de France, socio-démographie et identité*. Paris: Editions du CNRS.

Cohen, E. (2002). *Les juifs en France, valeurs et identités*. Rapport au Fonds Social Juif Unifié, Novembre.

Cowen, Z. (1983). Isaacs, Sir Isaac Alfred (1855–1948). *In Australian Dictionary of Biography, Volume 9*. Melbourne: Melbourne University Press. Retrieved from: www.adb.anu.edu.au/biography/isaacs-sir-isaac-alfred-6805.

CST (2015). Antisemitic Incidents January-June 2015. Retrieved from: www.cst.org.uk/data/file/0/e/Incidents_Report_-_Jan-June_2015.1438092642.pdf.

Della Pergola, S. (2014). World Jewish Population, 2014. *In* Dashefsky, A., & Sheskin, I. M. (eds.) *The American Jewish Year Book, 2014, Vol. 114*. Dordrecht: Springer, 301–93.

Dubnov, S. (1936), *Précis d'histoire juive*. Paris: Éditions du Cerf, 320.

Equality Challenge Unit. (2011). *Religion and belief in higher education: The experiences of staff and students*. London: Equality Challenge Unit.

Friedman, M. (1991). *Haredi society*. Jerusalem: Jerusalem Institute for Israel Studies.

Frischer, D. (2008). *Les enfants du silence et de la reconstruction, la Shoah en partage*. Paris: Grasset, 630.

Fundamental Rights Agency. (2013). Discrimination and hate crime against Jews in EU member states: Experiences and perceptions of anti-Semitism. Retrieved from: www.fra.europa.eu/sites/default/files/fra-2013-discrimination-hate-crime-against-jews-eu-member-states-0_en.pdf.

Goldberg, S.A. (1993) (ed.), *Dictionnaire encyclopédique du Judaïsme*. Paris: Éditions du Cerf, 1635.

Goldlust, J. (2004). Jews in Australia: A demographic profile. *In* Levey, G., & Mendes, P. (eds.), *Jews and Australian politics*. Brighton: Sussex Academic Press, 11–28.

Gordon, M., & Grattan, M. (2011). He restored Australia's faith: Sir Zelman Cowen dies at 92, *Sydney Morning Herald*. Retrieved from: www.smh.com.au/national/he-restored-australias-faith-sir-zelman-cowen-dies-at-92-20111208-1olqj#ixzz3uoIkgysr.

Graham, D. (2013). Institute for Jewish Policy Research 2011 Census Results (England and Wales): A Tale of Two Jewish Populations (July). Retrieved from: www.jpr.org.uk/documents/2011%20Census%20results%20-%20A%20Tale%20of%20Two%20Jewish%20Populations.pdf.

(2014). The Jewish Population: Key Findings from the 2011 Census. Retrieved from: www.artsonline.monash.edu.au/gen08/download/Australian-Census-2011.pdf.

Graham, D., Schmool, M., & Waterman, S. (2007). Jews in Britain: A Snapshot from the 2001 Census. Jewish Policy Research Report no.1. Retrieved from: www.jpr.org.uk/documents/Jews%20in%20Britain:%20A%20snapshot%20from%20the%202001%20Census.pdf.

Jewish Policy Research. (2012). 2011 Census Results (England and Wales): Initial Insights about the UK Jewish Population (December 12). Retrieved from: www.jpr.org.uk/documents/2011%20Census%20results%20(England%20and%20Wales)%20-%20Initial%20insights%20about%20the%20UK%20Jewish%20population.pdf.

Jewish Virtual Library. (2016). Retrieved from: www.jewishvirtuallibrary.org/jsource/Society_&_Culture/newpop.html.

Johnson, P. (1989). *Une histoire des Juifs*, Paris: Éditions Jean-Claude Lattès, 681.

Jones, J. (2011). Report on anti-Semitism in Australia. Australia/Israel & Jewish Affairs Council (November). Retrieved from: www.aijac.org.au/news/article/report-on-antisemitism-in-australia-november-201.

Kahn-Harris, K., & Gidley, B. (2010) *Turbulent times: The British Jewish community today*. London: Continuum.

Kay, A. (2012). Occupational preferences and expectations of ultra-orthodox men in Israel. *In* Caplan, K., & Stadler, N. (eds.), *Haredim in Israel: From survival to success. Influences and trends*. Jerusalem: Van Leer Jerusalem Institute (Hebrew), 165–75.

Kay, A. (2015). The place of work in the eyes of Israel Haredi Men. *In Conference on Haredi employment: Between policy and reality*. The Open University of Israel, 2 March.

Levey, G., & Mendes, P. (eds.) (2004). *Jews and Australian politics*. Brighton: Academic Press.

Loewenthal, K.M. (2012). Mental health and mental health care for Jews in the diaspora, with particular reference to the UK, *The Israel Journal of Psychiatry and Related Sciences*, 49 (3), 159–66.

Medding, P. (2006). Zionism and Australian Jewry before 1948: The battle for ideological and communal supremacy. *Jewish Political Studies Review*, 18, 3–4 (Fall). Retrieved from: www.jcpa.org/article/zionism-and-australian-jewry-before-1948-the-battle-for-ideological-and-communal-supremacy/.
Nathan, J. (2015). *Report on anti-semitism in Australia 2015*. Edgecliff: Executive Council of Australian Jewry.
Ono (2010). *The Ono Report on special populations at the workplace*. Kiryat Ono: The Ono Academic College.
Rutland, S. (2005). *The Jews in Australia*. Cambridge: Cambridge University Press.
Samuels, M. (2010). *Inventing the Israelite. Jewish fiction in nineteenth-century France*. Stanford, CA: Stanford University Press, 323.
Sarzin, A., & Sarzin, L.M. (2010). *Hand in Hand: Jewish and Indigenous people working together*. Darlinhurst: NSW Jewish Board of Deputies, 10–12.
Savy, N. (2010). *Les Juifs des romantiques. Le discours de la littérature sur les Juifs de Chateaubriand à Hugo*. Paris: Belin, 256.
Schnapper, D. (1987). Les limites de la démographie des Juifs de la diaspora. *Revue Française de Sociologie*, XVIII, 319–32.
Schnapper, D., Bordes-Benayoune, C., & Raphaël, F. (2009). *La condition juive en France: La tentation de l'entre-soi*. Paris: Presses Universitaires de France, collection Le Lien Social, 140.
Staetsky, L.D., & Boyd, J. (2014). *The exceptional case? Perceptions and experiences of anti-Semitism among Jews in the United Kingdom*. London: Institute for Jewish Policy Research.
Sue, E. (1983). *Le Juif errant*. Paris: Laffont.
Swirski, S., Konor-Atias, E., & Zelingher, R. (2015). Israel: A Social Report, Adva Institute. Retrieved from: www.adva.org/en/category/annual-publications/social-report/.
The Australian Bicentenary Authority, New South Wales Council. (1988). *New South Wales Bicentennial Oral History Project*. State Library of NSW, Mitchell Library, Transcripts: MLMSS 5163.
The Independent. (2015). The new anti-Semitism: Majority of British Jews feel they have no future in UK, says new study. Retrieved from: www.independent.co.uk/news/uk/home-news/the-new-antisemitism-majority-of-british-jews-feel-they-have-no-future-in-uk-says-new-study-9976310.html.
Thornton, M., & Luker, T. (2010). The new racism in employment discrimination: Tales from the global economy, *Sydney Law Review*, 32(1), 1–27.

Valfort, M.A. (2015). *Discrimination religieuse à l'embauche, une réalité*. Paris: Institut Montaigne, 142.
Victorian Equal Opportunity and Human Rights Commission. (2013). Cultural Diversity in the Workplace – A Guide for Employers Working with Jewish Employees. Retrieved from: www.humanrightscommission.vic.gov.au/index.php/our-resources-and-publications/know-your-responsibilities-brochures/item/519-cultural-diversity-in-the-workplace-a-guide-for-employers-working-with-jewish-employees.
Winock, M. (2004). *La France et les Juifs de 1789 à nos jours*. Paris: Éditions du Seuil, 409.

7 | Hinduism, Religious Diversity, and Spirituality at Work in India

RADHA R. SHARMA AND RANA HAQ

Introduction

Sanskrit:
Om SarveBhavantuSukhinah
SarveSantuNir-Aamayaah
SarveBhadraanniPashyantu
MaaKashcid-Duhkha-Bhaag-Bhavet
Om ShaantihShaantihShaantih"

Translation:
Om, May All become Happy
May All be Free from Illness
May All See what is Auspicious
May No one Suffer
Om Peace, Peace, Peace!
(*Source*: Kanchi Periva Forum)

This chapter begins with a prayer from the scriptures, as is a common practice in the Hindu traditions when starting something. In fact, every day in India begins with some form of a religious activity or ritual of some kind or another for most Indians. India is a highly religious and spiritual country where religion constitutes an integral, integrated, and essential part of daily life. Although Hinduism is the dominant religion, Islam, Christianity, and Judaism are also practiced. In addition, India is the birthplace of three other religions: Buddhism, Jainism, and Sikhism. Regardless of which particular religion one follows in India, religious practices and rituals are ubiquitously incorporated into everyday activities and celebrated every day in Indian society. The aim of this chapter is to advance the understanding of the complexity of multi-religious, multi-cultural, multi-lingual diversity in India and efforts to respectfully accommodate religion in Indian workplaces. It contributes to the literature on religion and spirituality in the workplace by providing insights into Hinduism in particular and its influence on managing religious diversity in Indian society and workplaces. Therefore, we first highlight Hinduism as the primary religion in India, presenting its main symbols and philosophy, followed by the vast array of religious diversity in India, and finally discuss the various ways in which it is accommodated in Indian society and workplaces.

Religion and Spirituality

Mitroff and Denton (1999) define spirituality as "the basic feeling of being connected with one's complete self, others and the entire universe" (p. 83). Krishnakumar & Neck (2002) sees a link between workplace spirituality and creativity, honesty, trust, personal fulfillment, and increased commitment to organizational goals. Spirituality also leads to a higher awareness of self and others and could lead to a personal vision or meaning in life (Mitroff & Denton, 1999). Mitroff, in his address to the Academy of Management in 1998, referred to spirituality as "the desire to find ultimate purpose in life and to live accordingly" (Cavanagh, 1999). Pawar (2009) suggests that spirituality for an individual is an affective and cognitive experience of spiritual connection to work and workplace. At the organizational level, it is the practice of spiritual values as part of organizational culture, therefore, affects behaviors, decisions, and resource allocation. Although some research reveals that organizations with voluntary spirituality programs have had higher profits and success (Karakas, 2010, p. 92), spirituality is not supposed to be used as an administrative/managerial tool to manipulate employees for increasing the financial performance of the organization. This is advocated by scholars cautioning on the potential misuse or abuse of spirituality in the workplace (Fernando, 2005).

Karakas posits that there are many definitions of spirituality at work but there is none that is universally accepted (Karakas, 2010). "Spirituality is distinguished from institutionalized religion by being characterized as a private, inclusive, non-denominational, universal human feeling, rather than an adherence to the beliefs, rituals or practices of a specific organized religious institution or tradition" (Karakas, 2010, p. 91). There is evidence of growing spirituality around the world in a number of multinational corporations in the form of prayer groups, inter-faith dialogue, reflection sessions, meditation exercises, yoga sessions, and servant leadership development programs under their diversity initiatives, religious accommodations, or corporate social responsibility (CSR) policies for enhancing organizational performance and profitability. However, from the secular perspective, religious and spiritual beliefs are considered to be a personal and private matter raising "negative connotations with the focus often being religious militantism, dogmatic prejudices, uncompromising and excluding attitudes, and religious worship practices and ceremonies disrupting organizational life and performance" (Bendl & Gröschl, 2015, p. 1).

The Context

A description of Hinduism would be incomplete without a discussion of religious diversity in India, which is a multi-religious, multi-cultural, and multilingual country with a 1.21 billion population (Census of India, 2011). Throughout India's history, religion has been an important part of the country's culture, and a vast majority of Indians associate themselves with a religion. Religious diversity and religious tolerance are both established in the country by law and custom. The terms Hindu and Hinduism have been described as geographical terms for those who lived near the river Sindhu (a Sanskrit word for the river Indus) in India (Stratton & Narayanan (2006, pp. 10–11)). The word Hinduism was used to describe the lifestyle of these people, which later took the form of the Hindu religion.

India, a 5,000-year-old civilization, has *Hinduism* as its dominant religion, as well as three other religions which have evolved over the years, viz., *Buddhism, Jainism*, and *Sikhism*. Hinduism is pantheistic, which "may be understood positively as the view that God is identical with the cosmos, the view that there exists nothing which is outside of God" (Owen, 1971: 74). It is also polytheistic – a belief in many Gods/deities; however, many Hindus explain that the Gods are various forms of a single Supreme Being, *Brahman*. Brahman has three forms, the "trinity" – the creator called *Brahma*, the preserver called *Vishnu*, and the destroyer, *Mahesh*, popularly called *Shiva*, two of which are believed to have had human incarnation (*avatar*) on earth to save the good from the evil (Radhakrishnan, 1956). Given the variety of these views, many Hindus believe "The Truth is One, but different sages call it by different names" (*Rig Veda* 1.164.46). As people find it difficult to understand the abstract God, they rely on different symbols/God/Goddesses, and follow a variety of rituals. Thus religious diversity is a part of Hindu religion. There are several Hindu scriptures in the form of *Vedas* and *Upnishads*, which go back to 3,000–5,500 years. These scriptures are believed to be what God said, and are considered to be divine truth that was revealed to some seers who chose to remain anonymous.

They passed on their vision of the truth to their disciples in oral form. The date of the writing of the Vedic literature is not known, but Vedic culture is believed to have started in India between 2000 and 1500 BC (Paul, 1987), and Hinduism emerged from the Vedic religion (Hoiberg, 2000). The Hindu religion is also referred to as *Vedic Religion, Vedic Dharma*, or *Sanatana Dharma*.

India has been pruned and churned up over centuries through the influence of foreign cultures which came to the country for political or commercial reasons. This has led to the emergence of a culture which is marked by (a) a pluralistic world view, (b) a synthesizing mindset and (c) high context sensitivity. The pluralistic world view implies that, by and large, Indians are open to new ideas and influences, and adopt the values, norms, beliefs, and practices of other cultures. The aspect of a synthesizing mindset yields that Indians either integrate influences from diverse cultures (if) acceptable to their culture; if not, they simply allow these differences to co-exist. "In the 8th century Arab incursions began, followed by a Turkish invasion in the 12th century. India had Mughal rule from 1526 to 1857 followed by the British rule …" (Sharma & Abraham, 2012). The British East India Company came to India in 1608 for trading with the Indian subcontinent "with its own private armies, exercising military power and assuming administrative functions" (Birdwood, 1893). The East India Company had a long lasting impact on the subcontinent in terms of colonial control, economy, culture, and language.

Indians allowed early immigrants and invaders to retain their religions and cultures (despite differences). Consequently one comes across consistency, inconsistency, as well as opposing components in Indian culture. As regards high context sensitivity, Indians adapt their behavior/responses according to the situation/context. The indigenous mindset retained ancient Hindu culture, and at the same time integrated/shared the culture of others (who entered/ruled India) where it was compatible. The colonial experience was different; the British Empire adopted a bureaucratic style of amoral familism (Banfield, 1958, p. 89). This had a significant impact on people's religious mindset. "The education during the ancient period was influenced by the country's indigenous theory of knowledge based on Indian Philosophy … It was aimed at holistic development and manifestation of divinity in the learner and not merely transfer of information." The Universities of Nalanda and Takshashila imparted education in fields like astronomy, astrology, religion theology, ethics, values, arithmetic, law, metaphysics, medical science, economics, and politics (Sharma & Pardasani, 2013, pp. 83–104).

In 1835 India witnessed the introduction of a modern system of education by the British, replacing its ancient system; colleges and universities were set up in 1837 (Porter, 1967). People considered the indigenous mindset and religion to be obstacles in their growth

Hinduism, Religious Diversity, and Spirituality at Work in India 181

and development, and started shunning the acquisition of knowledge embedded in *Vedic* literature and seeking Western knowledge and the English language (over Sanskrit) to become modern. This led to the disintegration of indigenous schooling, called *Gurukulum*, and a higher education system aimed at discovering oneself for the attainment of "true" knowledge from Vedic literature (Sharma & Pardasani, 2013, pp. 83–104).

Important Symbols in Hinduism

There are many ancient symbols in Hinduism but the most popular ones used at workplaces are described below (Ancient Symbols).

Om or Aum: Om comprises of three letters: A, U, and M; it is a symbol and a syllable. It is a sound which is believed to have been present at the time of the creation of the universe and is considered sacred. All important mantras start with *Om*. It is considered to be as powerful word and syllable as "Brahman," with all words, mantras, and sounds. People also use it during meditation. It is a sacred word for other religions too, viz., Buddhists, Jains, and Sikhs. People use this popular symbol at workplaces on their desks, or in lockets or rings for good luck.

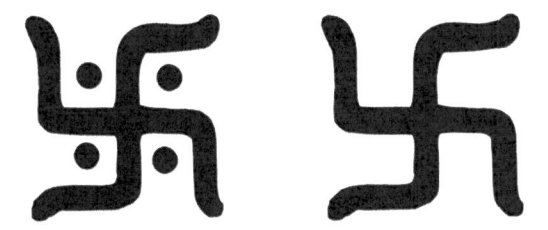

Swastika: The word Swastika is derived from a Sanskrit word *sv* (well) + *asti* (is). Archaeological evidence of swastika-shaped ornaments has been dated to the Neolithic period and was first found in the Indus valley civilization of the Indian subcontinent. The *swastika* is an ancient symbol which is a sign of good fortune, luck and well-being among the Hindus. Its four angles or points also symbolize the four directions or *Vedas*. This symbol is often drawn on the floor with colors or flower petals on special occasions. It represents honesty, truth, purity, and stability. Like *Om*, people use this symbol at workplaces, at the entrance, in the cash office or on tables. It is also used as an ornament.

Sri Yantra: *Sri Yantra* is used to symbolize the bond or unity of both the masculine and the feminine divinity, which is supposed to bring good fortune. Also called *Shri Chakra*, it is a symbol characterized by nine interlocking triangles that radiate from a central point. The symbol contains four upright triangles representing the masculine side or *Shiva*; while the five inverted triangles represent the feminine or the *Shakti* (divine mother). It can also mean the unity and bond of everything in the cosmos.

Religious Diversity Management Practices at the Workplace

India became independent from British occupation in 1947. Its constitution, adopted in 1950, declares it a secular democratic republic granting equality to all to practice their religious belief. According to the 2011 Indian census, Hindus constitutes 80% of the total population, whereas Muslims, Christians and Sikhs constitute 14%, 2.3%, and 1.7% respectively. Buddhists, Jains, Zoroastrians, Jews, and Baha'is constituted less than 1% of the population each (Census of India, 2011). It is important to note that, unlike secularism in France and in the province of Quebec in Canada, where it is defined as the separation of religion (private sphere) from the state (public sphere), secularism in the Indian context means that the constitution protects religious freedom in India by granting equal respect to all religions and prohibits discrimination on the basis of religion, requiring workplaces to accommodate the religious beliefs and practices of their employees.

People from various religions are free to keep religious symbols like the *Bible, Quran, Granth Sahib,* or pictures of their religious places or deities on their desk, dress according to their religious beliefs, and wear religious symbols as ornaments. Religious intolerance in the form of disrespect to another religion is punishable by law. The government is empowered to ban religious organizations that incite friction between communities or indulge in terrorism or similar activities. Nevertheless, despite these protections, religion based riots and conflicts have occured in the history of India, hence, people need to be cautious about the slightest provocation.

The major religious texts of Hindus are four Vedas, 18 Puranas, Smiritis, Ramayan, Mahabharat, and Bhagvad Gita, which contain knowledge, wisdom, and timeless teachings for the realization of self, victory of good over evil, preservation of the cosmos (water, earth, nature, etc.), and the well-being of the society and the world at large. "Vasudhaiv Kutumbakam," implying "world is a family," is the Indian ideology from the Upnishads (Mahōpaniṣad- VI.70–73). India is a collectivistic culture and the Hindu religion focuses on peace, harmony, and welfare for all. Vedic teachings relate to philanthropy, self-realization, concern for others, sharing of one's wealth with the disadvantaged, service to community, and protection of the cosmos. Influenced by these values, Indian organizations have been engaged in philanthropic/community development activities for centuries long before these concepts were introduced in management. Thus companies in India run schools/center for girls/women from poor communities, support welfare schemes, and offer scholarships to socially/economically disadvantaged children of all the ethnic groups for the inclusive growth of society and protection of the environment.

Principles from Bhagvad Gita at Indian Workplaces

The spiritual traditions of India offer wholesome spiritual foundation to the modern era and also provide practical wisdom to lead a stress-free and fulfilling life. Gandhi (2009) called Bhagvad Gita, a sacred Sanskrit scripture of Hindus, "The Gospel of Selfless Action." Bhagvad Gita provides four main paths that people choose as an approach to life to reach the ultimate goal, union with the Supreme (*Brahman*). Yoga is not a physical exercise, as is commonly thought; it is a lifestyle which lays down some steps to reach this ultimate goal. The four paths are

(i) Karma Yoga (ii) Gyan Yoga, (iii) Raj Yoga, and (iv) Bhakti Yoga. Karma yoga, which is prevalent at the Indian workplaces, is explained below.

1. **Karma Yoga**

Karma Yoga is the discipline of action and is generally adopted by people who are outgoing. This principle teaches that a person has control only over one's efforts/actions and not over the reward, as this may be controlled by external factors. This belief helps people focus on the task and not be obsessed with the reward.

"कर्मण्येवाधिकारस्तेमाफलेषुकदाचन।
माकर्मफलहेतुर्भूर्मातेसङ्गोऽस्त्वकर्मणि॥"

Karmanye Vadhikaraste, Ma phaleshu kada chana,
Ma Karma Phala Hetur Bhurmatey Sangostva Akarmani

(Bhagvad Gita, Ch. 2: 47)

Translation: To action alone hast thou a right and never at all to its fruits; let not the fruits of action be thy motive; neither let there be in thee any attachment to inaction. (Mehta, 2006)

Selfless devotion to work is not only highly satisfying intrinsically but it sublimates oneself. In a fair system one would be rewarded but if, for some reason, one cannot be, with karma yoga belief, one does not feel dejected or leave the job. Some people mistake *karma yoga* for fatalism, but it is not. It could possibly be one of the reasons for the low rate of turnover in Indian organizations, in general. This phenomenon of intrinsic motivation would be very different from the Western theories of motivation and operant conditioning, where one works for a reward or reinforcement and feels frustrated/dejected when the reinforcement/reward is not achieved. Thus external reinforcement dependent motivated behavior often leads to low productivity or employee attrition. Parboteeah et al. (2009) conducted a survey of 44,030 people in 39 countries and found that Buddhism, Hinduism, Christianity, and Islam are all positively related to intrinsic and extrinsic work values.

Another powerful concept at the Indian workplace is *Arthashashtra* written by Kautilya during the fourth century BC, grounding the art of governance on *nyaya* (justice) and *dharma* (ethics) as the two key pillars for success, now known as organizational justice theory and ethics (Rai, 2005, p. 388). Other relevant concepts from Bhagvad Gita relevant to the Indian workplace are discussed in the following paragraphs (Sharma, 2011, pp. 10–11).

2. Swadharma (Performing one's duty)

   Swadharma, articulated in *Bhagvad Gita*, states that individuals should perform the duties and responsibilities assigned to them with a positive mindset and effectiveness, treating it as their *dharma* (ethics). They should not overstep into others' roles and responsibilities as it would create conflict in the organization.

3. Loksangraha (Collective mindset)

   Loksangraha (lok=people; and *sangraha*=holding together) means that actions of an individual or organization should be in the collective interest of the people/society. Inclusive growth which is the pivotal agenda across organizations in the Indian economy, is based on the ideology of *loksangraha* from Bhagvad Gita.

4. Parasparam Bhavayantaha (Affinity and interdependence)

   A society depends on the interdependence of its constituents – the individuals and the organizations. Affinity and interdependence are essential to live in harmony and thrive in an organization or a society, and pave the way for cooperation and co-existence despite differences in values, beliefs, and cultures. India is a country of diversity where diversity exists in various forms such as – religious, geographic, linguistic, caste, and culture. Indian organizations have managed diversity at the workplace all along with the principle of *Parasparam Bhavayantaha*. This principle is also gaining ground in different forms of diversity management programs in the culturally diverse globalized world.

5. Cosmic Collectivism

   This ancient view based on Hindu mythologies comprises of cosmic collectivism (the assumption that the universe consists of diverse forms and elements), hierarchical order, and spiritual orientation. Hierarchical order signifies that all things within the universe are arranged in order of being superior or inferior to the other. Spirituality is considered to enable people to rise above their physical and material well-being to spiritual well-being or well-being of the soul. Rai (2005) presents the role played by the Hindu religion in forming the business values and ethics in India: "As can be seen in the Indian organizations, hierarchical perspective, the power play, preference for personalized relationship, social networking through own–other dichotomy and collectivistic orientation, play a significant role in determining organizational effectiveness in India." He posits "The salient ethical dimensions of sharing, respect for age, social networks, selfless work, ... necessity of hierarchical levels, role and responsibility of leader, ... and interpersonal relationships have significant impact on the personality of its constituents and these, in turn, are likely to manifest in the workplace as attitudes and behaviours" (Rai, 2005, p. 388).

In a scholarly review of the human resource management (HRM) literature in India, Pio (2007) explains that centuries-old Hindu traditions are still prevalent in India, such as the social stratification system of caste, which continues to have significant implications, both explicit and implicit, in Indian HRM policies and practices such as recruitment, selection and promotion. *Karma* (destiny) is the belief that one must bear the consequences of one's actions from the present and past lives lived; *Dharma* (righteous duty) gives precedence in importance to family over professionalism; *Bhakti* (devotion) is the worship of deities and at the temple of work; *Guru* (the teacher), is revered, as learning is highly valued (Pio, 2007, p. 322). These are some religious Hindu beliefs that overflow into organizational life, leading to behaviors of submissiveness, fatalism, clan orientation with in-groups, and out-group distinctions and power consciousness (Amba-Rao et al., 2000).

India is a highly collectivist society (Hofstede, 1980), with much emphasis on in-group and out-group categorization, whereby individuals are often driven by the need to take care of those in their in-group, which is typically made up of extended family and friends. Indeed, India is ranked as one of the most collective in-group countries, where individuals' need to take care of the in-group may sometimes supersede the organization's formal rules. These issues matter a lot in the Indian workplace and individuals tend to seek small groups to identify with, and are often mistrustful of others who may be different in some way (Sahay & Walsham, 1997).

Social Hierarchy and Networks

Influenced by the hierarchical nature of Hinduism, the caste system and respect for age, superior-subordinate relations are extremely complex in Indian organizations where paternalism, hierarchy, legitimate authority, and loyalty are all valued, as employees are expected to obey, take orders, and follow instructions with blind faith and without question (Varma & Budhwar, 2013). Hinduism is based on strict codes of relationships: *guru-shishya* (teacher-student), *maa-beta* (mother-child), *bhakta-bhagwan* (god-devotee), and *malik-sevak* (boss-employee) (Pio, 2007). The family and community supersedes the individual, parents often influence the career/profession of the children, parents-in-law often decide whether their daughter-in-law will be allowed to pursue her education or career after marriage, etc. It is expected that one will behave unquestioningly within the boundaries of one's status in the family, community, and society to maintain peace and harmony, even if it is at the cost of personal ambitions and aspirations. Personal sacrifice for the good of family and community is valued, above all loss with hope of better rewards in the afterlife, leading to a rather fatalistic world-view (Sparrow & Budhwar, 1997). This strict code of relationships is also reflected in the caste system, which is based on a hierarchal division of labor. Socio-demographic characteristics are given great importance – thus age, education, occupation, and family background influence one's place in the Indian family, workplace, and society.

Nuclear and extended family dynamics are complex and critical in India, making work-life balance issues all the more important for employees and managers alike. The nuclear family is defined as the husband, wife, and children. The extended family includes each of these on both maternal and paternal sides: the parents, grandparents, aunts, and uncles, as well as nieces and nephews. However, the father-in-law and mother in-law receive more importance, even above the needs of the nuclear family at times. There is high pressure on the couple and their nuclear family to honor and respect family ties by participating in important religious/ceremonial occasions every year if the family is in the same city/town. If the extended family lives in another city/town, people often commute to be together on important family events like marriage, religious festivals, the birth of a child, death, and so on. Therefore, most Indian workplaces are quite willing to accommodate requests for such work-life balance events.

According to social capital theory (Bourdieu & Waquant, 1992) this resource is acquired through different kinds of relationships in families, organizations, neighborhoods, communities, and caste, including vertical and horizontal social networks. Social capital at Indian workplaces has not been documented in the Indian management literature but plays an important role in HRM functions. "HRM in India is strongly influenced by social relations, political affiliation, informal networks, and one's caste and religion" (Cooke & Budhwar, 2015, p. 346). A common

Indian behavior is to ask for a person's last name to determine their clan or caste and lineage. Personal recommendations and requests for favors are mutually supported with an understanding that the favor will be returned in the future.

The Indian Hindu caste system is based on the traditional division of labor. *Brahmins* were engaged in teaching/advising and knowledge pursuits; *Kshtriyas* were warriors; *Vaishyas* were trading communities; and *Shudras* were engaged in manual labor. Indian business is dominated by the traditional trading communities, by religion (such as the Parsi, or Hindu *banias* (a caste engaged in business) with surnames such as Gupta and Agarwal), and sometimes by the geographic origin of those engaged in traditional business/trades (Gujaratis, Punjabis, Rajasthanis, and Marwaris). There are strong corporate business families (such as Tata, Birla, Mahindra, Jindal, and Bajaj) from different religions. Parsi (also written as Parsee) descend from the Persian Zoroastrians community which migrated from Greater Iran to Gujarat and Sindh (India) between the eighth and tenth century and settled there (Hodivala, 1920). Business families often arrange strategic marriage alliances and are generally managed by multiple generations of family members and close family friends. Blood and caste relations and community ties are all important aspects of personal identity and social networks in India, with powerful implications for the workplace.

Indians have held strong beliefs in astrology and numerology right from the Vedic era. A horoscope is made at the time of birth, keeping in view planet positions, which help make predictions about an individual's life. Belief in God, destiny, and astrology are commonplace in India even now, both in the private and public lives of most Hindu managers and employees. Consequently, many people start their day with a daily *aarti* or *puja* (ritualistic prayers) at home or at work. Sharing and distributing *prasaad* (religious sweet offerings) on *shubhavsar* (special occasions) such as birthdays, graduation, weddings, and religious events are commonplace. Serious attention is paid to the timing of special occasions for invoking divine blessings based upon religious *mahurat* (auspicious dates and times) guided by Hindu priests based on astrology and numerology. These are often accommodated in the workplace. Religion-based charity and philanthropy is prominently evidenced through the temples, hospitals, schools, and other institutions established by rich business conglomerates as a commonly practiced way of giving back to society.

Numerous Hindu holidays are celebrated in India, the major ones being *Holi* (the festival of colors) and *Diwali* (the festival of lights), which are recognized as gazetted or mandatory holidays. Diwali is like Christmas for Hindus, when gifts are exchanged not only with family but also with friends. Some organizations provide bonuses, while others offer gifts to employees. Some Hindu festivals such as *Karva Chauth* (the festival of a wife fasting all day to pray for her husband's long life) and *Raksha-bandhan* (the festival to strengthen the bond between brothers and sisters) are observed as restricted or limited optional holidays (see Appendix). Many of these also have an important impact on the workplace. For example, bonuses on Diwali are an important marker of how much the employees are valued by their employer. In fact, when workers at a Japanese company in India – Honda Motorcycle and Scooters India Ltd. – were given a lower-value than expected Diwali gift, it led to the formation of a labor union which went on strike, resulting in violence and a major financial loss to the company (Saini, 2007).

Religion and Spirituality at Work

India is a secular country by its constitution, but is ingrained with religious values and beliefs. Several facets from Indian spiritual traditions have been analysed by Pardasani et.al. (2014), Sharma and Pardasani (2015) and Sharma and Taneja (2013) for understanding workplace spirituality and religious diversity and their application in effective HRM.

Due to the significant presence of multiple religions in India, religious differences are respected by law and by custom, although occasionally inter and intra-religious tensions and conflicts do erupt, impacting people and communities. At the time of reconstruction of India after independence, Mahatma Gandhi was concerned about discrimination based on caste, religion, and gender (Varshney, 2002). These were, therefore, addressed while drafting the Indian Constitution, which was adopted by the Indian parliament in 1950 and continues to be the most authoritative document. Crowne (2013) posits that poverty sometimes plays a key role as a backdrop that can lead to ethnic violence. There are some sensitive issues; Hindus, for example, worship the cow and consider it sacred; therefore the slaughtering of cows raises emotions and sometimes arouses tension among the believers (*Times of India*, 2015). Similarly, pork is not sold in most restaurants to respect the feelings of the Muslim community. Generally, religion-based dietary restrictions are respected in most Indian homes and workplaces. People of diverse religions have been living and working together in harmony for centuries, evidencing religious tolerance derived from the Hindu principle of "interconnectedness." People in general and employees (managers or employees alike) prominently display religious symbols and practices in their daily personal and professional lives, which provides undisputed evidence of the presence of religious identity and intersectionality in the workplace, with many implications for individuals and organizations.

The Indian workplace has the mixed influences of ancient Hindu mythologies, the indigenous mindset, colonial experiences, and globalization. Many companies celebrate major festivals such as Christmas, Eid, Holi, and Diwali by organizing special events for the employees. Religious rituals such as reciting prayers or hymns, worship, *yagna* (invocation of deities with mantras), or reading of religious texts, are performed on special occasions such as opening of a new business/store/office for good luck and welfare. As prayers are a daily ritual in the lives of most Indians, there are prayer rooms for various faiths in some offices at Mahindra and Mahindra Tech. Though JP Morgan does not have a prayer room, Muslim employees use one of the meeting rooms for prayers (Layak, 2015). Some companies, such as Starbucks and Tata, allow their staff to do a little religious ceremony or prayer of their choice when opening stores every morning. The Birla group employs Hindus, Parsis, Muslims, and Buddhists and takes special care of their dietary needs (Layak, 2015). Yoga and meditation classes are offered in some organizations during the workday or over the weekend, in which employees from all the religions participate on a voluntary basis. It is worth noting that India defines secularism differently from the French concept of secularism (laïcité) also dealt with in this volume (see Chapter 10, Banon and Chanlat). The Indian concept of secularism refers to equality for all religions and does not require any separation of religion from public life, "while the French concept of secularism requires a complete separation of religion (which is considered a personal and individual choice) from public spheres of activity (including work and education)" (Patel, 2010:286). The Appendix provides a list of Indian government holidays (both mandatory and optional) for 2015, covering all the religions. This evidences that secularism is practiced at Indian workplaces in letter and spirit. A review of 140 articles on spirituality and performance in organizations yields that spirituality improves employees' performance and organizational effectiveness in three ways: (i) it enhances employee well-being and quality of life, (ii) it provides a sense of purpose and meaning at work, and (iii) it gives a sense of community and inter-connectedness (Karakas, 2010, p. 92). This is seen in practice at Indian workplaces; thus spirituality can be leveraged effectively by HR managers, practitioners, and policy makers to promote religious tolerance at the workplace.

Companies in India run schools/centers for girls/women from poor communities, support welfare schemes, and offer scholarships to socially/economically disadvantaged children of all the ethnic groups for the inclusive growth of society and protection of environment. The government offers free school education and scholarships to pursue further education for girls and minority communities from economically weaker sections of the society for their educational development. To give a boost to such activities on a large scale, the Government of India introduced the Companies Act 2013, whereby companies are required to spend 2% of their three-year average annual net profit on corporate social responsibility (CSR) activities (India code, 2013). This has led to the creation of separate CSR departments or positions in the HR or Corporate Communication Departments. Articles 15, 16, and 39 of the Indian Constitution grant equality to all in public employment irrespective of religion, race, language, or gender (*GK Today*, 2015).

Conclusion

This chapter has illustrated the vast array of religious diversity in India and ways that it is accommodated in the workplace broadly by the provision of religious holidays and prayer rooms, and respecting dietary restrictions and dress codes in order to allow everyone to practice their religion on a daily basis and to avoid religious conflict in Indian society and workplaces. The reality is that religious diversity is ingrained in the Indian society, culture, and psyche. When there are incidents of religious intolerance and extremism, tensions arise and flare up very quickly into communal conflict inciting senseless behaviour. Therefore, upon independence, the Constitution of India took a secular approach, in that it guarantees freedom of worship, prohibits discrimination on religious grounds, and treats all religions with equal respect. Consequently, Indian organizations manage religious diversity through both formal and informal policies and practices respecting all religions, and cultivate a climate of religious tolerance and accommodation in the workplace.

India is a highly diverse religious society with strong religious traditions and values manifested in the day to day personal and work lives of the majority of Indians, resulting in a significant impact on workplace policies and practices. In addition, as a high context culture with a strong emphasis on hierarchy and interpersonal relationships, there are many levels at which social, cultural, and religious demands influence formal and informal workplace policies and practices in Indian organizations, although empirical evidence of this in Indian diversity management literature is rather limited. India's religious, linguistic, geographic, ethnic, cultural, and socioeconomic diversity is more complex in its breadth, depth, and scope than any other country in the world. This makes workplace policies and practices complicated at many levels of sensitivity, understanding, coverage, and implementation. In terms of religion, Hinduism is not a homogeneous religion as there are many different sects, beliefs, and practices within it. While the caste system originates from Hinduism, casteism is a universal Indian issue today (Haq, 2010). India is constitutionally a secular nation with equal respect for all religions and there are no reservations based on religion *per se* (Haq, 2010:182). However, there still remain many challenges, as conflicts over India's reservations policy are a common occurrence and require greater sensitivity at the social level and the workplace. Tolerance for religious diversity, which has been a strength in Indian culture, needs to be refocused at the social level, although manifestations of religious diversity seem to be generally accepted at the workplace. Indians have coexisted in harmony over the centuries with full freedom to practice their faith in the public and private realm. Religion plays an important role in the everyday lives of Indians at home and at work with significant influence on their personal and social identification and interaction amongst each other. Despite the differences, it is commonplace for Indians to attend each others' religious ceremonies, celebrations, and festivals such as Holi, Diwali, Eid and Christmas, as well as weddings and funerals with due respect. This chapter fills a gap in the management literature linking Hinduism, spiritual principles, and religious diversity management practices for the peaceful co-existence of a variety of diverse religious groups in the Indian workplace, and can offer insights to other countries facing issues of religious accommodation in society and the workplace.

Appendix

Central Government Holiday List for 2015

The government of India – Ministry of Personnel, Public Grievances and Pensions (Department of Personnel and Training) sends out an annual memo on Holidays to be observed in Central Government Offices during the year. Each employee is granted fourteen Gazetted or Compulsory Holidays (mandatory for most employers, such as government offices, schools, banks) plus any three holidays to be chosen by employees from the list of twelve Restricted Holidays for a total of seventeen holidays per year.

Table 7.A1. *List of annual gazetted and restricted holidays in India*

List of fourteen gazetted (mandatory) holidays:		
1.	Republic Day	National
2.	Independence Day	National
3.	Mahatma Gandhi's Birthday	National
4.	Buddha Purnima	Buddhist
5.	Christmas Day	Christian
6.	Dussehra (Vijay Dashmi)	Hindu
7.	Diwali (Deepavali)	Hindu
8.	Good Friday	Christian
9.	Guru Nanak's Birthday	Sikh
10.	Idu'lFitr	Muslim
11.	Idu'lZuha	Muslim
12.	Mahavir Jayanti	Jain
13.	Muharram	Muslim
14.	Prophet Mohammad's Birthday (Id-E-Milad)	Muslim
List of twelve restricted (optional) holidays:		
1.	An Additional Day for Dussehra	Hindu
2.	Holi	Hindu
3.	Janamashtami (Vaishnavi)	Hindu
4.	Ram Navami	Hindu
5.	MahaShivratri	Hindu

(*cont.*)

Table 7.A1. *(cont.)*

6.	Ganesh Chaturthi	Hindu
7.	MakarSankaranti	Hindu
8.	RathYatra	Hindu
9.	Onam	Hindu
10.	Pongal	Hindu
11.	Sri Panchami / Basant Panchami	Hindu
12.	Vaisakhi/Vaisakhadi/Bhag Bihu/MashadiUgadi/Chaitra Sukladi/Cheti Chand/GudiPadava/Navratra/Nauroz/Chhath Pooja/CarvaChauth	

Source: Government of India, Ministry of Personnel, Public Grievances and Pensions (Department of Personnel and Training). Retrieved from: http://rajyasabha.nic.in/rsnew/Calander/2015_holidays.pdf.

References

Amba-Rao, S. C., Petrick, J. A., Gupta, J. N. D., & Von der Embse, T. J. (2000). Comparative performance appraisal practices and management values among foreign and domestic firms in India. *International Journal of Human Resource Management*, 11(1), 60–89.

Ancient symbols. (n.d.). Hindu symbols. Retrieved from: www.ancient-symbols.com/hindu-symbols.html.

Banfield, E. C. (1958). *The moral basis of a background society*. Glencoe, IL: The Free Press.

Bendl, R., & Groschl, S. (2015). Introduction. In Bendl, R., & Groschl, S. (eds.), *Managing religious diversity in the workplace: Examples from around the world*. Surrey: Gower Publishing.

Birdwood, G. C. M. (1893). *The register of letters, etc. of the governor and company of merchants of London trading into the East Indies, 1600–1619*. London: B. Quaritch.

Bourdieu, P., & Waquant, L. (1992). *An Invitation to Reflexive Sociology*. Cambridge: Polity Press.

Cavanagh, G. (1999). Spirituality for managers: context and critique. *Journal of Organizational Change Management*, 12(3), 186.

Census of India (2011). Retrieved date of retrieval from: www.censusindia.gov.in/2011census/C-01.html.

Cooke, F. L., & Budhwar, P. (2015). Human resource management in China and India. IN: Handbook of human resource management in emerging markets. Horwitz, F., & Budhwar, P. (eds.) *Research Handbooks in Business and Management Series*. Cheltenham (UK): Edward Elgar.

Crowne, W. (2013). Ethnicity as a Source of Conflict in India. Retrieved from: www.e-ir.info/2013/04/24/ethnicity-as-a-source-of-conflict-in-india/.

Fernando, M. (2005). Workplace spirituality: Another management fad? In Adams, A., & Alkhafaji, A. (eds.), *Business research yearbook: Global business perspectives, Vol. XII*. Florida: International Academy of Business Disciplines.

Gandhi, M. (2009). *The Bhagavad Gita according to Gandhi*. Berkeley: North Atlantic Books, ISBN Paperbac9781556438004. https://27pebh3agxku3bgo3k10r6k0-wpengine.netdna-ssl.com/wp-content/uploads/books/the-bhagavad-gita-according-to-gandhi.png.

GK Today. (2015). Retrieved from: www.indiacode.nic.in/acts-in-pdf/182013.pdf.

Government of India – Ministry of Personnel, Public Grievances and Pensions (Department of Personnel and Training). Retrieved from: www.rajyasabha.nic.in/rsnew/Calander/2015_holidays.pdf.

Haq, R. (2010). Caste based quotas: India's reservations policy. In Jawad Syed and Mustafa F. Özbilgin (eds.), *Managing cultural diversity in Asia: A research companion*. Cheltenham, U.K.: Edward Elgar Publishing, 166–91.

Hodivala, S. (1920). *Studies in Parsi history*. Bombay, India.

Hofstede, G. (1980). *Culture's consequences. International differences in work related values*. Newbury Park, CA: Sage.

Hoiberg, D. (2000). *Students' Britannica India*. Popular Prakashan, New Delhi, India.

India code. (2013). Retrieved from: http://indiacode.nic.in/acts-in-pdf/182013.pdf. Retrieved on March 2016.

Kanchi Periva Forum. Retrieved from: www.periva.proboards.com/thread/9136/mangala-slokam#ixzz3nyu9yepR. July 8, 2017.

Karakas, F. (2010). Spirituality and performance in organizations: A literature review. *Journal of Business Ethics*, 94, 89–106.

Krishnakumar, S., & Neck, C. P. (2002). The "what", "why" and "how" of spirituality in the workplace. *Journal of Managerial Psychology*, 17(3), 153–64.

Layak, S. (2015). How India Inc.'s workplaces are accommodating employees' religious and cultural needs. *Economic Times*. Retrieved from: www.articles.economictimes.indiatimes.com/2015-03-15/news/60137448_1_vegetarian-india-inc-av-birla.

Mehta, J. M. (2006). Samkhya theory and Yoga practice, The Bhagavadgita, Verse 47, Chapter 2. *In Essence of Maharishi Patanjali's Ashtang Yoga*. Delhi: Pustak Mahal, 23.

McShane, S., Glinow, M. A. V., & Sharma, R. (2011). *Organizational behavior: Emerging knowledge & practice for the real world*. New Delhi, India: McGraw-Hill, 665.

Mitroff, I. I., & Denton, E. A. (1999). A study of spirituality in the workplace. *Sloan Management Review*, 40, 83–92.

Owen, H. P. (1971). *Concepts of Deity*. London: Macmillan.

Parboteeah, K. P., Hogel, M., & Cullen, J. (2009). Religious dimensions and work obligations: A country institutional profile model. *Human Relations*, 62(1), 119–48.

Pardasani, R., Sharma, R. R., & Bindlish, P. (2014). Facilitating workplace spirituality: Lessons from Indian spiritual traditions. *Journal of Management Development*, 33(8/9), 847–59.

Patel, T. (2010). Confronting discrimination through affirmative action in India: Playing the right music with the wrong instrument. In Syed, J., & Özbilgin, M. (eds.), *Managing cultural diversity in Asia: A research companion*. Cheltenham: Edward Elgar, 278–306.

Paul, S. N. (1987). *The meek and the militant: Religion and power across the world*. London: Zed Books, ISBN 10: 1931859248.

Pawar, B. S. (2009). Individual spirituality, workplace spirituality and work attitudes: An empirical test of direct and interaction effects. *Leadership & Organization Development Journal*, 30, 759–777. DOI:10.1108/ 01437730911003911.

Pio, E. (2007). HRM and Indian epistemologies: A review and avenues for future research. *Human Resource Management Review*, 17, 319–35.

Porter, W. P. (1967). Secondary Education in India. *The High School Journal*, 50(4), 192–8.

Radhakrishnan, S. (Ed. 1956). *The Cultural Heritage of India*. Calcutta: The Ramakrishna Mission Institute of Culture.

Rai, H. (2005). The role of Hinduism in global India and Her business ethics. *In* Capaldi, N. (ed.), *Business and religion: A clash of civilizations?* Salem: Scrivener Press.

Sahay, S., & Walsham, G. (1997). Social structure and managerial agency in India. *Organization Studies*, 18(3), 415–44.

Saini, D. S. (2007). Declining labour power and challenges before trade unions: Some lessons from a case study on private sector unions. *Indian Journal of Labour Economics*, 49(4), 652–77.

Sharma, R. R. (2011). cf. McShane, S., Glinow, M. A. V., & Sharma, R. *Organizational behavior: Emerging knowledge & practice for the real world*. New Delhi, India: McGraw-Hill, 665.

Sharma, R. R., & Abraham, P. (2012). Leveraging Human Capital for Business Growth. In Michael Biron et al. (Eds.), *Global HRM Casebook, HR Ambassadors' Program*. New York & London: Academy of Management, Routledge, 276–88.

Sharma, R., R., & Pardasani, R. (2013). Unshackling management education through a Trishul approach. In Pathak, P., Sharma, R. R., & Singh, S. (eds.), *Reinventing the Society: Search for a Paradigm*. New Delhi, India: Macmillan, 83–104.

Sharma, R. R., & Pardasani, R. (2015). Management of religious diversity by organizations in India. In Groschl, S., & Bendl, R. (eds.), *Managing religious diversity at the workplace*. Surrey, England: Gower, 223–38.

Sharma, R. R., & Taneja, S. (2013). Indian Ethos as humanistic management principles: A case study of a family business organization, In: Khan, S., & Wolfgang, A. (eds.), *World Humanism: Cross-cultural perspectives on ethical practices in organizations*. USA: Palgrave Macmillan, 178–93.

Sparrow, P. R., & Budhwar, P. (1997). Competition and change: Mapping the Indian HRM recipe against worldwide patterns. *Journal of World Business*, 32, 224–42.

Stratton, J. H., & Narayanan, V. (2006), *The life of Hinduism*. Berkeley: University of California Press, 10–11.

Times of India. (2015). Beef ban – Bollywood reacts on Twitter. Retrieved from: http://timesofindia.indiatimes.com/entertainment/hindi/bollywood/Beef-ban-Bollywood-reacts-on-Twitter/photostory/46453554.cms.

Valea, E. (n.d.). The divine incarnation in Hinduism and Christianity. Retrieved from: www.comparativereligion.com/avatars.html.

Varma, A., & Budhwar, P. S. (2013). Human resource in the Asia-Pacific: agenda for future research and policy. In Varma, A., & Budhwar, P. S. (eds.), *Managing human resources in Asia-Pacific* (2nd ed.). (Global HRM). Abingdon (UK): Routledge, 281–7. DOI: 10.4324/9780203157053.

Varshney, A. (2002). Ethnic conflict and civic life: Hindus and Muslims in India. Retrieved from: www.carnegiecouncil.org/studio/multimedia/20020924/index.html.

8 | *Buddhist* Brahmaviharas *and Religious Diversity at Work*

EDWINA PIO

If you think you are too small to make a difference ... try sleeping with a mosquito!

(XIV Dalai Lama)

Introduction

Buddhism is one of the major religions in the world and through the centuries the words compassion and meditation have been associated with it. In the international arena there are a number of Buddhist individuals who have made a significant impact on the lives of numerous people worldwide and have also received universal acclaim. The XIV Dalai Lama, Tenzin Gyasto (1935–), the religious, spiritual, and political leader of Tibet living in exile in India and awarded the Nobel Peace Prize in 1989 believes in a smile, laughter, action, and compassion. Imagine if each of us actively and on a regular basis sought to make a difference in diversity at work – billions of individuals on a compassionate endeavor for inclusion and honoring difference! In the current century, the Dalai Lama is one of the most eminent proponents of Buddhism. Some famous individuals linked to Buddhism, who can provide sources of inspiration, include S. N. Goenka (1924–) the founder of the *vipassana* retreat with courses around the world; Thich Nhat Hanh (1926–) born in Vietnam and trained in the Zen tradition, who has written countless books on Buddhism which blend Zen with Theravada mindfulness; and Aung San Sui Kyi (1945–) the Burmese political figure who earned the Nobel Peace Prize in 1991.

Eight out of 10 people or 84% of the 6.9 billion people worldwide identify with a religious group. Many religious groups are concentrated in the Asia-Pacific region – Hindus (90%), Buddhists (99%), folk/traditional religions (90%), and members of other religions (89%); 75% of those unaffiliated also live in the Asia-Pacific region, as well as 75% of the world's Muslims (Pew Research Centre, 2012). Yet the formal study of religion has taken time to reach fields such as management and organization, though this has slowly started evolving with the importance of place, identity, and practices in business, society, and politics (Pio, 2014; Brunn, 2015). The total population of Buddhists in the world, based on a 2010 estimate, is 487,540,000 or 7.1% of the world's population (Pew Research Centre, 2012). The 10 countries with the largest number of Buddhists are China, Thailand, Japan, Burma (Myanmar), Sri Lanka, Vietnam, Cambodia, South Korea, India, and Malaysia. Interestingly, Buddhism was the first religion to use paper for writing its holy scriptures, and as Buddhism spread to countries such as Korea and Japan, papermaking followed (Monro, 2014). Buddhism prized learning and a number of renowned universities were built around monasteries, such as the ancient Nalanda University in the fifth century CE and Vikramasila in the eighth–ninth century CE. Buddhism also encouraged the mercantile class and the numerous caves spread throughout India are evidence of trade routes and caves as rest houses for merchants, mendicants, and travellers, as well as houses of prayer, meditation, and scripture where monks resided (Pio, 2010).

The purpose of this chapter is to present the multiple interpretations and heterogeneity in the performance of Buddhism at work. Work in organizations encompasses aspects such as leadership and decision making, gender, mindfulness, and enlightened workplaces. In the context of religious diversity, work also embraces how various religions are viewed and how, for example, Buddhism views other religions. This chapter is structured as follows: first the conceptual foundation is presented; next some of the major beliefs in Buddhism are described. This is followed by a discussion of Buddhism in organizations. Finally a critical management lens is used to explicate two scenarios – persecution by Buddhists, and inclusion by Buddhists and their impact on religious diversity at work.

Conceptual Foundation

In moving beyond conceptualizations of diversity as primarily contributing to the bottom line and organizational goals, Litvin (2006) interrupts the "taken-for-grantedness" of socially constructed, normalized meanings of diversity, through alternative understandings that move beyond the business case and economic profitability. She suggests four life-affirming possibilities for organizations to consider:

1. Organizations enrich the lives of their members.
2. Organizations serve as a medium for individuals to pursue their personal goals.
3. Organizations facilitate the achievement of community, since human beings organize themselves in groups not only to get things done, but also to overcome uncertainty and to achieve community.
4. Organizations enable individuals to pursue goals which individuals cannot do alone, and thus organizations can contribute to the totality of human happiness by providing meaning and through the creation of a just society.

Organizations can create the right circumstances for their people to grow, develop, learn, and connect with each other through mutual learning and cooperation. This necessarily involves an understanding of historical legacies and a critical understanding of power, as well as faith-based traditions and societies (Pio et al., 2013). Hence, "diversity work hinges on committing time and effort to process: to exploring one another's points of view and working out agreements on how to proceed with the task at hand ... for the organization, successful diversity work translates to change in the organizational power structure" (Litvin, 2006, p. 89). Thus rather than individuals being the means to achieve organizational goals, the organization is a means and an instrument to serve its members and society's needs through creating and sustaining inclusive, equitable places of work.

Each of the four life-affirming organizational possibilities can be linked to the ancient Theravada view of the Divine states or *Brahmaviharas* from the oldest written Buddhist source, the Pali Canon. The four *Brahmaviharas*, utilizing the ancient Buddhist Pali language, are *metta* or love, *karuna* or compassion, *mudita* or empathy, and *upekkha* or equanimity (Pio, 1986, 2013). Religious diversity in Buddhism can be seen as offering organizations and individuals the following possibilities:

1. *Metta* or love, when organizations endeavor to enrich their members holistically;
2. *Karuna* or compassion, when organizations facilitate and enable their members to achieve their personal goals;

3. *Mudita* or empathy, when organizations help their members achieve community;
4. *Upekkha* or equanimity/the zero point between pain and pleasure, so that organizations can effectively, and without exclusive self-interest, serve their members and society in creating a more just, equitable world order.

Since 2013, Metta conventions have been held yearly with the aim of promoting the practice of *metta* and bringing like-minded people together through acts of compassionate love (Metta convention, 2015). In 2014 a *metta* convention, titled "healing of hearts," was held in Sri Lanka and in 2016 a *metta* convention titled "connecting of hearts," was held in Australia. *Metta* is the wish for all sentient beings to be well and happy. It is also referred to as boundless, or universal love – a love that transcends all barriers such as caste, color, or creed (Metta convention, 2015).

The expression of faith in the workplace is increasing and in the current century there is a growing endeavor by scholars and practitioners to link the East-West religious context and management, as faith based traditions and their wisdom are seen as a pipeline to the future (Pio et al., 2013; Pio, 2014).

Context and Beliefs

Much has been written about Buddhism, and the Buddhist holy scriptures are a treasure trove of wisdom for both individuals and organizations. Buddhism originated in India about 2,500 years ago (sixth century BC) and was taught by Siddhartha Gautama, the Buddha. Buddha means "the enlightened one" and in Buddhism *dhamma* (Pali) or *dharma* (Sanskrit) or the path to inner peace as a move away from suffering and worldly illusion, is the main focus. There is a call to empty oneself of all negativity such as anger, fear, and desire. Among the many beliefs in Buddhism are the three gems, the three universal truths, the four noble truths, the eightfold noble path, and the law of dependent origination or chain of causation, all leading to the goal of *nirvana*, which is enlightenment based on deep moral change and purification of self (Nakamura, 1976; Smith, 1991; O'Donnell, 2006). There are a number of pathways to *nirvana*, including compassion and various forms of meditation such as *vipassana*.

Buddhist beliefs concerning the nature of the universe are intertwined with karma and rebirth; in order to escape from the cycle of birth and rebirth, one needs to avoid extremes and live a life of patience, kindness and non-attachment to worldly aspects.

The three gems are: Buddha (the enlightened one), *dhamma* (the Way/the scriptures/the good and moral life), and *sangha* (community including Buddhist monks and nuns).

The three universal truths: *dukkha* or suffering, *anicca* or impermanence/everything is in a constant state of flux, *anatta* or non-self/there is no permanent self.

The four noble truths are: Suffering, which involves all life; Craving, which is the origin of suffering; Cessation of craving, which is the cure for suffering; and the Middle way, which means the avoidance of extremes, through following the Eightfold noble path.

The Eightfold noble path consists of: right views, right aspirations, right speech, right conduct, right livelihood, right effort, right mindfulness, and right concentration.

The chain of causation consists of 12 aspects, starting with ignorance or lack of knowledge, because of which we suffer and go through the process of birth, death, decay, and suffering.

The earliest form of Buddhism is known as Theravada Buddhism or way of the elders and is practiced in a number of countries including Sri Lanka, Laos, Cambodia, and Thailand, and, it is based on the earliest Buddhist texts, the Pali Canon – the *Tipitaka*. Mahayana Buddhism is practiced across the globe, it consists of many variations of the earliest form of Buddhism, including the development of the *bodhisattva* or compassionate beings, and it is observed in the USA, China, Vietnam, Nepal, Korea, Japan, and Tibet. Mahayana Buddhism has many forms, such as Tibetan Buddhism, Zen Buddhism, and Won Buddhism. For example, Zen Buddhism is practiced in countries such as Japan and is known for its *haiku* (poetry) and *koan* (riddle/paradox).

The Buddhist pantheon consists of numerous gods and goddesses, such as Ambitabha or the Buddha of Infinite light; Avalokitesvara or the Lord who looks down is a popular Buddhist celestial being; Hotei the Laughing Buddha, Kwan Yin the goddess of compassion, and Tara the mother of liberation representing success in work (Bhattacharyya, 1958; Jordan, 2004). The goddesses are "dynamic and complex entities" (Shaw, 2006, p. 4) who support individuals in a variety of ways, such as protection against every mortal danger, support for mental purification, knowledge, and spiritual awakening and can be linked to the feminine divine.

In order to explicate the heterogeneity in Buddhism, a country exemplar, that of the little island nation of New Zealand, situated in the Pacific Ocean, is presented. Buddhism arrived on the shores of New Zealand in 1863 in the form of Chinese immigrants arriving to work in the gold mines. These Chinese gold miners' religious practices involved folk religion with elements of Buddhist influence (Viradhammo, 1990). Buddhism, however, remained a private family matter, behind closed doors, excluded from public discourse by cultural prejudice. The arrival of explicit Chinese forms of Buddhism had to wait until the mid-1980s with a new wave of Chinese immigrants (Kemp, 2007).

Buddhism has grown rapidly in New Zealand, with the 1966 census indicating 652 Buddhists, the 1986 census showing 6,516 individuals, the 2006 census indicating 52,392 individuals, and the 2013 showing 58,404 Buddhists, or 1.5% of the New Zealand population (Morris, 2012; Statistics New Zealand, 2014). Prior to the 1970s, Buddhist presence in New Zealand was insignificant except for a northern Maori sub-tribe who claimed to have ancestry going back to Tibet, the Chinese gold miners of 1863 in Otago province who had cultural practices nuanced with Buddhism, and the Theosophical Society who played host to meetings of Buddhist speakers and immigrants from 1893 (Kemp, 2007).

The Buddhist Society of New Zealand was one of the earliest recorded associations to be formed in 1956 (Spuler, 2002). In New Zealand, Buddhism was "a type of 1960s alternative spiritual group" (Ellwood, 1993, p. 214). "At best, individuals were exploring Buddhism in informal home meetings, or experimenting with meditation techniques, or reading the Beat poets of America" (Spuler, 2002, p. 140). The 1970s witnessed many monks and teachers arriving in New Zealand, like Karma Tenzin Dorje Namgyal Rinpoche of the Karma Kagyu lineage, Zen Master Joshu Sasaki Roshi, founder and Abbot of Rinzai-ji, Lama Thubten Yeshe, and Lama Thubten Zopa of the Foundation for the Preservation of the Mahayana Tradition (Kemp, 2007). With increasing interest in meditation in New Zealand, groups started forming based on a variety of traditions (Spuler, 2002), significant numbers of New Zealanders adopted Buddhist practices and teachings (Morris, 2012), and several monasteries were constructed. One of the earliest monasteries established was Bodhinyanarama, a Thai Forest Tradition monastery established near Wellington in 1986 (Spuler, 2002). Its affiliated centers were the Auckland Buddhist Vihara in Mt. Wellington, Auckland, and the Vimutti Buddhist Monastery, founded in 1980 in Bombay, South Auckland (Morris, 2012).

Following the Immigration Policy Review of 1986 and the Immigration Act (1987), immigrants from many of the Asian Buddhist countries arrived in New Zealand. These Buddhists came from Cambodia, Vietnam, Taiwan, China, Thailand, Sri Lanka, Hong Kong, and Korea, bringing various traditions of Buddhism with them (Nattier, 1998). The "Statement of Religious Diversity in New Zealand" (Human Rights Commission, 2009) has been endorsed by a wide range of faith communities and includes freedom of religion, conscience, and belief, freedom of expression, the right to safety and security, and the right to reasonable accommodation of diverse religious practices in various settings. New Zealand has been ranked as the world's fourth most peaceful country in the Global Peace Index and the second best country in which to do business, based on the World Bank's *Doing Business Report* (World Bank Group, 2015). Available sources indicate Buddhist organizations in the civil society sector, such as the Fo Guang Shan temple, which has activities for education, culture, charity, and dharma propagation (Fo Guang Shan, n.d.). However, there is a lack of sources indicating Buddhist organizations in the business sector. This could be due to the fact that Buddhism, while being the third largest religion in New Zealand, does not have specific Buddhist business organizations, as their adherents may prefer to start social organizations while working in business organizations. It is also possible that this may be because these Buddhist individuals believe that they can make a more meaningful difference through the civil society sector.

In fact, relative to those who practice other religions, Buddhists are less likely to see positive societal contributions from entrepreneurship (Carswell & Rolland, 2004). There is some descriptive data that may indicate that those who practice Buddhism perceive that entrepreneurship is less important for society, relative to those from other religions. The value base of some forms of Buddhism are focused more upon things beyond the world than within it, thus behavior is only thought of as helpful if it helps the individual find a way to *nirvana* (Eckel, 1998). The next section elucidates the practice of Buddhism in organizations.

Buddhism in Organizations

This section will touch on Human Resource Management in China, Japan, South Korea, Thailand, and Japan in the subsection regions and countries. This is followed by information on leadership and decision-making, gender, mindfulness, and enlightened workspaces.

Steve Jobs (1955–2011) is credited with fusing his meditation practice and design in the company he co-founded (Apple) and is said to have been deeply influenced by Buddhist practices. Jobs wished to stay hungry and foolish, reminiscent of Zen haiku and paradox. He chose the unconventional name of a fruit, apple, for his technology company and the ubiquitous use of Apple products has changed the way the world is today, possibly making the management of religious diversity both more challenging and more possible. For his obituary, *The New York Times* wrote "You touched an ugly world of technology and made it beautiful" (Markoff, 2011).

Redmond (2015) writes of Kazuo Inamori (1932–), the 85-year-old billionaire, entrepreneur, management guru, and Buddhist priest, and the man who established the electronics giant Kyocera Corporation more than five decades ago. Inamori notes that if you want eggs, take care of the hen and if you bully or kill the hen, it's not going to work. Inamori printed a small book for each staff member clearly outlining his philosophies and pledging the company's devotion to the growth of each staff member along with the social significance of their work and the importance of being humble and doing the right thing. He insists that company leaders should seek to make all their employees happy both materially and intellectually. Inamori's work is infused with the Buddhist idea of *shojin* which means elevating the soul through devotion to a task. Both Steve Jobs and Kazuo Inamori display the four *brahmaviharas* in their organizational processes and products.

There are a number of organizations in the civil society sector, or not-for-profit organizations founded on Buddhist principles. For example the Atisha Buddhist Centre in Australia which provides opportunities for meditation and study for people to develop their wisdom and compassion (Atisha Buddhist Centre, 2017). Buddhist Peace Fellowship cultivates compassionate action to serve as a catalyst for socially engaged Buddhism – they embrace a triple treasure of compassionate action through learning/community, speaking/communication and doing/collaboration (Buddhist Peace Fellowship, 2012).

Soka Gakkai International is Buddhism in Action for peace and believes in empowering individuals toward positive global change (Soka Gakkai International, 2015). The Sarvodaya organization in Sri Lanka, with a total budget exceeding USD 5 million and 1,500 full time employees check consistency between budget and number of employees (+ expenses) focuses on peace-making, community building, and economic development strategies through macro and micro interventions based on Buddhism and Gandhian thought (Sarvodaya, 2017).

Explicitly Buddhist organizations focusing exclusively on business goals are hard to locate, but there are a few studies which show how Buddhism is practiced in organizations and which can serve as pathways for understanding Buddhism and religious diversity in organizations as well as in Buddhist regions and countries.

Regions and Countries

The heterogeneity and multiple interpretations of Buddhist scriptures and teachings merges with country culture and organizational culture in research on Buddhist regions/countries. Rowley et al. (2004) argue that China, Japan, and South Korea represent a regional cluster where there is geographic and cultural closeness and openness to similar economic pressures and a degree of convergence in HRM. Four key areas of HRM are considered: flexible resourcing, employee development, performance-based rewards, and enterprise-focused employment relations. In China there was movement from the iron rice bowl (*tie fan wan*) and hereditary inheritance of jobs (*dingti*) in State Owned Enterprises (SOEs) till the late 1980s followed by more market-based resourcing and limited connections (*guanxi*). In Japan there has been life-time employment, though in the current situation younger workers look to be promoted based on skills rather than seniority. Training is regularly undertaken and promotion is a function of both training and seniority.

In Korea, lifetime employment was prevalent with strong internal labor markets and extensive employee development. In all three countries, the change has been from lifetime secure employment towards more flexible resourcing patterns, with remuneration moving from seniority based to skills and performance based systems. Yet there are differences in all three countries, dependent on the level and pace of change with the inextricable connections of history and culture, openness to western HRM practices and the management of ethnicity and diversity due to the increase of people mobility. Hence there is need for cross-cultural training both within these countries as well as for MNC's working in these countries. While there is some degree of convergence in HRM, the dynamism and complexity of each area needs to be carefully considered (Rowley et al., 2004).

Thailand is a Buddhist country with 95% of the population belonging to this group and the profession of Theravada Buddhism, though they also have the concept of *sanuk*, which means to have fun and enjoy life (Lawler & Atmiyanandana, 2003). There are two types of domestically owned firms in the private sector – family enterprises (where HRM are simple, informal and based on personal relationships) and Thai-owned corporations (which continue to be rooted in personal connections, though there is a greater reliance on strategic HRM). In general companies in Thailand are fairly relaxed with reference to rules, a large majority of workers have relatively low education and training, and pay continues to be on the basis of personal characteristics such as age, gender, social background, and connections. The values of *krieng jai* and *bunkhun* or deference and reciprocity continue to dominate organizations in Thailand.

In Japan, people are growing less religious and less numerous. In the October 2015 issues of *The Economist*, an article titled "Religion in Japan – Temples of Doom" indicates how Buddhism has for centuries been the religion of choice at funerals – at USD 24,700 among the priciest in the world – as well as for spiritual care for the bereaved. But with this high cost, automated indoor cemeteries are becoming more popular, for example the Koukokuji Buddhist Temple in Tokyo has an automated indoor cemetery with over 2,000 small altars to store the deceased's ashes. In an effort to remain relevant, earthly pleasures are encouraged as in Vowz, a Tokyo bar which has Buddhist priests behind the counter, for spiritual awakening can come in many forms and this bar believes that they provide the opportunity (*The Economist*, 2015a).

A huge statue of Guanyin the Buddhist goddess of mercy has been set up in Sanya overlooking the South China Sea and this statue has become a draw card for tourists and a money spinner (*The Economist*, 2015b). In China, Buddhism is big business and since the 1980s new shrines have sprung up in numerous places in China, for example the 128 meter Spring Temple Buddha in the province of Henan, with a plan for 10 more mega-Buddhas around the country (*The Economist*,

2015b). China's Buddhism is also going global with the Shaolin temple in Henan planning to build a USD 297 million, 500-bed hotel complex and temple, including a martial arts academy and a 27-hole golf course in Australia. Undoubtedly some Buddhists are unhappy about the commercialization of their faith, as they insist that religion is not for show, it is for practicing.

Leadership and Decision-making

The *Rajadhamma* or Kingly duties for leaders (Dalai Lama & van den Muyzenberg, 2008) involve 10 virtues, which are: *Dana* or generosity; *Sila* or morality/ethical behavior; *Parricaga* or unselfishness/altruism; *Ajjava* or honesty/integrity; *Maddava* or gentleness/avoiding arrogance; *Tapa* or self-restraint/self-control; *Akkhoda* or non-anger/ free from hatred and staying calm in confusing situations; *Avihimsa/ ahimsa* or non-violence; *Khanti* or patience/forgiveness; and *Avirodhana* or avoiding prejudice/ fairness. These 10 virtues can be subsumed under the four *brahmaviharas* as shown in the research on Buddhist leaders in business.

Van den Muyzenberg (2014) discusses the utilization of Buddhist concepts for leaders of businesses in the context of Buddhism. He notes that the Buddhist scriptures exhort their followers that for businesses, once there is success, it must be enduring, and wealth should be appropriately distributed. Furthermore, individuals should be truthful, generous, and exercise self-control; and where profit is concerned, one part should be used for ease and convenience, two parts for businesses, and one part should be saved for adversity. Buddhist precepts can be utilized for three main organizational situations (Dalai Lama & Van den Muyzenberg, 2008; Payutto, 2010): firstly, for reducing conflicts and tensions within an organization through an understanding of the cause and effect principle and the Buddhist holistic view and the removal of negative emotions and cravings for more power; secondly, for coping constructively with criticism and defensive behavior through a more careful understanding of Buddhism, and discussing anger and its side effects; thirdly, training the mind through various mindfulness methods such as *vipassana*. Buddhism emphasizes that managers and professionals should be "aware of their intentions and motivations and the effects of their decisions and actions on all stakeholders" (Van den Muyzenberg, 2014, p. 748).

Buddhist leaders tend to rely on their faith as a source of guidance, for example thinking of the five Buddhist precepts (abstain from harming living beings, stealing, sexual misconduct, lying, and intoxication) when taking decisions; engaging in worshiping statues of Buddha at work as well as daily collective meditation, annual pilgrimage, and Holy Scripture chanting (Fernando & Jackson, 2006). Law et al. (2014) looked at the influence of Buddhism on Chinese corporate leaders in Malaysia and found that these leaders reported peace of mind, letting go, and unselfishness as part of their management processes in their organizations.

Through mindfulness, compassion, and self-expansion, based on the practical wisdom of Buddhism, decision making can be enhanced at the individual, group, and organizational levels. In this respect, the Buddhist law of dependent origination, or the *paticcasamuppada*, which deals with cause and effect and interdependence, facilitates judicious decisions (Vallabh & Singhal, 2014). Compassion can be seen as organizational citizenship behavior with a culture of information sharing, resulting in better decision-making in organizations. Additionally, mindfulness can regulate stress and following Buddhist wisdom can lead to a happier and more responsible society and environment.

Kumarasinghe and Hoshino (2010), in their study on middle managers in Sri Lanka, note that "wealth sharing is a widely used traditional motto in Sri Lanka" (p. 10). Additionally, these authors note that the Buddhist *Sigalovada Sutta* states that employers should minister to employees by assigning them work based on their strengths, supplying them with food and wages, looking after them when they are ill, profit sharing, and leave and special allowances. On the other side of the coin, employees need to be content with what has been given to them, work well, and praise and spread the fame of their employer. Yet, collectivistic leadership, communication, or decision making as displayed in Sri Lanka in this study, did not influence economic performance, and the authors urge the need for further exploration of the role of religion and its influence in organizations.

In the research on Buddhist leadership and decision-making in organizations, while there is evidence of the first three *brahmaviharas* or *metta, karuna,* and *mudita,* there does not seem to be evidence for the fourth *brahmavihara uppekha* or equanimity. Perhaps through reaching this fourth *brahmavihara*, organizations can create more harmonious and wise forms of leadership which honor all aspects of diversity.

Gender

The gendered construct of respectable femininity or behavioral expectations in workplaces, streets, and/or homes is played out in career accounts of Sri Lankan women (Fernando & Cohen, 2014). Fernando and Cohen's (2014) study sample consisted of 24 highly skilled socially privileged women, of whom 21 belonged to the majority ethnic-religious group in Sri Lanka and consisted of Sinhalese Buddhists. The women in this sample explained how "conforming to society's ideals of respectability was critical to their hierarchical advancement" (Fernando & Cohen, 2014, p. 157). For example, avoiding extensive interactions with casual male acquaintances, which would be regarded as inappropriate, as would be being seen alone with a man out of office hours and not on official premises; maintaining a physical and emotional distance from men; not being seen alone at night with men despite the fact that the office had a number of evening functions and social gatherings. Thus networking with men sometimes made these women nervous and they were "conservative in exchanging their business cards with men since they did not want to risk their good reputation" (Fernando & Cohen, 2014, p. 157). However, the organizations also allowed women to leave earlier than men when there were after-hours meetings, indicating their endorsement of respectable femininity. Interestingly these rules primarily applied to early- and mid-career women rather than older women. Yet gendered moral behavior is a powerful dimension in women's career progression in this Buddhist country. However, we note that this moral behavior could be a mix of societal expectations for how a religion is interpreted, and in this case the geographical context of Sri Lanka as a South Asian country may play a major role for both women and men.

Gunawardana (2014) discusses voice from the perspective of socio-cultural contexts and the day-to-day culturally embedded realities experienced by female workers in Sri Lanka in export processing zones. Management encouraged and preferred informal personalized methods, social interaction, and agency through individualized voice mechanisms rather than broader collective forms such as trade unions, though "gendered recruitment practices were relied on to negate the desire to exercise voice" (Gunawardana, 2014, p. 464). Dimensions such as kinship, age, and authority through sociocultural elements determined the way voice was expressed.

In the context of the USA, Hayashino and Tsong (2014) discuss the interwoven nature of religion among Buddhist Asian-American women, where there is a blend of cultural, contextual, social, and religious roles and expectations. In navigating aspects of discrimination such as racism, these women use their faith to fight against oppression and to enable empowerment.

The role of women as expressed through Buddhist practice seems ambiguous and cultural mores dominate the expression and practice of the *brahmaviharas*.

Mindfulness

Mindfulness is a form of mediation derived from Buddhism and involves cultivating a direct active awareness of experienced phenomena, so that one is fully in the present moment. Mindfulness involves a non-judgmental awareness and insight generation, and is traditionally practiced in the context of spiritual development (Gordon et al., 2014). Individuals who undergo mindfulness meditation may be able to transfer the locus of control for stress to internal metacognitive and attentional resources rather than to the external work conditions (Gordon et al., 2014).

Shonin et al. (2013), in their review of mindfulness and other Buddhist-derived interventions, discuss how mindfulness can facilitate the development of compassion which can lead to improvements in levels of tolerance, cooperation, and interpersonal skills and a more balanced level of organizational identification through a re-evaluation of life's priorities.

Individuals of any faith or non-faith can benefit from the utilization of mindfulness practices, which can result in the alleviation of suffering, though it is essential to honor the Buddhist ethos from where such practices are derived. Such practices can lead to more gentleness and compassion, and they do not threaten other belief systems (Bowen et al., 2015).

In an intensive study with 10 participants, Shonin and Van Gordon (2015) show how the use of mindfulness practices can lead to a number of positive benefits for organizations. Benefits include changing attitudes towards work, improved job performance, well-being at work, a richer quality of communication, greater confidence in decision-making, remaining centered and calm under pressure, more autonomy and attention pertaining to the job, as well as an enhanced strategic outlook.

Loy (2003) writes of the empty nature of corporations in the globalized world, noting that for Buddhists the sense of self is not apart from the world and genuine enlightenment translates as a compassion for all sentient beings and the need to control greed. This stance would fulfill all four *brahmaviharas*, whereby loving kindness creates compassionate action and empathy, resulting in equanimity for self, the team, organizations, and society.

Enlightened Workspaces

Wagner (2009) discusses the frugal and ascetic lifestyle of the Buddhist monks who travelled to China on the silk route over 2,000 years ago, the importance of consciousness and meditation as the route to enlightenment, and the later developments of the *bodhisattva*, who is concerned about other people and devotes her/his life to the enlightenment of other.

The early Buddhist pluralistic attitude was inclusive, based on the Pali Nikayas, where the cultivation of humility and inquisitiveness was critical but firmly rooted in ethical and doctrinal aspects of Buddhism (Velez de Cea, 2013). Velez de Cea questions exclusivist readings of the Pali texts, which can be problematic to inclusiveness and often suggest arrogance and a low desire for open dialogue. Truong (2013) emphasizes the importance of mutual understanding between Asia and Europe and the significance of social justice in Buddhism through social engagement.

Metcalf and Hateley (2001) suggest becoming an enlightened worker through self-improvement, staying focused, establishing priorities, keeping commitments, and making the workday worthwhile. Enlightened work relationships can be cultivated, thus creating an enlightened workplace. These authors encourage individuals to believe that the Buddha exists in every individual. The Buddha mind, which is on a journey of awakening and insight, and asking oneself what the Buddha would do, enables us to tap into our own consciousness and our true nature, keeping in mind that each path is unique.

Gallagher (2012) writes of five mantras for the workday if Buddha was CEO and CSO (chief spiritual officer): every day is a good day (the past is gone and the future is not yet, therefore focus on nowness);

nothing wanting, nothing extra (avoiding categories of too much and too little); be kind to yourself first (the purpose of life is to be happy); it is fine to be wealthy (use wealth properly for good ends); and the fifth mantra is: other people's troubles are other people's problems (stay out of other people's karma and take care of your own, but also love your problem people).

Thus organizations can use Buddhism to embrace diversity from a number of angles, including gender, religious heterogeneity, and individual differences. As one interpretation of Buddhism states (Chung, 1994, p. 115): "Some people are intelligent, and other people are not. Some bamboo is tall, while other bamboo is short. Short or tall, intelligent or not, neither is good nor bad. Tall bamboo has its good points, and short bamboo has its good points."

A Critical Management Lens on Buddhism

In the preceding sections various positive aspects of Buddhism have been described and discussed. However, if one uses a critical lens on the diversity of Buddhist practices, there are some examples which starkly display exclusion, where some Buddhists exclude and persecute adherents who are not Buddhist. One example is the situation of the Rohingya Muslims, who have faced terror and violence in the Buddhist country of Myanmar/Burma.

Rohingya Muslims have been the butt of violence and hateful rhetoric from the Buddhist majority in the state of Rakhine, have suffered the cost more than 100 lives and over 100,000 made homeless with sectarian violence spreading across Myanmar (*The Economist*, 2013, 2015d). The Rohingyas are being called the most persecuted minority in the world, unable to claim citizenship in Myanmar or in any other country. Human rights groups are concerned that the situation is desperate that there may be a grave risk of mass atrocities and even genocide. However, in countries like India and Indonesia, Muslims have been helping the Rohingyas through donations and religious solidarity.

Another example of exclusion is in Sri Lanka where there has been violence against Christians by Buddhists who have attacked Christian churches and clergy (Bouma et al., 2010). Bloody battles in two of the Buddhist majority countries, Thailand and Sri Lanka, have attracted world attention. In Thailand the unrest has been in the

Malay-Muslim provinces. In Sri Lanka the battle has been between Sinhalese Buddhists and Tamils, who are mostly Hindus. The Bodu Bala Sena, literally meaning Buddhist force in Sri Lanka, preaches a doctrine of intolerance against a minority Islamic population, who are about 10% in the country (*The Economist*, 2015d).

Yet Buddhism is also an inclusive religion, and proof for this comes from the Dalit Buddhists in India. Clear View Project (n.d.) discusses "Ambedkar's Children" or Indian Buddhists, who are among the poorest of the poor with low levels of literacy and from the untouchable castes, who converted to Buddhism through the influence of Dr. Bhimrao Ambedkar in the 1950s as a political and social assertion. These individuals are known as neo-Buddhists, Dalits, or Ambedkarites, and the taint of being outcasts and untouchables in the Hindu caste system seems to continue as a stigma in their lives, despite their conversion to Buddhism (Thorat, 2009; Beltz, 2015). There are approximately 8 million Buddhists in India, of whom about 90% are Dalits. Dr. Ambedkar was himself an untouchable, but managed to earn a doctorate from Columbia University and the London School of Economics, but on his return to India was shunned by individuals who believed that if they even touched him, they would be "polluted" – the general feeling prevalent among Hindus about untouchables.

Dr. Ambedkar was the prime architect of the Indian constitution and organized the mass conversion of Dalits to Buddhism, fighting for their civil rights through his words and actions. The word *dalit* means people who are broken to pieces/suppressed – another word for them is *Harijan* or children of Hari or the god Vishnu, which was a term popularized by Mahatma Gandhi. A few organizations such as the Trailokya Bauddha Mahasangha Sahayaka Gana (TBMSG), Karuna Trust, Nagaloka, or the Nagarjuna Training Institute, and Navayan, have been working with the Dalits with various projects to develop Dalit women's leadership, to build solidarity amongst individuals and organizations, and to fight social discrimination through legal and constitutional means. The Indian government, over the last few decades, has also introduced legislation and other educational/social/employment measures to better the situation of Dalits, for example the Ambedkar Gram Vikas Yojna (Thorat, 2009). Undoubtedly, such country examples of inclusion and exclusion impact how organizations will treat adherents of various faiths.

Walls (2012) emphasizes that believing in Buddhism is like believing in a proven process of learning, where the purpose of wealth is for material comfort and security, mental well-being, and inner freedom. Thus in practicing the right livelihood, one has to live with love and compassion, and one's actions should not harm self and/or others. Short-term bottom line profit does not lead to long-term well-being.

Tibetan Buddhism relies on the XIV Dalai Lama, who has used his enormous prestige to urge Tibetans to refrain from violent resistance in Tibet, which is under Chinese rule, leading to the exile of the Dalai Lama from Tibet and his current residence in India (*The Economist*, 2015c). Since China took over Tibet in 1950, it has systematically suppressed Buddhist culture, persecuted its followers and destroyed monasteries and works of art (*The Economist*, 1992). Yet through collectors in Russia and America, the sacred art of Tibet, displaying wisdom and compassion, was seen through an exhibition at London's Royal Academy. Buddhist art is anonymous, highly schematic, and is often contemplative with a beatific stillness, enigmatic smiling features, and perfectly harmonious bodies – the ideal for future Buddhahood among humanity.

In the day-to-day organizational oppressions and generosities and the micro (individual), meso (organizational), and macro (societal) levels within which organizations and religious diversity are embedded it is important to remember that from a Buddhist point of view, love can conquer all and love can be the starting point and the ending point – the alpha and omega – for crumbling and stone walling discrimination, inequality, and oppressions, and embracing difference and diversity. In fact being in love with each other and with society and our planet can preserve our fragile earth for our children and future generations. As the Zen haiku by Shiki (Peter Pauper Press, 1960) indicates:

Tremendous forces ...
Stone-piled fence
All tumbled down
By two cats in Love.

Summary

This chapter has presented information on Buddhist beliefs and practices through the conceptual foundations of life-affirming possibilities and the *brahmaviharas*. The four *Brahmaviharas*, utilizing the ancient Buddhist Pali language are *metta* or love, *karuna* or compassion, *mudita* or empathy, and *upekkha* or equanimity. Among the many beliefs in Buddhism, are the three gems, the three universal truths, the four noble truths, the eightfold noble path and the law of dependent origination or chain of causation, all leading to the goal of *nirvana*, which is enlightenment based on deep moral change and purification of self. In order to explicate the heterogeneity in Buddhism, a country exemplar, that of the little island nation of New Zealand, situated in the Pacific Ocean, was presented. Regarding Buddhism in organizations, Human Resource Management in China, Japan, South Korea, Thailand, and Japan was offered. This was followed by information on leadership and decision-making, attitudes towards women, mindfulness, and enlightened workplaces. Next a critical lens on the diversity of Buddhist practices was applied with country examples on exclusion and inclusion.

References

Atisha Buddhist Centre. (2017). Welcome to Atisha. Retrieved from: www.atishacentre.org.au.

Beltz, J. (2015). The making of a new icon: B. R. Ambedkar's visual hagiography. *South Asian Studies*, 31(2), 254–65.

Bhattacharyya, B. (1958). *The Indian Buddhist iconography*. Calcutta: K. L. Mukhopadhyay.

Bouma, G., Ling, R., & Pratt, D. (2010). *Religious diversity in Southeast Asia and the Pacific*. New York: Springer.

Bowen, S., Bergman, A., & Witkiewitz, K. (2015). Engagement in Buddhist meditation practices among non-Buddhists: Associations with religious identity and practice. *Mindfulness*. doi: 10.1007/s12671-015-0420-9.

Brunn, S. (2015). Changing world religion map: Status, literature and challenges. *In* Brunn, S. (ed.), *The changing world religion map: Sacred places, identities, practices and politics*. London: Springer, 3–69.

Buddhist Peace Fellowship (2012). About BPF. Retrieved from: www.buddhistpeacefellowship.org/about-bpf/.

Carswell, P., & Rolland, D. (2004). The role of religion in entrepreneurship participation and perception. *International Journal of Entrepreneurship and Small Business*, 1(3), 280–6.

Chung, T. S. (1994). *Zen speaks – Shouts of nothingness*. London: Anchor Books, Doubleday.

Clear View Project. (n.d.). Ambedkar's children: Indian Buddhism reborn among the Untouchables. Retrieved from: www.clearviewproject.org/indiabuddhismrising.html.

Dalai Lama, H. H., & Van den Muyzenberg, L. (2008). *The leader's way: Business, Buddhism and happiness in an interconnected world.* London, UK: Nicholas Brealey.

Eckel, M. D. (1998). Is there a Buddhist philosophy of nature? *In* Cohen, R. S., & Tauber, A. I. (eds.), *Philosophies of nature: The human dimension: In celebration of Erazim Kohák.* Dordrecht: Springer Netherlands. 53–69.

Ellwood, R. S. (1993). *Islands of the Dawn: The story of alternative spirituality in New Zealand.* Hawaii: University of Hawaii.

Fernando, W., & Cohen, L. (2014). Respectable femininity and career agency: exploring paradoxical imperatives. *Gender, Work and Organization*, 21(2), 149–64.

Fernando, M., & Jackson, B. (2006). The influence of religion-based workplace spirituality on business leaders' decision-making: An inter-faith study. *Journal of Management & Organization*, 12(1), 23–39.

Fo Guang Shan. (n.d.). Fo Guang Shan North Island New Zealand. Retrieved from: http://fgs.org.nz/english/aboutus.aspx.

Gallagher, B. J. (2012). Buddha CEO: Five mantras for your workday. *Huffington Post* (January 5). Retrieved from: www.huffingtonpost.com/bj-gallagher/buddha-ceo-five-mantras-f_b_1466016.html.

Gunawardana, S. (2014). Reframing employee voice: A case study in Sri Lanka's export processing zones. *Work, Employment and Society*, 28(3), 452–68.

Hayashino, D., & Tsong, Y. (2014). Buddhism and Taoism in the lives of Asian American women. *In* Bryant-Davis, T., Austria, A., Kawahara, D., & Willis, D. (eds.), *Religion and Spirituality for Diverse Women: Foundations of Strength and Resilience.* Santa Barbara, CA: Praeger, 139–58.

Human Rights Commission. (2009). Statement on Religious Diversity (2nd edn.). Retrieved from: www.hrc.co.nz/files/5314/2387/7075/27-Aug-2009_09-44-53_Religious_Diversity_09_Web.pdf.

Jordan, M. (2004). *Dictionary of Gods and Goddesses* (2nd edn.). New York: Facts on File Inc.

Kemp, H. (2007). How the Dharma landed: Interpreting the arrival of Buddhism in New Zealand. *Journal of Global Buddhism*, 8, 107–31.

Kumarasinghe, S., & Hoshino, Y. (2010). The role and perceptions of middle managers and their influence on business performance: The case of Sri Lanka. *International Business Research*, 3(4), 3–16.

Law, K., Soo, K., & Mohammad, F. (2014). An examination of the influence of Buddhism philosophy on Malaysian Chinese corporate leadership. *International Journal of Academic Research*, 6(4), 151–61.

Lawler, J., & Atmiyanandana, V. (2003). HRM in Thailand: A post-1997 update. *Asia Pacific Business Review*, 9(4), 165–85.

Litvin, D. (2006). Diversity – Making space for a better case. *In* Konrad, A., Prasad, P., & Pringle, J. (eds.), *Handbook of workplace diversity*. London: Sage, 75–94.

Loy, D. (2003). *The Great Awakening: A Buddhist social theory*. Somerville, MA: Wisdom publications.

Markoff, J. (2011). Apple's visionary redefined digital age. *Business Day, The New York Times*, October 5. Retrieved from: www.nytimes.com/2011/10/06/business/steve-jobs-of-apple-dies-at-56.html?pagewanted=all&_r=1.

Metcalf, F., and Hateley, G. (2001). *What would Buddha do at work?* Berkley, CA: Seastone.

Metta Convention. (2015). Retrieved from: www.mettaconvention.org/metta.

Monro, A. (2014). *The paper trail: An unexpected history of the world's greatest invention*. London: Allen Lane.

Morris, P. (2012). Diverse religions – Buddhists. Te Ara – The encyclopedia of New Zealand. Retrieved from www.teara.govt.nz/en/diverse-religions/page-3.

Nakamura, H. (1976). The Basic teachings of Buddhism. *In* Dumoulin, H. and Maraldo, J. (ed.), *Buddhism in the modern world*. New York: Macmillan, 3–34.

Nattier, J. (1998). Who is a Buddhist? Charting the landscape of Buddhist America. *In* Prebish, C. S., & Tanaka, K. K. (eds.), *The Faces of Buddhism in America*. Los Angeles and London: University of California Press, 183–95.

O'Donnell, K. (2006). *Inside world religions*. Oxford: Lion Hudson plc.

Payutto, P. (2010). Buddhism and the business world: The Buddhist way to deal with business. Chandran Publishing House. Retrieved from: www.watnyanaves.net/uploads/File/books/pdf/buddhism_and_the_business_world_the_buddhist_way_to_deal_with_business.pdf.

Peter Pauper Press. (1960). *Cherry blossoms – Japanese haiku series III*. Mount Vernon, NY: The Peter Pauper Press.

Pew Research Centre. (2012). Forum on religion and public life. Retrieved from: www.pewforum.org/global-religious-landscape.aspx.

Pio, E. (1986). The Brahmaviharas of early Buddhism. *India past & present*, 3, 35–50.

 (2010). Religious Merchants? Entrepreneurship in India. *In* Dana, L.-P. (ed.). *Entrepreneurship and Religion*. MA, USA: Edward Elgar, 27–42.

(2013). *Parables through Brahmaviharas: Compassionate nudging in the teaching-learning praxis*. Florida, USA: Inaugural Teaching learning conference, Academy of Management (August).

(2014). *Work & Worship*. Auckland: Auckland University of Technology.

Pio, E., Waddock, S., Mangaliso, M., McIntosh, M., Spiller, C., Takeda, H., Gladstone, J., Ho, M., & Syed, J. (2013). Pipeline to the future? Seeking wisdom in indigenous, eastern and western traditions. *In* Neale, J. (ed.), *Handbook of Faith and Spirituality in the Workplace: Emerging Research and Practice*. Arkansas, USA: Tyson Centre for Faith and Spirituality in the Workplace, University of Arkansas. New York: Springer, 195–221.

Redmond, T. (2015). The Buddhist Priest who became a billionaire snubbing investors. Retrieved from: www.bloomberg.com/news/articles/2015-11-04/the-no-1-business-rule-of-this-billionaire-and-buddhist-priest.

Rowley, C., Benson, J., & Warner, M. (2004). Towards an Asian model of human resource management? A comparative analysis of China, Japan and South Korea. *The International Journal of Human Resource Management*, 15 (4–5), 917–33.

Sarvodaya. (2017). About. Retrieved from: www.sarvodaya.org/about.

Shaw, M. (2006). *Buddhist goddesses of India*. Princeton, NJ: Princeton University Press.

Shonin, E., & Van Gordon, W. (2015). Managers' experiences of meditation awareness training. *Mindfulness*, 6, 899–909.

Shonin, E., Van Gordon, W., Slade, K., & Griffiths, M. D. (2013). Mindfulness and Other Buddhist-derived Interventions in Correctional Settings: A Systematic Review. *Aggression and Violent Behavior*, 18, 365–72.

Smith, H. (1991). *The world's religions*. New York: HarperOne.

Soka Gakkai International. (2015). About Us. Retrieved from: www.sgi.org/about-us/sgi-timeline.html.

Spuler, M. (2002). The development of Buddhism in Australia and New Zealand. *In* Prebish, C. S., & Baumann, M. (eds.). *Westward Dharma: Buddhism beyond Asia*. Berkeley, CA: University of California Press, 139–51.

Statistics New Zealand. (2014). Religious Affiliation. Retrieved from: www.stats.govt.nz/Census/2013-census/profile-and-summary-reports/quickstats-culture-identity/religion.aspx.

The Economist. (2013). Fears of new religious strife; Buddhism v Islam in Asia. July 27, p. 35. Retrieved from: www.economist.com/news/asia/21582321-fuelled-dangerous-brew-faith-ethnicity-and-politics-tit-tat-conflict-escalating.

(2015a). Religion in Japan – Temples of doom, October 31, p. 25. Retrieved from: www.economist.com/news/asia/21677261-japans-buddhist-temples-are-going-out-business-temples-doom.

(2015b). Buddhism and business: Zen and the art of moneymaking. Retrieved from: www.economist.com/news/china/21656215-local-officials-make-packet-religion-self-denial-zen-and-art-moneymaking.

(2015c). The Golden Urn: Banyan. March 21, p. 38. Retrieved from: www.economist.com/news/china/21646795-even-china-accepts-only-dalai-lama-can-legitimise-its-rule-tibet-golden-urn.

(2015d). The most persecuted people on earth? The Rohingyas. June 13, p. 40. Retrieved from www.economist.com/news/asia/21654124-myanmars-muslim-minority-have-been-attacked-impunity-stripped-vote-and-driven.

Thorat, S. (2009). *Dalits in India*. New Delhi: Sage.

Truong, T-D. (2013). "Asian" values and the heart of understanding: A Buddhist view. *In* Cauquelin, J., Lim, P., & Mayer-Koenig, B. (eds.), *Asian values: Encounter with diversity*. New York: Routledge, 43–69.

Vallabh, P., and Singhal, M. (2014). Buddhism and Decision Making at Individual, Group and Organizational Levels. *Journal of Management Development*, 33(8/9), 763–75.

Van den Muyzenberg, L. (2014). The contribution of Buddhist wisdom to management development. *Journal of Management Development*, 33(8/9), 741–50.

Van Gordon, W., Shonin, E., Zangeneh, M., & Griffiths, M. (2014). Work-related mental health and job performance: Can mindfulness help? *International Journal of Mental Health and Addiction*, 12, 129–37.

Velez de Cea, J. A. (2013). *The Buddha and Religious Diversity*. London: Routledge.

Viradhammo, A. (1990). Buddhism. *In* Donovan, P. (ed.), *Religions of New Zealanders*. Palmerston North: Dunmore, 33–4, 43–5.

Wagner, J. (2009). Secularization: Confucianism and Buddhism. *In* Wiegandt, K., & Joas, A. (eds.), *Secularization and the World Religions*. Liverpool: Liverpool University Press, 141–59.

Walls, J. (2012). Corporate craving and Buddhist compassion: Is there a middle path for Buddhist business? Buddhistdoor global. Retrieved from: www.buddhistdoor.net/features/corporate-craving-and-buddhist-compassion-is-there-a-middle-path-for-buddhist-business.

World Bank Group. (2015). Doing business – economy rankings. Retrieved from www.doingbusiness.org/rankings.

PART III
Regional Approaches

9 | Spirituality and Workplace Diversity Practices in Africa

KURT A. APRIL, THABO MAKGOBA, AND DION A. FORSTER

Introduction

Diversity management, which is well established as a concept in many industrialized economies, has not been understood in its broadest sense within most African workplaces. Additionally, an uncritical adoption of Westernized diversity management practices within Africa leaves it vulnerable to the further exploitation of human potential through maximum-extraction managerialist philosophies (April & Blass, 2010). From the perspectives of spirituality and religion in the workplace, such narrow, morally questionable and resource-leveraging ideologies rob the African worker of his/her relationship to the sacred, hindering the deeply meaningful possibilities that difference and diversity can potentially offer them and the workplace. Diversity, and its multiple manifestations in the workplace are not problems to be solved by management, or pathologies (Costea & Introna, 2004) which need to be eradicated – but rather necessary conditions for allowing individual and communal spiritual growth. It is for this reason that we will discuss diversity in its broader sense within the African workplace, citing three cases of lived experience that illustrate the complex intersections of spirituality and workplace diversity in, and for, Africa. Spirituality, and notions of spiritual consciousness, permeate virtually every aspect of Africans lives, including their home lives, their interactions in families, communities, as well as in their workplaces – it affects how they think, what they value and how they are likely to behave (Paris, 1995; Forster, 2010a,b; Ngunjiri, 2016).

Literature Review and Theoretical Framework

The term "diversity" has been described variously in the academic literature as, for example, multiculturalism associated with visible characteristics such as race and ethnicity (Mendoza-Denton & Espana, 2010), individual differences within cultural contexts such as age, status, ability, sexual orientation, immigration status, thinking styles, psychological profiles, education, and national origin (Hicks, 2003; April & Shockley, 2007; Herring, 2009), and, visible and invisible social identity groups such as religious and spiritual identity, class, immigration status and ethnicity (Schaeffer & Mattis, 2012). Schaeffer and Mattis (2012) claim that such identities impact on: (1) the representation of individuals in private and public spheres, (2) individuals' access to opportunities and resources, and (3) their intellectual, social, economic, physical, and socio-political welfare (Uygur & Aydin, 2015).

Spirituality, another invisible aspect in the diverse context of work, is increasingly gaining importance in business and management research (Kutcher et al., 2010; Doran & Natale, 2011). This is particularly important in the African context where, in general terms, religion and spirituality remain important aspects of individual and social identity with implications for all spheres of life (including economics and work life). John Mbiti (1990) notes that "African peoples experience modern changes as a religious phenomenon, and respond to it in search of a stability that is fundamentally coloured by a religious outlook" (p. 257). The literature on religion in Africa largely supports this view. There are two important aspects of this statement that require some consideration. First, the notions of Africa and the African are often viewed too simplistically or narrowly from outside of the continent. A single African religious or cultural identity is a significant oversimplification of this vast and diverse continent and its people. There are a multitude of social, cultural, and religious differences among the persons and groups that inhabit the African continent. The cultures of Southern, Eastern, Western, and Northern Africans differ greatly; so too do their traditional and contemporary religious beliefs and practices (Mbiti, 1990, pp. 256–7; Bongmba, 2012, pp. 14–15). Indeed, there is no single Africa, African culture, or African religion. Yet, while this is true, there are some religious traits and spiritual characteristics that bear similarity across large cultural and geographic sectors of the continent. This is the second aspect of the above quote that deserves some consideration. Africans, in large measure, tend to be religious in outlook. African traditional religions, and the Abrahamic faiths (primarily Christianity and Islam), are widespread and influential in the formation of individual and social identity on the African continent (Mbiti, 1990, p. 257; Forster, 2010b, pp. 243–4; Bongmba, 2012, pp. 14–15). The dualism that exists between faith and life in some parts of the western world is largely foreign to the African person (Thorpe, 1991). Identity and meaning are deeply shaped and informed by tacitly held and overtly practiced religious convictions that inform ethics, social identity, economic, and political ideals (Forster, 2010a,b; Bongmba, 2012, pp. 430–43). Africa is a deeply religious continent, even though the religious convictions differ regionally. The construction of meaning in the face of adversity is often framed in religious symbolism, language, and rituals (Mbiti, 1990, p. 257; Bongmba, 2012, p. 430). The continuum of life between material reality and spiritual reality is of great importance for African communities and persons. Thorpe (1991) sums up this worldview as follows:

> [h]ealth, balance, harmony, order, continuity are all key words. They not only describe a desirable present condition for individuals and the community, but also represent the goal towards which people constantly strive. This ideal needs to be maintained not only within the visible community but equally in relation to the invisible community, conceptualized as spiritual powers (e.g., the ancestors). (p. 111)

Thus, since African religion and spirituality are such an important consideration for identity and meaning making, they should be considered in relation to workplace diversity.

To understand "spirituality," Ashforth and Pratt (2003) suggest that we use the following major dimensions. First, *transcendence of self*, which they define as a connection to something greater than oneself (e.g., other people, causes, nature, and belief in a higher power); second, *holism and harmony*, which they associate with authenticity, balance, and perspective; and third, *growth*, which they regard as the realization of one's aspirations and potential. The combination of these concepts is best described by Evans (1990), who views spirituality as connected to what I am (identity) and what I must become (meaning, control, and growth).

In their desire for a more humane workplace, many individuals are defining themselves as "seekers" (Lofland & Stark, 1965), who are less willing to consign their spirituality to non-work hours and domains (Ashforth & Pratt, 2003). The seekers are thus searching for spiritual fulfillment, especially in work settings (Forster, 2014; Mitroff et al., 1999). Giacalone and Jurkiewicz (2003) define "workplace spirituality" as organizational values promoting employees' experience of transcendence and facilitating their sense of being and connection to others. They further describe workplace spirituality in terms of practical and ethical utility, the former producing better work outputs and the latter ensuring that such work is held within a moral framework. Table 9.1 highlights the various aspects that make up

Table 9.1 *The dimensionality of spirituality*

Spiritual dimension	Description	Source
Spiritual well-being	The affirmation of life in a relationship with God, self, community, and environment. Nurtures and celebrates wholeness.	Ellison (1983)
Spiritual transcendence	(a) The capacity of individuals to stand outside of their immediate sense of time and place to view life from a larger, more objective perspective.	Piedmont (1999)
Spiritual development	The process of incorporating spiritual experiences that result ultimately in spiritual transformation.	Chandler & Holder (1992)
Spiritual wellness	(b) The openness to the spiritual dimension that permits the integration of one's spirituality with the other dimensions of life, thus maximizing the potential for growth and self-actualization.	Westgate (1996, p. 27)
Spiritual needs	Any factors necessary to establish and/or maintain a person's dynamic personality relationship with God (as defined by that individual) and out of that relationship to experience forgiveness, love, hope, trust, and meaning and purpose in life.	Stallwood & Stoll (1975, p. 1088)
Spiritual distress	A disruption of the life principle that pervades a person's entire being and that integrates and transcends one's biological and psycho-social nature.	Kim et al. (1987, p. 314)
Spiritual intelligence	Abilities and competencies that may be part of an individual's expert knowledge. These include the capacity to transcend the physical and material, the capacity to be virtuous, and the ability to experience heightened states of consciousness, sanctify everyday experience, and utilize spiritual resources to solve problems.	Emmons & Crumbler (1999)

Table 9.1 (cont.)

Spiritual dimension	Description	Source
Spiritual (religious)	The extent to which individuals reflect on their faith and beliefs.	Leak & Fish (1999)
Spiritual growth and self-consciousness	Reflective of the gratification of individual needs, especially "belonging" and those of a higher order, such as a "sense of achievement."	Burack (1999)
Spiritual health	(c) Its optimal function is the enhancement of spiritual oneness with whatever a person considers to be more than oneself as an individual with reason, experience, and intuition; the ongoing development of an adherence to a responsible ethical system.	Stroudenmire et al. (1986)

Source: Giacalone & Jurkiewicz, 2003.

the definition of workplace spirituality (spirituality) as connected to the following variables: well-being, transcendence/meaning, personal identity, other dimension of life, needs, personal safety, belonging, and self-consciousness.

Clegg and Bailey (2009) suggest that a helpful approach to "integrating spirituality in the workplace is through sacred or ultimate or whole-system values which enable the human spirit to grow and flourish." They point out that an additional benefit of these "time-honored, life-affirming, and unifying values, are that they can also enhance profit and productivity" as well as the furtherance of "truth and trust (which liberate the soul), freedom and justice (which liberate creative and co-creative genius), creativity and innovation, collective harmony and intelligence, wholeness, synergy, deeper meaning, and higher purpose" (2009, p. 1176). We intend to explore some of the personal testimony of issues of conflict that may result from exclusion in the workplace, resulting inequality of opportunity and resource access, as well as differing mental models. Within the context of the workplace, issues of spirituality and religion raise a central paradox: if the locus of spirituality is the individual and its focus, work organizations would not seem to be readily compatible with spiritual striving or spiritual-individual congruence. We have used the (interrelated) theoretical constructs of "palliative," "via media," and "transformative" as the categorizations through which we intend to discuss issues relating to such congruence, or lack thereof.

The Palliative Category

Authors, whom we broadly put into the *palliative category* of spirituality, include most religious mystics and current writers who write on spirituality, centered on the individual's interiority, and the individual's longing/feeling for self-actualization through cognitive development (Merton, 1961; Carson, 1992; Nouwen, 1994; Keating, 1999; Gibbons, 2000; Fluker, 2003; Runcorn, 2006; Rohr, 2013) – with some even linking it to cognitive development (Vaill, 2000; Wilber, 2001). How such thinking, feelings, values, and vocations are translated in the workplace and broader community is dependent on the definitional interpretations of the individual (Mitroff et al., 1999; Tischler, 1999; Olupona, 2000; Zohar, 2000; Lamont, 2002; Williams, 2004; Zohar & Marshall, 2004; Mbete, 2006; Volf, 2001). Writing from the perspective of sexuality in religion, Dunn and Ambige (2004, p. 68) offer the following definition:

… spirituality in general is grounded in the human search for ultimate reality and value, and finds expression in the basic attitudes and the practices that embody them. It embraces the whole of life, beginning with our intimate relationship with the God who made us and loves us. It pervades and transforms all aspects of our being, both mind and body. It embraces all our communal and interpersonal relationships, as it reaches out in service to others and commits us to justice.

Dunn and Ambige may have a potentially radical topic, but they are in fact, outlining a fairly conventional definition of spirituality as serving the individual in forming a connection with God (Hernandez, 2016; Williams, 1990; Nolan, 2006a) that is expressed in community (Thurman, 1984; Fluker, 2003; Williams, 2004), while still managing to present spirituality as an interpersonal concept with an intrapersonal locus of control (Hood, 1992; Lamont, 2002). This focus motivated the authors of this chapter to undertake an in-depth exploration of the possible "intra-individual" psychological processes (Jung, 1966) that may be at play in spiritual development (Williams, 1990; Goleman, 1998) and that may assist in defining workplace spirituality with more rigor.

There are various authors who have written about the psychological and psychosocial stages of development, for example, Piaget (1971), Kohlberg (1981), and Erickson (1995). In these same studies, there is a lack of consensus on moral or spiritual development (Vygotsky, 1978; Peck, 1980; Gilligan, 1998). Wilber (2000, p. 129) defines spiritual development as a linear process that involves the transpersonal, trans-rational attitude and the highest moral achievement. On the other hand, Capra (1982, p. 59) defines spiritual experience as an experience of the aliveness of mind and body as a unity. Goleman (1998) and Albert (2006) add yet another key dimension to consciousness development, and ultimately, spiritual development, called emotional intelligence. These authors (Capra, 1982; Goleman, 1998; Wilber, 2000; Albert, 2006) attempt to explore spiritual development within the nature–nurture debate, and link its development to the process of how, in particular, cognition develops. There are a few more authors in this palliative category who regard spiritual development as being the same as, or akin to, cognitive development. For example, Vaill (2000) states that spiritual intelligence is a process of wisdom that involves four elements, namely: (1) grounding in existence, (2) appreciation of openness of the human spirit, (3) understanding of human consciousness, and (4) an appreciation of the spirituality of humankind. Zohar and Marshall (2004), on the other hand, write of spiritual intelligence as a way by which we address and solve problems of meaning and value, or an intelligence with which we can assess our course of action as we wrestle with questions of good and evil. These authors argue that spiritual development has to do with our dreams, our aspirations, and our intuitive thinking (Olupona, 2000; Mbete, 2006). Zohar (2000), referring to spirituality and not spiritual intelligence, defines it as encompassing self-awareness, spontaneity, vision, and values (Mitroff et al., 1999; Tischler, 1999; Lamont, 2002). She adds that spirituality is about being holistic and compassionate, and enabling a celebration of diversity. Zohar (2000) further states that it is, nevertheless, field independent, as spirituality asks the "why" questions, reframing positive outcomes from adversity. She concludes that spirituality is about vocation. In sum, the palliative category views spirituality as a concept that has to do with interiority, as earlier described by Williams (2004), and as felt by the individual. How such feelings and vocation are translated in the community is dependent on the definitional interpretations of the individual (Zohar, 2000; Fluker, 2003).

What this summary does not address is what happens when an individual's vocation is nurtured by a value system different from that held by their community. This may include the value system(s) of organizations (Habermas, 1970). Who is responsible for regulating this vocation? Whose values should be upheld? We therefore turn to the "via media" approach which seems to offer a possible explanation here.

The via Media Category

Writers in the *via media category* (also known as the "inclusive approach") argue that spirituality cannot be limited to interiority, but rather should be linked to the wider context, and therefore key elements of spirituality as consisting of religion and God, and their relationship as expressed in community (Williams, 1982; Sheldrake & Fox, 1997; Sheldrake, 1998; Gibbons, 2000; Fluker, 2003; Forster, 2010a). These writers acknowledge that the phenomenon of spirituality lacks sufficient conceptuality, particularly as it relates to the workplace, pastoral care, and phenomenological and existential issues. They integrate an emphasis on a deity and palliative care with consideration of the communal context, thereby offering a continuum from the individual to the community, rather than an either/or model. The middle or "via media" authors view spirituality as a religious "accommodationist orientation" that places the individual's search for interiority in a broader communal context (Thurman, 1984; Wilber, 1998; Gibbons, 2000; Williams, 2004; Nolan, 2006a). There are also those in this category who reject religion, but appropriate its values, as described in Legge's (1995) normative category of spirituality. Those whom Legge (1995) classifies as secular seek to integrate the generic values of spirituality into the place of work. There are writers who urge a critical dialogue in this domain, but argue that this dialogue must accept the historical location of spirituality in the field of religion (William, 1982; Sheldrake, 1998; Howard & Welbourne, 2004). Nolan (2006a,b) concurs with the view expressed above, but from the perspective of human rights and the tenets of liberation theology in the context of South Africa. He defines the search for ultimate reality, or spirituality, as a revolutionary journey. In line with this, Wilber (2000) suggests that spirituality cannot merely be a private and personal enterprise that comforts and soothes the individual (Green, 2007), but that it must also lead to a radical transformation of the individual, enabling this individual to be an agent of social change in the world (Nolan, 2006b). Spirituality, viewed through this lens, is linked to human rights, ethics, and the tenets of liberation theology in post-colonial contexts in Africa (Williams, 1982; Sheldrake & Fox, 1997; Sheldrake, 1998; Gibbons, 2000; Wilber, 2000; Fluker, 2003; Nolan, 2006a,b; Tshaka, 2014). Spirituality is therefore understood as the whole spiritual experience, or orientation, of a person or group, involving their beliefs, ways of thinking, feelings, and relationships (Thurman, 1984; Venter, 2004; Forster, 2010a). When individuals suffer, their spiritual connection must move them to overcome their suffering for the benefit of all (Slosson Wuellner, 1998; Walters, 2001). Spirituality then becomes an all-encompassing concept, including behaviors and the attitudes and expectations that underlie behavior (Sheldrake & Fox, 1997; Thurman, 1981; Williams, 1990). There are scholars who would argue that, even though spirituality overlaps with ethics, it cannot be reduced to ethics alone (Sheldrake, 1998). From the "via media" perspective, spirituality is not exclusive, but "connects" with ethics (Sheep, 2006). Ethics enables spirituality to raise questions about the consequences of behavior (Fry, 2003), as well as issues of personal identity as they relate to the good of others (Goldsby et al., 1998; Goleman, 1998).

How does spirituality influence an individual whose social practices and policies degrade that individual's religious practices (Miller & Miller, 2002)? Resorting to Archbishop Williams' 1990 formulation of spirituality is useful at this stage. He affirms the notion that spirituality cannot be limited to interiority, but that: "it must seek to integrate all aspects of human experience, it must touch every area of human experience, public and social, painful and negative, even the pathological byways of the mind, and the moral and relational world ... spirituality is never abstract or pure in form" (cited in Sheldrake, 1998, p. 59). Williams (1990) suggests that spirituality cannot relate to a vacuum, but must shape and be inculturated by its encounter with its context (Shorter, 2006, pp. 10–13). His conceptualization not only assists in addressing the perceived dualism (Peck, 1980; Foucault, 1985) that usually exists between spiritual-scientific, technological-economic, and socio-cultural, but it also highlights the possible underlying value or motif of spirituality (Forster, 2010b). He emphasizes that spirituality pervades the whole spectrum of life, as we experience a sense of the aliveness of the mind and body as a unit (Capra, 1982). This experience of transcendent unity should not only mend the separation of mind and body (Merton, 1961; Peck, 1980), but also mend the split between the self and the world (Moe-Lobeda, 2002; Makgoba, 2005; Forster, 2010b).

The Transformative Category

Within the *transformative category* (also known as the "critical approach" or "prophetic approach") there is a general agreement that mainly rejects the relationship of spirituality to religion (Legge, 1995; Carrette & King, 2004; Kvarfordt & Sheridan, 2007). What is most important to this group is the premise that spirituality must move individuals compassionately to be agents of social change and justice in the world, to evaluate the material conditions of all in society (Sobrino, 1988; Ackers & Preston, 1997; Tischler, 1999; Bell & Taylor, 2001; Carrette & King, 2004; Kvarfordt & Sheridan, 2007), to confront the unfettered capitalism that alienates communities and individuals in its pursuit of profit (Groody, 2007), and that such agency should not be appropriated by religion (Ackers & Preston, 1997; Bell & Taylor, 2001; Gibbons, 2000; Howard & Welbourne, 2004). Writers in this group (e.g., Gibbons, 2000; Howard & Welbourne, 2004) argue that there cannot be neat distinctions between different facets of human experience, such as religious, secular, techno-economic, legal, or scientific. Individuals need to evaluate their material conditions holistically, along with the system that dictates relations among those conditions and other facets of their experience (Tischler, 1999).

Finally, writers in this third category are suspicious of an inclusive, global spirituality (Carrette & King, 2004), especially when it seems to be repackaged within a religious tradition (du Toit, 2006). They reject the "accommodationist orientation" and argue for a spirituality that is devoid of any religious connections.

Carrette and King (2004) argue that we need less emphasis on definitional issues, and more on confronting the unfettered capitalism that alienates communities and individuals in its pursuit of profit (Groody, 2007). The question still is: How can researchers, within the bounds and limitations of empiricism (Habermas, 1970, 1988), operationalize a spirituality of compassion and social justice? If spirituality cannot address this issue, including engaging with situations of economic injustice (Engelbrecht et al., 2005), then we must concede that there is a need for alternatives. Therefore, spirituality needs to be understood

Spirituality and Workplace Diversity Practices in Africa 233

to encompass all aspects of life (Cavanaugh, 1999). It should be transformative, and it needs to be liberated from its current captors (Boje, 2000; Gibbons, 2000). Perhaps venues such as African spirituality may provide an alternative conceptualization that could transform the whole discourse of spirituality (Forster, 2010b; Tshaka, 2014).

Having presented the three main conceptualizations of spirituality in the workplace (i.e. palliative, via-media, and transformative), we showed that spirituality, as the state and process of transcendence, is necessarily about the individual: extending the boundaries of self, striving for holism and harmony of self, and developing the self. Table 9.2 summarizes the description of the three categories discussed.

Individual Approaches to Religion, Spirituality and Work: Case Studies

Toledano and Karanda (2014) claim that studies of the individual journeys and subjective experiences of successful individuals are largely absent, and in particular the broader spiritual aspects of

Table 9.2 *Key features of the three conceptualizations of spirituality in the workplace*

Framework of spirituality	Key features
Palliative	• Has to do with interiority • Human search for ultimate reality • Serving the individual in forming a connection with God • Linked to "intra-individual" psychological processes • A linear process that involves the transpersonal, trans-rational attitude and the highest moral achievement • An experience of the aliveness of mind and body as a unity • Linked to emotional intelligence and cognitive development • Encompassing self-awareness, spontaneity, vision, and values • Being holistic and compassionate, and enabling a celebration of diversity

(*cont.*)

Table 9.2 *(cont.)*

Framework of spirituality	Key features
Via media	• Cannot be limited to interiority but rather linked to the wider context • Consisting of religion and God, and their relationship as expressed in community • Seculars seek to integrate the generic values of spirituality into the place of work • Historical location of spirituality located in the field of religion • Linked to human rights and the tenets of liberation theology in postcolonial contexts, such as in South Africa • Involving beliefs, ways of thinking, feelings, and relationships • Encompassing behaviors and the attitudes and expectations that underlie behavior • Not exclusive, but connected with ethics • Addressing the perceived dualism that usually exists between spiritual-scientific, technological-economic, and socio-cultural • Mending the separation of mind and body and of self and the world
Transformative	• Rejecting the relationship of spirituality to religion • Spirituality must move individuals to be agents of change in the world • Agency should not be appropriated by religion • Confronting capitalism that alienates communities and individuals in its pursuit of profit • Need to operationalize a spirituality of compassion and social justice • Can use models such as African spirituality in encompassing all aspects of life

these journeys (Reid et al., 2015). Pedagogy most often requires a phenomenological sensitivity to lived experience (lifeworlds) and a hermeneutic ability to make interpretive sense of the phenomena of the lifeworld in order to understand the relations of people to their unique environment. In her seminal work, Ngunjiri (2010, p. 183) profiles African and African-descent women, suggesting that spirituality is the modus operandi and raison d'être for their leadership and life. Unfortunately, Africa's workplace leaders' experiences are, in the main, described through the lenses of writers outside of Africa, and therefore the cases provided here help to situate some of the complexities of African life with respect to diverse, personal strivings within workplace contexts.

Methodology

Our three case studies are drawn from individuals who have deep personal, work connections with, or was born in and/or worked extensively in Africa. One of our respondents produced a relevant, self-reported piece about her situated-experience to this book chapter, during her MBA studies, and was recently asked for the anonymous inclusion thereof. We approached two other respondents (one providing permission to be named, and the other requested to stay anonymous) to write their own personal stories (in rich and thick descriptions), and to also self-report their lived experiences with respect to the role of spirituality within their personal- and work lives (phenomenological orientation), i.e., apart from grammatical edits (and anonymising in two cases), each of the case studies are in the words of the case respondents, and this was done to retain the authenticity of "voice" in the case studies.

Case Study 1: Samantha King

An Introduction to the Case Study

With respect to the palliative understanding of spirituality within the workplace, we see a number of problems that could arise when individuals have to suppress, alter or deny their intra-personal locus of control, interiority and/or personal value systems (spiritual core) in order to serve larger workplace dynamics and values, which may not be akin with their own. In our work, we find that there are many successful executives going through extreme mental stress and anxiety, but, because of the stigma of mental disease and fear of feeling less than capable, do not speak up about it. Samantha King (affectionately known around the globe as Sammy), Global Head of Executive Development in an international bank, had the courage to share her authentic and powerful narrative and covers a number of important issues: the lure of the economic machine (and the personal cost of narrowly defined apparent-success), the challenges of international work, the difficulty of balancing being a mom/wife/executive, the never-mentioned mental and emotional downside of continuous stress, the resilience it takes to overcome health and life's challenges, the gendered nature of work, the importance of spirituality/community/support/partner/friends, and the need to make constructive choices. The personal narrative that follows is illustrative of the palliative category of spirituality. The reader may find it helpful to keep the summary of the key features of palliative spirituality at hand (outlined in Table 9.2).

Sammy King's Narrative

The Build-up
Never take a person's dignity: It is worth everything to them, and nothing to you.
Frank Barron (in Storlie, 2015, p. 87)

October 2008   As the world melted into the global financial crisis, I must be one of the only people who missed it completely as I disappeared into oblivion with my own meltdown. I seemed to hit a wall, rather overwhelmed by competing commitments as I just failed to adapt to the reality of a fast changing and unbelievably uncertain world. That is a bit of a problem for humanity, if that happens, as this "new normal" as the Chinese call it, is not likely to calm down. As my dear Mum said at this point, "Sam, take all the time you need to recover, because you've worked so hard to earn this!" So how on earth did I get there, as a psychology graduate and executive coach, who should have known better?

October 1989 to October 2007   Always enthusiastic at home and work, I am known for volunteering for everything and rising to unusual challenges. Career-wise, I found myself the perfect niche, ironically as a creative change architect, cross-cultural facilitator, and leadership coach. My most privileged job is to invite leaders to tell their authentic stories to engage others' hearts, minds and souls, with a passion and purpose and to help them connect more meaningfully with their company's highest purpose. I have always been proud of being a bit of rare commodity, a so-called "high potential" pioneer, a mad mother of four beautiful children with an international career and a patient (and adventurous) husband who does the same. I was often told that I was a great role model. How wrong they were!!

I am offering my story now, showing the key factors leading up to cancer, a breakdown, and the self-care steps I have since taken to try and ensure that history does not repeat itself. It is so hard for me to make myself vulnerable in writing, as I'm always self-critical – but if it helps anyone to avoid the mistakes I made, it would be worth it. So this story is for anyone out there, setting goals too high, struggling to manage too much life, or drowning in a myriad of roles and the expectations of others, despite your best intentions. Whatever you do, don't forget you, and don't lose touch with your soul.

In summary, after 18 years of working, I had developed a few habits and self-beliefs that were unknowingly compromising my own health, formed from a horrible cocktail of ingredients: an extreme work dedication and devoted love of my company, a need to prove I was worthy or nearly equal, and, a need to belong and stay rather than walk away. Furthermore, I was probably too externally referenced with a desire to be appreciated by "those who mattered" (foolishly, even a few who I didn't respect!). Throughout my career, there have been many great leaders I loved working for, whom I was totally inspired by, but I also lost the ability to know that sometimes you just have to say no, or even let people down. Finally, all this was topped with a dose of motherhood guilt and never ending work tensions. We had tried everything to manage our four lovely kids, so they never suffered: by then, I had taken a total of five years off and sometimes worked part-time, and have a rare husband who has always starred in the extremely-high-contribution-at-home stakes, such as doing the household cooking and food shopping. I had every chance to make this work, everything to be grateful for.

My highly productive public CV contrasted with an emerging underground CV, hiding a different reality. I now suspect that working in manufacturing in mostly male business teams had unwittingly eaten away at my confidence and self-belief. Having privately dealt with gender-related incidents over my career had led to a certain kind of very low emotional exhaustion. In 2004, I passed my company's external agency job selection panel with flying colors except for scoring a fat zero for emotional resilience. That should have been a warning sign. Living with regular threats of redundancy and mistrusting climates had also taken its toll. Overall, I developed an unhelpful habit of shutting off emotions to say "I'm fine." Consequently, I found myself working superhuman hours, particularly over a two-year period from 2006 to 2008, with intense international travel under high pressure in an extreme culture.

March 2007 A day after moving house, I take one of my children to the doctor for suspected Autism Spectrum Disorder (ASD), which becomes increasingly evident as we try to move schools. The scary world of special needs and the prejudice the world has against your child had just been entered. We were shocked by how quickly society can potentially reject children through thoughtless comments and institutional decisions, and the power schools have in these processes. It's a lonely and confusing new journey, yet we are living with an intense need to understand, defend, protect and help our child. Thankfully we have some advantage with my psychology background. However, like any parents, we just struggle to do our best in a complex system. After late nights of mammoth research and paperwork, our child is soon diagnosed and awarded a high level of weekly support by September.

My support networks shift, it takes a while to build them in the new village, but my church, families with three to four children, and now those also with ASD become a common feature that is a huge blessing. Now I seem to keep visiting a vast array of GPs who hand out sleeping tablets, which, with a combination of vitamin supplements, I have learnt to feed my habit of either sleeping only three hours a night or completely working through the night to cope with the work pressures and redundancy worries. I must have looked dreadful. Interestingly, the only one I remember commenting one day was the outsourced IT crew who apparently wanted to call for site medical services as they thought I was going to collapse one morning. As someone with stamina who ran a marathon at 21, I've always considered myself a bit of an ox ... my body felt like it was carrying on, so why be lazy?! You have to keep going.

October 2007 One more exhausting but very silly incident happens in the workplace. Suddenly the next day, for the first time ever, I cannot go into work. I sit at home, mindless, soulless and almost catatonic, for nearly three months, I have no idea what will happen next. As the main earner, the fear of losing my job, the house – all are my fault, was added pressure. I just sit engulfed with my fears, reaching no-one and asking for no help. For once in my life I am mostly alone – for an extrovert, this is an acute trauma! Ironically stopping work then possibly saved my life, as I soon visit the doctor with symptoms I had ignored for years.

Not Quite So Invincible

Whatever happens to your body, your soul will survive, untouched ...
                                                J. K. Rowling (2014, p. 60)

January 8, 2008 With a clatter of pots and pans, and squabbles over who would set the table, this was an ordinary night in the King household. I could hear them chatting, joking and preparing dinner, our four kids and my husband were cooking, with my Mum staying with us. I was sitting in our office with a gut wrenching torment – how could I find easier words – that kept our world safe – than the ones the doctor had just given me? "You've got cancer" ... The words you dread and never imagine will apply to you. Should I hide it from them? Braver folk do. I also remember feeling somewhat angry, for losing my apparent inherited right to live to over 90 – as my two grannies had! It was a lot to take in.

Having sought family help, good options opened up of course. Fortunately, my surgeon was a world renowned breast cancer expert and trusted colleague of my father-in-law, who had also had a lifelong career as a professor of research in breast cancer. I knew I was damn lucky. I had access to the National Health Service (NHS, UK) with great treatment and the best advice. A few shocks along the way: I didn't expect to have to make decisions. I thought doctors just told you what to do when it got serious. Having a quick and simple operation to remove the cancer was a no brainer, but awaiting results to see what would be next for two to three weeks was agony. I remember looking up awful pictures of mastectomies, desperately afraid, and feeling the deep shock of not wanting to trust or live in your own body any more. "Me" might attack me. So who was "me," if not your body?! You are forced into a world of thinking thoughts you never knew existed.

Throughout my life, I've had a strong faith buttressed on my spirituality, but sometimes it disappears into the darkness, only to leap back like a bright light. Each time a tragedy has occurred, if I just hold on long enough to breathe and look up, I notice a guardian angel appears. It's a "God-incident" that I met my life partner the year before my only brother took his own life. Then, little guardians, the pediatrician happened to be changing her teapot the day our three-year old daughter eye-butted a crystal vase in a department store. Then, to support my cancer, God invites me to a new Bible home group a week before I get my cancer news, with not less than three wiser loving women, each of whom had survived breast cancer. Then the angel in the hospital the night I had my own cancer operation! I awoke from my post-operative slumber around midnight in an almost empty, small ward, to see a lovely lady sitting upright in bed with a bright light over her head, in a kind of halo effect. She was apparently in her fifties and having follow-up treatment after a mastectomy. We both had the same fabled surgeon, everyone's hero, which brought us immediately into shared understanding. Through my nervous hyper chatter, she sensed my fear of a second operation like hers, if I had to. She kindly showed me her surgery and I was amazed at what an incredible job he had done. He's known for fighting for women's rights to have the best immediate reconstruction treatment, if they wish to, so you never wake up "without." It's funny to suddenly feel deeply grateful and lucky in dire moments like these. The rollercoaster of emotions had really begun.

In my very fortunate case, I was told yes it was cancer but all perfectly contained and removed. But, "Mrs King, would you be wanting the radiotherapy now to remove the risk of recurrence or leave it till later to zap yourself when/if it returns – because you can only ever do it once?" Statistics were given to me but nothing went in. I lost the ability to hear and remember. I had already started recording the short sharp sessions with doctors, to replay and help me understand. I researched for hours into the early hours of the morning on the Internet, reading papers I could never understand. I worried, I tormented, I prevaricated. Eventually my wise oncologist made sense to me.

I was only 39 – hopefully, I had years ahead with my youngest only aged three, and I wanted to live my main life with the least risk and worry possible. So I went for the radiotherapy. I learnt how very few decisions in life really matter, only those that are truly irreversible.

Another shock was how cancer affects friendships. At the time you need them the most, people can respond in surprising ways, as some back off and some step up most generously. New and old lifelong buddies brought food, picnics, practical moments – I was especially grateful for the ones who took care of my kids and husband, not just me. Saying that, at the time, I also remember feeling inadequate – letting the kids down. Learning to ask for help and take it was not something I had yet mastered!

I chose to be gradually open with friends but protectively private from work. In mostly all male teams, where I felt vulnerable, I didn't want them to know at first what kind of cancer it was. Then later, only as I knew more about my positive cancer destiny, I shared with those I trusted to find out that many had experienced the pain of loved ones around them. I found that deep human truth, that connecting on real things is a true gift. You don't need to say anything. To those who had lost close family members, I was inconsolably useless. Their grief became mine. Then, I had real limits to how much I could hold others' pain.

So my life chapter became one of fighting and wanting to live longer and more. I got into a routine, even brought my kids along to view me being zapped in the machine. Seeing people of all ages with cancer every day has profound effects, and I always knew I had been through nothing compared to those who were going through chemotherapy, which I thought of as "real cancer," mine was "just pretend."

Work-wise, another guardian angel had stepped in to give me a great project, with unending flexibility and support to help my recovery. This gave me a positive focus, and I even attended a large global event I'd helped to arrange just a few weeks after the operation. I was so keen to never give up trying, although it was probably such behavior that got me ill in the first place.

But the seven weeks of nearly daily radiotherapy took its toll on me, surprisingly. Much older women were bouncing back, but I was living a life of misery, exhausted by the increasing effort of trying not to sleep through school pick up time. I hated what, to me, felt like begging for help – I probably didn't make it clear, as people were only too willing. At night I hated the sensation of my body burning, so I couldn't sleep. I felt so guilty for not coping, and it just got worse. I totally lost sense of time as every minute became painful and yet months went by. I have little memory of being a mother at that time, such a horrible, scary thought. They were so young (four, eight, nine, 11 years), I am sure we must have had lovely cuddly and caring moments. Actually I do remember them bringing tea and thoughtful snacks on a plate to me, which made me feel guilty. However, mostly, and so sadly, I remember that the noise of just the family having fun, never mind being irritable, had begun to be excruciating for me. I am sure it was hell for them to be neglected. Bless them all for coping without me and forgiving my absence.

Preliminary Reflection

Sammy King's narrative illustrates the complex intersection of personal well-being, work pressure, and gender dynamics. In this narrative one can identify numerous characteristics of a palliative spirituality. These include the search for ultimate reality in the midst of daily expectations and pressures, the "intra-individual" psychological processes at work in the midst of this traumatic life moment, as well as the development and emergence of aspects of emotional intelligence, self-awareness, the reshaping of values, and the appreciation of diversity.

Case Study 2: SM2 – Senior Manager 2 (Congolese-American)

An Introduction to the Case Study

With respect to the via media category of spirituality, we will use the case of SM2, a Congelese-American Project Manager, to discuss the real and perceived problems, and inner and outer "conflict," that arise when people encounter attitudes, behaviors and mental models/constructs with which they fundamentally disagree, or which serve to belittle them (Thurman, 1981; Slosson Wuellner, 1998; Williams, 1990; Walters, 2001). SM2 has lived in Germany for the past eight years, and has worked as Consultant Engineer for a German engineering firm. Prior to moving to Germany, she worked as a Design Engineer in the state of Texas (USA). She has recently started a company that focuses on smart and clean energy technology solutions, which she is looking at implementing in Africa. As suggested in the introduction to the previous case study, it would be helpful to keep the summary of the key features of the via media category of spirituality at hand while reading this case study (refer to Table 9.2).

SM2's Narrative

Spirituality has always played a very important role in my private life, and also in my professional life. I was baptized in the Catholic Church at the age of twelve, after I asked my parents for it. Very often, the sacrament of baptism is administered to babies in the Catholic Church. My paternal grandmother used to take my brother and I to mass on Sundays. I still had memories of how lively mass was celebrated in the Democratic Republic of Congo. We danced to all the songs, except the *Kyrie eleison* [A liturgical prayer meaning: "Lord, have mercy"].

Over time, my parents grew dissatisfied with the Catholic mass celebration, as they did not feel fed on the word of God and, in their words, the Bible was not made alive. They converted to a form of evangelical celebration, where the focus was on the Word (the Bible) and less on man-made rituals. I learned a lot about how to live according to the Word, and applying the Word to any situation in which I found myself. I applied religious teaching and values at school – praying before exams, asking for good grades, and loving my neighbour. I learned to become tolerant – I went to mass with my catholic friends and to the evangelical church with my evangelical friends.

When I started my tertiary studies, at the Polytechnic Faculty of Mons in Belgium, I was so absorbed by the demands of engineering school that my spiritual life took a back seat. Masses in Belgium were very dull, and mostly attended by elderly people. Engineering school was tough and I could not manage to get good grades – I ended up failing the first year of my studies. I had a second chance to repeat the year, which I did and I failed again. At that point in my life, I thought that I knew exactly what the reasons were for my failure. I was a smart girl and very good at subjects like Mathematics and Physics. After all, that was the main reason I decided to go to engineering school in the first place. Of course, my dad's influence (he was a qualified engineer) played a key role in helping me make that choice. In my most difficult times of failure, I felt that I needed to reignite my prayer life again. I began asking God to assist me to achieve good grades – there was an inner knowing that I had to put God first in my life again, otherwise I would not be able to achieve my dream of becoming an engineer.

I then decided to get my spiritual life back on track while going to both Catholic masses and evangelical celebrations.

Once again, I applied to an overseas university and got admitted to the University of Texas at Arlington, where I graduated with a Bachelor of Science in Electrical Engineering. After graduation I started working at an energy plant in the state of Texas. My work life was very demanding. But, despite the rigorous schedule, I still managed to go to church on Sundays. It always seemed that the gentle hand of the Lord guided me and supported me in all my projects and assignments. I seemed to be very much appreciated by my peers and superiors.

The same atmosphere continued as I moved to go and work for a German consulting firm in Germany. I wanted a change and I wished to acquire new skills, while being exposed to other challenges professionally and, of course, to discover a different culture and work with new levels of diversity. For seven years, superficially, and on the periphery, things went very well. However, when I decided to become more involved in the company, something changed.

I have always been a double-minority (a black woman, and an African) in my studies in engineering, where I worked at the energy plant, and again at the consulting firm in Germany. It has never bothered me and, on the surface, I was not aware of any overt discrimination against me. However, recently my level of awareness was raised.

The southern part of Germany is a very conservative region. People in the region hold on tightly to family values (values shaped over time with people similar to themselves), and they have a strong sense of their southern, regional identity. There was a prominent ethnic group in the region in which I worked in Germany. Most of my friends were not very supportive of my decision when I announced that I was moving to that region to work. In fact, this decision has cost me my marriage, as my now ex-husband refused to join me there. Besides having run into some difficulties finding an apartment in the beginning of my stay, and experiencing some extra scrutiny when operating in public (e.g., presenting my credit card at certain points of sale) life appeared fine to me – since such stumbling blocks have been the norm for me in my engagements around the globe.

Then came the time where I thought I needed to be more involved at more senior levels at work. I considered taking a two-year break to study for an MBA at Harvard Business School. I starting campaigning for company support, and I was positively surprised that my company was willing to pay for 20% of the school fees. I was not very keen on interrupting my career while going to school, so I chose to go for the Executive MBA at Oxford University instead. I made sure that the company management was well informed of my desires to take on a leadership role, with more responsibilities upon graduation. I met up with the company CEO and CFO to let them know of my plans. They seemed to be very supportive at first. However, I had a sense that some of my co-workers, and direct managers, seemed intimidated by my ambitious proactivity in seeking to climb the corporate ladder. My direct boss was, however, quite surprised when I told him that I had been accepted into the Oxford MBA program – as if it was impossible for me (or someone like me) to make it to Oxford.

At the time I was the project manager of a hydro-power refurbishment project in Haiti, which I managed from Germany. An interesting opportunity opened up, as the client asked for the project manager to be permanently based in Haiti. I volunteered to go. I had been involved in that project for almost two years by then. I did not realize it at the time, but the division management saw it as an opportunity to get me away from head-office for a while. I negotiated for a better relocation package than what I was offered initially, but unfortunately my request was not honoured. I later learned that a white man was hired for that position and got more than what I asked for it terms of the relocation package. I ended up getting a warning for having refused to honour my employment contract. That meant that my career, and any prospects for professional growth and development in the company, came to a dead end, both in the present and potentially in the future also (given the company's usual practice). I was shifted off interesting projects at work. I very much liked my job. Being passed over for working on interesting and important projects felt like a death sentence to me. I kept reminding myself that it was all because of the fact that I was too engaged, too motivated, and wanting too much. Nevertheless, the quiet time at work allowed me to focus more of my time on my three-year-old daughter, as well as my studies.

I never gave up hope. My parents also prayed for me a lot. I had a deep sense of peace knowing that God was in control and everything would be just fine. As a matter of fact, what seemed like a curse was, in fact, a blessing. As I mentioned earlier, I was able to spend more time on my school assignments and I had time to explore other career opportunities. I took a leave of absence, and travelled to Nigeria to work with a classmate on an energy project there. I returned to work six months later and I was reintegrated into the team with an interesting project to work on. Just a few days after the reintegration, my department manager called me into his office. I thought I was going to be "put in my place" or even be fired. I prayed and asked God for wisdom and courage. Regardless of the outcome of that meeting I was going to be stronger and not show any tears. To my surprise, I was offered a promotion to the sales division. That was also the typical promotion career path for engineers in that company. That is what I had always been asking for, and I wondered why they finally gave it to me.

A colleague, who was promoted to the sales division a few years back, wanted to return to the engineering department. There was therefore the need for someone who spoke French to help out in the Francophone Africa sales division. I was finally promoted to what I thought was going to get me on the path to upper management – until I received a letter stating that I was going to do it for only three months, and then would need to go back to the engineering division. In the history of the company, it was the first time that a black person made it to that division. I felt that I had all that it took to succeed in that position – I spoke perfect French, I had been with the company for almost eight years at the time, I was well networked within the company, and I was Francophone African working for the Francophone African division of the company. It was a perfect match, but the position came with restrictions. Why wasn't I being given the full passport to perform? I had a micro-manager boss who did not trust in my capabilities as an engineer and either did not value the great education I was getting from Oxford University or felt threatened by it. I finally left the company.

Throughout my life, my spirituality has played a great role in fighting overt and less conscious forms of discrimination and, because of my faith, I have chosen to not confront the perpetrators with anger, nor with hate, but rather with courteousness and respect, and tried to use my good work to sway their beliefs and assumptions about people like me. It is a burden one carries, and it can be quite tiring – but, I cannot get away from my gender, my skin colour, nor my Africanness. My dad once told me that life is tough and even more so when you are black, and that I would always have to work harder than everybody else simply to get less than everybody else. These were my "truths."

In the beginning, I did just that and worked very hard. But, as I have matured as a person as well as in my spiritual journey, I have realized that I do not need to prove anything to anyone, and I am less willing to do so. My mantra is: I work as hard as I need to, and the only person I am in competition with is me.

I see the love of God in all human beings and, if somebody has a problem with me being black or being a woman, I am not willing to make it my problem. I would attribute the opportunities I have been given in life to the blessings passed down from the generations that have gone before me. Even though, at times (in fact, many times), it feels hard to carry on with one's mission in life, there are moments when a silent force simply propels me to unimaginable heights where difficult situations are resolved without a lot of effort.

Preliminary Reflection

SM2's narrative offers a very helpful insight into some of the characteristic aspects of a via media spirituality in the life of a high-potential working person who has faced significant social challenges. One is able to identify how she moves from a limited interiority into making meaning in her wider context, bringing together her beliefs, and her communal identity. This case study shows a person who is overcoming the dualism between faith and life and, as a result of this shift, is able to create meaning that brings wholeness to herself and the community in which she functions.

Case Study 3: SM3 – Senior Manager 3 (South African)

An Introduction to the Case Study

With reference to the transformative category of spirituality in the workplace, we will use a case to highlight some of the problems that could arise when organizations attempt to create false distinctions between different facets of human experience, as well as what happens when social, economic, and political expectations are not met in the broader society and in the workplace. SM3, a Senior Manager at a global financial services firm and based in their offices in South Africa describes how "social change" and "justice," or the lack of it, are experienced by an educated black woman in democratic South

Africa. Once again, it would be most helpful for the reader to keep the summary of the key features of transformative spirituality at hand upon reading this case study (see Table 9.2 above).

SM3's Narrative

On the morning of the 27th of April 1994, I remember waking up to the eerie silence of an empty house. "Everybody including your grandma will wake up early in morning to go vote. Tomorrow is a big day for us," my dad had said the day before. I could not vote on the day as voting was only possible for those who were 18 years old and older. The day marked a new era in South Africa, an era of independence, democracy, freedom, solidarity and re-routing the destiny of an entire nation from a dark past. It was a day of black and white, where both blacks and whites stood together proclaiming democracy. It could easily have been a day for the bullet, but instead, it was a landmark in the inauguration of South Africa's non-racial democracy. One could say that finally our country, South Africa, had turned around to see the light. It had come out of the darkness of the cave in which it was a prisoner for long years and ascended to the intelligible realm of Plato's Allegory of the Cave. South Africa had turned away from ignorance to true knowledge of equality and non-racism.

The 27th of April 1994 renewed my perceptions about South Africa. In my view, the acquired democracy brought about equality and equal opportunities. I would no longer be seen as inferior because of my skin color. It was a day of possibilities. "The sky is the limit. You can be whatever you want to!" my dad said.

I remember a day when career counselors in Matric (the final year of high school) visited us. I informed the counselor of my desire to become an accountant one day. "Don't you want to pursue medicine, teaching or education instead?" she asked. I asked why. She replied by saying that careers in finance or accountancy are not meant for black people. This bothered me a great deal. I shared my discussion with my dad, who told me to ignore the statement and I did just that. I started my Bachelors in Commerce (BCom) degree. As I did not have an accounting background, I battled with accountancy. I remember having a conversation with a career advisor who blatantly told me that I should reconsider doing my BCom over a longer period instead of the usual four years, since she felt that I was definitely not going to succeed. There were very few black students who made it through the first year of BCom. Were my perceptions of freedom, equality, non-discrimination and non-racialism brought on by the events of 27th of April 1994 merely shadows cast by objects illuminated by firelight, just like the shadows seen by Plato's prisoners in the cave? Were they a far cry from reality? A lot seemed to have changed and yet nothing seemed to have changed, the stereotypical thinking that a person of color was inadequate was very much alive, just as it was before that big day. My hero who I proudly call my father, Nelson Mandela, spoke the truth when he said "After climbing a great hill, one only finds that there are many more hills to climb."

I completed my BCom degree and enrolled to do my audit internship in one of the "big four" audit firms in South Africa. To my surprise, I was the only black woman accepted into the internship. Discussions from a colleague revealed that I was accepted into the internship because I studied at the University of Cape Town (UCT) and showed a great deal of potential. Did that mean that had I studied in another institution, I would not have been accepted? I wondered. I qualified as a chartered accountant two years later. Since I wanted to specialize in taxation, I enrolled for a BCom Honors degree in Taxation. I joined a tax division in a law firm where I started as a consultant, and made it through the ranks to become the first black equity partner. My chartered accountancy and an honors degree in tax rendered me a qualified black, the "new black woman," as per Ella Louise Bell in her article "The bicultural life experience of career-oriented black women" (Bell, 1990).

Plato refers to the highest stage of knowledge, as the knowledge of Good. What has this meant to me in the context of needing to be highly qualified as a necessity for leadership? My reality of whether a high level of academic qualification is a necessity for leadership in the professional context has been shaped by the history of South Africa, my background, where I come from as a black child to a black family.

My reality is that my education (the number of qualifications that I have) speaks before me and opens opportunities for me to be heard, for judgment precedes me by reason of being black. I am given an opportunity because I am a Chartered Accountant and have an Honors degree in Tax. Now that it is common knowledge that I am doing an MBA at UCT, I get those who did not greet before saying, "Hi SM3." But for my qualifications, I would be perceived as "another black." My qualifications say "she probably has potential," "she is a better black citizen and she is not like all the other blacks," and "she may have something clever to say or contribute." It is sad that my qualifications are the knock at the door of the house of being a respected human. I do matter. I am also competent, just like anybody else. My qualifications are like a scream for me to be heard. In my journey, my reality has been that, in order to be considered or recognized as a leader, a high level of education is critical for it serves as a signal for my competence.

Certain scholars have produced literature in an attempt to assist organizations, which desire to have a discrimination-free workplace, use the whole talent pool by valuing diversity, and design tailored measures to reduce stereotyping. Whilst there may be policies such as equal opportunity and affirmative action, the scholars have discovered that these are not enough, the problems black women encounter in their professional worlds have to be looked at, as they march through the doors of organizations. "Awareness of racism and accompanying legislative avenues of litigation have to some extent lessened expression of blatant racist actions, such as being called *Kaffir* [a derogatory South African racial slur] or Negro, however, the outcome has been more insidious, subtle and pervasive ways to reinforce racism," notes Hite (1996) in "Black women managers and administrators: Experiences and implications." Now, it is no longer blatant racism but rather "everyday racism," "aversive racism," "institutional racism" where the deceptive tactics are difficult to identify. In order to more fully understand the issues, black professional women face, they have to be interviewed.

This isolation, coupled with the inescapability and pervasiveness of institutional racism in most work environments requires resilience, internal strength, confidence, spiritual conviction (coupled with forgiveness), and impeccable skills. I have come to realize that one of the weapons I have, in order to have a voice, is a high level of education. As Nelson Mandela noted "Education is the most powerful weapon which you can use to change the world" (in Hargreaves et al., 2010, p. 148).

Preliminary Reflection

In SM3's narrative one is able to identify some of the characteristics of a transformative spirituality at work. While there is a clear expression of spirituality, it is not coupled with a religious grouping or religious tradition. She shows through her spirituality that she bears a strong sense of responsibility to work for change in an unjust working environment. This form of meaning-making not only places the problems and challenges within their proper context, it also shows how the individual can transcend these problems by drawing upon resources of spiritual value that stem from culture, history, and other aspects of non-religious inspiration.

The three case studies presented in the previous section served to explicate key features and characteristics of the three conceptualizations of spirituality in the workplace. While there are some common traits that are identifiable in the three narratives, such as transcendent meaning, greater personal resilience, and an intersection between spirituality and ethics, each narrative highlighted different forms of spirituality in the workplace; namely, palliative spirituality, via media spirituality, and transformative spirituality. Furthermore, these case studies illustrate the complexity of navigating intersectional aspects such as gender, race, social identities, societal expectations, and the various roles associated with being a professional African woman who has experienced challenge or adversity in her personal life or in the world of work. The case studies show how religion and/or spirituality helped each of them to navigate such struggles, prejudices and discrimination in their respective work environments and personal lives. Spirituality, whether explicitly religious or not, served to enable the women not only to navigate personal and professional crises, but even to succeed and flourish in spite of these challenges.

Organizational Approaches

As the previous sections have shown, the role of spirituality in the context of work is very important. It is increasingly acknowledged in business and management research (Kutcher et al., 2010; Doran & Natale, 2011). This urges researchers in business and management to question how spirituality is understood and practiced in work organizations. Although spirituality is intensely personal, it does not need to be private (Palmer, 1994; Scott, 1994) and although spirituality tends to be idiosyncratic, it is often predicated on shared experiences, values, and beliefs. A typical organization espouses a certain identity and attendant goals, values, beliefs, and norms; that is, it stands for something. What the organization stands for provides potential spiritual hooks for the individual, particularly for connection and growth.

```
Enabling          Partnering         Directing
organizations  →  organizations  →   organizations

●─────────────────────●─────────────────────●
Individual           Mutual            Organization
                  Relative control
```

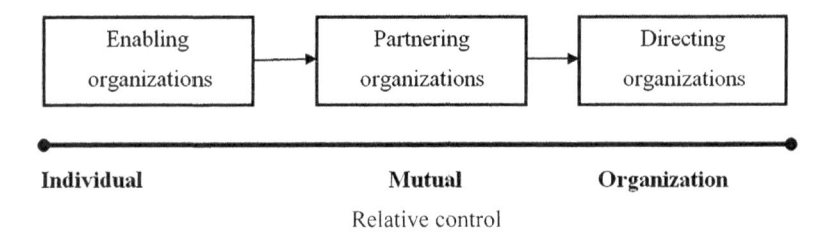

Figure 9.1 Spirituality continuum within organizations
Source: Ashforth & Pratt, 2003.

Palmer (1994) and Scott (1994) argue that what organizations stand for can be conceptualized in terms of a continuum, ranging from those that involve relatively high individual control (enabling organizations) to those that involve relatively high organizational control (directing organizations). In the middle of the continuum, we find partnering organizations, which are characterized by mutual control between the individual and the organization. This continuum (as depicted below in Figure 9.1) applies to organizations that are receptive to spirituality.

The Enabling Model

In the continuum from enabling to directing, enabling organizations are those which acknowledge that many individuals are defining themselves as seekers and are less willing to consign their spirituality to non-work hours and domains (Mitroff et al., 1999). Enabling organizations acknowledge spiritual striving and allow individuals to discover their own idiosyncratic transcendence, through prayer, meditation, journaling, or retreats.

The essence of enabling is personalization. This allows the individual to make a choice about whether or not they want to undertake a spiritual journey at work. Personalization could enable a sense of spiritual fulfillment congruent with the workplace that enabled it. Personalization could further foster a diverse environment wherein organizations can affirm, rather than shun, creativity. Diversity, while being celebrated, however, can foster practices that make members feel unlike others in the organization, thus weakening the individual–organization bond

(April & April, 2009). This may lead to possible interpersonal conflict and alienation, according to Ashford and Pratt (2003).

Enabling organizations may also encourage many diverse requests, raising troubling questions about whether and where to draw the line (Ashford & Pratt, 2003). Furthermore, as Ashford and Pratt (2003) note, the permissiveness of enabling organizations may actually cause some individuals to feel an implicit pressure to display their spirituality in the workplace, or to conform to the spiritual practices of their superiors or peers. By taking the case of religious diversity in Lebanon, Al Ariss (2010) shows how enabling structures and organizations can be problematic when individuals are expected to conform to taken-for-granted rules of 17 officially existing Christian and Muslim confessions. Therefore, what is an idiosyncratic, voluntary activity may gain normative momentum and seem constraining in the context of employment relations.

The Directing Model

This end of the continuum represents high organizational control, with a strong organizational culture that provides clear and distinct hooks for spiritual striving. These organizations can be "top down" in approach: constantly seeking to define who one is (identity) and who belongs (membership); what matters (values) and what is to be done (purpose); how and why things hang together to constitute "reality" and "truth" (ideology); and, how individuals are embedded in that reality and connected to what matters and what is to be done (transcendence) (Ashford & Pratt, 2003).

In recruitment and selection, directing organizations emphasize person–organization (P–O) fit over technical skills, or person–job fit (Schneiders, 2000). They socialize individuals using a cyclical process of sense-breaking and sense-giving (Weiss, 1999). They further challenge the incoming identities, values, and beliefs of recruits via sense breaking, thus fomenting a desire for change. In sense-giving, managers and peers model the espoused culture, and recruits are encouraged to form personal attachments to these models.

Strong cultures breed strong commitment by screening out those whose commitment is only half-hearted, and encouraging a sort of emotional contagion among those who remain. Directing organizations may facilitate a deep sense of spiritual fulfillment, spiritual community and belonging, workplace identification, and wholeness, leading to enhanced motivation and organizational citizenship behavior (Ashford & Pratt, 2003).

On the other hand, weariness and lack of creativity may also characterize these organizations, in conjunction with pressure applied to individuals who may not have internalized the organization's cosmology. Lack of creativity may induce myopia, resistance to change, arrogance, and a degree of fundamentalism that will eventually not serve organizational goals.

The Partnering Model

The partnering model represents a middle ground, or territory of shared control, where power is not understood as a zero-sum proposition. The middle ground may represent high individual control and high organizational control. Its spirituality is a meld of active bottom-up and top-down processes that are not legalistic or mechanistic in manner. Spirituality is jointly authored, or socially constructed, as members explore their spirituality within a facilitative context. In these organizations, values are emergent and open-ended, and there are opportunities for the individual and organization to co-evolve (Ashford & Pratt, 2003).

In partnering organizations, leaders seek to serve rather than lead their followers. This servant leadership allows the incorporation of enabling values, such as a holistic approach to work, self-awareness and development, empowering and collaborating, true listening, and constructive feedback (Greenleaf, 1977). As in the case of transformational leaders, articulating a vision and inspiring trust are critical. In these organizations, trustees exchange personal and communal stories that explore the institution's identity, culture, and future and enhance each trustee's deeper, idiosyncratic connections with the institution (Fleming, 2001). In short, the personal becomes the communal, and vice versa (Ashford & Pratt, 2003).

This way of socially constructing spirituality is empowering, leading to personalization of spirituality and possibly to spiritual fulfillment and personal development. Because individuals and organizations co-evolve, both are likely to remain more adaptable than in the directing model, and the organization is less likely to lose external legitimacy. The disadvantage of this model is that it can easily turn into the directing model, depending on whose interest drives the process.

In sum, just as spirituality cannot be completely institutionalized without compromising its locus and focus, so institutions cannot be completely "spiritualized" without sacrificing their collective and corporeal form (Ashford & Pratt, 2003). Institutions may approximate spirituality through an array of approaches that differ in the degree of control exercised by the organization. Given the inherent incompatibility between spirituality and organizational concerns, perhaps attempts to link them tightly will always involve a trade-off. Success in approximating spirituality for some members may necessitate failure in achieving certain organizational interests.

Conclusions

The turbulent contemporary work environment is driving new ways of thinking and transforming work arrangements. Africa is also facing these forces at present. However, the intersections of the economic, political, cultural, and religious distinctive to the African context complicate notions of spirituality and workplace diversity. The African religious milieu can be characterized as overtly religious (Jenkins, 2011) – yet having a diversity of religious groups, and a myriad of spiritualities (as Case Study 2 showed). Having to make meaning from an African spiritual perspective, within the globalized reality of the world of work, may require a careful navigation of cultural values, personal aspirations, and social expectations (seen in Case Studies 2 and 3). Moreover, the consequences of colonization and unjust social, economic, and political systems (such as *Apartheid* in South Africa) still have significant effects on identity and meaning in both the private and the public spheres of life (as seen in Case Study 3). In contrast to the kinds of resources required to function in a Western context (such as those described in Case Study 1), the African working person still faces far greater challenges when it comes to race, gender, and societal expectations.

It does not help that there are naïve notions of a single African identity, or a single African spirituality. Concepts of intersubjective identity ethics, infused by Christianity (such as contemporary expressions of the philosophy of *Ubuntu* found in parts of Southern Africa) differ significantly from forms of communal identity found in North African communities that have been deeply formed by Islam (Forster, 2010a; Jenkins, 2011). When an African works in a Western country, or a company whose culture is Westernized, there is an added layer of nuance and complexity to social relations and spiritual identity.

However, what all three case studies showed is that people seek to be part of something greater than themselves. The search for meaning and the need to be part of something greater than oneself have been posited as the major motivations for the identifying of individuals with organizations (Ashford & Pratt, 2003). The P–O fit, though, would almost inevitably be incongruent, especially if the values, beliefs, and practices of the individual and the organization are markedly at odds. According to Reid et al. (2015), while "spirituality" remains difficult to define, it is generally considered to be a psychological characteristic that refers to creating a meaningful life, aspiring towards spiritual growth, connecting with the transcendental (Zinnbauer et al., 1999, p. 895), and holding positive views of work (Mayer & Viviers, 2014); it is also associated with inner peace (Chatters, 2000). Our cases demonstrate a catalytic engagement with spirituality in the African context (Paris, 1995) to mean, as Phipps (2012, p. 181) describes, personal experiences that transform or alter one's foundational outlook in order to place one's experiences in a context larger than the self.

Today, most organizations want people to serve a purpose, not just to have a job (Kelemen & Peltonen, 2005). The challenge is to create an opportunity for workers to personalize their experiences in collaboration with the organization. In other words, work should serve as a source of enjoyment, satisfaction, and fulfillment, whereby purpose and meaning are more closely tied to what we do. This new way of conceiving of work emphasizes, "why we do what we do rather than how we do what we do" (Richards, 1995, p. 65). This implies a search for meaning, an aspiration beyond instrumentality, towards a deeper self-knowledge or transcendence to a higher level. Therefore, what is spiritual can also be understood in terms of emotions internalized and personal feelings of meaning, purpose, knowing, and being. These felt emotions serve to energize action. Spirit for them is thus a form of energy. Thus, spirituality expresses itself behaviorally and cognitively (Richards, 1995). In such an understanding, spirit represents an inner source of energy, and spirituality is the outward expression of that force.

How we experience our work becomes increasingly central to our lives because it serves as a "source of spiritual growth, suggesting that organizations need to meet the meaning needs of their members" (Richards, 1995, p. 115). People bring their whole selves to work and seek to integrate their work into their whole lives. This integration is more readily accomplished if personal values are congruent with organizational values. Some assert that workplaces that allow people to remain true to their beliefs in daily work will become the only companies that make a profit, because they create a context for creativity and innovation (Dorsey, 1998).

References

Ackers, P., & Preston, D. (1997). Born again? The ethics and efficacy of the conversion experience in contemporary management development. *Journal of Management Studies*, 34(5), 677–701.

Al Ariss, A. (2010). Religious diversity in Lebanon: Lessons from a small country to the global world. *In* Özbilgin, M., & Syed, J. (eds.), *Managing cultural diversity in Asia: A research companion*. New York: Edward Elgar Publishing, 56–72.

Albert, R. (2006). *From Newton to Heisenberg: Spiritual intelligence and business leadership*. Unpublished manuscript.

April, K., & April, A. (2009). Reactions to discrimination: Exclusive identity of foreign workers in South Africa. *In* Özbilgin, M. (ed.), *Equality, diversity and inclusion at work: A research companion*. Cheltenham: Edward Elgar Publishing Limited, 216–28.

April, K., & Blass, E. (2010). Ethical leadership required to lead a diverse Europe. *In* Matiaske, W., Costa, S., & Brunkhorst, H. (eds.), *Contemporary perspectives on justice*. München, Mering: Rainer Hampp Verlag, 183–201.

April, K., & Shockley, M. (2007). *Diversity: New realities in a changing world*. Basingstoke: Palgrave Macmillan.

Ashforth, B. E., & Pratt, M. G. (2003). Institutionalized spirituality: An oxymoron? *In* Giacalone, R. A., & Jurkiewics, C. L. (eds.), *Handbook of workplace spirituality and organizational performance*. Armonk, NY: M. E. Sharpe, 93–107.

Bell, E. L. (1990). The bicultural life experience of career-oriented black women. *Journal of Organizational Behavior*, 11(6), 459–77.

Bell, E., & Taylor, S. (2001, July). The resacralization of work. *In Proceedings of critical management studies conference*, Manchester, United Kingdom.

Boje, D. (2000). Post-Spiritual capitalism. *Journal of Organizational Studies*, (August), 5–9.

Bongmba, E. K. (2012). *The Wiley-Blackwell companion to African religions*. Malden, MA: John Wiley & Sons.

Burack, E. H. (1999). Spirituality in the workplace. *Journal of Organizational Change Management*, 12(4), 280–92.
Capra, F. (1982). *The turning point: Science, society and the rising culture*. London: Flamingo.
Carrette, J. A., & King, R. (2004). *Spirituality and the new world order*. Canada: Routledge Taylor and Francis Group.
Carson, D. A. (1992). *A call to spiritual reformation*. UK: Intervarsity Press.
Cavanaugh, G. F. (1999). Spirituality for managers: Context and critique. *Journal of Organizational Change Management*, 12(3), 186–99.
Chandler, C. K., & Holden, J. M. (1992). Counselling for spiritual wellness: Theory and practice. *Journal of Counselling and Development*, 71, 168–76.
Chatters, L. (2000). Religion and health: Public health research and practice. *Annual Review of Public Health*, 21, 335–67.
Clegg, S., & Bailey, J. R. (2009) *International encyclopedia of organization studies*. London: SAGE Publications.
Costea, B., & Introna, L. (2004). *Self and other in everyday existence: A mystery not a problem* (Working Paper 2004/020). UK: Lancaster University Management School, 1–24.
Doran, C. J., & Natale, S. M. (2011). Empatheia and caritas: The role of religion in fair trade consumption. *Journal of Business Ethics*, 98, 1–15.
Dorsey, D. (1998). The new spirit of work. *Fast Company*, 16, 125–34.
Dunn, J., & Ambige, C. (eds.). (2004). *Living together in the church: Including our differences*. Toronto: ABC Publishing.
Du Toit, C. W. (2006). Secular spirituality versus secular dualism: Towards post-secular holism as model for a natural theology. *HTS*, 62(4), 1251–68.
Ellison, C. (1983). Spiritual well-being: Conceptualisation and measurement. *Journal of Psychology and Theology*, 11(4), 330–40.
Emmons, R., & Crumbler, C. (1999). Religion and spirituality? The roles of sanctification and the concept of God. *The International Journal for the Psychology of Religion*, 9(1), 17–24.
Engelbrecht, A., Van Aswegen, C., & Theron, T. (2005). The effect of ethical values on transformational leadership and ethical climate in organizations. *South African Journal of Business Management*, 36(2), 19–26.
Erickson, R. J. (1995). The importance of authenticity for self and society. *Symbolic Interaction*, 18(2), 121–44.
Evans, C. S. (1990). *Soren Kierkgaard's Christian psychology: Insights for counselling and pastoral care*. Grand Rapids, MI: Zondervan.
Fleming, D. (2001). Narrative leadership: Using the power of stories. *Strategy & Leadership*, 29(4), 34–7.
Fluker, W. E. (2003). Dangerous memories and redemptive possibilities: Reflections on the life and work of Howard Thurman, 1984.

Critical Review of International Social and Political Philosophy, 7(4), 147–76.

Forster, D. A. (2010a). A generous ontology: Identity as a process of intersubjective discovery – An African theological contribution. *HTS*, 66(1), 1–12.

——— (2010b). African relational ontology, individual identity, and Christian theology: An African theological contribution towards an integrated relational ontological identity, *Theology*, 113(874) 243–53.

——— (2014). Called to work: a descriptive analysis of Call42's research on faith and work in South Africa: original research, *Koers*, 79(2), 1–9.

Foucault, M. (1985). *The use of pleasure*. New York: Pantheon Books.

Fry, L. W. (2003). Toward a theory of spiritual leadership. *The Leadership Quarterly*, 14(6), 693–727.

Giacaclone, R. A., & Jurckiewicz, C. L. (2003). Towards a science of workplace spirituality. *In* Giacolone, R. A., & Jurkiewicz, C. L. (eds.), *Handbook of workplace spirituality and organizational performance*. Armonk, NY: ME Sharpe.

Gibbons, P. (2000). *Spirituality at work: Definitions, measures, assumption and validity claims, spirituality at work reader*. Toronto: Academy of Management.

Gilligan, C. (1988). *Mapping the moral domain: A contribution of women's thinking to psychological theory and education*. Cambridge, MA: Harvard University Press.

Goldsby, M. G., Neck, C. P., & Gerde, V. W. (1998). Inner leadership: A social cognitive-based approach toward enhanced ethical decision-making. *Teaching Business Ethics*, 2(3), 229–47.

Goleman, D. (1998). *Working with emotional intelligence: Why it can matter more than IQ*. New York: Bantam Books.

Green, M. (2007). *In search of spirituality: Finding a way through the spiritual maze*. Oxford: Monarch Books.

Greenleaf, R. (1977). *Servant leadership: A journey into the nature of legitimate power and greatness*. New York: Paulist Press.

Groody, D. G. (2007). *Globalization, spirituality and justice*. New York: Orbis Books.

Habermas, J. (1970). *Towards a rational society: Student protest, science, and politics*. Oxford: Blackwell Publishers Ltd.

——— (1988). *On the logic of the social sciences*: Cambridge: Polity Press.

Hargreaves, A., Lieberman, A., Fullan, M., & Hopkins, D. (2010). *Second international handbook of educational change*. New Jersey, NJ: Springer Science & Business Media.

Hernandez, W. (2016). *Henri Nouwen: A spirituality of imperfection*. New York: Paulist Press.

Herring, C. (2009). Does diversity pay? Race, gender and the business case for diversity. *American Sociological Review*, 74(2), 208–24.

Hicks, D. A. (2003). *Religion and the workplace: Pluralism, spirituality, leadership*. Cambridge: Cambridge University Press.

Hite, L. M. (1996). Black women managers and administrators: Experiences and implications. *Women in Management Review*, 11(6), 11–17.

Hood, R. W. Jr., (1992). Sin and guilt in faith traditions: Issues for self-esteem. *In* Schumaker, J. F. (ed.), *Religion and Mental Health*. New York: Oxford University Press, 320.

Howard, S., & Welbourne, D. (2004). *The spirit at work phenomenon*. London: Azure.

Jenkins, P. (2011) *The next Christendom: The coming of global Christianity*. Oxford, Oxford University Press.

Jung, C. G. (1966). *The practice of psychotherapy: Essays on the psychology of the transference and other subjects* (Collected Works Vol. 16). Princeton, NJ: Princeton University Press.

Keating, T. (1999). *Awakening*. New York: The Crossroad Publishing Company.

Kelemen, M. L., & Peltonen, T. (2005). Spirituality: A way to an alternative subjectivity? *Organization Management Journal*, 2(1), 52–63.

Kim, M. J., McFarland, G., & McLane, A. (1987). *Pocket guide to nursing diagnosis*. St. Louis, MO: Basic Books.

Kohlberg, L. (1981). *Philosophy of moral development*. Cambridge, MA: Harper and Row.

Kutcher, E. J., Bragger, J. D., Rodriguez-Srednicki, O., & Masco, J. L. (2010). The role of religiosity in stress, job attitudes, and organizational citizenship behavior. *Journal of Business Ethics*, 95, 319–337.

Kvarfordt, C., & Sheridan, M. (2007). The role of religion and spirituality in working with children and adolescents. *Results of a National Survey*, 26(3), 1–23.

Lamont, G. (2002). *The spirited business*. London: Hodder and Stoughton.

Leak, G. K., & Fish, S. B. (1999). Development and initial validation of a measure of religious maturity. *International Journal for the Psychology of Religion*, 9, 83–103.

Legge, K. (1995). *Human resource management: Rhetorics and realities*. Basingstoke: Macmillan.

Lofland, J., & Stark, R. (1965). Becoming a world-saver: A theory of conversion to a deviant perspective. *American Sociological Review*, 30(6), 862–75.

Makgoba, T. (2005). *Connectedness*. Cape Town: Pretext.

Mayer, C., & Viviers, R. (2014). Following the word of God: Empirical insights into managerial-perceptions of spirituality, culture and health. *International Review of Psychiatry*, 26, 302–14.

Mbete, M. (2006). *Ibuyambo: A pilgrimage towards a spiritual cooked in African pots*. Durban: Methodist Publishing House.

Mbiti, J. S. (1990). *African religions & philosophy*. London: Heinemann.

Mendoza-Denton, R., & Espana, C. (2010). Diversity science: What is it? *Psychological Inquiry*, 21(2), 140–45.

Merton, T. (1961). *New seeds of contemplation*. New York: New Directions Publishing Corporation.

Miller, W. C., & Miller, D. R. (2002). *Spirituality: The emerging context for business leadership*. Austin, Texas: Global Dharma Center.

Mitroff, I. I., Denton, E. A., & Ferguson, T. (1999). *A spiritual audit of corporate America: A hard look at spirituality, religion, and values in the workplace*. San Francisco, CA: Jossey-Bass Publishers.

Moe-Lobeda, C. D. (2002). *Healing a broken world*. Minneapolis, MN: Fortress.

Ngunjiri, F. (2010). *Women's spiritual leadership in Africa*. New York: SUNY Press.

Ngunjiri, F. W. (2016). "I am because we are:" Exploring women's leadership under Ubuntu worldview. *Advances in Developing Human Resources*, 18(2), 223–42.

Nolan, A. (2006a). *Jesus today: A spirituality of radical freedom*. New York: Orbis Books.

(2006b). *Unpublished retreat addresses. To the Southern African province of the society of the sacred mission*. Durban: Compiled by Moakes and Motaung.

Nouwen, H. J. M. (1994). *The wounded healer: Ministry in contemporary society: Text complete and unabridged*. London: Darton, Longman and Todd.

Olupona, J. K. (ed.) (2000). *African spirituality: Forms, meanings, and expressions. World spirituality, v. 3*. New York: Crossroad.

Palmer, P. J. (1994). Leading from within: Out of the shadow, into the light. In Conger, J. (ed.), *Spirit and work: Discovering the spirituality in leadership*. San Francisco, CA: Jossey Bass, 19–44.

Paris, P. J. (1995). *The spirituality of African peoples: The search for a common moral discourse*. Minneapolis, MN: Fortress Press.

Peck, S. (1980). *The road less travelled*. London: Arrow Books.

Phipps, K. A. (2012). Spirituality and strategic leadership: The influence of spiritual beliefs on strategic decision making. *Journal of Business Ethics*, 106(2), 177–89.

Piaget, J. (1971). *The child's conception of the world*. London: Routledge & K. Paul.

Piedmont, R. L. (1999). Does spirituality represent the sixth factor of personality? Spiritual transcendence and the five-factor model. *Journal of Personality*, 67, 985–1013.

Reid, M., Roumpi, D., & O'Leary-Kelly, A. M. (2015). Spirited women: The role of spirituality in the work lives of female entrepreneurs in Ghana. *Africa Journal of Management*, 1(3), 264–83.

Richards, D. (1995). *Artful work: Awakening joy, meaning and commitment in the workplace*. San Francisco, CA: Barrett-Koehler.

Rohr, R. (2013). *Falling upward: A spirituality for the two halves of life*. New York: John Wiley & Sons.

Rowling, J. K. (2014). *Harry Potter and the deathly hallows*. London: Bloomsbury.

Runcorn, D. (2006). *Spirituality workbook*. London: Society for Promoting Christian Knowledge.

Schaeffer, C. B., & Mattis, J. S. (2012). Diversity, religiosity and spirituality in the workplace. *Journal of Management, Spirituality & Religion*, 9(4), 317–33.

Schneiders, S. M. (2000). Religion and spirituality: Strangers, rivals or partners? *Santa Clara lectures*, 6(2), 1–16.

Scott, K. T. (1994). Leadership and spirituality: A quest for reconciliation. In Conger, J. (ed.), *Spirit and work: Discovering the spirituality in leadership*. San Francisco, CA: Jossey Bass, 63–99.

Sheep, M. L. (2006). Nurturing the whole person: The ethics of workplace spirituality in a society of organizations. *Journal of Business Ethics*, 66(4), 357–75.

Sheldrake, P. (1998). *Spirituality and theology – Christian living and the doctrine of God*. London: Darton, Longman and Todd Ltd.

Sheldrake, R., & Fox, M. (1997). *Natural grace: Essays on science and spirituality*. London: Bloomsbury Publishing.

Shorter, A. (2006). *Toward a theology of inculturation*. Eugene, OR: Wipf and Stock Publishers.

Slosson Wuellner, F. (1998). *Feed my sheep*. Nashville, TN: Upper Room Books.

Sobrino, J. (1988). *Spirituality of liberation: Toward political holiness*, Maryknoll, NY: Orbis Books.

Stallwood, J., & Stoll, R. (1975). Spiritual dimensions of nursing practice. In Geland, I. L., & Passos, J. Y. (eds.), *Clinical nursing*. New York: MacMillan.

Storlie, T. A. (2015). *Person-centered communication with older adults: The professional provider's guide*. New York: Elsevier Academic Press.

Stroudenmire, J., Batman, D., Pavlov, M., & Temple, A. (1986). Validation of a holistic living inventory. *Psychological Reports*, 57, 577–8.

Thorpe, S. A. (1991). *African traditional religions: An introduction*. Pretoria: University of South Africa.

Thurman, H. (1981). *Meditations of the heart*. Boston, MA: Beacon Press.

Tischler, L. (1999). The growing interest in spirituality in business -a long-term socio-economic explanation. *Journal of Organizational Change Management*, 12(4), 273–80.
Toledano, N., & Karanda, C. (2014). Leading, self, teams and organizations from a female perspective: An exploration of women leaders' journey. *African Journal of Business Management*, 8(20), 972–80.
Tshaka, R. S. (2014). A perspective on notions of spirituality, democracy, social cohesion and public theology. *Verbum et Ecclesia*, 35(3), 1–6.
Uygur, S., & Aydin, E. (2015). Religious diversity in the workplace. *In* Syed, J., & Özbilgin, M. (eds.), *Managing diversity and inclusion: An international perspective*. London: SAGE Publications Ltd.
Vaill, P. (2000). Introduction to spirituality for business leadership. *Journal of Management Inquiry*, 9(2), 115–16.
Venter, E. (2004). The notion of Ubuntu. *Communication in Philosophy and Education*, 23, 149–60.
Volf, M. (2001). *Work in the spirit: Toward a theology of work*. Eugene, OR: Wipf and Stock.
Vygotsky, L. S. (1978). *Mind in society*. Cambridge, MA: Harvard University Press.
Walters, K. (2001). *Practicing presence – The spirituality of caring in everyday life*. Wisconsin, WI: Sheed and Ward.
Weiss, W. H. (1999). Leadership. *Supervision*, 60(1), 4–10.
Westgate, C. E. (1996). Spiritual wellness and depression. *Journal of Counselling and Development*, 75(1), 26–35.
Wilber, K. (1998). *The marriage of sense and soul integrating science and religion*. New York: Random House.
  (2000). *Integral psychology*. Boston, MA: Shambalala.
  (2001). *A theory of everything: An integral vision for business, politics, science, and spirituality*. Boston, MA: Shambhala.
Williams, R. (1982). *Resurrection*. London: Darton, Longmann and Todd.
  (1990). *The wound of knowledge: Christian spirituality from the new testament to St John of the cross*. London: Darton, Longmann and Todd.
  (2004). *The wound of knowledge*. London: Darton, Longmann and Todd.
Zinnbauer, B., Pargament, K. I., & Scott, A. B. (1999). The emerging meanings of religiousness and spirituality: Problems and prospects. *Journal of Personality*, 67, 889–919.
Zohar, D. (2000). *Spiritual intelligence*. London: Cygnus Books.
Zohar, D., & Marshall, M. I. (2004). *Spiritual capital*. London: Bloomsbury.

10 The French Principle of Laïcité[1] and Religious Pluralism in the Workplace: Main Findings and Issues

PATRICK BANON AND JEAN-FRANÇOIS CHANLAT

Introduction

Since the beginning of the twenty-first century, the movement of people has become global (Héran, 2007; Mouhoud & Oudinet, 2007; Gedde & Scholten, 2016). We are living a veritable cultural revolution, what Claude Lévi-Strauss (2013) did not hesitate to call, in a text, recently republished, a "world civilization," notably due to the global economy, the mobility of individuals, the free circulation of ideas, and the Internet. Within this great social process, we have observed in recent years an increase in religious demands in many democratic countries, who, as in the case of France, thought they had settled the question once and for all. Sometimes heated debates begin to emerge around numerous, often high-profile articles in the media, which question the principle of "laïcité," the French version of secularism and integration of people from different backrounds (Bowen, 2007; Banon, 2008, 2016; Laborde, 2008; Sciberras, 2010; Barth, 2012; Languille, 2015; Weil, 2015) within a debate that pits, on the one hand, advocates of a post-secular age who want to lift restrictions on the expression of religious beliefs in public spaces, against, on the other hand, defenders of what might be called a naturalist secularism (Stavo-Debauge et al., 2015).

---

[1] The term "laïcité" is often approximately translated as secularism. However, "laïcité" represents the constitutional principle of separation between the Church and State. State employees and public service organizations must show strict neutrality in their behavior and appearance, and the French Republican ethos includes a certain way of behaving around this issue in broader social life which relates to the history of France, notably the French socio-historical movement to free itself from the control of the Catholic Church (Champion, 1993; Haarscher, 1996; Pena-Ruiz, 2003; Bowen, 2007; Schnapper, 2007; Delfau, 2015; Weil, 2015).

Inside this now very interconnected world, the proliferation of information networks delivers in effect to our door spiritual offerings from all backgrounds. It is estimated that, today, 4,000 forms of belief and tens of thousands of deities exist (Banon, 2008; Machelon, 2006). Although some studies indicate that one should not exaggerate the significance of religious demands in France, it remains the case that the proportion of conflicts in companies based on religion is growing (Institut Randstad & Ofre, 2014, 2015, 2016) and the challenge to democracies and organizations cannot be underestimated. For it is not a matter here of asking the question of the place religions should have, but rather how to organize the equitable coexistence of a diversity of cultural expectations, traditions, and religions in a multicultural society with a secular character – in French, "le principe de laïcité" (the principle of secularism) (Bowen, 2007; Schnapper, 2007; Laborde, 2008; Delfau, 2015; Languille, 2015; Stavo-Debauge et al., 2015; Weil, 2015). The tragic events that we have witnessed in recent years in many parts of the world, and recently in France, while strongly marking our consciousness lead our societies to question our ways of being together (Kepel, 2015). For if we know from history and anthropology that religious systems and thought have accompanied and forged humanity for millennia (Durkheim, 1912, 1915 [2008]; Hervieu-Léger & Willaime, 2001), the current globalization has not only served to emancipate cultures and religions from their land of initial development, it has also necessitated a change of era.

This text, based on a comparative analysis of different countries and an analysis of legal decisions in the arena of employment, tries to give some understanding of this issue. The structure of the chapter will be the following: after a reminder of the actual situation in relation to religious expression in our countries, particularly in France, we will present: (1) the issue of religions' visibility, (2) the countries' diverse responses: freedom of choice or equality of rights based on a study of legal decisions, (3) the larger issue of religious expression in the public space according to secular principles, in particular the French variations, and (4) the case of the so-called "tendency companies." In our conclusion, we identify the impact of the "laïcité" principle on a pluralist society, come back to the innovative character of French secularism in relation to this issue, and give a warning about the risk of the spread of religiously driven companies in the coming years.

Religious Expressions' Diversity in the Workplace: A Growing Trend

Spiritual rules, developed contemporaneously to the agricultural revolution, nearly 10,000 to 15,000 years ago, organized our societies around the sacredness of the land, the cycle of seasons, and the social status of people based on appearances, resemblance, and differences. Taking part in the desecration of the earth, modernity, and the ensuing globalization imposes a mutation in religions rendering archaic and obsolete their historically life-regulating prescriptions (Banon, 2008, 2016).

The relationship to "the other" requires one to be humanized and equal. The different, the foreigner, who comes from another country, who does not have the same skin color, who follows particular traditions or claims a different sexual orientation, has today in many democratic societies, the same rights as those born in the host country; and equal rights between men and women has become imperative for any self-respecting democracy (Schnapper, 2007). In other words, from an anthropological point of view, we are indeed witnessing a fragmentation of religion and an attempt to restructure according to a new social and political environment (Hervieu-Léger, 2001), which is characterized by both religious globalization, a convergence of concerns about the human condition, and by questioning the principle of secularism, notably in its French version. The challenge is not for a society to deconstruct religions or traditions but to meet their expectations using a democratic language (Laborde, 2008; Bowen, 2009; King et al., 2009; Delfau, 2015; Gröschl & Bendl, 2015; Klarsfeld, 2016; Languille, 2015; Le Monde, 2013; Stavo-Debauge et al., 2015; Weil, 2015).

The management of the diversity of religious practices, coexisting in a shared territory, has thus become indispensable, each country responding differently according to its history, its waves of settlement, and its main religion. Currently, 84% of people in the world indeed identify with a religious group and 77% of the world population declare themselves a member of one of the five major religions or spiritual beliefs: Christianity, Islam, Hinduism, Buddhism, and Judaism. Sixteen percent of the population identify as religiously unaffiliated (Pew Research Center, 2013). All models of society are therefore faced with the coexistence of cultural and religious diversity (real, virtual, or imagined) and inevitably, with the possible expression of both the nostalgia for a sacred territory and of competition with other identities who claim it.

This encounter involves a number of potentially problematic questions: first, how to organize collective time in a multicultural society? Then, how to deal with the partial privatization of the collective space for individual purposes? How to manage the intrusion of an external moral system of prescriptions into the workplace? Can such an external moral system be presented as a set of "higher principles" in the implementation of the employment contract?

Time-space, geographical space, and social space are now subject to these external pressures, which exert a direct internal influence on company performance. This involves a certain number of other questions: is this a redistribution of power of certain religious traditions in the space of a company thus far secularized? Is it a religious awakening in the face of the new realities of a diverse society? Is it the expression of an identity weakened by the loss of connection with a territory of reference? Is it, yet, a competition between different models of society, one privileging cultural freedom for each community, the other favoring equal rights for each individual?

One point shared by these models is the fact that there is no state which is not historically organized around rituals, worship, and holy commandments, serving to cement the collective and inspire social principles: social acts and the status of women and men, citizens and foreigners. "No state has ever been founded without a religious basis," wrote Jean-Jacques Rousseau three centuries ago in *The Social Contract*, Book IV, Chapter 8, "Civil Religion" (1762). It is based on this socio-historical observation that we next study how these universal shocks affect the world of organizations, and in particular that of private-sector organizations; and what space we can leave for these cultural particularities in the collective space of the private sector organization, in particular in France.

The Workplace on the Front Line of the Globalization of Religions

The world of work in Western countries, including the private and public sectors, is today the front line of finding the response to this question of the fragmentation of collective space and time, and even to the question of the alteration of societal principles believed to ensure social cohesion. In the public sector, particularly in the French case, the problem arises less obviously as a result of the 1905 law, which governs the principle of French secularism. This principle was extended to the educational realm for students and teachers from elementary public school through high school in 2004 (Languille, 2015; Weil, 2015).

However, two sectors (private and voluntary) are not subject to the principle of secularism. Strictly speaking, the French principle of "laïcité" is, as Guy Coq (2003) recalled, drawing inspiration from the definition of Ferdinand Buisson (1878), "the recognition of the autonomy of society and the state in relation to any religion." Leaders of organizations in these sectors must now respond to numerous questions that arise daily about how to manage peculiar demands and to preserve individual freedom of belief and religion, while ensuring social cohesion and collective interest, as the jurisprudence on this issue remains unclear. Based on what criteria should a manager appreciate, support, and at times restrict religious freedom?

The new realities of the world we have just briefly evoked, indeed make any decision in this area increasingly complex. Decision-making is especially difficult as the intensity of the practices of certain religions appears to weaken, while that of other religions seems to progress (Tincq, 2013). In France, for example, according to the latest data available at the time of the writing, 50% of French managers have already been confronted with religious requests. In 2015, 23% of respondents declare regularly facing a question associated with religious behavior in the company, this rate having doubled in a year, and the proportion of conflicts in the company based on religion tripled over three years, then increased by 50% in 2016 (Institut Randstad & Ofre, 2015, 2016). However the most worrying issue is that nearly a third of Muslims in France place religious law above the law of the republic, and this proportion climbs to 50% among the younger part of the sample, people who will very soon enter the workplace (Institut Montaigne, 2016).

As we recall from numerous studies in the contemporary world, the coexistence of more than 4,000 beliefs and religions and tens of thousands of deities, leads to as many cosmologies and "ideal" social models evolving in the same space. Such a phenomenon is accentuated by the Internet. In fact, more than 2 billion active Internet users on social networks – that is 28% of the global population – approach in one click, cultures that they never could have met nor interacted with before in the same proportions (Dassetto 1996; Institut Sociovision 2014; Meeker, 2015). The deterritorialization of cultures (Deleuze & Guattari, 1972; Warnier, 1999) makes obsolete the principle of the "law of the land" to privilege the universalism principle of equal human rights regardless of the culture of origin. Elsewhere is now here and everywhere (Chanlat, 1994; Banon, 2008; Chanlat, Davel & Dupuis, 2013). This new proximity to elsewhere has important consequences in questioning even the principle of cultural relativism. But the question remains unanswered of the prevalence of traditions and value systems of one territory over other traditions and practices attached to other territories. "Does this mean we have to live this way?" Claude Lévi-Strauss (2013) questioned in recently republished text.

With concrete coexistence or exchanges in the virtual world of social networks, the conditions are created for grand societal disparity (Banon & Chanlat, 2014). Gods, people, and traditions, once attached to a sacred territory, are now destined to coexist in multicultural territories, and to adapt to the new realities of the world with all the contradictions that can result. Even if history shows some experience of religious diversity in some geographical areas, it also shows that this diversity can sometimes lead to terrible events, as in India or elsewhere. While long ago, attached to a sacred land, to a heroized people and to a religion guaranteeing a privileged relationship with supernatural powers, *homo religiosus* (Eliade, 1969a) now aspires to be at once a citizen of the world, and to claim a local, or even tribal, attachment, real or fantasized. In fact, if man is, without a doubt, incapable of a total desacrilization of identity (Durkheim, 1912, 1915 [2008]; Eliade, 1969b), the Republic reaches towards the sacred within a national territory, which now leads us to recall the importance of this notion of territory.

Territory, Workplace, and Religious Expressions

Every human being and/or every social activity is always registered in time-space. Organizations and businesses surely do not escape this imperative (Chanlat, 1990). They, by registering in a space, themselves create a collective and personal space for those who work in them (Fischer, 1990; Hassard, 1990; Chanlat, 2006; Clegg & Kornberger, 2006). What do we observe today in this regard in terms of religious practices?

73% of the world population still lives in the territory where their religion is the majority religion (Pew Research Center, 2015). Religious belief systems are historically attached to a people and to a territory. Thus, the attachment to the land was once defined as the identity of a person. The question was not therefore "who are you?" but "where are you from?" For example, the term "Jew," *Yehudi* in Hebrew, stemming from *Yehudah* (Judah), did not first designate belonging to the Jewish religion, but the inhabitants of Judea (Sarfati, 1997). The citizen of Athens was, in turn, supposed to be "born of the earth" and not of women. The men of the same group were thus of the same blood and were related to each other by a common mother, their country (Loraux, 1981). As we can see, in ancient times, collective identity is guaranteed by membership in a matrix territory. The closeness of a society refers to a likeness, to the same divine protector, to a common language, to the same food, and to an appearance serving as window of the soul; and difference was then seen as strange, even foreign – and thus a potential source of chaos. Yet, it is very much the difference and how the other sees the self, which reveal identity (Arendt, 1951 [2004]; Laing, 1961; Honneth, 1995). No identity can be had without encountering the other. "We never exist in the singular," wrote Levinas (1982, p. 50).

Today, as, in modern democracies, diversity is a characteristic of social life (Özbilgin & Tatli, 2008; Chanlat & Özbilgin, 2016); the loss of an original territory of reference can create a sentiment of isolation, weakening identities and pushing for a greater visibility based on new imaginary cultural territories (Kepel, 2012; Lagrange, 2013; Stavo-Debauge et al., 2015; Banon, 2016). In such a context, private life is not intended to be subject to collective judgment, as can be observed in traditional societies. The exigency of visibility seeks first to express itself in the collective life, to meet the eyes of "the other" and thus confirm its identity.

The globalization of the current economy contributes to this deterritorialization of cultures which has led to a deconsecration of the territories. The religious proliferation that ensues intensifies competition for individual freedoms of opinion, conscience, and belief. This unprecedented pluralism differs according to the societal, religious, and philosophical heritage of different regions of the world. This is an upheaval that does not lead to the disappearance of religious expression, but contrarily to its revitalization; a reality distorted in certain countries, such as France, by the overrepresentation of a population not affiliated to any religion (Tincq, 2013), of which 44% can be found in Western Europe and 43% in Pacific Asia (Pew Research Center, 2015). This religious presence in territories that seemed to have eliminated it challenges both officials and citizens (Bouchard & Taylor, 2008;

Stavo-Debauge et al., 2015), notably in France (Schnapper, 2007; d'Iribarne, 2013; Languille, 2015; Weil, 2015).

From this point of view, it is no longer necessary today to associate the sacred with a behavior insofar as this behavior is considered as part of the religious: a religion not limited to a belief or practice of a sect. Today, in the new context of globalization, the definition of religion also incorporates elements of the societal offering it proposes. In this context, what companies must take into consideration is not, therefore, the relevance of such or such religion or belief, but rather the compatibility of its related traditions with collective interest, since the company itself is subject to principles of economic and social coherence of its own. In other words, the company does not manage beliefs but guarantees the equality of its employees before a general rule: social cohesion and optimal operational performance.

So we are not living with a new religious dynamic, but rather a process of readjustment of religion in this globalized world. The question is therefore no longer summarized by one religion, but concerns them all, and this adjustment asks new questions such as: how to define one's territory in a space without borders? How, in a multicultural and secular democracy, to define one's identity, while all identities possess an equal right to expression?

Human organizations, and private businesses in particular, as ultimate meeting places of all human differences around a collective project, raise the question of managing a diversity of cultural heritages, with respect to individual freedom of conscience, religion, and worship, while seeking optimal operation, and the equalizing of rights and obligations between different people. Spinoza (1677 [1842]) already affirmed a long time ago that the exercise of worship and the expression of all forms of piety should be measured against collective interest. This is indeed the same question asked today in private and public businesses. Resulting in two key questions for which our societies are currently seeking answers: the question of visibility and that of secularism or "laïcité" in France.

The Question of the Visibility of Religion

The concept of visibility, which has been debated in France since the French Revolution, has also been debated in recent years in many Western countries, with the initial focus on the behavior of Muslims in public space (Dassetto, 1996), notably in France, which has the largest community of Muslims in Europe, with one quarter of European Muslims living there (Tribalat, 2013; Godard, 2015). It carries with it additional implications. First, religious expression is associated with celebrations and festivals which require appropriate accommodation, the definitive anchoring of the second and third generation immigrants into Western societies, leading those who practice to claim such visibility in public space. Second, religious visibility refers to the stereotyping that followed the events of September 11 in New York, certain immigrant workers being from now on identified as Muslims, and having thus been associated with fanaticism and terrorism. Finally, a third meaning refers to the questions of social recognition, developed firstly by the thought leaders of multiculturalism (Kimlycka, 2001; Taylor, 2009), and secondly, by the philosophers of critical theory (Honneth, 1995, 2012).

In other words, as recalled by Philippe Gonzalez,

The visibility of Muslims can therefore be broken down into three meanings: (1) a Muslim presence still more marked in urban areas in connection with the mutations of immigration; (2) problematic media framing that generates effects of negative reputation due to international events; (3) a third implication is for the question of social recognition resulting in the appropriation of public space. (2015, p. 253)

So these meanings are especially important in a world where migration flows intensify, where the Islamic religion is growing, and where the attacks made on behalf of this religion are increasing. It must be remembered, however, that the question of visibility is not only a question relevant to the Muslim religion in France.

The loss of cultural distance with a sacred territory of reference, real or imagined, can weaken individual identities and lead to more visible faith-based behaviors in host societies (Languille, 2015). This will be even more the case when host societies no longer know how to convey the fundamentals of their living together. Some, like France, have left some of their suburbs drift apart from the rest of society. We speak in such cases of a growing social crisis in which identity issues play a key role (Lagrange, 2010; Tribalat, 2013; Kepel, 2014, 2015; Godard, 2015).

This social crisis requires clear decisions in a confused situation. This is not a crisis in the sense of a disaster but an acceleration of symptoms that are indicative of a paroxysmal situation. The principles on which our societies are organized seem challenged in many places and in different national contexts. Either this *krisis* leads to the birth of a new world organized around an ethics of differences, privileging diversity and equality of rights and opportunities, working towards a compensation of inequalities suffered and a dynamic of differences (Héritier, 2007; Özbilgin & Tatli, 2008; Chanlat & Özbilgin, 2016; Klarsfeld, 2016); or the fear of the other, the defiance with regard to difference can lead to a resacralization of territories, the fragmentation of collective space, and a return to the archaic scale of differences, which evaluate the rights and obligations based on appearances and their assumed complementarities. The corporate world lives this *krisis* directly, notably in France (Barth, 2012; Banon et al., 2013; Galindo & Surply, 2013; Banon & Chanlat, 2014).

Until a few years ago, geographical distance helped to minimize cultural distances. Exoticism anesthetized ethical and societal disruptions. What happened elsewhere stayed elsewhere; a way also to favor a comfortable principle of tolerance without having to feel responsible for the other. Claude Lévi-Strauss recalled that geographical difference contributed to a form of indifference towards female genital mutilation (FGM, or excision) For example, FGM "did not disturb Western consciousness, when it was practiced far away, in an exotic country with whom we did not maintain relations" (Lévi-Strauss, 2013, p. 90). Religious customs and practices can coexist when they are assigned to a distant land. But nowadays, these distant territories no longer exist. As we have already underlined, elsewhere is here and is also everywhere. The responsibility towards others becomes an ethical condition for the intercultural relationships that ensue. Female genital mutilation, early and forced marriage, discrimination, and other archaic traditions become the responsibility of all, regardless of distance, leading to discussions around a central question: in our own democratic societies, which of the two should take precedence, freedom or equality?

Freedom and/or Equality Facing a Religious Demand: Diverse Responses

The changes we have just mentioned are emerging situations that question not only our legal foundations, but also our ways of thinking about social life. As the following cases will show, the answers to this question can be quite variable according to the national contexts concerned. This provokes new questions. If we begin with the most favorable to religious demands, we will see that the legal decisions are frequently inconsistent.

First Case: Protective Helmets in the United Kingdom and Canada

In 1973, British Parliament made the wearing of a helmet on motorcycles compulsory, which forced Sikhs to remove their turbans in order to wear a helmet. As this obligation was presented at that time by the representative authorities of Sikhism as an indirect discrimination, a new legislation was adopted in 1976, exempting Sikhs from wearing helmets (*Motor-Cycle Crash Helmets; Religious Exemption Act*). If an equivalent exemption came into effect in Canada (Bouchard & Taylor, 2008), such an initiative is highly unlikely in France, whose model does not allow the granting of differential rights based on a religion when doing so may prove to be ultimately detrimental to the person concerned (Weil, 2015).

However, such an equality requirement seems to have been echoed recently in Ontario. In 2014, this Canadian province indeed overturned the exemption granted to Sikhs not to wear helmets while on a construction site or on a motorcycle. In a letter addressed to the Canadian Sikh Association, Ontario's prime minister, Kathleen Wynne, while declaring she understood the religious importance of wearing turbans for Sikhs, added that such an exemption violated the safety of individuals; thus herein safety prevails over religious practice. Her stance seemed to contradict a decision adopted in 2010 by the Court of Human Rights of Ontario, which recognized that Home Depot had discriminated against Deepinder Loomba, a Sikh security guard, by requiring him to remove his turban and wear a protective helmet. The employee refused, arguing that exposing his hair in public was forbidden by his religion, despite the defense of the company concerned, noting that "The law on occupational health and safety requires that helmets be worn at all times on the sites" (*Loomba* v. *Home Depot Canada Inc.*, [2010] O.H.R.T.D. No. 1422 (QL) (Ont. H.R. Trib.).

The same year, the Ontario Court of Justice had refused to grant a motorcyclist of the same faith an exemption to drive his motorcycle without a helmet. While supported by the Commission of Human Rights of Ontario, the plaintiff, Baljinder Badesha, had contested a violation received in September 2005 while driving his motorcycle without a helmet (R. c. Badesha, 2008, O.J. N° 854, Ont. C. J.). In another judgment in 1999, the Court of Human Rights of British Columbia, another Canadian province, confirmed the right of a Sikh wearing the turban and to ride a motorcycle without a protective helmet, and concluded its decision by affirming that the discrimination involved by mandating the helmet in spite of the obligation to wear a turban was not justified by the marginal increase of risk for the person or increased medical costs for society. It was therefore the motorcyclist without a protective helmet who would face alone the risk in question (*Dhillon v. British Columbia*; Ministry of Transportation & Highways, 1999, 35 CHRR D/293).

For some French researchers and legal experts, the British and Canadian models of religious freedom and equality, despite their often contradictory decisions, seem now incompatible with the existing legal model in France. In this model, the obligation to guarantee optimal safety for all citizens takes precedence over religious practice, under the principle of individual equality before collective regulations, whereas, according to the Anglo-Saxon model, in the name of freedom, Sikhs seem less protected by the state than those faithful to other religions. Would the life of a Sikh have less value under Anglo-Saxon rule? The question posed here is that of the priority accorded to "freedom" over equality.

Second Case: The Case of Behavior and Religious Symbols in Several Developed Countries, an Inconsistent Jurisprudence

In the domain of religious requests, the workplace is a laboratory for the entire society. This is all the more true given that today, as noted previously, religious requests have increased in the workplace, particularly in France. In the current environment, however, reducing our reflections only to Islam would be misleading.

In effect, since the French law of 1905 on the separation of the church and the state, there have been hundreds of court decisions by the French "Cour de Cassation," the highest French Court, relating to religious expression in the workplace, concerning Judaism, Catholicism, Protestantism, and now, Buddhism, Sikhism, and Islam. All religions have indeed the potential to develop an "orthodox" or "fundamentalist" vision and practice (Stavo-Debauge et al., 2015). We know the amount of religious practice in France: 41% of Muslim people declare they are observant and 71% say they observe Ramadan (an increase of 11% compared with 1989 (IFOP-La Croix, 2011)) and 12.7% of French Catholics declare themselves observant (Fourquet & Le Bras, 2014). Such results indicate neither that people of Muslim faith will move toward fundamentalist behavior, nor that 87.3% of the non-observant Catholics are totally disconnected from the Judeo-Christian model of society. They indicate that a pool from which a possible resurgence of more rigorist practices exists and could create difficulties for management when orthodox practice is growing among these religions.

Faced with religious demands, as we have seen, states do not all react in the same way but rather according to their legislation, their history, or their demography. Court decisions in this area can thus vary, or often be contradictory, with no common position prevailing. In such a context, the existing jurisprudence cannot therefore dictate decision-making without risk to managers, as we will now discuss in more detail, based on a certain number of recent legal decisions made in different countries, especially in France.

In 2014, in the spirit of the First Amendment, which prohibits the United States Congress from passing law restricting religious freedom and the liberty of expression (Lacorne, 2007), the Supreme Court of the United States authorized prayers at the municipal council of the city of Greece in the state of New York, judging them "conforming to the heritage and tradition of the country" (*Galloway and Stephens* v. *Greece municipality & John Auberger*, case 12-696, 2014). In 2015, on the other hand, the Supreme Court of Canada banned the recitation of prayers from the municipal councils of the Quebec town of Saguenay, while no charter clearly states the obligation of the religious neutrality of the State, and refused at the same time to comment on the presence of the crucifix in the deliberation room, considering it as a reminder of the Catholic "heritage" of the Province (*Mouvement laïc québécois* v. *Saguenay (Ville)*, 2015 CSC 16, 2R.C.S.3, dossier: 35496).

In France, the administrative tribunal of Nantes requested the dismantling of the Nativity scene, installed in the space of the Vendée General Council during the Christmas period, considering the Nativity scene a "religious symbol," violating "the neutrality of public service with respect to religions." It is clear that the heritage dimension of the Nativity scene had not been raised here by the court, despite the arguments of the General Council who estimated that "the respect for secularism is not the abandonment of traditions and the breaking with cultural roots." On October 13, 2015, the Administrative Appeals Court of Nantes, conforming to the recommendations of the Observatory of Secularism, "cancelled" this Court decision. In its ruling, the Administrative Appeals Court of Nantes considered that the Nativity scene, although "constituting subjects representing Mary and Joseph accompanied by shepherds and magi surrounding the bed of the infant Jesus" to fit in the part of the tradition relative to the preparation of the family celebration of Christmas and does not take the nature of a "religious emblem" (Jugement du tribunal administratif de Nantes, November 14, 2014, Fédération de Vendée de la libre pensée, N° 1211647).

On July 16, 2015, the administrative tribunal of Montpellier decided to leave the nativity scene installed in the town of Béziers in place, because it did not give rise to "disturbing the public order," and did not constitute "proof of infringement of the principles of secularism and neutrality" of the Town Hall. The tribunal found that the prohibition under Article 28 of the law of 1905 does not concern all of the objects having religious significance, but only those which "symbolize the reclamation of religious views." Only objects having a "clearly symbolic" character fall within the scope of the prohibition, taking into account the criterion of the "presentation asserting religious signs," also retained by the State Council in a decision of July 17, 2005 (N° 259806), recommended on April 7, 2015 by the Observatory of Secularism (l'Observatoire de la Laïcité, a public advice body related to the French Government).

However, the Association of Mayors of France in its guide for "good secular conduct" (2015) addressed to local elected officials, condemns even the presence of Nativity scenes Town Halls, as "incompatible with secularism" (Tribunal administratif de Montpellier – 5ème chambre – *"la Ligue des droits de l'Homme"* v. *Commune de Béziers*, N° 1405625, Audience, June 30, 2015), a contradictory position to the opinion of the Minister of the Interior who in 2007 declared that: "the principle of secularism does not impose on local authorities to disregard the traditions arising from religious faith which, without constituting the exercise of worship, are nevertheless more or less directly attached to it."

At the European level, the European Court of Human Rights has, for its part, already accepted the asymmetry between religions on the basis of local cultural criteria, deciding, for example, that the crucifix installed in public schools or in forums representative of the State is a symbol of national culture rather than a case of religious proselytism; it could not therefore request their removal on the basis of their religious characteristics. Moreover, as, in 2005, an Italian court had already ruled that the crucifix could be present in the polling stations relevant to the State, in 2007, the Italian Minister of Justice decreed that the crucifix could be displayed in government buildings since it was a symbol of Italian culture and values – a decision which, in 2011, the European Court of Human Rights upheld, arguing that the crucifix is essentially a passive symbol in secular schools and that there was no violation of the right to an education, such as defined in the European Convention (*Case of Lautsi and Others v. Italy*, ECHR, N° 30814/06, March 18, 2011).

If the presence of religious symbols in certain public spaces brings, as we have just seen from these different court decisions, a variation in judgments, the wearing of the headscarf arouses the same types of reactions, and is appreciated differently in Germany, Belgium, Switzerland, the United Kingdom, or France. Let us see for illustrative purposes, some examples drawn from such European countries' case law.

In Germany, a recent decision, rendered March 13, 2015, by the Constitutional Court, ruled that the general prohibition of religious expression determining "the external appearance of teachers in public schools" was not compatible with the freedom of religion provided in the fundamental German Law of 1949 (Jones, 2015). For the constitutional judges, wearing a veil or head covering is not a "sufficiently concrete danger," which calls into question the neutrality of the State, or is disruptive to the proper functioning of a school. This decision of the Karlsruhe Court reversed an earlier decision of the Constitutional Court in 2003, when several German Länders, in this case those of Bavaria, of Bade-Württemberg and Hessen, had banned wearing the veil for teachers and professors within the grounds of public schools. The question regarding the potential ban on headscarves and all other religious symbols by German pupils, on the other hand, has not been raised.

In Belgium, a judgment from January 15, 2008, of the Brussels Labor Court (R. G. N° 48695, *Yamma v. S.A.C.*) upheld the dismissal of a bookstore's saleswoman for serious misconduct, motivated by the

The French Principle of Laïcité 279

wearing of a headscarf. In 2013, a judgment of the Tongres Labour Tribunal admitted that the decision of HEMA (a Dutch store chain) to dismiss a temporary worker established directly a distinction on the basis of the manifestation of a religious conviction. The same court seemed to suggest, however, that the private company had the right to claim "neutrality," just as a public service does. In other words, if an internal regulation, imposing a specific dress code, had been enforced in the company, there would not be grounds for discrimination based on religious beliefs.

In 2001, in the judgment of Lucia Dhalab against Switzerland (February 15, 2001), the European Court of Human Rights ruled inadmissible the appeal of a teacher in a public school in Geneva against a decision of the board of primary education, which prohibited her from wearing the Islamic headscarf in the exercise of her professional duties. The Court agreed with the public school, on the basis of the vulnerability of students between four and eight years of age; the wearing of a headscarf by a teacher being detrimental to the religious sentiments of the students and their parents and thus the principle of religious neutrality of the school. In the United Kingdom, however, Muslim headscarves and Sikh turbans are accepted at "state school", especially following the decision in 1983 by the House of Lords, which established that their prohibition would amount to racial discrimination.

Third Case: The French "Baby Loup" Nursery

In France, the highly publicized case of the Baby Loup nursery in Mantes-la-Jolie, added to the confusion in this domain. In December of 2008, returning from a parental leave, the associate director of the nursery made a request to the Director relating to her desire to wear the veil. Since the internal rules, established collectively, prohibited the wearing of any religious, philosophical, or political symbol, the Director did not accept this request. However, the associate director continued to wear a veil. The Director decided to lay off the associate director, then dismissing her for serious misconduct on December 19, 2008. The internal code of conduct of this establishment clearly prohibited the wearing of religious symbols in the name of the principle of "laïcité" (neutrality). Alleging unfair dismissal, the employee then appealed the HALDE (Upper authority for the fight against discrimination [Haute autorité de lutte contre les discriminations], created by the French government and integrated today into the Defender of Rights, the French Ombudsman), then the Employment Tribunal, claiming more than 80,000 euros in damages and interest. After having received a positive opinion from the HALDE, the Employment Tribunal of Mantes-la-Jolie upheld her dismissal for serious misconduct. The judgment recognized "repeated insubordination" of the employee. Thereafter, the Versailles Court of Appeals upheld the decision of the Employment Tribunal (October 27, 2011) and underlined in its own decision that the Baby Loup nursery must "ensure neutrality of staff with the aim to welcome all the children of the quarter, regardless of cultural or religious belonging, and that these children given their age do not have to be confronted with ostentatious manifestations of religious affiliation." The dismissal of the employee does therefore not adversely affect her religious freedom, and restrictions imposed in this case by the employer were justified by the task performed and proportionate to the objective sought.

On the March 19, 2013, the Social Chamber of the Cour de Cassation overturned the decision of the Appeals Court of Versailles, and therefore the dismissal of the employee of the Baby Loup nursery. However, the same day, a second decision of this Court upheld the dismissal of an employee who worked for the CPAM (Health Insurance Fund [Caisse primaire d'assurance maladie]) and who wanted to wear a "religious" headdress, clearly presenting them as belonging to a faith community. By that decision, the Court of Cassation extended the principle of secularism, by imposing the neutrality of civil servants to private bodies, charged with a public service mission. "The principles of neutrality and secularism of public service are applicable to all public services, including when they are provided by private bodies," held the Court de Cassation (Banon & Chanlat, 2014, 2015).

The Baby Loup nursery appealed the judgment of the Court. On November 27, 2013, the Paris Court of Appeal confirmed the judgment of the Employment Tribunal of Mantes-la-Jolie, confirming the dismissal's validity. On June 25, 2014, the plenary assembly of the Cour de Cassation put an end to four years of proceedings, and issued a decision confirming the one made by its social chamber in 2013. The Court recalled that, according to the Labor Code, a private company, or an association in the case of the nursery, can restrict the freedom of employees from displaying religious beliefs, if doing so is justified by "the nature of the task performed" and if the measure is "proportionate

The French Principle of Laïcité 281

to the objective sought." Now, Baby Loup had adopted internal rules, which stated that "the principle of freedom of conscience and religion of each member of staff cannot hinder respect for principles of secularism and neutrality that are applied in the exercise of all activities." The purpose of the nursery being to support childcare impartially, without distinction of opinion "and to work for the social and professional integration of women ... without distinction of political or religious opinion," the dismissal was therefore confirmed (Arrêt, June 25, 2014 N° 612 Assemblée plénière N° de pourvoi: E1328369).

As we have seen, the confusion of judgment decisions relating to the wearing of religious symbols, notably of the veil or turban, in the workplace led the Social Chamber of the Cour de Cassation to turn towards the Court of Justice of the European Union in April 2015 asking for clarification of the contours of the Directive of 2000, which sought to establish a general framework for fighting against discrimination in the domain of work, based on religion or belief, disability, age, or sexual orientation and its views on the relationship between religious freedom and the commercial interest of the company. (Arrêt N° 630, April 2015 (13-19.855) – Cour de Cassation – Chambre sociale).

The examples in this field are numerous; here is a final exemplary case which also led the Cour de Cassation to turn to the European Union Court of Justice for interpretation of what constitutes "an essential and determinant professional requirement."

The Fourth Case: Micropole Universe

Recruited in 2008 as a design engineer by Micropole Universe, a consulting company, specialized in engineering and training, an employee was dismissed in 2009 after having been rejected by a client, Groupama in Toulouse, where she was conducting an information services training session. "Following this intervention," explains the employer in the dismissal letter addressed to the employee and cited by the Cour de Cassation, "the client informed us that the veil, that you effectively wear every day, had bothered a number of their employees. They also asked that there be 'no veil the next time'" (Letter of dismissal from the employer Micropole Universe to the employee dated June 22, 2009, quoted *in extenso* by the Cour de Cassation). If the employer had in fact stated, upon the recruitment of this engineer, to respect fully the principle of religious freedom for all, it was added that once in contact internally or externally with clients of the company, in the interest and for the development of the company, her veil may not be worn at all times. The young woman having refused to commit to removing it, was dismissed without notice, and filed a suit with the Employment Tribunal of Paris, arguing that her termination constituted discrimination by reason of her religious convictions. The judgment of May 4, 2011 sided with the employer, holding that the dismissal was for a real and serious cause. The Court of Appeals of Paris, by a judgment on April 18, 2013, upheld the judgment. The Cour de Cassation, in turn, examined the case and recalled several times in its reasoning of April 9 "that the restrictions to religious freedom must be justified by the nature of the task to be performed, must correspond to an essential and professional determinant requirement as long as the objective is legitimate and the requirement proportionate." This is the reason why the Social Chamber requested an opinion from the European Court (Arrêt N° 630, April 9, 2015 (13-19.855) – Cour de Cassation -Chambre sociale).

The question the Cour de Cassation put to the Court of Justice of the European Union is indeed one facing many corporate managers today. In this latter case, does the desire of a client firm to no longer benefit from the services of an employee, engineer, wearing a headscarf, constitute an essential and determinant professional requirement? Do the commercial interests of the company constitute a legitimate criterion of the restriction of religious freedom? Referring as well to "values of efficacy" (Sachs, 2010), the fault of the employee could be characterized by the negative effects their conduct has "on the operation of the company" (Soc. 3/04/1981, Droit ouvrier, 1982, p. 168). However, as there exists no clear definition of the interests of the company, especially as the accounting realities can be interpreted in different ways (Colasse, 2015), and as the "common good" does not necessarily reflect the addition of individual interests, the legitimate criteria for restriction of religious freedom in France, let alone elsewhere in Europe, remains to be defined.

In the French context, restricting religious freedom in the workplace should in effect respond to legitimate criteria, justified by the task to be performed and proportionate to the objective sought. In order to do this, following current case law, a certain number of criteria already exist which limit employee freedom: compliance with health and safety rules, prohibition of proselytism, prohibition of discrimination (including with respect to religious beliefs), prohibition of imposing on others in accordance with one's own religious requirements, compliance with obligations related to the mission entrusted to the employee, and defined by the employment contract, compatibility of the religious practice with the proper functioning of the company's services, the good organization of the team to which the employee is integrated, and the commercial interest of the company. Note here that, regardless of the criterion applied, the burden of proof that there is no discrimination remains the company's responsibility (Banon et al., 2013; Banon & Chanlat, 2014).

Another element to consider here is the zone of cultural and religious expression to which the behavior in question refers. (1) Is it an individual behavior that only has an effect on the person him or herself and his or her privacy? (2) Is this a behavior that would have a direct effect on the functioning of the company and its social cohesion by promoting a social fragmentation based on religious practices of certain employees (dietary restrictions, conspicuous symbols or attire, partial privatization of collective space, grouping together fellow believers in the company)? (3) Are these accommodation requests during working hours, which naturally affect other employees' working hours, and more broadly in the organization of collective time (festivals, prayers, holidays)? (4) Is it a behavior that would directly cause harm to the commercial interest of the company (breach of the employment contract, refusal to reconsider behavior with regard to clientele, or jeopardizing the image of the company)? (5) Is it a behavior that challenges certain basic principles of society (gender equality, diversity, proselytizing, and discrimination)?

All of these issues have led many authors to reflect on the larger question, which is that of the place that the principle of secularism should occupy in the public space.

In the case of Micropole Univers in France and similarly G4S Secure in Belgium, the Court of Justice of the European Union concluded on March 14, 2017, that a company can be allowed, through its internal rules, to impose on its employees a principle of neutrality in the context of their professional activities. However, the CJUE (ECJ) stressed that prohibition of religious, philosophical, or political emblems must obey a principle of objectivity, and be justified by, for example, the fulfilling of professional duties, security, or hygiene. Furthermore, the requirement of a customer is not sufficient to impose a principle of neutrality on employees (Arrêts C-157/15 Achbita, Centrum voor Gelijkheid van kansen en voor racismebestrijding / G4S Secure Solutions and C-188/15 Bougnaoui et Association de dêfense des droits de l'homme (ADDH) / Micropole Univers).

Public Space, Religious Expression, and Secularism

Today, notably in France, the principle of secularism is not only perceived as a political claim, and a rampart against communitarian temptations, but appears also increasingly as a claim coming from the managerial world. In line with what exists in the state sphere, secularism in the business sphere would not require employees to renounce their beliefs, but would limit the expression of religious beliefs in the space-time of work. This would be a way of avoiding not only competition between practices but also the guilt felt by members of the faith with moderate observance in relation to those with the most rigorous practice. Secularism thus appears as a barrier to both discrimination and proselytizing, and the guarantee of equal treatment of employees, notably between believers and nonbelievers.

It is in this spirit, for example, that the recycling group, Paprec, adopted in agreement with all employees a Charter of "Laïcité" on February 10, 2014. Article 5 of the Charter stipulates that "Laïcité in the corporate setting implies that staff members have a duty to maintain neutrality: they must not express their political and religious convictions in the exercise of their work," adding in its article 7: "The wearing of symbols or clothing by which staff members conspicuously show religious affiliation is not authorized" (Paprec, 2015).

Note that this initiative has no binding legal significance, and that this Charter of Laïcité cannot, under current legal circumstances, be integrated into the internal regulations of the company. Note also that the claim of terminology "Laïcité" in the corporate setting has no legal foundations, since French secularism concerns to date neither the private sphere, nor the company under common law, but only the State and its remit, including companies of public service, or private or community organizations of public interest (Delfau, 2015; Languille, 2015; Weil, 2015; Portier, 2016).

The Act of December 9, 1905, of Separation of Church and State outlines in effect clear principles that have constitutional value since the 1st Article of the Constitution of October 4, 1958, states that: "France is an indivisible Republic, laïque (secular), democratic and social." The principles of the 1905 Law ensure the freedom of conscience and guarantee the freedom of religious exercise, under the sole restrictions enacted in the interest of public order (Article 1). The Republic does not recognize, pay, nor subsidize any religion (Article 2). Religions and their ministers nevertheless remain under the supervision of the State, since Article 35 prohibits speeches or writings designed to resist the execution of laws or legal acts of the public authority. And according to Article 31, proselytism and any pressure of any nature to exercise or abstain from observing religion are prohibited.

The European Convention on Human Rights, meanwhile, stipulates in its Article 9 that the freedom to manifest one's religion or beliefs shall be subject only to such restrictions as are prescribed by law, and constitute necessary measures, in a democratic society, for public safety, the protection of public order, public health or morals, or the protection of rights and freedoms of others, and in its Article 9:2, "freedom of thought, conscience and religion." If these questions and debates are particularly vivid in France, they are also present in other countries, notably in Europe. The debate around secularism is not therefore exclusively French.

In Europe, as can be observed, there coexist three models of relations between religion and the State: the model of "separation-cooperation" or of "active neutrality," which is found in Germany, Belgium, Austria, Spain, Italy, and Switzerland; the "State-Church" regime, which is found in England, whose sovereign is also head of the Anglican Church; and in Greece, Iceland, Finland, and Denmark, which subsidize Orthodoxy for the first, and the protestant Lutheran Church, for the other three (the Danish Parliament voted in 1947 against the opinion of the majority of clerics, in favor of granting women access to the function of pastor); and the "strict separation" regime, which is found in France, the Netherlands, and Ireland (Haarscher, 1996; Rambaud, 2011).

France is therefore not the only country concerned with the debate of the place of religion in workplace, in the State's sphere or even at school. France is not the only State in Europe to enunciate a principle of secularism. But we can observe differences between these three models: some advocating a strict separation between the state and religion, others seeking to give religions a place in the space of the State, a distinction which relates historically to the dominant religion in these European countries, notably Protestantism or Catholicism (Champion, 1993). If the French, British, German, Belgian, Swiss, or Nordics have different approaches of religious pluralism according to their history, we must also note that since June 2013, the European Union has discussed these different models and tested their potential convergence; and that the European Court ruled in favor of the decisions of the French Parliament to prohibit full face cover (including the burka) in public spaces, declaring that these provisions did not violate the European Convention on Human Rights, and that the motive of co-existence invoked in particular one of its conditions: showing one's face can be legitimately invoked by the French legislator to regulate this practice and preserve public safety. Therefore, the absolute prohibition is not disproportionate to the objective pursued; the question of the acceptance or rejection of the complete covering of the face in public space constituted, according to the Court, a societal choice. As Constantin Languille (2015, p. 129) has written: "the full and entire respect of human rights may have as a consequence the destruction of common rules without which it is not possible to live together."

Such a decision very well shows, once again, the tension between freedom and equal rights as it is experienced in each society, starting from its own definition of living together. Beyond the specific case of full face cover, the question of secularism in Europe inevitably opens up the debate on religious demands that arise today in the workplace, while being related to the manner in which each country historically sees the relationship between public and religious space. This is what we will now focus on in terms of what is happening in France.

French Variations on Secularism Principles

In a recent survey, 83% of French people believe that "the company must remain a neutral place and not take into consideration claims of a religious order," as with, for example, an arrangement of working time which allows religious practice. The French largely privilege religious neutrality, not only at the level of the State and public services as the law already requires, but in society in general and at the company level in particular. This view is widely shared among all religious denominations, 87% of Catholics, 79% of Protestants, 92% of Jews, and 69%

of Muslims approving this stance. In addition, the number of French in favor of the expression of religious faith at work is declining; there was in effect 23% in 2013 compared to 30% in 2010 (a reduction of seven percent) who considered "normal to adapt the location, working hours or collective catering to accommodate religious practice" (Observatoire Sociovision de la Société française, 2014).

Eighty-two percent of the French also believe "religious symbols must remain discreet in public;" compared to 79% in 2013. The judgment, however, differs according to religious affiliation. Thus, 49% of people of the Catholic faith accept "the need to find food suitable for all religious precepts in the canteen," while 88% of people of the Muslim faith think along these lines, and 55% of all French people. French secularism remains an "essential value" for 78% of the French. Even if they do not all feel this to the same extent, religion is reaffirmed as relevant in the private domain. Seventy-nine percent of the French indeed think that "as religion is a private matter, signs of religious affiliation should remain discreet in public" (Institut sociovision, 2014). But even in France itself, not everyone assigns the same meaning to "laïcité".

As mentioned above, the principle of French secularism is a complex concept whose direct translation into English does not exist. In English, for example, the terms used to express this principle are "secularism" and "pluralism." But in France the diversity of the interpretations of "laïcité" (French secularism) is not limited only to the dynamics of secularization, but also creates a link to the social, historical, and heritage, among all the cultural backgrounds involved (Champion, 1993; Pena-Ruiz, 2003; Delfau, 2015; Weil, 2015). By allowing everyone to free themselves from their social community of reference, French secularism fixes an historical continuity close to a collective identity. As the French historian, Patrick Weil (2015, p. 160), recently recalled, "what is the identity of France ... ? ... it is the construction, by generations of French, of a common social and political history which gives specific references and has shaped our identity." In France, denying the principle of "laïcité" (secularism) can be perceived at a macro level, as a refusal to be part of the nation, in the political sense of the word, and in the world of work, would be to refuse to be part of the collective project that the company represents. By putting religious affiliation above citizenship, the collective interest is placed second. This is not acceptable in the French context (Champion, 1993; Pena-Ruiz, 2003;

Delfau, 2015; Weil, 2015) but perhaps, also in many other countries. As Constantin Languille again recalled,

> If the function of the nation is to unite across differences, it is unlikely that human rights can achieve the same result insofar as their purpose is to protect precisely the differences from the pressure of the majority. The sense of community can hardly be based on something that separates. The difficulty results from the fact that human rights are not transcendent: they allow the definition of a sphere where everyone can show their subjectivity but cannot constitute the common reference that transcends individual differences and establishes the community by supporting a sense of belonging. This function characterizes only the nation. Knowing whether we can do without such a common principle is the burning question of our time ... the response to the question of the possibility of cosmopolitanism is primarily philosophical: we must make a judgment on what keeps the world human. Is horizontal solidarity, resting on inclusive collective decision-making and mechanisms of social insurance, sufficient to ensure living together? Or do human beings need a verticality that transcends differences and unites hearts, so that they feel they belong to the same political community? Can political bonds be emancipated from all transcendence? (2015, p. 130 and p. 134)

Heir to the spirit of the French Revolution and consolidations by the Third Republic, reaffirmed later in the establishment of the Constitution of the Fifth Republic, it is Citizenship that is ultimately in question here, but not all Republicans perceive in citizenship the same obligations, duties, and rights. Jean Jaurès, one of the leading figure of the French left, already affirmed in 1904 that "the Republic must be secular and social. It will remain secular if it knows how to remain social".

The differences in appreciation of what is or is not the principle of French secularism are therefore not new. Since the 1789 Revolution, confusion has been instilled in successive stages, following the Law of separation of Church and State, about the neutrality of the public service, and today, questions concerning religious pluralism (Costa-Lascoux, 1996; Haarscher, 1996; Delfau, 2015).

This confusion can even be found at the heart of public service companies. For example, the project of the "Laïcité" charter of French Social Security, while reaffirming in its Article 6 the strict obligation of neutrality to which public services are subjected (2015), suggests in the same document that the restrictions on wearing religious symbols "are justified by the nature of the task to be performed, and proportionate to the objective sought." The RATP [Paris Public Transportation Authority] felt, in turn, the need recently to specify the principles of French secularism and neutrality of the company in a practical guide. The employment contracts of the employees indeed states that "RATP being a company of public service bound by the principle of neutrality, you agree to prohibit all attitude or wearing conspicuous signs that may indicate an affiliation to any religion or to some unspecified philosophy" (RATP, 2013, p. 6). Yet, in this same guide, RATP eludes the question of men who refuse to shake hands with women (or vice versa), noting that the company cannot codify greetings, this refusal "can only give rise to disciplinary sanction" (RATP, 2013, p. 16).

This behavior is nevertheless a discriminatory act recognized by the courts. In May 2013, an employee of the city of Brussels was thus dismissed because of his refusal to shake hands with a work colleague given that his religion "forbids him to touch women." The Court of The Hague ruled on April 10, 2012, that the refusal to shake hands with women is "unacceptable," and constituted "a violation of gender equality." The Utrecht court ruled in the same direction on January 9, 2013. France refused French nationality to a Moroccan national because of his "discriminatory attitude with regard to women." He specifically refused to shake hands with a female agent who received him at the Prefecture on the grounds that it was against his religion (July, 2010). The Cour de Cassation also found that the negative context of refusing to shake a woman's hand, justifies dismissal among other elements (Cour de Cassation, Social Chamber, N° 08-41239, November 10, 2009). In other words, the refusal to signal civility does not identify a simple cultural difference, but rather a religious norm (Nounckele & Christians, 2013). This behavior has therefore no place in the space of a public service company, subject to secularism principles.

As this is a discriminatory practice, this behavior has no place, either, in the space of a firm governed by private law. Accommodating the wearing of religious signs and even indirectly legitimizing religious behavior in the space of public service, contributes without a doubt to the confusion that reigns on this subject. The distinction between territories which should be neutral, and those in which religious expression can manifest freely, must indeed be clarified. A former French prime minister has otherwise proposed that violating the principle of secularism in public service qualifies as an "offense obstructive to 'laïcité' [secularism]" (Juppé, 2016).

"Laïcité of separation" versus "open laïcité": it is always in the name of secularism that some want the neutralization of the collective space, and others want the acceptance of religious expressions in their diversity. It should be recalled here again that, contrary to what some people think, the French principle of secularism is not the refusal of religion. French secularism is neither atheist nor faithful to a religion, but it is a-religious, the believers and the unbelievers being treated equally (Pena-Ruiz, 2003; Delfau, 2015; Weil, 2015; Portier, 2016). Neither a Republican religion, nor opposing religions, French secularism accepts all forms of religion, but refuses the irruption of their regulations against the remit of the State. Guarantor of the unity and indivisibility of the Republic (Constitution of 1793, Article 1), French secularism rejects any religious practice that may fragment the nation, opposing the communities that create it, creating social schisms that promote the legitimacy of a differential right according to religious culture. French secularism is not "against" religious or customary practice, but decides where and when it is possible. It is not up to religious thought systems to define what falls under the principle of secularism, but for secularism to define the space of expression of traditions of religious inspiration and thus the State, guaranteeing both the unity of the nation and of individual rights. As recently stated one American commentator, Paul Berman,

> Republican secularism is not, after all, merely a negative concept, useful for fending off religious fanatics. Republican secularism is a positive principle. It offers something to the individual. This is citizenship. In its French version, republican secularism says to every individual: "Human and citizen rights are your own rights, regardless of what some church might say". The aspirations of the French Republic are open to you, as well as to everyone. These are the aspirations of the French Revolution. You have access to political freedom and a modern education and a modern culture and an advanced welfare state. At least, you ought to have access, and, if you find that you do not, you have a right to march in the streets and to vote for the political party that speaks for you. You have a right to be a Muslim, or to adhere to any other religion, or to none, and this right is yours precisely because, as a citizen of France, you enjoy rights on the broadest of scales. The French republican idea, with its secularism – this idea is, in short, grander than anything the Islamists can offer. The Islamist ideal is an ugly and

deceptive promise. It is a self-oppression. But the French republican ideal is a liberation – at least, in principle" (2016, p. 3).

It is the reason for which, in November 1903, George Clemenceau, a leading French senator, rejected the idea of an "integral laïcité," seeing in it the risk of "only escaping the Church to fall into the hands of the State" (1903); Jean Jaurès in turn condemned "all that could resemble a breach of freedom of worship." During the debates of 1905 on the law of separation of the Church and State, two factions were opposed: on the one hand, proponents of atheistic secularism – that is to say those in favor of the abolition of religions, deeply influenced by the model of the abolition of the monarchy; on the other, supporters of inclusive secularism, protector of religions – that is to say those favoring a secularism of religious coexistence in the Republic. This struggle is still alive today. Even if the model of atheistic secularism was rejected in 1905 by the French Parliament by a large majority, many incorrectly associate French secularism and atheism, and imagine that after liberation from the monarchical yoke, humanity must break free from the shackle of religion. This anti-religious secularism has become today a proposal for managing religious diversity in certain spheres of the workplace.

The above-mentioned charter of "laïcité," adopted by Paprec, had the advantage of concretely posing the question of the place of secularism and thus religions in a company under private law. In fact, as we have seen, the legal uncertainty that goes hand in hand with conflicts of a religious order disarms managers and promotes demands for accommodation of religious practices. Managers have the feeling of having to choose between two only attitudes: either acceptance, and support of requests of a religious order; or taking the risk of being accused of discrimination in cases of non-acceptance.

This is why the vast majority among them now call for a clarification of the rules for managing religious practices; and by clarification, they most often imply the extension of secularism principle to non-State entities. In effect, among more than 800 SME managers (encountered in groups of 10 to 20 over two years) with whom we exchanged views on religious practices in the workplace, almost all of them demanded the right to benefit from the secularism principle reserved for the State (Banon et al., 2013). This is also the case for French employees.

If 55% of employees say they have a connection to religion, 84% of the French "agree," of which 60% "strongly agree" that "the company must remain a neutral place and not take into consideration claims of religious order" (BVA, 2013; Observatoire Sociovision, 2014; Institut Randstad & Ofre, 2016). French secularism rejects any religious practice that may fragment the nation, pitting the communities that compose it against one another, creating social schisms, sometimes geographic or temporal, or, worse, which promote the legitimacy of a differential right according to religious culture. It is in this spirit that in 2011 the High Council for Integration (which ceased operating in 2012) filed an opinion on "Religious expression and secularism in the workplace," proposing to augment the Labor Code with an article authorizing companies to adopt internal rules relative to the prohibition of clothes, the wearing of religious symbols, and religious practices in the company with the purpose of maintaining a certain neutrality in the space of the company, all while guaranteeing everyone's freedom of belief. This opinion did not result in an evolution of the law in this domain. But the question of the restriction of religious freedom arises today with even more acuity, particularly through the extension of the principle of secularism in a company under private law.

The HALDE affirmed in 2008 that "the principle in the private sector is that of freedom of conscience and religious liberty, which includes that of manifesting religion. The company cannot be built in a neutral or secular place in the absence of a statutory rule that restricts such fundamental freedom" (HALDE deliberation N° 2008-10 from January 14, 2008). Until now, the secularism principle has stopped at the doors of the enterprise and the freedom of religion figures among fundamental freedoms. To put in question these two principles has direct effects on the French model, which raises equality to the rank of essential condition for veritable freedom. "The principle of French secularism designated the attitude of the State towards the religious. It is not applicable to civil society" (Huglo, 2014, p. 6).

Under current regulations, the company under private law is not authorized to discriminate in the name of promoting any secularism. To extend the principle of "laïcité" to the private (non-State) workplace may seem in the short term a good response to help managers deal with an unprecedented diversity of cultures and religious traditions at the workplace. Some indeed consider secularism as a social project in itself, but we must not forget that such a principle is not a goal, but primarily a means towards better co-existence in equality of rights and separation of spheres.

The Concept of Enterprise of "Conviction" or "Tendency"

Establishing a concept of secularism with variable scope makes it lose its specificity as a pillar of the French Republic. From a fundamental principle, French secularism would be reduced to a simple philosophical principle. This secularism then risks being perceived as a tendency, as well as all other religious or political beliefs (Aldigé, 2013). In other words, if the company of the "secular" tendency is authorized to reduce the religious freedom of its employees, it will be difficult to avoid the right of companies of "religious" tendency to impose their own religious regulations on their employees too.

Extending the domain of secularism in companies under private law could lead to the proliferation of peer companies, meaning companies animated by a philosophical principle or "tendency," religious or political. Creating the conditions for legal discrimination could favor the development of communitarian businesses, creating veritable schisms in a Republic founded on the principle of indivisibility. Extending the principle of secularism throughout the workplace would lead to a result inverse to the one sought; that is to say social sectarianism, accompanied by geographic and social fragmentation, which inevitably leads to cultural schisms; that which is indeed integrated in the definition of this notion of companies of conviction or "tendency."

The notion of "tendency" companies (a term borrowed from German law and from the notion of *tendenzbetriebe* meaning "convictional" or religious business, advocating a doctrine or an ethics, is recognized by the European legal framework. Article 4 of the European Directive 2000/78/CE of November 27, 2000, provides more flexibility of the principle of non-discrimination at work in the name of "the right of churches and other public or private organizations whose ethos is founded on religion or beliefs ... to require of those working for them an attitude of good faith and loyalty towards the ethics of the organization."

Despite the lack of implementation of this part of the European directive into French law, this notion derived from case law is already taken into account and allows justification of violations of equality and the freedom of conscience of employees. Thus, in 1978, the Cour de Cassation judged that the dismissal following the divorce and remarriage of a teacher, employed in a private Catholic institution, was justified, since religious convictions had been mentioned in the employment contract (Dame ROY case, public audience, May 19, 1978, N° 76-41.211). Divorce not being authorized by the religious rule of the institution of employment, the teacher had thus, according to the Court, broken the moral contract with her employer. Yet, freedom of marriage is a fundamental constitutional principle. Marriage is a union governed by civil law and not by religious law. Everyone possesses the freedom to marry or not to marry and no one can punish a person for having exercised this right. This is not however what is expressed in the judgment of the Plenary Assembly "Dame Roy" (Cour de Cassation, public audience, May 19, 1978, N° 76-41211).

The second case is that of a professor of the Protestant Theological faculty of Montpellier, who was dismissed due to disagreements with certain elements of the ideology of the establishment. In 1986, the Cour de Cassation Social Chamber asserts that Article L 122-45 (which forbids discrimination) of the Labor Code does not apply "when the employee, who was hired to perform a task implying that they are in communion of thought and faith with their employer, disregards the obligations resulting from this commitment" (the Cour de Cassation, November 28, 1986 – Reformed Church of France /Demoiselle Fisher, bull. N° 555). In other words, in this case, the employee had the obligation to act in communion of thought and faith with their employer. The Cour de Cassation considered in its judgment that although there was an employment contract, Article L 122-45 should not apply due to the religious nature of his functions, positing in principle that the end-purpose of the organization constitutes a legitimate reason for discrimination.

A third case is that of an employee dismissed for adultery. Responsible for monitoring compliance with *Kosher* (food prohibitions and Jewish religious obligations), this Jewish supervisor was fired for not having respected the religious commandment prohibiting adultery, which presents herein the question of the boundary between private life and professional life. This employee, given his professional status and religious responsibilities, would appear to have demonstrated an exemplary piety and therefore accepted the restrictions on his private life without "power to avail himself of the freedom of a private life in order to keep his job" (Toulouse Employment Tribunal [Conseil des Prud'hommes de Toulouse], June 23, 1995, Cahiers prud'homaux, 9/1995, p. 159; judgment of August 17). A decision that joins the analysis of the German Court of Justice, justifying the dismissal without notice of a German employee of the Mormon Church for adultery; this decision being reaffirmed by the European Court of Human Rights on appeal for the same reason: "the incompatibility of his extra-marital relationship with the increased duties of loyalty he had contracted towards the Church as director for Europe of the public relations department perhaps contributing to the loss of credibility of their employee" (*Obst v. Germany*, European Court of Human Rights, 425/03, September 23, 2010).

A restriction that remains at least arbitrary if one believes the case of another *Kosher* Jewish supervisor, dismissed for having been absent for 25 days for the funeral of his brother in Israel (conforming to Jewish law). The employer had then considered that only a statutory period of three days leave was authorized for family bereavement. The Paris Court of Appeal nevertheless considered the dismissal unjustified, taking into consideration the spiritual environment of the company and the fact that the Consistory of Paris had proposed a replacement to the company: "Considering that the employer gave the restaurant ... its specific character founded on the strict observance of Jewish law, considering that the contractual relations supposed equal commitment of the parties to Jewish law, and the reciprocal concern to apply it without restriction even beyond the scope of the assignment of ritual supervision" (Judgment of the Paris Court of Appeal, N° 90556, May 25, 1990). This consideration was nevertheless insufficient to allow a pastor of a church to dismiss his sacristan who, for religious reasons, refused to work on Sundays, the "sacred" day of rest (Tribunal du travail, Rennes, July 8, 1993, Cahiers prud'homaux, 7/1994, p. 111).

Finally, a recent decision of the United States Supreme Court warns of potential discrimination in the notion of "tendency" organizations. Based on the "Religious Freedom Restoration Act" adopted in 1993, the Supreme Court established in fact in its judgment of June 30, 2014 the profitmaking notion of a "tendency" organization, finding that a commercial company enjoys the same constitutional right to religious freedom as a person, thereby creating a differential right between female and male employees.

The first case is that of Hobby Lobby Stores, a chain store specializing in the sale of articles of decoration. The Green family of Oklahoma founded the company in 1972 with the following philosophical strategy: "Honouring the Lord in all its activities, leading the company in accordance with biblical principles." The second case is that of the company of Conestoga, specializing in furniture, closets, and kitchens.

Founded in 1964, in Pennsylvania by devout Mennonite Christians, the company aims to "ensure a reasonable profit in accord with their Christian heritage." These two companies refused to provide contraceptives, some of which belong to the category of "morning-after pills," as part of their employees' healthcare coverage, on the ground that such contraceptives are tantamount to abortion. The judgment of the Supreme Court, through two decisions (*Burwell* v. *Hobby Lobby Stores, Inc., et al.*, N° 13-354, 2014; and *Conestoga Wood Specialties Corp* v. *Burwell*, N° 13-356, 2014), by upholding the religious freedom of companies and their leaders, has thus restricted the freedom of their employees. This is a perverse effect equivalent to the exemption in the law that allowed Sikhs, as we have shown above, to not wear a construction or motorcycle helmet. This is a right conferred in the name of religious freedom, which eventually may be unfavorable to individuals, and creates inequalities of rights and treatment between persons. The development of such a moral contract, superior to the contract of employment, thus creates the conditions of differential rights between employees according to their employer.

The proliferation of companies "of tendency" imposing religious values-based management disrupts the sacred/profane balance. Considering the secularism principle as one tendency among others would make our companies leap back into a time when religious law prevailed over any other rule. From this point of view, the establishment of such companies would be without a doubt entail the worst adverse effect: that of an extension of the principle of secularism in the entire workplace.

Conclusion

As we have seen, every culture, belief and tradition expresses many particularities, sometimes conflicting with fundamental principles of democratic societies. Trying to satisfy all requests in the name of tolerance can create an approximate and malleable sense of human right. The logician and mathematician, Kurt Gödel, wrote, when he appeared before the American commission of citizenship, "If we extend the unrestricted tolerance, even for those who do not tolerate anything ... then tolerance will be destroyed, and tolerance will be destroyed with us" (2013). The rigidity of belief and the pressure of traditions inevitably lead to a "legitimate" inequality between individuals, and to the trivialization of a process of exclusion, or self-exclusion from the collectivity of a company. A certain number of errors are thus to be avoided.

The first mistake would be to reduce an individual to his or her community of origin, to recognize a different law for them on the pretext of their cultural heritage. This would caricature them, describing them on the basis of stereotypes and depriving them of personal liberty of conscience and the right to equality. This is an aspect emphasized by many authors (Lahire, 2006; Banon, 2008, 2016; Pierre & Mutabazi, 2010).

The second would be to evaluate religious diversity, proceeding by the association of ideas, without seeking to know the impact of the particularities of the collective concerned. There are behaviors that could be problematic for living together. For example, when a colleague refuses to shake hands with a woman because she is a woman, it recognizes explicitly the social differentiation of the sexes and the marginalization of women. Such behavior is incompatible with the definition of living together in a secular republic and reinforces the idea that women are *de facto* impure; which is the true element behind this behavior.

The third error is to imagine that beliefs, rites, and religious symbols are ethnic identification when a religion is not an ethnic group, and when belief is not transmitted genetically but by membership. We must therefore distinguish the collective rights of an ethnic group from those of religious expression in the workplace. The company finds itself therefore in a dilemma: to adapt to individual particularities and disappear in an inevitable fragmentation until the concept of social cohesion itself becomes a distant myth; or to reject multiculturalism, and disappear for having given up the universal values of human rights, freedom of conscience, and worship which built the same society. The question therefore arises of the degree of recognition of individual expectations vis-à-vis the coherence of collective expectations. Any organization or company finds itself faced with two evident contradictions: how do we make choices without discriminating? And, on what basis do we forge a just opinion about a religious request without having to enter into a religious debate?

We have just highlighted that knowledge in both religion and human rights, as well as solid ethical reflection, become crucial elements for making decisions that are both enlightened and just. There are in fact still too many decisions founded on ignorance and lack of reflection.

When we see that a large municipality in Ontario has removed the Christmas tree of the City Hall lobby in order to avoid offending different sensibilities, we measure how far we still have to go in some cases. The Christmas tree is not religious, and neither is Santa Claus, both of which, incidentally, were opposed by the Catholic Church when introduced (Lévi-Strauss, 2013).

Promoting the coexistence of differences therefore requires a distancing from the relevance of a cultural or religious expectation. Anthropology of the social context concerned then becomes a key element in order to measure the effects of these differences on the persons themselves and on the collectivity in which they are situated (Chanlat, Dameron et al., 2013; Chanlat, Davel et al., 2013; D'Iribarne, 2008, 2014). This posture is similar to that of John Dewey who considered that religion had no place in the management of public affairs for two main reasons. (1) The method for religion to establish its values and to form its beliefs does not lend itself to the open and public investigation specific to the management of public affairs. (2) Religious language only plays a role in religious life animated by the faith that enlivens it. Therefore, believers are not entitled to impose their ideals on a community of citizens under the pretext that they are dictated and guaranteed by a sacred or transcendent higher power (Dewey, 2011; Quéré, 2015).

In other words, as French philosopher Louis Quéré underscored, "in order to participate in the learning and identification of purposes and values in the treatment of public issues, they [believers] must adopt an ethical attitude. This requirement is as costly for non-believers as for believers" (2015, p. 143). Dewey, as a naturalist pragmatist philosopher and advocate of social democracy, puts forward what is termed today "social reflexivity," which is particularly pertinent in his view, based as it is on a method that excludes dogmatic beliefs.

In times of "war of the Gods," as Max Weber called it, and of the surge of religious fundamentalism in society, the principle of secularism is undoubtedly one that guarantees this ethic of inquiry urged by John Dewey (Quéré, 2015). Dewey made an interesting distinction between religion and the religious. While religion refers to "a particular body of beliefs and practices that have an institutional organization, more or less constraining" (Dewey, 2011, p. 93), the religious, meanwhile, refers not to a religious experience but to a quality of experience, that is to say to a set of attitudes which produce a harmonization of the self with the surrounding universe. Accordingly, one must free the religious from religion (Dewey, 2011; Quéré, 2015).

From this point of view, French secularism is an ongoing social innovation system. An antidote to the confinement of individuals to their community of reference (real or imagined), an emancipator from custom and traditional social organizations, secularism, in its French version, by its capacity to create a shared space of reference, is intended to accompany the expression of an individual identity (Weil, 2015; Banon, 2016; Fourest, 2016;). A territory of reference in a globalized world where the territories of identification seem to evaporate, secularism has meaning only because it is not integral. It is a kind of application of the distinction established by Dewey between religion and the religious.

In the French model of an indivisible, secular, democratic and social Republic (Schnapper, 2007; Weil, 2005, 2015; Delfau, 2015; Banon, 2016; Fourest, 2016; Portier, 2016), the state is neutral and individuals are unique and singular persons. They are not elements of a whole, but a whole in themself. If, in the state sphere, the law is clear, only demanding to be applied in case of deviation, this is not the case in the non-state workplace, which is strictly governed by private law.

As we have seen in this last case, French "laïcité" must not be extended to the private setting. It should instead provide criteria for supporting or restricting religious freedom in the workplace. This involves giving managers the freedom to make choices calmly, clarifying principles, simplifying decision making, and adapting criteria to the activity of the company, to its image and to its social/commercial interest. The recent proposals of the Badinter Committee on the redesign of the French Labor Code follow this line of thought: "the freedom of employees to manifest their beliefs, including those which are religious, can be subject to restrictions only if they [the restrictions] are justified by the exercise of other fundamental rights and freedoms or by the necessities of the proper functioning of the company and if they are proportionated to the objective sought" (Badinter, 2016, Article 6). This would be a way to ensure that everyone is working towards corporate performance without religious convictions disrupting economic performance and internal social peace.

References

Aldigé, B. (2013). Le champ d'application de la laïcité: La laïcité doit-elle s'arrêter à la porte des crèches. *Recueil Dalloz*, 14(7551), 956.

Arendt, A. (1951 [2004]). *The origins of totalitarianism*. New York: Schocken.

Badinter, R. (2016). *Rapport sur la réforme du code du travail*. Paris: République française.

Banon, P. (2008). *La révolution théoculturelle*. Paris: Presses de la Renaissance.

— (2014). Alimentation sacrée et restauration collective: Pour mieux comprendre les particularismes alimentaires d'inspiration religieuse et leur gestion dans l'entreprise. Paris: Cahier de recherche, Chaire Management et diversité, université Paris-Dauphine.

— (2016). *Marianne en péril: Religions et laïcité, un défi français*. Paris: Presses de la Renaissance.

Banon, P., Chanlat, J-F. (2014). La diversité religieuse et culturelle dans les organisations française contemporaines. *In* Dauphine Recherche Management, *L'état des entreprises*, Paris: La Découverte, 9–13.

— (2015). La diversité religieuse et culturelle dans les organisations contemporaines: constats et proposition d'un modèle d'analyse et d'action pour le contexte français. *In* Guenette, A-M., Mutabazi, E., von Overbeck Ottino, S., & Pierre, P., (eds.), *Management interculturel, altérité et identités*. Paris: L'Harmattan, 119–50.

Banon, P., Chanlat, J-F., Périac, F., Bouville, G., (2013). *Etat des lieux PME diversités, Représentations, perceptions et pratiques*. Paris: Rapport de recherche, Opcalia, chaire Management et diversité de l'université Paris-Dauphine et institut des sciences de la diversité.

Barth, I. (ed.). (2012). *Management et religion*, Paris: EMS éditions.

Berman, P. (2016). Why the French Ban the Veil. The secular republic debates how best to contain and suppress the Islamist movement. *Tablet*, August 29.

Bouchard, G., & Taylor, C. (2008). *Fonder l'avenir. Le temps de la conciliation, rapport abrégé, Commission de consultation sur les pratiques d'accommodements reliées aux différences culturelles*. Québec: Gouvernement du Québec.

Bowen, J. (2007). *Why the French don't like headscarves: Islam, the state and public space*. Princeton: Princeton University Press.

BVA. (2013). *La laïcité*, Poll, March 22.

Champion, F. (1993). Entre laïcisation et sécularisation. Des rapports Eglise-Etats dans l'Europe communautaire. *Le Débat*, 5(77, novembre-décembre), 40–63.

Chanlat, J-F. (ed.) (1990 [2005]). *L'individu dans l'organisation, Les dimensions oubliées*. Ste Foy: Les Presses de l'université Laval, Paris: Eska.
  (1994). Towards an anthropology of organizations. *In* Hassard, J., & Parker, M. (eds.), *New theory of organizations*. London: Routledge, 155–89.
  (2006). Space, organization and management: A socio-historical perspective. *In* Clegg, S., & Kornberger, M. (eds.), *Space, organization and management theory*. Liber: Copenhagen Business School Press.
Chanlat, J-F., Dameron, S., Dupuis, J-P., de Freitas, M-E., & Ozbilgin, M. (2013). Management et diversité: lignes de tension et perspectives (Introduction au numéro spécial, *Management et diversité*. *Management International*, 17 (printemps), 5–13.
Chanlat, J-F., Davel, E., & Dupuis, J-P. (eds.) (2013). *Cross-cultural management, culture and management across the world*. London: Routledge.
Clegg, S., & Kornberger, M. (eds.) (2006). *Space, organization and management theory*, Liber: Copenhagen Business School Press.
Clemenceau, G. (1903). Discours sur la liberté, *Journal Officiel, Assemblée Nationale*, November 17.
Colasse, B. (2015). *Dictionnaire de comptabilité Compter/conter l'entreprise*. Paris: La Découverte.
Costa-Lascoux, J. (1996). *Les trois âges de la laïcité*. Paris: Hachette.
Coq, G. (2003). *Laïcité et république. Le lien nécessaire*. Paris: Editions du Félin.
Dassetto, F. (1996). Visibilisation de l'islam dans l'espace public. *In* Bastenier, A., Dassetto, F. (eds.), *Immigrations et nouveaux pluralismes: Une confrontation de sociétés*, Bruxelles: De Boeck-Wesmael, 179–208.
Deleuze, G., Guattari, F. (1972). *L'anti-Œdipe, Capitalisme et schizophrénie (vols. 1 and 2)*. Paris: Les Éditions de Minuit.
Delfau, G. (2015). *La laïcité, défi du XXIème siècle*. Paris: L'Harmattan.
Dewey, J. (2011). *Une foi commune*. Paris: La Découverte.
D'Iribarne, P. (2008). *Penser la diversité du monde*. Paris: Seuil.
  (2013). *L'Islam devant la démocratie*. Paris: Gallimard.
  (2014). *Theorizing National Cultures*. Paris: AFD éditions.
Durkheim, E. (1912). *Les Formes élémentaires de la vie religieuse*. Paris: Alcan.
  (1915 [2008]). *The elementary forms of religious life*. Oxford: Oxford University Press.
Eliade, M. (1969a). *Le sacré et le profane*. Paris: Gallimard.
  (1969b). *La nostalgie des origines*. Paris: Gallimard.
El Mouhoud, E. M., & Oudinet, J. (eds.) (2007). *L'Europe et ses migrants. Ouverture ou repli?* Paris: L'Harmattan.

Fischer, G.-N. (1990). Espace, identité et organisation. *In* Chanlat, J.-F. (ed.), *L'individu dans l'organisation, Les dimensions oubliées*. Ste Foy: Les Presses de l'université Laval, Paris: Eska, 165–84.

Fourest, C. (2016). *Le génie de la laïcité*. Paris: Grasset.

Fourquet, J., & Le Bras, H. (2014). *La religion dévoilée, Nouvelle géographie du catholicisme*. Paris: Fondation Jean Jaurès.

Galindo, G., & Surply, J. (2013). Quel processus d'apprentissage de la gestion du fait religieux dans les entreprises françaises? *Management international*, 17, printemps, 37–49.

Geddes, A., & Scholten, P. (2016). *The politics of migration and immigration in Europe (2nd edn.)*. London: Sage.

Godard, B. (2015). *La question musulmane en France. Un état des lieux sans concessions*. Paris: Fayard.

Gödel, K. (2013). *In* Feferman, S., Dawson, J.W., Cole Kleene, S., Moore, G.H., Solovay, R.M., & van Heijenoort, J. (eds.), *Collected works. Vol I: Publications 1929–1936* Oxford: Oxford University Press, 1–37.

Gonzalez, P. (2015). Montrer les minarets pour imposer une Suisse "chrétienne." Les sources évangéliques d'une initiative populaire. *In* Stavo-Debauge, J., Gonzalez, P., & Frega, R., (eds). *Quel âge post-séculier? Religions, démocraties, sciences*. Paris: Editions EHESS, 249–84.

Gröschl, S., & Bendl, R. (2015). *Managing diversity in the workplace, examples from around the world*. London: Routledge.

Haarscher, G. (1996). *La laïcité*, Paris: PUF.

Hassard, J. (2007). Pour un paradigme ethnographique du temps de travail. *In* Chanlat, J.-F., (ed). *L'individu dans l'organisation, Les dimensions oubliées*. Ste Foy: Les Presses de l'université Laval, Paris: Eska, 215–30.

Héran, F. (2007). *Le Temps des immigrés*. Paris: Seuil.

Héritier, F. (2007). *Masculin-Féminin*. Paris: Éditions Odile Jacob.

Hervieu-Léger, D. (2001). *La religion en miettes ou La question des sects*. Paris: Calmann-Lévy.

Hervieu-Léger, D., Willaime, J-P. (2001). *Sociologies et religion: Approches classiques*. Paris: Presses universitaires de France.

Honneth, A. (1995). *The struggle for recognition: The moral grammar of social conflicts*, Cambridge: Polity Press.

(2012). *The I in we: Studies in the theory of recognition*. New York: Wiley.

Huglo, J.-G. (2014). Entretien, *Semaine Sociale Lamy*, 15–77.

IFOP-La Croix. (2011). *Enquête sur l'implantation et l'évolution de l'Islam de France*. Paris: IFOP-La Croix.

Institut Montaigne. (2016). *Un Islam français est possible*. Paris: Rapport.

Institut Sociovision. (2014) *Une demande de discrétion religieuse dans la vie collective* Paris: Étude.

Institut Randstad, Ofre (2014). *Le travail, l'entreprise et la question religieuse*. Paris: Étude.

(2015). *Le travail, l'entreprise et la question religieuse*, Paris: Etude.
(2016). *Le travail, l'entreprise et la question religieuse*, Paris: Étude.
Jean, J. (1904). "Pas d'autre issue." In *La Dépêche du Midi*, 15 août.
Jones, T. (2015). Constitutional Court strikes down absolute headscarf ban, *DW*, March 13, p5.
Juppé, A. (2016). Entretien, *Journal du Dimanche*, January 3.
Kepel, G. (2012). *Quatre-vingt-treize*. Paris: Gallimard.
(2014). *Passion française. La voix des cites*. Paris: Gallimard.
(2015). *Terreur dans l'Hexagone, Genèse du djihad français*. Paris: Gallimard.
Kimlycka, W. (2001). *Politics in the Vernacular: Nationalism, Multiculturalism, Citizenship*. Oxford: Oxford University Press.
Klarsfeld, A. (2016). A Review of Gröschl, S., & Bendl, R., (eds.), Managing religious diversity in the workplace: examples from around the world. *Equality, Diversity and Inclusion: An International Journal*, 35(no 2), 169–72.
King, J.E., Bell, M.P., & Lawrence, E. (2009). "Religion as an aspect of workplace diversity: an examination of the US context and a call for international research", *Journal of Management, Spirituality and Religion*, 6(no 1), 43–57.
Laborde, C. (2008). *Critical republicanism. The hijab controversy and political philosophy*. New York: Oxford University Press.
Lacorne, D. (2007). *De la religion en Amérique*. Paris: Gallimard.
Lagrange, H. (2010). *Le déni des cultures*. Paris: Seuil.
Lahire, B. (2006). *La culture des individus, Dissonances culturelles et distinction de soi*. Paris: La Découverte.
Laing, R.D. (1961). *The self and others*. London: Tavistock Publication.
Languille, C. (2015). *La possibilité du cosmopolitisme*. Paris: Gallimard.
Lévi-Strauss, C. (2013). *Nous sommes tous des cannibals*. Paris: Seuil.
Levinas, E. (1982). *Ethique et infini*. Paris: Fayard.
Loraux, N. (1981). *Les enfants d'Athéna. Idées athéniennes sur la citoyenneté et la division des sexes*. Paris: F. Maspero.
Machelon, J.-P. (2006). *Les relations de cultes avec les pouvoirs publics*. Paris, La Documentation française. Collection des rapports officiels.
Meeker, M. (2015). "Internet Trends 2015-Code Conférence." KPCB Report, in Glokalde, 1(no 3), May 2015.
Nounckele, J., Christians, L. L. (2013). La main invisible entre civilité et religion. Chaire de droit des religions, Université Catholique de Louvain, July 4.
Observatoire Sociovision de la Société française (2014). *Une demande de discrétion religieuse dans la vie collective*. Note d'analyse.
Özbilgin, M., & Chanlat, J-F. (editors), (2017), *Management and Diversity: Perspectives from Different National Contexts*, London: Emerald Publishing Limited.

Özbilgin, M., & Tatli, A. (2008). *Global diversity management an evidence based approach*. London: Palgrave Macmillan.

Paprec (2015). *Charte de la laïcité*. Paris, Paprec.

Pena-Ruiz, H. (2003). *La Laïcité. Textes choisis*. Paris: GF-Flammarion.

Pew Research Center (2015). *Religion & public life project*. Washington: Pew Research Center.

Pierre, P., & Mutabazi, E. (2010). *Les discriminations*. Paris: Le cavalier bleu.

Portier, P. (2016). *L'Etat et les religions en France, Une sociologie historique de la laïcité*. Rennes: Presses universitaires de Rennes.

Quéré, L. (2015). Religion et sphère publique au prisme du naturalisme pragmatiste. *In* Stavo-Debauge, J., Gonzalez, P., Frega, R. (eds.), *Quel âge post-séculier? Religions, démocraties, sciences*. Paris: Editions EHESS, 113–45.

Rambaud, T. (2011). Introduction. *Société, droit, et religion*, 1(1), 7–9.

RATP. (2013). *Laïcité et neutralité dans l'entreprise, Guide pratique à destination des managers*. Paris: RATP.

Rousseau, J-J. (1762 [2011]). *Du contrat social*. Paris: Poche.

Sachs, T. (2010). *L'intérêt de l'entreprise en droit du travail*. Paris: Séminaire: "Propriété de l'entreprise", Collège des Bernardins.

Sarfati, G. E. (1997). L'étymologie sociale du mot juif. *Mots*. 50(1), 138–42.

Schnapper, D. (2007). *Qu'est-ce que l'intégration?* Paris: Gallimard.

Sciberras, J.-C. (2010). Travail et religion dans l'entreprise: Une cohabitation sous tension, *Droit Social*, 1, 72–5.

Seksig, A. (2011), *Avis: Expression religieuse et laïcité dans l'entreprise*. Paris, Rapport September 1, Haut conseil à l'intégration.

Stavo-Debauge, J., Gonzalez, P., & Frega, R. (2015). *Quel âge post-séculier? Religions, démocraties, sciences*. Paris: Editions EHESS.

Spinoza, B. (1670 [1842]). *Traité théologico-politique*. Paris, Caute, Digitalized by Serge Schoeffert & David Bosman – édition H. Diaz.

Tincq, H. (2013). *France, les religions et la laïcité?* Paris: Le Monde.

Tribalat, M. (2013). *Assimilation. La fin du modèle français*. Paris: éditions du Toucan.

Warnier, J-P. (1999). *Construire la culture matérielle, L'homme qui pensait avec ses doigts*. Paris: Presses Universitaires de France.

Weil, P. (2005). *La République et sa diversité*. Paris: Seuil.

(2015). *Le sens de la républiques*. Paris: Seuil. Retrieved from: www.oyez.org/cases/2013/12-696.

11 *Lessons from the Academy: Concordia College's Journey toward Religious Pluralism*

JACQUELINE BUSSIE AND
MICHELLE LELWICA

> We must embrace the religious diversity that comes with our commitment to religious freedom, and as we move into the new millennium we must find ways to make the differences that have divided people the world over the very source of our strength here in the US.
> ~ Diana Eck, *A New Religious America*

Who are we as an institution and as an organization? Who do we want to become? How can our institution best serve its religiously diverse constituents by embracing the multiple worldviews, gifts, and creativity they bring to the table? In a world where daily news headlines scream religious conflict, how can our organization foster a workplace characterized by interreligious cooperation? How might such cooperation promote organizational flourishing? This chapter explores these pressing questions by taking as its case study Concordia College, an undergraduate residential liberal arts college of the Evangelical Lutheran Church in America (ELCA) located in Moorhead, Minnesota. While our case study addresses the specific challenges and opportunities of a higher education institution on its journey toward religious pluralism, the lessons we have learned along the way proffer practical wisdom that will prove illuminative for any mission-driven organization or business on a similar trajectory.

It is August 2012, and Dr Eboo Patel, founder and president of Interfaith Youth Core (IFYC) and Concordia's first Forum on Faith and Life guest speaker, has just given the convocation keynote address. A mother whose daughter is considering a Religion major sits in a religion professor's office and puzzles, "I don't get it. Why would a Christian college have a Muslim convocation speaker?" Her tone is curious, not confrontational. It's not the first time this question will be asked, nor will it be the last, and not always so kindly. In fact, the increased frequency of the question compels us to collectively respond with intentionality to the deeper questions that ground it, namely: What does it mean for an institution to embrace religious pluralism, and how does this embrace relate to and/or challenge an institution's mission and identity? What specific actions must an institution take to embrace religious diversity as a source of strength rather than division?

Religious Diversity as a Fact of Life, Religious Pluralism as an Institutional Goal

Intentionally exploring such questions is crucial for the health of any workplace in our nation today. As Dr. Diana Eck, the director of Harvard University's Pluralism Project, observes, "The United States has become the most religiously diverse nation on earth" (Eck, 2001, p. 4). While most organizations (perhaps especially higher education institutions) aim to foster understanding and respect for human diversity, strangely and regrettably this aim rarely if ever extends to religious diversity. As Patel notes, "While higher education has stepped forward to do the hard – even heroic – work engaging diversity issues related to race, gender, ethnicity, and sexuality, religious identity has too frequently been dismissed or treated with derision ... Yet religion is at the heart of national debates and global politics" (Patel, 2015, n.p.). Religion is also central to many people's core values and identity. Arguably, many workplaces in America fail to engage this form of diversity. As a result, they not only neglect key aspects of the lives of their employees, shareholders, and clients or customers, but they miss an opportunity to be part of a larger movement that is reshaping the social, cultural, and religious landscape of twenty-first century America: the movement toward interfaith understanding and cooperation.

Concordia's interfaith journey toward religious pluralism has been guided by Eck's distinction between religious diversity and religious pluralism. *Religious diversity* is a fact of life in our global society: Jews, Hindus, Atheists, Muslims, Buddhists, Christians, people from a variety of less well-known faith traditions, and those who identify as "spiritual-but-not-religious" live and work side by side, and/or they are connected by a vast array of technologies. In this context, *religious pluralism* involves intentional dialogue and cooperation among people who orient around religion differently (Eck, 2006). Organizationally, pluralism may entail creating workplaces that welcome, engage, and affirm diverse religious beliefs and practices, inclusive of those who do not hold any religious beliefs or affiliations. As the distinction between religious diversity and religious pluralism suggests, religious pluralism – the harnessing of religious diversity as a rich resource for working toward the common good – is an ongoing, deliberate, and not-always-tidy process. It is as much a voyage across unknown terrain as it is an arrival at a terminus. It is not for the faint of heart, the unadventurous, or those bound to a parochial past.

A pluralist approach to religious diversity is critical for addressing the challenges and opportunities of twenty-first century organizations, companies, and institutions. Avoiding or ignoring religious differences, tip-toeing around them, or approaching them in an exclusivist manner, are outdated methods for dealing with this diversity. As Eck observes,

No one would dream of operating in the business or political world with ideas about Russia, India, or China that were formed 50, 100, or 500 years ago … The old time religion is not "good enough" unless those of us who claim it are able to grapple honestly and faithfully with the new questions, challenges, and knowledge posed to us by the vibrant world of many living faiths. (Eck, 2001, p. 24)

Organizational leaders need new strategies and perspectives for engaging religious diversity in the workplace not only to pre-empt or navigate conflicts that emerge in relation to such differences, but also to engage their creative potential to advance institutional/organizational goals.

Embracing these challenges and opportunities, Concordia College has publicly committed to the journey of religious pluralism. Our engagement in interfaith work is a direct response to the "changing US religious landscape," as it is described by a recent survey by the Pew Research Center. Whereas the number of self-identified Christians has declined (from 78.4% in 2007 to 70.6% in 2014), the number of those belonging to non-Christian traditions has increased (4.7% in 2007 to 5.9% in 2014). The most dramatic change, however, is the growing number of those who are not religiously affiliated (16.1% in 2007 to 22.8% in 2014), especially (though not exclusively) among young adults. Interestingly, these developments are happening around the country among people who are demographically diverse (Pew Research Center, 2015).

Both our local community and our student body reflect these broader trends. The once predominantly Lutheran Midwestern town of Fargo-Moorhead where Concordia is located now has over 6,000 Muslims (and two mosques), about 100 Jews (and three synagogues), nearly 3,000 Hindus, roughly 1,000 Buddhists, approximately 1,000 self-described secular individuals, a small but thriving Baha'i community of about 45 members, and 28 Yazidis, one of our newest religious refugee groups (Meyers, 2016). Reflecting these demographic changes, Concordia's campus has also become more diverse. As one might expect at a Christian affiliated college, a sizable majority of our students in 2014 (64%) reported some form of Christian religious identity, but that was down from 89% in 2007 (the same comparative period studied by the Pew Research Center). Interestingly, a significant number (13.9%) among the remainder identify as atheist or agnostic. Also worth noting is that roughly a third of our students have switched religious affiliation since coming to Concordia, and about the same percentage self-describe as "spiritual but not religious" (Martinson & Copeland, 2014; O'Connor, 2015) Instead of ignoring this rich and evolving diversity, we have sought to value and engage it as an opportunity to re-examine our identity and mission as a church-related institution that seeks to serve the wider world.

In this process of re-examination, we aim to avoid the two dangerous pitfalls on either end of the institutional identity-crisis continuum (Bussie, 2014). On the one end of the continuum, we are not interested in jettisoning who we are as an institution, as if our spiritual heritage is a source of shame – i.e. we were once a Lutheran school, but that doesn't mean anything to us now. On the opposite end, we have no interest in defining our identity in negative or exclusivist terms – i.e. by hiring only Lutheran faculty, teaching exclusively Lutheran students, or seeking to convert all students to Lutheranism. Alternatively, we seek continually to explore, define, and express our identity in ways that are simultaneously rooted in our mission and open to reinterpreting that mission in a manner that respectfully responds to the actual needs of our diverse students.

Chapter Preview

The authors of this chapter have been integrally involved in Concordia's journey toward religious pluralism. Dr. Jacqueline Bussie is the director of Concordia's Forum on Faith and Life, and Dr. Michelle Lelwica is chair of Concordia's Religion Department. Our story in this chapter maps our quest to become a community that is both intentionally grounded in the college's mission and genuinely pluralist in its policies and practices. It describes ten *deliberate practical steps* Concordia College has taken to infuse the campus ecology with the goal of religious pluralism and thereby live out its public commitment to interfaith understanding and cooperation. In brief, these steps include:

1. Identify and engage core institutional assets for the journey toward religious pluralism;
2. Craft curricula and language that promote religious pluralism;
3. Adopt intentional hiring practices;
4. Develop a strong institutional infrastructure;
5. Consult national experts to glean best practices;
6. Empower students;
7. Incorporate diverse voices in organizational policy;
8. Assess campus climate/workplace regarding religious diversity and modify policies and practices based on assessment findings;
9. Establish a public interfaith identity by means of an official Interfaith Cooperation Statement and community engagement programming;
10. Risk innovation.

Shaped by specific challenges and opportunities in the academy, Concordia's interfaith journey has implications for any organization, business, or institution that seeks to create a workplace that flourishes *not in spite of – but because of –* religious diversity.

Infusing Religious Pluralism across the Campus Ecology

Step 1: Identify and Engage Core Institutional Assets

Because it is an educational institution, Concordia has several built-in assets and advantages as it pursues the path of religious pluralism. As a liberal arts college of the Evangelical Lutheran Church of America, we are an institution that takes religious faith seriously as a significant dimension of human life and cultures. In fact, all of our students are required to take two courses in religion, both of which aim to foster basic religious literacy (i.e., knowledge and critical thinking about religious beliefs, practices, and institutions) as well as examination of one's own spiritual convictions and/or worldview. These courses play a significant role in fulfilling Concordia's mission to educate students to be thoughtful, informed, and responsible global citizens who positively "influence the affairs of the world" (Concordia College, 2016b). While this mission was articulated decades before the interfaith movement had gained momentum, we have come to see it as an asset on our journey toward pluralism as we recognize that interreligious literacy and skills for dialogue are key components of the responsible global citizenship Concordia seeks to foster in its students.

Undoubtedly, one of the biggest advantages Concordia has in cultivating the interfaith dimension of this mission is its Religion faculty's commitment to the academic study of religion. This approach to teaching and learning about religion is designed to cultivate students' capacity to examine religious faith with a curious mind and open heart. It enables them to:

- analyze religions' function in human lives and cultures;
- recognize religions' potential as vehicles for cruelty as well as compassion;
- ask critical questions about the social implications of seemingly personal religious beliefs and practices;
- appreciate the diverse stories, symbols, moral teachings, and institutions humans have created to connect them to their ultimate values and to guide them in their daily lives;
- struggle to make sense of and respond to the reality of suffering; and
- wonder about the ultimate purpose of existence.

In other words, the courses that all Concordia students are required to take are designed to help them learn about, explore, understand, and critically analyze religions *without promoting or requiring adherence to a particular creed*. Put differently, our classrooms affirm academic freedom when it comes to investigating questions of faith. Such an approach fosters an environment in which students can develop and articulate their own views about religion in dialogue with course materials, their professors, and each other – *without fear of coercion*. Ultimately, this approach to religion provides a natural foundation for interreligious understanding and dialogue because its aim is not to judge, indoctrinate, or convert but to learn about and better understand the complex, varied, and dynamic character and functions of religion.

While most companies, organizations, and institutions do not have the luxury of having employees who are trained in the academic approach to studying religion, it may be possible to invite specialists in this area to share their knowledge and skills for engaging religious diversity with employers and employees. Religion faculty from local colleges and universities may be consulted or hired to lead religious diversity training for workers and corporate leaders who seek to foster both literacy and skills for dialogue across religious differences.

Whether in the classroom or in the workplace, fear of judgment, indoctrination, and/or coercion can make discussions about religious differences difficult at best, and potentially explosive at worst. In this light, Concordia's Religion department's foundational commitment to academic freedom when it comes to exploring religious values and viewpoints may be more than an internal advantage we have as a religiously affiliated liberal arts institution. It may also provide a model for approaching religion – namely, in a curious-minded, open-hearted, and analytical way – that is fruitful for any workplace that seeks to engage religious diversity as a resource rather than an obstacle to organizational flourishing.

Just as religions are themselves dynamic – Eck suggests they are more like rivers than stones (Eck, 2001, p. 22) – so too our approach to teaching about them has evolved over the years, responding to changes within and beyond the academy. By the turn of the millennium, public discourse about religion had become deeply polarized in the West. New Atheists declared religion to be the nemesis of civilization, while religious fundamentalists viewed secularism as synonymous with "Satan." Growing divisions among people who orient around religion differently in the USA, alongside ongoing conflicts involving religion around the world, prompted Concordia's Religion faculty to intensify our efforts to promote religious pluralism.

Step 2: Craft Intentional Curricula and Language That Promote Religious Pluralism

As a second step in this fortified effort, we decided to revise our first required Religion course (Religion 200), which all Concordia students take, by increasing its focus on interreligious literacy and skills for interfaith dialogue. Prior to 2002, Religion 200 was called "Christianity and the Religious Life." As this title suggests, its content focused primarily on various aspects of the Christian tradition, and "religious life" was defined mostly (though not exclusively) in relation to Christianity. Without abandoning attention to Christianity, we committed to expanding course materials to include more learning about other traditions. Specifically, we aimed to introduce students to at least one non-Christian religion in significant depth, and we renamed Religion 200: "Christianity and Religious Diversity." This new title was significant not only because it reflected substantive content changes in the course, but also because it communicated to students and to a broader public our commitment to religious pluralism. "Christianity and Religious Diversity" unapologetically expressed our belief that learning about different religions is valuable and necessary for thoughtful and informed global citizenship – and, that this learning need not come at the expense of studying one's own tradition, which, for most of our students, was (and still is) Christianity.

One lesson we learned in revising this core course and changing its title is that the movement to religious pluralism requires deliberate effort. Since most faculty in our department had expertise primarily in the study of Christianity (i.e., in Christian history, theology, or biblical studies), increasing attention to religious diversity in Religion 200 required some serious homework on our part: reading, researching, attending conferences, talking with peers at other institutions to learn more about traditions outside our expertise. The result of such intentional efforts has been not only more complex and informed understandings of Judaism, Islam, Buddhism, and Hinduism among Concordia's Religion faculty, but also a richer view of Christianity in relation to those traditions. Needless to say, we pass the fruits of our labors on to our students, the majority of whom now tell us they enjoy and even take pride in gaining knowledge about religions and worldviews other than their own.

In fact, many of our students are intrigued by the possibility of thinking about religious differences in ways that do not presume the superiority of one tradition and the corresponding need for "others" to convert. A number of them express relief upon learning that it is possible to wholeheartedly affirm the truths of their own spiritual tradition or worldview without assuming that all people on earth must adopt them. Moreover, these students are genuinely grateful to acquire the interfaith skill of gaining deeper insight into the particularity of their own religious traditions and commitments through conversations with others with divergent beliefs and devotions. One of the texts Dr. Michelle Lelwica uses when she teaches Religion 200 – Karen Armstrong's *Twelve Steps to a Compassionate Life* (Armstrong, 2011) – encourages this process of cultivating self-knowledge through the process of learning about diverse spiritual traditions. Students also appreciate gaining basic knowledge about these traditions – e.g., about the Five Pillars of Islam, the two different meanings of "jihad," the Four Noble Truths of Buddhism, the role of deities in the Hindu tradition, the Confucian concepts of *ren* or *li*, the significance of the Torah in Judaism, the key differences between Protestant, Catholic, and Orthodox Christian teachings, and so forth.

As an extension of the work we do to foster interreligious literacy in the classroom, several Religion faculty also lead study abroad trips for students to places where they experience cultural and religious diversity first hand – in countries as diverse as Egypt, South Africa, Italy, Greece, Turkey, Israel, and Jordon. These embodied encounters with diverse people and their worldviews, customs, architecture, food, landscapes, rituals, life struggles, and stories foster the kind of three-dimensional interfaith learning that is impossible to get from a book. Paradoxically, students' first-hand experiences with religiously diverse worlds help them appreciate the common existential questions and humane values that connect spiritual traditions. As the Dalai Lama observes,

On the metaphysical level, all major religions confront the same perennial questions: Who am I? Where do I come from? Where will I go after death? On the level of living a good life, all the faith traditions turn to compassion as a guiding principle. They use different words, invoke different images, root themselves in different concepts. But what they have in common is far more than what divides them, and their differences form the potential for a tremendously enriching dialogue, rooted in a marvelous diversity of experience and insight. (His Holiness the Dalai Lama, 2010, p. x)

To be sure, there are moments in this learning process that are difficult for some students. For those who grew up learning that religion is strictly about what you believe, that only one belief is correct, and that it is thus imperative to convince others to adopt that belief, the academic study of multiple religions can be difficult, disorienting, and even disturbing. With time, however, and with supportive and sensitive prodding from both their professors and their classmates, most students come to appreciate the value of a pluralist classroom precisely because their views are considered valuable – if particular – assets in the conversation. Many enjoy the challenge of taking seriously the religious perspectives of others while remaining true to their own beliefs and commitments. Some are genuinely puzzled about why they did not have the opportunity to learn about diverse religions sooner. "Why didn't they teach me this in Sunday school?" is a common question, and, "Kids should learn about different religions in high school" is a frequent suggestion. Fortunately, it's never too late to learn about diverse religions and to practice religious pluralism. On the whole, the sometimes challenging but always lively exchanges about and across different religions and worldviews that take place in our classrooms is proof that such diversity need not be an obstacle to building mutual relationships and respectful understanding.

Step 3: Adopt Intentional Hiring Practices

Our decision in 2002 to modify the content and title of Religion 200 to increase attention to religious diversity was prompted not only by growing animosity among people with different religious commitments, but also by the terrorist attacks of September 11. If most Americans knew little about Islam prior to this defining moment in world history, the harmful consequences of such ignorance became apparent almost as soon as the dust from the crumbled buildings settled. Widespread stereotypes of Muslim men as probable terrorists, of Muslim women as horribly oppressed, and of Islam in general as a religion of violence made Muslims in the USA (and those perceived to be Muslims) vulnerable to verbal and physical abuse. Since one of the best ways to counter stereotypes is to educate people about the complexity and diversity within the group being targeted, Concordia Religion faculty knew we had a particular responsibility to teach our students about Islam. In redesigning Religion 200, we devoted a significant portion of the course to teaching about Islam. Our curricular development in this area emphasized *both* common Muslim patterns of belief and practice (e.g., the oneness of God, submission to God through prayer and other observances) *and* the vast diversity within this tradition (e.g., nearly all incidents of violence committed in the name of Islam have emanated from radical [Takfiri] Wahhabi/Salafi and Deobandi traditions within Islam, while the vast majority of Sunni and Shia Muslims practice their faith through acts of peace, justice, and compassion). In addition to devoting more curricular attention to Islam, we launched an international search for a scholar specifically trained in the study of Islam – someone who could not only teach our students about this tradition but who could further enrich our own understanding.

This hiring decision represented another significant step on our journey to religious pluralism – one that expressed our growing commitment to the interfaith enterprise. Those of us involved with this decision knew about the benefits of intentional hiring practices when it comes to ethnic, racial, and/or gender diversity; we simply extended this line of thinking to include the area of religious diversity.

The first scholar/teacher of Islam who joined our faculty – a brilliant, soft-spoken Pakistani-American Muslim who wore traditional clothing and a thick, neatly shaven beard – brought a dimension to learning about Islam that neither students nor faculty could get from a book. His broad and deep knowledge about religion – not just Islam, but Judaism and Christianity as well – and his very presence made such a positive impression on our students and on us that when he left our department to take a position in Pakistan in 2005, we knew immediately that we would seek to replace him with someone with similar training. Fortunately, we were able to hire another brilliant yet humble Muslim scholar/teacher who, coincidentally, was also of Pakistani descent and whose expertise continues to enrich students and faculty alike. While this Muslim colleague teaches a few upper-level courses on Islam, significantly, he also teaches "Christianity and Religious Diversity," as well as other upper-level courses (e.g., "American Religions," "Religion, Violence, and Nonviolence"), and a first-year seminar entitled "Surviving Progress," which focuses on environmental issues. This colleague's scholarly and personal grounding in his own faith tradition, combined with his deep knowledge about and openness to learning/teaching about the beliefs, practices, stories, and worldviews of other religions, further strengthens the pluralism our department fosters and our institution embraces.

Step 4: Develop a Strong Intentional Infrastructure: The Forum on Faith and Life

In addition to the steps Concordia has taken to engage its assets, modify curriculum, and make intentional hiring decisions that promote religious pluralism, the college has also taken significant strides at the institutional level. One of the boldest and most effective of these has been the creation of a more *intentional infrastructure*, namely, the establishment of the Forum on Faith and Life in 2011. Founded with the help of a generous grant from the Lilly Endowment, the Forum on Faith and Life functions as the institution's interfaith and ecumenical resource center. Building upon the college's basic character and aims, the Forum on Faith and Life's mission is to "foster a deeper and more compassionate understanding of one another across traditional boundaries" by creating "opportunities for genuine encounter with the intra-faith and interfaith neighbor" (Concordia College, 2011).

Undoubtedly, the Forum on Faith and Life has helped transform our campus and enabled Concordia to take its commitment to pluralism to the next level. Wisely, Concordia perceived "the next level" to be unattainable unless interreligious work received (1) substantially greater resource and budget allocation, (2) an intentional oversight "house" at the institutional level, (3) a reduced teaching-time tenured faculty director whose specific directive was to help foster and sustain a climate of pluralism for the college as a whole, and (4) outspoken administrative support and leadership. With the groundbreaking 2011 start-up of the Forum and hiring of its inaugural director, Dr. Jacqueline Bussie, Concordia accomplished all four of these necessary steps. As Concordia College president Dr. William Craft officially explained that same academic year in the new strategic plan, *Whole Self, Whole Life, Whole World*: Concordia will "promote inter-faith conversation and service as a primary function of our identity as a college of the church" (Concordia College Board of Regents, 2012). Instead of paying mere lip service to this commitment, the administration continues to provide the Forum with its own operating budget, even at a time of institutional frugality. Walking the talk of its commitment to religious diversity has helped make Concordia an interfaith leader in higher education.

What makes Concordia's interfaith resource center especially innovative and unique within the landscape of higher education is that its director is not only a religion professor but also a public theologian rooted in the spiritual heritage of the college. This decision alone sends a strong public relations message that increased involvement in interreligious cooperation, service, and learning, does *not* represent an abandonment of our institution's valued heritage, but instead a revivification of that heritage for enhanced relevance in the current era of increased pluralism. As interfaith activist Rabbi Abraham Joshua Heschel once pithily explained: "The problem to be faced is how to combine loyalty to one's own tradition with reverence for different traditions" (Heschel, 2011, p. 125).

As a Lutheran theologian, the director of the Forum on Faith and Life is tasked with helping the college provide a clear articulation for internal and external constituents of the theological legitimacy of pluralism within the Lutheran tradition. Fortunately, a growing number of resources within the Lutheran heritage support interfaith dialogue, cooperation and pluralism. The ELCA statement on "Ecumenical and Inter-Religious Relations" is one such resource (ELCA, 1991). In addition, the Lutheran World Federation has a strong emphasis in Interfaith Dialogue (ELCA, 2016). Recently, an entire issue of *Intersections* (a publication that features articles by and primarily for members of the 26 colleges and universities of the ELCA) explored the relationship of the interfaith movement to this denomination, and included an invited article written by Dr. Bussie, examining Concordia as a case study for interfaith work in Lutheran higher education (Bussie, 2014). In that article, Bussie argues that Luther's resistance to the either/or mold – with his designation of human beings as *simul justus et peccator* (simultaneously righteous and sinner) – theologically empowers Lutherans to be adept at "simul"/*both-and* thinking and therefore enables them to embody Heschel's stated paradox of both rootedness and reverence. In that same article, Bussie also shares the prophetic words of former ELCA Presiding Bishop Mark Hanson, "We are called to be stewards of unity within diversity in a culture which confuses unity with uniformity" (Bussie 2014, pp. 36–7).

Misperceptions about who belongs and who does not arise with renewed vigor in today's us-vs.-them culture, where religious identity is often assumed to be a polarizing and exclusivist force. In 1991, in a social statement on ecumenism, the ELCA intentionally discouraged polarization by overtly stating its relationship to other Christian traditions in this manner: "It is a communion where diversities contribute to fullness and are no longer barriers to unity ... The diversities are reconciled and transformed into a legitimate and indispensable multiformity [i.e., diverse expressions of Lutheran faith] within the one body" (ELCA, 1991). The Lutheran tradition therefore, advocates for *harmony within heterogeneity* – not unity through uniformity.

This guiding principle of reconciled diversity is a healthy precept to adopt in any workplace, and one which Concordia's Director of the Forum on Faith and Life has extracted from the tradition and used repeatedly in various publications and lectures to theologically ground Concordia's interfaith work.

Much to our delight, after only five short years (2011–16), the creation of intentional infrastructure embodied in the Forum on Faith and Life has garnered national recognition for our college as a vanguard institution for interfaith excellence in higher education. As evidence, consider the following. Dr. Jacqueline Bussie, Director of Concordia's Forum on Faith and Life, was invited to speak on a three-person panel entitled "Interfaith Engagement: A Liberal Arts Imperative," at the Association of American Colleges and Universities Annual Conference in Washington, DC in January, 2015. That some month, Concordia President William Craft was invited to deliver a plenary lecture at the Council of Independent Colleges on the theme of interfaith work's importance in higher education. At the White-House sponsored President's Interfaith Campus Challenge conference in September 2014, Dr. Eboo Patel, in his plenary address highlighting the best practices of ten national vanguard interfaith higher education institutions, named Concordia College first as exemplary in articulating and grounding interfaith work in the school's larger identity and mission. These examples illustrate how religious diversity can become an asset when it is institutionally supported and intentionally engaged, rather than ignored or politely avoided. Indeed, Concordia College is proof that such engagement can not only affirm institutional mission, but reinterpret that mission in ways that promote organizational flourishing while contributing to the common good.

Step 5: Consult the Experts: Partnership with Interfaith Youth Core

The very first action taken by the Forum on Faith and Life was to enlist the aid of the most well-respected experts in interfaith cooperation in higher education, the Interfaith Youth Core (IFYC). Founded by Dr. Eboo Patel in 2002, IFYC's mission is simple yet ambitious: to move interfaith cooperation from niche to social norm, starting with college campuses. In 2011, Concordia entered into a fruitful partnership with IFYC for two years, during which time IFYC served as outstanding consultants to our organization, providing helpful advice with regard to national best practices. Without their constructive feedback, we would most likely never have gleaned the aforementioned national recognition with regard to our interfaith efforts. Perhaps the best guidance offered by IFYC was the careful instruction to be sure to infuse the entire campus ecology with the goal of religious pluralism. After thoughtful critical reflection upon our own institutional needs and culture, we implemented this advice through the following five critical steps, which constitute the remainder of this essay.

Step 6: Empower Students – Interfaith Scholars and Better Together

Concordia harnessed the rich diversity of its greatest asset – our students – by empowering them to voice, engage, and act. To do so, we instituted an Interfaith Scholars program, and approved a first-ever on-campus chapter of IFYC's Better Together Interfaith Alliance, a student organization dedicated to interfaith service and dialogue (Interfaith Youth Core, 2016). Concordia's Interfaith Scholars are students from diverse disciplines and religious/non-religious traditions who, as the Forum on Faith and Life interns, receive a fellowship to engage in interfaith studies research, coordinate interfaith programming and service projects, and serve as liaisons between Fargo-Moorhead's religious communities and the college. Selected yearly from an ever-increasing pool of excellent applications, the Interfaith Scholars are exemplary students who are frequently called upon to represent the college regionally and nationally. For the last three years in a row, for example, Concordia's Interfaith Scholars presented their scholarship at national venues including the prestigious National Council on Undergraduate Research and the American Academy of Religion. One Interfaith Scholar was even invited to introduce the Dalai Lama during his 2013 visit to Minneapolis, Minnesota for the Nobel Peace Prize Forum.

For the past two years, Concordia's Interfaith Scholars and Better Together students have organized a community-wide service project that has brought together over 100 youth from eight religious traditions to construct 500 toiletry kits needed for the homeless staying overnight in area shelters. This service project of religious cooperation attracted substantial positive media attention to our institution, including featured spots on the television evening news, radio, and local newspaper. As a result of these successful events, Concordia's Better Together students won one of IFYC's four national awards in both 2013 and 2014. Together, Concordia's Interfaith Scholars and Better Together students have made Concordia's work in interreligious diversity a point of distinction for the college, a source of both pride and enhanced recruitment possibilities.

Notably, the college's Interfaith Scholars as well as the Better Together co-presidents come from different religious and non-religious traditions; by virtue of their shared leadership across difference, these students serve as powerful role models for pluralism. For example, in 2015, one of the Interfaith Scholars was a Lutheran and the other was an atheist; their shared leadership symbolized Concordia's simultaneous commitment to its own Lutheran tradition as well as its dedication to welcoming its growing number of secular students. Importantly, this intentionally inclusive, joint leadership also demonstrates that in spite of media stereotypes and gloomy presages of inevitable culture wars, people who orient differently around religion are perfectly capable of collaborating to achieve common good, without negating their differences or allowing them to escalate into conflict. Equipped with interfaith knowledge and skills, these student leaders model a kind of inclusive leadership that enables people to discover shared goals and values, and empowers them to prioritize doing over doctrine, and collaboration over creed (Bussie, 2011, pp. 30–5).

Step 7: Incorporate Diverse Voices into Organizational Policy: The President's Interfaith Advisory Council

Rather than remain aloof from the interfaith groundswell on campus, Concordia's president created an Interfaith Advisory Council to support it. Chaired by the director of the Forum on Faith and Life, this 22-member President's Interfaith Advisory Council (PIAC) includes diverse faculty, staff, students, and administrators from across the institution who serve as an advisory board to the president and greater campus on all matters related to interfaith engagement. Such a board could easily be emulated within any workplace. The key is to fashion it according to the principle and practice of pluralism. For example, when the director of the Forum on Faith and Life issued invitations to serve on the council, one faculty member mentioned that he would love to be on the council, but then confessed, "I'm an atheist, and I've always felt like an outsider on this campus, so I don't think you want me." The director replied, "That's exactly why the college needs you to be on it. Your voice needs to be heard."

If welcoming diverse voices is essential to the success of a cross-institutional committee like the PIAC, so is the inclusion of leaders from the oft-forgotten offices such as Advancement and Enrollment (whose staff on most campuses rarely if ever have direct contact with faculty, much less matriculated students). One of our Advancement officers on the PIAC became such an articulate advocate of interfaith work that she brought in the college's first gift earmarked for the Interfaith Scholars program. She confided that Concordia's journey toward pluralism allowed her to build relationships with alumni and donors who previously felt alienated by a more parochial understanding of our Lutheran heritage. Lessons learned? *Be intentional about engaging members from all sectors of your workplace community in religious pluralism conversations and efforts.* Interfaith collaboration is an opportunity for building bridges across different sectors of a company or institution. Indeed, many old organizational wounds might be healed and undiscovered resources reclaimed by an explicit invitation of belonging and by deliberate actions to unsilo folks from various branches across the institution.

Step 8: Is Our Organization Where We Want It to Be? Religious Diversity Assessment and Subsequent Modifications

Concordia performed an initial baseline assessment of our campus religious climate (and we plan to assess again every three to five years). As one of 25 schools participating in the 2012 Campus Religious and Spiritual Climate Survey (CRSCS) national pilot, Concordia discovered numerous unknown strengths as well as areas for growth. We discovered to our delight, for example, that our students place an incredibly high value on learning about diverse religious traditions, with 99% of students reporting a medium-to-high pluralism orientation. But we also discovered – much to our shame – that not all of our students saw our campus climate as hospitable. 38% of secular and non-religious students reported feelings of coercion or a lack of acceptance toward their beliefs. Our secular students and their faculty and staff allies leveraged this crucial information as evidence that our institution urgently needed to establish a secular student organization, an organization that had previously been denied official recognition at Concordia because it was understood to be "inconsistent" with our school's Lutheran identity and Christian heritage. In 2013, Concordia established its first-ever Secular Student Alliance, which has supported and served the needs of many students. Without having taken the step of assessment, this change in favor of pluralism would in all likelihood never have occurred.

Additionally, our assessment revealed that many faculty, staff, and students would like to receive more training with regard to religious diversity and pluralism. Prior to the establishment of the Forum on Faith and Life, almost no professional development or training was offered on campus with special attention to religious diversity. As a result of this assessment outcome, we implemented (1) annual Better Together student-led training sessions on religious diversity for Residence Life staff, (2) summer faculty development workshops on interfaith studies and cooperation and (3) an Interfaith Educators program, in which Better Together students visit nearly 20 sections of the required "Christianity and Religious Diversity" courses per year and offer peer-led interactive modules on pluralism and interfaith engagement.

Lessons learned? *Don't fear assessment*. Courageous assessment is particularly essential for Concordia given its roots in the Reformation tradition of *semper reformanda* (always reforming), which Martin Luther helped to establish in the sixteenth century. But this principle has relevance beyond Lutheran institutions. Organizations cannot know what areas in their daily operations and communal life might need reform until they intentionally ask their members for feedback. Concordia's outside-consultant-led focus groups revealed, for example, that some members of our campus were deeply dissatisfied with the lack of accommodations for their non-Christian religious holidays with regard to exams and paid time off. Moreover, our assessment data consistently showed that those at the college within the majority tradition (Christians) overestimated the satisfaction level of those from minority traditions (e.g., atheists, Muslims). Though it may be uncomfortable, such evidence is crucial since it tells us where we need to put more effort as we seek to create a more welcoming campus environment. Because they are not anonymous, conversations with management and supervisors cannot be expected to yield authentic measures of job satisfaction. Individuals experience varying degrees of comfort when it comes to discussing religious identity. Prior to doing our strategic and targeted assessment, we had virtually no idea how those not in the privileged majority were actually experiencing our campus climate. Without the CRSCS survey as an anonymous means of evaluating our campus's religious climate, we would not have been able to identify, much less address, misperceptions, unspoken concerns, and unmet needs.

In your particular workplace, when was the last time the managers and CEOs asked staff and clients in a safe and anonymous way if their diverse religious needs are being accommodated? Has your organization ever formally asked this question? Assessment is not for the timid or uninventive, for undoubtedly it will reveal some unpleasant organizational truths that will require creative solutions. But remember, doing assessment is akin to using a GPS (Global Positioning System). As any GPS user knows, heading anywhere new requires an accurate understanding of your current location – of where you now stand. When it comes to fostering pluralism in the workplace, baseline assessment and regular, sustained, follow-up inventory and evaluation of strengths and weaknesses are perennially necessary. No organization should ever stop asking its members the question, "Are we where want to be with regard to religious pluralism, and if not, what strategies can we take to get there?"

Step 9: Establish a Public Interfaith Identity: Interfaith Cooperation Statement and Community Engagement Programming

Another challenging yet transformative step on our journey toward pluralism was the articulation of a succinct thoughtful answer to the question raised in the anecdote appearing at the beginning of this essay: "Why does a Lutheran college commit itself to interfaith cooperation, dialogue and service?" Many of us on campus knew intuitively that our college's many interfaith curricular and co-curricular activities somehow expressed who Concordia is in the twenty-first century, but we still had not, in unison and in relation to our mission and Lutheran tradition, answered the inquisitive parent's question: *why?*

Although some of us across campus had our own individual answers to this query, any business major could easily have diagnosed our woeful lack of consistent messaging. And while some academics may frown on "messaging" as the for-profit concern of corporations and not colleges, our interfaith work has taught us that consistent messaging really matters. Why? If you do not know as a community who you are and articulate why you do the things you do, tragic misperceptions fill the gaps the same way weeds grow in lawns and gardens – precisely in those areas that have been neglected. A consistent message enables us, for example, proactively to address the potential anxieties and questions of a prospective student, who tells an admissions representative or faculty member, "I am Muslim/Buddhist/Baha'i/atheist. I am worried I won't fit in at Concordia. Is there really a place for me here?"

To pre-empt misperceptions about what it means to be a religiously affiliated college in a religiously polarized society, the Concordia President's Interfaith Advisory Council (PIAC) decided to construct an official college statement on interfaith engagement and pluralism. After a year of wordsmithing, focus groups, countless meetings, and broad-based consensus building across all levels of the campus ecology, the end result was a sentence we cherish for its connections both to our specific educational mission and to the ELCA's values:

Concordia College practices interfaith cooperation because of its Lutheran dedication to prepare thoughtful and informed global citizens who foster wholeness and hope, build peace through understanding, and serve the world together. (Concordia College, 2015)

Members of the PIAC were thrilled to discover not only that a group of people in an academic setting could unanimously agree to a one-sentence answer to any question (miraculous!), but also that the process of answering the particular question – why interfaith at Concordia? – evoked some fascinating and long overdue conversations. None of us will forget the meeting wherein an extraordinarily lively yet respectful debate broke out over the statement's subordinate clause, "because of its Lutheran dedication." Several Christian members of the group argued for the milder subordinate conjunction "guided by," but – perhaps contrary to expectations – an atheist student and a Muslim faculty colleague argued compellingly for the unequivocal phrasing "because of." The Muslim colleague passionately insisted, "I want to know that there will *always* be a place for me here ... that I belong here because this place is Lutheran, not because some folks might possibly be 'guided' to create a space for me ... or not." In the end, she (along with our atheist student) persuaded everyone in the room.

Also surprisingly, many participants in the statement's construction openly expressed gratitude merely for inclusion in the dialogue. Many of us sensed that we were part of a conversation in which who we are as a community was in the process of being determined by us collectively, rather than handed down to us as pre-ordained by strangers from the past. Lesson learned? *The process of creating a pluralism statement for your organization is as informative and necessary as the actual statement itself.* Let the process surprise you and perhaps even help facilitate understanding and reconciliation amongst your divergent constituents.

As the IFYC states in its document *Leadership Practices for Interfaith Excellence*, "a campus' public interfaith identity complements its internal strategy" (Patel et al., 2015). Without a doubt, an official pluralism statement like Concordia's strengthens an organization's public interfaith identity. Concordia has already begun utilizing its interfaith engagement statement on its website, recruitment materials, and conversations with donors, with great success. Moreover, as Concordia's interfaith praxis statement makes clear, our institution of higher learning seeks to distinguish itself in the marketplace through its interfaith initiatives, *not in spite of*, but *because of* its identity as a college of the ELCA. For any organization seeking to make institutional change, a transparent explanation to valued constituents that the change is authentically grounded in the institution's mission and identity is crucial to mitigate misinformed resistance.

In addition to the interfaith engagement statement, another crucial way that Concordia has established its public identity as an institution hospitable to pluralism is through active interfaith community engagement, including high-profile interreligious speakers and co-curricular programming. These activities are essential, for they bring theory to praxis, and prove that we are not paying mere lip-service to religious diversity. The Forum on Faith and Life has been intentional in planning a signature speaker series for students and the broader public that either focus on a non-Christian tradition or that feature scholars and/or activists who represent religious minorities. For example, the Forum's annual speaker series has brought to campus Nobel Peace Prize Winner and interfaith activist Leymah Gbowee; renowned author, humanist chaplain and interfaith leader Chris Stedman; Indigenous ecofeminist author and activist, Winona LaDuke; and Dr. Eboo Patel, founder and president of IFYC. Both Gbowee and Patel drew huge audiences of nearly 900 attendees, many of whom were from the surrounding Fargo-Moorhead area, and many of whom remarked that they were surprised (and thrilled) to see Concordia doing this new pluralism programming. Concordia's curricular and co-curricular interfaith events, such as public lectures, serve a dual purpose of nurturing interfaith understanding on campus while creating bridges between our campus and the local community.

Concordia also collaborates with community partners to host a Religious Diversity in the Workplace conference for local business leaders, a bi-annual Interfaith Chapel Week with Baha'i, Buddhist, and Native American speakers, and regular interfaith events such as a "Meet Your Muslim Neighbor" panel, a Buddhist Mindfulness & Meditation Retreat, and an "Ask an Atheist" panel. Faculty in the Religion department also regularly welcome scholars from around the country to give lectures on topics relating to religious diversity. In addition, they invite religiously diverse guest speakers from the local community to their classes, take students on field trips to local and regional religious sites (e.g., mosques, synagogues, orthodox churches, and Hindu temples) where they interact with people whose spiritual worldviews differ from their own. The Forum on Faith and Life hosts faculty book reads on interfaith texts, and the year that Eboo Patel was Concordia's convocation speaker, all incoming first-year students read his book *Acts of Faith* as the summer book read. Events such as these not only enhance interfaith learning among students, faculty, and staff on campus, but they are also important public relations opportunities. Through such high-profile, broad-reaching events, Concordia establishes itself to external and internal constituents both locally and nationally as an institution that prioritizes pluralism.

Step 10: Risk Innovation: Developing an Interfaith Studies Minor

Tenth and finally, as mentioned above, the authors of this essay applied and won (in 2014) one of ten national grants distributed by the Teagle Foundation to higher education institutions seeking to establish interfaith studies minor course sequences. (At the time of this writing, less than a dozen institutions nationwide have such programs [Freedman, 2016; Silverman, 2016].) Interfaith Studies is an emerging interdisciplinary field that examines "the multiple dimensions of how individuals and groups who orient around religion differently interact with one another, and the implications of these interactions for communities, civil society, and global politics" (Patel, 2013). It is an academic field that has a practical aim of developing a cadre of professionals who can "responsibly engage the world" as interfaith leaders (Concordia College, 2016a). In our vision, an Interfaith Studies minor combines rigorous academic study that promotes interreligious literacy with the cultivation of skills for dialogue so as to empower interfaith leaders to engage the religious diversity of our world to positive ends.

Ultimately, we envision that Concordia students who graduate with this minor will be future educators, public servants, health care professionals, business people, communications specialists, musicians, writers, and social workers (to give some examples) whose interfaith literacy and skills prepare them to navigate the challenges and opportunities of religious diversity in the workplace to constructive ends. In this way, the Interfaith Studies minor we are creating links Concordia's journey toward religious pluralism to a broader – indeed global – movement to create a more peaceful society.

Grant co-directors Lelwica and Bussie, along with an interdisciplinary committee of students and faculty, worked throughout the 2014–15 academic year to draft a proposal for an interdisciplinary Interfaith Studies minor at Concordia. In the fall of 2015, Concordia's Faculty Senate unanimously approved this proposal. The strong buy-in and interest from faculty across the disciplines seeking to teach in the new, innovative minor is indicative of broad enthusiasm for interfaith engagement. Remarkably, 28 faculty from 11 different disciplines – including Business, Education, History, Political Science, Psychology, Communications, Philosophy, and Religion, among others – submitted their courses to be included in the minor! Lesson learned? *Risking innovation pays off*. Members of your workplace community might be more ready for creative change than you think. Moreover, a burgeoning number of foundations and philanthropic organizations like the Teagle Foundation, the Ford Foundation, and the Luce Foundation are beginning to fund inventive projects that foster religious diversity training and interreligious competencies for leadership and service in a pluralistic world. We expect this number to grow in the future. Drawing upon these resources and the practical strategies and lessons offered in this chapter, your organization could become a leader in this nascent field.

The enthusiasm surrounding the creation of an Interfaith Studies minor at Concordia did not happen overnight. It is the result of decades of a committed journey to interreligious pluralism. Thanks to previous steps we've taken along the way, Concordia faculty clearly support the vision that responsible citizenship requires developing a framework, knowledge base, and skills set to help religiously diverse individuals and communities build mutual respect, fruitful relationships, and collaboration for a more just and compassionate world. Together with our students, staff, and administration, we have come to see that promoting interfaith literacy and skills for dialogue are essential elements of our mission to teach students to cultivate inquiry instead of ignorance, reconciliation instead of division, and the common good instead of conflict.

Concluding Reflections

In *Living Buddha, Living Christ*, Vietnamese Zen Master, peace activist, and poet Thich Nhat Hanh describes an exchange that occurred at a conference of theologians and religion professors. A conference leader addressed the assembly: "We are going to hear about the beauties of several traditions, but that does not mean that we are going to make a fruit salad." In response, Hanh gently observed: "Fruit salad can be delicious!" Analyzing the incident, Hanh explains: "I do not see any reason to spend one's whole life tasting just one kind of fruit. We human beings can be nourished by the best values of many traditions" (Hanh, 1995, pp. 1–2). Hanh does not advocate that people abandon their particular spiritual heritage. Nor does he recommend making a smoothie from our religious differences. Instead, his fruit salad image implies that organizations can be nourished when their constituents' distinct perspectives and traditions are brought into conversation with each other in ways that honor the particular beauty and integrity of each.

Few of us live and work in a world that consists entirely of apples or oranges. Sadly, the widespread polarization and misunderstanding about religious differences generates a good deal of "fruit salad" (and/or "smoothie") anxiety. But, as Concordia's journey toward religious pluralism demonstrates, this needs not be the case. Whether religious diversity is a blessing or a burden largely depends on the perspective we cultivate. Organizational and educational practices that help constituents approach such diversity with curiosity, understanding, respect, and appreciation are crucial for creating a workplace in which different loyalties and worldviews are assets rather than liabilities. Institutional support for the kinds of steps we have described in this chapter is critical for their success. Intentionally rooting the interfaith journey in an organization's mission is a powerful way to promote the wondrous alchemy of continuity and change that enables an organization – and the individuals who serve it – to flourish.

References

Armstrong, K. (2011). *Twelve steps to a compassionate life*. New York: Alfred A Knopf.

Bussie, J. (2011). Reconciled diversity: Reflections on our calling to embrace our religious neighbors. *Intersections*, 33, 30–5.

(2014). Interfaith Understanding at Lutheran Colleges and Universities. *Intersections*, 40, 34–7.

Concordia College. (2011). Forum on Faith and Life Mission Statement. Retrieved from: www.concordiacollege.edu/directories/offices-services/forum-on-faith-and-life/.

(2015). Interfaith Cooperation Statement. Retrieved from: www.concordiacollege.edu/studentlife/spiritual-life/.

(2016a). BREW (Becoming Responsibly Engaged in the World). Retrieved from: www.concordiacollege.edu/academics/brew/.

(2016b). Our Mission. Retrieved from: www.concordiacollege.edu/about/our-mission/.

Concordia College Board of Regents. (2012). Whole Self, Whole Life, Whole World: The Plan for Concordia College 2012–2017. Retrieved from: www.concordiacollege.edu/about/our-mission/strategic-plan/.

Eck, D. (2001). *A new religious America: How a "Christian country" has become the world's most religiously diverse nation*. New York: HarperCollins Publishers.

(2006). What is Pluralism? The Pluralism Project, Harvard University. Retrieved from: http://pluralism.org/pluralism/what_is_pluralism.

ELCA (Evangelical Lutheran Church in America). (1991). The Vision of the Evangelical Lutheran Church in America. Retrieved from: www.download.elca.org/ELCA%20Resource%20Repository/The_Vision_Of_The_ELCA.pdf.

(2016). Public Theology and Interreligious Relations. Retrieved from: www.lutheranworld.org/content/public-theology-and-interreligious-relations.

Freedman, S. G. (2016). A laboratory for interfaith studies in Pennsylvania Dutch country. *The New York Times* (April 29). Retrieved from: www.nytimes.com/2016/04/30/us/alaboratory-for-interfaith-studies-in-pennsylvania-dutch-country.html.

Hanh, T. N. (1995). *Living Buddha, living Christ*. New York: Riverhead.

Heschel, A. J. (2011). *Essential Writings*. Heschel, S. (ed.). Maryknoll, NY: Orbis.

His Holiness the Dalai Lama. (2010). *Toward a true kinship of faiths: How the world's religions can come together*. New York: Doubleday Religion.

Interfaith Youth Core. (2016). Better Together. Retrieved from: www.ifyc.org/about-better-together.

Martinson, R., & Copeland, A. (2014). *Worship, faith, and spiritual practice project: Final report*. Moorhead, MN: Concordia College.

Meyers, D. (2016). Fargo-Moorhead's Center for Interfaith Projects (email correspondence).

O'Connor, J. (2015). Concordia's Office of Institutional Research.

Patel, E. (2013). Toward a field of interfaith studies, *Liberal Education*, 99(4). Retrieved from: www.aacu.org/liberaleducation/2013/fall/patel.

(2015). In promoting campus diversity, don't dismiss religion. Retrieved from: www.chronicle.com/article/In-Promoting-Campus-Diversity/228427/.

Patel, E., Bringman Baxter, K., Silverman, N. 2015). Leadership practices for interfaith excellence in higher education, liberal education. Association of American colleges and universities. Retrieved from: www.aacu.org/liberaleducation/2015/winter-spring/patel.

Pew Research Center. (2015). Changing US Religious Landscape. Retrieved from: www.pewforum.org/2015/05/12/americas-changing-religious-landscape/pf_15-05-05_rls2_1_310px/.

Silverman, N. (2016). Interfaith Youth Core. Email correspondence about the number of interfaith studies minors in the United States as of May 2016.

12 | Religious Diversity in the Canadian Workplace: The Case of Muslims

HANIFA ITANI AND YUSUF M. SIDANI

Introduction

The last few years have witnessed a growth of anti-immigration sentiment in many Western societies. For Muslims, the problem is more profound. They do not only have to face a general anti-immigration feeling among a portion of Western populations; they also have to cope with an increasing trend of Islamophobia triggered by recent political events emerging out of an increase in terrorist activities and the greater involvement of Western powers in Middle Eastern political and military affairs (Ogan et al., 2014). Anti-immigration attitudes against various races and religions are well documented (e.g., Ben-Nun Bloom et al., 2015). Yet what is becoming more evident both in popular media and in scholarly circles is a rise of Islamophobic attitudes and behaviors that have led to challenging contexts for Muslim populations living in the West (Kunst et al., 2012; Creighton & Jamal, 2015). Waves of work-related anti-Muslim prejudice were witnessed in many Western countries even before September 11, 2001 (Jefferys, 2015); it has only become worse since.

This chapter tackles the challenges that face Muslims in the Canadian workplace. It is acknowledged at the outset that Canada offers a very diverse context, not only for Muslims, but also for other ethnicities and religious minorities. Compared to other Western countries, Canada has been very successful in creating an "overall inclusive society" (Griffith, 2015), in schools, workplaces, and other societal institutions. The past few decades have been positive for visible minorities (Ng et al., 2014). Yet, perceived discrimination remains an issue (Griffith, 2015). The Canadian experience, with all its many successes and some shortcomings, reflects a case that needs to be continuously revisited and assessed.

Visible Minorities

According to the Employment Equity Act (1995), visible minorities include all individuals (excluding aboriginal people) who are nonwhite in color or non-Caucasian in race. This category includes a rising proportion of the population in Canada as most immigrants are nonwhite and non-Caucasian. Visible minorities are expected to approach 31% of the population by 2031 (Statistics Canada, 2016). Visible minorities are more likely to report discrimination or injustice in the workplace (Baklid, 2004), and they "fare worse in Canada's labour markets than do their similarly aged and educated white counterparts" (Pendakur, 2005). A large portion of visible minorities are recent immigrants, and immigration often comes with lots of life pressures on new comers and their families. Travel, relocation, and trying to come to terms with how to live in a new society and new culture often pose significant challenges. Immigrants often find it hard to transfer their prior work expertise into the workplace due to credential recognition problems (Becklumb & Elgersma, 2008) and requirements for a "Canadian experience" (Buzdugan & Halli, 2009). Discrimination has also been cited as a problem that faces new immigrants (Krishnan & Berry, 1992; Creese & Ngene Kambere, 2003; Fuller-Thomson et al., 2011; Chaze & Robson, 2014), including Muslims.

Problems that face visible minorities do not only pertain to finding a job – "glass doors" – but also to problems of getting promotion and development opportunities after they get hired – "glass ceilings" – (Pendakur & Woodcock, 2010). This seems to affect visible minorities irrespective of whether they are new immigrants (first generation) or were born in Canada (second or higher generations). The interplay of race, gender, ethnicity, and religion presents more problems for certain individuals. This results in persistent pay gaps despite reported improvements (Swidinsky & Swidinsky, 2002). Lapses in economic integration and pay equity are reported even as people get better skilled and become language savvy (e.g., Skuterud, 2010; Grady, 2011; Pendakur & Pendakur, 2011). Swidinsky and Swidinsky (2002) noted the heterogeneity of workplace experiences for visible minorities, which makes it necessary to explore labor market challenges within each ethnicity and/or religion. With the exception of white Caucasian Canadian converts to Islam, most Muslims belong to the "visible minority" group in Canada. This makes most Muslims subject to similar challenges and pressures that face other categories that belong to visible minorities. Yet, on top of those challenges is a growing set of problems that Muslims face stemming from how they are positioned in the minds of many non-Muslims due to recent political events connecting Islamic practice with violence and terrorism. While Muslims are fast to brush away such perceptions, the societal and workplace impacts of those perspectives contribute to the marginalization of Muslims in many Western societies (Pauly, 2016).

Canadian Workplace

It is well acknowledged that Canada's multicultural experience has been fruitful on many fronts. The multiculturalism model in Canada aims at ensuring that no minorities are downgraded to operate on the periphery of society or treated as second class citizens (Fleras, 2015). Canada has been fairly successful with such efforts; the 2015 composition of the liberal government is evidence of the extent to which Canada will go in advancing a diverse society. Discriminating against any person because of their religious affiliation is illegal. The *Canadian Charter of Rights and Freedoms* (Charter, 1982) explicitly mentions religion and ethnicity as two categories where discrimination is strictly prohibited:

Every individual is equal before and under the law and has the right to the equal protection and equal benefit of the law without discrimination and, in particular, without discrimination based on race, national or ethnic origin, colour, religion, sex, age or mental or physical disability. (Section 15(1), p. 3)

Problems, however, exist despite the open culture and progressive laws, especially for Muslims. In a study about job opportunities for Muslim immigrants in the Greater Toronto area, it was found that 75% had not been able to find a job two years after they immigrated into Canada. This is despite the fact that most come under the "professional worker" category with long work experience that is apparently not well recognized in the Canadian workplace (ISCC, 2014).

Muslims in Canada

According to the 2011 census, Muslims comprise 3.2% of the Canadian population but that number is expected to increase to about 6.6% in 2030 (Lewis, 2011; Environics, 2016). This is a significant growth compared to the 0.9% of the Canadian population in 1991 (Janhevich & Ibrahim, 2004). Most Muslims live in metropolitan areas with over 40% of them living in the greater Toronto area. Muslims generally belong to a younger age bracket compared to other Canadians. Muslims are ethnically diverse and most belong to a visible minority group. About 37% come from South Asia, 21% from Arab descent, and about 14% are West Asians (Janhevich & Ibrahim, 2004).

In a 2016 survey targeting Muslims, it was found that the vast majority of Muslims in Canada are proud to be Canadian (Environics, 2016). Those results were higher than the non-Muslim populations. Other earlier surveys also found that Muslims do not perceive that other Canadians are hostile to them (Adams, 2007). Muslims were found to share the views of other Canadians regarding the need to report extremist violent activities within their communities. The vast majority of Canadian Muslims identified with moderate views of their religion, and had no sympathy for those involved in violent activities. The overall conclusion of the study displayed that Canadian Muslims have lots in common with their counterparts, especially other immigrant groups of various religions and ethnicities. Yet challenges are many, and they often find their way to the workplace. In tandem with the political events and terrorist attacks, Muslims have been increasingly facing challenges, irrespective of their political or religious views or levels of religiosity. In a 2012 survey, 42% of Canadians agreed with the statement "if there is discrimination against Muslims, it is mainly their fault." In the same survey, a whopping 70% of French Canadians indicated that Muslims cannot be trusted (Boswell, 2012). This is an indicator that Muslims have to continuously face an environment that is overwhelmingly distrustful of them and less tolerant of their existence in Western societies. This is similar to what is happening in many corners of the Western world. Idilby (2014) talks about the status of Muslims in America, which would also describe their situation in many other Western societies:

Muslims are the only minority about whom mainstream public figures, journalists, politicians, and academics can make outlandish, outright racist, xenophobic remarks and continue as respected, credible public figures; in some quarters, making those remarks can actually further one's career. (p. 131)

Canadian Muslims are generally better educated than the rest of the Canadian population as they score higher in terms of post-secondary education. Those above-average education levels, however, do not correspond to higher earning powers. Muslims earn less than average compared to other Canadians. In addition, the latest 2011 census showed that the unemployment rate for Muslims was around 13.9% compared to 7.8% for the Canadian population as a whole. There are many explanations for this discrepancy including the higher incidence of new immigrants with no Canadian experience. This renders their experiences prior to immigrating to Canada virtually useless. Some studies, however, affirm that, beyond "Canadian experience," discrimination could be core to such disparities (Janhevich & Ibrahim, 2004). When comparing Muslim unemployment rate to other religious minorities who also come from immigrant populations, it is clear that Canadian Muslims have a higher unemployment rate (13.9%) compared to Hindus (10.1%), Sikhs (9.4%), and Buddhists (9.4%). Although those statistics pertain to the 2011 census and may not reflect what is actually happening years after such figures were released, there is no evidence that such trends, in terms of disparities, have reversed.[1] On the contrary, evidence would suggest that challenges still exist in the workplace as far as Muslim employees are concerned.

Studies have also shown that female Canadian Muslims face additional challenges. In a study about immigrant Muslim women, Ruby (2012) noted that many veiled Muslim women encountered discrimination stemming from them being stigmatized. Still, the study affirmed that Muslim participants reported that adopting aspects of the Canadian culture enhanced their lives: "In crafting their identities, all of the informants demonstrated forms of agency in spite of tremendous constraints" (p. 92). In a report by the Canadian Council of Muslim Women (CCMW), it was asserted that compared to other faith communities with similar demographic and education profiles, female Muslims in Canada face more obstacles in the work force (Hamdani, 2014). This is despite the fact that more and more of those entering the labor force are born in Canada, graduated from Canadian Universities, and are proficient in English and/or French. In 2011, the unemployment rate among Muslim females aged 15 years and older peaked to 16.7% compared to a Canadian female national average of 7.4%. Visible minorities, with an unemployment rate reaching 10.9%,

---

[1] A census was conducted in 2016 but results were not available at the time this chapter was written.

also fared much better than female Muslims. The only group with lower unemployment rate than that of Muslim women was that of the Indigenous women – who practice traditional spirituality. All of this is despite the fact that proportionally twice as many Muslim women in Canada – compared to Canadian women – have pursued careers in STEM (science, technology, engineering, and math), and twice as many are proficient in both English and French. Even when female Muslims find work, they are underpaid. In 2010, working Muslim women earned 36% less than all working women in Canada – a median income of $15,763 compared to a median of $24,606 for all the Canadian female working force. Muslim females with a graduate degree (Masters, Doctorate, or professional) earned 16.1% less than the female national average. One explanation for this disparity could be attributed to underemployment. Many Muslim women are not able to find work in their chosen fields of specialization, so they end up working in unrelated professions which are irrelevant to their expertise and which pay less (Hamdani, 2014). All of this portrays a dismal picture for female Muslim Canadians whose visible affiliation could be argued to be a challenge as they try to integrate in jobs that fit their skills and that pay them on a par with their counterparts.

Studies on Diversity Regarding Muslims in Canada

Very few studies have assessed the status of Muslims in Canada especially pertaining to workplace challenges. In an early study about Muslim men of Ethiopian origin, some complained about discrimination despite being skilled and well educated (Gibb, 1998). Adams (2007) noted that Muslim participants in his study expressed some concerns about discrimination and unemployment, yet they believed that they were the least likely in any Western country to be subject to attitudes hostile to Islam. This reaffirms the notion that Canada is one of the most tolerant of Western countries for religious diversity. Still, some studies indicate that Muslims experienced changes to their cultural safety due to the events of 9/11 where suddenly they became a visible minority in the media spotlight (Baker, 2007). The events that happened in the Western world starting in 9/11 and many other parts of Europe, including the 2015 terrorist attacks in Paris have only complicated the issue for Muslim immigrants and contributed to their increased stigmatization.

In a study by Lubuto Mutoo (2001), questionnaires sent to employers even before September 11, 2001, regarding discrimination practices met with a dismal response rate (about 9% – 19 responses out of 197). This shows that many employers are hesitant to share their company policies as to how to treat immigrants coming from a certain ethic minority or religion. Yet the small number who responded reflected a sad situation, whereby a third declared they would refuse to hire an "Arab" or a person from the Maghreb (Arabs from West Africa). This is – reportedly – a conservative figure, as very few employers would have the courage to express such racially prejudicial sentiments openly (Bouchard et al., 2002). Moreover, after 9/11 some employers called agencies asking them not to refer Arabs to them for employment; some job seekers even asked to change their names. Helly (2004) notes that discrimination is manifested in many forms, including, first, refusing to receive or take into consideration Arabs or Muslims due to the perceived incompatibility between their social habits and company cultures. Second, also according to Helly, there are instances of refusing to hire some job applicants due to an "unacceptable French accent" or "bad attitude." This puts significant hurdles before first generation immigrant Muslims, even if they are professionally qualified with a mastery of the language, albeit without a "good" accent. Third, Muslims are overwhelmingly unable to get into employment networks. Such networks are essential for career development and ascension into organizational hierarchies. Finally, discrimination also takes place when already employed Muslims are subjected to intimidating work environments where they are requested to compromise an important religious custom, in terms of appearance or behavior, or they are subjected to harassing remarks.

In sum, many studies have uncovered increasing challenges for Muslim minorities in Western workplaces. Authors of a study conducted in the Northeast USA, where Muslims were found to receive one-third fewer responses from employers, concluded that:

Among the specific religions, Muslims received the most job discrimination. The mere addition of the word "Muslim" to a job application dropped the total number of employer contacts by 33–41%, depending on the coding of rote responses. Muslims also experienced weaker employer preference – scoring lowest on the employer preference index. (Wright et al., 2013, p. 121)

Media Reports

It is important to reaffirm here that the above studies do not negate the fact that, compared to many other Western countries, Canada stands out as a more welcoming and more tolerant country for diverse workplaces that offer reasonable accommodation to religious and ethnic minorities including Muslims. This is despite some problems that are often addressed quickly in line with Canadian laws and heritage. We present below some of these challenges as reported in the media. Such incidents should – of course – neither be taken out of their own contexts, nor generalized regarding all Canadian workplaces. They do, however, tell stories of continuous challenges that often differ in intensity and frequency from one Canadian province to another.

Welcoming the Hijab in the Police Force

News reports in 2013 indicated that the Edmonton Police Service would allow for a uniform that accommodates a form of the female veil worn by veiled Muslim women (Brean, 2013). The understanding is that the hijab (headscarf) will follow certain guidelines, including being worn under the standard police cap. Likewise, in 2011, the Toronto police indicated that they were proactively looking forward to recruiting their first veiled Muslim officer after a headgear policy had been approved (QMI Agency, November 17, 2011). Such moves did not come without objections and were not uniform across Canada. French-speaking Quebec seemed to be following France's lead, banning all religious symbols including Muslim hijabs and Sikh turbans (Allemandou, 2013). The proposed Quebec Charter of Values, which was supposed to include such stipulations, was not passed, but in the wake of the terrorist attacks in Europe, it seems to have "come back from the dead" (Kheireddine, 2015).

Accommodating Muslims Causes Uproar

In 2011, a memo was sent to public service managers in Ontario and ended up being forwarded to 120,000 employees. The memo encouraged workers to be sensitive and accommodating towards their Muslim coworkers during Ramadan, the Muslim holy month of fasting. Some non-Muslim workers were enraged by the memo which created intense controversy (QMI Agency, September 25, 2011). Some groups faulted the Ontario government for giving "preferential treatment to Muslims." Ministry officials responded by indicating that similar measures were taken in comparable instances, and that memos and publications regarding accommodation needs have already been sent in the past for other religious groups including the Jewish observances of Rosh Hashanah and Yom Kippur, the Hindu festival of Diwali, in addition to Christmas and Easter (QMI Agency, September 27, 2011).

"No Hijab Permitted Here"

A few years ago, Women Working with Immigrant Women conducted a study called "No Hijab Permitted here" to document what Muslim women wearing the veil experience when they apply for jobs and at the workplace (Persad & Lukas, 2002). The results concluded that Muslim women wearing the hijab faced "obvious examples of discrimination" (p. 40). It showed that veiled women are supplied with incorrect information regarding the availability of jobs, are blocked from equal opportunities to apply for jobs, are made to "feel invisible and unwelcome when applying," are dismissed from jobs as a consequence of wearing the hijab, and are sometimes harassed in the workplace due to their religious attire. Moreover, veiled Muslim women "experienced discrimination in all sectors regardless of their age, skin colour, experience in Canada, accent, mannerisms and education" (p. 3). Some women reported that they were told by employers to remove their "head cap" or "hijab," while others faced verbal harassment regarding prayers, religion, and culture.

As an example of the problems facing veiled women, eight veiled female Muslim workers filed complaints at the Canadian Human Rights Tribunal against Universal Parcel Services (UPS), with the help of the Workers' Action Center (WAC) and other community organizations. Those women had been working for two years at UPS as temporary agency workers. The women later applied for permanent positions where they were supposed to do exactly the same type of work. However, UPS stated that their clothing presented a "health and safety issue." This, according to the women, was never mentioned during the two years of their temporary employment. They were told they could take the job on the condition they wore shorter skirts. The women refused and were left without any job. They filed complaints at the Canadian Human Rights Commission, against what they believed to be "discrimination based on gender and religion." According to those women, they were never asked whether they could perform other jobs at the company where their clothing wouldn't pose any issue, nor were they asked about their skills and past experiences.

On November 18, 2008, the case was settled out of court. One of the women, Dales Yusuf, stated in her testimony: "I am not only fighting this for myself, I am fighting this so that my daughter knows she has the freedom to live and work in a society where she can be free. And where she can fight against an injustice like this also" (Workers' Action Centre, 2008, p. 2). This case reflects the barriers faced by Muslim workers, "especially whose clothing identifies them as Muslims." Moreover, it underlines the many shortcomings of the law when it comes to temporarily employed staff, constituted mainly of ethnic minorities and immigrant workers.

Two Case Studies

The following two case studies are taken from a larger study we are currently conducting about workplace diversity in Canada (see Boxes 12.1 and 12.2). These two cases are illustrative. The study aims to explore the various experiences of Canadian Muslims, the vast majority of whom are immigrants. Due the nature of the study, a snow-balling technique was used which gave us the opportunity of meeting people from various backgrounds and different countries of origin. The first case is that of a female – Najat – originally from Lebanon, who was a permanent citizen at the time of the interview. Najat wore a headscarf when she came to Canada, but found difficulties in finding a job. She decided to take the headscarf off and – as she indicated – things became easier after she had made that decision. On the other hand, there is the case of Hamada, originally from Egypt. He reported no problems with him being Muslim in terms of getting access to employment opportunities. The only challenges he reported were ones many new immigrants face, such as the need to have Canadian experience before getting a relevant job. These two cases are just two examples of the varying positive and negative experiences that Canadian Muslims face in the workplace.

The overall conclusion that we have so far is that the Canadian workplace is perceived to be very welcoming of religious diversity,

> **Box 12.1 Najat**
>
> **Najat** (33; Female; Canadian permanent resident, originally from Lebanon)
>
> **How do you find Canada in terms of workplace diversity?**
> Compared to Europe, Canada is considered receptive of cultural and religious diversity. Meanwhile, Muslims pose a specific exception due to the terrorist attacks that took place in some parts of Canada, Australia, and France. The rules in Canada protect people from different religions, cultures, and ethnic groups. No one has the right to ask you about your religion during an interview and you have the right to sue them if they do, but you cannot change people by putting these rules on paper. In general, media is promoting stereotyping.
>
> **How about your first job?**
> I found my first job through an immigrant center ... At my arrival, I was wearing a scarf and the [chief administrator] of the school where I applied for work asked me if I can take it off because the kids are not used to see veiled women. Parents were not so friendly with me and I had to do double efforts to prove that I am a hard worker. What I did to cope with those challenges was simply taking off my scarf ... After taking off my scarf, interviews were easier to me since no one can know my background.
>
> **How do you find diversity in Canada as far as Muslims are concerned?**
> When Muslims don't show any signs of their religion (female scarf for example), people are usually very friendly to them even if they know that they are Muslims ... It is my personal story; I feel more approachable and accepted after taking the scarf off.

with some exceptions. For Muslims who do not show signs of visible religious affiliation or religiosity, things tend to be easier. For those, other problems may emerge not particular to their religions or levels of religiosity but which relate more to their ethnic origins and skin colors. The experience of Muslims would sometimes differ depending on their ethnic origins. For many Lebanese or Syrians, who could come across as white Europeans due to their skin color, few problems could emerge as their religiosity is not "visible." For other Muslims who come from visible ethnicities, such as those coming from African countries or the Indian subcontinent, problems of ethnicity become

> **Box 12.2 Hamada**
>
> Hamada (36; Male; Canadian, originally from Egypt)
>
> **How do you find Canada in terms of workplace diversity?**
> I find Canada is very receptive for cultures and religious diversity. I am satisfied with the legislations as I think they protect my religious group and other religious groups as well and provide freedom to practice our religious practices.
>
> **How about your first job?**
> The only challenge I have faced when I arrived to Canada is the so called Canadian experience. Actually the law prevents recruiters and companies from using this term, but still you can hear it a lot on your first job that you don't have the Canadian experience. My company was very receptive and my colleagues were very receptive. It was a diverse company; there were different religious groups and cultures. It was normal for them to accept me as a new member of the company.
>
> I don't think my cultural or my religious background has imposed any challenge for me in finding my job as my skill was the only challenge to be used.
>
> **How do you find diversity in Canada as far as Muslims are concerned?**
> Our whole company is diverse; you can find people from different backgrounds, different countries, different cultures, and different religious groups. It's really very diverse. As a result of that, everybody is receptive for other cultures, I think managers and employers are accepting for all religious diversity and groups and they are also keen to celebrate with different religious groups their occasions, and to show that they are so welcome for them.
>
> We don't have any veiled woman in our company, and I'm not sure what is the reason for that, whether [because they] are not accepting of them or because nobody has applied; I can't judge this. I don't think wearing a veil results in any challenge for Muslim women to find a job. A lot of veiled women find jobs in organizations; even at the airport when you arrive, you find employees working and they are actually veiled.

similar to others of similar origins who might not even share the same religious affiliation.

This poses specific problems for veiled Muslim women. The veil, as a visible symbol of a woman's religious affiliation, poses considerable challenges in terms of finding a job or even of being taken seriously as a worker. From previous work on the veil (Sidani, 2005; Syed & Pio, 2010), we know that the veil often poses considerable problems for Muslim women as they negotiate their identities through internal struggles and also with external stakeholders such as potential employers, managers, and coworkers. This is perhaps one of the many things at the junction of politics, religion, and gender that prompted Sheema Khan, a Canadian Muslim woman (veiled herself) to express at the eve of the 2015 Canadian election the following sentiment: "50 years in Canada, and now I feel like a second-class citizen" (Khan, 2015). The 2015 election results which brought a more diverse and liberal government will most likely move such sentiments in a more positive direction. As it stands at the time of this writing, the Canadian cabinet represents a diversity of affiliations, religions, and ethnicities that may make people of color and various ethnicities and religions more comfortable.

How Muslim Organizations Deal with Diversity Issues

Many Muslim organizations have been active in promoting diversity in the workplace that is inclusive of Muslims and accommodating to their religious needs. Three of these organizations, which are active and have been portrayed in various media outlets, are the National Council for Canadian Muslims, the Muslim Council of Montreal, and the Canadian Council of Muslim Women.

The National Council of Canadian Muslims published a guide titled "An Employer's Guide to Islamic Religious Practices" (Guide, 2014). The guide targets employers irrespective of their religions with the aim of promoting better understanding between employers and their Muslim employees. The guide introduces the basic Muslim rituals and briefly explains the demands that this puts on employers. For example, it is noted to employers that only two of the five daily Muslim prayers fall within the 9–5 daily schedule, and each prayer takes 10–15 minutes. They indicate to employers that this makes conducting prayers – within the lunch hour and the daily break – not disruptive of daily work schedules.

The council also published a "My Rights at Work Document" which explains to Canadian Muslim employees their rights to accommodation in the workplace, the obligations for employers, how to ask for accommodation in a flexible and realistic manner, and how to act if they feel their rights are being violated. By approaching both employers and Muslim employees, the Council has been trying to help both parties work together to find solutions and foster common understanding and tolerance leading to reasonable accommodation that does not cause undue hardship to employers.

The Muslim Council of Montreal (MCM) has also been very active in relation to issues of school and workplace diversity for Muslims. The MCM, on several occasions, was active in initiatives to address racism and discrimination. It called for "stricter accountability within the media for propagating hate and stereotypes against minority communities and for an establishment of checks and balances to regulate media fairness, especially within Canadian media outlets that are publicly financed" (MCM, 2006). The MCM was also vocal against banning Muslim girls from playing sports because of their hijab, labeling such actions as discriminatory, which "only seems to push Quebec backward" (MCM, 2007). Most relevant to workplace diversity was the move by the Parti Québécois government's plans to introduce a Quebec Charter of Values which would have prohibited employees from wearing religious symbols in the workplace. While such charter is not solely directed at Muslims, Muslims in Quebec saw this as being overwhelmingly directed at Muslim women wearing the hijab, which would stop them from properly integrating in the workplace. The MCM issued a statement indicating that "to deny them the opportunity to work in public sector jobs because of their religious convictions will only serve to prevent their meaningful contribution, participation and integration in society" (MCM, 2013). The MCM has also been working with employers to help create an environment of accommodation for Muslim employees and found that "most are very accommodating [which] fosters an atmosphere of loyalty" (Brunschot, 2006).

A third example is the Canadian Council of Muslim Women (CCMW), which is an organization that aims to promote Muslim women's identity in Canada, ensuring their equity, equality, and empowerment. They strive to help women understand their rights and responsibilities in the diverse Canadian society, and encouraging religious diversity in the workplace is one of their aims. The council publishes resources, hosts events, issues position statements on various issues, and manages a network of chapters all over major Canadian cities. Issues of religious accommodation represent one of the many issues the CCMW is involved in, which also include Muslim family laws, diversity among Muslims, and anti-Semitism.

The CCMW was also vocal against the proposed Quebec Charter of Values, quickly detailing its negative ramifications. The charter, which proposed limitations on religious symbols and clothing, was criticized for its negative implications for workplace diversity, especially for Muslim women. Shaheen Ashraf, Secretary of the CCMW, noted that the charter would have negative implications for Muslim women and workplace diversity in Quebec as "the province could face an exodus of young professionals who will choose religion over so-called PQ [Parti Québécois] values" (CTV News, 2013).

Organizational Issues

Organizational responses to dealing with Muslim employees vary. There are many examples of Canadian workplaces making special accommodations for Muslim employees in terms of giving them space and time for daily prayers, revisiting the work schedules during Ramadan, or accepting the Muslim clothing attire for women.

The Canadian *Globe and Mail* reported in 2012 on the intersection of faith and work, during the month of fasting, asking Canadian Muslim workers about their experiences (Bitonti, 2012). The responses ranged from "everyone in the office is being nice and accommodating" to people reporting the real challenges they face as they try to keep their fast at the same time as trying to fulfil their work duties. Salam Elmenyawi, president of the MCM, reported that most businesses are increasingly accommodating to the special needs of Muslim employees. He asserted that such accommodation had positive impacts on businesses. Such impact was reiterated by Carolyn Grossi, who worked at the time as senior operations manager for IBM at Kelly Services in Toronto: "accommodating religions makes good business sense ... In tight labour markets like this, if we can do anything to keep our employees happy and to accommodate their requests, we [would do it]" (Brunschot, 2006). Another example is the BMO financial group, which acknowledges diversity for various faiths and lifestyles (Vancouver Province, 2007). The Group holds information sessions so that people from different faiths know about the practices of others to be able to better accommodate them in work activities. During the month of Ramadan, the group usually plans for key activities to take place with consideration for their Muslim employees.

An increasing number of human resource (HR) professionals and job specialists are thus taking note and issuing guidance regarding religious diversity in the Canadian workspace. Advice ranges from "how to request religious accommodation at work" (Ali, 2013) to "how to accommodate religious diversity at work" (Levitt, 2015). Two sets of recommendations seem pertinent, one for employees and the other for employers. Nobes (2012), for example, issued a list of recommendations to HR professionals in Canadian organizations to make the job environment more accommodating to Muslim employees, especially during the month of Ramadan. Those included giving proper consideration to leave requests, providing alternate flexible work schedules, providing them with a private place for their breaks and prayers during the workday, and accommodating more breaks than usual.

Organizational and HR experts have increasingly issued recommendations to Muslim workers and the organizations in which they work (see Tables 12.1 and 12.2) to facilitate integration and promote diversity. Such recommendations revolve around the need for Muslim employees to be able to recognize organizational demands while still understanding their rights in the workplace. For organizations, the recommendations revolve around the notion that accommodation is not only the right thing to do from an ethical and equity standpoint, but it is often the right things to do from a practical results-oriented perspective in today's diverse workplaces. It would be best to understand those recommendations in line with Berry's model (1997), where mutual accommodation results in harmonious integration. Non-dominant groups, Muslims in this case, adopt the basic values of the host society, while at the same time the host society becomes prepared to reasonably alter societal institutions to accommodate the needs of diverse minority groups (Berry, 1997).

Conclusion

The composition of the Canadian population is changing due to waves of immigration, and Muslims represent a growing minority in that society. The Canadian workplace is generally diverse, open, and tolerant. Yet, fully integrating Muslims in the economic sphere requires bold steps that encourage inclusion and discourage stereotyping and discrimination. As Muslims continue to face challenges prompted by political events, they need to continue to demonstrate that they

Table 12.1 *Facilitating integration of Muslim workers and diversity: What Muslim workers need to do*

1. Understand your rights. Understand the Canadian laws that protect religious freedom of expression and practice and do not give away your religious beliefs.
2. Research the organization and its diversity policy before you join.
3. Ask directly for religious accommodation. Give employers enough time to deal with your request and do not expect ideal accommodation.
4. Do not ask for extensive breaks for prayers. If you have a special need to take more than 15 minutes for each prayer, discuss this with your employer. Consider fitting the noon prayer during your lunch break.
5. During the month of Ramadan, notify your employer that you are observing the fast if you feel this might interfere with your productivity.
6. During Ramadan, discuss with your employer whether you would be allowed to take a shorter lunch break and leave earlier.
7. Express your willingness to fill in for other employees of other faiths during their own holidays.
8. Express your willingness to make up for lost time in a fair and transparent manner.
9. If you are a Muslim woman observing the hijab, consider choosing a head cover that would not conflict with the company policy for professional attire. For example, be willing to accommodate your employer's request to shy away from certain flashy colors if this does not fit the organizational culture.
10. Some organizations may be willing to come up with a head cover policy. Be willing to serve on any committee or provide feedback on what would be the best policy from an organizational perspective in a way that does not compromise your religious beliefs and practice.

Sources:
- Woog, D. Retrieved from: www.career-advice.monster.ca/in-the-workplace/workplace-issues/religious-accommodation-in-the-workplace-canada/article.aspx
- Ovais, R. (2015). Ramadan In the Workplace. Retrieved from: www.muslimmoms.ca/ramadan-in-the-workplace/
- Alli, N. (2010). Retrieved from: www.cnmag.ca/issue-35/478-work-how-to-request-religious-accommodation-at-work-n00
- Authors' input

Table 12.2 *Facilitating integration and diversity of Muslim workers: What employers need to do*

1. Understand Canadian laws that prohibit discrimination in the workplace.
2. Work on developing a clear diversity policy that includes aspects of religious accommodation.
3. Provide time for religious holidays and prayers. Negotiate in good faith with employees making up time for missed work.
4. If accommodation creates significant hurdles for employment, discuss this with the employee concerned to work out a solution. If all else fails, and accommodation will create "actual undue hardship and not merely convenience" then you might need to discuss this with your employment lawyer (Levitt, 2015). According to the Canadian Human Rights Commission "To prove undue hardship, you will have to provide evidence as to the nature and extent of the hardship."
5. In the specific case of Muslims, daily prayers that would interfere with a 9:00 to 5:00 schedule are two. Each should take about 10–15 minutes which could easily fit within usual breaks in the daily schedule. Request for extensive breaks (for example, a request for 30 minutes for each prayer during a workday) are not warranted. If the employee nevertheless asks for longer breaks, address how he/she would make up for lost time.

Sources:
– Levitt. H. (2015). Retrieved from: www.financialpost.com/m/search/blog.html?b=business.financialpost.com/2015/03/09/530200/&q=Bear&o=336.
– Canadian Human Rights Commission (2013). Retrieved from: www.chrc-ccdp.ca/eng/content/duty-accommodate.
– Authors' input

represent an important and relevant component of the society in which they are living and working. Muslim organizations have an important role to play in educating both Muslim Canadians and business organizations about the rights and duties of their employees pertaining to issues of workplace accommodation. For Canadian business organizations, Muslims – similar to other religious minorities – have a lot to offer. Yet Muslim workers often require certain accommodation that should not, if implemented properly, stand in the way of productivity and business functioning. On the contrary, business organizations that help employees grow at all levels, including the spiritual level, will have much to gain in terms of employee engagement, commitment, and loyalty. Ignoring such needs, or failing to address them in an appropriate manner, would not make them go away; it would just make it harder on both organizations and the people they employ.

References

Adams, M. (2007). Muslims in Canada: Findings from the 2007 Environics survey. Retrieved from: www.policyresearch.gc.ca, 19–26.

Ali, N. (2013). Work: How to request religious accommodation at work. *Canadian Newcomer Magazine*, March 31. Retrieved from: www.cnmag.ca/issue-35/478-work-how-to-request-religious-accommodation-at-work-n00.

Allemandou, S. (2013). Canada split over hijab-style Muslim police uniform, *France 24*, December 10. Retrieved from: www.france24.com/en/20131209-edmonton-canada-police-uniform-islamic-veil-women-quebec-secular-muslim.

Baker, C. (2007). Globalization and the cultural safety of an immigrant Muslim community. *Journal of Advanced Nursing* 57(3), 296–305.

Baklid, B. (2004). The voices of visible minorities: Speaking out on breaking down barriers. *Conference Board of Canada*. Retrieved from: www.triec.ca/uploads/368/voices_of_visible_minorities.pdf.

Becklumb, P., & Elgersma, S. (2008). Recognition of the foreign credentials of immigrants. *Parliament of Canada*. Retrieved from: www.parl.gc.ca/Content/LOP/researchpublications/prb0429-e.htm#measuring.

Ben-Nun Bloom, P., Arikan, G., & Courtemanche, M. (2015). Religious social identity, religious belief, and anti-immigration sentiment. *American Political Science Review*, 109(2), 203–21.

Berry, J. W. (1997). Immigration, acculturation, and adaptation. *Applied Psychology*, 46(1), 5–34.

Bitonti, D. (2012). How Muslim Canadians cope with work, hot days and fasting during Ramadan. *The Globe and Mail*, August 05. Retrieved from: www.theglobeandmail.com/life/how-muslim-canadians-cope-with-work-hot-days-and-fasting-during-ramadan/article4461815/.

Boswell, R. (2012). More than half of Canadians mistrust Muslims, poll says. *Postmedia Network Inc.* Retrieved from: www.canada.com/life/More+than+half+Canadians+mistrust+Muslims+poll+says/6331705/story.html.

Bouchard, H., Chang, Y., & Raffa, R. (2002). Emploi et immigration dans la capitale nationale. *Vivre Ensemble*, 11(38), 8–11.

Brean, J. (2013). Edmonton police set to unveil official hijab that Muslim officers can wear on duty. *National Post*, November 24. Retrieved from: www.news.nationalpost.com/news/canada/edmonton-police-set-to-unveil-official-hijab-that-muslim-officers-can-wear-on-duty.

Brunschot, A. (2006). The prayer room does good: Feeling the pressure from a culturally diverse workforce, companies are making room for religion at work. *National Post*, 18.

Buzdugan, R., & Halli, S. S. (2009). Labor market experiences of Canadian Immigrants with focus on foreign education and experience. *International Migration Review*, 43(2), 366–86.

Charter. (1982). The Canadian Charter of Rights and Freedoms. *Government of Canada Publications*, Retrieved from: www.publications.gc.ca/collections/Collection/CH37-4-3-2002E.pdf.

Chaze, F., & Robson, K. (2014). In control of life chances? Visible minority immigrants and sense of mastery. *Journal of Immigrant & Refugee Studies*, 12(3), 161–71.

Creese, G., & Ngene Kambere, E. (2003). What colour is your English. *Canadian Review of Sociology and Anthropology*, 40, 565–73.

Creighton, M. J., & Jamal, A. (2015). Does Islam play a role in anti-immigrant sentiment? An experimental approach. *Social Science Research*, 53, 89–103.

CTV News (2013). Values charter slammed as a diversion, a solution to a problem that doesn't exist. September 10. Retrieved from: www.montreal.ctvnews.ca/values-charter-slammed-as-a-diversion-a-solution-to-a-problem-that-doesn-t-exist-1.1448534.

Environics. (2016). Survey of Muslims in Canada 2016. The Environics Institute for Survey Research. Retrieved from: www.environicsinstitute.org/.

Fleras, A. (2015). Multicultural media in a post-multicultural Canada? Rethinking integration. *Global Media Journal – Canadian Edition*, 8(2), 25–47.

Fuller-Thomson, E., Novack, A., & George, U. (2011). Health decline among recent immigrants to Canada: Findings from a nationally-representative longitudinal survey. *Canadian Journal of Public Health*, 102(4), 273–80.

Gibb, C. 1998. Religious identification in transnational contexts: Being and becoming Muslim in Ethiopia and Canada. *Diaspora: A Journal of Transnational Studies*, 7(2), 247–69.

Grady, P. (2011). How are the children of visible minority immigrants doing in the Canadian labour market? *Global Economics Limited*, January 11, retrieved from http://global-economics.ca/immigration_2nd_generation_nhs.htm

Griffith, A. (2015). *Multiculturalism in Canada: Evidence and anecdote*. Ottawa, Canada: Anar Press.
Guide (2014). *An employers guide to Islamic religious practices*. National Council for Canadian Muslims. Retrieved from: www.nccm.ca/wp-content/uploads/2014/03/NCCM-Employer-GUIDE-PF.pdf.
Hamdani, D. (2014). Canadian Muslim women: A decade of change – 2001 to 2011. Canadian Council of Muslim Women, Toronto, Canada. Retrieved from: www.ccmw.com/canadian-muslim-women-a-decade-of-change-2001-to-2011/.
Helly, D. (2004). Are Muslims discriminated against in Canada since September 2001? *Canadian Ethnic Studies*, 36(1), 24–47.
Idilby, R. T. (2014). *Burqas, baseball, and apple pie: Being Muslim in America*. New York: Macmillan.
ISCC (2014). Muslim migrants in Canada – victims of undeclared racism and discrimination. Retrieved from: www.islamicsupremecouncil.com/muslim-migrants-in-canada-victims-of-undeclared-racism-and-discrimination/.
Janhevich, D., & Ibrahim, H. (2004). Muslims in Canada: An illustrative and demographic profile. *Our Diverse Cities*, 1, 49–56.
Jefferys, S. (2015). The context to challenging discrimination against ethnic minorities and migrant workers at work. *Transfer: European Review of Labour and Research*, 21(1), 9–22.
Khan, S. (2015). Fifty years in Canada, and now I feel like a second-class citizen. *The Globe and Mail*, October 7. Retrieved from: www.theglobeandmail.com/globe-debate/fifty-years-in-canada-and-now-i-feel-like-a-second-class-citizen/article26691065/.
Kheireddine, T. (2015). Quebec Charter of Values comes back from the dead. *National Post*, January 22. Retrieved from: www.news.nationalpost.com/full-comment/tasha-kheiriddin-quebec-charter-of-values-comes-back-from-the-dead.
Krishnan, A., & Berry, J. W. (1992). Acculturative stress and acculturative attitudes among Indian immigrants to the United States. *Psychology and Developing Societies*, 4(2), 187–212.
Kunst, J. R., Tajamal, H., Sam, D. L., & Ulleberg, P. (2012). Coping with Islamophobia: The effects of religious stigma on Muslim minorities' identity formation. *International Journal of Intercultural Relations*, 36(4), 518–32.
Levitt, H. (2015). Unlike the courts, employers must accommodate religious diversity. *Financial Post*, March 9. Retrieved from: www.financialpost.com/m/search/blog.html?b=business.financialpost.com/2015/03/09/530200/&q=Bear&o=336.

Lewis, C. (2011). Number of Muslims in Canada predicted to triple over next 20 years: study, Canadian CRC. January 31. Retrieved from: www.canadiancrc.com/Muslim_Population-Census_Canada_Statistics_growing-National_Post_31JAN2011.aspx.

Lubuto Mutoo, V. (2001). *Discrimination raciale en milieu de travail dans la region métropolitaine de Quebec*. La Ligue des droits et des libertés du Quebec, Montreal.

MCM. (2006). *Muslim Council of Montreal to appear before Commission on Racism and Discrimination in Quebec City*. Muslim Council of Montreal, September 27. Retrieved from: www.muslimcouncil.org/en/2006/09/muslim_council_of_montreal_to_appear_before_commission_on_racism_and_discri.html.

(2007). *Muslim Council of Montreal dismayed by discrimination at Tae Kwon Do tournament in Quebec*, Muslim Council of Montreal, April 15. Retrieved from: www.muslimcouncil.org/en/2007/04/muslim_council_of_montreal_dismayed_by_discrimination_at_tae_kwon_do_tourna.html.

(2013). *Muslim Council of Montreal slams proposed PQ Charter of Values as discriminatory and ready to challenge in court*, Muslim Council of Montreal, August 30. Retrieved from: www.muslimcouncil.org/en/2013/08/muslim_council_of_montreal_slams_proposed_pq_charter_of_values_as_discrimin.html.

Ng, E., Haq, R., & Tremblay, D. G. (2014). A review of two decades of employment equity in Canada: progress and propositions. *In* Klarsfeld, A., Booysen, L., Ng, E., Rooper, I., & Tatli, A. (eds.), *International Handbook on Diversity Management at Work: Country Perspectives on Diversity and Equal Treatment*, 46–67, Cheltenham: Edward Elgar Publishers.

Nobes, C. (2012). Ramadan has started, is your workplace accommodating? *HRM Canada*, July 23. Retrieved from: www.hrmonline.ca/hr-news/ramadan-has-started-is-your-workplace-accommodating-124030.aspx.

Ogan, C., Willnat, L., Pennington, R., & Bashir, M. (2014). The rise of anti-Muslim prejudice: Media and Islamophobia in Europe and the United States. *International Communication Gazette*, 76(1), 27–46.

Pauly, R. J. (2016). *Islam in Europe: Integration or marginalization?* New York: Routledge.

Pendakur, K. (2005). *Visible minorities in Canada's workplaces: A perspective on the 2017 projection*. Issues 5-11 of Working paper series (Research on Immigration and Integration in the Metropolis), Simon Fraser University, British Columbia, Canada.

Pendakur, K., & Pendakur, R. (2011). Color by numbers: Minority earnings in Canada 1995–2005. *Journal of International Migration and Integration*, 12(3), 305–29.

Pendakur, K., & Woodcock, S. (2010). Glass ceilings or glass doors? Wage disparity within and between firms. *Journal of Business & Economic Statistics*, 28(1), 181–9.

Persad, J. V., & Lukas, S. (2002). No hijab is permitted here. Women working with immigrant women. Retrieved from: www.atwork.settlement.org/downloads/no_hijab_is_permitted_here.pdf.

QMI Agency. (2011). Ramadan memo creates controversy. *Toronto Sun*, September 25. Retrieved from: www.torontosun.com/2011/09/25/ramadan-memo-creates-controversy.

—— (2011). More religious pamphlets for government workers. *Toronto Sun*, September 27. Retrieved from: www.torontosun.com/2011/09/27/more-religious-pamphlets-for-government-workers.

—— (2011). Toronto police still seeking Muslim recruit. *Toronto Sun*, November 17. Retrieved from: www.torontosun.com/2011/11/17/toronto-police-still-seeking-muslim-recruit.

Ruby, T. F. (2012). *Immigrant Muslim women and the hijab: Sites of struggle in crafting and negotiating identities in Canada*. An unpublished Master of Arts thesis, University of Saskatchewan, Canada.

Sidani, Y. (2005). Women, work, and Islam in Arab societies. *Women in Management Review*, 20(7), 498–512.

Skuterud, M. (2010). The visible minority earnings gap across generations of Canadians. *Canadian Journal of Economics/Revue canadienne d'économique*, 43(3), 860–81.

Statistics Canada, (2016). Ethnic diversity and immigration. Retrieved from: www.statcan.gc.ca/pub/11-402-x/2011000/chap/imm/imm-eng.htm.

Swidinsky, R., & Swidinsky, M. (2002). The relative earnings of visible minorities in Canada: New evidence from the 1996 Census. *Relations Industrielles/Industrial Relations*, 57(4), 630–59.

Syed, J., & Pio, E. (2010). Veiled diversity? Workplace experiences of Muslim women in Australia. *Asia Pacific Journal of Management*, 27(1), 115–37.

Vancouver Province. (2007). Businesses accommodate fasting Muslim employees, September 23. Retrieved from: www.working.com/vancouver/resources/story.html?id=521db895-1acb-499a-b25d-68c86f33e3f7.

Workers' Action Centre. (2008). *Up against a giant: Campaign backgrounder*. Retrieved from: http://www.workersactioncentre.org/wp-content/uploads/xnew-downloads/bg_ups_eng.pdf.

Wright, B. R., Wallace, M., Bailey, J., & Hyde, A. (2013). Religious affiliation and hiring discrimination in New England: A field experiment. *Research in Social Stratification and Mobility*, 34, 111–26.

13 | Religious Diversity at Work in the Asia-Pacific Region

EDWINA PIO AND TIMOTHY PRATT

Introduction

Asia-Pacific is a far reaching geographical region, largely surrounded by water and linked by commerce (Bouma et al., 2013). The region spans from Mongolia in the North East, to New Zealand in the South West and comprises a basin of considerable diversity with respect to topographies, climates, economies, cultures, and religions (Asia Pacific Forum for Environment and Development, 2010). Over the last 40 years it has experienced considerable economic growth, in part due to its rich natural environment (United Nations ESCAP, 2014). In 2014 it was estimated that the region comprised 4.3 billion persons who represented 60% of the global population. This includes individuals from the world's two most populated countries, China and India, but also the small Pacific Island nations of Nauru with around 10,000 inhabitants, and Tuvalu, which has a resident population of 1,200. Furthermore, between 2000 and 2014 the number of persons living in the region increased by 573.7 million and expanded by just under 1% in 2014 (United Nations ESCAP, 2014).

The concept of religion generally involves "a system of beliefs and practices primarily centerd around a transcendent reality, either personal or impersonal, which provides ultimate meaning and purpose to life" (Meister, 2008, p. 2). The various religions constitute pathways for "experiencing, conceiving and living in relation to an ultimate divine Reality which transcends all our varied visions of it" (Hick, 2008, p. 11) and thus there is religious pluralism. Within such pluralism is soft pluralism or the manifestation of the Real through many traditions and no tradition holds the complete truth; whereas in hard pluralism all the traditions are "equally valid paths to salvation and equally authentic modes of experience of a Real which is a completely unknowable postulate of religious life" (Ward, 2008, p. 37).

In the current century, religious diversity translates as a negotiation of religious beliefs within different contexts such as the social, cultural, institutional (Giordan, 2014), and organizational, as many individuals bring their whole selves to work. International migration has resulted in the spread of various religions in countries around the world, thus creating a mosaic of cultures, a plurality of religions, and a varied work ethos (Yang, 2014). Religious pluralism may mean that institutional levels of involvement, including those of a legal nature, will be critical to regulate diversity and can be translated as "the social arrangement that protects both individual freedom and group equality in religious affairs" (Yang, 2014, p. 51). This involvement is likely to vary between countries and "is a continuous process of negotiation and re-negotiation, in an ongoing effort to maintain and preserve the boundaries between the different social spheres in a world that makes these boundaries ever more porous and fragile" (Giordan, 2014, p. 9). Religious pluralism can also refer to four overlapping aspects (Beckford, 2014, p. 21): empirical forms of diversity in relation to religion (distinct faith traditions and heterogeneity within religions); normative or ideological views about the positive value of religious diversity (ecumenism, religious literacy, etc.); the frameworks of public policy, law, and social practices which accommodate, regulate, and facilitate religious diversity; and relational contexts of everyday interactions between individuals and groups identified as religious.

Five diversity megatrends (Pio, 2014) are of relevance in the context of religious pluralism. The first one is demographic patterns or the increasing global mobility of individuals based on economic migrations, ecological migration, wars, and refugee status. The second megatrend is religious growth; as multiple religions are diffusing historical religious monopolies. The third megatrend is corridors of commerce with the BRICS countries (Brazil, Russia, India, China, South Africa) and the Asia-Pacific region gaining ascendance along with halal markets. The next megatrend pertains to human rights based on a fusion of the sacred and secular, accommodation, and good faith. The fifth and final megatrend is the whole self at work with increasing numbers of individuals living 24/7 lives and the integration of work and life.

With pluralism and diversity megatrends as a backdrop, this chapter will present the countries in this great landmass with the nomenclature Asia-Pacific region and beliefs of specific religions. Next, five randomly chosen country examples will be touched upon, specifically Australia,

Japan, New Zealand, the Pacific Islands, and South Korea, incorporating religion at work and the need to be sensitive as well as draw boundaries for religious diversity in organizations. This will be followed by organizational and managerial practices of relevance to religious diversity and concluding comments.

The Asia-Pacific Region

While defining boundaries for the region is somewhat arbitrary, the Statistical Yearbook for Asia and the Pacific (United Nations ESCAP, 2014) divides the area into five sub-regions. Within these groupings are a total of 58 countries that occupy around 30% of the world's land mass. An overview of the five sub-regions and their countries is outlined below (Table 13.1).

Table 13.1 *The sub regions and countries of Asia-Pacific*

Country	Population	GDP USD per capita
East and North-East Asia (ENEA)		
DPR of Korea	20.2 (million)	$582
Hong Kong	7.3 (million)	$36,827
China	1,393.8 (billion)	$6,070
Japan	127 (million)	$46,838
Macao	575.5 (thousand)	$78,275
Mongolia	2.9 (million)	$3,673
Republic of Korea	49.5 (million)	$23,052
South-East Asia (SEA)		
Brunei Darussalam	423.2 (million)	$41,127
Cambodia	15.4 (million)	$944.4

Table 13.1. *(cont.)*

Country	Population	GDP USD per capita
Indonesia	252.8 (million)	$3,557
Lao PDR	6.9 (million)	$1,369
Malaysia	30.2 (million)	$10,422
Myanmar	53.7 (million)	$1,126
Philippines	100.1 (million)	$2,587
Singapore	5.5 (million)	$52,141
Thailand	67.2 (million)	$5,775
Timor-Leste	1.2 (million)	$4,835
Viet Nam	92.5 (million)	$1,716
South and South-West Asia (SSWA)		
Afghanistan	31.3 (million)	$682.8
Bangladesh	158.5 (million)	$882.2
Bhutan	765.6 (thousand)	$2,509
India	1,267.4 (billion)	$1,516
Iran	78.5 (million)	$7,217
Maldives	351.6 (thousand)	$7,770
Nepal	28.1 (million)	$656.2
Pakistan	185.1 (million)	$1,201
Sri Lanka	21.4 (million)	$2,816
Turkey	75.8 (million)	$10,653

(cont.)

Table 13.1. *(cont.)*

Country	Population	GDP USD per capita
North and Central Asia (NCA)		
Armenia	3.0 (million)	$3,351
Azerbaijan	9.5 (million)	$7,383
Georgia	4.3 (million)	$3,632
Kazakhstan	16.6 (million)	$12,455
Kyrgyzstan	5.6 (million)	$1,183
Russian Fed	142.5 (million)	$14,178
Tajikistan	8.4 (million)	$953.1
Turkmenistan	5.3 (million)	$6,469
Uzbekistan	29.3 (million)	$1,801
Pacific		
American Samoa	55.3 (thousand)	No data
Australia	23.6 (million)	$67,869
Cook Islands	20.7 (thousand)	$14,918
Fiji	887 (thousand)	$4,572
French Polynesia	279.8 (thousand)	$26,113
Guam	167.5 (thousand)	No data
Kiribati	103.9 (thousand)	$1,745
Marshall Islands	52.8 (thousand)	$3,773
Micronesia (Federal States)	103.9 (thousand)	$3,165
Nauru	10.1 (thousand)	$12,022

Table 13.1. *(cont.)*

Country	Population	GDP USD per capita
New Caledonia	529.8 (thousand)	$38,869
New Zealand	4.6 (million)	$38,399
Niue	1.3 (thousand)	No data
Northern Mariana Is	54.5 (thousand)	No data
Palau	21.1 (thousand)	$10,271
Papua New Guinea	7.5 (million)	$2,187
Samoa	191.8 (thousand)	$3,607
Solomon Islands	572.9 (thousand)	$1,837
Tonga	105.5 (thousand)	$4,429
Tuvalu	9.9 (thousand)	$4,042
Vanuatu	258.3 (thousand)	$3,040

The Asia-Pacific region hosts a variety of religions, so much so that the Pew Research Center (2015a) describes it as the most religiously diverse region of the globe. Bouma et al. (2013) contend that the region's traditional mix of spirituality and faith has included Buddhism, Islam, Hinduism, and a number of indigenous folk religions. However, over recent centuries, the area has also been influenced by various Christian missionary endeavors from Europe and the United States of America (Pio, 2014). More recently, numerous new religious groups such as Soka Gakkai (Fisker-Nielsen, 2012) have emerged. By 2010, 78.8% of the region's population affiliated with at least one faith-based group. The spread of religious diversity can be seen in Figure 13.1.

It is estimated that by 2050 the overall number of those domiciled within the region that possess no religious affiliation will have fallen

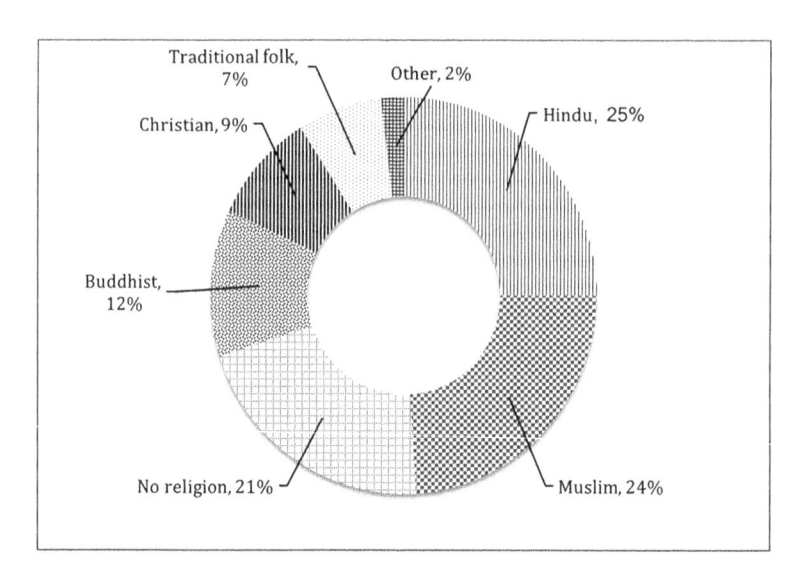

Figure 13.1 Religious affiliation in Asia-Pacific 2010 (Pew Research Center, 2015c)

from 21% to 17%, or 838 million persons (Pew Research Center, 2015b). This indicates that religious expression within the region is expected to intensify. The growth of religious interest can be attributed to a combination of migration, trade, missionary endeavor, tourism, and the growth of information technology that is utilized to communicate respective religious messages (Manderson et al., 2012). Demographic projections also indicate that the religious preference of those in the Asia-Pacific region will change during the first half of the millennium. Current trajectories suggest that Buddhists will decline from 12% to represent only 9.6% or 476 million of the total population. Similarly, folk religions are anticipated to experience decline from 9% to 7.4% or 367 million. However, Christianity will expand from 7.1% to 7.7% or 381 million. The region's two dominant religions of Hinduism and Islam will also expand so that the Muslim community will be represented by 29.5% or 1,458 million and the Hindu faith by 27.7% or 1,370 million (Pew Research Center, 2015d).

Beliefs

Within the religious plurality of this region, the beliefs of five religions are summarized (O'Donnell, 2006; Pio, 2014). These religions have been chosen as exemplars which highlight the breadth of spiritual diversity across the region. They include both dominant and small minority expressions of faith. Therefore, in alphabetical order we overview: Christianity, Hinduism, Islam, Sikhism, and Zoroastrianism.

Christianity

Christianity is a faith based on Jesus also known as Christ (Greek) and Messiah (Hebrew), which means the anointed one. Christians believe that Christ is God and their holy scripture is the Bible. For Christians, God stepped into the world and became man, was crucified and then resurrected to save the world. Christianity began around 4 BC to 33 BC as a Jewish movement in Galilee, today's Israel, which was part of the Roman Empire. Christianity spread throughout the Roman Empire and also reached Persia, India, and China. It became the faith of Europe and with the spread of the Portuguese, Spanish, and British Empires became the faith of many peoples in the far flung corners of the globe. The faith revolves around concepts of humility, forgiveness, service, and divine grace. The main Christian symbol is the cross, to commemorate the crucifixion of Christ. Christians believe in one God.

The Bible consists of 39 books known as the Old Testament, and 27 books known as the New Testament. Christians have many denominations, such as Roman Catholics, Greek Orthodox, Coptic Christians, Anglicans, Baptists, and Presbyterians. The Roman Catholics revere Mary, the mother of Jesus, and also pay respect to a pantheon of saints. Many Christians believe in Ecumenism from the Greek word *oikoumenos*, translated as the inhabited world, meaning to work together in unity. Christians are known for their work with the under-privileged, such as working with the indigenous peoples in India, and the poor in Latin America through prayer, worship, and political protest, known as liberation theology. Christians can worship anywhere, but as a group or congregation they tend to worship in a church. Christians celebrate Christmas (December 25), Easter (usually in March/April) and Pentecost (usually in June). Christian symbols include the cross, the rosary, pictures of saints, and Mother Mary. The current head of the Catholic Church, Pope Francis, has played a major role in inter-religious harmony and stresses doing business by doing good with a focus on humility and the less fortunate who are often in the lower socioeconomic strata of society.

Hinduism

Hinduism is the name given to a wide variety of beliefs and practices that reflect the history of the many regional and local traditions of India. The Hindu festive calendar, which is lunar, includes *Holi* (spring harvest festival), *Navratri* (a nine-night celebration of the goddess *Shakti*), and *Diwali* (the festival of lights). Hinduism includes a pantheon of over a thousand gods and goddesses such as *Brahma* the creator, *Vishnu* the preserver, *Shiva* the destroyer, *Ganesha* a guardian for preventing evil things, *Lakshmi* the goddess of wealth, and *Saraswati* the goddess of learning. There are many ways to reach salvation, such as through yoga, and various traditions to practicing Hinduism, such as vegetarianism, *ahimsa* or non-violence, and *nishkamakarma* or the meritless deed. This religion has a rich tapestry of scriptures including the *Vedas, Upanishads, Ramayana, Mahabharata,* and *Bhagavad Gita. Dharma* or righteous duty is important to Hindus, as is also *karma* or destiny.

The cow is considered sacred, as is also Mother *Ganga* or the river Ganges, which flows in Northern India. The practice of dowry and the caste system continue in Indian society but are practices which many Hindus do not adhere to. There is also a preference for male children. Hindus refer to the place of work as the *Shram Mandir* or temple of work. Religious expressions of Hinduism include symbols such as images or pictures of various gods and goddesses, for example *Ganesha, Krishna, Lakshmi, Saraswati,* the symbol *Om,* and hymns such as the *Gayatri mantra,* or recitation of the *Bhagavad Gita.*

Islam

The etymology of Islam is from the Arabic *slm,* which means peace or submission. Muslims believe that they should submit to the will of God and thus find peace. The word Allah is the Arabic word for God, and Islam propagates one God, with His will revealed to the Prophet Muhammad, expressed in the Holy book of the Muslims, the Quran. God cannot be represented in human form, and the symbols of Islam include the five pointed star representing the five pillars of Islam and the new star rising over the crescent moon suggests the rise of Islam. Muslims believe God is holy, transcendent, compassionate, and merciful. Muslims recite the Quran, generally in Arabic, and look to it for guidance and peace. The five pillars of Islam are: the confession of faith (*shahadah*), prayer (*salat*), alms giving (*zakat*), fasting (*saum*), and pilgrimage (*hajj*). Muslims are instructed to pray five times a day and fasting takes place during Ramadan and generally lasts for 29–30 days and takes place during daylight hours. Before prayer, Muslims are exhorted to wash with cleansing rituals using water, so that they can be externally clean and thus show respect before they pray to God. Mosques are Muslim places of worship, literally places of prostration, and there are no statues or paintings, but adornment consists of Arabic verses from the Quran. Muslims have prayer beads, comprising 99 beads threaded on a string, to help recite the 99 names of God.

Islam has two major festivals: Id-ul-Fitr, which comes at the end of the month of Ramadan, and Id-ul-Adha, which means festival of sacrifice, when an animal, for example a sheep, goat, cow, or camel, is sacrificed and the meat shared between family, friends, and the poor. Dress codes and modesty laws are a source of debate. Sunnis and Shias form the two main sects of Islam, though there are numerous other subsects and denominations such as the Sufis, the Wahabis, the Deobandis, and the Salafis.

Sikhism

Sikhism was founded in Punjab in the Indian subcontinent, by Guru Nanak when he had a mystical experience in 1499. The holy book of the Sikhs, the Guru Granth Sahib consists of hymns (Gurbani) composed by the Sikh gurus as well as Hindus and Muslims. Sikhs celebrate four main *gurpurbs* or important days in the life of one of their gurus: Guru Nanak's Birthday, Vaisakhi, Diwali, and Hola Mahalla or a festival for military training and exercise. Sikhs worship in a *gurdwara*, translated as the doorway to the guru, and acknowledge a lineage of 10 gurus or teachers, beginning with Guru Nanak (1469–1539).

Sikh men traditionally wear a *dastaar* (turban) and have a full beard. Sikhs subscribe to the five Ks or the *panj kakkar*: *kachchera* (wearing full undergarments, indicating self-discipline, as well as in previous centuries for running and combat); *kara* (wearing an iron bangle on the right wrist, referring to *dharma* or order); *kes* (unshaved and uncut hair symbolizing saintliness, dating back to Guru Nanak); *kanga* (carrying a hair comb, to keep oneself neat); and the *kirpan* (a small dagger, symbol of self-reliance). Sikhs are exhorted to be both worldly as well as seekers of God. A Sikh should have true discipline to exist in this world yet to be a hermit; to work hard for earning one's money but to remember God and to live by the teachings of the Guru Granth Sahib. Sikhs' generosity is evidenced in their *langar* or communal kitchens, where they feed many people.

Zoroastrianism

This ancient faith from Persia, modern Iran, was an early form of monotheism, with the symbol Ahura Mazda, the Wise Lord riding the solar disk with outstretched wings. Zarathustra, more commonly known as Zoroaster (Greek name) was the founder of this religion, which he called Daênâ Vañuhi, meaning the "Good Conscience." Followers of Zarathrustra believe that fire symbolizes purity and wisdom: the wisdom to know the right from the wrong, the wisdom to speak the truth no matter what, to treat people who work with you respectfully whether they are your subordinates or your colleagues, and the wisdom to see through posers and pretenders. The religion has always been very progressive and is inclusive. It gives man and woman equal status and knows no barriers related to sex, race, or color. The teachings of Zoroastrianism can be summed up in one word, "asha," which means piety or holiness, purity, truth, righteous conduct, and living in harmony or divine order.

Central to Zoroastrianism is the belief in a sole creator god, Ahura Mazda, the dichotomy between good and evil and the doctrine of Good Thoughts, Good Words, and Good Deeds. Zoroastrians are committed to gender equality, higher education, wealth creation through the creation of dynastic excellence, and community activities – all of which have contributed to the justifiably high regard in which individuals are held both within their own community and amongst the wider community internationally. The Zoroastrian scriptures are the Avesta, which contain the Gathas or divine songs of Zarathustra to Ahura Mazda. Zoroastrians have few rituals, apart from the symbolism of the sacred fire which represents holiness and the light of God. Festivals are in celebration of nature and there is a strong ethos of care for the environment, for example Navroze or New Year festival on the first day of spring.

Country Examples

Australia, Japan, New Zealand, the Pacific Islands, and South Korea have been selected, as in many ways they exemplify religious diversity in the Asia-Pacific region. These countries are listed alphabetically and each is described through research and data pertaining to religious diversity.

Australia

Prior to colonization, Aboriginal culture comprised more than 250 languages. Each of these groupings had their own understandings concerning spirituality. Therefore, the indigenous spirituality of Australia is "incredibly diverse" (Bunbury, 2014). Mudrooroo (1995) contends that central to Aboriginal spirituality is the sense of oneness or connectedness. Here, all objects are living; animals, plants, and rocks each have a soul and share of the same spirit. Upon death the soul is reborn and returns to earth as a human, animal, plant, or rock. Land is also of significance. It is here that the power of ancestral spirits resides and these may be drawn upon for strength. Therefore, importance is placed on looking after the land, which is not owned but is rather seen as the owner of all, the Mother of humanity. It is from the land that food, culture, spirit, and identify are sourced (Knight, 1996). Aboriginal spirituality is expressed in artworks, music, and ceremony (Grant, 2004).

In 2014, Australia accommodated a population in excess of 23 million persons (United Nations ESCAP, 2014). Christianity is the country's dominant religion, having a following of 67% of the population or 15 million (Pew Research Center, 2015d). The roots of Christian faith in Australia lie in its British colonization, which began in the nineteenth century and brought with it the Church of England (Breward, 1988) along with a variety of smaller Christian denominations. Despite its current strength, Christianity in Australia is expected to continue its decline to 46% by 2050 (Pew Research Center, 2015d). In part, this is due to the country's immigration policy changes that were progressively introduced during the 1960s and 1970s, allowing many nationalities and religions entry into the country. Buddhists and Muslims each make up around 2.5% of the Australian population. The trajectory of both these religions is towards growth. By 2050 Buddhism is predicted to reach 3.1% of the population and Muslims will represent

4.9% of all Australians. Similarly, Hinduism will expand from 1.4% to 2.3% (Pew Research Center, 2015d).

Those unaffiliated with religious groups currently account for 24.2% of Australians. This number is expected to substantially increase by 2050 so that it will exceed 40% (Pew Research Center, 2015d). Organizations are embedded within the societies in which they function and exist. Anti-terrorism laws and fears of radical Islam have meant that managing minority religious and ethnic groups in Australia is an area of growing concern with wide ranging influences on social cohesion and political contingencies (Richardson, 2013), as well as impacting organizations.

Although Islam is a heterogeneous religion, no reliable data exists to identify numbers involved in its various subsects within Australia (Akbarzadeh & Roose, 2011). Bendle (2007) contends that Saudi Arabia has invested heavily in supporting educational and religious activities including the building of Mosques, which promote the causes and beliefs of the Sunni Wahabi. Milani and Possamai (2015) discuss Islam with reference to two Sufi orders, the Khaniqahi (Nimatullahi) and Haqqani (Naqshbandi). The applied nature of Sufism and its non-definitive practices are appealing both intellectually and sociologically to both Muslim and non-Muslim converts and such an interpretation of Islam can operate well in various social and public spheres. Sav et al. (2009) discuss work-life conflict and work-life facilitation among employed Australian Muslim men. In managing a diverse workforce, the experiences of work-life balance are important, along with an understanding of non-work roles. These authors stress the importance of programs that aim to reduce conflict at work, so that there is less of a spillover of work into non-work roles. Moreover, flexibility and control were important for diversity management and facilitated fulfilling religious obligations.

The beliefs of Arabic-speaking religious leaders regarding the causes of mental illness and the use of medication for treatment are discussed in a novel study by Youssef and Deane (2013). Where necessary, it is important that in respecting religious diversity, organizations can have recourse to guidance from appropriate clerics for employees who may face various stresses which may tilt them towards mental illness. Additionally, these leaders also need to be better educated regarding medication and various other possible actions in the Australian context.

Religious organizations and their clergy have been the focus of research on religious diversity, for example prison chaplaincy and work engagement among church leaders. Prison chaplaincy pertaining to correctional services in Australia, is an important component of sometimes forgotten workplaces, for example prisons as organizations and prison ministries as part of church and other religious organizations. The detailed study by Carey and Del Medico (2014) indicates that chaplains need more support and appreciation for the work they do and the relevance and importance of their work needs to be emphasized as it impacts on the well-being of the prisoners, and the wider community. Aspects that such organizations can look into involve pastoral assessments, pastoral ministry, counseling, education and welfare, ritual worship, coordination with state authorities, community relations and support, and crucially teamwork between the various levels of hierarchy in religious organizations so that the prison chaplains do not function in isolation. Such considerations can ensure that the "work of chaplains can be instrumental in helping to bring about positive change – not only for the benefit of prisoners but also for the correctional system itself and fundamentally the community to which the majority of inmates return" (Carey & Del Medico, 2014, pp. 1797–8).

In examining spirituality and work engagement among church leaders, Miner et al. (2015) focus on positive indicators of mental health at work. Where there were appropriate performance feedback mechanisms and spiritual and job resources, such as spiritual retreats, there was an increase in work engagement of church leaders. A variety of organizations can look into providing such facilities for their members, as it is possible that spirituality and work engagement can motivate and increase the commitment of individuals in various kinds of organizations (Pio, 2014).

Another organization where the beliefs of various members in the community are crucial is the police. Carpenter et al. (2015) discuss the role of the police and the importance of their organization being aware of the cultural and religious differences when dealing with death and the need to have other lenses besides a criminal one in such investigations. Furthermore, it is important to note that "death investigations are almost always challenging, emotional and disruptive to the professional persona of police" (p. 12). They discuss vulnerable populations such as the elderly, Indigenous people, and individuals from lower socioeconomic strata of society and the varying emotional work required by police at the death scene, and stress the need for "effective, considerate and sensitive death investigation" (p. 2). Individuals from the Jewish and Muslim faiths, as well as Indigenous people, are the groups most impacted by "the legislative requirement, variously enacted in all Australian states, that a family's religious and cultural status and concerns about the non-consensual medico-legal autopsy be communicated to the police at the time of the death notification" (p. 9). Training and awareness can ensure that police have the skills and knowledge for such investigations so that both the police are protected and the trauma of families is allayed.

Not-for-profit organizations such as faith-based agencies and social workers represent another area of religious diversity in organizations. Crisp (2013) discusses the issues of expectations of the users of such services pertaining to participation in religious activities and religious proselytization in the Australian context. It is worth noting that in Australia such services by the Catholic Church can be availed of and are provided to individuals irrespective of their faith, with a focus on those communities and individuals who are most in need. Additionally, many of the social workers who work in these Catholic agencies do not necessarily identify with their employer's religion, but are attracted by the ethos of the agency (for example *caritas*, or care), despite the fact that the position may be less well paid than in other agencies in the welfare sector.

With reference to the health sector, Daher et al. (2015) discuss pharmacists, and the need for knowledge and sensitivity in serving a population who are culturally and religiously diverse. Examples include patients' concerns during times of fasting, as well as the possibility of animal ingredients in the medication. Dealing with such issues involves appropriate medication management and the importance of understanding the patients' perspectives. In like manner, in the context of religious diversity, it is necessary for biomedical practitioners to understand, acknowledge, and appreciate the spiritual belief systems through which patients feel supported, thus enhancing overall patient management. In coping with and managing chronic illness, it is important to note that individuals draw on their spirituality to manage their daily lives. There were four dimensions to these belief systems which enhanced well-being positively (Unantenne et al., 2013): coping and support, acceptance, healing, and finally health and subjective well-being, which then influenced treatment and the patient's condition and resilience.

Focusing on the norms regarding food habits and practices in four faith communities, Judaism, Hinduism, Buddhism, and Islam, Nath et al. (2013) discuss how individuals negotiate food issues based on their religious beliefs. This included how food was selected, prepared, and certified. Organizations need to take into consideration these practices and beliefs so that all communities are catered for and as a consequence their perceptions of respect by the organization and colleagues can increase (Nath et al., 2013; Razzaque & Chaudhry, 2013).

Crossman (2015), in her grounded study of spiritual diversity in globalized Australia suggests that there is a high level of individual spiritual eclecticism and dynamism in the experience of spirituality. She urges the utilization of common values to manage spiritual diversity and to foster inclusiveness in organizations. These common values included honesty, tolerance, respectfulness, caring, and a sense of connectedness such as safe spaces. Inter-personal tolerance among various faith groups was also raised in the study, as for example lack of wine consumption by Muslims and the need to respect their practices; Jehovah's Witnesses and their views on blood transfusions; and Indigenous people's views, particularly with respect to mining. Crossman suggests that discussions around the common values could "be incorporated into goal statements, recruitment criteria, and other organizational activities with periodic evaluations of their relevance and effectiveness" (p. 73).

Japan

Japan was inhabitated by 127 million people in 2014 (United Nations ESCAP). Whilst the country contains a wide range of indigenous folk religions, its population has also embraced Buddhism, Daoism, Confucisiam, and Christianity, whilst also giving expression to a number of novel religious groups (Bouma et al., 2013). These include Happy Science (Okawa, 2014) and Soka Gakkai; the latter of which claims to have in excess of 17 million members (Shimazono, 2004). Despite Japan's historical diversity with respect to faith, only two religions hold significance for more than 1% of its population. Christianity attracts 1.6% or 2 million people and Buddhism, which is the dominant faith, attracts 36.2% or 46 million people. While Christianity is projected to rise to 2.4% by 2050, those affiliated with Buddhism are likely to decline to just over 25% (Pew Research Center, 2015d).

Of all the Asia-Pacific countries, Japan has the highest percentage of population that is without religious faith. In 2010, 57% or 72 million persons held no religious affiliation. This number is projected to rise to 68% by 2050 (Pew Research Center, 2015d). Even though the Japanese may define themselves as not religious as in being members of religious institutions, they are nonetheless practitioners of rituals and religious festivals and they have a belief of spirits within nature. There exists the Buddha-nature in all creatures, including organic and inorganic objects such as the sun, rocks, caves, flowers, and rivers, thus emphasizing the inseparable union of man and nature with the spiritual world or *kami-sama*. Aesthetic and spiritual values can serve as strong motivators for individuals in the Japanese system, resulting in conservation of rural landscapes and biodiversity, deeply embedded in the Shinto religion, according to a study by Kieninger et al. (2013).

Zhong (2014) discusses religious freedom of the Meiji era and the Constitution of 1889, in particular the 28th article, which deals with conditional freedom of religious belief. This 28th article deals with freedom which is not prejudicial to peace and order and not antagonistic to the duties of individuals as subjects. Through a detailed analysis of historical documents, he argues how this conditional religious freedom facilitated the construction of the modern nation-state and the individual as a subject citizen. He shows how the idea of religion, which was synonymous with Christianity, came into being when the treaties of the Tokugawa *bakufu* or feudal government with military dictatorship, was signed with Western powers in the 1850s. Shinto was re-categorized as a religious Shinto and a political Shinto, "to bring the private religion and imperial authority together in the legal framework of the Constitution" (Zhong, 2014, p. 62). Thus "the Meiji state succeeded in incorporating conditional freedom of religious belief into the constitutional formulation, a formulation that provided the fundamental legal structure for a political state even while that very state was at the same time authorized by the sacred yet non-religious authority of the emperor as the sovereign of the Japanese nation-state" (Zhong, 2014, p. 67).

Japanese society happily integrates the religious and cultural so that a person may be born with Shinto rites, married with Christian practices and when the individual dies the burial rites are likely to be Buddhist (Coslett, 2015). Not having specific domains for religion and secular there is great emphasis put on values such as reciprocity and self-sacrifice (Fitzgerald, 2003).

The philosophy of Honda is "providing joys to the world through new challenges and the realization of dreams" (Honda, 2015). The organization believes in equality, which means to recognize and respect individual differences – an individual's race, gender, age, religion, national origin, educational background, social, or economic status has no bearing on the individual's opportunities.

The text of the Toyota Global Vision (Toyota, 2015):

Toyota will lead the way to the future of mobility, enriching lives around the world with the safest and most responsible ways of moving people. Through our commitment to quality, constant innovation and respect for the planet, we aim to exceed expectations and be rewarded with a smile. We will meet challenging goals by engaging the talent and passion of people, who believe there is always a better way. (p. 1)

In the Toyota Code of Conduct, it is clearly stated that the organization believes in moderate participation in political and/or religious activities by its employees and does not wish to interfere with individual's religious activities.

In the health sector, Malloy et al.'s (2014) study of religiosity and ethical ideology of physicians shows how religion influences physicians' choices. Japanese physicians have low religiosity rates and this is perhaps because a large proportion of the Japanese people claim no personal religion, despite the fact that the vast majority show high levels of belonging and practices in line with Buddhism or Shinto. Moreover, ethical relativism or the ethical rightness based upon the context was higher for Japanese physicians in contrast to those from other countries in the study, for example Canada and Ireland. The authors note that while Japan is culturally homogenous, the people use situational context and in their practices move seamlessly between Buddhism, Shinto, and Confucianism. This therefore can bring into question the basis on which decisions are made by physicians, and if their education does not provide them with adequate tools, then they may turn to their own experiences and cultural and religious foundations for making decisions regarding patients. Therefore, at work and in training, there may be a need to "broaden the scope of medical curricula to include social science and humanities content in order to give physicians an expanded capacity for decision-making" (Malloy et al.,

2014, p. 253). Here we note that appropriate training opportunities are crucial for a more sensitive implementation of religious diversity in organizations, as also indicated in a study on suicide prevention and the role of clergy, who may be relied on for counselling and comfort in instances of extreme organizational stress.

Additionally, in a study on suicide prevention, utilizing the role of American Christian clergy and Japanese clergy pertaining to suicide prevention Hirono (2013) notes that at work, this clergy had a lack of financial resources, time, and training opportunities, and suggests that there should be a stronger nexus between clergy and mental health professionals. While there were some differences in the perceptions of these two groups of clergy based on intra-denominational differences, in general they believed that "life was a gift from God or Buddha, and we do not have a right to quit it" (Hirono, 2013, p. 11).

Ghanbarpour (2015) provides a lucid account of the origins and current developments of Christianity in Japan, which has been in practice for over 400 years, since the mid-sixteenth century initiated by Jesuit missionaries. She shows how Christianity was initially spread through the support of the warlord Oda Nobunaga (1534–82), as he sought to undermine the warrior monks in major Buddhist temple complexes. But his successor and the Tokugawa rulers banned it through suppression decrees and persecuted Christians, resulting in two centuries of suppression. However, a group of Christians called *kakure Kirishitan* or hidden Christians preserved their practices, liturgy, and prayer, and survived the purges to reunite with other Christians when missionaries re-entered Japan in the mid-nineteenth century. Nagasaki has traditionally been a Christian center and there are about 20,000 *kakure Kirishitan* living there.

Between 1870 and 1930 there was a "kind of renaissance for Japanese Christianity as the number of converts increased and Christian institutions spread" (Ghanbarpour, 2015, p. 2031). The Japanese people were keen to avail of Western education which was available in various Christian institutions and Christian reformers spread the idea of equal education for both males and females. In the post-war years after 1945, Christianity again grew exponentially, though the growth also emphasized Christian's loyalty to the state despite Christianity being a foreign religion. Furthermore, a number of Christian practices have been incorporated into Buddhist and Shinto based religions such as in marriage ceremonies which may be held in a chapel or church with a "priest" who may be a non-ordained white male European, Australian, American, or New Zealander, specifically hired for this purpose. Christianity has "contributed an important legacy to Japanese history and continues to influence contemporary Japanese culture and society" (Ghanbarpour, 2015, p. 2044), as well as multinational corporations and several companies in Japan which often show a blend of various religious values in their vision and mission statements.

New Zealand

For Māori, the indigenous inhabitants of New Zealand, individuals possess a spirit or *wairua* and the spiritual dimension of one's life, their *taha wairua* is central and is integrated across every aspect of their existence (Benland, 1988). Thus, Cody (2004) contends that spirituality is infused within all Māori culture *(Tikanga)*, as is captured in the essence of understanding behind the word *Māoritanga*.

The Māori word *mana* refers to spiritual authority, or the power of the gods over daily concerns in the lives of individuals (Patterson, 1992). For example, when someone falls ill, not only are plants used to facilitate healing but alongside these natural medicines, spiritual ceremonies, and prayers or *karakia* are also conducted. *Mana* is protected through *tapu* or by setting aside that which is sacred (Marsden, 1975). Here it is believed that balance is restored. Thus *Taha wairua* impacts not only a person's beliefs but also their values and their practices. Moeke-Maxwell et al. (2012) suggest that spirituality is understood to be the cornerstone of Māori health and well-being.

The concept of *wairua* extends beyond humans and includes all aspects of the environment (Ministry of Justice, 1998). Furthermore, *wairua* extends beyond the current life of Māori and continues into the afterlife.

In common with Australia, New Zealand was colonized by Europeans who brought with them the Christian faith of their homelands (Tennant et al., 2008). This perhaps explains why the majority (57%) or 2.5 million (Pew Research Center, 2015d) of its population adhere to Christianity. As with Australia, New Zealand's immigration policies (Parliamentary Counsel Offices, 1987) paved the way for an influx of nationalities and religions (Pio, 2014). However, for many inhabitants, New Zealand is a secular country in that 37% of the population are not affiliated with any religion (Pew Research Center, 2015d). In line with these figures, the New Zealand Government released a statement on religious diversity (Human Rights Commission, 2007). The document emphasizes that the country holds no official religion, that all residents are entitled to freedom of religious belief and expression, that all faith communities and their members have a right to safety and security and that all reasonable steps should be taken to accommodate religious belief and practices in education, work, and public service.

It is expected that by 2050 the Hindu, Buddhist, and Muslim religions within New Zealand will have each doubled in size (Pew Research Center, 2015d). Those unaffiliated with religious faith will expand to 45% of the total population and correspondingly, Christianity is expected to decline to 45% of the total population (Pew Research Center, 2015d).

Pio (2014) presents a meticulous empirical study on minority faiths – Hindus, Muslims, Indian Christians, Zoroastrians, and Sikhs in New Zealand. While the study showed differences among each of the religions, overall there was a strong preference for living and working in New Zealand rather than in their countries of origin, despite the fact that there was more that could be done and needed to be done in organizations with reference to religious diversity.

Hinduism is one of the fastest growing religions in New Zealand, with Hindus making up 2.1% of the population. Hindus, in the research of Pio (2014), felt that New Zealand organizations are actively trying to recognize various religions and to support celebrations of important events, such as Diwali. She found that many organizations are aware that Hindus may be vegetarian. Additionally, some Hindus spoke about how colleagues in their organizations make fun and refer to Hindus as "holy cow" and some had negative experiences when they displayed in their offices images of their Gods and bemoaned the lack of cultural and religious sensitivity in organizations. There was also concern expressed over grieving and burial customs and if employers would be willing to understand their religious worldviews.

Indian Christian is a combination of Indian ethnicity and Christian religious affiliation and they constitute 0.4% of the New Zealand population. Indian Christians strongly acknowledged the benefits they derived in New Zealand from having westernized names, a western dress sense, fluency in English with the ability to understand English proverbs and phrases as also to celebrate festivals both in the religious and cultural sense such as Christmas and Easter. The Indian Christians felt that their religious needs were well looked after in organizations. Indian Christians believe that their faith and religion requires them to be the best that they can in each of their roles – as a citizen, a manager, a colleague, and at home.

Muslims form 1.09% of the New Zealand population. Organizations are slowly working towards accommodating and accepting Muslims and their religious beliefs through organizational flexibility, particularly during Ramadan, and allow employees to work varying hours to facilitate their fasting times. Many managers understand the need by Muslims for time off for prayers and they are also aware of Muslim food habits. Some organizations have provided separate prayer rooms for Muslims to offer prayers, and many organizations recognize the need for women to wear traditional attire like the veil or headscarf and are prepared to allow it. However, what organizations do not like are surprises. For example, when candidates make no mention of special attire during recruitment, but after the contract has been signed or after working for a few weeks in the role, the new employees raise the topic of accommodating their special needs. A number of Muslims have faced racial comments or queries, linking all Muslims to terror attacks in various parts of the world, and many Muslims have experienced discrimination on religious grounds.

Sikhs constitute 0.45% of the New Zealand population. Sikhs believe that organizations in New Zealand are interested in learning about other religions and cultures. However, many Sikhs felt that their physical appearance, as in their visible diversity discriminators such as a turban and beard, made it difficult for them to get work.

Zoroastrians, also known as Parsis, are just 0.02% of the New Zealand population. Due to their appearance (fair-skinned), mode of dressing, and command over the English language, there has been a very high acceptance in tandem with many happy experiences in New Zealand for Zoroastrians. Overall while Zoroastrians believed that there was a strong acceptance of them in organizations, they found it very difficult to climb the corporate ladder.

Pacific Islands

The Pacific Islands extend over a large area of the Pacific Ocean. As with the label "Asia Pacific," the term "Pacific Islands" is ambiguous, having different meanings dependent on context. It may exclusively refer to islands within the Pacific that were colonized by Europeans and Americans. Alternatively, the term is used to define the collective of Australasian islands including Taiwan, Indonesia, Micronesia, Polynesia, and the Myanmar Islands (William Collins, 1995). In line with the Statistical Yearbook for Asia and the Pacific (United Nations ESCAP, 2014), the Pacific Islands includes 21 countries. These include both Australia and New Zealand, along with the 19 small island nations of American Samoa, the Cook Islands, Fiji, French Polynesia, Guam, Kiribati, the Marshall Islands, Micronesia, Nauru, New Caledonia, Niue, the Northern Mariana Islands, Palau, Papua New Guinea, Samoa, the Solomon Islands, Tonga, Tuvalu, and Vanuatu.

The composition of religious diversity within the Pacific in 2010 was 73% Christian, 1.84% Buddhist, 1.76% Hindu, 1.76% Muslim, and less than 2% for all other religions combined, with 19% of the collective population having no affiliation with any religion (Pew Research Center, 2015d). Bouma et al. (2013) assert that due to the strongly Europeanized cultures that dominate within both Australia and New Zealand, neither of these countries naturally fit in the cluster of Pacific Islands. When they are removed from the percentages of religious diversity within the area, the remaining 19 small island nations contain a Christian population of 95% of all persons living in the area.

One of the smallest countries in the Pacific (and the world) is Tuvalu. It comprises a series of nine atolls, the highest of which is five meters above sea level (CIA, 2017). The nation is home to less than 10,000 people (United Nations ESCAP, 2014), of which 96% are Polynesian (CIA, 2017). It is one of the least developed countries in the world, receiving 61.5% of its revenue through official development assistance programs (United Nations ESCAP, 2014). Other income is secured through fishing exports, licences to fish within its territorial waters, through remittances from family members abroad, and subsistence farming (CIA, 2017). Missionaries from the London Missionary Society arrived on Tuvaluan shores during the mid-1860s and the entire population was converted to Christianity by 1878. The Catholic Church arrived during the mid-1940s but attracted only a very small following of 120 persons. Scattered across the eight atolls that are habitable within Tuvalu, are also small numbers of Baha'i, Jehovah's Witnesses, Mormons, Open Brethren, Seventh Day Adventists, and The Assemblies of God (CIA, 2017; Bouma et al., 2013). The Constitution of Tuvalu (2008) defines the state as one based on Christian principles; however, persons are not to be discriminated against based on their religion. Therefore, freedom of religious belief and practice is recognized, and attendance at religious education or ceremonies is voluntary.

Fiji stands in contrast to Tuvalu as the Pacific's largest country. It lies directly South of Tuvalu and has a population of 887,000 persons (United Nations ESCAP, 2014). Indigenous Fijians (*iTaukei*) arrived from Melanesia over 3,000 years ago (Robertson & Sutherland, 2001) and currently comprise around 57% of the population. A further 37% are Indian Fijians, with the balance of residents coming from Rotuman, European, Chinese, and other Pacific Islands (Fiji Bureau of Statistics, 2015). Bouma et al. (2013) note that Christianity was established in Fiji by European traders and Missionaries. The first denomination to settle was Methodism in 1835. Shortly thereafter, the Catholic Church was established, in 1844, and then the Anglican and Presbyterian denominations began proselytizing in the 1860s. Hinduism, Islam, and Sikhism were also introduced during the 1800s as Indian indentured laborers arrived to work on plantations in 1879.

The conversions of the Western High Chief Cakobau and then shortly afterwards, the Eastern High Chief Ma'afu to Methodism that led to this Christian denomination becoming the historical religious stronghold of the *iTaukei* and the ruling class of Fiji (Bouma et al., 2013). The Methodist church continues to be the country's strongest religious force, having some 290,000 adherents. The Hindu, Santan sect has over 194,000 devotees and the Catholics some 69,000 followers. Collectively 87% of the Christian population are *iTaukei*, while virtually all Hindu, Muslim, and Sikh followers are Indian Fijians (Fiji Bureau of Statistics, 2015). Due to the numeric strength of the Christian population and its connection with the ruling *iTaukei*, who control governance within the country (Srebrnik, 2002), Christianity is recognized as the official religion of Fiji (Newland, 2006). So much so, that the Sunday Observance Decree (1987) was passed in parliament. This required all residents to forego work, trade, recreation, entertainment, and public gathering on Sundays so that they could worship (Heinz, 1993). This decree was later rescinded in 1989.

Currently, the Constitution of the Republic of Fiji (2013) ensures religious freedom and that persons are not to be discriminated based on their religion, and attendance in religious education or ceremonies is voluntary. However, this does not imply that religious tension in non-existent within the country. Recently Fiji has experienced a number of political coups that have been ethnically motivated, largely by the *iTaukei*, to ensure Indian Fijians are kept from the legislative chambers of power. Srebrnik (2002) contends that much of this political unrest has religious overtones. For example, in 1987 the Methodist Lay Preacher Colonel Rabuka took control of Parliament and in so doing claimed that he was divinely inspired (Heinz, 1993). Additionally, George Speight's coup in 2000 overtly appealed to the Christian church for support. The 2006 coup led by Frank Bainimararama aimed to neutralize the political gains achieved by Speight for the Christian *iTaukei*. In response, the Methodists condemned the revolution as treasonous. Similarly, the Christian Mission Fellowship and the Roman Catholic Church strongly advocated that the coup was illegal (Newland, 2007).

South Korea

The Korean Republic (South Korea) is home to 49.5 million persons (United Nations ESCAP, 2014). The dominant faith is Christianity, attracting 29.4% or 14 million people, followed by Buddhism with a 22.9% share of followers. While the projection is for Christianity to expand its reach to 33.5% by 2050, adherents of Buddhism will fall to 18.1% (Pew Research Center, 2015d). Forty-six percent of the Korean Republic's residents are affiliated with no religion and this figure is expected to remain relatively static between now and 2050 (Pew Research Center, 2015d).

Lee et al. (2012) discuss how Confucian, Zen Buddhist, and Taoist concepts of the interrelatedness of everything in the universe influences how ecotourism is managed and practiced in South Korea. Self-cultivation and harmony extend beyond nature and also embrace the social and economic development and modernization of the country and thus where necessary modification of the landscape.

Jeon et al. (2013) discuss spiritual leadership in the South Korean context. Workplace spirituality is a component of organizational values and culture whereby spiritual leadership through hope/faith, altruistic love, and membership adds to inner life and individual life satisfaction. Such spiritual leadership is possible irrespective of Judeo-Christian and Confucian religious traditions in the South Korean context. Such leadership can be enhanced through providing meditation and prayer rooms in organizations, as well as meditation, mindfulness walking, and yoga. This can be extended to ensuring that individuals perceive their work as meaningful, feel connectedness with coworkers, customers, and the community, and feel that their work is appreciated. Leadership development programs can involve reflection on the vision and mission of the organization intertwined with hope/faith in how the vision could be played out.

The five country/region examples provide vivid illustrations of how religiously diverse the Asia-Pacific region is. The next section presents organizational tips for relevant managerial practices in the context of the rich diversity of this region.

Organizational and Managerial Practices

Based on comprehensive empirical data that explored the perspectives of both employers and employees, Pio (2014) identified five organizational and managerial practices that are of relevance in the negotiation and management of religious diversity. These are:

1. Crafting Policies that incorporate religious diversity into the human resource management systems as well as the overall strategic direction and implementation of the organization. This may include policies on dress code, food at various functions and appropriate symbolism displayed in offices and corridors of the organization.
2. Talent management, with socialization processes that legitimize differences and thus also actively seek out diverse individuals for recruitment and selection into the company. Furthermore, religious diversity could be included in planning for job enhancement, career progression, and psychological capital, as for example in the export of certain products and processes to specific targeted markets.
3. Engaging voice or listening to different voices and incorporating their suggestions and requests into aspects such as dress code, etiquette, and symbols. This can also include aspects of health and safety so that all members of the organization feel safe.
4. Learning and development so that there are structural institutional processes put into place, that serve as the bedrock for mindful negotiation and civility. This may consist of maintaining a dynamic learning environment to encompass religious diversity, including aspects of religious diversity in induction programs, and visiting different religious shrines as an immersive experience.

5. Augmenting media to ensure that communication is inclusive, respectful, and supportive. This may include a calendar of religious festivals. Care is also needed in the messages communicated regarding the world we operate in and perceived "flash points," such as terrorism and refugees.

The above five practices are broadly universal, and are based on Pio's (2014) empirical research on religious diversity in New Zealand. While the research was done in a specific geographical context, they can be implemented in any organization, irrespective of the country in which the religions exist and irrespective of the nature of the organization.

Concluding Comments

Religious diversity in organizations calls into question the distinction between the sacred and secular. Tenzin Gyasto, the fourth Dalai Lama, encourages interreligious harmony and notes that irrespective of whether a person practices religion or not, "the spiritual qualities of love and compassion, patience, tolerance, forgiveness and humility and so on are indispensable ... and properly employed it [religion] is an extremely effective instrument for establishing human happiness. In particular, it can play a leading role in encouraging people to develop a sense of responsibility towards others and of the need to be ethically disciplined" (Gyasto, 2008, p. 80). He notes that lack of appreciation of other faith traditions is the biggest obstacle to interreligious harmony and emphasizes dialogue with various faith traditions and thus, diversity can be very enriching. However, he underscores the importance of genuinely practicing one's own religion and applying those teachings in all aspects of our lives.

In the extremely diverse and large land-mass of Asia-Pacific, it is impossible to go into details of each of the countries or religions which exist, many of them peacefully with each other as do the people in various organizations within those countries. However, this chapter has sought to present some aspects of this diversity, as an introduction into an appreciation and possibly understanding of distinct faith traditions. In fact religion in organizations can be exemplified by "the many instances when we have been humbled by kindness, listened to the music in our hearts and celebrated life with generosity, grace and gratitude" (Pio, 2014, p. 107).

Summary

This chapter has sought to present information on the broad swathe of religions in the vast geographical area known as the Asia-Pacific. Religious pluralism is a defining characteristic of this region, the most religiously diverse in our planet, with considerable economic growth and consisting of 60% of the world's population. A table depicting the flags, population, and GDP of each of the countries in this region was presented. This was followed by an outline of the beliefs of five religions – Christianity, Hinduism, Islam, Sikhism, and Zoroastrianism. Next, country examples were described through relevant research and data. The selected countries were Australia, Japan, New Zealand, The Pacific Islands, and South Korea.

Finally, we suggested that five managerial and organizational practices may be employed for relevant and meaningful managerial practices pertaining to religious diversity within Asia Pacific or for that matter any geographical context across the globe. These included: (1) crafting human resource policies that incorporate religious diversity; (2) developing talent management processes which legitimize differences and seek out diverse individuals for recruitment as employees; (3) engaging different voices into the decision making processes of the organization, including the development of its culture; (4) maintaining a dynamic learning and development environment that encompasses religious diversity; and (5) augmenting media to ensure that communication is inclusive, respectful, and supportive. By adopting these policies, organizations facilitate building a sense of responsibility for self and others, and endorse the value of ethical practices.

References

Akbarzadeh, S., & Roose, J. M. (2011). Muslims, multiculturalism and the question of the silent majority. *Journal of Muslim Minority Affairs*, 3, 309–25.

Asia Pacific Forum for Environment and Development (2010). *APFED II final report*. Kanagawa: Asia Pacific Forum for Environment and Development.

Beckford, J. A. (2014). Re-thinking religious pluralism. *In* Giordan, G., & Pace, E. (eds.) *Religious pluralism: Framing religious diversity in the contemporary world*. New York: Springer, 15–30.

Benland, C. (1988). *The S-factor: Taha wairua. The April report: Future directions. Report of the Royal Commission on Social Policy Vol. III, Part One.* Wellington: Government printer, 449–61.

Bendle, M. F. (2007). Secret Saudi funding of radical Islamic groups in Australia. *National Observer*, Autumn, 7–18.

Bouma, G. D., Ling, R., & Pratt, D. (2013). *Religious diversity in Southeast Asia and the Pacific.* Dordrecht: Springer.

Breward, I. (1988). *Australia: The most godless place under heaven?* Melbourne: Beacon Hill.

Bunbury, S. (2014). Warwick Thornton in conversation with God. *Sydney Morning Herald*, September 1.

Carey, L. B., & del Medico, L. (2014). Correctional services and prison chaplaincy in Australia: An exploratory study. *Journal of Religion and Health*, 53, 1786–99.

Carpenter, B., Tait, G., Quadrelli, C., & Thompson, I. (2015). Investigating death: The emotional and cultural challenges for police. *Policing and Society*, 26(6), 698–712.

CIA. (2017). World Factbook: Tuvalu [Online]. CIA. Retrieved from: www.cia.gov/library/publications/the-world-factbook/geos/tv.html.

Cody, P. (2004). *Seeds of the word: Nga Kakano O Te Kupu: The meeting of Māori spirituality and Christianity.* Wellington: Steele Roberts.

Constitution of the Republic of Fiji. (2013). Fiji. Retrieved from: www.paclii.org/fj/Fiji-Constitution-English-2013.pdf.

Coslett (2015). Japan: The most religious atheist country. Retrieved from: Accessed 31 July 2017.

Crisp, B. R. (2013). Social work and faith-based agencies in Sweden and Australia. *International Social Work*, 56, 343–55.

Crossman, J. (2015). Eclecticism and commonality in employee constructions of spirituality. *Journal of Management, Spirituality & Religion*, 12, 59–77.

Daher, M., Chaar, B., & Saini, B. (2015). Impact of patients' religious and spiritual beliefs in pharmacy: From the perspective of the pharmacist. *Research in Social and Administrative Pharmacy*, 11, e31–e41.

Fiji Bureau of Statistics. (2015). *Population and demography* [Online]. Fiji: Fiji Bureau of Statistics. Retrieved from: www.statsfiji.gov.fj/index.php/social/9-social-statistics/social-general/113-population-and-demography.

Fisker-Nielsen, A. M. (2012). *Religion and politics in contemporary Japan: Soka Gakkai youth and Komeito.* New York: Routledge.

Fitzgerald, T. (2003). "Religion" and "the secular" in Japan. Retrieved from: www.blog.gaijinpot.com/japan-religious-atheist-country/.

Ghanbarpour, C. (2015). Legacy of a minority religion: Christians and Christianity in contemporary Japan. *In* Brunn, S. D. (ed.) *The changing* world religion map: Sacred places, identities, practices and politics. Dordrecht: Springer Netherlands, 2025–44.

Giordan, G. (2014). Pluralism as legitimacy of diversity. *In* Giordan, G., & Pace, E. (eds.) *Religious pluralism: Framing religious diversity in the contemporary world*. New York: Springer.

Grant, E. K. (2004). *Unseen, unheard, unspoken: Exploring the relationship between Aboriginal spirituality and community development*. Thesis, University of South Australia.

Gyasto, T. (2008). Interreligious harmony. *In* Meister, C. (ed.), *The philosophy of religion reader*. London: Routledge.

Heinz, D. (1993). The Sabbath in Fiji as guerrilla theatre. *Journal of the American Academy of Religion*, 61, 415–42.

Hick, J. (2008). Religious pluralism and the pluralistic hypothesis. *In* Meister, C. (ed.) *The philosophy of religion reader*. London: Routledge.

Hirono, T. (2013). The role of religious leaders in suicide prevention. *Sage Open*, 3. 1–11.

Honda. (2015). *Honda philosophy* [Online]. Retrieved from: www.world.honda.com/profile/philosophy/.

Human Rights Commission. (2007). *Religious diversity in Aotearoa New Zealand*. Wellington: Human Rights Commission.

Jeon, K. S., Passmore, D. L., Lee, C., & Hunsaker, W. (2013). Spiritual leadership: A validation study in a Korean context. *Journal of Management, Spirituality & Religion*, 10, 342–57.

Kieninger, P. R., Penker, M., & Yamaji, E. (2013). Aesthetic and spiritual values motivating collective action for the conservation of cultural landscape: A case study of rice terraces in Japan. *Renewable Agriculture and Food Systems*, 28, 364–79.

Knight, S. (1996). *Our land our life, card*. Canberra: Aboriginal and Torres Strait Islander Commission.

Lee, Y., Lawton, L. J., & Weaver, D. B. (2012). Evidence for a South Korean Model of Ecotourism. *Journal of Travel Research*, 52(4), 520–33.

Malloy, D. C., Sevigny, P. R., Hadjistavropoulos, T., Bond, K., Mccarthy, E. F., Murakami, M., Paholpak, S., Shalini, N., Liu, P. L., & Peng, H. (2014). Religiosity and ethical ideology of physicians: A cross-cultural study. *Journal of Religion and Health*, 53, 244–54.

Manderson, L., Smith, W., & Tomlinson, M. (2012). *Flows of faith: Religious reach and community in Asia and the Pacific*. New York: Springer Science & Business Media.

Marsden, M. (1975). God, man and universe: A Māori view. *In* King, M. (ed.), *Te Ao Hurihuri: The world moves on*. Wellington: Hick, Smith and Sons Ltd.

Meister, C. (2008). General introduction. *In* Meister, C. (ed.), *The philosophy of religion reader*. New York: Routledge (pp. 1–4).

Milani, M., & Possamai, A. (2015). Sufism, spirituality and consumerism: The case study of the Nimatullahiya and Naqshbandiya Sufi orders in Australia. *Contemporary Islam*, 1, 1–19.

Miner, M., Bickerton, G., Dowson, M., & Sterland, S. (2015). Spirituality and work engagement among church leaders. *Mental Health, Religion & Culture*, 18, 57–71.

Ministry of Justice. (1998). *He Hinatore ki te Ao Māori – A glimpse into the Māori world: Māori Perspectives on Justice*. Retrieved from: www.justice.govt.nz/pubs/reports/2001/Māori_perspectives/foreword.html.

Moeke-Maxwell, T., Te Awekotuku, N., & Nikora, L. W. (2012). The Māori way of living and dying. *In Death Down Under Conference*. Conference held at University of Otago, Dunedin, New Zealand.

Mudrooroo. (1995). *Us mob: History, culture, struggle: An introduction to indigenous Australia*. Sydney: Angus & Robertson.

Nath, J., Henderson, J., Coveney, J., & Ward, P. (2013). Consumer faith. *Food, Culture & Society*, 16, 421–36.

Newland, L. (2006). Fiji. *In* Ernst, M. (ed.), *Globalization and the re-shaping of Christianity in the Pacific Islands*. Suva: Pacific Theological College.

(2007). Religion and politics: The Christian churches and the 2006 coup in Fiji. *10th Pacific Islands Political Studies Association*.

O'Donnell, K. (2006). *Inside world religions*. Oxford: Lion Hudson plc.

Okawa, R. (2014). *The basic teachings of happy science: A happiness theory on truth and faith*. Japan: IRH Press Co. Ltd.

Parliamentary Counsel Offices. (1987). *Immigration Act*. Wellington: Parliamentary Counsel Office.

Patterson, J. (1992). *Exploring Māori values*. Palmerston North: The Dunmore Press Limited.

Pew Research Center. (2015a). *Compare Asia Pacific* [Online]. Washington, DC: Pew Research Center. Retrieved from: www.globalreligiousfutures.org/regions/asia-pacific/religious_demography-/?affiliations_religion_id=0&affiliations_year=2010.

(2015b). *Global religious diversity* [Online]. Washington, DC: Pew Research Center. Retrieved from: www.pewforum.org/2014/04/04/global-religious-diversity/.

(2015c). *Global religious futures project: Asia Pacific* [Online]. Washington, DC: Pew Research Center. Retrieved from: www.globalreligiousfutures.org/regions/asia-pacific.

(2015d). *Religious composition by country, 2010–2050* [Online]. Washington, DC: Pew Research Center. Retrieved from: www.pewforum.org/2015/04/02/religious-projection-table/2050/percent/Asia-Pacific/.

Pio, E. (2014). *Work and worship*. Auckland: Faculty of Business and Law, Auckland University of Technology.

Razzaque, A. M., & Chaudhry, S. N. (2013). Religiosity and Muslim consumers' decision-making process in a non-Muslim society. *Journal of Islamic Marketing*, 4, 198–217.

Richardson, J. T. (2013). Managing minority religious and ethnic groups in Australia: Implications for social cohesion. *Social Compass*, 60, 579–90.

Robertson, R., & Sutherland, W. (2001). *Government by the gun: The unfinished business of Fiji's 2000 coup.* Sydney: Pluto.

Sav, A., Harris, N., & Sebar, B. (2009). Work–life conflict among Australian Muslim men and women in South-East Queensland. *Equality, Diversity and Inclusion: An International Journal*, 32, 671–87.

Shimazono, S. (2004). *From salvation to spirituality: Popular religious movements in modern Japan.* Melbourne: Trans Pacific Press.

Srebrnik, H. (2002). Ethnicity, religion and the issue of aboriginality in a small island state: Why does Fiji flounder? *The Round Table*, 364, 187–210.

Tennant, M., O'Brien, M., & Sanders, J. (2008). *The history of the non-profit sector in New Zealand.* Wellington: Office for the Community and Voluntary Sector.

The constitution of Tuvalu. (2008). Retrieved from: www.tuvaluislands.com/const_tuvalu.htm.

Toyota. (2015). *Vision & philosophy* [Online]. Retrieved from: www.toyota-global.com/company/vision_philosophy/toyota_global_vision_2020.html.

Unantenne, N., Warren, N., Canaway, R., & Manderson, L. (2013). The strength to cope: Spirituality and faith in chronic disease. *Journal of Religion and Health*, 52, 1147–61.

United Nations capitalise. (2014). *Statistical yearbook for Asia and the Pacific 2014.* Herndon, VA: United Nations Publications.

Ward, K. (2008). Truth and the diversity of religions. *In* Meister, C. (ed.), *The philosophy of religion reader.* London: Routledge.

William, C. (1995). *Collins atlas of the world.* London: Harper Collins.

Yang, F. (2014). Oligopoly is not pluralism. *In* Giordan, G., & Pace, E. (eds.), *Religious pluralism: Framing religious diversity in the contemporary world.* New York: Springer.

Youssef, J., & Deane, F. P. (2013). Arabic-speaking religious leaders' perceptions of the causes of mental illness and the use of medication for treatment. *Australian and New Zealand Journal of Psychiatry*, 47, 1041–50.

Zhong, Y. (2014). Freedom, religion and the making of the modern state in Japan, 1868–89. *Asian Studies Review*, 38, 53–70.

PART IV

Organizational Approaches

14 | Organizational Approaches to Religious Diversity in the Workplace

TIMOTHY EWEST

Introduction

This chapter presents a religious diversity workplace integration framework posited by Miller (2007) and later adapted by Miller and Ewest (2015) which this chapter suggests is a better alignment with organizational practices and The Universal Declaration of Human Rights, Title VII, and Employment Equality Framework Directive requirements. As a means for comparative analysis, this chapter considers the various historical challenges to civil rights as outlined in Title VII, to which organizations have had to adjust in order to accommodate their employee's religious practices. These historical challenges include: Ethnicity (in the 1960s), equality of woman (in the 1970s), the changing nuclear family (in the 1980s), and gender orientation (in the 1990s) (Miller & Ewest, 2015). The framework presented is theoretically anchored in Symbolic Management theory (Ashforth & Vaidyanath, 2002; Roberge et al., 2011). Symbolic Management theory is a way management presents a picture with certain parameters or frames, and portrays the desired organization to its members and other stakeholders (Fiss & Zajac, 2006). The strength of this perspective is that it aids in finding a common frame of reference for individuals to understand and identify a proposed organizational culture which allows employees to find commonalities among differences, or specifically in this case diversity within faith or religious groups.

The proposed faith integration framework posits four frames to assess how well an organization accommodates religious diversity in regards to religious or faith accommodation requests, formal organizational policies, and employee wellness. The four frames within the framework are: Faith avoiding, faith based, faith safe, and faith friendly. These frames are placed within an assessment rubric assessing: Organizational policy, accommodation requests, and employee well-being. The recommended frame within the framework is "Faith-Friendly." The faith friendly frame addresses Title VII requirements for religious accommodation in the United States (and tacitly The Universal Declaration of Human Rights), but also goes beyond this by developing polices that regard a person's religion as a means to employee wellness and corresponding organizational benefits. The faith friendly frame goes beyond the minimum requirements of The Universal Declaration of Human Rights, Title VII and Employment Equality Framework Directive because it seeks out employee's faith needs and understands and embraces the corresponding benefits associated with empowering the diverse faith traditions within the workplace.

The chapter presents two case studies, The Paprec Group and PacMoore Corporation, as a means to understand the various frames in a diagnostic fashion. Each of these companies assertively incorporates one of the frames into their business practices and branding. The framework provides the reader with a tool to diagnose which frame they believe each company is using, and making recommendations in regards to The Universal Declaration of Human Rights, Title VII, and Employment Equality Framework Directive accommodation requirements and corresponding policy requirements. The chapter resolves by presenting the findings from one organization that the author considers to be faith friendly, that is, they have met all the criteria presented in the assessment rubric for being a faith friendly company and compares this to a random sample. The survey reports the findings of self-perceived satisfaction in regard to how employees believe how their organization honors their faith tradition with respective policies, their ability to accommodate their faith needs, and finally their consideration of themselves as human beings. The survey was part of a larger assessment, whose findings will not be discussed in this chapter, that was designed to determine how employees integrate their faith into the workplace through their religiously motivated behavior manifested in ethics, verbal or symbolic expression, or finding purpose in their work or enriching faith practices.

Contextual Considerations

How does the modern workplace respond to the growing presence of religion? While religion has declined in some places, such as Europe,

Table 14.1 *Equal opportunity commissions claims based on religious grounds*

Year	Religious claims filed
2012	3,811
2013	3,721
2014	3,549

globally the number of people who identify with a major world religion is predicted to rise from its present level of 80% to 85% by 2050 (Johnson, 2010). This reality is coupled with the reality that many employees are less willing to leave their faith and its corresponding expression outside of the workplace (Mitroff & Denton, 1999; Nash & McLennan, 2001; Hicks, 2003; Williams, 2003; Fogel, 2004; Giacalone & Jurkiewicz, 2005; Hart & Brady, 2005; Miller, 2007; Miller & Ewest, 2013c).

Many developed countries, like the United States, are becoming less religiously uniform and becoming more religiously diverse and pluralistic. This new complex religious reality is going to require the attention of human resource departments, diversity managers, and managers at every level. Within the United States the reality is demonstrated by a growth in Equal Employment Opportunity Commission (EEOC) claims pertaining to religious discrimination (Atkinson, 2004). Globally, organizations will need to develop an understanding of how organizational policies should best be designed to respect those of diverse faith traditions. If organizations are not able to address these issues, the default will be for individuals to best determine what is the appropriate level of expression of their faith in the workplace (Gregory, 2011).

In the United States, recent claims cited by Equal Employment Opportunity Commission (EEOC), the federal agency that administers and enforces civil rights laws against workplace discrimination, would suggest faith expression in the workplace is a growing concern. There were 4,151 religious claims filed with the EEOC during the 2011 fiscal year, a 9.5% increase on 2010. In subsequent years, total claims filed have dipped below the 2011 high, but these numbers are staggering compared with the 1997 number of 1,709 claims. See Table 14.1.

Further, the two largest categories of EEOC religious claims in the workplace have consistently centered on accommodation requests for time off (for prayer and/or special holiday observances) and issues around clothing (Estreicher & Gray, 2006; Greenwald, 2012). This could suggest the historically and statistically Christian-dominated workforce is unfamiliar with the issues, practices, rituals, and beliefs of many non-Christian traditions, resulting in possible mismanagement of religious accommodation requests (Greenwald, 2012).

Within developed countries, the challenges before organizations go beyond this simple depiction of internal organizational management decisions, since religion is regarded as a universal human right. Organizations will need to consider both voluntary approaches to honoring human rights as manifested in faith or religious expressions, as well as adherence to external accountability measures such as the Universal Declaration of Human Rights, Employment Equality Framework Directive, and, in the United States, Title VII considerations (Campbell, 2006).

What may be of encouragement is that some suggest that today's organizations within developed countries are more willing to partner with employees and take responsibility to respect employees' religious freedom (White, 2011). In developed countries, organizations before 1950 emphasized the rights of the employer, in contrast to the 1960s and 1970s, when organizations began to emphasize the rights of the employee (White, 2011).

Religion: An Aspect of Our Humanity

Regardless of how organizations respond, what cannot be refuted is that a person's faith or religious tradition is part of their human identity (Richards & Bergin, 1997; Hart & Brady, 2005). A person's faith or religious tradition is vital to how individuals create meaning for themselves and ultimately is vital in how one forms their personal identity (Emmons, 2003; Wuthnow, 2005). Yet, while business should recognize this trend and adhere to the legal requirements as mandated by their nation, they may still miss the vital constructive aspects of bringing faith into the workplace (King & Holmes, 2012). Research has demonstrated that there are numerous positive effects that integration of faith and work can have on the workplace, such as on important life outcomes (Walker, 2013); organizational commitment (Pawar, 2009; Bodia & Ali, 2012); productivity (Duchon & Plowman, 2005; Chen et al., 2012); job satisfaction (Hall et al., 2012); ethics

(Weaver & Argle, 2002; Emerson & McKinney, 2010); and, finally, job retention and job involvement (Milliman et al., 2003; Pawar, 2009).

Yet, the prevailing assumption of the modern workplace is that there must "be a wall of separation between a person's beliefs and the workplace" (Kelly, 2008, p. 42). The "wall" of separation is perceived to be important because we do not all share the same worldview. Some believe that secularization has also influenced management theory so it has become individualist and materialistic (Dyck & Schroeder, 2005). The governing attitude of the modern workplace can be best understood as one that supports a necessary decline in religious faith since it interferes with organizational processes (Berger, 1969; Wilson, 1982; Ashforth & Vaidyanath, 2002; King, 2012).

And, while sociologists continue to consider the degree, scope, or existence of secularization in greater society, it would be difficult to contend that many organizations are in reality committed to secularization within their own walls (Goldblast, 2000; Ashforth & Vaidyanath, 2002; Seales, 2012). The impact on employees are potentially numerous, but most notable is the tendency for workers to compartmentalize their religious faith while at work. Yet, other organizations take the opposite perspective, in that they embrace a more holistic approach and recognize their employees' personal lives including various attributes, such as race, sex, gender orientation, and religious faith (Ashforth & Vaidyanath, 2002; Gull & Doh, 2004; Johnson, 2007; Vasconcelos, 2010).

Religious Diversity and Human Rights

Organizations which take a more holistic approach understand the vital role religious faith can play in the development of personal meaning and identity (Emmons, 2003; Wuthnow, 2005), and ultimately understand religion as an aspect of their employees' human rights. Human rights should be understood as a set of moral imperatives, that critique law and legal systems (Campbell, 2006); moral imperatives that are granted to people simply because they are human (Morsink, 2009). Internationally, the United Nations adopted the Universal Declaration of Human Rights (United Nations, 2009) to establish a baseline of universal respect and value for all human persons. Within this declaration, Article 2 affirms that every human is to be entitled to all the rights and freedoms with respect to religion. The Universal

Declaration of Human Rights addresses religious human rights in Article 18, stating:

Everyone has the right to freedom of thought, conscience, and religion; this right includes freedom to change his religion or belief, and freedom, either alone or in community with others and in public or private, to manifest his religion or belief in teaching, practice, worship and observance. (United Nations, 2009)

As a demonstration of the United Nations' commitment to ensure that human rights are upheld, they established The Global Compact, which is the world's largest global citizenship initiative, representing over 100 countries. The Global Compact carries with it a series of commitments organizations promise to fulfill, including a specific commitment to take responsibility in areas of human rights, labor, the environment, and anti-corruption. Most companies that participate, 79%, do so because they believe it will increase trust in their company (United Nations, 2010).

In the United States, a similar set of laws are intended to protect the religious human rights of individuals. Title VII of the Civil Rights Act of (1964) makes it unlawful for employers to discriminate against an employee in regards to the employee's religious faith; employers must accommodate all reasonable requests from employees having to do with their religious beliefs or practices. However, the employer does not have to accommodate those requests which create an undue burden on the workplace (employer) (Gregory, 2011). The fear is that if organizations do not take a more proactive role in accommodating the religious rights of their employees of faith, they will become more marginalized, resulting in increased legal and social religious challenges (Witte & van der Vyver 1996; Atkinson, 2000; Schley, 2008; Gregory, 2011). Similar human rights considerations and corresponding legal measures have been adopted in the European Union under the Employment Equality Framework Directive of 2000 and were implemented in the United Kingdom (UK) in 2010 (Kramar & Syed, 2012). Some research suggests that laws in the UK are moving away from a focus on non-discrimination against minority groups to one that considers how to create equity among groups by considering the scope of positive action (Barnard & Hepple, 2000).

However, many countries have institutionalized accommodation of religious practices that are held by the majority national religion. For example, in predominantly Muslim countries, accommodations for daily prayer are anticipated, as are certain financing practices. However, in many countries the challenge will be twofold: the first being how to address accommodation requests from employees who come from minority religions, and the second coming from organizations which have not been proactive and simply have no idea how to become proactive.

However, globally, organizations have had to learn, or are learning to respect the human rights of their employees. Issues such as child labor, women in the workplace, and ethnic divisions are issues organizations located within China, South Africa, and Korea are familiar with, and they can recognize progress in meeting and addressing those challenges. Within the United States, there is a pattern of organizations observing the lapse in human rights issues and putting in place organizational practices and policies to accommodate and correct the lapse in employees' human rights (Miller, 2010; see Table 14.2). That organizations have recognized human rights violations and found ways to accommodate those human rights issues is a promising indication of the ability of organizations to recognize and accommodate employees' religious human rights.

Diversity Management

It is important to note that globally, not all organizations are mandated by law, contractual pressure, or ethical mandate to accommodate human rights. Therefore, it may be important to find voluntary approaches such as "diversity management," which is used to protect historically underutilized and discriminated groups (Gagnon, & Cornelius, 2000; Bassett-Jones et al., 2007). Yet, there is a considerable amount of opacity on how employers can best respect employees' religious rights. One managerial philosophy, known as Symbolic Management (Ashforth & Vaidyanath, 2002; Roberge et al., 2011), may provide a means for both employees and employers to envision a diversity strategy. Borrowing from social identity theory (Taifel & Turner, 1986) and self-categorization theory (Turner et al., 1987), which both focus on commonalties among groups, Symbolic Management is a management philosophy that frames or portrays the desired organization as an ideal

Table 14.2 A pattern of organizations observing human rights issues

Year	Social issue	Corresponding business issue
The 1960s – the "race-friendly" decade.	The 1960s were fraught with a great deal of social turmoil and anti-establishment protest, with racial discrimination at the forefront.	One of the defining social and business issues of this decade was the civil rights movement, which dramatically changed company recruitment, development, and promotion practices.
The 1970s – the "female-friendly" decade.	Women have long fought for equal rights and treatment in the marketplace. These efforts culminated in the 1970s with the proposed Equal Rights Amendment (ERA) to the Constitution.	Although the ERA failed, it contributed to changes in the way companies addressed such topics as equal pay and equal opportunity for women in the marketplace.
The 1980s – the "family-friendly" decade.	The traditional image of the "nuclear family" fell apart during the 1980s, replaced by single parents, blended families, and dual-career couples.	Women entered the workforce in increasing numbers. Often both parents worked, and finding daycare for their children and flexible work hours became a major business issue.
The 1990s/2000s – the "gender orientation-friendly" decade.	This decade saw the beginning of more overt and organized activism by the LGBT (lesbian, gay, bisexual, and transgendered) community.	This manifested itself in businesses having to consider same-sex partner medical benefits, recruitment practices, and adoption policies.
The 2000s and beyond – the "faith-friendly" decades?	Employees wanted increasingly to bring their whole selves to work, including their faith, and were no longer satisfied to sublimate that part of their human identity or live a bifurcated life, leaving their spiritual side at home or in the parking lot.	This initially raised concerns over proselytizing, discrimination, and harassment. But issues of dietary considerations, religious garb, and prayer requests have become the newer touchstones of concern. This parallels a growing corpus of research that suggests that faith-friendly workplaces (Miller, 2007) and "respectful pluralism" (Wuthnow, 2005) might benefit employees and employers alike.

Source: Miller & Ewest, 2015

group to its members or stakeholders (Fiss & Zajac, 2006). Diversity programs which foster or emphasize commonalities among groups have strong diversity outcomes (Brewer & Brown, 1998; Brewer & Gaertner, 2004). Another term used for the same phenomenon is the word "Frame," which is understood as the activity of attributing a perspectival model to guide mangers. For Bolman and Deal (2008), a frame "involves matching mental maps to circumstances" (p. 12). Researchers have developed numerous theories as a means to depict or frame how organizations should be or are positioning themselves in regards to religion in the workplace (see Table 14.3). Yet many of the established theories within management science fail to consider organizational practices such as the creation of policies, nor do they provide direct consideration of aforementioned established national and international human rights laws, and finally they do not address religious expressions; instead they focus on the "values" of organizations or "Social Responsibility."

Table 14.3 *Organizational frames for faith and work*

Authors	Organizational frames
Ashforth and Pratt (2010)	• The "enabling organization" is not interested in imposing a specific worldview on employees and may or may not consider work to be an integral part of the employees spiritual activity. • The "directing organization" has low individual control and high organizational control that "effectively imposes its preferred cosmology on individuals, a cosmology that is intimately tied to the mission and practices of the organization itself" (p. 49). • The "partnering organization" that has high individual control and high organizational control. This approach respects that workplace spirituality is both a "bottom-up and a top-down process, although not in a mechanistic or legalistic manner" (p. 52). Spirituality is believed to be a social construction which is created through the free interchange of beliefs.

(*cont.*)

Table 14.3 *(cont.)*

Authors	Organizational frames
Giacalone and Jurkiewicz (2010)	• The "parallel stance" understands spirituality and the workplace as being separate and different worlds. The two exist, but one has no impact on the other. • The "adversarial stance" sees spirituality and the workplace as not belonging together, creating antagonism and hostility. • The "integrative stance" sees spirituality and the workplace as being potentially connected, even suggesting causal relationships between faith and work.
Mitroff and Denton (1999)	• Hypothesize five organizational models of spirituality at work (the religion-based organization; the evolutionary organization; the recovering organization; the socially responsible organization; and the values-based organization). They conclude by prescriptively recommending a less specific and more generic conception of spirituality at work called the "hybrid-type organization" as best for the workplace.

Source: Miller & Ewest 2015

Four Organizational Approaches

The proposed Faith-Friendly Scorecard is a framework which acts as a rubric to assess how good organizations perform in regards to religious or faith accommodation requests, formal organizational policies and employee wellness. The four frames within the framework are: Faith avoiding, faith based, faith safe, and faith friendly. See Table 14.4.

A Faith-Avoiding Organization

Faith-avoiding companies advocate for a secular workplace, and see any inclusion of a person's religious faith to be problematic, prone to creating adversity and counterproductive to the purposes of the

Table 14.4 *Faith-friendly scorecard*

	Religious accommodation	Formal policies	Fatal dualism
Faith-avoiding	Requests are suppressed or may not be accommodated, company practices secularization. May not be meeting Title VII requirements. Holidays, while they follow the Christian calendar, are given secular names, unwittingly institutionalizing Christian traditions. No diversity frame is used to manage or guide the organizational culture.	Proactively connecting faith and work is rejected. Religious objects, rituals, religious expression are prohibited by policy. Religion as motivation as behavior is questioned, secular neutrality is championed. Religious expression is associated with harassment, fundamentalism, or extremism. Secular neutrality is believed to ensure equal footing for all religious traditions.	Is often practiced, as management signals that faith/spirituality is solely a personal matter with no role or place in the workplace. Positive effects of spirituality and religious religion such as organizational commitment, productivity, job satisfaction, and job retention may be in jeopardy, for those with strong religious convictions.
Faith-based	Requests are accommodated and promoted but often appear to favor one religious tradition. Themes from the promoted religion are used to incentivize activities, including sales and employee gatherings. Diversity frames focus on tolerance of those outside the predominant religious tradition, and greater adherence to the predominant frame.	Are proactively embraced, yet typically privilege one tradition over others. Many of the policies can be tacitly rooted within the tradition such as days taken off, garb expectations, religious expression, and personal motivation. They are anchored in the dominant faith tradition.	Is avoided for some by promoting the privileged tradition, while those from other traditions might feel compelled to practice compartmentalization. For those within the promoted faith tradition there is increased positive effects. Organizational commitment, productivity, job satisfaction, and job retention may be in jeopardy.

(*cont.*)

Table 14.4 (*cont.*)

	Religious accommodation	Formal policies	Fatal dualism
Faith-safe	Requests are met as necessitated by law, with priority given to avoiding undue burden on or disruption to the business and avoiding costly litigation. Diversity frames focus on tolerance of and understanding of those with varying religious traditions, encouraging greater identity with the predominant faith tradition.	Accommodate religious practices as necessitated by law, but fall short of embracing it. Policies are designed to avoid litigation, and provide accommodation for most issues providing they do not put an undue burden on the workplace. Most policies unwittingly support institutionalized Christian traditions in regards to holidays, professional dress, and religious practice.	May be less likely for those whose faith/spiritual needs are satisfied through some religious accommodations. Positive effects of spirituality and religion are mediated by religious adherence and expectations rooted in religious self-identity. For those with low adherence and religious expectations, there is minimal mediating (negative) effect.
Faith-friendly	Requests are respected, where employers seen as valued, and seeks out religious and spiritual needs of employees, going beyond letter of law seeing multifaceted workplace benefits. Diversity frames focus on understanding and agreement between those with varying religious traditions.	Support practices that proactively embrace all religious faith traditions, with equal respect and consideration given to each, including atheists. Formal policies are constructed, reviewed, and updated by employees who represent various faith traditions.	Avoided by encouraging the integration of faith and work for all religious/spiritual employees from various traditions. Positive effects of spirituality and religion are clearly seen: organizational commitment, productivity, job satisfaction, and job retention.

Source: Miller & Ewest, 2015

workplace. With the use of this frame, the organization forces employees to practice a type of fatal dualism, whereby employees are required to leave their religious faith outside the door of their workplace (Miller & Ewest, 2015). This perspective may represent the present disposition of organizations in developed countries. Yet, surprisingly, this perspective is also supported by key management authors in the Academy of Management. Mitroff and Denton (1999), whose research subjects indicated religion is perceived as pejorative, viewing religion as a highly inappropriate form of expression and topic within the workplace. Mitroff (2003) personally states, "I still believe that formal, organized religion has very little, if any, role to play in the workplace" (p. 378), because he believes religion is divisive.

However, while the use of this frame may avoid the division sometimes created by religious practice in the workplace, it also can create paranoia because the religiously devoted employees may feel they are being treated unjustly. And, even if this frame does protect some employees from offensive religious expression of some, it ignores legitimate demands from the religiously devout employees, which could result in litigation where a nation's laws prohibit such discrimination (Gregory, 2011).

A Faith-Based Organization

Alternatively, faith-based companies are clearly grounded in one particular faith tradition. This frame or perspective seeks to align the company's mission with the values of their religious faith tradition. Companies which are faith-based are typically privately owned, and the founder's faith tradition can play a significant role in promoting the faith within the workplace. The fact is that many faith-based companies view their religious belief as being central to and the main purpose of their business model and their financial success, even at the risk of creating discriminatory policies and practices (Miller & Ewest, 2015).

While favoring one religious tradition may not be illegal and in some countries is required (e.g., Sharia law) the faith-based company runs the risk of privileging some and discriminating against or even aggressively proselytizing to those from other religious faiths. The faith-based company may even wish to ensure the centrality of their faith and favor and promote those who agree with the leadership's faith perspectives and beliefs. Moreover, employees who hold a different faith tradition to that of their employer may be forced to hide their own faith tradition, feel excluded or simply feel marginalized (Aadland & Skjørshammer, 2012; Miller & Ewest, 2015).

A Faith-Safe Organization

Faith-safe companies choose to tolerate their employees' faith traditions, but do not embrace or encourage religious expression. These companies recognize that there is a legal or humane requirement to accommodate at least the minimum standards pertaining to Title VII and other relevant international laws and guidelines that recognize religion as a human right. These companies accommodate religious requests because they wish to mitigate risk of lawsuits and/or desire employees to feel valued (Miller & Ewest, 2015).

But this frame doesn't encourage or proactively seek out their employees' religious faith practices because the organization doesn't understand religious faith as an organizational asset or a valued aspect to organizational diversity. One result is that faith-safe companies may not have specific policies for people of faith, yet have set up policies for other protected or marginalized groups (e.g., race, gender, age), raising questions of fairness for people of religious devotion (Miller & Ewest, 2015).

A Faith-Friendly Organization

The faith-friendly company is like the faith-safe company because it acknowledges the importance of faith in the life of employees and wishes to accommodate those employees, but more importantly this frame also seeks to go beyond what is expected by relevant laws and international guidelines. The faith-friendly company goes beyond minimal legal requirements and international guidelines and embraces religious faith in ways that are consistent with other diversity and inclusion practices. And, consistent with research findings, the company understands the advantages of including religion with and alongside other diversity issues. These advantages include: Organizational commitment (Pawar, 2009; Bodia & Ali, 2012); productivity (Duchon & Plowman, 2005; Chen et al., 2012); job satisfaction (Hall et al., 2012); ethics (Weaver & Argle, 2002; Emerson & McKinney, 2010); and, finally, retention, and job involvement (Milliman et al., 2003; Pawar, 2009).

Organizational Approaches to Religious Diversity in the Workplace 403

The primary way a faith-friendly company demonstrates their commitment to seeing religion as an aspect of human rights and diversity is by constructing workplace policies which are welcoming and inclusive, not favoring one religious tradition over the other. The faith-friendly company understands the vital role religion plays within the lives of many employees (Emmons, 2003; Wuthnow, 2005). Therefore, faith-friendly companies seek to include all people of religious faith and understand their religious expression as something to embrace and respect alongside other aspects of diversity (Miller & Ewest, 2015).

Cases for Discussion

The two cases that follow both depict examples of one of the frames within the four aforementioned frames. The cases were found using web based search engines using Boolean operatives, and selected not because they were an exact fit, but instead are generally "representative" of one of the four frames; The Paprec Group represents a faith-avoiding company and the PacMoore Corporation represents a faith-based one.

The Paprec Group

The French company The Paprec Group, began in 1995 by Jean-Luc Petithuguenin when he took over a small paper recycling company with 45 employees. Petithuguenin was convinced that recycling market had great potential and set to become one of the most important enterprises for the twenty-first century. Through aggressive investment policies the Paprec group acquired advanced industrial technology which allowed it to enter into new recycling markets such as plastics, e-waste, and selective collection. The Paprec group today also has numerous environmental services that include collecting household waste, public bins, and sorted waste. Finally, they offer delegated management of waste collection and sorting facilities, including management of facilities for nonhazardous waste storage (Paprec Group Raw Material Producer of the 21st Century).

With solid leadership, The Paprec Group's dynamic growth and innovation has attracted over 20,000 industrialists to participate in Paprec recycling, resulting in them becoming one of the key players in the world of recycling and waste management (Paprec Group Raw

Material Producer of the 21st Century). The respect that the Paprec Group has for the environment is mirrored in their respect for individuals. Paprec seeks out individuals who adhere to the same set of founding values that establishes the company's market presence. The driving philosophy of the company is stated in the following, "We believe in human rights and believe in the Enterprise." Paprec desires employees who seek excellence, professionalism, and mutual respect.

Jean-Luc Petithuguenin, in order to maintain this respect of individuals and fight against discrimination, asked all of its current 4,000 employees (from 56 different nationalities) to agree to practice a newly adopted "Charter of Secularism" (see Table 14.5). The Paprec group anticipates that the charter will move the company beyond present French laws, which prohibit the wearing of conspicuous religious symbols in schools. Moreover the charter seeks to resonate with the philosophy of secularism within French society, which intends to create freedom for people to believe or not believe freely (The Charter For Secularity and Diversity).

PacMoore Case Study

In 1985 Bill Moore left Procter and Gamble to take a leadership role at this father's company, George Meyer Company. Bill became aware of a need within the food industry for a reliable and capable manufacturing partner. Bill spent the next 20 years growing the company to meet the industries needs of packaging, blending, spray drying, and extrusion (Management Team).

Today the PacMoore Corporation, an American company, is a progressive and reliable food-contract packaging and processing business located in Hammond, Indiana. The company's contract manufacturing capabilities include blending, sifting, spraying, and turnkey processing, all of which enable the company to meet almost any requirement for food and dry ingredients. PacMoore, led by Bill Moore, employs 300 people, processes an estimated 250 million pounds of ingredients each year and generates annual sales over $35 million.

For the leadership at the PacMoore Corporation, their organization goes beyond simple social responsibility or respect for employees. "For PacMoore, Business a Mission (BAM) is not simply a social responsibility campaign – it is a calling we have been given as Disciples of Jesus Christ." The leadership at PacMoore understand the business they are

Table 14.5 *Charter of secularism adopted by a French recycling company*

The Paprec Group Charter for Secularism and Diversity
The Paprec Group, which welcomes and protects all forms of diversity, invites its stakeholders to respect the following principles to promote harmonious collective living.
Preamble: France is an indivisible, laic, democratic and social Republic. It ensures legal equality for all citizens, all over its territory. It respects all creeds.
As a laic entity, the Republic organizes the separation of State and religions. With regard to religious or spiritual convictions, the State is a neutral entity. There is no State religion.
The secularism of the Republic guarantees the freedom of conscience of all citizens. Everyone is free to believe or not.
Secularism allows proper citizenship, while conciliating everyone's freedom with the equality and fraternity of all, in the best interest of the nation.
1. Organizational secularism provides employees a common and shared frame of reference, promoting corporate cohesion, respect for all diversities, and living together.
2. Organizational secularism provides stakeholders conditions to forge their personality, exercise their free will and exercise their citizenship. It protects from any proselytism and any pressure that would prevent one from making his/her own choices and practicing a given activity in a serene environment.
3. Organizational secularism supports freedom of expression of employees within the limits of proper company management, as well as the respect of republican values and pluralism of convictions.
4. Organizational secularism implies rejection of all forms of violence and discrimination, guarantees equality between Men and Women, and is based upon a culture of respect and understanding of each other.
5. Organizational secularism implies that employees have a duty of neutrality: they should not express their political or religious beliefs during the exercise of their work.
6. According to law, no one can use his or her religion to refuse to perform his or her mission or to disrupt the smooth running of the business.
7. Within the company and the exercise of their functions, the rules of life of associated with different work spaces, as described in the policy handbook of each branch, are respectful of secularism. Thus, the wearing of signs or dress codes by which employees overtly manifest a religious affiliation is not allowed.
8. Through their reflections and mutual respect, employees sustain within the company the founding values associated with the Diversity Promotional Group.

Source: www.paprec.com/en/actualite/paprec-implements-a-charter-secularism

committed to as a mission, the term "Business as Mission" conveys how their Christian faith is integrated into their business practices. BAM is the building and sustaining of profitable businesses that create jobs, allowing them to form relationships with their employees, customers, and salespersons through which they are able to share the message of Jesus Christ with those who are interested.

Although making a profit is still the overarching goal of the company, CEO Bill Moore believes the company's mission is much deeper, broader, and eternal. This sense of an eternal mission in the company started 15 years ago when Moore became convinced that his faith shouldn't be confined to Sundays only. He decided to bring his faith to work and use the company he leads to change the lives of employees, customers, suppliers, and even farmers in Uganda. CEO Bill Moore states, "The concept of mission is very important to us, we use the company as a platform to bring the Gospel of Jesus Christ to all the people we can ... our business is a mission field" (Shorr, 2012, p. 21). It is the company's purpose to live fully committed to love, serve, and honor Jesus Christ and the company's mission to supply 5,000 jobs to low-income communities around the world by 2020.

The PacMoore Corporation has five core values that hold the company and their employees together – faith, family, integrity, respect, and excellence – all of which encourage employees to grow spiritually at work. The company employs seven Christian workplace chaplains that regularly help and care for employees. "Our job is to shepherd employees, care for them and love them. If an employee is facing a difficult family situation, an ethical dilemma at work, or one of a thousand other problems that can descend upon us, we are at hand to provide prayer, comfort and counsel" (Shorr, 2012, p. 21). The company also sponsors numerous activities and programs to help employees grow in their spirituality. The company's mission also extends beyond its local community and is working to help farmers in Uganda to produce products for market.

Assessing with "Faith-Friendly Scorecard"

While neither of these companies is a perfect fit within one of the four frames, the purpose of the framework is to act as a guide in assessing where companies are seeing religion as an aspect of human rights and diversity by constructing workplace policies which are welcoming and inclusive, nor favoring one religious tradition over the other. And, depending on where they fall within the "Faith-Friendly Scorecard," the assessment provides a better understanding of the organizational risk and corresponding benefits associated with the use of their present organizational frame.

Does Faith-Friendly Frame Make a Difference?

The Faith-Friendly Frame and accompanying scorecard are theoretical propositions, but does the adoption and use of the frame within organizational life make a difference in organizational life for employees? Preliminary research conducted by myself and my research colleague, Dr David W. Miller of the Princeton University Faith and Work Initiative suggests it does in the perception of employees, and with this positive perception comes increased employee commitment.

Methodology

Preliminary Research was conducted in order to understand whether "faith-friendly companies make a difference" on employee perceptions by focusing on two samples of employees, one drawn from a faith-friendly organization, the other one drawn from a random sample of alumni. The first organization was regarded as a faith-friendly company, sampled a large manufacturing organization in the United States, and had 5,828 respondents. Specifically, the company met all the criteria within the Faith-Friendly Scorecard: it had formal organizational policies which both accommodated and embraced their employees' religions and they saw an employee's religion as an aspect of employee wellness. The faith-friendly company also had chaplaincy programs, of which chaplains came from various faith traditions (Imams, Pastors, Priests, Rabbis, etc.) as well as social workers. The second sample was a randomized sample from an alumni group of more than 1,500, which represented individuals from various organizational frames, and had 176 respondents. The random sample was taken from a group of college alumni who were working full time at various occupations. Permission was obtained from both Institutional Research Boards of participating institutions. All responses were kept confidential, respondents could stop the survey at any time and responses were only obtained with written consent of the participant. The questions were collected via an online survey tool and the responses were loaded into Statistical Package for the Social Sciences (SPSS).

Research Findings

From the research findings, presented in Table 14.6, the majority of respondents (90%) believed in God, and self-identified as a Christian

Table 14.6 *Comparison of employees' attitudes in a faith-friendly company and in a random sample*

Random sample (N = 176)		Faith-friendly companies (N = 5828)	
Do you believe there is a God, a higher power of some nature, or gods?			
Yes	83.5%	Yes	92.5
No	16.5%*	No	3.5*
Which of these most closely describes your tradition or beliefs?			
Christianity	90.0%	Christianity	89.7*
I believe that my organization is aware of my religious faith needs.			
Strongly Disagree	4.0	Strongly Disagree	3.9
Disagree	15.9	Disagree	10.3
Undecided	17.0	Undecided	14.7
Agree	31.3	Agree	51.9
Strongly Agree	17.6*	Strongly Agree	18.8*
I believe that my organization is accommodating of my religious faith needs.			
Strongly Disagree	.6	Strongly Disagree	2.6
Disagree	5.1	Disagree	5.6
Undecided	13.6	Undecided	14.9
Agree	44.9	Agree	54.8
Strongly Agree	21.6*	Strongly Agree	21.4*
I believe my organization embraces my religious faith identity at work.			
Strongly Disagree	2.3	Strongly Disagree	3.5
Disagree	14.2*	Disagree	7.8*
Undecided	22.2	Undecided	18.6
Agree	29.5	Agree	50.5
Strongly Agree	17.6*	Strongly Agree	18.9*

Table 14.6 (cont.)

Random sample (N = 176)		Faith-friendly companies (N = 5828)	
At work I have experienced discrimination, harassment, or discomfort due to my religious faith.			
Strongly Disagree	55.7	Strongly Disagree	52.2
Disagree	22.7	Disagree	34.7
Undecided	1.1	Undecided	4.8
Agree	5.7	Agree	6.0
Strongly Agree	.6*	Strongly Agree	0.5*
The organization I work for has formal policies which prevent me from expressing my religious faith at work.			
Strongly Disagree	35.2	Strongly Disagree	38.4
Disagree	27.3	Disagree	45.5
Undecided	12.5	Undecided	9.6
Agree	9.1	Agree	4.5
Strongly Agree	1.7*	Strongly Agree	1.0*
My company has a culture that discourages me from expressing my religious faith at work.			
Strongly Disagree	29.5	Strongly Disagree	38.5
Disagree	34.7	Disagree	44.5
Undecided	7.4	Undecided	9.1
Agree	13.1	Agree	6.4
Strongly Agree	1.1*	Strongly Agree	1.5*
Does your organization allow you to freely integrate your religious faith with work?			
Yes	56.3	Yes	85.1
No	29.5*	No	12.7*

*totals less than 100% are due to non-response.

faith. The underrepresentation of other religious traditions is a limitation to this research, and thus this research should be considered exploratory and not universally applicable. But, when both groups were asked if the organization was aware of their religious needs the random sample self-reported agreement or strong agreement at 48.9%

compared with 70.7% of the faith-friendly company. When asked if their religious faith was accommodated, the random sample self-reported "agreed" or "strongly agreed" at 66.5% compared with 76% of the faith-friendly companies self-reporting agreement or strong agreement. When asked if their organization embraced their religious faith, the group from the random sample "agreed" or "strongly agreed" at 47%, compared with the faith-friendly sample at 69.4%. When asked if the employee had experienced discrimination or harassment, both scored roughly the same with both "agreed" or "strongly agreed," the random sample scoring at 6.3% and the faith-friendly sample at 6.5%. When both groups were asked if the organization had any policies that prevented them from expressing their religious faith, the random sample either "agreed" or "strongly agreed" at 10.8% and the faith-friendly group reported 5.5%. When the two groups were asked if the company's culture discouraged them from expressing their faith at work, the random sample "agreed" or "strongly agreed" with the statement at 14.1%, compared with 7.5% of respondents of the faith-friendly employee. Finally, when asked the binary question of whether their company allows them to freely integrate their religious faith in the workplace, 56% of the random sample said "yes," compared with 85.1% of the faith-friendly sample.

Implications/Directions for Future Research and Practice?

This research is exploratory and the frames presented in this chapter would benefit from further research. However, the hope is that the presentation of the Faith-Friendly Frame and corresponding Faith-Friendly Scorecard will allow organizational managers and managers to consider alternative organizational structures to better respect and embrace employees' religious faith tradition alongside other human rights considerations.

The data raises many questions as to the effects moderating and mediating variables have on survey responses. However, with the exception of harassment and discrimination, one thing would require further exploration: how faith-friendly companies appear to have more employees that self-report more organizational attention to their religious faith. The Faith-Friendly Frame which fosters this self-perception may then begin to foster greater employee wellness and in turn result in the aforementioned benefits of integrating religious faith within the workplace and potentially contributing to work life balance (Syed & Ozbilgin, 2015).

Conclusions and Considerations

The chapter considered the importance of diversity philosophies and how these philosophies allow for the development of organizational frames (perspectives) that would allow for the inclusion of and respect for religion within the workplace and in doing so honor individual human rights (e.g., race, gender, sex). The chapter proposes an organizational framework, presenting four different "frames" as a means to structure and guide managerial policy. The organizational frames of faith-avoiding, faith-based, faith-safe, and faith-friendly represent the various organizational frames or strategies organizations use to manage the ongoing human rights issues relating to human religious beliefs. The chapter resolved by explaining research which suggests the use of the Faith-Friendly Frame may have positive effects on religious employees' self-perceptions.

References

Aadland, E., & Skjørshammer, M. (2012). From God to good? Faith-based institutions in the secular society. *Journal of Management, Spirituality & Religion*, 9(1), 83–101.

Ashforth, B. E., & Pratt, M. G. (2010). Institutionalized spirituality: An oxymoron? *In* Giacalone, R. A., & Jurkiewicz, C. L. (eds.), *Handbook of workplace spirituality and organizational performance*. New York: M.E. Sharper, Inc., 93–107.

Ashforth, B., & Vaidyanath, D. (2002). Work organizations as secular religions. *Journal of Management Inquiry*, 11(4), 359–70.

Atkinson, W. (2000). Divine accommodations: Religion in the workplace. *Risk Management*, 47, 12–17.

(2004). Religion in the workplace: Faith versus liability. *Risk Management*, 15(12), 18–23.

Barnard, C., & Hepple, B. (2000). Substantive equality. *The Cambridge Law Journal*, 59(3), 562–85.

Bassett-Jones, N., Brown, R., & Corneulis, N. (2007). Delivering effective diversity management through effective structures. *System Research and Behavioral Science*, 24(1), 59–67.

Berger, P. L. (1969). *The sacred canopy: Elements of a sociological theory of religion*. Garden City, NY: Doubleday.

Bodia, M. A., & Ali, H. (2012). Workplace spirituality: A spiritual audit of banking executives in Pakistan. *African Journal of Business Management*, 6(11), 3888–97.

Bolman, L., & Deal, T. (2008). *Reframing organizations: Artistry, choice and leadership*. San Francisco, CA: Jossey Bass.

Brewer, M. B., & Brown, R. J. (1998). Intergroup relations. *In* Gilbert, D.T., Fiske, S.T., & Lindzey, G. (eds.), *The Handbook of Social Psychology*, 554–94.

Brewer, M. B., & Gaertner, S. L. (2004). Toward reduction of prejudice intergroup contact and social categorization. *In* Brewer, M.B., & Hewstone, M. (eds.), *Self and social identity*, 298–318.

Chen, C. Y., Yang, C. Y., & Li, C. I. (2012). Spiritual leadership, follower mediators, and organizational outcomes: Evidence from three industries across two major Chinese societies. *Journal of Applied Psychology*, 11 (4), 227–68.

Civil Rights Act of 1964 § 7, 42 USC §2000e et seq. (1964). Retrieved from Equal Employment Opportunity Commission website: www.eeoc.gov/laws/statutes/titlevii.cfm.

Duchon, D., & Plowman, D. (2005). Nurturing spirit at work: Impact on work unit performance. *The Leadership Quarterly*, 16(5), 807–33.

Dyck, B., & Schroeder, D. (2005). Management, theology and moral points of view: Towards an alternative to the conventional materialist-individualist ideal-type of management. *Journal of Management Studies*, 42, 705–35.

Emerson, T., & McKinney, J. (2010). Importance of religious beliefs to ethical attitudes in business. *Journal of Religion and Business Ethics*, 1(2), 1–14.

Emmons, R. (2003). *The psychology of ultimate concerns: Motivation and spirituality in personality*. New York: Guilford Press.

Estreicher, S., & Gray, M. (2006). Religion and the US workplace. *Human Rights: Journal of the Section of Individual Human Rights & Responsibilities*, 33(3), 17–21.

Fiss, P. C., & Zajac, E. J. (2006). The symbolic management of strategic change: Sense giving via framing and decoupling. *Academy of Management Journal*, 49, 1173–93.

Fogel, R. W. (2004). *The escape from hunger and premature death, 1700–2100: Europe, America, and the third world*. Cambridge: Cambridge University Press.

Gagnon, S., & Cornelius, N. (2000). Re-examining workplace equality: The capabilities approach. *Human Resource Management Journal*, 10(4), 68–87.

Giacalone, R., & Jurkiewicz, C. (2005). From advocacy to science: The next steps in workplace spirituality and research. *In Handbook of psychology of religion and spirituality*. New York: Guildford Press.
  (2010). *Handbook of workplace spirituality and organizational performance*. Armonk, NY: M.E. Sharpe, Inc.
Goldblast, D. (2000). *Knowledge and the social sciences theory method and practice*. Routledge Publications.
Greenwald, J. (2012). Religious discrimination claims rising. *Business Insurance*, 46(7), 3–18.
Gregory, R. (2011). *Encountering religion in the workplace: The legal right and responsibilities of workers and employers*. Ithaca, NY: Cornell University Press.
Gull, G., & Doh, J. (2004). The "Transmutation" of the organization: Toward a more spiritual workplace. *Journal of Management Inquiry*, 13(2), 128–39.
Hall, M., Oates, K., Anderson, T. L., & Willingham, M. M. (2012). Calling and conflict: The sanctification of work in working mothers. *Psychology of Religion and Spirituality*, 4(1), 71.
Hart, D., & Brady, N. (2005). Spirituality and Archetype in organizational life. *Business Ethics Quarterly*, 15(3), 409–28.
Hicks, D. (2003). *Religion and the workplace: Pluralism, spirituality, leadership*. Cambridge Press.
Johnson, A. (2007). Mary Parker Follett: Laying the foundations for spirituality in the workplace. *International Journal of Public Administration*, 30(1), 425–39.
Johnson, T. (2010). A statistical approach to the world's religions adherents, 2000–2015. *In* Melton, J. G., & Bauman, M. (eds.), *Religions of the world: A comprehensive encyclopedia of beliefs and practices, Vol. 1*. Santa Barbara, CA, lv–lix.
Kelly, E. (2008). Accommodating religious expression in the workplace. *Employee Responsibilities and Rights Journal*. 20(1), 45–56.
King, J. (2012). (Dis)Missing the obvious: Will mainstream research ever take religion seriously? *Journal of Management Inquiry*, 17(3), 214–24.
King, J. E. Jr., Bell, M., & Lawrence, E. (2009). Religion as an aspect of workplace diversity: An examination of the US context and a call for international research. *Journal of Management, Spirituality & Religion*, 6(1), 43–57.
King, J. E., & Holmes, O. (2012). Spirituality, recruiting and total wellness: Overcoming challenges to organizational attraction. *Journal of Management, Spirituality & Religion*, 9(3), 237–53.
Management Team, Pacmore Corporation, retrieved 7-30-2017 from www.pacmoore.com/management-team/.

Miller, D. W. (2007). *God at work: The history and promise of the faith at work movement*. New York: Oxford University Press.

——— (2010). The Faith-Friendly company: An idea whose time has come? In Stackhouse, M. L., Hainsworth, D. K., & Paeth, S. (eds.), *Public theology for a global society: Essays in honor of Max L. Stackhouse*. Grand Rapids, MI: W.B. Eerdmans, 74–86.

Miller, D. W., & Ewest, T. (2013). The present state of workplace spirituality: A literature review considering context, theory, and measurement/assessment. *Journal of Religious & Theological Information*, 12(2), 29–54.

——— (2015). A new framework for analyzing organizational workplace religion and spirituality. *Journal of Management, Spirituality & Religion*. Advance online publication. doi: 10.1080/14766086.2015.1054864

Milliman, J., Czaplewski, A. J., & Gerguson, J. (2003). Workplace spirituality and employee work attitudes: An exploratory empirical assessment. *Journal of Organizational Change Management*, 16(4), 426–47.

Mitroff, I. (2003). Do not promote religion under the guise of spiritualty. *Organization*, 10(2), 375–82.

Mitroff, I., & Denton, E. (1999). *A spiritual audit of corporate America: A hard look at spirituality, religion, and values in the workplace*. San Francisco, CA: Jossey-Bass Inc.

Morsink, J. (2009). *Inherent human rights*. Philadelphia, PA: University of Pennsylvania Press.

Nash, L., & McLennan, S. (2001). *Church on Sunday, work on Monday: A guide for reflection*. San Francisco, CA: Jossey-Bass.

Paprec Group Raw Material Producer of the 21st Century. From Recycling Paper to the Waste Management: The History of Paprec Group. N.p., n.d. Web. 30 July 2017.

Pawar, B. S. (2009). Individual spirituality, workplace spirituality and work attitudes: An empirical test of direct and interaction effects. *Leadership and Organizational Development Journal*, 30(8), 759–77.

Richards, P. S., & Bergin, A. E. (1997). *A spiritual strategy for consulting and psychotherapy*. Washington, DC: American Psychosocial Association.

Roberge, M. É., Lewicki, R. J., Hietapelto, A., & Abdyldaeva, A. (2011). From theory to practice: Recommending supportive diversity practices. *Journal of Diversity Management*, 6(2), 1.

Robinson, R., Franklin, G., & Hamilton, R.H. (2011). Workplace religious accommodation issues for adherents of Islam. *Business Studies Journal*, 3(2), 41–50.

Schley, D. (2008). Legal aspects of Spirituality in the workplace. *International Journal of Public Administration*, 31, 342–58.

Seales, C. (2012). Corporate Chaplaincy and the American workplace. *Religion Compass*, 6(3), 195–203.

Shorr, B. (2012). Finding mission in your business. *Christianity Today*, May 21. Retrieved from: www.christianitytoday.com.

Syed, J., & Ozbilgin, M. (eds.) (2015). *Managing diversity and inclusion: An international perspective*. Chicago, IL: Sage.

Taifel, H., & Turner, J. C. (1986). *The social identity theory of intergroup behavior. In* Worchel, S., & Austin, W.G. (eds.), Chicago, IL: Nelson-Hall, 7–24.

Turner, J. C., Hogg, M. A., Oakes, P. J., Reicher, S. D., & Wetherell, M. S. (1987). *Rediscovering the social group: A self-categorization theory*. Hoboken, NJ: Basil Blackwell.

United Nations. (2009). Universal declaration of human rights. Retrieved from: www.un.org/en/documents/udhr/index.shtml.

Vasconcelos, A. F. (2010). Spiritual development in organizations: A religious-based approach. *Journal of Business Ethics*, 93(1), 607–22.

Walker, A. (2013). The relationship between the integration of faith and work with life outcomes. *Journal of Business Ethics*, 25(3), 453–61.

Weaver, G., & Argle, B. (2002). Religiosity and ethical behavior in organizations: A symbolic interactionism perspective. *Academy of Management Review*, 27(1), 77–97.

White, R. (2011). Drawing the line: Religion and spirituality in the workplace. *In* Park, P. (ed.), *Handbook of the psychology of religion and spirituality*. New York: The Guildford Press, 185–96.

Wilson, B. R. (1982). *Religion in sociological perspective*. Oxford: Oxford University Press.

Williams, O. (2003). *Business, religion, & spirituality: A new synthesis*. Notre Dame: University of Notre Dame Press.

Witte, J., & van der Vyver, J. (eds.). (1996). *Religious human rights in global perspective: Religious perspectives*. The Hague: Martinus Nijhof.

Wuthnow, R. (2005). *America and the challenges of diversity*. Princeton, NJ: Princeton University Press.

15 | From Diverse Frameworks to Diverse Attitudes towards Religion at Work: Focus on the French Case

GÉRALDINE GALINDO AND HÉDIA ZANNAD

The Baby Loup affair in France, that of Ewaida and McFarlane in Great Britain, and that of Abercrombie & Fitch in the USA, are representative of the rapid development of religious issues at work all over the world in recent years. Today, debates about the expression of religious beliefs do not stop at the companies' door; for several years, businesses have been struggling with the issue of how to respond to religious claims at work (for example religious bias complaints have increased by over 69% in the last 12 years in the USA, according to Schaeffer & Mattis (2012)). More and more employees no longer want to park their souls at the door, and need to bring their whole selves to work (Clair et al., 2005; Miller, 2007). Indeed, this "deep level side of diversity" (Harrison et al., 1998) has become an important question for companies. The phenomenon appears in the form of requests or even demands concerning food, clothing, the organization of both prayer times and working time and attitudes, particularly relations between the sexes (Galindo & Surply, 2010). Increasingly, employees for whom religious identity is important are finding it necessary to express their beliefs publicly, including those in private firms (Gebert et al., 2014).

Faced with these issues, several observations are shared by many Western countries. First, the religious landscape is changing drastically in every country, since the increased population flows around the world are resulting in the increasing globalization of religion (Machelon, 2006). Second, national laws are very often based on principles of freedom and non-discrimination. Third, the "meaninglessness" of work felt by increasing numbers of employees (Kinjerski & Skrypnek, 2004) is leading increasing numbers of them to claim their full identity (Miller, 2007) and thus to attempt to make their faith part of their working life. Finally, whilst statistics tend to show that the number of problematic cases remains small (9% of religious questions in French companies), they are subject to significant media interest and have potentially strong societal consequences (Gebert et al., 2014).

In the workplace, these points of convergence take the form of shared concerns about how to understand and respond to staff claims in this area. In the face of these more or less pressing employee expectations, it is important to study how firms can respond to them and on what they can base their responses.

This chapter discusses why firms respond in very different ways to their employees' expectations in terms of religious expression. More specifically, we investigate the legal and informal foundations on which companies base their responses.

The first part of the chapter discusses the various frameworks that condition company strategies. The second section studies the French context in more detail, analyzing the positions taken by major firms and their different ways of responding to their employees' claims.

Frameworks for the Religious Question in Western Companies

Religion is defined in countless ways. All of these definitions refer to two of its features, the belief in an invisible world (or a supra-empirical reality) together with shared ritual observances related to this belief. Religion has been an integral part of many societies since the Palaeolithic period according to some (Lenoir, 2008).

The notion of religion appears in the constitution and legal texts of many Western countries. In their policy, companies can refer to legal settings and to informal principles. All these references are subject to interpretation and uncertainty.

Formal Frames of Reference

Religion represents each person's capacity to believe or not to believe. In many Western countries, such as the United States, Canada, the United Kingdom, Germany, or France, religion is directly linked to the concept of freedom. This principle is one of the pillars of Western society, and a yardstick for private firms. Naturally this leads us to think about how each person's freedom can coexist with that of those around him, and about the equality of each person's freedom and beliefs.

The Principle of Freedom

It is the foundation of the constitution of many states. Several examples show the central role of freedom in legal texts:

Article 9 of The European Human Rights Convention takes up Article 18 of the Universal Declaration of Human Rights, and specifies:

> Everyone has the right to freedom of thought, conscience, and religion; this right includes freedom to change his religion or belief and freedom, either alone or in community with others and in public or private, to manifest his religion or belief, in worship, teaching, practice and observance.

In France, Article 10 of the Declaration of the Rights of Man and of the Citizens (1789) states that "No one may be attacked for their opinions, even religious, provided that their expression does not harm public order as established by the law."

Article 4 of German Basic Law states that "Freedom of belief and conscience and the freedom to confess religious and philosophical beliefs are inviolable" and its second paragraph guarantees "freedom of religious practice."

In the autumn of 2012, the new Icelandic Constitution added to the traditional total religious freedom, the fact that every person has the right to religious observance in accordance with their personal beliefs.

These texts commit firms to recognize the right of each of their employees to freedom of belief and freedom of observance. However, the types of belief concerned differ significantly between countries. In France, for example, this freedom is limited to recognized religions which requires the existence of a subjective component (a belief or faith in a divinity) and an objective component (which embodies the first; in other words a community that comes together for the observance of this belief), whilst other countries such as Canada and the United Kingdom take a broader view and include sectarian movements. The United States shares this broad view and has implemented measures aimed at guaranteeing this freedom, such as the International Religious Freedom Act (IRFA), adopted in 1998, which established the Commission on Religious Freedom (USCIRF) and an ambassador for religious freedom.

Thus, all countries share the idea that employees of private firms should feel free in their beliefs and practices. In this sense, they are considered as individualities.

The Principle of Equality

It extends the principle of freedom in our opinion by adding to it a relative dimension. Indeed, freedom of belief and expression stops when it begins to impinge on that of other people. While Western societies are traditionally anchored in certain religions (Christianity, Orthodox religions, Judaism, Islam, and to a lesser extent Buddhism), they have to attempt to manage this diversity and the emergence of other kinds of beliefs. The challenge here is to guarantee equal treatment for believers and non-believers, whatever they believe or do not believe in (within the limits defined by each country).

For example, Article 7 of the Universal Declaration of Human Rights states that "All are equal before the law and are entitled without any discrimination to equal protection of the law. All are entitled to equal protection against any discrimination in violation of this Declaration and against any incitement to such discrimination."

In the United Kingdom, the Equality Act of 2010 forbids direct or indirect discrimination, harassment, and victimization in areas such as the provision of goods and services, employment, and education. For private firms, this equality means that they must not give precedence to one belief over another and therefore must not discriminate against some employees for whatever they believe or do not believe in. These two principles, one of which involves a positive right (equality) and the other a negative right (non-discrimination) are indissociable in the field of religion.

In the context of private firms, French labour law (Article L.1121-1) states that "no one may restrict another's rights and individual and collective freedom in any way that is not justified by the nature of the tasks they have to accomplish or is not proportionate to the aim of the restriction."

In the name of this quest for equality and non-discrimination, some countries, such as Canada and the USA have recourse to the principle of reasonable accommodation: "reasonable accommodation when the employer finds a fair balance between the demands imposed by business operations and the employee's religious freedom. The employer must therefore, for the sake of equality, attempt to accommodate the employee's religious practices."

These pillars are part of many developed Western countries and are the ultimate basis for company policy. Their understanding of religious belief encourages firms to accept religious claims or, at least, to seek a compromise. The aim is to move towards "respectful pluralism" (Hicks, 2003) and successfully accommodate everyone, whatever their religious convictions. Indeed, firms have to guarantee positive rights such as freedom and equality, and establish negative rights to fight against religious discrimination. These strong legal principles represent solid foundations companies can use to manage religious beliefs at work. They can see these principles as reference points or to the contrary as sources of contradictions. Even if, in the great majority of cases – whatever the country or the organization – what is sought is a balance between these two principles, generally one of them becomes the starting point for discussion and dominates the other, creating, *de facto*, tension. Indeed, while these principles provide easy answers to some employees' religious demands concerning the principles of freedom or non-discrimination, in other cases they can place firms in a more difficult position.

Some organizations believe that legal principles are sufficient. However, case law suggests this is not true and decisions can vary, sometimes in favor of freedom. For example, AT&T in the United States was ordered to pay $1.3 million for dismissing two employees in a customer services department who had taken time off to attend a Convention of Jehovah's Witnesses with the argument that they did not have to choose between their work and their beliefs (US EEOC, 2009).

Other Types of Arguments

In the face of religious demands, companies can refer to organizational and individual arguments that are not legal obligations, but rather convenient anchors.

Individual Identity

Religion is considered as a series of associated beliefs and practices, chosen (or not) by each individual. It can be considered as a "controllable aspect of identity" that everyone can reveal (or not). Thus, some people decide to keep their beliefs for themselves – "intrinsic religion" – whereas other people need to express their religion as a way of belonging to a community – "extrinsic religion" – (Allport, 1966) and so acquiring a social identity (Tajfel & Turner, 1986) that they do not necessarily find in the company. In the workplace, employees can decide whether to separate, merge, or balance their professional and personal identity (Sainsaulieu, 1992; Kreiner et al., 2006). Increasing numbers of workers seem to want a holistic life (theorized in Miller's (2007) "Integration Box") that merges, among other things, faith and work, but they have few resources to help them in this aim (Miller & Ewest, 2013). Revealing one's religion can be seen as a voluntary choice resulting from a need to be considered as a "whole person" at work (Mitroff & Denton, 1999; Clair et al., 2005; Hart & Brady, 2005). Thus, religion is moving away from deep-level identity towards surface-level identity and can generate conflicts, and accusations of proselytism or discrimination (Gebert et al., 2014). Framing religion in relation to identity positions the issue at an individual level, i.e. how each person considers religion in his/her professional and personal life. However, it also positions religion at a collective level, as a vector of social belonging.

Firms may refer to individual expectations about whether to reveal the different facets of one's identity. They can even encourage them in a particular direction through the HR and diversity policies they implement.

Corporate Policies
At work, religion echoes other human resource management issues, and can fall within the scope of other previously established policies. Firstly, a growing number of companies have introduced and developed diversity policies. These policies can be viewed as reactive (associated with costs and short-term responses) or proactive (as a long-term strategic asset in line with the business case approach (Cox & Blake, 1991)). Religious diversity can thus be considered as one type of diversity that has to be managed for better performance (Cui et al., 2015), even if many consider it as the "bête noire" of this type of policy. Secondly, religious demands may "resonate" with work/life balance policies. Some companies attempt to separate their employees' professional and private lives, whereas others, on the contrary, promote a more integrated view, and others again take a middle course, with a policy of respect (Kirchmeyer, 1995). These policies take a collective management approach to the religious question.

Grey Areas for Firms with Regard to These Frameworks

Each of the principles mentioned above represents a frame of reference for private companies in many Western countries. However, as

Table 15.1 *Levels and uncertainty of the frameworks used by firms to manage religious issues*

Principles	Frameworks used by private firms	Questions
Legal register		
Freedom	Guarantee: – employees' freedom to believe or not – freedom of religious expression – fair and equal treatment	Sincerity of religious beliefs? How far can freedom of expression go?
Equality	Fight against discrimination linked to employees' religious beliefs	How can all employees be treated impartially?
Other registers		
Individual identity	Understand employees' overall identity Estimate the collective identity created by religious belief	What sides of the identity have to be managed? What are the roles of this identity at work?
Corporate policies	Integrate religion with other policies already implemented or initiated: Diversity or work/life balance	Is religion another dimension to relate to existing policies? Is it an extension of already initiated policies?

the following table shows, these principles also raise questions about how they can be converted into clear guidelines.

Implications of These Diverse Principles

Table 15.1 highlights the types of risk firms face (Ghumman et al., 2013). The decision to accept, refuse, or accommodate can be seen by other employees as unfair privileges enjoyed by groups of believers or disbelievers. To guarantee freedom of religious belief and observance may establish disparate treatment through specific measures for

Individual level	Individual/collective	Collective
- Freedom	- Equality	Corporate policy
- Individual identity	- Non-discrimination	

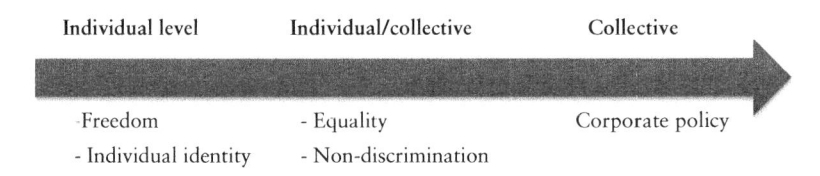

Figure 15.1 The different levels of the principles for managing religious issues in the workplace

those who reveal their identity to the detriment of those who do not. To treat everyone impartially may also create "undue hardship" (as it is commonly described in the USA). All these frames of reference can thus become starting points for corporate "micro-inequality" by extracting common law in the name of religion. For example, in 2015 in Indiana, the "Religious Freedom Restoration Act" was signed in order to give business owners a stronger legal defense if they refuse to serve lesbian, gay, bisexual, and transgender customers and want to cite their faith as justification for their actions, stirring the emotions of many.

Different Viewpoints

Some of these principles are rooted in an individual perspective (freedom and individual identity) whilst others, at the other end of the spectrum, refer to the collective corporate dimension (policy implementation). Between these two extremes, some principles consider the individual in relation to the group and introduce the notion of the relative importance of the various frameworks (equality and non-discrimination). They express the limits within which people wish to contain religious issues: either individual or, on the contrary, those of the broader corporate community (see Figure 15.1).

Whilst these principles seem to be sufficient, they leave companies with "grey areas." These areas of uncertainty, which can also be seen as providing firms with leeway for their action, come from the different foundations (and sometimes lack of clarity) of the principles.

Different Answers Identified in Companies

Regarding how companies deal with all these frameworks, scholars propose some typologies in order to analyze company attitudes to religious questions. Mitroff & Denton (1999) identify five different manners for US companies to be religious and/or spiritual: religion-based, evolutionary, recovering, socially responsible, and value-based organizations. This typology mainly helps to distinguish the different ways in which religion and/or spirituality are considered in US companies. Grossman (2008) extends this research and pinpoints three types of company according to their leaders' convictions: faith-frosty (the less religious expression there is at work, the better), faith-focused (faith provides underlying values that motivate and guide the organizations), faith-friendly (inclusion and integration of all religious beliefs are promoted). In line with these categorizations, Giacalone and Jurkiewicz (2010) describe three types of relationship between spirituality and the workplace: a parallel, an adversial, or an integrative relationship, while Ashforth and Pratt (2010) also define three types of organizations: enabling, directing, and partnering.

More recently, Miller & Ewest (2015) investigate corporate actions and attitudes toward workplace spirituality and propose an integrative structure understanding organizational attitudes, policies, and practices: faith-avoiding, faith-based, faith-safe, faith-friendly, as detailed in Table 15.2.

To deal with religion in the workplace, firms have to find a balance between the different principles with which they must comply. Nonetheless, areas of uncertainty and liberty remain. All these typologies underline the crucial role of leaders and the diversity of organizational responses to religious issues in the workplace. But these researches are based on companies based in the United States, where faith is an "umbrella" term (Miller, 2007; Miller & Ewest, 2015) that includes all forms of beliefs, i.e. religious and spiritual ones. We think that it could be interesting to investigate these frames of attitudes in the French context where the definition of religion is narrower and the attitudes towards it more regulated by law.

The French Exception: Evidence from Diversity Guides

Research Context

Whilst around 1% of the complaints received in 2014 by the Defender of Rights (Défenseur des Droits) concerned religion in private employment (9% of these are perceived by company actors as resulting in conflict according to the OFRE & Randstad, 2016 survey), the French

Table 15.2 *Typology of faith-orientations and their implications in the workplace*

	Descriptions	Principles
Faith-avoiding	No religious accommodation	Corporate policies based on secularization theory
Faith-based	One predominant religion and some accommodations for the others	Corporate policies rooted within one religion
Faith-safe	Tolerance and understanding of various religious beliefs with a predominant religion	Law (diversity is promoted in order to avoid undue burden or costly litigation) Equality of all employees Identity of all employees
Faith-friendly	Accommodations for various religious traditions	Freedom Diversity of identities at work

Source: Miller & Ewest (2015).

context is particularly interesting with regard to this issue. The subject, which was long considered a "blind spot," has come into the spotlight.

The Influence of the Principle of *Laïcité*

In France, the Law of 1905 officially separated the Church from the State, removing all religious power from the State and all political power from the Church (in fact, nine countries have a form of separation between religion and State: Cuba, Mexico, Uruguay, Venezuela, Portugal, Turkey, India, and Japan). This principle of *Laïcité* (The French word for "secularism" referred in Chapter 10) means that the State may neither promote nor favor one religious opinion over another, and at the same time protects the religious freedom of its citizens: "it must lead neither to uniformity nor to the negation of differences" (p. 5, according to the for Integration in 2011 High Council). Despite this precise definition, the principle is often viewed in one of two ways. Tolerant *Laïcité* implies that all religious beliefs are respected and accepted in the name of equality by the government. Exclusive *Laïcité*

> **Box 15.1 The French and *Laïcité* (IFOP Survey, 2015)**
>
> The French consider *Laïcité* (46%) as the foremost republican value, well ahead of universal suffrage (36%), freedom of association (8%), or the freedom to establish political parties or trade unions (5% each). For 51% of respondents, it is chiefly perceived as "the possibility for all citizens to observe their religion." Meanwhile 25% consider it chiefly as "the prohibition of manifesting religious affiliation in public services."

is also associated with neutrality and so with the denial of any kind of religion in the public sphere. These multiple interpretations lead to some confusion about the scope of this principle. Whatever the conception of *Laïcité*, it does not apply to private companies. It remains influential, however, and is often mentioned by the High Council for Integration as a principle that should enable situations encountered in firms to be decided upon: "It enables us to create a society, to live together rather than just side-by-side, *Laïcité* must, with the help of education, be present and serve as a reference in the workplace" (p. 7).

This concept, specific to France, raises as many questions in France as in other countries. Although some countries have adopted similar principles of secularism (for example *Kulturkampf* in Germany), the French position appears unique and debatable.

A Strict Understanding of Religion
Whilst the French State recognizes no religion, six major religions are recognized in the country: Catholicism, Islam, Protestantism, Judaism, Orthodoxy, and Buddhism. Whilst other beliefs, such as Zen Buddhism, Taoism, and Shamanism are not forbidden, many more movements than in the United Kingdom or the United States, are considered to be sects, for example the Church of Scientology and the Jehovah's Witnesses. France is therefore far from those English-speaking countries that recognize a wide-range of beliefs. Canada is emblematic of these countries; it recognizes traditional native beliefs and other religions such as the Anglican Church of Canada, Jainism, and Raëlism.

Evolving Religious Beliefs
Since ethnic and religious statistics are forbidden in France, and the protection of freedom of religion guarantees that the Census cannot

ask questions on this subject (Law of January 6, 1978), only estimates are available of the changing landscape of religious belief. According to surveys based on extrapolations made from respondents' declarations, there are around 48% Catholics, 6% Muslims, 2% Protestants, 1% Buddhists, and 1% Jews in France (Sociovision Observatory, 2016). Meanwhile the rate of atheism, estimated at 63%, is very high (Win Gallup International, 2012). Thus, the French history of using immigration to meet labour demands (Al Ariss & Özbilgin, 2010) has resulted in the diversification of religious belief among the working population.

Safeguards Implemented
In the face of the uncertainty described above, France has gradually introduced reference points, or rather limits, for businesses. The HALDE (The Supreme Anti-discrimination and Equality Authority, Deliberation N° 2009-117 of April 6, 2009), one of the remits of the Defender of Rights since 2011, has detailed the admissible restrictions to religious freedom at work (the respect of safety and hygiene rules, proselytism, aptitude for work, organization of work, and the firm's commercial interests). Meanwhile the internal regulations cannot include elements that impair the freedom of the employees (Law of August 4, 1982).

France has also been caught for several years now between its principles and its historical traditions, and between changes not only in terms of the diversification of belief, but also in terms of the way the founding principle of *Laïcité* is apprehended. The Charlie Hebdo terrorist attacks in January 2015 highlighted the questions that contemporary society is facing over the place it gives to religion.

Methodology

This research was initiated in 2009 to investigate the issue of religious management in large non-state firms in France. To explore this "taboo" subject, we collected three types of qualitative data (see Figure 15.2).

Large French companies have chosen to concentrate on the way those receiving different religious claims can interpret this facet of identity. The role of the guides is to establish certain standards to be integrated into the organization's culture (see extracts in Appendix). They also aim to allow all employees to avoid interpreting religious belief at work individually and subjectively. We collected guides of how to manage religious diversity in the workplace from companies

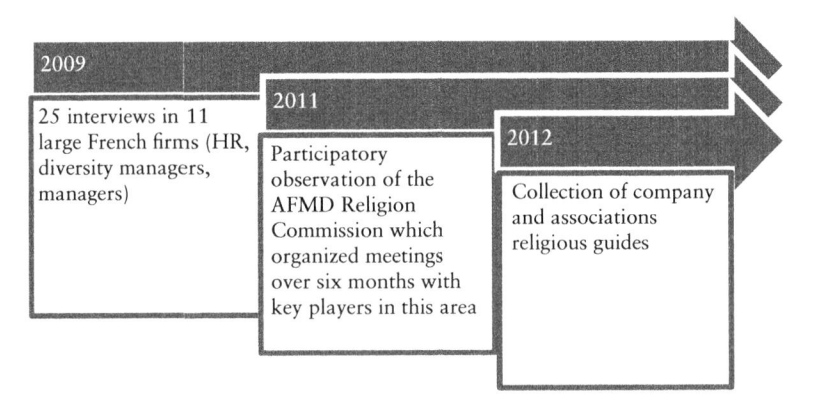

2009
25 interviews in 11 large French firms (HR, diversity managers, managers)

2011
Participatory observation of the AFMD Religion Commission which organized meetings over six months with key players in this area

2012
Collection of company and associations religious guides

Figure 15.2 The phases of the religious French guides project

Table 15.3 *Profile of French firms of our research*

Firm	Sector	Staff
Casino	Retail	330,000
EDF	Electricity distributor	110,000
La Poste	Services (postal, banking, and mobile telephony)	240,000
Orange	Mobile telephony	170,000
RATP	Public transport	56,000
Valeo	Automotive parts supplier	79,000
Veolia	Water, waste, energy, and transport management	318,000

in different sectors, as detailed in the Table 15.3 below. Major large French firms have led this initiative. We collected the guides of almost all the firms that had produced them in France. For the others, we interviewed diversity managers, and obtained information on the contents of these guides in line with those studied.

We also studied the guides produced by other organizations (AFMD, ORSE, Alliance du Commerce, IMS Entreprendre).[1] We complemented this data with secondary data, by investigating, for example,

---

[1] AFMD: French Association of Diversity Managers; ORSE: Observatory on Corporate Social Responsibility; Alliance du Commerce: Trade Alliance; IMS-Entreprendre: IMS-Entrepreneurship, an employer think tank.

the discourses produced by the State Defender of Rights, the MEDEF (French employers' umbrella association), the Observatory of *Laïcité*, and the Economic, Social, and Environmental Council on this topic. We analyzed and triangulated this data (Miles & Huberman, 2003) using secondary data (minutes of meetings of the AFMD diversity commission and press articles) and primary data to better understand the positioning of these firms and the types of discourses produced. We analyzed the data in the guides thematically based on the criteria we had already established, isolating the topics in each text in order to compare them with the other texts dealing with similar topics (Ghiglione & Matalon, 1991).

Managerial Guides Highlighting the Complexity of Responses in France

Faced with the "feelings of injustice" of their employees, the major French firms listed above produced guides with the aim of finding collective responses to a topic that previously had usually been dealt with at individual level. These guides express the three attitudes we had identified in the first phase of our research (Galindo & Surply, 2010, 2013).

Discourses Related to Accommodation

Some large firms position themselves in line with the notion of reasonable accommodation. Reasonable accommodation is not only a French-Canadian concept but one widely used across all of Canada, the United States and more generally Anglo-Saxon countries. Their discourses tend to encourage managers to respond to religious demands on a case-by-case basis. As EDF states, it is important to "find a compromise between individual and collective needs and between the expectations of employees and the requirements of the enterprise, and to deal with each case objectively in its context."

At the individual level, we observe two types of arguments. The first is linked to the integration of professional and personal identities:

The first series of criteria concern the protection of the individual: the freedom of others (prevention of proselytism); safety and hygiene. EDF will take into account the non-respect of safety measures as applied to classified equipment (EDF). *We should remember that religion and its expression are based on individual choices, concerning which the enterprise should not interfere* (Orange). *In the name of their religious convictions, may a postman or woman change their behaviour depending on the sex of the person they address or their colleagues? Such an attitude is of course, a matter for individual freedom. However, it may be sanctioned when it causes problems with the organisation and operation of the department* (la Poste).

At the organizational level, as with the attitude of acceptance, diversity is considered as a source of enhanced performance and the need to balance private and professional life:

Personal convictions … rarely cause debate at EDF, since we all feel so strongly that the company's performance is based on the respect of others, their skills and their solidarity, within our work teams. (EDF)
The practice of fasting is an individual choice. The organisation of work takes precedence, and there is no obligation to respond in the affirmative to a modification of working hours. However, you are advised to be "flexible" and to take into account the possibility that employees may be tired. (Orange)

At societal level, finally, the guides stress the application of the law and respect of religious practices:

[We must] respect religious convictions and expression strictly in accordance with the law (the wearing of visible religious symbols, prayer during breaks, taking leave for religious reasons, when compatible with the requirement of operations) and sanction deviant behaviour (excessive proselytism, harassment for pseudo-religious reasons). (Orange)

These attitudes use all the frameworks to justify the search for case-by-case solutions. Freedom, equality, individual identity, and corporate policies are all used to understand each situation in its context.

Discourses Related to Refusal
RATP and Paprec are emblematic of this attitude, which we describe as refusal. It is based almost exclusively on *Laïcité* as a synonym of neutrality. Neutrality is seen as overriding all other considerations: "The principle of neutrality to which RATP conforms, as a public service enterprise, cannot accept on its premises behavior revealing clearly an agent's adherence to any religion." In 2014, Paprec, a French industrial waste-recycling

firm, published its "Laïcité and Diversity Charter" to combine respect for all and religious neutrality (according to its management). Its Article 7 states that "wearing signs or clothing by which staff clearly manifest their religious affiliation is not authorized" in the firm. This type of argument leads to the separation of personal and professional identity and the consideration of religion as an intimate affair: "People are not considered individually but more as part of a workforce, from a perspective that unifies people" (French Association of Diversity Managers Guide, p. 96). "Freedom of belief does not mean freedom of religious expression. RATP, as a public service operator, requires the application of the principle of neutrality as the basis of its community life."

The principle of *Laïcité* dominates such guides, which refuse to take into account their employees' religious practices. Employees must reserve religious aspects of their identity for their private life, and may not include them as part of their professional identity. Freedom of belief and expression is presented as going no further than the door of firms who adopt this position.

Discourses Related to Acceptance

We have observed the position of acceptance in the field. However, it is not illustrated in guides, since by definition, explanations are not necessary when everything is accepted; no limits are set for allowable claims. In our research, however, we discovered different arguments proposed by firms that take this attitude (in their transcripts). The first is that diversity is a source of enhanced performance, and in particular the inclusion of every kind of belief. The aim of this attitude is to reflect the beliefs of the firm's clientele. Subsidiaries of Anglo-Saxon firms in France often take such a position (Pepsi-Cola and IBM for example). The second argument is the fear of stigmatizing Islam – since both in the section of the guide concerning practical responses and that providing additional information, all religions are mentioned, but Muslim practices are clearly the main focus. More broadly, the fear of discrimination leads these firms to accept everything and to accept their employees' overall identity without distinction. Small and Medium Entreprises, which often prefer to deal with this issue informally, also take this approach. Such an attitude is based on two principles: individual freedom, including within the company, and the desire for impartial treatment of all employees (associated with the fear of discrimination).

Table 15.4 *The arguments presented in French corporate guides*

	Accommodation	Refusal	Acceptance
Freedom			
Equality & non-discrimination			
Laïcité			
Identity			
Corporate policy			

N.B.: The more the color of the cell of the table is dark gray the more this argument is used by companies.

The Links between Attitudes and Learning Effects

Different attitudes are based on different arguments. As underlined by Table 15.4, the attitude of accommodation uses arguments linked to individual identity and existing policies concerning the promotion of diversity and work/life balance. In this approach, legal frameworks remain secondary, and serve to limit such accommodation. The attitude of refusal is clearly justified by *Laïcité*, whilst that of acceptance is more strongly rooted in the principle of freedom, and to a lesser degree in the principles of equality, identity, and corporate policy.

While these three attitudes correspond to ideal types, they reveal the different perspectives of private organizations with regard to this issue. The large firms that produced the guides we studied mostly have an intermediate position of accommodation. This situation reflects their learning curve, which we can describe as "emerging" (Galindo & Surply, 2013). Whilst some of these large firms initially ignored the issue of religion, gradually they initiated discussion and action, notably through their guides, to move towards shared practices at every level of the organization. Many of them moved away from extreme positions (refusal or acceptance) towards an intermediate position, accommodation. By realizing the limits of referring either only to the law or only to individual identity, or only to society, these firms are attempting today to understand all these contextual elements and develop concrete solutions.

Religion in the Workplace: The French Exception?

The principle of *Laïcité* is a French particularity. It could lead the French to view religion in the workplace differently from other countries. Indeed, although *Laïcité* does not apply to private firms, it permeates their practices to a significant degree. The guides refer to it systematically, either to justify neutrality or to recall the importance of *Laïcité* in French society and its lack of relevance in private companies. *Laïcité* is therefore a framework that constantly affects the way people consider freedom and equality. The temptation to refer to the neutrality associated with *Laïcité* incites some firms (such as Paprec, mentioned above) to limit freedom of religious conscience. It is quoted when firms attempt to justify barely tenable positions involving refusal or acceptance. In our opinion, the fact that *Laïcité* is an integral part of French culture makes it possible for firms to publish these guides (for example, Grossman (2008) proposes that only 2% of US firms have a formal, distinct policy on this subject, without mentioning whether this includes publishing a guide). Indeed, freedom of belief is frequently challenged by the notion of *Laïcité* within society, and therefore, naturally, in private enterprises. Such guides do not exist in other countries (to the best of our knowledge), except at the national level (the Equal Employment Opportunity Commission (EEOC) in the United States, for example). We believe that this unique feature of French business life conveys the desire of these firms to formalize their responses and to control any attempted "faith at work movement" as observed for example, in the USA (Miller, 2003).

Whilst *Laïcité* as such does not exist elsewhere, it does inspire other countries. In 2013, the Parti Québécois initiated a national debate by proposing a "Charter for Laïcité," which was abandoned but has now been relaunched and is supported by public opinion. Business in the province of Quebec is still far from secular, and the requirement for reasonable accommodation persists; but it appears that the principle of *Laïcité* inspires society and raises questions for companies. This very French principle appears to be spreading to other countries, as a foil or, on the contrary, as an ideal new solution.

Whilst this subject is relevant to all firms in Western countries, attitudes are very different between countries. Grossman (2008) identifies, for example, three types of position in the USA. Firms such as Coca Cola Bottling Co. and Austaco Ltd. are clearly faith-focused, making their leaders' faith a value and a guiding principle for the firm's management. Others are faith-frosty; they try to limit religious expression in the firm as much as possible. A third group of firms is faith-friendly; they promote diversity of belief and try to include different expressions in line with the "faith at work movement" (Miller, 2003). Whilst these last two categories correspond respectively to the positions of refusal and acceptance identified in France, the first of them translates the unique feature of the USA as a "nation of believers," where 70% of the population declare their affiliation to a religion (Grossman, 2008). In this case, the principle of freedom seems to dominate corporate policy, whereas French firms hesitate between freedom, equality, and Laïcité.

All Western countries look for reference points to deal with an increasing variety of religious claims. France is unique in its strong reliance on the principle of Laïcité, which, although it does not apply to private firms, remains a frame of reference for many company heads and employees and even, today, for other countries.

Conclusion

Our research contributes to fill the gap in the literature identified by King et al. (2009) regarding the analysis of religious diversity within organizational units. It underlines that most of Western firms deal with religious claims in terms of both legal frames of reference and informal principles. These principles, whose definitions are vague, leave room for interpretation. Thereby, our work calls for their reconsideration as symbols of three dimensions: societal, organizational, and individual. The investigation of these nested levels of analysis shows the limits of each one taken alone but also the difficulties of reconciling them.

Facing these grey areas, we show that companies adopt three different positions in line with previous typologies in the US context (described before). Our focus on the French context allows us to show that some firms are in a position of denial (or "faith-avoiding" in the continuum of Miller & Ewest, 2015) with a neutrality argument inspired in France by the principle of Laïcité. Recently strengthened this position in France, by inscribing in the New Labor Law (or Law El Khomri, July 2016), the Article 1 bis A introduces the right to inscribe the principle of neutrality in companies rules and regulations. If this tendency of excluding religion from work exists, we observe in the same time the evolution of many French private firms from a refusal or acceptance position to an accommodation one. This evolution demonstrates the learning process of these organizations in the face of this complex area of management. But we do not find any correspondence with the "faith-based" (Miller & Ewest, 2015) or "religion-based" (Mitroff & Denton, 1999) types in our research. Firstly, the faith of a company's founder does not imply the dissemination of his or her values to their employees. Businesses linked with religious issues can also justify this position; these "tendency organisations" are essentially associations, unions, or groups (political parties, churches, or other religious groups) in which ideology, morality, philosophy, or policy is expressly advocated. Secondly, there is a strict definition of faith associated in France with the six main religions.

Our research provides evidence of interactions and identifications of societal, organizational, and individual principles and of the three stances towards religion in the workplace. It also questions the roles of management tools. Indeed, many firms attempt to determine guidelines to ensure that their responses are consistent. The guides produced by French firms reflect the different views they use to justify their arguments and the way they respond to religious claims. These documents shed light on the different positions taken by firms and the way they consider societal, organizational, and individual issues. They have a responsibility to help those who receive such claims to manage them. Nonetheless, our research suggests that we should not overestimate the influence of these guides. The managers or employees we interviewed in some firms were not aware of their existence, or did not refer to them, preferring to find their own local solutions. This paradox, whereby the tools are produced but the users are either unaware of them or do not use them, raises questions about the best way to help managers to respond to their subordinates' religious expression. Thus, this result confirms the limited scope of the management tools described by scholars (Aggeri & Labatut, 2010).

This perspective opens new avenues for research. From a managerial point of view, we would question the role of management tools in dealing with religious diversity. In our opinion, the guides are a sign of the increasing awareness of major private organizations interested in taking up this issue and in considering it as a type of diversity that they need to manage. They also reveal the attitudes adopted by each firm towards the subject. Their scope appears uncertain, however. It would be interesting to compare the effect of the training and guides used in each firm.

Like all categorizations, our typology of French companies' positions towards religion at work, risks suffering from "conceptual rigidity" (Miller & Ewest, 2015, p. 322). Our objective is to help managers and leaders to position their firms in a continuum of attitudes regarding this complex topic. Besides, this typology is dynamic. Companies can move from one position to another for many reasons: new leaders, contexts or problematic cases ... It would be interesting to follow some of them during their evolution in order to analyze the causes and consequences of this process.

Finally, if the French case is sometimes considered as specific because of its restrictive definition of religion and its principle of *Laïcité*, our research underlines the difficulties associated with this last concept. It emphasizes that the principle of *Laïcité* disrupts the principle of freedom, even in the private business sector. While the use of *Laïcité* appears to complicate the situation in France, it is beginning to be studied in other Western countries, or may even be inspiring them. These countries also face the limitations of freedom and the particular requests of their employees with their broad range of beliefs. At the same time, business and more widely French society are increasingly looking towards Anglo-Saxon reasonable accommodation. Perhaps this situation, in which the general model of *Laïcité* and the particular model based on individual freedom are sources of inspiration for each other, announces the emergence of a hybrid model shared by all Western private firms.

Appendix

Guide 4, Quote 1

What is the attitude to adopt to manage issues related to religion in the company?

Respect religious convictions and expression strictly according to the law (wearing visible religious signs, prayer during breaks, taking leave for religious reasons when it is compatible with the needs of the department) and sanction irregular behavior (excessive proselytism, harassment for pseudo-religious reasons).

If the image of the firm is at risk, particularly its brand image (wearing visible religious signs): look for reasonable accommodation.

Guide 4, Quote 2

In my team I have employees who ask that when they are fasting nobody should eat near them, even a biscuit, what can I do to maintain a good team spirit?
The observance of a fast is an individual choice, it is important to remind everyone that this choice must not be imposed on others and that each member of the team is free to act as he/she wishes, as long as the internal regulations are strictly respected. It is important to discuss this topic with the employees concerned to find an agreement. However, in no case can religious observance constrain other employees who do not wish it.

Guide 5, Quote 1

Can an employee wear apparent religious clothing or signs?
No. You should refer to the principle of neutrality clearly mentioned in his/her contract to remind the employee that he/she has undertaken "to avoid any attitude or wear any visible sign that might reveal affiliation to any religion or philosophy."

Guide 7, Quote 1

In the canteen, if employees who do not eat pork for religious reasons refuse to let colleagues who do sit with them, this is an act of discrimination obstructing the freedom of conscience of the other employees: it must therefore be stopped.

References

Aggeri, F., & Labatut, J. (2010). La gestion au prisme de ses instruments. Une analyse généalogique des approches théoriques fondées sur les instruments de gestion. *Finance Contrôle Stratégie*, 13(3), 5–37.

Al Ariss, A., & Özbilgin, M. (2010). Understanding self-initiated expatriates: Career experiences of Lebanese self-initiated expatriates in France. *Thunderbird International Business Review*, Jul/Aug, 52(4), 275–85.

Allport, G. W. (1966). The religious context of prejudice. *Journal for the Scientific Study of Religion*, 5, 447–57.

Ashforth, B. E., & Pratt, M. G. (2010). Institutionalized spirituality: An oxymoron? *In* Giacalone, R. A., & Jurkiewicz, C. L. (eds.), *Handbook of workplace spirituality and organizational performance*. New York: M. E. Sharper, 93–107.

Cui, J., Jo, H., Na, H., & Velasquez, M. G. (2015). Workforce diversity and religiosity. *Journal of Business Ethics*, 128, 743–67.

Clair, J. A., Beatty, J. E., & Maclean, T. L. (2005). Out of sight but not out of mind: Managing invisible social identities in the workplace. *Academy of Management Review*, 30(1), 78–95.

Cox, T., & Blake, S. (1991). Managing cultural diversity: Implications for organizational competitiveness. *Academy of Management Executive*, 5(3), 45–56.

Equal Employment Opportunity Commission (US EEOC). (2009 July 31). AT&T pays $1.3 million to satisfy judgment in religious discrimination lawsuit, from www.eeoc.gov/eeoc/newsroom/release/7-31-09.cfm.

Galindo, G., & Surply, J. (2010). Quelles régulations du fait religieux en entreprise? *Revue Internationale de Psychosociologie*, November, 16(40), 29–55.

(2013). Quel processus d'apprentissage de la gestion du fait religieux dans les entreprises françaises? *Management International*, Janvier, 17, 37–49.

Gebert, D., Boerner, S., Kearney, E., King, J. E., Zhang, K., & Song, L. J. (2014). Expressing religious identities in the workplace: Analyzing a neglected diversity dimension. *Human Relations*, 67(5), 543–63.

Ghiglione, R., & Matalon, B. (1991). *Les enquêtes sociologiques: Théories et pratique*. Paris: Armand Colin.

Ghumman, S., Ryan, A-M., Barclay, L. A., Karen, S., & Markel, K. S. (2013). Religious discrimination in the workplace: A review and examination of current and future trends. *Journal of Business and Psychology*, 28(4), 439–54.

Giacalone, R., & Jurkiewicz, C. (2010). *Handbook of workplace spirituality and organizational performance*. Armonk, NY: M. E. Sharpe.

Grossman, R. J. (2008). Religion at work. *HR Magazine*, December, 27–33.

Harrison, D. A., Price, K. H., & Bell, M. P. (1998). Beyond relational demography: Time and the effects of surface- and deep-level diversity on work group cohesion. *Academy of Management Journal*, 41(1), 96–107.

Hart, D., & Brady, N. (2005), "Spirituality and archetype in organizational life," *Business Ethics Quarterly*, 15(3), 409–28.

High Council of Integration (Haut Conseil à l'Intégration). (2011). *Expression religieuse et Laïcité dans l'entreprise* [Religious expression and Laïcité in firms], Advice, Paris, 26.

Hicks, D. A. (2003). *Religion and the Workplace Pluralism, Spirituality, Leadership*. Cambridge: Cambridge University Press, 222.

IFOP Survey. (2015). Les français et la Laïcité [French and the Laïcité], February.

Jurkiewicz, C. L., & Giacalone, R. A. (2004). A values framework for measuring the impact of spirituality on organizational performance. *Journal of Business Ethics*, 49, 129–42.

King, J. E., Bell, M. P., & Lawrence, E. (2009). Religion as an aspect of work place diversity: An examination of the US context and a call for international research. *Journal of Management, Spirituality and Religion*, 6(1), 43–57.

Kinjerski, V., & Skrypnek, B. (2004). Defining spirit at work. Finding common ground. *Journal of Organizational Change Management*, 17, 165–82.

Kirchmeyer, C. (1995). Managing the work-nonwork boudary: An assessment of organizational responses. *Human Relations*, 48(5), 515–36.

Kreiner, G. E., Hollensbe, E. C., & Sheep, M. L. (2006). On the edge of identity: Boundary dynamics at the interface of individual and organizational identities. *Human Relations*, 59, 1315–41.

Kutcher, E. J., Bragger, J. D., Rodriguez-Srednicki, O., & Masco, J. L. (2010). The role of religiosity in stress, job attitudes, and organizational citizenship behavior. *Journal of Business Ethics*, 95, 319–37.

Lenoir, F. (2008). *Petit traité d'histoire des religions*, Essais coll. Points, 374.

Machelon, J-P. (2006). Les relations des cultes avec les pouvoirs publics. *Ministère de l'Intérieur et de l'aménagement du territoire*. La documentation Française, Collection des Rapports Officiels, September, 83.

Miles, M. B., & Huberman, A. M. (2003). *Analyse des données qualitatives* (Translation of the 2nd US edn.). De Boeck Université.

Miller, D. W. (2003). The faith at work movement. *Theology Today*, 60(3), 301–10.

(2007). *God at work: The history and promise of the faith at work movement*. New York: Oxford University Press.

Miller, D. W., & Ewest, T. (2013). Rethinking the impact of religion on business values: Understanding its reemergence and measuring its manifestations. *Journal of International Business Ethics*, 3(2), 49–57.

(2015). A new framework for analyzing organizational workplace religion and spirituality. *Journal of Management, Spirituality & Religion*, 12(4), 305–28.

Mitroff, I., & Denton, E. (1999). *A spiritual audit of corporate America: a hard look at spirituality, religion, and values in the workplace*. San Francisco, CA: Jossey-Bass.

OFRE & Randstad Survey. (2016). *Firm, work and religion* (L'entreprise, le travail et la Religion), Survey, 32.

Sainsaulieu, R. (1992). *L'entreprise une affaire de société*. Paris: Presse de Sciences Po, 352.

Schaeffer, C. B., & Mattis, J. S. (2012). Diversity, religiosity, and spirituality in the workplace. *Journal of Management, Spirituality & Religion*, 9(4), 317–33.

Sociovision Observatory. (2016). Les Français et leurs croyances [The French and Their Beliefs], May, 31.
Tajfel, H., & Turner, J.C. (1986). The social identity theory of intergroup behavior. *In* Worchel, S., & Austin, L. W. (eds.), *Psychology of intergroup relations*. Chicago, IL: Nelson-Hall, 7–24.
US EEOC. (2009). United States Equal Employment Opportunity Commission, Annual Report on the Federal Work Force, https://www.eeoc.gov/federal/reports/fsp2009/upload/FY-2009-Annual-Report.pdf
Win Gallup International. (2012). *Global index of religiosity and atheism*. 25.

16 Resilient Leadership and Tempered Radicalism: Navigating the Intersections of Race, Gender, Nationality, and Religion

FAITH WAMBURA NGUNJIRI AND
KATHY-ANN C. HERNANDEZ

Introduction

What happens when religious identity intersects with gender, race/ethnicity, nationality, and other social identities in the professional lives of women in the US academy? Our chapter interrogates how we experience academic careers at the intersection of these various identities. As researchers have argued, "within American society, the spiritual dimension of our lives has traditionally been regarded as intensely personal, an innermost component of who we are that lies outside the realm of appropriate discussion or concern within business and academic contexts" (Lindholm & Astin, 2006, p. 64). However, this self limiting taboo is slowly lifting; both in popular press and academic environments, there appears to be a discernible hunger for appropriate (i.e. not obnoxious) ways of "fostering spirituality and an associated hunger for spiritual growth" (ibid., p. 64). Higher education is, as Lindholm and Astin argue, "a critical focal point for responding to the question of how we balance the 'exterior' and 'interior' aspects of our lives more effectively" (p. 64). Further, they add that "existing research indicates that developing people's abilities to access, nurture, and give expression to the spiritual dimension of their lives impacts how they engage with the world and fosters within them a heightened sense of connectedness that promotes empathy, ethical behavior, civic responsibility, passion, and action or social justice" (p. 64). The internal or interior aspects refer to the spiritual or existential dimensions of life; the exterior refers to work, actions, behavior, etc.

Our focus in this chapter is to explore faith-work integration, discussing the strategies we use to leverage the different aspects of our identity in support of our leadership aspirations. Using an intersectional framework (Crenshaw, 1989; Sanchez-Hucles & Davis, 2010), we investigate how our various identities are implicated in our experiences of both privilege and discrimination within higher education in the United States. Both of us have experiences as students in both secular and religiously affiliated predominantly white institutions (PWIs), but the bulk of our work experience is within religiously affiliated institutions, what we shall hitherto refer to as Christian Higher Education (CHE) institutions.

As management and education scholars, we borrow from both disciplines in theorizing and unpacking our experiences. Our work is informed by our interests in women's leadership experiences in higher education, particularly women who are differentially positioned due to their social identities, in our case, our being, at a minimum, black, immigrant, Christians in PWIs in the USA (Hernandez et al., 2015). As scholars who hold multiple social identities, we illustrate how race, ethnicity, national origins, gender, and religious/spiritual identities intersect in our experiences navigating the predominantly white higher education context within the United States. As immigrants from Kenya and Trinidad; as tenured faculty members; as Christians; as women who, upon coming to the United States to pursue higher education, suddenly found ourselves identified as black or African American due to our phenotype; as wives to African American men; and as mothers; our experiences can illustrate life at the intersections of multiple identities. Most of the studies on spirituality and religion in the workplace do not employ an intersectional framework, thus our collaborative autoethnography work can add a missing dimension to the extant literature.

We begin by discussing intersectionality as the theoretical framework undergirding our study and situate our work in the management, spirituality, and religion literature. We then we describe the present study and ensuing themes that emerged from our collective data collection and meaning making process.

Intersectional Theoretical Framework

Kimberle Crenshaw, a legal scholar, is credited with having popularized the term intersectionality, in her landmark work unpacking the experiences of women of color and domestic violence (Crenshaw, 1989, 1991). Since then, the term has been utilized by scholars from a diverse range of disciplines, particularly feminist studies, women's studies, ethnic studies, sociology, and psychology, to describe and problematize the issues of diverse people's experiences at the nexus of various social identities, and to explicate their experiences of discrimination in social and organizational life (Collins, 1999; Shields, 2008; Hulko, 2009). Such scholars argue that discrimination and oppression due to social identities often involve more than one identity; it involves the intersections, the nexus, or to use Patricia Hill Collin's term, a *matrix* of domination (Collins, 1999, 2008).

Intersectionality as a concept highlights the complexity of experiences of differentially positioned individuals at the intersection of race, gender, class, and other identities. Recently, organization and management scholars have begun using an intersectional framework to interrogate the experiences of women and people of color, in areas such as their struggles with the glass ceiling and advancement as leaders (Ospina & Foldy, 2009; Sanchez-Hucles & Davis, 2010; Sang et al., 2013). However, such studies in management remain quite few, with most scholars utilizing a single frame, such as race, or gender (Richardson & Loubier, 2008; Ospina & Foldy, 2009; Rosette & Livingston, 2012). Intersectionality

Provides a critical lens to interrogate racial, ethnic, class, ability, age, sexuality, and gender disparities and to contest existing ways of looking at these structures of inequality, transforming knowledges as well as the social institutions in which they have found themselves. (Dill & Zambrana, 2009, p. 1)

This chapter joins the small but growing body of research in using an intersectional framework to narrate the experiences of two black women within organizational life, particularly looking at race, gender, nationality, and religion. Building on prior work with another colleague (Hernandez et al., 2015), we go further in interrogating and narrating our experiences with being *minoritized* individuals within religious institutions of higher learning. In the previous study, even though we focused on race, gender and nationality in the published article, in the data collection process, religion/spirituality emerged as salient to our experiences. However, we were asked to remove that section from the paper during the review process. As such, we welcome the opportunity to reposition our religiosity/spirituality in its rightful place – we recognize it as both a source of strength as well as a point of contention in the academy. The central question guiding our interrogations is: How are we, Faith and Kathy-Ann, able to integrate our spiritual identity with our personal and professional calling as foreign-born, black female leaders in the predominantly white academy?

Spirituality, Religion, and Work

Within the management literature, spirituality and religion became topics of conversation in the late 1990s, as researchers began to ask questions about the role that these play in the world of organizations (see for example, Fairholm, 1997; Fort, 1997; Fry, 2005, 2008; Fry & Whittington, 2005; Fry et al., 2005; Jackson, 1999; Mitroff and Denton, 1999). Mitroff and Denton's (1999) work was particularly intriguing as a pioneering study into how managers and executives integrated spirituality into the management of organizations. Their study revealed participants discomfort with the idea of religion at work, fearing that religion could be disruptive to work. Further, participants in their study shared their discomfort with bringing their souls to their workplace:

On the one hand, they wished fervently that they could express more of themselves in the workplace, but ... were terrified to do so. They were worried if they did express their souls, they would end up selling them to their organizations ... On the other hand, if they didn't express more of themselves in the setting where they spend the vast majority of their waking time, then the development of their souls would be seriously stifled, possibly even halted. (p. 7)

Mitroff and Denton argued for the need to integrate spirituality into management, including the ability to recognize individuals full personhood at work, to be motivated by higher level needs (not just money), to express their creativity and intelligence, and to find higher meaning through their work. Mitroff and Denton's work was foundational to many of the empirical studies that emerged in the 2000s with a clear focus on spirituality and religion in the field of management studies.

Management and spirituality scholar Margaret Benefiel's conceptualization of spirituality connects well with our own experience. Benefiel argues that

A major change is taking place in the personal and professional lives of leaders as many of them more deeply integrate their spirituality and their work. Most would agree that this integration is leading to very positive changes in their relationships and their effectiveness. (Benefiel, 2005, p. 724)

Benefiel's (2005) account of the leader's spiritual transformation journey is particularly helpful in informing and explaining our own experiences. She draws on a five stage model of individual spiritual transformation, that can be summarized thus:

1. First half of the journey
   Stage I: Awakening – individual becomes aware of spiritual reality and adopts spiritual practices
   Stage II: Transition – Individual has difficulty with spiritual practices, feels isolated and frustrated, questions path

2. Second half of the journey
   Stage III: Recovery – individual discovers new way of relating to God (or ultimate reality), adopts new spiritual practices, and experiences renewed joy
   Stage IV: Dark night – Individual finds spiritual practices ineffective, goes through a time of deeper questioning and sense of isolation
   Stage V: Dawn – individual experiences new sense of connectedness, alignment, and new ways of making meaning.

Benefiel (2005) explains that at stage V, "leaders who live predominantly in this place are more available to the needs of the people they serve, and more available to their organizations. Because their egos have been relativized to the higher good, they can use their skills and energy to serve the good of the organization as a whole, rather than using them to fill their own ego needs" (p. 735). This kind of understanding of spiritual development is helpful in unpacking some of our own experiences as black immigrant women academics working in environments where we experience racist microaggressions – it helps to unpack both why we choose to stay and/or when we choose to move on, it explicates the underlying framework that undergirds our choice to do so.

Spirituality among African Ascended People

Several studies provide evidence of the salience of religiosity/spirituality and positive outcomes for African ascended people – that is, people who have African ancestry whether they reside in Africa or the vast African Diaspora – especially in light of the intersecting struggles with racism, sexism, and classism. As Dantley (2005) argues, "spirituality has given people of color the impetus to create, innovate, and transform infirming and deprecating conditions with which they have had to contend" (p. 655). Further, "African American spirituality is the internal grounding of many Black people's ontology or sense of being. It crafts a sense of self and provides the impetus to resist forms and practices of dehumanization and oppression that are sometimes promoted by the dominant culture" (p. 657).

Other researchers similarly agree that for many people of African ascent, spirituality is a deeply integral part of our identity, and an important source of our meaning making in the context of struggle (e.g., Allison & Broadus, 2009; Cozart, 2010; Dillard et al., 2000). Spirituality and religious participation enhance physical and emotional well-being among African Americans (Levin et al., 2005; Zavala et al., 2009); the social support engendered in a faith community minimizes the effect of race-related stress (Utsey et al., 2008); and spirituality contributes to cultural resilience and the ability to cope with adversity as part of a community (Brown & Tylka, 2011; Utsey et al., 2007). In sum, religious/spiritual connection can act "as an emotional support and guidance, a source of stress relief and comfort, and a way for participants to access and then address their challenges" (Teti et al., 2012, p. 529).

By religious identity, most management, spirituality and religion scholars often indicate the specific rituals, beliefs, and practices associated with specific religious institutions (Fry, 2003). On the other hand, spirituality often refers to the broader deeper connections amongst human beings, the divine, and nature, connections that go beyond religious affiliations (Fry, 2003). Whereas some scholars and practitioners are uncomfortable with studying and discussing religion in relation to work – attempting to separate spirituality from religion because many individuals now identify as spiritual but not religious (Lindholm & Astin, 2006) – our own spiritual identities are deeply tied to our religious identities, and thus, need not be separated. We are religious and spiritual. We sometimes use the terms interchangeably. Chiorazzi (2015) quotes Jacob Olupona observation that, "African spirituality simply acknowledges that beliefs and practices touch on and inform every facet of human life, and therefore African religion cannot be separated from the everyday or mundane" (Chiorazzi, 2015, para. 15). Peter Paris agrees, arguing that "religion permeates every dimension of African life ... the ubiquity of religious consciousness among African peoples constitutes their single most important common characteristic" (1995, p. 27).

It is imperative to continue explorations of spirituality amongst people of African heritage in the continent and the diaspora, in this case, two immigrant women faculty members in PWIs, to uncover the role spirituality plays both in our struggle against domination and racist microaggressions, and in our understanding and use of power and privilege. The approach we selected for our study, a collaborative autoethnography, was chosen because it enabled us to stay true to ourselves and honor our experiences as subjects as we interrogate a phenomenon that has larger socio-cultural consequences.

Collaborative Autoethnography

We employed collaborative autoethnography (CAE) to interrogate our experiences and reveal, through this first person approach, the role of spirituality in navigating the intersections of race, gender, national origins, and other identities. CAE is a qualitative research method that allows researchers to "work in community to collect their autobiographical materials and to analyze and interpret their data collectively to gain a meaningful understanding of sociocultural phenomena reflected in their autobiographical data" (Chang et al., 2013, pp. 22–3). Though still a nascent addition to the field of social science research, it is gaining recognition as a valuable tool of inquiry that is malleable to academic rigor (Hughes et al., 2012) and to interrogations of life in various sociocultural contexts, always aimed at problematizing the status quo and dehegemonizing inquiry (Tillman, 2009; William-White, 2011). CAE is particularly sensitive to the need for relational authenticity in research, acknowledging the vulnerability that individuals experience in difficult institutional contexts, and articulating shared meaning making of collective realities (Hernandez & Ngunjiri, 2013). The process begins with a shared agreement about the boundaries of the research project, in this case, a focus on our individual and collective experiences as marginalized individuals in PWI contexts, exploring both the challenges and opportunities inherent in that marginality.

Autoethnographers range from those who recognize the story as analysis, as stories evoke emotional responses from their readers (Ellis, 1997) to those who employ a more analytical approach to explicitly connect their stories to socio-cultural and organizational issues (Anderson, 2006). We situate this autoethnographic exploration in the middle of that continuum – we expect to evoke emotional responses to some of the more difficult stories about microaggressions and oppressions in academia as well as to add our experiences to the larger conversation about the experiences of people like us.

Our choice in using first-person qualitative research in the form of CAE is a political choice to both legitimize and highlight the appropriateness of the personal in capturing the complexity of our experiences. Indeed, there is a growing recognition of the need for qualitative approaches in leadership studies like ours. For example, Lund Dean and colleagues have observed:

> It has been generally established that the positivist, empiricist methodological model is not only insufficient for SRW [spirituality, religion and work] research, but may actually harm the discipline by *inauthentically* [emphasis added] measuring and analyzing crucial SRW variables such as spirit, soul, faith, God, and cosmos. (Lund Dean et al., 2003, p. 379)

As such, we view our choice of a method that focuses on us as both subject and object of our inquiry as well-suited to authentically capturing the complexities of how we integrate our spiritual and work identities as black women in the academy. Below we describe the data collection and analysis processes we utilized to unpack our experiences at the intersections.

Data Collection and Analysis

The data for this paper come from several sources collected over the last seven years. Specifically, we draw on culturegram activities in which we visually mapped out our salient identities, self-reflective writing inspired by both current events (e.g., the recent Ferguson, Missouri and related race crises in the United States), and focus group discussions, which were collected for the aforementioned CAE project. Further, data come from reflexive journals, where we engage in narrating and reflecting on our experiences in the classroom, with student evaluations, interactions with colleagues and other daily examples of microaggressions. The third source of data is work that we have done with another colleague, which we presented at a leadership conference (Ngunjiri et al., 2014).

Data were analyzed on two levels: independently and collaboratively. After the first phase of data collection, we exchanged our individual writing and independently extracted themes and made suggestions of areas for further probing. In reading the scripts, we compared focus group discussion data with our written documents to independently code meaningful ideas in response to the question: "What are the areas of convergences/divergences in our experiences?" Extensive discussions helped us to negotiate and condense final themes. We condensed overlapping and redundant codes into broad themes with supporting text segments relevant to our central research question. Being mindful that autoethnographic work faces unique ethical challenges which include the reliance on personal self-disclosures that implicate self and others with the potential to cause harm, we implemented relevant ethical guidelines to protect ourselves as well as the unknowing participants in our self-stories (Ellis, 2007; Catham-Carpenter, 2010; Hernandez & Ngunjiri, 2013).

Findings

In the following sections, we first discuss our spiritual/religious identity as the nexus for the strategies we employ to successfully navigate the academy. Then we discuss in turn the strategies that emerged from this exploration: turning challenges into opportunities, becoming tempered radical, and developing spiritual resiliency.

Religious/Spiritual Identity

As explained previously, as people of African ascent, our spiritual and religious identity are deeply intertwined. Our spiritual identity emerged as critical to our ability to persist in the face of overwhelming challenges. In the context of this study, we recognized spirituality and religiosity as overlapping constructs (see Moberg, 1990). Our expressions of spirituality converged in a mutual understanding of spirituality as the "personal, subjective side of religious experience" (Hill & Pargament, 2003, p. 64). We each identify as protestant Christians, and as both religious and spiritual women. In our conversations about coping, it was the "personal, subjective side" of our faith walk irrespective of denominational affiliation in which we were able to identify areas of commonalities.

Firstly, spirituality tempers our responses to the real or perceived injustices we face often at the intersection of being both black and female. Our spirituality allows us to process our anger in intentional ways; it provokes us to channel that anger into paths of advocacy and action. For example, in recounting the challenges we face in academe our ability to cope coalesced around an understanding that our responses should be congruent with our faith walk. For instance, Kathy-Ann, when trying to decide if she should or should not respond to injustices, shared the following with Faith

In thinking about how and if to respond – I am guided by my faith. I heard Maya Angelou say once that it is human to be angry at injustice, but that you should not allow it to make you bitter. Instead I think you use that anger to propel you to a more just way of being – that informs practice, and helps others do better.

Consistent with this tempering of our responses is the construction of a tri-partite lens – a merger of our gendered, cultural/ethnic, and spiritual lens – for interpreting our experiences. For example, Faith observed that having "a racialized identity can be a burden. It can lead us to act/think in ways that are not necessarily healthy; it becomes easier to personalize issues even where they need not be personal." However, adding a spiritual lens to our analysis provides a somewhat neutral space to understand our experiences as perhaps not colored by gender, or race, or gender times race, but in the wider context of human experiences. In so doing, we are able to choose our battles carefully.

Secondly, spirituality fuels our righteous indignation to fight against injustice as part of our spiritual calling. We recognized that this functional aspect of our spiritual identities exists in tension with the tempering function. While spirituality tempers our responses to perceived injustices against us, it also propels us to fight non-negotiable injustices as part of a spiritual mandate to not only advocate for ourselves but also for those who will follow. For example, Kathy-Ann talks about being aware of this larger mandate on her life:

That necessitates that I act against injustice, if I fail to do so I am left with a feeling that I have "let down the cause." And so I am constantly balancing the tempering and igniting functions of my spiritual self as I decide whether to respond to injustices. It becomes part of my story – when, another young black woman I am mentoring, asks me questions about the academy and how to make it – if there are racial and gender issues, how do I navigate them? And so, I realize I am writing my answers to her by the way I respond to these challenges/experiences.

Relatedly, our spiritual identities help us to see our positions in the academy as having a larger purpose. As such, we find personal satisfaction in acting in accordance with this larger purpose at the intersection of our spiritual, gendered and cultural ethnic statuses even though we are aware of injustices against us in our current context. From a dominant spiritual perspective, both of us teach at Christian religiously affiliated universities where we feel a strong connection to our institutions and the mission they espouse. Kathy-Ann remains convinced that "though not always well implemented, I see my commitment to ideals of the university to live out its mission as an extension of my faith." Likewise, Faith's personal mission is congruent with that of her current university. We share this commitment to a larger calling. However, we do feel the weight of this responsibility by virtue of our minority status at the intersection of our various identities. When we started collecting autoethnographic data in 2008, we were working at the same institution, before Faith changed jobs in 2013. Faith is the only black female faculty at her institution as of September 2016. Kathy-Ann is one of only a handful of black female faculty at her institution. As such, we are very much aware that our positions come with responsibilities to advocate for ourselves, to mentor others, and also to be pioneers in paving a more equitable path for those to follow. Our spirituality enables us to employ the following tempered radical strategies, and it enables us to survive and thrive in spite of overt and covert racist/sexist microaggressions that we face in the academy.

Turning Challenges into Opportunities

The challenges that women of color face at the intersection of race and gender in the academy have been well documented (Jean-Marie et al. 2009; Brown & William-White, 2010; Robinson & Clardy, 2010). However, most of the literature focuses on pathologizing the experiences of people of color in the academy, by highlighting the challenges and microaggressions with scant focus targeted at the navigational strategies (Hernandez et al., 2015) or points of victory. In explicating the intersection of our spiritual identity with our various selves, we were able to uncover the critical role that it plays in helping us get over, or get through the challenges we experience in those intersections (Tillman, 2012).

We have faced the gamut of challenges ranging from inequitable pay, overloaded course work and service requirements, feeling unsupported, being the recipient of harsh student evaluations, lack of recognition for our accomplishments, and various instances of microaggressions (see for example, Hernandez et al., 2015; Ngunjiri et al., 2014). Microaggressions involve daily, often subtle actions and statements said to people of color by white people, as opposed to Jim Crow or other forms of overt racism (Solorzano, 1998; Solorzano et al., 2000) – microaggressions include questions such as "where do you come from," or the statement "you speak very well" that serve to remind us, to let us know that "you don't belong here." These challenges are consistent with the findings reported by other scholars (for example, Turner, 2002; Sanchez-Hucles & Davis, 2010).

However, we recognize our spiritual identity as the fulcrum that emboldens us to utilize these challenges as fuel for the fire to excel in academia, first as graduate students, and now as tenured faculty leaders. Rather than allow the challenges to overwhelm us or simply accept the status quo, we have empowered ourselves to work passionately to become change agents within our institutional contexts even as we advanced through tenure and promotion.

It is challenging to find opportunities to engage in research at teaching universities where women of color constitute a small minority. Hence, we have sought out collaborators within and beyond our institutions. That is how we started working together with a third colleague on CAE projects, as three immigrant faculty working at the same institution, producing several conference presentations and publications together (e.g., Chang et al., 2013; Hernandez et al., 2015; Ngunjiri et al., 2010). This same impetus led us to start working together on this project, this time focusing on our common experiences as foreign-born black women of faith in academia. Through this collaborative effort, we have earned the reputation of being "researchers" at our institutions, being sought out by other faculty and students for advice on publications and presentations. Faith was the first director of research, helping to spearhead research and publications at her previous department, while Kathy-Ann served in a similar role for the school of education at the same institution. Our efforts have helped to support and encourage faculty and graduate students in their scholarship endeavors within that "teaching" [higher teaching load, lower research and publishing expectations] institution.

We also find it challenging to find mentors and/or sponsors in our various contexts. However, we have been resourceful in seeking out mentors beyond our institutions. At the same time, because of this awareness of our own limitations and our spiritual calling, we seek out opportunities to mentor others in the academy, both colleagues and our students, and especially students of color and international students. The products of some of these efforts are presentations and publications with students who are now better positioned to seek out careers in the academy (see for example, Ngunjiri et al., 2010; Ngunjiri & Christo-Baker, 2012; Hernandez & Murray-Johnson, 2014, 2015). In contemplating the outcomes of mentoring, Faith reflected on two of her proud academic "mama" moments:

I am so proud of both Maggie and Priscilla. Watching them work so hard to turn each of their dissertations into a book, both of which demonstrate African women's use of spiritual leadership practices to lead within challenging circumstances. It feels like we have gone full circle. My first book, and now their first books, all focusing on the passions that connect us around women and leadership, and the role of spirituality in the meaning making and resiliency of leaders. Both of their books are now in print (Ndlovu, 2016, Madimbo, 2016) through the Palgrave Studies in African Leadership series that I co-edit. These are proud mama moments for me.

Through mentoring, we lead by example to show students how to advance and thrive in spite of the challenges they face. Where it is in our power, we advocate for students and other people of color in our institutions and the wider academy in order to effect change, a theme that we discuss in more depth below under tempered radicalism.

Overall, we find that our spirituality empowers us to reconfigure, strategize and confront injustices so that we are able to not only advance towards our goals but also to effect change irrespective of external realities. To do this effectively, we have become resilient leaders who have been "refined as by fire" at the nexus of our various identities.

Developing Resiliency

Resiliency is the capability to bounce back, and to grow after experiencing adversity (Ramsey & Blieszner, 1999; Christman & McClellan, 2008, 2012). As black women in the academy, our ability to survive and thrive is linked to our capacity to persevere, to get through and get over, keeping our eyes on the prize that is tenure, promotion, and more importantly, leaving a legacy for students of color (Tillman, 2012). Resiliency for us involves "adaptive and coping strategies that forms and hones positive character skills" (Christman & McClellan, 2012, p. 650), giving us the ability to cope with the microaggressions that we face as a matter of course in academia. Without resilience, we would have given up and walked away, or worse, stayed but experienced psychological and physical health issues. The protective factors that have enabled us to survive and thrive include our ability to face the structural injustices with hope rather than anger, our ability to engage in a paradigm shift so that we see our whole lives in focus – as mothers, wives, siblings, coaches, consultants – as opposed to merely as professors, our ability to stand up and advocate for ourselves and others, and even the growing wisdom that enables us to choose when/if to respond to injustices or not.

On the other hand, it is challenging to be resilient in the face of constant adversities in the academy. In particular, we are aware of an undercurrent of being presumed incompetent (Muhs et al., 2013). Kathy-Ann remembers being praised publicly by a senior administrator at a faculty and student gathering with the compliment:

"Kathy-Ann has successfully taught the class XXX!" I was humiliated. The irony was that I had been teaching in higher education for more than ten years, and I had just been promoted to full professor, but here I was being applauded for successfully teaching a course as if that in itself was a major accomplishment for *me*.

Experiences like these invoking subtle racism and sexism, make us poignantly aware of the burden we bear to work twice as hard with no assurance that our work will receive the recognition or affirmation that it deserves. Moreover, this overworking can cause workaholic tendencies. Having support systems outside of our academic environments provides the necessary checks and balances; we lean on spouses and loved ones to say to us, "You need to stop now! That is enough already!" or "You are working too hard!" Being mothers and wives, having extended family that we care for gives us that avenue for experiencing our non-academic selves.

As with other resilient individuals, we have learned, through intense spiritual introspection and engaging in dialogue with others who are similarly positioned, and with the support of our significant relationships, to "transform pain into growth and achieve fulfillment in personal and professional domains" (Whatley, 1998, p. 4, as cited in Christman & McClellan, 2012, p. 651). Thus, rather than succumb to the microaggressions, we have learned to overcome, to succeed in the midst of, and in spite of, the challenges we face in academia. In addition, as Christman and McClellan (2012) argue, we have learned "to develop patience, tolerance, responsibility, compassion, determination, and risk taking" (p. 650).

To illustrate Christman and McClellan's point above, Faith remembers facing racist and sexist behavior from a white middle-aged male student who told her she was

"Too young to have so much control over the curriculum." She reflected on her feelings from that encounter: I reacted with anger and indignation, confronting the program director for allowing such overtly discriminatory and unwarranted comments to go unchallenged. The student had emailed him complaining about me, that I was working the class too hard, and questioning why I should have such power and control. That was in 2009. Today, when I see comments in evaluations that essentially identify the student as a white male, complaining about being uncomfortable being under the authority of a black female professor, I no longer react with anger. Recently, I read the following comment from a student on my course evaluation: "As a white non-religious male, I am very uncomfortable in her class." Did I respond in anger? No. I now treat such feedback as par for the course. However, I also ensure that I write commentary about that in my self-evaluations for tenure and promotion, so that the committee does not fail to notice the racist and sexist nature of such comments and the likelihood of lower scores from such students.

Such is the experience of women and minority faculty in most higher education contexts within the US (Smith, 2007).

Finally, Christman and McClellan (2012) state that "resiliency develops and substantiates self-awareness and identity. As individuals encounter adversity, they navigate potential response – to fight or flee" (p. 651). We have each been at this crossroad and have asked ourselves the question: "Should I stay or should I leave?" For Faith, "this meant leaving my previous [toxic] environment and joining a more affirming institutional context that would help advance my professional and research goals." For Kathy-Ann, "that meant coming to terms with my current institutional contexts due to the demands of my life overall (i.e. familial roles that limit geographic mobility), and finding additional income through consulting." We recognize that as long as we are minoritized, we have limited choices for more affirming academic contexts than where we are currently located. The reality we face is that sometimes leaving and starting over is not the most pragmatic choice. We each have to discern our individual limits and to make the choice that best fits our personal goals, professional aspirations, and familial realities.

In this way, the nexus of being black, female, spiritual/religious, and the interaction of these identities with the roles that we play, all contribute to our ability to persevere, stay strong, overcome, "get over," and succeed in both academia and our personal lives. For us, being resilient is also linked to our ability to function as tempered radicals, change agents in our institutional contexts.

Engaging Tempered Radicalism

Meyerson and Scully (1995) first used the term tempered radical to describe people who find themselves at odds with the dominant culture, and who choose agentic responses to disrupt unfair arrangements and change the status quo. Tempered radicals, according to Meyerson (2001) function as outsiders within their organizations, and operate along a continuum of five possible responses: resisting quietly and staying true to self, turning personal threats into opportunities, broadening impact through negotiation, leveraging small wins, and organizing collective action. Other actions that found to be consistent with tempered radicals in the African context include: intercultural boundary spanning, resourcefulness and creative problem solving, maturity in leadership, and leveraging the outsider/within positionality (Ngunjiri, 2010). These four approaches enable tempered radicals to be effective in being both authentic in their identity (as women, as people of color) and as leaders in their organizations or communities, in contexts that often involve risk-taking and an ethic of care.

For us, tempered radicalism emerged as the approach we utilize for leading at the intersections. In a sense, we came to the realization that tempered radicalism comes about with maturity in leadership, as well as experience and understanding of the institutional and wider social context in which we enact our lives. On the one end of Meyerson's continuum is the response of staying true to oneself and at the other end is the response of collective action. Consistent with this approach, there are times when we choose silence and staying true to ourselves, other times we voice our values (Creed, 2003) and speak up against the microaggressions and inequitable treatment we endure. Knowing which response to take – voice or silence – is driven by pragmatism and prudence borne out of our experience in academia. Early in our experience as international students in the United States, we did not know enough to be able to always actively voice our dissent against microaggressions or racist statements. Take for example this story from Kathy-Ann's life:

Coming here, and finding out that, just by virtue of my skin color and my cultural ethnicity, which I didn't realize before, it came with baggage that I had to carry. I had to prove myself ... I worked for this Caucasian, it was the first time I was working for a Caucasian. And I managed her office. I wrote a report and she said, "you write very well for someone from the Caribbean!" Maybe she meant to compliment me but I felt offended, but I didn't know what "from the Caribbean" meant to her. Did she perceive me as not competent just because I came from the Caribbean? ... or this other time, driving to Gary, Indiana and my boss saying, "I don't understand these people, [referring to black people] but you, you are different."

In these early experiences, Kathy-Ann did not respond. She remained silent – there was too much to process in the moment about what was being said and the intended meaning behind such comments. Later, after having many such experiences,, she was aware that in these moments, she had a clear choice – to remain silent or to speak out. We both had those kinds of early experiences, where silence was the only response, borne more out of not really knowing how to engage as we were coming to terms with a different construction of blackness for us in this context (see for example Hernandez & Murray-Johnson, 2015). In private, we would talk through these kinds of experiences with fellow international students and American minority students trying to understand the racism and ethnocentricity that elicited them. And with time, silence could be more of an intentional choice, as in "that does not deserve a response." Thus we moved from silence because of lack of knowledge and understanding, to silence as choice and more agentic behavior on the Meyerson continuum, quiet resistance and staying true to ourselves.

On the quiet resistance end of the continuum, Meyerson recognizes that quiet actions are motivated by either a desire to be ones authentic self, or as first steps towards initiating change in the context. This backstage work, acting behind the scenes in ways that may remain invisible, requires "enormous fortitude and personal conviction" (Meyerson, 2001, p. 51). Such actions include some already mentioned above, such as mentoring and helping others in the organizational context, enacting values and beliefs outside of work (e.g., consulting, coaching), connecting with others in other organizations to network and share resources, all aimed at enabling us to be authentically black immigrant women and effective in our various roles.

In the middle of Myerson's five strategies continuum are three strategies that we discuss here and illustrate with one example that demonstrates how they overlap in real life situations: turning personal threats into opportunities, broadening impact through negotiation, and leveraging small wins. Our ability to turn personal threats into opportunities is a very important strategy we employ to thrive in the midst of the micro aggressions. Agency, the ability to make choices about how to respond to situational variables, enables us not to be silenced, or to appear to collude with the oppressive systems.

The strategy of broadening impact through negotiation requires "seeking out the broader issues embedded" in our encounters at the intersections (Meyerson, 2001, p. 79). Meyerson recommends looking at these encounters as opportunities to negotiate, "think in terms of competing interests, differing positions and concerns, distinct sources of influence, and alternative framing of issues" (p. 79). That enables us to not merely advocate for ourselves as individuals; instead, we advocate by locating our experiences within the broader institutional context.

In leveraging small wins, we are empowered by every little successful effort. For example, when a publication leads to better appreciation in the department for supporting faculty research goals. Or the win of getting an appropriate office ensures that the unfair treatment will not happen to the next person down the line, because it becomes a learning opportunity for the department leader in how not to treat those who are different. Each small win empowers us for future and further action.

This example helps to demonstrate how tempered radical strategies overlap. Kathy-Ann tells her story to illustrate:

> I found myself in a situation where a colleague took my intellectual property without asking (course syllabus and course content); moreover, that same colleague then asked me to meet with him during my vacation break so

he could be even better prepared for the upcoming semester. I was dumbfounded by both his actions and request.

After the incident I choose to remain silent and did not broach the topic with him. My thinking was that the act was more an indication of his character and values than mine – nor did I think that he could bring to the syllabus the spirit and conviction that I could. I chose to remain silent and convicted in my own understanding that here was a counter example of what I valued as a professional at the nexus of my spirituality and cultural ethnic identity-integrity and professional courtesy. I would probably have remained silent except as is often the case, said colleague in a separate incident again stole my ideas and initiative and presented it to superiors as his ideas. That was when I made the decision to voice.

Though I was still tempted to brush this off as a minor offense, the more I thought about it, the more I realized that such actions were artifacts of an institutional culture where taking others work without asking, was normative. To be able to effect change in the status quo, I had to intentionally rebel against it. So I seized the opportunity to demand respect from him for both my personal and professional boundaries. I let him know that I would be happy to meet with him after my vacation, and subsequently had a private discussion with him about professional courtesies in the academy. Was this a major win for me? Not at all! But it was a small win against a threat which I was able to turn into an opportunity to begin changing the institutional culture one battle at a time.

This example illustrates silence as a choice, as opposed to the earlier example where silence was fueled by a sense of powerlessness and not fully understanding the context. In this case, Kathy-Ann was silent at first reading this as a character flaw. But on further reflection, she realized that it was also an issue of institutional culture, at which point it became necessary to voice her values. It became necessary to use this incident to turn a personal threat into an opportunity to teach about personal and professional boundaries, to counter institutional culture. This small win could then become part of a larger goal of changing a culture where taking others intellectual property was quite common.

Finally, engaging in collective action is a very empowering strategy, because it helps us to not feel alone, and to put our resources together for bigger impact than we could achieve individually. For example, by working collaboratively in projects, we have found ourselves being more productive as researchers, as we provide each other with accountability in addition to sharing both the load and the resources. Further, collective action does often translate to encouraging each other, lifting each other up when our individual energies are flagging from the efforts of dealing with daily racial microaggressions, providing one another with the support we need to keep going.

These five strategic approaches are further fueled by our ability to act as intercultural boundary-spanners and leveraging our outsider/within positionality (Ngunjiri, 2010), so we can represent and advocate for our groups within our institutional contexts. As we have grown and matured as leaders, we find that it has become easier to differentiate between the battles we should fight, and those we should leave alone in order to win the war. That is, our capacity for critical spirituality or practical wisdom has been enhanced by our maturity as leaders. Dantley defines critical spirituality thus:

The element of critique and deconstruction of undemocratic power relations is blended with spiritual reflection grounded in an African American sense of moralism, prophetic resistance, and hope in order to form the viscera of this hybrid theoretical construct called critical spirituality. (Dantley, 2003, p. 5)

Thus critical spirituality gives us the tools to critique, to deconstruct, it provides us with the practical wisdom to discern our responses to situations and events pragmatically and authentically. Further, being resourceful in our problem solving, including reframing issues, recognizing a higher purpose, knowing whom to call to think through situations, and just overall having one another as sources of support has enabled us to thrive in spite of, and in the midst of the racist/sexist discrimination we are exposed to in PWIs.

Discussion

Living at the intersections of race, gender and national origins, within the context of PWIs in the United States requires that we have the skill set and competency to thrive in the midst of, rather than the absence of challenges to our authority as leaders. As people of African ascent living in the United States, we have found that our spiritual identity and religious communities provide us with the life affirming sustenance that we need to engage in our teaching, research and scholarship in a way that honors who we are, in spite of and in the midst of, challenges to our authority as academics.

These findings are consistent with the work of other scholars (Dillard et al., 2000; Allison & Broadus, 2009; Cozart, 2010; Alston & McClellan, 2011). Our spiritual identity is the impetus that tempers our responses to injustices, ignites our indignation in the face of injustices, and enables us to see a bigger purpose for our professional calling that is consistent with our faith walk. It is from this integrated understanding of our spiritually centered selves that we are able to employ the three strategies that we have discussed here: turning challenges into opportunities, engaging tempered radicalism, and developing resiliency to overcome the impacts of racial and sexist microaggressions that exist in our institutional contexts.

As indicated above, ours is a critical spirituality (Dantley, 2005) enacted through the three strategies enumerated. As Dantley (2005) offers, our "faith is prophetic in that it argues that what we see is a current reality, surely there is an antithesis, a response or future yet to be realized" (p. 6). Indeed, for us, having faith that things can be better, that racist and sexist microaggressions are not inevitable, is what fuels our agency towards change. As a matter of course, tempered radicalism demands action, whether quiet or collective action, towards bringing about a more just social arrangement. While we are not always successful in our efforts, our faith empowers us to keep advocating and advancing change. Our spirituality fuels that tempered radicalism, convicting us of the need to act not only on our own behalf, but also on behalf of others, present or future. Our faith communities provide us with an avenue for, at a minimum, letting off steam after racist or sexist encounters.

Our spirituality empowers us in our ability to reframe situations, to see the bigger picture, and to have a sense of calling and purpose in our work. This aspect of spirituality is well covered in the leadership and spirituality literature (Dantley, 2003; Delbecq, 2004; Duchon & Ploman, 2005; Fry, 2013). We recognize how our careers, including the institutions where we choose to work, are part of a higher calling on our lives to serve others with our intellectual gifts (Delbecq, 2004; Hernandez, 2011; Ngunjiri, 2011). Indeed, finding each other at the same institution and working together since our initial meeting has been a real gift, a way for both of us to actualize our call to academia as we recognized "we are more powerful as a community than we can be as individuals ... the inconveniences and tensions of joint scholarship could be accepted knowing that the benefits would outweigh the difficulties" (Delbecq, 2004, p. 646). When the challenges of being immigrant black women in the academy threaten to overwhelm us, we can rest in the knowledge that this is what we have been called to for this season of our lives.

Our spiritual maturity has been instrumental in anchoring our meaning making process as black women in the US academy, giving us the practical wisdom that enables us to serve our students, engage authentically with our colleagues, and be available to our external constituents as professionals without giving up our identities. Spiritual maturity (Benefiel, 2005) affords us the prudence and patience to navigate unjust social arrangements, and craft, as Dantley (2005) argues, creative responses to the challenges we face to our authority as professors and leaders in academia. We attempt to "rock the boat without falling out" (Ngunjiri, 2007) as spirited tempered radicals in PWI contexts. Our spiritual maturity is the key to crafting effective navigational strategies that enable us to thrive in spite of, and in the midst of, the racism, ethnocentrism, and sexism that causes the microaggressions we face daily.

Implications for Theory and Practice

First person research endeavors such as ours help to illuminate the lived experiences of a limited number of people, by going deep into their stories and analyzing those stories. Such approaches provide viable alternatives to positivistic research paradigms for individuals like us who are differently positioned. By employing CAE, we are able to engage in research that allows us to stay true to who we are and honors our experiences, which may have larger socio-cultural implications. However, such stories are not aimed at generalization. Rather, autoethnographic projects enable researchers to unpack experience and illuminate theory. In this case, our CAE exposes our experiences as immigrant black women faculty in PWIs, illustrating how our spirituality and religious identity serves as a buffer against the stresses of racisms and sexism. Seen in light of similar studies that critique the intersectional realities of those who are different from the dominant culture (e.g., Brown & William-White, 2010; Tilley-Lubbs, 2011; William-White, 2011), our study can help in suggesting the need for institutional changes that would bring about better, more just, social arrangements.

At a theoretical level, our CAE illuminates intersectionality theory in praxis – that is, what it means to be black, female, immigrant, and other identities – in particular organizational settings; in our case, PWI contexts. Thus, it brings intersectionality theory to life in the lived experience of two minoritized individuals. In illuminating theory, studies such as ours help to enhance the validity of such theories, because good theory reflects reality (Witz, 2007).

One can draw implications from our study in relation to others who are differentially placed, perceiving lessons that other differentially positioned individuals could resonate with and perhaps emulate. We have highlighted how our spirituality and religious identity enables us to engage with our work of teaching, research and service, and how these intersect with our non-academic roles, setting the example for future generations of black women scholars, and other minorities, in navigating the academic landscape (Dillard, 2006; Alston, 2012; Hernandez et al., 2015).

Finally, we recognize that our spirituality and religious identity can be seen in light of the broader topic of this book; in the sense that specifically, for us, it helps us to successfully navigate an often hostile context, and be productive, and successful academics in the midst of challenging realities. That is, for us, our spirituality and religious identity supports our ability to perform, to produce, and to persist. Without the challenges to our authority as academic leaders and professors, perhaps we would be a little less resilient, perhaps we would not have learned to become tempered radicals invested in the goals of institutional change, perhaps we would not have learned how to turn our challenges into learning opportunities. In other words, our story should be seen as an example of navigating nefarious organizational contexts by being all of who one truly is – a raced, gendered, classed … and spiritual/religious being.

References

Allison, A. M. W., & Broadus, P. R. B. (2009). Spirituality then and now: Our journey through higher education as women of faith. *New Directions for Teaching & Learning*, 2009(120), 77–86. doi: 10.1002/tl.379.

Alston, J. A. (2012). Standing on the promises: A new generation of Black women scholars in educational leadership and beyond. *International Journal of Qualitative Studies in Education*, 25(1), 127–9. doi: 10.1080/09518398.2011.647725.

Alston, J. A., & McClellan, P. A. (2011). *Herstories: Leading with the lessons of the lives of Black women activists*. New York: Peter Lang.

Anderson, L. (2006). Analytic autoethnography. *Journal of Contemporary Ethnography*, 35(4), 373–95. doi: 10.1177/0891241605280449.

Benefiel, M. (2005). The second half of the journey: Spiritual leadership for organizational transformation. *The Leadership Quarterly*, 16(5), 723–47.

Brown, A. F., & William-White, L. (2010). "We are not the same minority:" The narratives of two sisters navigating identity and discourse at public and private white institutions. *In* Robinson, C. C., & Clardy, P. (eds.), *Tedious journeys: Autoethnography by women of color in academe*. New York: Peter Lang, 149–76.

Brown, D. L., & Tylka, T. L. (2011). Racial discrimination and resilience in African American young adults: Examining racial socialization as a moderator. *Journal of Black Psychology*, 37(3), 259–85.

Catham-Carpenter, A. (2010). "Do thyself no harm:" Protecting ourselves as autoethnographers. *Journal of Research Practice*, 6(1). Retrieved from: http://jrp.icaap.org/index.php/jrp/article/view/213/222.

Chang, H., Ngunjiri, F. W., & Hernandez, K. C. (2013). *Collaborative autoethnography*. Walnut Creek: LeftCoast Press.

Chiorazzi, A. (October, 2015). The spirituality of Africa. Interview with Professor Jacob Olupona. Harvard Divinity School. Retrieved from: www.hds.harvard.edu/news/2015/10/07/spirituality-africa#.

Collins, P. H. (1999). Moving beyond gender: Intersectionality and scientific knowledge. *In* Ferree, M. M., Lorber, J., & Hess, B. B. (eds.), *Revisioning gender*. Thousand Oaks: Sage, 261–84.

(2008). *Black feminist thought: Knowledge, consciousness, and the politics of empowerment*. New York: Routledge.

Cozart, S. C. (2010). When the spirit shows up: An autoethnography of spiritual reconciliation with the academy. *Educational Studies*, 46(2), 250–69. doi: 10.1080/00131941003614929.

Creed, W. E. D. (2003). Voice lessons: Tempered radicalism and the use of voice and silence. *Journal of Management Studies*, 40(6), 1503–36. doi: 10.1111/1467-6486.00389.

Crenshaw, K. (1989). Demarginalizing the intersection of race and sex: A black feminist critique of antidiscrimination doctrine, feminist theory, and antiracist politics. *The University of Chicago Legal Forum*, (140), 139–67.

(1991). Mapping the margins: Intersectionality, identity politics, and violence against women of color. *Stanford Law Review*, 43(6), 1241–99.

Christman, D., & McClellan, R. (2008). "Living on barbed Wire:" Resilient women administrators in educational leadership programs. *Educational Administration Quarterly*, 44(1), 3–29. doi: 10.1177/0013161x07309744.

Christman, D. E., & McClellan, R. L. (2012). Discovering middle space: Distinctions of sex and gender in resilient leadership. *Journal of Higher Education*, 83(5), 648–70.

Dantley, M. E. (2003). Purpose-driven leadership: The spiritual imperative to guiding schools beyond high-stakes testing and minimum proficiency. *Education and Urban Society*, 35(3), 273–91.

(2005). Faith-based leadership: Ancient rhythms or new management? *International Journal of Qualitative Studies in Education*, 18(1), 16.

Delbecq, A. L. (2004). How the religious traditions of calling and spiritual friendship shaped my life as a teacher/scholar. *Management Communication Quarterly*, 17(4), 621–7. doi: 10.1177/0893318903262292.

Dill, B., & Zambrana, R. (2009). Emerging intersectionality: Race, glass, and gender in theory, policy and practice. Retrieved from: www.scribd.-com/doc/88390007/Bonnie-Thornton-Dill-amp-Ruth-Emid-Zambrana-Emerging-Intersections-Race-Class-And-Gender-in-Theory-Policy-And-Practice.

Dillard, C. B. (2006). *On spiritual strivings: Transforming an African American woman's academic life*. Albany, NY: State University of New York Press.

Dillard, C. B., Abdur-Rashid, D., & Tyson, C. A. (2000). My soul is a witness: Affirming pedagogies of the spirit. *International Journal of Qualitative Studies in Education*, 13(5), 447–62.

Duchon, D., & Ploman, D. A. (2005). Nurturing the spirit at work: Impact on work unit performance. *The Leadership Quarterly*, 16(5), 807–33.

Ellis, C. (1997). Evocative autoethnography: Writing emotionally about our lives. *In* Tierney, W., & Lincoln, Y. (eds.), *Representation and the text: Re-framing the narrative voice*. Albany, NY: SUNY, 115–39.

Ellis, C. (2007). Telling secrets, revealing lives: Relational ethics in research with intimate others. *Qualitative Inquiry*, 13(1), 3–29. doi: 10.1177/1077800406294947.

Fairholm, G. W. (1997). *Capturing the heart of leadership: Spirituality and community in the new American workplace*. Westport, CT: Praeger.

Fort, T. L. (1997). Religion and business ethics: The lessons from political morality. *Journal of Business Ethics*, 16(3), 263–73.

Fry, L. W. (2003). Toward a theory of spiritual leadership. *The Leadership Quarterly*, 14(6), 693–727.

(2005). Toward a theory of ethical and spiritual wellbeing, and corporate social responsibility through spiritual leadership. *In* Giacalone, R. A. (ed.), *Positive psychology in business ethics and corporate social responsibility*. Charleston, NC: IAP, 47–83.

Fry, L. (2008). Spiritual leadership: State-of-the-art and future directions for theory, research and practice. *In* Biberman, J., & Tishman, L. (eds.), *Spirituality in business: Theory, practice and future directions*. New York: Palgrave, 106–23.

(2013). Spiritual leadership and faith and spirituality in the workplace. *In* Neal, J. (ed.), *Handbook of faith and spirituality in the workplace*. New York: Springer, 697–704.

Fry, L. W., Vitucci, S., & Cedillo, M. (2005). Spiritual leadership and army transformation: Theory, measurement, and establishing a baseline. *The Leadership Quarterly*, 16(5), 835–62.

Fry, L. W., & Whittington, J. L. (2005). In search of authenticity: Spiritual leadership theory as a source of future theory, research and practice on authentic leadership. *In* Gardner, W. L., Avolio, B. J., & Walumbwa, F. (eds.), *Authentic leadership theory and practice: Origins, effects and development*. Oxford, UK: Elsevier Science, 183–200.

Hernandez, K. C. (2011). Spiritual introspection and praxis in teaching and assessment. *In* Chang, H., & Boyd, D. (eds.), *Spirituality in higher education: Autoethnographies*. Walnut Creek, CA: Left Coast Press, 163–79.

Hernandez, K. C., & Murray-Johnson, K. (2014). Towards a new construction of blackness: Being a black immigrant woman in US academe. Paper presented at the American Educational Research Association, Philadelphia, PA, April 2014.

Hernandez, K. C., & Murray-Johnson, K. (2015). Towards a different construction of blackness: Black immigrant scholars on racial identity development in the United States. *International Journal of Multicultural Education*, 17(2), 53–72. Retrieved from: www.dx.doi.org/10.18251/ijme.v17i2.1050.

Hernandez, K. C., & Ngunjiri, F. W. (2013). Relationships and communities in autoethnography. *In* Adams, T. E., Ellis, C., & Holman Jones, S. (eds.), *Handbook of autoethnography*. Walnut Creek: Left Coast Press, 262–80.

Hernandez, K. C., Ngunjiri, F. W., & Chang, H. (2015). Exploiting the margins in higher education: A collaborative autoethnography of three foreign-born female faculty of color. *International Journal of Qualitative Studies in Education*, 28(5), 533–51. doi: 10.1080/09518398.2014.933910.

Hill, P. C., & Pargament, K. I. (2003). Advances in the conceptualization and measurement of religion and spirituality. *American Psychologist*, 58(1), 64–74.

Hughes, S., Pennington, J. L., & Makris, S. (2012). Translating Autoethnography Across the AERA Standards: Toward understanding autoethnographic scholarship as empirical research. *Educational Researcher*, 41(6), 209–19. doi: 10.3102/0013189x12442983.

Hulko, W. (2009). The time-and context-contingent nature of intersectionality and interlocking oppressions. *Affilia*, 24(1), 44.

Jackson, K. T. (1999). Spirituality as a foundation for freedom and creative imagination in international business ethics. *Journal of Business Ethics*, 19(1), 61–70.

Lindholm, J. A., & Astin, H. S. (2006). Understanding the "interior" life of faculty: How important is spirituality? *Religion & Education*, 33(2), 64–90.

Levin, J., Chatters, L. M., & Taylor, R. J. (2005). Religion, health and medicine in african americans: Implications for physicians. *Journal of the National Medical Association*, 97(2), 237–49.

Lund Dean, K., Fornaciari, C. J., & McGee, J. J. (2003). Research in spirituality, religion and work: Walking the line between relevance and legitimacy. *Journal of Organizational Change Management*, 16(4), 378–95.

Madimbo, M. (2016). *Transformative and engaging leadership: Lessons from indegenous African women*. New York: Palgrave McMillan.

Meyerson, D. E. (2001). *Tempered radicals: How people use difference to inspire change at work*. Boston: Harvard Business School Press.

Meyerson, D. E., & Scully, M. A. (1995). Crossroads tempered radicalism and the politics of ambivalence and change. *Organization Science*, 6(5), 585–600.

Mitroff, I. I., & Denton, E. A. (1999). *A spiritual audit of corporate America: A hard look at spirituality, religion, and values in the workplace* (1st edn.). San Francisco: Jossey-Bass Publishers.

Moberg, D. (1990). Spiritual Maturity and Wholeness in the Later Years. *Journal of Religious Gerontology*, 7, 5–24. doi: 10.1300/J078V07N01_02.

Muhs, G. G. y., Niemann, Y. F., Gonzalez, C. G., & Harris, A. P. (eds.) (2013). *Presumed incompetent: The intersections of race and class for women in academia*. Boulder, CO: University of Colorado Press.

Ndlovu, P. (2016). *Discovering the spirit of Ubuntu leadership: Compassion, community, and respect*. New York: Palgrave Macmillan.

Ngunjiri, F. W. (2007). Rocking the boat without falling out: Spirited tempered radicals as agents of community transformation. *UCEA Review*, XLVI(3), 1–4.

(2010). *Women's spiritual leadership in Africa: Tempered radicals and critical servant leaders*. Albany: State University of New York Press.

(2011). Studying spirituality and leadership: A personal journey. In Chang, H., & Boyd, D. (eds.), *Spirituality in higher education: Autoethnographies*. Walnut Creek, CA: Left Coast Press, 183–98.

Ngunjiri, F. W., & Christo-Baker, E. A. (2012). Breaking the stained glass ceiling: African ascended women's strategies for thriving as leaders (Editorial). *Journal of Pan African Studies* 5(2). Available at www.jpanafrican.com/vol5no2.htm.

Ngunjiri, F. W., Hernandez, K. C., & Chang, H. (2010). Living autoethnography: Connecting life and research [editorial]. *Journal of Research Practice*, 6(1). Available at http://jrp.icaap.org/index.php/jrp/article/view/241/186.

Ngunjiri, F. W., Hernandez, K. C., & Elbert, C. (2014). Resiliency at the intersections: Black women faculty surviving and thriving in the academy. Paper presented at the American Educational Research Association, Chicago, IL, April 16–20.

Ngunjiri, F. W., Madimbo, M., Ndlovu, P., & Aziz, A. (2010). Studies on female leadership in three African settings. Panel of Papers presented at International Leadership Association annual meeting, Boston, October 28.

Ospina, S., & Foldy, E. (2009). A critical review of race and ethnicity in the leadership literature: Surfacing context, power and the collective dimensions of leadership. *The Leadership Quarterly*, 20(6), 876–96.

Paris, P. J. (1995). *The spirituality of African peoples: The search for a common moral discourse*. Minneapolis: Fortress Press.

Ramsey, J. L., & Blieszner, R. (1999). *Spiritual resiliency in older women: Models of strength for challenges through the life span*. Thousand Oaks: Sage Publications.

Richardson, A., & Loubier, C. (2008). Intersectionality and leadership. *International Journal of Leadership Studies*, 3(2), 142–61.

Robinson, C. C., & Clardy, P. (2010). *Tedious journeys : autoethnography by women of color in academe*. New York: Peter Lang.

Rosette, A. S., & Livingston, R. W. (2012). Failure is not an option for Black women: Effects of organizational performance on leaders with single versus dual-subordinate identities. *Journal of Experimental Social Psychology*, 48(5), 1162–7. doi: 10.1016/j.jesp.2012.05.002.

Sanchez-Hucles, J. V., & Davis, D. D. (2010). Women and women of color in leadership: Complexity, identity, and intersectionality. *American Psychologist*, 65(3), 171.

Sang, K., Al-Dajani, H., & Ozbilgin, M. (2013). Frayed careers of migrant female professors in British academia: An intersectional perspective. *Gender, Work & Organization*, 20(2), 158–71. doi: 10.1111/gwao.12014.

Shields, S. (2008). Gender: An intersectionality perspective. *Sex Roles*, 59(5), 301–11.

Smith, B. P. (2007). Student ratings of teaching effectiveness: An analysis of end-of-course faculty evaluations. *College Student Journal*, 41(4), 788.

Solorzano, D. G. (1998). Critical race theory, race and gender microaggressions, and the experience of Chicana and Chicano scholars. *International Journal of Qualitative Studies in Education*, 11(1), 121–36.

Solorzano, D., Ceja, M., & Yosso, T. (2000). Critical race theory, racial microaggressions, and campus racial climate: The experiences of African American college students. *Journal of Negro Education*, 69(1/2), 60–73.

Teti, M., Martin, A. E., Ranade, R., Massie, J., Malebranche, D. J., Tschann, J. M., & Bowleg, L. (2012). "I'm a keep rising. I'm a keep going forward, regardless:" Exploring black men's resilience amid sociostructural challenges and stressors. *Qualitative Health Research*, 22(4), 524–33.

Tilley-Lubbs, G. A. (2011). The coal miner's daughter gets a PhD. *Qualitative Inquiry*, 17(8), 720–2. doi: 10.1177/1077800411420669.

Tillman, L. C. (2012). Inventing ourselves: an informed essay for Black female scholars in educational leadership. *International Journal of Qualitative Studies in Education*, 25, 119–26. doi: 10.1080/09518398.2011.647728.

Turner, C. S. V. (2002). Women of Color in Academe. *The Journal of Higher Education*, 73(1), 74–93. doi: 10.1080/00221546.2002.11777131.

Utsey, S. O., Bolden, M. A., Lanier, Y., & Williams III, O. (2007). Examining the role of culture-specific coping as a predictor of resilient outcomes in african americans from high-risk urban communities. *Journal of Black Psychology*, 33(1), 75–93.

Utsey, S. O., Giesbrecht, N., Hook, J., & Stanard, P. M. (2008). Cultural, sociofamilial, and psychological resources that inhibit psychological distress in African Americans exposed to stressful life events and race-related stress. *Journal of Counseling Psychology*, 55(1), 49–62.

Whatley, A. (1998). Gifted women and teaching: A compatible choice? *Roeper Review*, 21(2), 117–24. doi: 10.1080/02783199809553942.

William-White, L. (2011). Dare I write about oppression on sacred ground [Emphasis Mine]. *Cultural Studies=Critical Methodologies*, 11(3), 236–42. doi: 10.1177/1532708611409535.

Witz, K. G. (2007). "Awakening to" an aspect in the other: On developing insights and concepts in qualitative research. *Qualitative Inquiry*, 13(2), 235–58. doi: 10.1177/1077800406295634.

Zavala, M. W., Maliski, S. L., Kwan, L., Fink, A., & Litwin, M. S. (2009). Spirituality and quality of life in low-income men with metastatic prostate cancer. *Psycho-Oncology*, 18, 753–61.

Index

Aarti (puja), 188
Abbas, Tahir, 41
Abbasid Era (Islam), 112, 113, 118
Abercrombie & Fitch, 5, 416
Abraham, Philip, 180
Abrahamic faiths, Africa, 224
Abu Musa, 111
accommodations, 42, 61–63, 170, 389, 429–30
  acceptance, 431
  denial, 434
  ethics of, 346
  faith-focused, 433
  faith-friendly, 434
  faith-frosty, 434
  India, 177, 182, 187, 190–92
  institutionalized for religious majorities, 395
  intermediate position, 432
  multiple diversity strands, 126
  New Zealand, 204
  organizations, 434
  reasonable, 419–20, 429
  refusal of, 430–31
  religion-based, 4, 11–12, 15, 23, 43, 45, 46, 52, 62, 66, 74, 75, 152, 156–58, 157, 167, 178, 272, 281–84, 289, 291, 322, 375, 391, 394, 398, 436
    Canada, 338–43, 345
      Muslims, 343–45, 345–46
    France, 268, 274–75, 287
    Israel, 167
    New Zealand, 374
    Title VII, U.S., 390, *See also* Title VII
  U.S., balance of, 67
  workplace, 43
action, collective, 459
Acts of Faith (Patel, Eboo), 326
advocacy, 451

Afghanistan, women in business, 114
Africa, 20, 223–57
  Abbasid Era power, 113
  Abrahamic faiths, 224
  business, seekers, 225
  diversity, 20
    regional, 224
  post-Abbasid era, 113
  religiosity, profound, 224
  spirituality, 223–33
    business, and, 224–25
    defined, 225
    growth, 225
    holism, harmony, 225
    seekers, 225
    transcendence of self, 225
  Western exploitation of, 223
African ascent, 460
age, 210, 371, 455
  as a human right, 87
  respect for, 186
agnostics, U.S., 63–64, 308
Ahmadi sect (Pakistan), 50
Ahura Mazda, 364
Al Jahiz, Abu Othman Ibn Omer, 111, 112
Al Kindy, Al Mugdad Ibn Omer, 112
Al-Andelesy, 118
Al-Farsi, Sulyman, 112
Ali, Abbas J., 119
Ali, Imam, 111
Ali, Maulana Muhammad, 117–18
Ali, Terry, 6
Allah, 362
Allegory of the Cave, Plato's, 248–49
Al-Maki, 119
Al-Maki, Abu Talb, 115
Al-Mawardi, 108, 115
Ambedkar, Bhimrao, 214–15
Ambidge, Chris, 228

Ambitabha, 202
American Telephone & Telegraph (AT&T), 44
America's Changing Religious Landscape, 63
Amnesty International, 109, 114–15
Angelou, Maya, 450
anthropology, 127
Anti-Defamation League, 141, 171
Anti-Discrimination Board Conciliated Cases Reports (ADB) NSW, 150
Anti-Discrimination Committee, 6
anti-religious perspectives, 24
anti-Semitism, 5, 18, 123, 127, 130, 132, 133, 141, 146, 152, 158–59, 163–65, 164–65, 171, 344
 Australia workplaces, 150–53
 Christian-based, 134
 Europe rankings, 165
 France, 160
 spread of via colonialism, 42
 violent, 131–32
apatheism, 61
Apostle Paul, 84
Apple, Inc., 205
Arabs, 118
 India, invasion of, 180
 Israel, workers in, 124
 Ommeyade era, 113
 pre-Islam, 112
 working in Haredi environments, 169
Argentina, anti-Semitic violence, 131
Aristotle, 96
Armstrong, Karen, 313
aroha (Maori), 73
Arthashashtra, 184
Ashforth, Blake E., 225, 253–55, 253
Ashkenazi Jews, 153, 168
Ashkenazi Judaism, 170
Asian-Americans, income and education gap, 129
Asians, 167
 discrimination, 152
Asia–Pacific region, 14–15, 21, 354–81, 356–60
 Australia, 365–69
 demography, 198, 354, 359–60
 diversity, religious, 359–61
 Japan, 369–73
 New Zealand, 373–75

Pacific Islands, 375–78
 religious diversity management, 379–80
 South Korea, 378–79
Astin, Helen S., 441
astrology, India in, 188
atheism, 5, 60, 69, 311
atheists, 42, 44, 45, 62, 308
 discrimination against, 46, 61
 U.S., 63–64
Auckland Buddhist Vihara, 204
AUM. *See* OM
Aung San Suu Kyi, 198
Australia, 170, 365–69
 Aboriginal peoples, 73, 365
 British invasion of, 146
 demography, 365–66
 diversity, prison population, 367
 education and employment demography, Jewish, 148–50
 employment gender gap, Jews and, 148–50
 health care, 368–69
 Islamic pluralism, 366–67
 Jews, 145–53
  demography, 146–50
  employment demographics, 148–50
  workplace aspects, 150–53
 law enforcement, 367–68
 spiritual diversity, 369
 workplace issues, 151–53
Australia/Israel & Jewish Affairs Council, 152
Australian Human Rights Commission (AHRC), 150–51
Autism Spectrum Disorder (ASD), 238
autoethnography, collaborative (CAE), 447–48, 462
Avalokitesvara, 202
Avesta, 364
avoda (Judaism), 140
Avtar, 179
Azaan, 112

Baby Loup nursery (France), 279–81, 416
Badinter Committee, 299
Baghdad, 111
Baha'i, 308
Baha'i, U.S., 64

Bahrain, 127
Bailey, James R., 227
Bailey, John, 337–38
Bainbridge, William Sims, 40
Bainimararama, Frank, 378
baptism, 86, 92, 97, 243
Baptists, 361
Barbers
   Abbasid Era power, 113
Bataclan, shooting in, 131
Bay, Darlene, 91
Belgium, 165
   anti-Semitic violence in, 132
Bell, Ella Louise, 249
Bender, Courtney, 46
Bendl, Regine, 178
Benedict XVI, Pope, 94, 97
Benefiel, Margaret, 444–45
Berger, Peter L., 99–100
Bergin, Allen E., 92
Berman, Paul, 290–91
Berry, John W., 346
Better Together Interfaith Alliance, 319
Bhagavad Gita, 183–86, 362
Bhakti, 186
Bhakti Yoga, 184
bias
   conformist, 69
   in-group, 62
   prestige, 69
   teliological, 69
Bible, 183, 243, 361
   Exodus, 98
Bicentennial Oral History Project (New South Wales), 152
biculturalism, 72
bigotry, 116
Bilal, 112
Birdwood, George, 180
Birla group, 190
Blum, Léon, 164
BMO financial group, 345
Board of Deputies (UK), 153
Boas, Franz, 127, 139
Bodhinyanarama, 204
bodhisattva, 202, 212
Bolman, Lee G., 397
Brahman (Hinduism), 179, 181, 183
Brahmaviharas (Buddhism), 19, 198, 200–1, 205, 208, 209, 211, 215–16

British Airways (BA), 6, 44, 48, 98–99
British East India Company (India), 180
Brunei, corporations in, 2
Brussels Jewish Museum, 131
Brussels Labor Court, 278
Bruton, Richard, 2
Buber, Martin, 84
Buddha, 201–2, 209, 212, 370, 372
Buddhism, 12, 13, 19, 177, 198–216, 266, 312, 359, *See also* Zen Buddhism
   beliefs, 201–5
   business, 215
   business elements, 204–6
   China, 207–8
   commercialization of, 207–8
   deities, 202
   demographics, global, 199
   diversity in, 212
   exclusivity within, 213–15
   gender in, 210–11
   history, 201–5
   human resource management, 205–6
   illusion, worldly, 201
   international demographics, 206–8
   Japan, 207
   leadership, 208
   Mahayana, 202
   mindfulness, 211–12
   negative aspects of, 213–15, 213–15
   New Zealand, 203–4
   organizational culture, 199–201
   origins, 179
   philosophy, 215
   pluralism in, 212
   positive aspects, 214–15
   scriptures, 199, 201–2
   South Korea, 378
   Sri Lanka, 209–11
      violence against Christians and Hindus, 213–14
   suffering, 201–2
   Thailand, 207
   Theravada, 202, 207
   Tibetan, 215
   U.S., 211
   violence against other sects, 213–14
   workplaces, 212–13
Buddhist Society of New Zealand, 203

Buddhists, 5, 157, 308
  Dalit, 214–15
  OM, 181
Budhwar, Pawan, 187
Buisson, Ferdinand, 268
Bund (humanistic Judaism), 123, 135
burka, 286
Burma (Myanmar), 198
Busdugan, Raluca, 332
business
  Buddhist principles-driven, 205–6
  conviction, companies of, 293–96
  diversity, 307
  France, secularism, 286–93
  French secularism, 284–85
  global fragmentation or unity, 273
  moderation in (Islam), 119
  normative ethics (Christian), in, 91
  performance in, 38
  repulsion of harm in (Islam), 118
  secularism, workplace, 286–93
  spirituality, 224–25
  spirituality and work, 251, 252–55
  tendency, companies, 293–96
  Thailand, 207
Bussie, Jacqueline, 308, 316, 317, 318, 327

Caliph
  fourth, Imam Ali, 111–12, 115
  second, Omer, 111
Campaign Against anti-Semitism (UK), 158
Canada, 20–21, 331–49, 331
  discrimination, religion-based illegal, 333
  Muslims
    demography, 333–34
    education, 334–35
    sentiments against, 334
    unemployment, 334–35
    women, 335–36
    workplace, 336–38
  religious freedom, 418
Canadian
  Muslim immigrants, assimilation, 334
Canadian Charter of Rights and Freedoms, 333

Canadian Council of Muslim Women, 335, 343–45
Canadian Human Rights Tribunal, 339–40
Cann, David E., 40
capitalism, 40, 162, 232
  global, 18, 106, 109, 120
  indigenous, 73
Capra, Fritjof, 229
Cargill, 5
Caritas in Veritate, 94
Carpenter, Belinda, 367
caste system, 201, 214–15, 362
  India, 186–88, 189, 192
catechism, 86
Catholic Church, 40, 243, 298
Catholicism, 86
  marriage, 293
Catholics, 5, 94
  U.S., 63–64
Cathy, S. Truett, 97–98
censorship, state-sponsored, 127
Central Asia, post-Abbasid era, 113
Central Europe, Jews from, 128
chain of causation, Buddhism, 202
Chang, Heewon, 447
Chaplin, Sherly, 44
charity, 96, 188, 204
  Islam, 117
Charlie Hebdo terrorist attacks, 427
Charter of Quebec Values, 343–45
Chaves, Mark, 40
Chick-fil-A, 17, 83, 97–98
  Closed on Sunday Policy, 97–98
child labor, 395
China, 206
  Buddhism, 207–8
  Tibet, occupation of, 215
  workplace issues, 395
Christ, 12, 84–85, 86, 92, 95–97, 97, 361
Christian moral identity, 99
Christianity, 12, 13, 17, 19, 40, 46, 83–100, 266, 359, 372
  beliefs, 361–62
  Buddhist violence, 213–14
  calendar, 156
  charity, 96
  colonialism, 361
  diversity of sects, 83

Index 475

eras, 91
ethics in faith integration, 89–92
Fiji, 377
global demographics, contemporary, 85
historical emergence, 84–85
identity, 92–97
India, 177
moral theology, 95
morals, 95
Nicene Creed, 85
origins of, 84
PacMoore Corporation, 406
Patristic period, 91
religious curricula, 311–14
South Korea, 378
tenets of, 85–87
tension with Judaism, 84
tensions with pluralism, 87–88
ties to Judaism, 130
U.S. workforce dominant, 392
workplace aspects, 46, 87–88, 92–94
workplaces, U.S., 66
Christians, 5, 42, 62, 157, 159–61, 308
anti-abortion in U.S., 63
identity, 84
Islam, early, 112
religious prohibitions in France, 160
U.S., 307
diversity growth, 64
fundamentalists, 63
Christians, Mennonite, 295–96
Christman, Dana E., 454, 455
Christmas, 189–90, 192, 339, 361
Chung, Tsai Chih, 213
Church of England, 365
church-state institutions, 40
church-state separation, 39
Civil Rights Act, 87
Civil Rights Act of 1964. *See also* Title VII
civil rights, historical challenges, 389
class, 39, 46, 62, 371, 463
Islam, 111
Islam, early, 108
Marxism, 138
religion and, 16
Clegg, Stewart, 227
Clemenceau, George, 291

clothing, religious, 3, 5, 15, 16, 20, 41, 44, 45, 61, 67, 89, 183, 274–75, 278–79, 279–81, 281–82, 281–84, 284, 286, 292, 315, 335, 338–43, 344, 363, 375, 392, 431, 437
Clovis, 159
Cohen, Laurie, 210
colonialism, 42, 231, 255
Hindu-Muslim violence, 42
Commission on Religious Freedom, 418
Community Security Trust (CST) (UK), 158
Companies Act (India), 191
compassion, 12, 19, 63, 198, 200, 201, 209, 211, 215, 229, 232, 310, 313, 315, 328, 380, 455
Concordia College, 20, 305–29
Conestoga, 295–96
conflicts, inter-religion
Christianity, 5
Hindus and Christians, 5
Muslims and Buddhists, 5
Muslims and Jews, 5
conflicts, intra-religion
Islam, 5
Judaism, 5
Sunni and Shia Muslims, 5
conformity, 69
Confucians, U.S., 64
Constantine, emperor, 85
Constitutional Court (Germany), 278
conversion, religious, 84, 128, 138, 139, 159, 214, 243, 308, 312, 332, 376
conviction, companies of, 293–96
Cooke, Fang Lee, 187
Coq, Guy, 268
core values, diversity in, 2
corporate "micro-inequality", 423
corporate policy, religious diversity, 421–23
corporate typologies, workplace discrimination, 423–24
countries with Muslim majorities (CMM), 105–6, 108, 109, 113, 120
Cour de Cassation (France), 275, 280–81, 280, 282, 289, 293, 294

Court of Human Rights of British Columbia, 275
Court of Human Rights of Ontario, 274–75
Cowen, Zelman, Sir, 146
Craft, William, 316, 318
creativity, 71, 107, 116, 178, 227, 252, 305, 307, 444, 446, 456
  lack of, 254
Crémieux, Adophe, 164
Crenshaw, Kimberle, 442
critical spirituality, 460, 461
Crossman, Joanna, 369
Crowne, William, 189
crucifixion, 96
Crusades, 83
culture, deterioration of, 270
culturegram, 448
Cuypers, Ilya R. P., 69, 72
Czech Republic, secularization in, 39

Dahlab, Lucia, 279
Dalai Lama, XIV, 198, 208, 215, 313, 319, 330, 380
Dalit Buddhists, 214–15
Dantley, Michael E., 445, 460, 461
Dark Ages, Christianity, 91
David, King, 84
Dawad, Mohamed Ibn, 111
Deal, Terrence E., 397
Deists, U.S., 64
Delbecq, Andre L., 461–62
Democratic Republic of Congo, 243
Denmark, anti-Semitic violence, 131
Denton, Elizabeth A., 178, 444
Deobandi Islam, 5, 6, 9, 29, 42, 314, 363
development, stages of, 229
Dewey, John, 298–99
Dhamma, 201–2
Dharma
  Buddhism, 201
  Islam (ethics), 184, 186
Diaspora, 170
Diaspora, African, 445
Dierksmeier, Claus, 94, 96
dietary elements, 43, 45, 49, 123, 156, 170, 190, 191, 283
Dill, Bonnie Thornton, 443

directing model of workplace spirituality, 253–54
disability, 44
discrimination, 16, 23, 37, 116, 141, 294, 410, 421, 460, *See also* anti-Semitism; class; ethnicity; gender; legal cases; LGBTQ; race; visible minorities; workplace
  absence of, 129
  after attacks, 6
  Asians, 152
  Buddhism, 213–14
  Canada, Muslims, 336–38, 340–43
  European workplaces, 281
  faith-based companies, 401
  France, higher ed, 163–64
  higher education, 442
  Hindu against Dalit Buddhists, 214–15
  intersectionality, 443
  LBGTQ, 423
  Muslims, 152
  organizational, 3–4
  religion-based, 3–4, 4, 41, 43
    atheists, 46
    Australia, 150–53
    Canada Muslims, 333, 334, 335–36
    Christian, 48
    Jewish, 156–57
    Muslim countries, 113–15
    rejection of in Islam, 115
    U.S., 46, 66–68
    UK, 42, 99
      Islamic penalty in, 43
  religious, 391, 394
    New Zealand, 375
  unperceived by majority, 157
  workplace, 52, 106, 227
displaced persons, European Australia, 146
diversity, 242, 252, 273
  adaptation to, 2
  Africa, 223–25
  benefits to corporations, 106–7
  Buddhism, 206, 212
  business, countries with Muslim majorities, 108
  creativity, 107
  definitions of, 223–24

Index 477

frames, 397
holistic approaches to, 37
India, 179
industrial countries, 37–46
inter-religious in U.S., 67
intra-religious in U.S., 67
Islam, 107, 112–13, 116–21
Islam, early era, 105
levels of, 67
megatrends, 355
organizations, 434
religion
　human rights, 393
religious, 306–8, 306, 377–78
　Africa, 255
　business, 307
　Canada, 336
　management, 379–80
　organizations, 434
religious and spiritual, 3
religious curricula, 311–14
religious, positive aspects, 37–38
schools, 344
spirituality facilitates, 229
U.S., demographic shifts, 64
workforce, 37
workplace, 266–67
workplace (Islam), 116
workplace Canada
　Muslims, 343–45
workplace management, 75
diversity management, 4, 395–98
　direct and indirect integration, 75
diversity paradoxes
　management of, 17
diversity research
　arguments against, 124–28
diversity, obstructions to, 109–10
Diwali, 189–90, 192, 339, 362, 363, 374
Dow, Douglas, 69, 72
dress codes, 3, 168, 191, 379, *See also*
　clothing, religious
Dreyfus Affair, 160
Dreyfus, Alfred, 160, 164
Druids, U.S., 64
Druze, U.S., 64
duality of structure, 38
Dukkha, 201–2
Dunn, Greig S., 228
Durkheim, Émile, 39, 69, 127, 139, 265, 269

East India Company, 180
Easter, 339, 361
Eastern Europe, 135
　Jews in, 145
Eastern Orthodox Church, 85, 94
Eck, Diana, 305, 306, 307, 311
Ecumenism, Christian, 361
EDI. *See* equality, diversity, and
　inclusion (EDI)
Educate Together model, 2
egalitarianism, 266, 271, 434
　Saudi Arabia, 108
Egypt, post-Abbasid era, 113
Ehsan (social justice, Islam), 12, 109, 116, 119–21
　business, 119–20
Eid, 192
eight-fold path, Buddhism, 201, 202
Elauf, Samantha, 5
Ellwood, Robert S., 203
Elmenyawi, Salam, 345
Emmons, Robert A., 92
emotional intelligence, 242
empathy, 19, 73, 74, 200–201, 201, 212, 216, 441
Employers Forum of Beliefs, 49
Employment Appeal Tribunal (EAT) (UK), 48
Employment Equality (Religion and Belief) Regulations, 47
Employment Equality Framework
　Directive, 87, 389, 390, 392, 394
Employment Equity Act, 332
employment gap, UK, 48
Employment Tribunal, 47
enabling model of workplace
　spirituality, 252–53
Enlightenment, 91
environment, pluralistic, 6
Epstein, Edwin E., 89
Equal Employment Opportunity
　Commission (EEOC) (U.S.), 15, 42, 44, 66, 391
equality, diversity, and inclusion (EDI), 126
　conference, 2009, 127
　conference, 2015, 127
　research, 128, 132, 135–37
equality, 20, 110, 248, 269, 273, 297, 346
　corporate policy, 419

equality (*cont.*)
  France, 162
  Islam, 111–12, 115, 120
  private firms, France, 419
  private firms, UK, 419
  religious freedom, 419–20
Equality Act of 2010 (UK), 42, 47, 419
Equality and Human Rights Commission (EHRC), 48
Equality Exchange Program (UK), 49
equanimity, 12, 19, 200, 201, 209, 212, 216
Erez, Miriam, 38
Erickson, Erik, 229
Ertug, Gokhan, 69, 72
Estonia, secularization in, 39
ethic, embodied, 92
ethical approach, normative, 90–92
ethics, 38, 51, 140
  Africa, 255
  Aristotelian, 96
  autoethnography, 449
  business, 90
  Christian faith integration, 89–92
  Christianity, in, 83, 99
  difference-centered, 273
  Islam, in, 106–21
  Islamic, 109–12
  moral, 90
  reason and cognition in, 91
  spirituality, 231
  theological, 90
ethnic groups, minority, 45
ethnic minorities, 15, 338, 340
ethnicity, 23, 62, 223, 306, 441
  and discrimination, 43
  and religion
    intersectionality, Jewish, 133–36
  as a human right, 87
  equanimity in, 111
  ethno-psychiatry, 134
  intertwined with religion, 46
  religion and, 16
ethnocentricity, 457
ethnography, 10
ethnology, 127
Etidal (moderation, Islam), 116, 118–19
Eurobarometer, 141
Europe
  active neutrality model, 285–86
  intrinsic rights, 418
  separation-cooperation model, 285–86
Europe, secularization in, 39
European Convention on Human Rights, 48, 285, 286
European Court of Human Rights (ECHR), 6, 48, 278, 279
European Group for Organizational Studies conference, 2013, 127
European Human Rights Convention, 418
European Union, 158, 394
  Court of Justice, 281
  Fundamental Rights Agency, 141
  Jewish economic standing, 133
  religious diversity in, 46
  secularism, 285–86
European Union Court of Justice, 282
Evangelical Lutheran Church in America (ELCA), 20, 305, 309, 317–18, 317, 324, 325
Eweida, Nadia, 6, 17, 44, 48, 83, 98–99, 416
Ewest, Timothy, 89
Executive Council of Australian Jewry, 152
existential spirituality, 230
Exodus, 98, 129
EY (formerly Ernst & Young), 6

Faith and Work initiative, Princeton University, 407
faith at work movement, 1, 433
faith integration framework, 14, 21, 389
faith-avoiding organizations, 398–401
faith-based communities, conservative, 45
faith-based organization, 401–2
Faith-Friendly Company study, 407–11
faith-friendly frame
  workplace positivity, 410
faith-friendly organizations, 402–3
  benefits, 402
Faith-Friendly Scorecard, 398
Faith-Friendly Scorecard, efficacy of, 406
faith-related identity development, 17

faith-safe organizations, 402
faith-work integration, 441
fatalism, 184, 186
Faulkner, Sandra L., 132
Fernando, Weerahannadige D. A., 210
Fiji, 377–78
  Christianity, 377
  coups, 377–78
  religious diversity, 377–78
financial crisis, global, 236
flexibility, organizational, 4
Fo Guang Shan, 204
Ford Foundation, 327
Forniciari, Charles T., 448
Forum on Faith and Life (Concordia College), 305, 309, 315–18, 316, 317, 318, 319, 320, 322, 325, 326, 329
Foundation for the Preservation of the Mahayana Tradition, 203
France, 11, 164–65, 170, 264–300
  anti-Semitic violence, 131–33
  business and religion, 271
  clinic for Shoah survivors, 134
  freedom, subjectivity and objectivity, 418
  Jewish demography, 161–62
  Jewish economic standing, 134
  Jews, 145, 159–65
    emancipation of, 160, 162, 164
    literary portrayals, 164–65
    regional treatment in, 160
  Jews, expulsion from, 160–61
  Law of 1905 (laïcité), 267, 275, 277, 284, 291, 425
  legal cases, 279–81
  Muslims, 268, 271–72
  religion-based violence in, 5, 13
  religions, recognized, 426
  religious favoritism in, 163–64
  religious freedom, 418
  secularism, 162, 290, 299
    workplace, 286–93
  visibility, religious, 271
  workplace
    accommodation perspectives, 23
    issues, 161–64, 267–69
Francis, Pope, 106, 361
freedom, 417–19
freedom, religious

corporate attitudes, 433
French Labor Code, 299
French Revolution, 160, 162, 271, 288, 290
Fuchs, Josef, 95, 99
functionalism, 38
Fundamental Rights Agency (EU), 141, 158–59, 164–65, 171

Gandhi, Mahatma, 183, 189, 214
Gati, Efrat, 38
Gaza and rockets war, 131
Gbowee, Leymah, 325
gender, 23, 43, 46, 133, 191, 238, 242, 246, 250, 251, 306, 335, 371, 441, 463
  as a human right, 87
  diversity research, 125–26
  employment gap in Australia, Jews and, 148–50
  equality, 266
  Hinduism, 362
  intersectionality, 443
  Islam, 110, 111, 114
  Islam, early, 108
  lack of civil rights for women, 127
  pay gap, 106
  Sri Lanka, 210–11
  U.S., religion data, 65
  workplaces, Islamic, 114
gender pay gap, 48
gender wage gap
  Canadian Muslim women, 336
Generation X, U.S.
  religious unaffiliation, 64–65
German Basic Law, 418
Ghanbarpour, Christina, 372
Giddens, Anthony, 38
Gidley, Ben, 153–54
Giordan, Guiseppe, 355
Global Compact, 394
Global Peace Index, 204
globalization, 38, 39, 107, 264–65, 266
  business, of, 105
God, 46, 69, 84, 85, 95, 96, 98, 108, 110, 112, 115, 123, 129, 179, 187, 188, 214, 228, 230, 240, 243, 245, 246, 247, 314, 361, 362, 363, 364, 372, 408, 445, 448

God at work movement, 1
goddesses
  Buddhist, 202, 207
  Hindu, 362
Gödel, Kurt, 296
gods, 269, 298, 373, 374
  Buddhist, 202
  Hindu, 179, 362
Goenka, S. N., 198
Gonzalez, Phillippe, 272
Gorsuch, Richard L., 69
graduation rates, 106
Granth Sahib, 183
Greek Orthodox Church. *See* Eastern Orthodox Church
Griffith, Andrew, 331
Gröschl, Stefan, 178
Grossi, Carolyn, 345
Guanyin, 207
Gulf States, foreign workers in, 113–15
Gunawardana, Samanthi J., 210
Guru, 186
Guru Granth Sahib, 363
Guru Nanak, 363
Gurukulum (India), 181
Gyan Yoga, 184
Gyasto, Tenzin, 380, *See* Dalai Lama, XIV

Hadith, 49, 107
haiku, 202, 205, 215
halal, 49, 189, 355
Halal, 156
HALDE, 279, 292, 427
Halimi, Ilan, 131
Halli, Shiva S., 332
Hanson, Mark, Bishop, 317
hāpai (Maori), 73
Haredi Judaism, 123–24, 154, 168–70
  Arabs in workplaces, 169
  gender roles and work, 168–70
  Israeli workforce in, 168–69
Harijan, 214–15
Harrison, David A., 416
Härtel, Charmine, 10
Harvard University Pluralism Project, 306
Hauerwas, Stanley, 94, 99
Hecht, Michael L., 132
Helly, Denise, 337

hermeneutics, 38, 94, 99, 234
  economic, 94
Hernandez, Kathy-Ann C., 447
Heschel, Abraham Joshua, Rabbi, 317
Hewlett Packard (HP), 46
Hick, Joanna, 354
High Council for Integration, 292
higher education, 441–63
  France, discrimination in, 163–64
  integrating faiths, 13
  leadership, 442
  minoritized individuals within, 443
higher education, Christian (CHE), 442
hijab, 3, 5, 16, 41, 45, 61, 278–79, 279–81, 281, 335, 338–43, 344, 375
Hinduism, 13, 46, 177–92, 266, 312, 359, 362
  beliefs, 179–81, 183–86, 188–92, 362
  caste system, 214–15
  holidays, 189–90, 192, 193–94
  India, 19
  origins of, 179–81
  symbols, 181–82
  teachings, 183–86
Hindus, 5, 43, 157, 198, 308
  U.S., 64
  education and income, 65
  religion switching, 65
Hirono, Tatsushi, 372
Hite, Linda M., 250
Hitler, Adolf, 151
Hobby Lobby Stores, 295–96
Hola Mahalla, 363
Holi, 189–90, 192, 362
holidays, religious, 3, 66, 156–57, 339
  Christian, 361
  Hinduism, 189–90, 192, 193–94
  India, 14, 193–94
  Judaism, 156
Holocaust. *See* Shoah
Holy Spirit (Christianity), 86
Home Depot, 274
homophobia, 41
Honda (Japan), 371
Honda Motorcycle and Scooters India Ltd, 189
Hotei, 202

Huglo, Jean-Guy, 292
human resource management (HRM), 8, 21, 66, 74, 109, 119, 121, 191, 346, 379
  Buddhism, 205–6, 206
  India, 186, 187, 189
human rights
  religious, 395
  religious diversity, 393
Human Rights Watch, 115
humanistic Judaism (*Bund*), 123
humanists, 95
Hungary, 165
Hyde, Allen, 337–38

Icelandic Constitution, 418
identity, 37, 45, 60–75, 139–40, 251, 431, 448, 463
  Africa, 255
  African, 225
  blackness, 457
  Christian, 84, 92–97, 99
  collective, 74
  complexity, 441–63
  concealable, 67–68
  desacralization of, 269
  ethical, 459
  ethnic, 297
  French, 162
  individual, 420–21
  Jewish, 126–28, 129, 132, 159, 162
  mapping, 448
  othering, 270
  personal, 231
  privilege and discrimination, 442
  race, gender, class, 443
  race, migration status, religion, 442
  racialized, 450
  religious, 1, 24, 28, 61, 99, 297, 306
    visible, 416
  religious development of, 68–69
  resilience, 455
  spiritual, 459, 460–61
  spiritual/religious, 446, 449–51
  stigmatism and, 67, 126
  tempered radicals, 456–60
  visible, 16, 67–68, 83, 121
  workplace, safety in, 75

identity, visible
  private and public sectors, 416
identity-based differences, 37–38
Idliby, Ranya Tabari, 334
Id-ul-Fitr, 363
Ikhwan-us-Safa (Brothers of Purity), 108
immigrants, 114
  Muslim countries, 109, 127
  U.S., religiosity in, 64
immigration, 39, 153, 331
  Australia, Jews to, 147–48
  New Zealand, 203
  sentiments against, 331
  UK trends, 61
Immigration Act (New Zealand), 204
Immigration Policy Review (New Zealand), 204
Inamori, Kazuo, 205
inclusion, culture of, 53
income inequality, 106
Independent, The, 158
India, 14–15
  British era, 180–81, 191
  Buddhism, 201
  caste system, 186–88, 189, 192
  Constitution of, 182, 189
  context sensitivity, 179–81
  Dalai Lama exile, 198
  Dalit Buddhism, 214–15
  demography, religious, 182
  diversity, 179
  ethnic violence, 189, 191–92
  family dynamics, 186–87, 186–88
  Hinduism, 19, 177–92
  history, 179
  holidays, religious, 189–90, 192, 193–94
  Mahindra and Mahindra Tech, 190
  management in, 75
  pluralistic worldviews, 180
  religious inclusiveness, 177
  secularism, constitutional, 182, 189, 190–92
  social hierarchy, 185–88
  violence in, 183, 192
  workplace, 189
India, Constitution of, 191–92

Indigenous peoples, 17, 60, 72–73, 73, 198
  Australia, 152
  Canada, 336
  Fiji, 377
  pattern thinking, 72
  relational knowledge, 73
  traditions, 13, 72–73
  worldviews, 74
Indonesia, 75
  management in, 75
  minority religions in, 15
Indus River, 179
inequality, collective and individual, 4
injustices, structural, 454
institutions, predominantly white (PWI), 442, 447, 460
Integration Box, identity, 421
integration, faith-work, 441
integrity
  academic, 459
intelligence, emotional, 229
intelligence, spiritual, 229–30
interconnectedness, 191, 225, 228–30, 228, 231, 256, 370, 378, 441, 445, 446
  Aboriginal beliefs, 365
  Buddhism, 201
  Hinduism, 190
  Indigenous peoples' beliefs, 72
  Maori values, 73
intersectionality, 48
Interfaith Advisory Council, 320–21, 324
Interfaith Cooperation Statement, 309
Interfaith Youth Core, 305, 318–20, 325
intergroup contact theory, 74
intermarriage, 65
International Religious Freedom Act, 418
intersectionality, 16, 23, 37, 52, 136, 190, 332, 345, 441, 442, 450, 460
  identity integration, 443
  Judaism, 133–36
  theory, 442–44
intolerance, 16
Iran, 113, 364
Iraq, 127
Ireland, 2

Isaac, 116
Isaacs, Isaac Alfred, Sir, 146
Islam, 3, 18, 19, 41, 46, 83, 105–21, 266, 312, 314, 359, 362–63, *See also* Deobandi Islam; Salafi Islam; Wahhabie Islam
  Aftica, North, 255
  Dafe almfsada (repulsion of harm), 116–21
  diversity
    as principle, 107
    in early era, 105, 107
    practices in, 112–13
  diversity in early era, 112–13
  doctrine, 8, 105–21
  Ehsan (social justice), 12, 109, 116, 119–21
  ethics, 106–21
  Etidal (moderation), 116–21
  Five Pillars of, 313, 362, 363
  India, 177
  Maslaha Aamah (public interest), 116
  mental illness, perspectives on, 366–67
  philosophy, 116
  political shifts in, 108–10
  scholars of, 105
  Sikhs, discrimination against, 5
  stereotypes of, 41
  Sunni-Shia binary, 9
  ties to Judaism, 130
  women, role of, 114
Islamic countries
  abuse of foreign workers in, 113–15
  religious and ethnic minorities in, 109, 114
Islamic eras
  contemporary, 113
  first, the Prophet and the Rightly Guided Caliphs, 112–13
  second, Ommeyade, 112–13, 118
  third, Abbasid, 112, 113, 118
Islamic pilgrimage, 49
Islamic State, 5
Islamophobia, 5, 41–42, 47, 331
Ismael, 116
Israel, 84, 127, 146, 164
  demography, 167–69

Index 483

economics in, 166–67
Jewish studies in, 124
Jews in, 145, 165–69
Labor Party, 170
poverty in, 128
workplace issues, 166–69
Israel–Palestine conflict, 5, 131

Jacobs, Joseph, 128
Jainism, 19, 177
  OM, 181
  origins of, 179
Jains, U.S., 64
Jajfel, Henry, 138
Japan, 206, 369–73
  Buddhism, 207
  Christianity, 372–73
  demography, 369–70
  health care, 371–72
  mental health, 372
  religion and culture, 370
  Shintoism, 370
Japanese Americans
  internment of, 28
Jaurès, Jean, 288, 291
Jehovah Witnesses, discrimination against, 45
Jesus, 84–85, 86, 92, 95–97, 97, 361, 404
jewelry, religious, 6, 44, 48, 99
Jewish law, 295
Jewish Museum, Brussels, 131
Jewish Policy Research (UK), 154
Jewishness, 124–42, 145, 160, 162, 166, 169–70
Jews, 5, 42, 115, 124–42, 134, 145–72, 308, *See also* anti-Semitism; Judaism
  Ashkenazi, 153
  Australia, 145–53
    demography, 146–50
    education attainment, 148
    employment demographics, 148–50
    employment gender gap, 148–50
    immigrant sources of, 147–48
    refugees in, 146
    workplace aspects, 150–53
  Black, 135–36
  contemporary condition of, 131

dietary constraints, 43, *See also* kosher
diverse religiosity, 46
EDI research, 132
Ethiopian, 135
ethnic identity only, 133
France, 145, 159–65
  demography, 161–62
  emancipation in, 160, 162, 164
  expulsion from, 160–61
  regional treatment, 160
identity
  disclosure or concealment, 126, 129, 132, 133–34, 139, 160, 162–64
  rejection, 127
immigrants
  study of, 139
  U.S., 135
  UK, 153
Islam, early, 112
Israel, 145, 165–69
  demography, 167–69
Jewish sources used against Jews, 129–30
literature, in, 164
Messiah, 84
oppression-privilege paradox, 133–36
orthodox, 5, *See also* Haredi Judaism
privilege-oppression paradox, 133–36
race, 136
reform, 5
secular, 147
Sephardi, 153
social justice activism, 138
socioeconomic variables, 128–29, 134, 168
statistical issues regarding, 125–26, 128–29, 132
stereotypes of, 41, 128, 130, 133, 136, 164–65, 165
U.S., 64–65, 131, 133
  education and income, 65
  religion switching, 65
  unions, 135
UK, 145, 153–59
  demography, 154–55
  employment demographics, 155

Jews (*cont.*)
  visible, 163–64
  workplace, 140–42
  workplace issues
    Australia, 151–53
    France, 161–64, 164–65
    Israel, 166–69, 164–65
    UK, 155–59
Jim Crow, 452
Jobs, Steve, 205
Jordan, workplace discrimination, 114
Joshu Sasaki Roshi, Zen Master, 203
Journal of Management Development, 136
JP Morgan, 190
Jubar, Saeed ibn, 112
Judaism, 3, 12, 13, 18–19, 124–42, 133, 136–38, 266, 312, *See also* anti-Semitism; Jews
  Ashkenazi, 168, 170
  avoda, 140
  Board of Deputies (UK), 153
  conversion and assimilation, 128, 138
  culture of, 124
  EDI research, 132
  France, 134
  global population data, 123, 125–26
  Haredi, 123–24, 154, 168–70
  identity disclosure or concealment, 159
  India, 177
  intersectionality aspects, 133–36
  justice, 137
  leadership, 137–38
  morals, 95
  research issues (tempered radical dilemma), 125–32
  Rosh Hashanah, 156, 339
  sacred texts, 129, 136, 137, 160, 313
  secular, 123
  secularism, 127, 133
  Sefardi, 167
  Sefardi Jews (Mizrachi), 170
  Shabbat, 138, 156, 159, 166
  study, emphasis on, 137
  tension with Christianity, 84
  tikkun olam, 137–38, 140
  United Synagogue (UK), 153
  work ethic, 137
  Yom Kippur, 156
justice, 111, 137

Kabbalah, 3, 34
Kahn Harris, Keith, 153–54
Kaitiakitanga, 73
Karakas, Fahri, 178–79
Karma, 186
Karma Kagyu, 203
Karma Tenzin Dorje Namgyal Rinpoche, 203
Karma Yoga, 183–85
karuna, 19, 200–201, 209, 216
Karva Chauth, 189
Kautilya, 184
Kelly, Eileen P., 393
Khan, Mr., 48–49
Kheireddine, Tasha, 338
King, Samantha (Sammy), 235–42
kippah, 16, 41, 45
Klarsfeld, Alain, 9
koan, 202
Kohlberg, Lawrence, 229
Korea, 206
  workplace issues, 395
kosher, 43, 123, 156, 294, 295
kotahitanga (Maori), 73
Kumarasinghe, Sriyalatha, 209
Kurds, 127
Kwan Yin, 202
Kyocera Corporation, 205

Labor Party (Israel), 170–71
Labour Law (Qatar), 114
LaDuke, Winona, 325
laïcité, 12, 14, 20, 162, 190, 264–300, 264, 265, 268, 271, 275, 277, 279, 284, 287–88, 288, 290, 291, 299, 425–26, 426, 427, 429, 430–31, 432, 433, 434, 436
  accommodation, reasonable, 436
  call for clarification of, 291
  exclusive, 426
  freedom, tension, 436
  French businesses, 284–85
  French schools, 268
  guiding philosophy, public sector, 433–34
  intolerant, 425–26

Index 485

private sector, 292–93, 426
  tolerant, 425
Languille, Constantin, 286, 288
leadership, Mosaic, 137–38
Leahy, John T., 92, 99
Lebanon
  foreign workers, abuse of, 114
  religious diversity, 253
legal aspects, 4, 20, 53
  countering past discrimination, 52
  discrimination in religious organizations, 47
  North America, 62
  Pakistan, 50
  workplace religiosity, 417
legal cases, 42, 265, 273–83, 401
  array of religion-based decisions, 275–79
  Australia, 150–53
  Belgium, 278–79
  Canada, Muslim women, 339–40
  Europe, 289
  France, 276–78, 279–81
    Micropole Universe, 281–84
  Germany, 278
  Italy, 278
  landmarks, 416
  religion, 293–96
  Switzerland, 279
  U.S., 5, 44
  UK, 44, 48–49, 99
Legge, Karen, 230
legislation, 4
  anti-discrimination, 416
  Quebec, visible minorities, against, 343–45
legislation, anti-discrimination, 42
Lelwica, Michelle, 309, 313, 327
Levinas, Emmanuel, 270
Lévi-Strauss, Claude, 127, 139, 264, 269, 273
LGBTQ, 28, 41, 43, 46, 266
  conservative restrictions on, 45
  diversity research, 125–26, 129
  oppression of, 138
  religious affiliation, U.S., 64
  workplaces, discrimination in U.S., 67
liberation theology, 230–31, 361
Lilly Endowment, 316

Lindholm, Jennifer A., 441
Lindley, Joanne, 43
literacy, interfaith, 20
Lithuania, *Bund* in, 123
Litvin, Deborah, 199–200
Living Buddha, Living Christ (Thich Nhat Hanh), 328
Livonia Dermatology, 6
Loksangraha, 185
London Borough of Lambeth, 49
Loomba, Deepinder, 274
Luce Foundation, 327
Lukas, Salome, 339
Luker, Trish, 151
Lund Dean, Kathy, 448
Luther, Martin, 322
Lutheranism, 308, 317–18, 320, 321, 322

Mahabharat, 183
Mahabharata, 362
Mahayana Buddhism, 202, 203
Mahesh (Hinduism), 179
Mahurat, religious (Hindu), 188
majority national religion practices, 395
Malay Muslim Monarchy, 2
Malaysia, 15
Malloy, D. C., 371–72
manaaki (Maori), 73
management
  cognitive complexity, 71–72
  diret and indirect integration, 75
  human resource (HRM). *See* human resource management (HRM)
  integration of spirituality, 444
  Maori values in, 73
  religious diversity, 28, 434
  religious diversity paradigm, 73–74
  socially responsible view, 12
  thinking, pattern and relational, 73
Mandela, Nelson, 249, 250
Maori, 73, 203, 373
Maori spirituality, 373
Maori values, 73
marginalization, 447
Marx, Karl, 39, 127, 138, 139
Maslaha Aamah (public interest, Islam), 116
mātauranga (Maori), 73

materialism, 39
matrix of domination intersectionality, 443
Maupassant, Guy de, 164
Mazumdar, Shampa, 71–72
Mazumdar. Sanjoy, 71–72
Mbiti, John S., 224
McClay, Wilfred M., 90
McClellan, Rhonda L., 454, 455
McFarlane, 416
McGee, James, 448
Mecca, 49
meditation, 178, 181, 190, 198, 378
Meeks, Wayne A., 95–96
Meiji era, 370
Meister, Chad, 354
Melayu Islam Beraja, 2
Melé, Domènec, 96
Mennonite Christians, 295–96
mentoring, 450–51, 452–53
Merriweather Woodson, Tarani, 136
Messiah, 84, 361
metta, 19, 200–201, 209, 216
Meyerson, Debra, 124–25, 456, 457–58
microaggressions, 23, 445, 448, 451, 452, 455, 457, 460, 461
  resilience, 458
Micropole Universe, 281–84
Middle Ages, 160
  Christianity, 91
Middle East, 131
  Jews in, 145
  tensions in, 158
Miller, David W., 24–28, 89, 407
mindfulness, 378
mindfulness (Buddhism), 208, 209, 211–12
minorities
  Arab, 15
  Chinese/Confucian, 15
  ethnic and religious, oppression of, 138
  India religious, 182
  invisible, 136
  Muslim, 15
  oppression of, Islam, 105
  religious, 325, 331, 348
  visible, 20, 332–33, 341, 342

Mitroff, Ian I., 178, 401, 444
moderation
  Buddhism, 202
  Islam, 116–21, 118–19
  Toyota, 371
modernism, 90, 139
Moore, Bill, 404–6
moral reasoning, 91
morale, damage to, 5
Mormons
  U.S., 64
Moses, 129
  as leader, 137–38
mudita, 19, 200, 209, 216
Mughal rule (India), 180
Muhammad, 49, 107–8, 109, 111, 112–13, 115–16, 117–18, 362
  diversity teachings, 110
Multi Faith Forum (UK), 49
Muslim Council of Montreal, 343–45
Muslim religion. *See* Islam
Muslims, 5, 13, 43, 46, 49, 62, 308, *See also* Islam
  accommodations, 431
  Asia–Pacific region, 199
  Canada, 20–21, 331–49
    education, 334–35, 334–35
    unemployment, 334–35
    women, 335–36
    workplace, 331–49
    workplace challenges, 336–38
  Deobandi, 5
  dietary constraints, 43, *See also* halal
  France, 268, 271–72
  India, 189, 190
  Israel, workers in, 124
  New Zealand, 375
  Royhinga, 213
  Salafis, 5
  Shia, 5
  stereotypes of, 314
  Sufis, 5
  Sunni, 5
  U.S., 29, 64
    religion switching, 65
  UK, 43, 47–48, 156–58
    prison population, 48
    unemployment rate, 48
    wage gap, 48
  Wahhabis, 5

Mutoo, Lubuto, 337
Myanmar/Burma, 198
    Buddhist violence, 213
mysticism, 3
mystics, 228

Naht Hanh, Thich, 328
National Council for Canadian
    Muslims, 343–45
National Health Service (NHS, UK),
    44, 239
nationalist right-wing parties, UK, 47
nationality, 23, 441
    intersectionality, 443
Native American religions, U.S., 64
Navratri, 362
Nazism, 134, 150, 160
Némirovsky, Irene, 164
Neuman, William, 106
neuroscience research, 62
neutrality
    organizational, 87
    secular, 88
New Agers, U.S., 64
New Zealand, 373–75
    Buddhism, 203–4
    demography, 373–75
    immigration, 373
    religious diversity, 374
    workplace, 374–75
Ngunjiri, Faith W., 9–10, 235, 447
Nhat Hanh, Thich, 198
NIC Hygiene Ltd, 48
Nicene Creed, 85–86
9/11 attacks. *See* September 11 attacks
Nirvana, 201, 204, 216
Nobel Peace Prize, 198, 325
Norenzayan, Ara, 68–70
normative ethical theory, 90–92, 95
numerology, India in, 188
Nyaya (justice), 184

Observatory of Secularism (France), 277
Oda Nobunaga, 372
Ollier-Malaterre, Ariane, 136
Olupona, Jacob, 446
OM (Hinduism), 181–82, 362
Ommeyade Era (Islam), 112–13, 118
oppression
    and privilege, paradox of, 133–36

optimism, Islam, 108, 117
Organisation for Economic
    Co-operation (OECD), 128
organization design
    pluralistic, 17
Organizational Diversity Learning
    Framework, 73–74
organizational frames, 411
organizational justice theory and
    ethics, 184
organizations
    Buddhist principles for, 199–201
    diversity, Canada, 345–46
    interreligious, 305
    pluralism, 307
    religion accommodating, 71
    religion dominant, 71
    religion included, 71
    religion insensitive, 71
    religious neutrality, 87
    spirituality in the workplace,
        251–52
    workplace spirituality models,
        252–55
othering, 7, 37, 129, 139, 266, 270,
    273
    identity, 270
Ottoman Empire, 113

Pacific Islands, 375–78
    Christianity, 376
    Fiji, 377–78
    religious diversity, 376
    Tuvalu, 376–77
PacMoore Corporation, 390, 404–6
    core values, 406
    faith-based, 403, 406
pagans, U.S., 64
Pakistan
    constitutional prohibitions against
        non-Muslims, 49
    discrimination in, 50
    religious diversity in, 49
Palestine–Israel conflict, 5, 131
Pali Canon (Buddhism), 200, 202, 212,
    216
palliative spirituality, 228–30, 235–42,
    242
panj kakkar, 363
Pantheism, Hinduism, 179

pantheists, U.S., 64
Paprec Group, 291, 390, 403–4, 430–31, 433
　faith-avoiding, 403
　human rights, 404
　secularism, 404
Paprec policy (French business), 284, 430
paradox theory, 17, 60, 70–74, 74
Parasparam Bhavayantaha, 185
Paris Public Transportation Authority, 289
Paris, Peter, 446
Parsis, 375
partnering model of workplace spirituality, 254–55
Patel, Eboo, 305, 306, 318, 325, 326–27
Patel, Taran, 190
paticcasamuppada (Buddhism), 209
patriarchy, 43
Patristic period (Christianity), 91
pattern thinking, 72–73
Paul, Apostle, 84
Pawar, Badrinarayan Shankar, 178
pedagogy, 234
Pentateuch, 169, *See* Torah
Pentecost, 361
Persad, Judy Vashti, 339
Persians
　Abbasid Era power, 113
　Islam, early, 112
personalization, 252–53
pessimism, Islam, 117
Peterson, Christopher, 94
Petithuguenin, Jean-Luc, 403
Pew Research Center, 63–66, 133, 307, 308
phenomenology, 38, 230, 234–35
　Christian, 92
Philippines, The
　management in, 75
　minority religions in, 15
Piaget, Jean, 229
Pilate, Pontius, 86
Pio, Edwina, 186
Plato, 91, 248–49
pluralism, 6
　Buddhism, 212
　religious, 14, 20, 40, 87, 212, 286, 288, 305–29, 305, 306–8, 317, 354–55
　steps toward, 309
　respectful, 420
Poland, *Bund* in, 123
polytheism, Hinduism, 179
polytheists, U.S., 64
Pope Benedict XVI, 94, 97
Pope Francis, 106, 361
Postconciliar period (Roman Catholicism), 94
poverty, 68, 128, 189
　India, 189
Prasaad, 188
Pratt, Michael G., 225, 253–55, 253
prejudice, 23
　lowering, 8
Presbyterians, 361
privilege, 18, 128, 129, 130, 131, 133–36, 140, 145, 210, 323, 361, 442, 447
　ethnic, 133
　racial, 133
productivity, 5
Promised Land, 129
Prophet, The. *See* Muhammad
Prophets of Judaism, 130
proselytism
　religious, 278, 285, 368, 377, 421, 429, 430
　workplace, 44, 282, 283, 284, 401, 427, 436
Protestant Church, 40, 85
Protestantism, evangelical, 243
Protestants, 5, 94
　legal cases, 294
　mainline, U.S., 63
Protestants, evangelical
　U.S., 63–64
Protocols of the Elders of Zion, The, 133
Puranas, 183

Qatar
　abuse of foreign workers, 109
　foreign workers, exploitation of, 114–15
Quéré, Louis, 298

Index 489

Quran, 49, 109, 110, 112, 115, 116, 183, 362
   diversity teaching, 108

Rabuka, Colonel, 378
race, 23, 43, 112, 133, 134, 135–36, 151, 191, 201, 223, 246, 247–49, 250, 251, 266, 306, 331, 371, 441, 442, 463
   definition of, Australia, 152
   diversity research, 125
   intersectionality, 443
   Islam, 110
   Islam, early, 108
   privilege, 133
   U.S., 139
race discrimination, 151
Rachi, 160
racism, 48, 211, 457
   Australia, 152
   overt, 452
   response to, 457
radicalism, tempered, 453, 461, 463
radicals, tempered, 124–32, 456–60
   African context, 456
   strategies, 456
Rai, Himanshu, 185–86
Raj (British), 42
Raj Yoga, 184
Raksha-bandhan festival, 189
Ramadan, 3, 45, 46, 276, 338, 345, 346, 363
Ramayan, 183
Ramayana, 362
Rastafarians, U.S., 64
Reformation, 91
Reformation, Protestant, 322
refugees, 380
   Jews in Australia, 146
relational knowledge, 73
religion, 133
   African, 445–47
   and ethnicity, 15–16
   and spirituality, 24, 69–70
      workplace integration, 75
   concept, 354
   definitions of, 69–70, 417
   demographics, global, 198
   fragmentation of, 266
   freedom of, 278

   freedom of, limits on, 433–34
   fundamentalism, 63, 275–76, 298, 311
   gender, class, and ethnicity, 16
   globalization of, 416
   internal and external logic of, 94
   intersectionality, 443
   intertwined with ethnicity, 46
   intrinsic, extrinsic, 420
   source of performance, 12–13
   tensions among, 11
religion and business
   France, 271
religion and ethnicity
   intersectionality, Jewish, 133–36
religions
   majority populations, 13, 15
   minority populations, 13, 15
religion-based discrimination, 41
religious affiliation
   visible, 20
religious diversity
   Asia–Pacific region, 21
   business impact, 391
   definitions of, 37, 67, 69–70
   faith-based organizations, 402
   global, 17
   integrated definition of, 60
   New Zealand, 374
   paradox theory, 70–74
   promotion of, 6
   UK, 46–49
religious equality
   India, 182
religious expression in the workplace, 43
religious freedom, 295
   workplace, 53
Religious Freedom Restoration Act
   discrimination, corporate, 423
Religious Freedom Restoration Act (U.S.), 295
religious freedom U.S., 295–96
Religious Landscape Study (Pew Research Center), 63
religious literacy, 309
religious majorities, 61
religious market theory, 40
religious minorities, 325, 331, 348
   Pakistan, 50
religious practices in the workplace, 44

religious switching, 65
religious symbols, 338–43, 404, *See* Symbols, religious
Report on the All-Party Parliamentary Inquiry into anti-Semitism (UK), 158
Repulsion of harm principle (Islam), 116–21
research, Faith-Friendly Company study, 407–11
resilience
  advocacy, 458
  identity, 455
resiliency, 453–56, 461
resilient leadership, 23
resurrection (Christianity), 84, 86, 361
rhetoric
  anti-minority in U.S., 28
Richards, Dick, 256
Richards, P. Scott, 92
Ricoeur, Paul, 94–95, 96, 99
Rinzai-ji, 203
Rohinga Muslims, 213
Roman Catholic Church, 378, *See also* Catholicism
  origins, 85
  Postconciliar period, 94
Roman Empire, 85, 159, 361
Rosh Hashanah, 156, 339
Rousseau, Jean Jacques, 267
Rowling, J. K., 239
Ruby, Tabassum F., 335
Russia, 127
  Bund in, 123
  Tsarist era statistics about Jews, 128

Sabbath. *See also* Shabbat
  Christian, 98, 167
  Islam, 3, 167
Safavid, 113
Salafi Islam, 5, 6, 9, 29, 42, 127, 314, 363
Salafi Islamic groups, 5
Samkhya theory (Bhagavad Gita), 184
Sanatana Dharma (Vedic religion), 179–80
Sangha, 202
Satan, 311
Satanists, U.S., 64
Saudi Arabia
  Islam, 108
  women in business, 114
Scientologists, U.S., 64
Scully, Maureen A., 124–25
Second Temple (Judaism), destruction of, 137
Secular institutions overtaking religious functions, 39–45
secularism, 38, 60, 127, 139, 147, 170, 178, 232, 251, 279–81, 295–96, 308, 311
  ascendency of, 39
  atheistic, 291
  corporate, 293–96
  Europe
    active neutrality model, 285–86
    separation-cooperation model, 285–86
  European Union, 285–86
  France, 14, 162, 264, 276–78, 290, 299
    business, 284–85
    private sector, 292–93
  Germany, 426
  inclusive, 291
  India (inclusive), 182, 189, 190–92
  neutrality, 430–31
  post-secularism, 264
  Quebec, 433
  workplace, 398
    France, 286–93
secularization, 61, 88
  management theory, 393
secularism
  management aspects, 75
Sefardi Jews (Mizrachi), 167, 170
self-categorization theory, 62
Seligman, Martin, 94
Sephardi Jews (UK), 153
September 11 attacks, 4, 41, 63, 272, 314, 331, 336–37
servant leadership, 7, 12, 178, 254
sexuality, 306
Shabbat, 138, 156–57, 159, 166
Shakti, 182, 362
Sharma, Radha R, 180
Shavuot, 157
Shaw, Miranda Eberle, 202
Sheldrake, Philip, 231
Shia Islam, 3, 28–29, 42, 363

Shiki, Masaoka (Masaoka Noboru), 215
Shinto, 370
Shiva (Hinduism), 179, 182, 362
Shoah, 134, 141, 145, 157, 160
shojin, 205
Siddhartha Gautama, 201
Sigalovada Sutta (Buddhism), 209
Sikhism, 19, 177, 363–64
    OM, 181
    origins of, 179
Sikhs, 43, 157, 274–75
    Australia, 151
    New Zealand, 375
    U.S., 64
Simmel, Georg, 127, 139
Simon Peter, 85
Sindhu (Indus River), 179
Singapore, minority religions in, 15
Sinhalese Buddhism, 210
Smiritis, 183
Smith, Adam, 40
social capital theory, 187
social identity theory, 62, 93, 94, 95, 99, 138, 395
social justice, 38, 51, 106, 116, 123, 124, 135, 183, 191, 200, 208, 212, 231, 232–33, 314, 361, 441
    Jews, 138
    Jews in Australia, 146
social media, 268
social reflexivity, 298
social responsibility, 38, 397
socialism, 123, 166
Sodexo UK and Ireland, 49
Soka Gakkai, 359, 369
Sophie's World (Jostein Gaarder), 91
South Africa, 247–49
    workplace issues, 395
South China Sea, 207
South Korea, 378–79
    Buddhism, 378
    demography, 378
    workplace spirituality, 378–79
Speight, George, 378
spiritual transformation stages, 445
spirituality, 223–57, 308, 463
    academia, 443
    Africa, 223
    African, 20
    African, types of, 20
    African-ascended people, 445–47
    and religion, 69
    business, 224–25
    corporate forms of, 178
    critical, 460, 461
    definition, 231
    empowerment, 453, 461
    higher education, 441
    Hinduism, 185
    identity, 460–61
    injustice, response to, 449–51
    manifest, 458
    maturity, 462
    palliative, 228–30, 235–42, 242
    spiritual intelligence, 229–30
    transformative, 247–51
    transformative category, 232–33
    via media, 230–32, 242–47, 247
    workplace, 2, 177, 178–79, 178, 227, 228, 233, 247, 251, 406
    workplace intersectionality, 442
spirituality in the workplace, 251–52, 252–55
    directing model, 253–54
    enabling model, 252–53
    partnering model, 254–55
spirituality sans religion, 232–33
Spuler, Michelle, 203
Sri Lanka
    Buddhism, 209–11
    Buddhist violence against Christians and Hindus, 213–14
Sri Yantra (also Shri Chakra, Hinduism), 182
Starbucks, 190
Stark, Rodney, 40
Statement of Religious Diversity in New Zealand, 204
Stedman, Chris, 325
Stefan, Reverend Florea, 92
stereotypes, 7, 23, 37, 53
    Christianity, 88
    Jews, 128, 130
    Judaism, 128
    persistence of, 130
    religious, 41
stereotyping, 41, 74
stigma theory, 88

structuralism, 38
structuration theory, 38
structure, duality of, 38
Sue, Eugène, 165
suffering, 211, 231, 310
Sufis, 363
Sufism, 3, 366
Sunni Islam, 3, 28, 42, 363
Supreme Court (Canada), 276
Supreme Court (U.S.), 276, 295–96
sustainability, 73
Swadharma, 185
Swastika (Hindu symbol), 181
Syed, Jawad, 9
symbolic interactionist perspective, 93
symbolic management, 395–97
symbolic management theory, 389
Symbolic Universe, 99–100
symbolism, religious, 225, 289
symbols, religious, 44, 48, 89, 179, 181–82, 183, 190, 275, 276, 278, 279–81, 281–84, 284, 289, 292, 361, 379, 431
Syria, 127

Talmud, 13, 136–37, 137, 168, 170
Tan, Siang-Yang, 69
Tanakh, 129
Tanzania, management in, 75
Taoists, U.S., 64
Tara, 202
Tata, 190
Teagle Foundation, 326, 327
tempered radical dilemma, 124–32
tempered radicalism, 461, 463
tempered radicals, 456–60
  African context, 456
  strategies, 456, 458
tendency, companies of, 293–96
tension, religion-based, 183
territory, conceptions of, 269–71
terror attacks
  U.S., California, 6
  U.S., New York, 4, 41, 63
terrorism, 272, 331, 333, 334, 336, 338, 341, 366, 375, 380, 427
  Islamist sectarian, 42
Thai Forest Tradition, 203–4
Thailand
  Buddhism, 207

Buddhist violence against Malay Muslims, 213–14
theodiversity and atheodiversity, 69
theory
  functionalism, 38
  intergroup contact, 74
  intersectionality, 442–44
  management, 7
  normative ethical, 90–92, 95
  organizational justice and ethics, 184
  paradox, 17, 60, 70–74, 74
  religious market, 40
  Samkhya, 184
  self-categorization, 62
  servant leadership, 7, 12
  social capital, 187
  social identity, 62, 93, 94, 95, 99, 138
  socioeconomic, 40
  stigma, 88
  structuralism, 38
  structuration, 38
  symbolic management, 389
Theosophical Society, 203
Theravada Buddhism, 198, 200, 202, 207
Thich Nhat Hanh, 198, 328
Thomson, Stanley Bruce, 88
Thornton, Margaret, 151
Thorpe, S. A., 225
Thubten Yeshe, Lama, 203
Thubten Zopa, Lama, 203
Tibet, 198, 203, 215
  Chinese occupation of, 215
Tibetan Buddhism, 202, 215
tika (Maori), 73
tikkun olam (repairing the world), 137–38, 140
Tipitaka (Buddhism), 202
Title VII, 389, 390, 392, 394, 402
Torah, 12, 129, 136–37, 160, 168, 169, 170, 313
Tour of Jewish History, A (Australia), 146
Toyota Global Vision, 371
transformative category of spirituality, 232–33
transformative spirituality, 247–51
Trinity (Christianity), 86

Trump, Donald J., 28
turban, 3, 274–75, 281, 338, 363, 375
Turkey, 113, 127
 India, invasion of, 180
Turks, Abbasid Era power, 113
Tuvalu, 376–77
Twelve Steps to a Compassionate Life (Karen Armstrong), 313

Ubuntu, 255
Ulrich, Peter, 90–92
unaffiliated, as a religious category, 13, 47, 270
 among U.S. LGBTQ, 64
 Asia–Pacific region, 198, 366
 Japan, 370
 Korea, 378
 U.S., 63–64, 307
 U.S. Jews, 133
unemployment rates
 UK Muslims, 48
unions, 135, 139, 150, 164, 189, 210, 426, 435
United Arab Emirates, 127
 exploitation of foreign workers, 114–15
United Kingdom (UK), 170
 Australia, invasion of, 146
 employment demographics, Jews, 155
 higher education, 155–58
 India, rule of, 180–81
 Jewish demography, 154–55
 Jews, 145
 Jews in, 153–59
 London, 98
 Muslim prison population, 48
 Muslims, intolerance to, 47
 religion demographic data, 46
 religious discrimination in, 42
 religious freedom, 418
 workplace issues, 155–59
United Nations, 393
United States
 Black Jews in, 135–36
 Buddhist women in, 211
 demographics
  Concordia College, 308
  religion, 63–64, 307
 diversity in, 106

education and income, Hindus and Jews, 65
election, 2016, 28
gender religion data, 65
Generation X, 64–65
higher education, 305–29
intermarriage, 65
Jewish economic standing, 134
Jews, immigrant, 135
minorities in, 28
religious discrimination, 66
religious diversity in, 62–67
religious freedom, 126, 418
secularization in, 39
separation of church and state, 276
unions, 135
workplaces, secular, 66
Universal Declaration of Human Rights (France), 87, 389, 390, 392, 393–94, 418, 419
Universal Parcel Services, 339–40
Upanishads, 179, 183, 362
upekkha, 19, 200–201, 216
uppekha, 209

Vaill, Peter, 229
Vaisakhi, 363
Van den Muyzenberg, Laurenz, 208–9
Vatican Council, Second, 94
Vedas, 179, 181, 182, 183, 362
Vedic era, 188
Vedic religion, 179–80, 183
via media spirituality, 230–32, 242–47, 247
Victorian Equal Opportunity Act (Australia), 153
Victorian Equal Opportunity and Human Rights Commission, 152
Vimutti Buddhist Monastery, 204
Vipassana retreat, 198
Virgin Mary, 86, 361
Vishnu (Hinduism), 179, 362
visibility, 270
 religious, 265
visible minorities, 20
 Muslims, 332–33, 334
visible religious affiliation, 20
visible religious identity, 45, 61
 France, 271–73
vocation, 229–31, 450, 461

wage gap
  Asian-Americans, 129
  gender, UK Muslim women, 48
  Gulf State foreign workers, 114
  Judaism, 137, 167–68
  religious, Muslims in UK, 48
  UK religion and ethnicity, 43
Wahhabi Islam, 5, 9, 29, 42, 127, 314, 363, 366
Walker, Donald F., 69
Wallace, Michael, 337–38
Ward, Keith, 354
Weber, Max, 39, 40, 298
Weil, Patrick, 287
Weller, Paul, 47
Werner, Andrea, 93
whakapapa (Maori), 73
Wheaton, Ken, 98
Wiccans, U.S., 64
Willard, Aiyana K., 69
Williams, Rowan (Archbishop), 231–32
women
  conservative restrictions on, 45
  diversity research, 129
  Haredi workforce, 168–69
  Jewish, UK employment demographics, 155
  oppression of, 138
  restrictions on
    Saudi Arabia, 108
    Sri Lanka, 210–11
Women Working with Immigrant Women, 339
Won Buddhism, 202
workers, foreign
  Asians in Israel, 167
  discrimination against in Islamic countries, 109, 114–15
Workers' Action Center, 339–40
workplace, 311, *See also* accommodations
  Australia, Jews in, 150–53
  barriers to visible minorities, 332
  Canada
    minorities, 333
    Muslims, 342
  challenge and empowerment, 451
  challenges
    higher education, 451

Christianity in, 92–94
discrimination, 227, 391
diversity, Canada, 345–46
diversity, Canada Muslims, 343–45
employee commitment, 407
empowerment, 452
ennui, 416
environment, expression in, 434
equity, 106, 200
ethnic divisions, 395
faith integration benefits, 392–93
faith, integration of, 88–90
France, Jews, 161–64
holistic approaches, 393
human rights, 411
human rights respected, 395
identity, 441–63
inclusion, 52
India, 189–91, 192
India spirituality, 183–86
interreligious, 305
Islamic women in, 114
Israel demographics, 166–69
Jews, 140–42
Jews in, 164–65
laïcité, 292–93
Muslims in Canada, 331–49, 336–38
New Zealand, 374–75
Persian Gulf, minority discrimination in, 114
pluralism, 307
positivity, faith-friendly frame, 410
religious contexts, 390
religious identity expression, 416
secular space, 393
spirituality, 444
spirituality and intersectionality, 442
spirituality in, 230
Sri Lanka, 210–11
U.S. diversity, lack of, 306
UK, Jews in, 155–59
visible minorities, 332
women in, 395
workplace issues
  Australia, Jews in, 151–53
  France, 164–65, 267–69
    Jews in, 161–64
  Israel, 166–69

reward motivation, religion-based, 184
UK, 158–59
UK, Jews in, 155–59
workplace spirituality, 178–79, 225
  Africa, 225
  South Korea, 378–79
World Bank's Doing Business Report, 204
World Court, the Hague, 289
World War I, 123
World War II, 28, 123, 170
  Jewish survivors of, 134
World War II, post, 164
Wright, Bradley R. E., 337–38
Wuthnow, Robert, 92
Wynne, Kathleen, 274

Yagna, 190
Yang, Fenggang, 355

Yardley, Jim, 106
Yasuo, Hoshino, 209
Yazidis, 308
yoga, 178, 190, 362, 378
Yoga (Hindu), 183–84
Yom Kippur, 156, 339
Yusuf, Dales, 340

Zambrana, Ruth Enid, 443
Zen Buddhism, 198, 202
Zhong, Yijiang, 370
Zionism, 166, 170
Zohar, Danah, 229
Zoroastrianism, 364–65
Zoroastrians, 188
  New Zealand, 375
  U.S., 64